# Circuit Analysis

with computer applications to
problem solving

The Intext Series in

**Circuits, Systems, Communications and Computers**

**Consulting Editor**

**S. C. Gupta**

Gupta, Bayless & Peikari—CIRCUIT ANALYSIS: With Computer Application
to Problem Solving
Ingels—INFORMATION AND CODING THEORY
Matsch—ELECTROMAGNETIC AND ELECTROMECHANICAL
MACHINES
Mickle & Sze—OPTIMIZATION IN SYSTEMS ENGINEERING
Sheng—INTRODUCTION TO SWITCHING LOGIC

# Circuit Analysis

## with computer applications to problem solving

**Someshwar C. Gupta**
*Southern Methodist University*

**Jon W. Bayless**
*Defense Communication Agency*
*System Engineering Facility*

**Behrouz Peikari**
*Southern Methodist University*

Intext Educational Publishers
College Division of **Intext**
*Scranton   San Francisco   Toronto   London*

ISBN  0-7002-2405-X

Copyright ©, 1972, International Textbook Company

Library of Congress Catalog Card Number:  70-177301

# Preface

This book is the outgrowth of class notes written for a two-semester sophomore/junior level course at the Southern Methodist University. This course was designed to integrate basic circuit analysis with the use of the digital computer as a tool.

Our objective in this text is to develop the basic principles of circuit analysis while at the same time introducing the computer as an aid in solving linear, nonlinear, and time-varying problems. In level and content the book is intended to provide a basic introduction to circuit theory and, in recognition of the fact that an introductory circuits course is often a basic course for many curriculums, to present techniques important to a wide variety of more advanced engineering topics.

Our particular method of presenting the computer material has been motivated by the belief that the student must learn the analytical part and then should be able to use simple numerical procedure to evaluate his results. Also, because the digital computer has become an essential analysis and design aid in all phases of engineering, including the analysis and design of electric circuits, it is desirable for the student to start using the computer as early as possible in his educational career. It should also be mentioned that students at the introductory level do not develop an appreciation for fully automated computer-aided analysis programs without first developing basic knowledge of circuit analysis and an understanding of how the computer can be used as a computational tool in problem solving. Hence throughout the text the student is motivated and encouraged to learn to write his own computer programs. The computer programs developed within the text range from a simple integration routine to programs that solve a set of simultaneous state equations. Each program is introduced by a short and intuitive discussion on concepts of numerical analysis which pertain to the particular program. In fact, all the computer material in the text is self-contained.

In Chapter 1 of this book we discuss the definition and properties of two-terminal elements, including nonlinear and time-varying. We develop a simple integration routine which can be used to compute the energy stored in a capacitor or an inductor. Kirchhoff's current and voltage laws are discussed in Chapter 2. Using elementary notions of network topology, a systematic procedure for writing a set of linearly independent KCL and KVL equations is developed. Loop and nodal analysis are also discussed in this chapter. Chapter 3 contains a detailed discussion of representation and specification of various signals commonly used in circuit analysis.

In Chapter 4 resistive linear and nonlinear networks and matrix representation of KVL and KCL are discussed. The concept of a matrix inverse is introduced and a computer program for multiplication of matrices and for solving a set of simultaneous equations is developed. Chapters 5 and 6 are devoted to transient analysis of first- and second-order circuits. The computer plot program is introduced in Chapter 6. In Chapter 7 we discuss the state-space approach to network analysis and give a step-by-step method for writing the state equations of a proper network. Analytic and numerical solution of state equations together with the corresponding computer program is also developed in this chapter.

The network impulse response and the convolution integral are discussed in Chapter 8, and a program for computer evaluation of convolution integral developed in this chapter. The Laplace transform method, sinusoidal steady-state analysis, and circuit analysis for other periodic waveforms are discussed in Chapters 9 through 11. The computer programs developed in these chapters are for root solving of algebraic equations, evaluation of network frequency response, and for evaluating Fourier series coefficients. Plot program is also used in many places. Discussion of two-port networks, network theorems, and a systematic procedure for analysis of large-scale networks are developed in Chapters 12, 13, and 14. There is a short discussion of complex numbers and complex variables in Appendix A. Answers to selected problems are given in Appendix B.

A one-semester course covering the conventional topics in introductory circuits can be taught from the material contained in Chapters 1–6, 9, and 10. For a two-quarter course, we suggest covering the essential topics in Chapters 1–10. The textbook can be covered easily in two semesters. We suggest the first seven chapters in the first semester and the last seven chapters in the second semester. If the book is used in a three-quarter course, Chapters 1 through 5 can be covered in the first quarter, Chapters 6 through 10 in the second quarter, and the remaining chapters in the third quarter. We assume that the students have completed work in elementary electricity and magnetism together with a freshman-level course in FORTRAN programming. Freshman-level calculus and some elementary knowledge of differential equations are also assumed. Introductory knowledge of matrices, determinants, and complex numbers is helpful but not necessary. It should be mentioned that the text can also be used if no computer applications are to be considered. In this case, all the sections or subsections involving computer programs can be omitted without loss of continuity.

We are indebted to the instructors who have taught the course from our class notes, in particular Prof. John Savage and Mr. Sam Houston. Their help in providing answers to the selected problems and proofreading the manuscript have been invaluable. We are also grateful to Prof. Charles M. Close of Rensselaer Polytechnic Institute, Kendel Su of Georgia Institute of Technology, Jack W. Lapatra of University of California, Davis, and L. Hasdorff of Virginia Polytechnic Institute, Blacksburg for their helpful suggestions and constructive comments. Finally, it is our pleasure to thank Patsy Wuensche, Carolyn Hughes, and Mary Lou Caruthers for the typing and preparation of the manuscript.

S. C. Gupta

J. W. Bayless

B. Peikari

November 1971

# Contents

# List of Computer Programs

## CHAPTER 1

# Basis of Circuit Analysis

## 1.1. INTRODUCTION

Circuit analysis, as one branch of electrical engineering, is based upon mathematical relationships which have been formulated to describe physically observable phenomenon. Just as Sir Isaac Newton worked to establish a mathematical description of gravitational effects, so also were Coulomb, Gauss, Lorentz, Faraday, Lenz, and other early workers in the field inspired by experimental observation to formulate mathematical descriptions of electrical and magnetic effects.

In circuit analysis we are concerned with four basic manifestations of electricity, namely, electric charge, $q(t)$, magnetic flux, $\phi(t)$, electric potential, $v(t)$, and electric current, $i(t)$. Here we assume that the reader has some familiarity with these concepts and merely state the basic relationship among them. There are four equations fundamental to circuit analysis; first

$$i(t) = \frac{d}{dt} q(t) \tag{1.1.1}$$

That is, the current through a circuit element is the time derivative of the electric charge. Since the unit of charge is coulomb, the unit of the current is coulomb per second. This unit is called the *ampere* (abbreviated amp) in honor of French physicist André Marie Ampère (1775–1836). Second,

$$v(t) = \frac{d}{dt} \phi(t) \tag{1.1.2}$$

The potential difference between the terminals of a circuit element for which the magnetic flux is the dominating factor is equal to the time derivative of the flux. The unit of the potential is webers per second, which is called *volts* (not abbreviated) in honor of Italian physicist Alessandro Volta (1745–1827). Next, the instantaneous power delivered to a circuit element, $p(t)$, is given by

$$p(t) = v(t)i(t) \tag{1.1.3}$$

1

where $v(t)$ and $i(t)$ are the voltage and currents of the element respectively. The unit of power is *watt*, named after the British engineer and inventor James Watt (1736–1819). Finally, the energy delivered to a circuit element over the time interval $(t_0, t)$ is given by

$$E(t_0, t) = \int_{t_0}^{t} p(\sigma)\, d\sigma \qquad (1.1.4)$$

or equivalently

$$E(t_0, t) = \int_{t_0}^{t} v(\sigma) i(\sigma)\, d\sigma \qquad (1.1.5)$$

where $E$ is given in watt-seconds or *joules* in honor of British scientist J. P. Joule (1818–98).

Equations 1.1.1 through 1.1.5 hold for any circuit element regardless of its nature. The relation between the voltage and current of an element, however, depends entirely on the physical nature of the element. The study of these relationships and the interconnection of the circuit elements is the objective of circuit analysis. In this chapter we first classify the circuit elements in four groups, resistive, capacitive, inductive and source elements and then study their voltage current relationships in detail. Before we start, we want to draw attention to Tables 1.1.1 and 1.1.2 which give the basic *units* and some other notations used in this text.

TABLE 1.1.1. INTERNATIONAL SYSTEM OF UNITS.

| Quantity | Unit | Symbol |
|---|---|---|
| Length | meter | m |
| Mass | kilogram | kg |
| Time | second | s |
| Temperature | degree Kelvin | °K |
| Electric charge | coulomb | C |
| Electric current | ampere | A |
| Voltage (potential difference) | volt | V |
| Electric resistance | ohm | Ω |
| Electric capacitance | farad | f |
| Magnetic flux | weber | wb |
| Inductance | henry | h |
| Energy | joule | J |
| Power | watt | W |

TABLE 1.1.2. MULTIPLES, SUBMULTIPLES, AND PREFIXES

| Multiples and Submultiples | Prefixes | Symbols |
|---|---|---|
| $10^{12}$ | tera | T |
| $10^{9}$ | giga | G |
| $10^{6}$ | mega | M |
| $10^{3}$ | kilo | K |
| $10^{-3}$ | milli | m |
| $10^{-6}$ | micro | $\mu$ |
| $10^{-9}$ | nano | n |
| $10^{-12}$ | pico | p |

## 1.2. BASIC TWO-TERMINAL CIRCUIT ELEMENTS

The symbolic representation of a two-terminal circuit element is shown in Fig. 1.2.1. The end points marked $A$ and $B$ represent the two terminals of the device which are available for interconnection with other

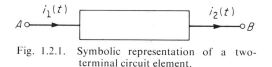

Fig. 1.2.1.   Symbolic representation of a two-terminal circuit element.

circuit elements. A basic property of two-terminal "lumped" elements is that the current entering one terminal is equal to the current leaving the other terminal at all times. More precisely, the two-terminal circuit element whose symbolic representation is given in Fig. 1.2.1 is said to be *lumped* if

$$i_1(t) = i_2(t) \qquad \forall t$$

where the symbol $\forall$ means "for all." Besides the current flowing through the element, we are interested in the voltage across the element. In order to establish voltage-current relationships, it is necessary to settle upon a sign convention.

*SIGN CONVENTION.* Voltage polarity on a circuit element is established arbitrarily by assuming one terminal is at a higher potential than the other. The terminal *assumed* to be of highest potential is marked with a + (plus) sign and the terminal assumed to be of lowest potential is marked with a − (minus) sign as shown in Fig. 1.2.2. In Fig. 1.2.2a, terminal $A$ is assumed to be of higher potential than $B$ and $v_1$ denotes the potential difference between $A$ and $B$; i.e.,

$$v_1 \triangleq v_A - v_B$$

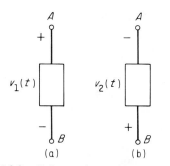

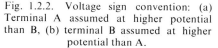

Fig. 1.2.2.   Voltage sign convention: (a) Terminal A assumed at higher potential than B, (b) terminal B assumed at higher potential than A.

where $v_A$ and $v_B$ denote the potentials at $A$ and $B$ respectively.   In Fig. 1.2.2b, terminal $B$ is assumed to be of higher potential than $A$ and $v_2$ denotes the potential difference between $B$ and $A$; i.e., $v_2 = v_B - v_A$. From these two definitions, it is obvious that at any time $t$, we have the relationship

$$v_1(t) \triangleq -v_2(t)$$

We are now in a position to establish a convention for the current direction relative to the assumed voltage sign convention.   Throughout the book we denote the direction of the current flow in a circuit element by an arrow and assume that the current enters at the $+$ (plus) terminal and leaves at the $-$ (minus) terminal.   This convention is shown in Fig. 1.2.3.   The relationship between the voltage and the current of a

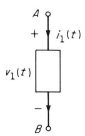

Fig. 1.2.3.   Current   direction   in   two-terminal circuit elements.

circuit element depends entirely on the nature of the element; on this basis, circuit elements are divided into four different categories: resistive, capacitive, inductive, and source elements.   In the rest of this section we examine some of the properties of a special class of circuit elements, namely, linear time-invariant, resistive, capacitive, and inductive elements.

### Linear Time-Invariant Resistor

The term *resistance* denotes the property of an element which converts electrical energy into heat energy.   Physical resistive elements vary in their electrical properties; some exhibit a large resistance, others exhibit a relatively small resistance.   An element which exhibits a predominant resistance characteristic is called a *resistor* and is often modeled by neglecting other electrical properties of the physical element.   Mathematically a resistor is modeled as a function relating the terminal voltage and current; more precisely, we have the following.

*DEFINITION.* A two-terminal element is said to be a linear, time-invariant resistor if its terminal voltage can be specified as a linear, time-invariant function of the terminal input current, i.e., the resistance property can be described mathematically by

$$v(t) = Ri(t) \tag{1.2.1}$$

where $R$ is the value of the resistance and is measured in ohms (symbolically written as $\Omega$), $i(t)$ is the value of the input current in amperes, and $v(t)$ is the value of the terminal voltage in volts. We can solve Eq. 1.2.1 for the current as

$$i(t) = \frac{1}{R} v(t) \tag{1.2.2}$$

or equivalently

$$i(t) = Gv(t) \qquad \therefore \; v(t) = \frac{i(t)}{G} \tag{1.2.3}$$

where

$$G \triangleq \frac{1}{R} \tag{1.2.4}$$

The quantity $G$ is called *conductance* and has units of $(\text{ohm})^{-1}$ which for convenience is denoted by mhos (symbolically written as $\mho$). Quite obviously, for a linear time invariant resistor, we can describe its terminal voltage-current relationship by either the parameter $R$ or $G$. When the term resistance or conductance is employed, linear time-invariance will be implied unless stated otherwise. The *v-i* relationship of a linear time-invariant resistor can be represented as a straight line going through the origin in the *v-i* plane. The slope of this line is the resistance $R$ of the resistor (see Fig. 1.2.4). When $R = 0$, the line is horizontal and $v = 0$ for all values of $i$. For this special case, the two-terminal resistor is said to be a *short circuit*. When $R = \infty$, the line is vertical indicating $i = 0$ for all values of $v$, in this special case the two-terminal resistor is said to be an *open circuit*. The schematic representation of a resistor, an open circuit

$$v_R(t) = R i_R(t) \qquad R = \frac{v_R(t)}{i_R(t)} = \frac{y}{x}$$

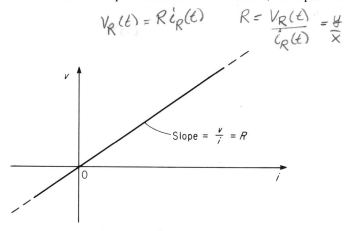

Fig. 1.2.4. Characteristic plot of voltage vs. current for a linear, time-invariant resistor with resistance $R$.

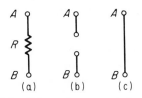

Fig. 1.2.5.   Schematic representation of (a)
resistor, (b) open circuit, (c) short circuit.

and a short circuit are shown in Fig. 1.2.5.  As indicated, an open circuit
between terminals $AB$ is shown as an incompleted line between the
terminals, while a short circuit is indicated by a completed line.

*Example 1.2.1*

Figure 1.2.6 shows a voltage waveform, $v_R$, as a function of time
which is observed at the terminals of a resistor of value $R$ ohms.  Calculate
$i(t)$ the current through the resistor if (a)  $R = 1$,  (b)  $R = 2$,  (c)
$R = \infty$ ohms.

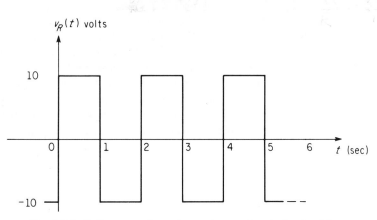

Fig. 1.2.6.  Voltage waveform observed across terminals of resistor.

*Solution*

Applying Eq. 1.2.2, we find

$$i_R(t) = \frac{v_R(t)}{R}$$

hence the current is found by dividing $v_R(t)$ by resistance values given.
These are shown in Fig. 1.2.7.

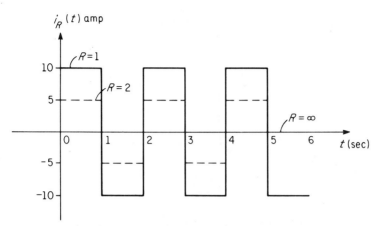

Fig. 1.2.7.   Current waveform through resistor for R = 1, 2, and ∞, Ω.

## Linear Time-Invariant Capacitor

The term *capacitance* is used to denote the property of an element which stores electric energy.  In a typical capacitance element this energy storage is accomplished by accumulating charges between two surfaces separated by an insulating material.  A parallel-plate capacitor is indicated schematically in Fig. 1.2.8.  In a linear time-invariant capacitor at any instant, the stored charge is related to the terminal voltage by

$$q(t) = Cv(t) \qquad (1.2.5)$$

where the quantity $C$ is called the *capacitance* of the element and is measured in farads (written symbolically as f) when the units of $q$ are

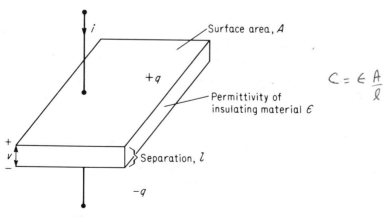

Fig. 1.2.8.   Parallel-plate capacitor.

$q(t) = C v_c(t)$

$C = \dfrac{q_c(t)}{V_c(t)} = \dfrac{y}{x}$

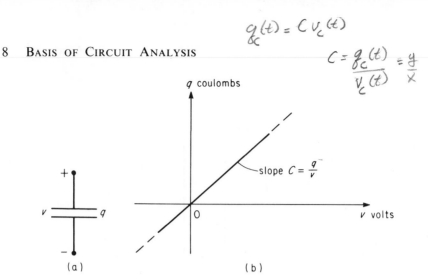

Fig. 1.2.9. (a) Symbolic representation of a linear time-invariant capacitor, (b) q-v characteristic of a linear time-invariant capacitor.

coulombs and the units of $v$ are volts. Equation 1.2.5 represents a linear, time-invariant relationship between the variables $q$ and $v$, which can be represented in the $q$-$v$ plane as a straight line going through the origin. The symbolic representation of a linear time-invariant capacitor and its $q$-$v$ characteristics are represented in Figs. 1.2.9a and 1.2.9b respectively. The capacitance of a linear time-invariant capacitor which is made up of two parallel plates can be found from

$$C = \epsilon \frac{A}{l} \tag{1.2.6}$$

where $\epsilon$ is the permittivity of the insulating material, $A$ the surface area of the plates, and $l$ the distance between two plates. Let us now give a precise definition of a linear time-invariant capacitor.

*DEFINITION.* A two-terminal circuit element is said to be a linear time-invariant capacitor if its electric charge $q$ is given as a linear time-invariant function of the voltage across it.

Since the electrical current flowing through a particular point in a circuit is the time derivative of the electrical charge, Eq. 1.2.5 can be differentiated to yield a relationship between the terminal current and the terminal voltage

$q(t) = C v(t)$

$$i = \frac{dq}{dt} = C \frac{dv}{dt} \qquad \frac{1}{C} \frac{dq}{dt} = \frac{dv}{dt} \tag{1.2.7}$$

Hence, the current through a two-terminal linear time-invariant capacitor is proportional to the voltage across it. The proportionality constant is the capacitance $C$.

Equation 1.2.5 can be written in the form

$$v(t) = \frac{1}{C} q(t) = Sq(t) \tag{1.2.8}$$

$v(t) = \dfrac{1}{C} \int i(t)\, dt$

where $S \triangleq \dfrac{1}{C}$ is called *elastance*. Either the capacitance or the elastance can be used to describe the charge-voltage relationship for a linear capacitor.

Let us now consider a simple example.

*Example 1.2.2*

For the voltage waveform $v_C(t)$ shown in Fig. 1.2.10, find the charge and current for a capacitor of value $C = 1/10$ farads.

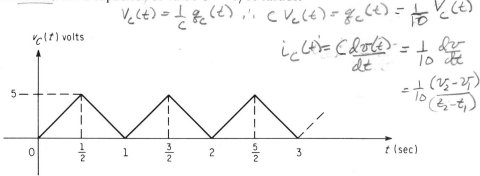

$$V_c(t) = \frac{1}{C} q_c(t) \; , \; \therefore \; C V_c(t) = q_c(t) = \frac{1}{10} V_c(t)$$

$$i_c(t) = C \frac{dv(t)}{dt} = \frac{1}{10} \frac{dv}{dt}$$

$$= \frac{1}{10} \frac{(v_2 - v_1)}{(t_2 - t_1)}$$

Fig. 1.2.10.   Voltage observed at capacitor terminals.

*Solution*

Applying Eqs. 1.2.5 and 1.2.7, we have $q_C(t) = \dfrac{1}{10} v_C(t)$ and $i_C(t) = \dfrac{1}{10} \dfrac{dv_C(t)}{dt}$. Hence the charge and current are as shown in Fig. 1.2.11.

It is often convenient to have a relationship for the capacitor voltage directly in terms of the current rather than the charge. We can obtain

$$i(t) = C \frac{dv(t)}{dt} \qquad \frac{1}{C} \int i(t) dt = \int dv(t)$$

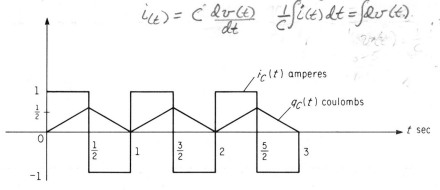

Fig. 1.2.11.   Charge and current waveforms for capacitor of Example 1.2.2.

such a relationship from Eq. 1.2.7 simply by dividing by $C$ and integrating both sides of the equation:

$$\frac{1}{C} \int i(t) \, dt + k = v(t) \tag{1.2.9}$$

where $k$ is the integration constant. The question arises as to what are limits of integration on the integral. Since we are evaluating the voltage at time $t$, the upper limit on the integral must be $t$. We assume that the integral is to be evaluated over some observation interval $(t_0, t)$ so that the lower limit is $t_0$. Thus

$$\frac{1}{C} \int_{t_0}^{t} i(\sigma) \, d\sigma + k = v(t) \tag{1.2.10}$$

This equation must hold at the beginning of the observation interval, i.e., at $t = t_0$; hence

$$\frac{1}{C} \int_{t_0}^{t_0} i(\sigma) \, d\sigma + k = v(t_0) \tag{1.2.11}$$

Equation 1.2.11 indicates that the integration constant must be equal to $v(t_0)$. Also since the integration variable is simply a dummy variable, we have used $\sigma$ rather than $t$ giving finally the desired relationship between terminal voltage and current for the capacitor

$$v(t) = \frac{1}{C} \int_{t_0}^{t} i(\sigma) \, d\sigma + v(t_0) \tag{1.2.12}$$

where $v(t_0)$ is referred to as the initial voltage across the capacitor under consideration.

*Example 1.2.3*

Consider a linear time-invariant capacitor with capacitance $C = 10^{-6}$ farad. Assume that initial voltage across this capacitor is $v_C(0) = 1$ volt. Find the voltage $v_C(t)$ at time $t \geq 0$ on this capacitor if the current through it is $i_C(t) = \cos(10^6 t)$.

*Solution*

Using Eq. 1.2.12 we get

$$v_C(t) = \frac{1}{10^{-6}} \int_0^t \cos(10^6 \sigma) \, d\sigma + 1$$

or

$$v_C(t) = \left[ 10^6 \, \frac{1}{10^6} \sin(10^6 \sigma) \right]_0^t + 1$$

Finally,

$$v_C(t) = 1 + \sin(10^6 t)$$

## Linear Time-Invariant Inductor

The term *inductance* is employed to denote the property of an element to store energy in a magnetic field. This energy storage is accomplished by establishing a magnetic flux within a ferromagnetic material. For example, Fig. 1.2.12 shows a simple inductor which is made by wrapping a

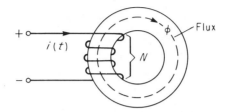

Fig. 1.2.12.   Iron-core inductor.

coil of wire around an iron loop. For a linear time-invariant inductor at any instant, the magnetic flux $\phi(t)$ is given approximately by the relationship

$$\phi(t) = \left[\frac{\mu N^2 A}{l}\right] i(t) \qquad (1.2.13)$$

where $\frac{\mu N^2 A}{l}$ is the inductance of the device and its units are henries (symbolically written as h). The inductance of a linear inductor is usually denoted by $L$, i.e.,

$$L \triangleq \frac{\mu N^2 A}{l}$$

where $\mu$ is the permeability, $l$ the mean length, $A$ the cross-sectional area of the magnetic core, and $N$ the number of turns of the coil.

Let us now give a precise definition of a linear time-invariant inductor.

*DEFINITION.* A two-terminal element is said to be a linear, time-invariant inductor if its magnetic flux is specified as a linear, time-invariant function of the terminal current, i.e.,

$$\phi(t) = Li(t) \qquad L = \phi(t)/i(t) = \psi/x \qquad (1.2.14)$$

where $\phi(t)$ is in webers and $i(t)$ is in amperes, and the units of the inductance parameter $L$ are henries.

The schematic representation of a linear time-invariant inductor together with the associated current, voltage, and flux directions are indicated in Fig. 1.2.13a. Its $\phi$-$i$ characteristic is plotted in Fig. 1.2.13b. By Faraday's law, the voltage at the terminals of the inductor is the time

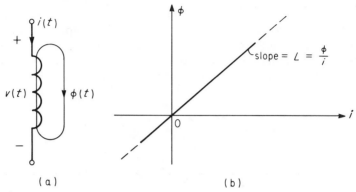

Fig. 1.2.13. (a) Schematic representation of a linear time-invariant inductor, (b) $\phi$-$i$ characteristics of a linear inductor with inductance $L$.

derivative of the flux

$$v(t) = \frac{d\phi}{dt} \qquad (1.2.15)$$

Combining this relationship with Eq. 1.2.14 gives the terminal voltage-current relation of a linear time-invariant inductor

$$v(t) = L\frac{di}{dt} \qquad di = \frac{1}{L}v(t)\,dt \qquad (1.2.16)$$

Integrating both sides of this equation yields

$$i(t) = i(t_0) + \frac{1}{L}\int_{t_0}^{t} v(\sigma)\,d\sigma \qquad (1.2.17)$$

where $i(t_0)$ denotes the initial current through the inductor.

*Example 1.2.4*

The current through a linear time-invariant inductor with inductance $L = 10^{-3}$ henry is given as

$$\cos 2x =$$

$$i_L(t) = 0.1\sin 10^6 t$$

Find the voltage $v_L(t)$ across this inductor.

*Solution*

From Eq. 1.2.16 we readily have

$$.1\cos 10^6 t \cdot 10^6$$

$$= 100\cos 10^6 t$$

$$v_L(t) = 10^{-3}\frac{d}{dt}[0.1\sin 10^6 t]$$

or

$$v_L(t) = 100\cos(10^6 t)$$

*Example 1.2.5*

For the voltage waveform shown in Fig. 1.2.14a, calculate the current through an inductor if $L = \frac{1}{2}$ henry and $i_L(0) = -2$ amperes.

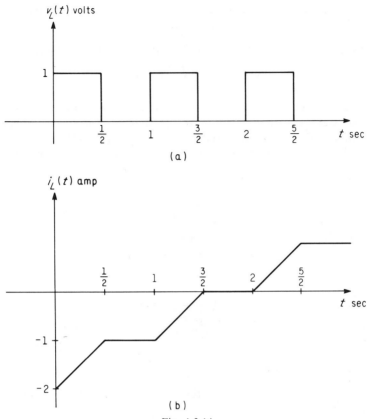

Fig. 1.2.14.

*Solution*

We employ Eq. 1.2.17 with $t_0 = 0$ and $1/L = 2$. Hence we have

$$i_L(t) = -2 + 2 \int_0^t v_L(\sigma) \, d\sigma$$

Recognizing the integral of $v_L(t)$ as the area under the waveform in Fig. 1.2.14a, the current waveform in Fig. 1.2.14b results. Note that the initial current $i_L(0)$ simply shifts the current waveform intercept on the vertical axis.

## 1.3. ENERGY CONCEPTS IN TWO-TERMINAL ELEMENTS

As mentioned previously the resistive, inductive, and capacitive elements relate respectively to dissipation of electrical energy in heat, storage of electrical energy in a magnetic field, and storage of electrical energy in an electric field. *Instantaneous power, which is defined as the time deriva-*

*tive of energy*, is given as the product of element voltage and current:

$$p(t) = v(t)i(t) \qquad (1.3.1)$$

The energy delivered to the element over the time interval $(t_0, t_1)$ is

$$E(t_0, t_1) = \int_{t_0}^{t_1} v(t)i(t)\,dt \qquad (1.3.2)$$

This energy can be either positive or negative, depending on the relative values and signs of $v(t)$ and $i(t)$. With the sign convention established for $R$, $L$, and $C$ elements, a positive value on the integral in Eq. 1.3.2 is associated with net energy flow into the circuit elements as shown in Fig. 1.3.1.

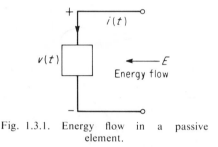

Fig. 1.3.1.  Energy  flow  in  a  passive element.

### Energy Dissipated in a Resistor

For a linear time-invariant resistor we have the voltage-current relationship

$$v(t) = Ri(t) \qquad (1.3.3)$$

$$p(t) = Ri(t)i(t) = Ri^2(t)$$
$$p(t) = v(t) \cdot v(t) \quad \left( R = \frac{1}{R} v^2(t) \right)$$

which gives the energy flowing into the resistor:

$$E(t_0, t_1) = R \int_{t_0}^{t_1} i^2(t)\,dt = \frac{1}{R} \int_{t_0}^{t_1} v^2(t)\,dt \qquad (1.3.4)$$

Since $i^2(t)$ and $v^2(t)$ are always greater than zero, Eq. 1.3.4 indicates energy always flows into a resistive element with positive resistance.

### Energy Stored in a Capacitor

For a linear time-invariant capacitor we have the voltage-current relationship

$$i(t) = C\frac{dv(t)}{dt} \qquad E = v \cdot i \qquad (1.3.5)$$

which gives the energy flowing into the capacitor:

$$E[t_0, t_1] = C \int_{t_0}^{t_1} \frac{dv(t)}{dt} v(t)\,dt \qquad (1.3.6)$$

With a simple change of variables we can write

$$E(t_0, t_1) = C \int_{v(t_0)}^{v(t_1)} v \, dv \tag{1.3.7}$$

or

$$E[t_0, t_1] = \frac{C}{2} [v^2(t_1) - v^2(t_0)] \tag{1.3.8}$$

Hence

$$E(t_0, t_1) = E(t_1) - E(t_0) \tag{1.3.9}$$

where $E(t_1) \triangleq \frac{1}{2} Cv^2(t_1)$ is the energy stored in the capacitor at time $t_1$ and $E(t_0) \triangleq \frac{1}{2} Cv^2(t_0)$ is the initial stored energy. Thus the energy flow into the capacitor can be positive or negative depending on whether or not $v^2(t_1) > v^2(t_0)$. If $v^2(t_1) < v^2(t_0)$, Eq. 1.3.8 indicates that over the interval $(t_0, t_1)$ the capacitor had a net flow of energy out from its terminals.

**Energy Stored in an Inductor**

For a linear time-invariant inductor

$$v(t) = L \frac{di(t)}{dt} \qquad L \int_{i(t_0)}^{i(t)} i \, di \tag{1.3.10}$$

which gives the energy flow into the inductor over the interval $(t_0, t_1)$ as

$$E(t_0, t_1) = L \int_{t_0}^{t_1} \frac{di(t)}{dt} i(t) \, dt = \frac{L}{2} [i^2(t_1) - i^2(t_0)] \tag{1.3.11}$$

Thus, depending on the relative values of $i^2(t_1)$ and $i^2(t_0)$, the net flow of energy over the interval $(t_0, t_1)$ can be either into or out of the inductive element. A negative $E(t_0, t_1)$ indicates that energy flows out of the terminals of the inductor under consideration.

In summary, energy flow is always into a resistive element with positive resistance indicating the resistor always absorbs electrical energy and dissipates it in the form of heat. Inductors and capacitors, on the other hand, can have energy flow out of their terminals when the energy stored in the magnetic or electric fields is released.

**Computation of Energy Using a Digital Computer**

We have seen above that the computation of energy requires a solution of the integral of the type

$$E(t_0, t_1) = \int_{t_0}^{t_1} v(t) i(t) \, dt \tag{1.3.12}$$

In the simple examples worked out above it was easy to compute this integral by analytical means. In many practical problems, however, the analytical solution of Eq. 1.3.12 is rather difficult and sometimes impossible. As an example let us compute the energy stored on a capacitor whose $q$-$v$ characteristics are given by

$$q = 1 + e^{\sin v}$$

The current through this capacitor is given by

$$i(t) = \frac{dq}{dt} = \cos v e^{\sin v} \frac{dv}{dt}$$

Consequently the amount of energy required to charge this capacitor from $v(t_0) = 1$ volt to $v(t_1) = 2$ volts is given by

$$E(t_0, t_1) = \int_1^2 v \cos v e^{\sin v} \, dv$$

The analytic solution of the above integral is not simple (try it!). In such situations we must resort to numerical methods to obtain an approximate solution of this integral. With the advent of digital computers this has become a relatively easy task and the integral can be computed with any desired accuracy.

We can rewrite Eq. 1.3.12 as

$$E(t_0, t_1) = \int_{t_0}^{t_1} f(t) \, dt \tag{1.3.13}$$

The right-hand side of Eq. 1.3.13 which is a *definite integral* can be easily programmed on a digital computer. There are a number of ways of numerically evaluating an integral but the one which is quite satisfactory for our purposes and which will be discussed here is Simpson's Rule of Integration. After discussing this, we will develop a computer program that carries out this integration.

### Simpson's Rule of Integration, a Numerical Method for Evaluation of a Definite Integral

Evaluation of the integral of Eq. 1.3.13 amounts to finding the area under the curve $f(t)$ from $t = t_0$ to $t = t_1$. We can divide the interval $(t_0, t_1)$ into $N$ equal intervals $(0, H), (H, 2H), \ldots, \{(N-1)H, NH\}$. Then we can write

$$\to T_2\left(\frac{N-2}{2}\right) + 2 = T_N$$

$$I = \int_{t_0}^{t_1} f(t) \, dt = \sum_{i=0}^{N/2-1} \int_{T_{2i}}^{T_{2i+2}} f(t) \, dt$$

where $T_0 = t_0$, $T_N = t_1$, and $N$ is even. Now we consider

$$I_i \triangleq \int_{T_{2i}}^{T_{2i+2}} f(t) \, dt \tag{1.3.14}$$

Let $f(t)$ be as shown in Fig. 1.3.2, choose any of these subintervals, say, $(T_{2i}, T_{2i+2})$.

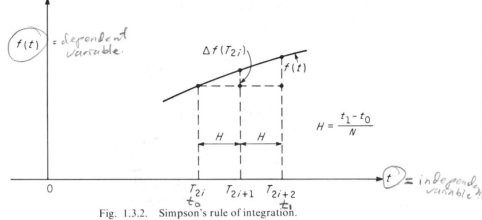

Fig. 1.3.2.   Simpson's rule of integration.

We can write for $T_{2i} < t < T_{2i+2}$:

$$f(t) \cong f(T_{2i}) + \frac{\Delta f(T_{2i})}{H}(t - T_{2i}) + \frac{\Delta^2 f(T_{2i})}{2H^2}$$
$$\cdot (t - T_{2i})(t - T_{2i+1}) \tag{1.3.15}$$

Substituting this $f(t)$ in $I_i$ and evaluating the integral, we get

$$I_i = H[2f(T_{2i}) + 2\Delta f(T_{2i}) + \tfrac{1}{3}\Delta^2 f(T_{2i})] \tag{1.3.16}$$

Where:

$$\Delta f(2T_i) = f(T_{2i+1}) - f(T_{2i}) \tag{1.3.17}$$
$$\Delta^2 f(2T_i) = f(T_{2i+2}) - 2f(T_{2i+1}) + f(T_{2i}) \tag{1.3.18}$$

Hence

$$I_i = \frac{H}{3}[f(T_{2i}) + 4f(T_{2i+1}) + f(T_{2i+2})] \tag{1.3.19}$$

Substituting in the original equation,

$$I = \int_{t_0}^{t_1} f(t)\,dt$$

$$= \sum_{i=0}^{N/2-1} I_i$$

$$\cong \sum_{i=0}^{N/2-1} \frac{H}{3}[f(T_{2i}) + 4f(T_{2i+1}) + f(T_{2i+2})] \tag{1.3.20}$$

where $t_0 = T_0$ and $t_1 = T_N$, $N$ being even.  Also $T_N = T_0 + HN$.

### Development of the Flow Chart for Computer Computation of a Definite Integral

From Eq. (1.3.20) we note that we need to know $T_0$, $T_N$, $H$, $N$ and $f(t)$ to evaluate the integral $I$. We also note that the term $f(T_{2i}) + 4f(T_{2i+1}) + f(T_{2i+2})$ is repetitive—that is, we have to compute it for each $i$ and hence can be done by a DO loop. We let

$$TA = T_{2i}$$
$$TB = T_{2i+1}$$
$$TC = T_{2i+2}$$

$SUM$ = Value of the integral (VIN) without $\dfrac{H}{3}$ factor

Before we start, $SUM = 0$. For the first period $i = 0$; that means $TA =$

Flow Chart of Integration Program

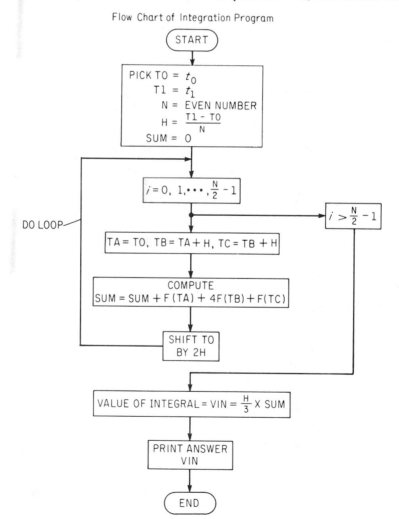

$TO$, $TB = TO + H = TA + H$, $TC = TO + 2H = TB + H$.   For the next period $i = 1$, we have to shift $TA$, $TB$, and $TC$ by $2H$.   We continue to do this until $i = N/2 - 1$.   Thus we have the flow chart as above.

The computer program based on the above flow chart is given below. Note that $C$ stands for the comment card inserted for better understanding of the computer program.

Computer Program for the Evaluation of a Definite Integral

```
C       THIS PROGRAM COMPUTES A DEFINITE INTEGRAL
C       USING SIMPSON'S RULE OF INTEGRATION,
C       CHOOSE N AS AN EVEN NUMBER,  NOTE THAT N
C       IS RESERVED FOR INTEGER NUMBERS IN FORTRAN
C       SO WE LET N = AN,
        THIS PART COMPUTES THE VALUE OF THE INTEGRAL(VIN)
        N = CHOSEN NUMBER
        AN = N
        TO = LOWER LIMIT OF THE INTEGRAL
        T1 = UPPER LIMIT OF THE INTEGRAL
C       THE FOLLOWING SECTION DEFINES THE FIRST TWO
C       BOXES OF THE FLOWCHART,
        H = (T1-TO)/AN
        SUM = 0,
        TA = TO
        TB = TA+H
        TC = TB+H
C       FTA IS THE GIVEN INTEGRAND F(T),T BEING REPLACED BY TA
C       SIMILARLY FTB AND FTC
C       THE FOLLOWING SECTION IS THE DO LOOP,
        M = N/2
        DO 10 I=1,M
        FTA = F(T), T REPLACED BY TA
        FTB = F(T), T REPLACED BY TB
        FTC = F(T), T REPLACED BY TC
        SUM = SUM+FTA+4,*FTB+FTC
        TA = TA+2,0*H
        TB = TA+H
        TC = TB+H
10      CONTINUE
C       THIS PART COMPUTES THE INTEGRAL AND PRINTS IT,
        VIN = SUM*H/3,
        PRINT 15,VIN
15      FORMAT (5X,'VIN IS ',F10,6,/)
        END
```

*Example 1.3.1*

Use the computer program to find the energy delivered to a linear time-invariant capacitor with capacitance $C = 1f$ from $t_0$ to $t_1$ if

(a)   $v(t) = t$,   $t_0 = 0$,   $t_1 = 5$ sec

(b)   $v(t) = te^{-t^2}$,   $t_0 = 0$,   $t_1 = 2$ sec

*Solution*

(a)   The current through this capacitor is given by

$$i(t) = C\frac{dv}{dt} = 1 \text{ amp}$$

Therefore

$$E(0, 5) = \int_0^5 t \, dt = \frac{25}{2} = 12.5 \text{ joules}$$

In this case the answer is trivial, however, let us use the computer program where we let $N = 10$. The result is easily obtained as given in the printout.

```
C       THIS PROGRAM IS FOR EXAMPLE 1.3-1A
C       THIS PROGRAM COMPUTES A DEFINITE INTEGRAL
C       USING SIMPSON'S RULE OF INTEGRATION.
C       CHOOSE N AS AN EVEN NUMBER.  NOTE THAT N
C       IS RESERVED FOR INTEGER NUMBERS IN FORTRAN
C       SO WE LET N = AN.
        N = 10
        AN = N
        T0= 0.
        T1 = 5.
C       THE FOLLOWING SECTION DEFINES THE FIRST TWO
C       BOXES OF THE FLOWCHART.
        H = (T1-T0)/AN
        SUM = 0.
        TA = T0
        TB = TA+H
        TC = TB+H
C       FTA IS THE GIVEN INTEGRAND F(T),T BEING REPLACED BY TA
C       SIMILARLY FTB AND FTC
C       THE FOLLOWING SECTION IS THE DO LOOP.
        M = N/2
        DO 10 I=1,M
        FTA = TA
        FTB = TB
        FTC = TC
        SUM   = SUM+FTA+4.*FTB+FTC
        TA = TA+2.0*H
        TB = TA+H
        TC = TB+H
   10 CONTINUE
C       THIS PART COMPUTES THE INTEGRAL AND PRINTS IT.
        VIN = SUM*H/3.
        PRINT 15,VIN
   15 FORMAT (5X,'VIN(JOULES) IS',F10.6/)
        END
```

```
        VIN(JOULES) IS 12.500000
```

(b)   Here again

$$i(t) = C \frac{dv}{dt} = e^{-t^2} + t e^{-t^2}(-2t) = e^{-t^2} - 2t^2 e^{-t^2} \text{ amp}$$

Hence

$$E(0, 2) = \int_0^2 e^{-2t^2}[t - 2t^3] \, dt$$

It is quite clear that here the Simpson's Rule of Integration offers a decided advantage because we cannot easily evaluate the integral exactly. We will use the computer program and assume $N = 16$.

```
C       THIS PROGRAM IS FOR EXAMPLE 1,3-1B
C       THIS PROGRAM COMPUTES A DEFINITE INTEGRAL
C       USING SIMPSON'S RULE OF INTEGRATION
C       CHOOSE N AS AN EVEN NUMBER,  NOTE THAT N
C       IS RESERVED FOR INTEGER NUMBERS IN FORTRAN
C       SO WE LET N = AN,
        N=16
        AN = N
        TO=0,
        T1=2,
C       THE FOLLOWING SECTION DEFINES THE FIRST TWO
C       BOXES OF THE FLOWCHART,
        H = (T1=T0)/AN
        SUM = 0,
        TA = TO
        TB = TA+H
        TC = TB+H
C       FTA IS THE GIVEN INTEGRAND F(T),T BEING REPLACED BY TA
C       SIMILARLY FTB AND FTC
C       THE FOLLOWING SECTION IS THE DO LOOP,
        M = N/2
        DO 10 I=1,M
        FTA = EXP(=2,*TA**2)*(TA=2,*TA**3)
        FTB = EXP(=2,*TB**2)*(TB=2,*TB**3)
        FTC = EXP(=2,*TC**2)*(TC=2,*TC**3)
        SUM  = SUM+FTA+4,*FTB+FTC
        TA = TA+2,0*H
        TB = TA+H
        TC = TB+H
     10 CONTINUE
C       THIS PART COMPUTES THE INTEGRAL AND PRINTS IT,
        VIN = SUM*H/3,
        PRINT 15,VIN
     15 FORMAT (5X,'VIN(JOULES) IS',F10,6/)
        END



        VIN(JOULES) IS   ,000706
```

*Example 1.3.2*

A linear time-invariant resistor of 4 Ω has a current through it given by $i(t) = \sin \pi t$. If $E(0) = 0$, find the energy dissipated in the resistor at $t = 1, 2, 3, 4, 5, 6$ sec, using the computer program.

*Solution*

Using Eq. 1.3.4, we have

$$E(t) = R \int_0^t i^2(t)\,dt = 4 \int_0^t \sin^2 \pi t\,dt$$

For using the computer program we note that

$$f(t) = \sin^2 \pi t$$
$$T0. = 0$$
$$T1 = t$$

We can choose $N = 16$. However, T1 is now not fixed so the above integral is *indefinite*. We can overcome the difficulty by having a DO loop around the total computer program developed earlier. We can insert cards

DO 14 J = 1,6

AJ = J

T1 = AJ

14 CONTINUE

We can also print T1 as well as the value of the integral. So the new print and formal cards are

PRINT 15, T1, VIN

15 FORMAT (5X, 'T1(SEC)IS', F10.6,' VIN (JOULES)IS', F10.6/)

Now we have the computer program of an indefinite integral and the results as given below.

Computer Program for Evaluation of an Indefinite Integral—an Example

```
c       THIS PROGRAM IS FOR EXAMPLE 1,3=2
c       THIS PROGRAM EVALUATES AN INTEGRAL WITH VARYING UPPER
c       LIMITS USING SIMPSON'S RULE OF INTEGRATION,
c       CHOOSE N AS AN EVEN NUMBER,  NOTE THAT N
c       IS RESERVED FOR INTEGER NUMBERS IN FORTRAN
c       SO WE LET N = AN,
        N=16
        AN=N
c       NOW WE HAVE THE DO LOOP FOR VARYING T1, THE
c       UPPER LIMIT
        DO 14 J=1,6
        T1=AJ
        AJ=J
        T0=0,
c       THE FOLLOWING SECTION DEFINES THE FIRST TWO
c       BOXES OF THE FLOWCHART,
        H = (T1-T0)/AN
        SUM = 0,
        TA = TO
        TB = TA+H
        TC = TB+H
c       FTA IS THE GIVEN INTEGRAND F(T),T BEING REPLACED BY TA
c       SIMILARLY FTB AND FTC
c       THE FOLLOWING SECTION IS THE DO LOOP,
        M = N/2
        DO 10 I=1,M
        PI=3,14159
        FTA=SIN(PI*TA)**2
        FTB=SIN(PI*TB)**2
        FTC=SIN(PI*TC)**2
```

```
     SUM  = SUM+FTA+4.*FTB+FTC
     TA = TA+2.0*H
     TB = TA+H
     TC = TB+H
  10 CONTINUE
C    THIS PART COMPUTES THE INTEGRAL AND PRINTS IT.
     VIN = SUM*H/3.
     PRINT 15,T1,VIN
  14 CONTINUE
  15 FORMAT (5X,'T1(SEC) IS',F10.6,
    13X,'VIN(JOULES) IS ',F10.6/)
     END
```

```
     T1(SEC) IS    .000000    VIN(JOULES) IS     .000000

     T1(SEC) IS   1.000000    VIN(JOULES) IS     .500000

     T1(SEC) IS   2.000000    VIN(JOULES) IS    1.000001

     T1(SEC) IS   3.000000    VIN(JOULES) IS    1.500001

     T1(SEC) IS   4.000000    VIN(JOULES) IS    2.000002

     T1(SEC) IS   5.000000    VIN(JOULES) IS    2.500002
```

## 1.4. OTHER CIRCUIT ELEMENTS

Not all physical devices can be described in terms of the three circuit elements we have discussed thus far. For example, we have not presented any element which represents a source of electrical energy. In order to model physical devices which are sources of electrical energy, we consider ideal voltage and current sources.

*DEFINITION.* An *ideal voltage source* is a two terminal element which maintains a terminal voltage $v(t)$ regardless of the value of the current flowing through its terminals.

Such a device is represented schematically as shown in Fig. 1.4.1a and b. Note that it is customary to take the associated current direction flowing *out of the* + (*plus*) terminal. A *v-i* plot of the terminal voltage-

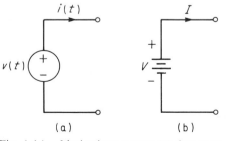

(a)                         (b)

Fig. 1.4.1.   Ideal voltage source: (a) time-varying, (b) time-invariant.

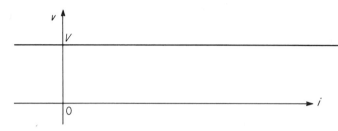

Fig. 1.4.2.   *v-i* characteristic of an ideal voltage source.

current relationship for an ideal voltage source is shown in Fig. 1.4.2. At any instant, the value of the terminal voltage is a constant with respect to the current value *i*. Whenever $v = 0$, the voltage source *v-i* characteristic is the same as that of a *short circuit*.

*DEFINITION.* An *ideal current source* is a two-terminal element which maintains a current $i(t)$ flowing through its terminals regardless of the value of the terminal voltage.

An ideal current source is represented schematically in Fig. 1.4.3.

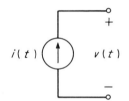

Fig. 1.4.3.   Ideal current source.

Again, as with the ideal voltage source, the associated current-voltage sign convention is such that the current flows out of the terminal marked $+$. The *v-i* characteristic of an ideal current source is shown in Fig. 1.4.4 which at any instant is simply a vertical line at $i = I$. When $I = 0$, the ideal current source has the same *v-i* characteristic as an *open circuit*.

In describing the circuit elements $R$, $L$, $C$ and ideal sources, we have limited our discussion to a special class of circuit elements: the class of elements with two terminals or *one-port* devices. Other types of circuit elements are available; for example, the *transformer* element shown in Fig. 1.4.5. A time-varying current, $i_1(t)$, flowing in winding 1 establishes a time-varying magnetic flux in the transformer core. This flux links winding 2 thus establishing a voltage $v_2$. The transformer shown in Fig. 1.4.5 has four terminals or *two ports* and could be expanded to include more terminals by simply adding additional windings.

A mathematical description of the voltage-current terminal relationships for the transformer are developed by considering the flux linkage

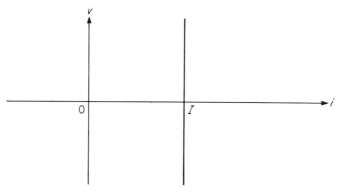

Fig. 1.4.4.    *v-i* characteristic of an ideal current source.

associated with the various windings. If we consider the two port transformer of Fig. 1.4.5, the total flux linking winding 1, $\phi_1$, can be visualized as being the sum of two components

$$\phi_1 = \phi_{11} \pm \phi_{12} \qquad (1.4.1)$$

$\phi_{11}$ being the flux linking winding 1 due to the current in winding 1, and $\phi_{12}$ being the flux linking winding 1 due to the current in winding 2. In Eq. 1.4.1 plus sign is adopted if the windings are in the same directions and the minus sign is adopted if the windings are in opposite directions. Similarly we can write the total flux linking winding 2, $\phi_2$, as the sum of two components

$$\phi_2 = \phi_{22} \pm \phi_{21} \qquad (1.4.2)$$

where $\phi_{22}$ is the flux linking winding 2 due to the current in winding 2 and $\phi_{21}$ is the flux linking winding 2 due to the current in winding 1. We note that the flux terms $\phi_{12}$ and $\phi_{21}$ may either reinforce or oppose the flux terms $\phi_{11}$ and $\phi_{22}$, respectively, depending on the physical relationships of the transformer winding. Hence $\phi_{12}$ and $\phi_{21}$ have algebraic signs, i.e., can be either a positive or negative quantity. As in the case of a linear

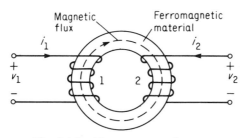

Fig. 1.4.5.    Elementary transformer.

inductor, we write the flux terms $\phi_{11}$ and $\phi_{22}$ as

$$\phi_{11} = L_1 i_1$$

and                                                                                                (1.4.3)

$$\phi_{22} = L_2 i_2$$

where $L_1$ and $L_2$ are called the *self-inductance* of winding 1 and winding 2, respectively.  The cross-flux terms $\phi_{21}$ and $\phi_{12}$ are written in a similar fashion:

$$\phi_{12} = M i_2$$

and                                                                                                (1.4.4)

$$\phi_{21} = M i_1$$

where $M$ is called the *mutual inductance* of the transformer and has units of henries but may be either positive or negative.  Since the voltages $v_1$ and $v_2$ are the time derivatives of the total flux in windings 1 and 2, respectively, we have from Eqs. 1.4.1 through 1.4.4

$$v_1 = \frac{d\phi_1}{dt} = L_1 \frac{di_1}{dt} \pm M \frac{di_2}{dt}$$

$$v_2 = \frac{d\phi_2}{dt} = \pm M \frac{di_1}{dt} + L_2 \frac{di_2}{dt}$$

(1.4.5)

Equation 1.4.5 represents the mathematical description of a transformer in terms of its terminal voltage-current characteristics.  When a transformer is used in developing a physical circuit, the quantities $L_1$, $L_2$, and $M$ are specified by the transformer manufacturer or alternatively can be measured in the laboratory.

The schematic representation of a transformer is shown in Fig. 1.4.6. Since it is not feasible to indicate the winding directions in such a diagram, a *dot convention* is employed to indicate whether the mutual inductance is positive or negative.  By convention, the mutual inductance is taken to be positive when both currents are directed either toward or away from the dotted terminal, and is negative when one current is directed toward the

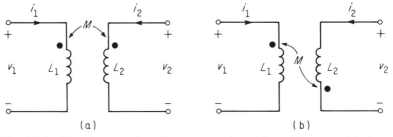

Fig. 1.4.6.  Transformer schematic representation: (a) positive mutual inductance, (b) negative mutual inductance.

dotted terminal and the other away from the dotted terminal. Thus in Fig. 1.4.6a the mutual inductance is positive while in Fig. 1.4.6b the mutual inductance is negative. Hence for Fig. 1.4.6a we have

$$v_1 = L_1 \frac{di_1}{dt} + M \frac{di_2}{dt}$$

$$v_2 = M \frac{di_1}{dt} + L_2 \frac{di_2}{dt}$$

$$(1.4.6)$$

and for the transformer shown in Fig. 1.4.6b we get

$$v_1 = L_1 \frac{di_1}{dt} - M \frac{di_2}{dt}$$

$$v_2 = -M \frac{di_1}{dt} + L_2 \frac{di_2}{dt}$$

$$(1.4.7)$$

There are other examples of two-port elements. A *gyrator* is a two-port circuit element which is represented schematically as shown in Fig. 1.4.7. The gyrator terminal voltage-current relationships are

$$v_1 = \alpha i_2$$

$$v_2 = -\alpha i_1$$

$$(1.4.8)$$

where $\alpha$ is a constant called the gyration constant.

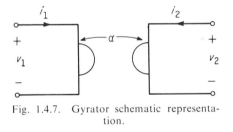

Fig. 1.4.7. Gyrator schematic representation.

Another important class of two-terminal elements are dependent sources. A *dependent voltage source* is a two-port circuit element whose voltage depends on the voltage or current of another circuit element. A *dependent current source* is a two-terminal element whose current depends on the current or the voltage of another circuit element. These dependent sources are usually used in electronic circuits which contain *transistors*. Figure 1.4.8 shows the schematic representation of a dependent voltage source.

So far we have considered only linear time-invariant resistors, capacitors, and inductors. In many practical applications, however, nonlinear and time-varying elements are found to be useful. In the next two sections we give a brief discussion of nonlinear and time-varying elements. The

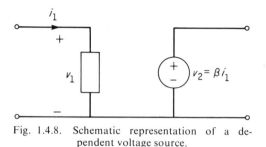

Fig. 1.4.8.   Schematic representation of a dependent voltage source.

emphasis will be mainly on their definitions and classifications. In future chapters we further discuss their properties and some of their applications.

### 1.5. NONLINEAR TWO-TERMINAL ELEMENTS

In this section we define nonlinear resistors, capacitors, and inductors in a precise manner and their voltage-current relationships.

**Nonlinear Resistors**

For our purposes we classify the nonlinear resistors into two categories, current-controlled resistors and voltage-controlled resistors.

A two-terminal element is said to be a *current-controlled* resistor if its

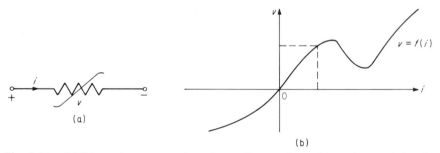

Fig. 1.5.1.   (a) Schematic representation of a nonlinear resistor, (b) $v$-$i$ characteristic of a typical nonlinear resistor.

terminal voltage is a single-valued function of its terminal current:

$$v = f(i) \qquad (1.5.1)$$

where $v$ denotes the terminal voltage and $i$ the terminal current, $f(i)$ is single-valued if to each $i$ there corresponds exactly one $v$ (see Fig. 1.5.1b).

Figure 1.5.1a shows a nonlinear resistor and Fig. 1.5.1b shows the $v$-$i$ characteristic of a typical nonlinear current-controlled resistor. There are numerous applications for such elements, some of which will be mentioned in future chapters.

A two-terminal element is said to be a *voltage-controlled* resistor if its terminal current is a single-valued function of its terminal voltage, i.e.,

$$i = g(v) \tag{1.5.2}$$

A typical example of a nonlinear voltage-controlled resistor is a *tunnel diode*. The *v-i* characteristic of such a diode is given in Fig. 1.5.2; tunnel diodes are used extensively in *electronic amplifiers* and *oscillators*.

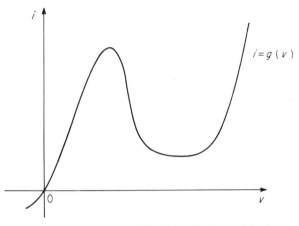

Fig. 1.5.2.    *v-i* characteristic of a typical tunnel diode.

It should be mentioned that a resistor can be both voltage-controlled and current-controlled. An example of such a resistor is the *pn-junction diode* whose terminal current $i(t)$ is given in terms of its terminal voltage $v(t)$ by

$$i(t) = \alpha(e^{\beta v(t)} - 1) \tag{1.5.3}$$

and its terminal voltage is given in terms of its terminal current by

$$v(t) = \frac{1}{\beta} \log\left(\frac{1}{\alpha} i(t) + 1\right) \tag{1.5.4}$$

The *i-v* characteristic of this diode is given in Fig. 1.5.3. In general, we can say that a nonlinear resistor is both voltage-controlled and current-controlled if its *v-i* or *i-v* characteristic is a monotonically increasing function. A special case of this nonlinear resistor is a linear resistor, since its *v-i* characteristic is a straight line through the origin with slope $R$. Properties of such a resistor were discussed in Sec. 1.2.

### Energy Dissipated in a Nonlinear Resistor

In order to compute the energy dissipated in a resistor we need to consider the expression for the instantaneous power

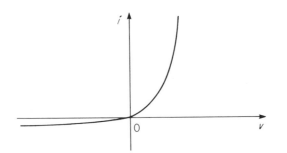

Fig. 1.5.3.   *i-v* characteristic of a *pn*-junction diode.

$$p(t) = v(t)i(t) \qquad (1.5.5)$$

For a voltage-controlled resistor, we have

$$i = g(v) \qquad (1.5.6)$$

and for a current-controlled resistor we have

$$v = f(i) \qquad (1.5.7)$$

Hence for these two cases respectively the instantaneous power becomes

$$p(t) = v(t)g[v(t)] \qquad (1.5.8)$$

and

$$p(t) = f[i(t)]i(t)$$

Concentrating on the current-controlled case, we will have a *v-i* characteristic such as shown in Fig. 1.5.4.  For any value of the current $i(t)$ we

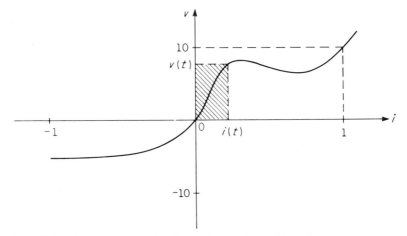

Fig. 1.5.4.   Current-controlled resistor characteristic with instantaneous power indicated.

find the instantaneous voltage value $v(t)$ on the characteristic curve. The instantaneous power $v(t)i(t)$ is then just the shaded rectangular area shown in Fig. 1.5.4. Knowing $i(t)$, it becomes possible to compute values for $v(t)i(t)$. For example, Fig. 1.5.5a shows a triangular current waveform applied to the current-controlled resistor of Fig. 1.5.4. The resulting voltage waveform is shown in Fig. 1.5.5b, and the instantaneous power is shown in Fig. 1.5.5c. Now to compute the energy dissipated in the resistor over a given interval $(t_0, t_1)$ all we have to do is to evaluate the area under

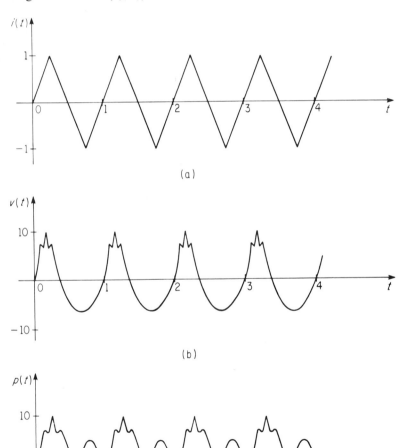

(a)

(b)

(c)

Fig. 1.5.5.   Plot of $i(t)$, $v(t)$, $p(t)$.

$p(t)$ over this interval. This evaluation can be done graphically or by use of a digital computer.

### Nonlinear Capacitors

In this case also we can classify nonlinear capacitors in two categories, voltage-controlled and charge-controlled.

A two-terminal element is said to be a *voltage-controlled* capacitor if the charge on it is a single-valued function of the voltage across it, i.e.,

$$q = f(v) \tag{1.5.9}$$

where $q$ is the charge in coulombs and $v$ is the voltage in volts. Figure 1.5.6a shows a nonlinear capacitor and Fig. 1.5.6b shows the $q$-$v$ characteristics of a voltage-controlled capacitor.

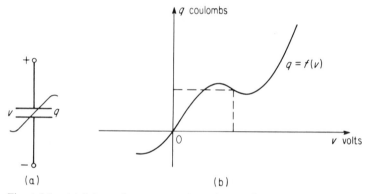

Fig. 1.5.6.   (a) Schematic representation of a nonlinear capacitor, (b) $q$-$v$ characteristic of a voltage controlled capacitor.

A two-terminal element is said to be a *charge-controlled* capacitor if the voltage across it is a single-valued function of the charge on it, i.e.,

$$v = g(q) \tag{1.5.10}$$

Figure 1.5.7 shows the $q$-$v$ characteristic of a charge-controlled capacitor.

As in the case of nonlinear resistors, there are nonlinear capacitors that are both charge-controlled and voltage-controlled. In this case, if the charge is given as a function of the voltage, then the voltage can be found as a function of the charge simply by inverting the function.

*Example 1.5.1*

Assume that a nonlinear capacitor is defined by

$$q = \alpha e^{\beta v}$$

This capacitor is both voltage-controlled and charge-controlled, since the

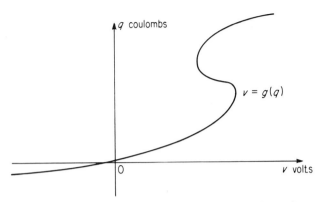

Fig. 1.5.7.    *q-v* characteristic of a charge-controlled capacitor.

voltage *v* can be written as a *unique* function of *q*, i.e.,

$$\frac{1}{\alpha} q = e^{\beta v}$$

or

$$\log \frac{1}{\alpha} q = \beta v$$

hence

$$v = \frac{1}{\beta} \log \frac{1}{\alpha} q$$

In general, if the *q-v* curve of a nonlinear capacitor is monotonically increasing the capacitor is both voltage-controlled and charge-controlled.

### Voltage-Current Relation of a Nonlinear Capacitor

In the beginning of this chapter we mentioned that the current through a capacitor is given by the derivative of the charge across it, i.e.,

$$i(t) = \frac{d}{dt} q(t) \qquad (1.5.11)$$

This equation is quite general; it holds for linear, nonlinear, and time-varying capacitors.

In the case of nonlinear capacitors, since *q* is usually given as a function of the voltage, we must use the chain rule for evaluating the current through the capacitors, i.e., Eq. 1.5.11 can be written as

$$i(t) = \frac{d}{dt} f(v(t)) \qquad (1.5.12)$$

Using the chain rule we get

$$i(t) = \frac{df(v)}{dv} \cdot \frac{dv}{dt}$$
(1.5.13)

*Example 1.5.2*

Consider a nonlinear capacitor which is defined by

$$q = v + \frac{1}{3}v^3$$

Let the voltage across this capacitor be

$$v(t) = \sin t$$

Find the current through this capacitor (see Fig. 1.5.8).

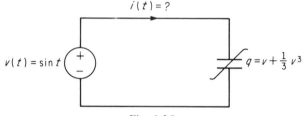

Fig. 1.5.8.

*Solution*

We have

$$f(v) = v + \frac{1}{3}v^3$$

then

$$\frac{df(v)}{dv} = 1 + v^2$$

and

$$\frac{dv}{dt} = \cos t$$

Then from Eq. 1.5.13 we get

$$i(t) = (1 + v^2) \cdot \cos t$$

and by substituting for $v$ we have

$$i(t) = (1 + \sin^2 t) \cos t$$

### Energy Stored in a Nonlinear Capacitor

Earlier in this chapter we mentioned that the energy delivered to a capacitor in the time interval $(t_0, t)$ is given by

$$E(t_0, t) = \int_{t_0}^{t} v(\sigma)i(\sigma)\,d\sigma$$

or equivalently

$$E(t) = \int_{t_0}^{t} v(\sigma)i(\sigma)\,d\sigma + E(t_0) \tag{1.5.14}$$

where $E(t)$ is the energy stored at time $t$, $E(t_0)$ is the initial stored energy, $v(t)$ is the voltage across the capacitor and $i(t)$ is the current through it. We can replace $i(t)$ in Eq. 1.5.14 by $i(t)$ given in Eq. 1.5.12 and, for the moment, assume that the initial stored energy is zero, i.e., $E(t_0) = 0$. Then Eq. 1.5.14 becomes

$$E(t) = \int_{t_0}^{t} v(\sigma) \cdot \frac{df(v)}{d\sigma} \cdot d\sigma \tag{1.5.15}$$

By a simple change of variable we get

$$E(t) = \int_{v(t_0)}^{v(t)} v\,df(v) \tag{1.5.16}$$

Equation 1.5.16 has a simple interpretation. Consider the $q$-$v$ curve of the nonlinear capacitor shown in Fig. 1.5.9; $v\,df(v)$ is the narrow strip shown. The energy delivered to the capacitor from $t_0$ to $t$ is then equal to the shaded area. The numerical value of the energy delivered to the capacitor from $t_0$ to $t$ is the same as the area of the shaded region.

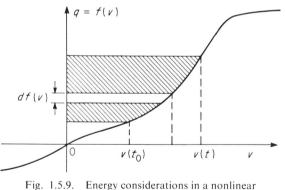

Fig. 1.5.9.    Energy considerations in a nonlinear capacitor.

*Example 1.5.3*

Find the energy required to charge a nonlinear capacitor from $v(t_0) = 1$ volt to $v(t) = 3$ volts if the $q$-$v$ relationship of the capacitor is given by

$$q = v + \tanh v$$

Use the integration computer program developed previously.

*Solution*

We use Eq. 1.5.16 to write

$$E(t_0, t) = \int_{v(t_0)}^{v(t)} v\, d[f(v)]$$

where

$$f(v) = v + \tanh v$$

We get

$$E(t_0, t) = \int_{1}^{3} v[1 + \text{sech}^2 v]\, dv$$

The integral is programmed easily if we let

$$t_0 = 1$$
$$t_1 = 3$$

and

$$f(t) = \text{integrand with } v \text{ replaced by } t$$
$$= t[1 + \text{sech}^2 t]$$

The computer program and the result is given below.

```
C        THIS PROGRAM IS FOR EXAMPLE 1,5=3
C        THIS PROGRAM COMPUTES A DEFINITE INTEGRAL
C        USING SIMPSON'S RULE OF INTEGRATION,
C        CHOOSE N AS AN EVEN NUMBER,  NOTE THAT N
C        IS RESERVED FOR INTEGER NUMBERS IN FORTRAN
C        SO WE LET N = AN,
         N=10
         AN=N
         T0=1,
         T1=3,
C        THE FOLLOWING SECTION DEFINES THE FIRST TWO
C        BOXES OF THE FLOWCHART,
         H = (T1=T0)/AN
         SUM = 0,
         TA = T0
         TB = TA+H
         TC = TB+H
C        FTA IS THE GIVEN INTEGRAND F(T),T BEING REPLACED BY TA
C        SIMILARLY FTB AND FTC
C        THE FOLLOWING SECTION IS THE DO LOOP,
         M = N/2
         DO 10 I=1,M
         FTA=TA*(1+1/COSH(TA)**2)
         FTB=TB*(1+1/COSH(TB)**2)
         FTC=TC*(1+1/COSH(TC)**2)
         SUM  = SUM+FTA+4,*FTB+FTC
         TA = TA+2,0*H
         TB = TA+H
         TC = TB+H
      10 CONTINUE
C        THIS PART COMPUTES THE INTEGRAL AND PRINTS IT,
```

```
      VIN = SUM*H/3,
      PRINT 15,VIN
   15 FORMAT (5X,'VIN(JOULES) IS',F10,6/)
      END
```

        VIN(JOULES) IS  4,34799A

## Nonlinear Inductor

A two terminal inductor is said to be nonlinear if $\phi$ is a nonlinear function of $i$, i.e.,

$$\phi = f(i) \tag{1.5.17}$$

where $\phi$ is the flux and $i$ is the current through the inductor. Figure 1.5.10a shows the symbol of a nonlinear inductor and Fig. 1.5.10b shows

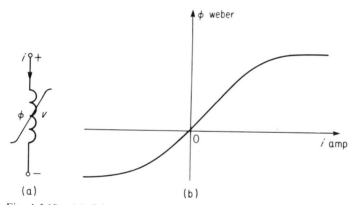

(a)  (b)

Fig. 1.5.10.  (a) Schematic representation of a nonlinear inductor,
(b) $\phi$-$i$ characteristics of a typical nonlinear inductor.

the $\phi$-$i$ curve of a typical nonlinear inductor. As in the case of nonlinear capacitors, we can define *current-controlled* or *flux-controlled* inductors. For many practical inductors, however, the $\phi$-$i$ curve is a multivalued function in both $i$ and $\phi$. This phenomenon of nonlinear inductors is called *hysteresis*. Figure 1.5.11 shows a typical hysteresis loop.

### Voltage Current Relation of a Nonlinear Inductor

In Eq. 1.2.15 the voltage across an inductor is given as the derivative of the magnetic flux with respect to time. This equation holds for linear, nonlinear, and time-varying inductors and is given by

$$v(t) = \frac{d}{dt}\phi(t) \tag{1.5.18}$$

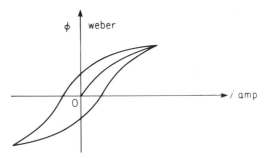

Fig. 1.5.11.   A hysteresis loop.

For a nonlinear inductor we replace $\phi(t)$ in Eq. 1.5.18 by $\phi(t)$ given in Eq. 1.5.17 to obtain

$$v(t) = \frac{d}{dt} f[i(t)] \tag{1.5.19}$$

Now by the chain rule we can write

$$v(t) = \frac{df(i)}{di} \cdot \frac{di}{dt} \tag{1.5.20}$$

*Example 1.5.4*

Consider a nonlinear inductor which is defined by

$$\phi = i + \tanh(i)$$

let the current through this inductor be

$$i(t) = \sin t$$

Find the voltage across it (see Fig. 1.5.12).

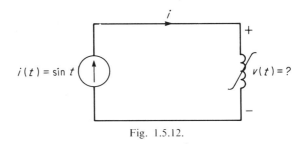

Fig. 1.5.12.

*Solution*

Here we have

$$f(i) = i + \tanh(i)$$

Therefore

$$\frac{df(i)}{di} = 1 + \text{sech}^2(i)$$

Using this result in Eq. 1.5.20 we get

$$v(t) = (1 + \text{sech}^2 i)\frac{di}{dt}$$

Now $i(t) = \sin t$; therefore $\dfrac{di}{dt} = \cos t$. Hence

$$v(t) = [1 + \text{sech}^2(\sin t)]\cos t$$

### Energy Stored in a Nonlinear Inductor

As in the case of nonlinear capacitors, the energy stored in an inductor is given by

$$E(t) = \int_{t_0}^{t} v(\sigma)i(\sigma)\,d\sigma + E(t_0) \qquad (1.5.21)$$

where $E(t)$ is the energy stored at time $t$, $E(t_0)$ is the initial stored energy, $v(t)$ is the voltage across the inductor and $i(t)$ is the current through it. Assume that $E(t_0) = 0$ and replace $v(t)$ from Eq. 1.5.19; then

$$E(t) = \int_{t_0}^{t} \frac{df(i)}{d\sigma} \cdot i(\sigma)\,d\sigma \qquad (1.5.22)$$

By a change of variable we get

$$E(t) = \int_{i(t_0)}^{i(t)} i\,df(i) \qquad (1.5.23)$$

As in the case of nonlinear capacitors, Eq. 1.5.23 can be interpreted as the numerical value of the shaded area shown in Fig. 1.5.13.

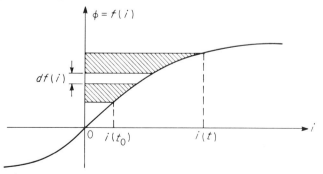

Fig. 1.5.13.   Energy considerations in a nonlinear inductor.

*REMARK.* Notice that for nonlinear elements the resistance $R$, capacitance $C$ or inductance $L$ *are not defined.*

## 1.6. LINEAR TIME-VARYING ELEMENTS

So far we have discussed only the circuit elements whose characteristics do not vary with time. There are, however, many practical circuits in which a resistor, capacitor or inductor is time varying. *Parametric amplifiers* are a good example of this case. In this section we briefly discuss the properties of a special class of time-varying elements, namely, linear time-varying two-terminal elements.

A *linear resistor* is said to be *time varying* if its resistance $R$ is a function of time, i.e.,

$$v(t) = R(t)i(t) \tag{1.6.1}$$

The $v$-$i$ characteristic of a time-varying resistor is a straight line through the origin with the slope $R(t)$. This slope varies with time (see Fig. 1.6.1).

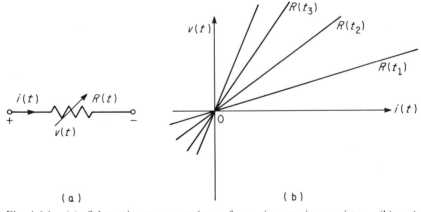

( a )                                        ( b )

Fig. 1.6.1.   (a) Schematic representation of a time-varying resistor, (b) $v$-$i$ characteristics.

A *linear capacitor* is said to be *time-varying* if its capacitance $C$ is a function of time, i.e.,

$$q(t) = C(t)v(t) \tag{1.6.2}$$

The current through a linear time-varying capacitor can be found by differentiating Eq. 1.6.2, since

$$i(t) = \frac{dq(t)}{dt}$$

then

$$i(t) = C(t)\frac{dv}{dt} + v(t)\frac{d}{dt}C(t) \qquad (1.6.3)$$

*Example 1.6.1*

Consider the capacitor shown in Fig. 1.6.2.  The capacitance $C(t)$ is given by

$$C(t) = C_0(1 + 0.5 \sin t)$$

The voltage across this capacitor is given by

$$v(t) = 2 \sin \omega t$$

Find the current through the capacitor.

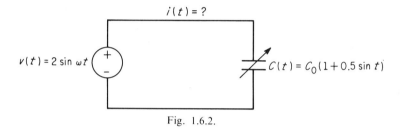

Fig. 1.6.2.

*Solution*

From Eq. 1.6.3 we get

$$i(t) = C_0(1 + 0.5 \sin t)(2\omega \cos \omega t) + (2 \sin \omega t)(0.5C_0 \cos t)$$

or

$$i(t) = 2\omega C_0 \cos \omega t (1 + 0.5 \sin t) + C_0 \sin \omega t \cos t$$

A *linear inductor* is said to be *time-varying* if its inductance $L$ is a function of time, i.e.,

$$\phi(t) = L(t)i(t) \qquad (1.6.4)$$

The voltage across a linear time-varying inductor can be found by differentiating the flux $\phi(t)$, since

$$v(t) = \frac{d\phi(t)}{dt} \qquad (1.6.5)$$

or equivalently,

$$v(t) = L(t)\frac{d}{dt}i(t) + i(t)\frac{d}{dt}L(t) \qquad (1.6.6)$$

*Example 1.6.2*

Find the voltage across an inductor, shown in Fig. 1.6.3, whose inductance is given by

$$L(t) = te^{-t} + 1$$

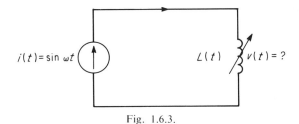

Fig. 1.6.3.

and the current through it is given by

$$i(t) = \sin \omega t$$

*Solution*

From Eq. 1.6.6 we get

$$v(t) = (1 + te^{-t})(\omega \cos \omega t) + (\sin \omega t)(e^{-t} - te^{-t})$$

or

$$v(t) = \omega \cos \omega t (1 + te^{-t}) + e^{-t} \sin \omega t (1 - t)$$

## PROBLEMS

**1.1.** In a certain linear time-invariant circuit element, 20 joules of energy is stored. Calculate the value of the element if the element is (a) an inductor carrying 2 amp of current (find $L$); (b) a capacitor with 500 volts across its terminals (find $C$).

**1.2.** For the capacitor shown, $v_C = \sin 2\pi t$. Calculate $i$ at the instants (a) $t = 0$, (b) $t = \frac{1}{4}$, (c) $t = \frac{1}{2}$, (d) $t = \frac{3}{4}$, (e) $t = \frac{7}{8}$, (f) $t = 1$.

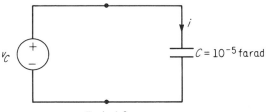

Prob. 1.2.

**1.3.** For the capacitor shown in Prob. 1.2, let $i = \sin 2\pi t$. Calculate $v_C$ at the instants (a) $t = 0$, (b) $t = \frac{1}{4}$, (c) $t = \frac{1}{2}$, (d) $t = \frac{3}{4}$, (e) $t = \frac{7}{8}$, (f) $t = 1$. Assume $v_C(0) = 0$.

**1.4.** The current through the linear time-invariant inductor shown is given by $i = \cos 2\pi t$. Calculate $v_C$ at the instants (a) $t = 0$, (b) $t = \frac{1}{4}$, (c) $t = \frac{1}{2}$, (d) $t = \frac{3}{4}$, (e) $t = \frac{7}{8}$, (f) $t = 1$.

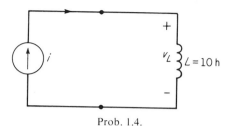

Prob. 1.4.

**1.5.** The current through the inductor of Prob. 1.4 is observed to be the function plotted here.

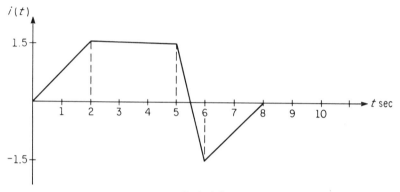

Prob. 1.5.

Plot the function $v_L(t)$ and indicate the values for (a) $t = 0^+$, (b) $t = 2^-$, (c) $t = 2^+$, (d) $t = 5.5$, (e) $t = 5.5^+$, (f) $t = 6$, (g) $t = 6.5$, (h) $t = 6.5^+$, (i) $t = 8^-$.

**1.6.** The element in the terminal pair $a$-$b$ in the figure is either an inductor or a capacitor. If $i = \cos 3t$ and $v = \sin 3t$, what is the element and its value if (a) $v = v_{ab}$; (b) $v = v_{ba}$?

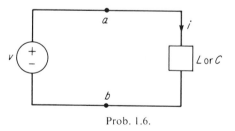

Prob. 1.6.

**1.7.** A 5-$\mu$f capacitor ($C = 5 \times 10^{-6}$) has an initial voltage of $V_0$ volts at $t = 0$ when the current waveform shown is applied. (a) Find and sketch $v_C(t)$ for (i) $V_0 = 0$, (ii) $V_0 = -5$ (iii), $V_0 = 5$. (b) Plot the power $p(t)$ for each condition i, ii, and iii. (c) Evaluate the energy stored at $t = 1, 2, \infty$ for each condition i, ii, and iii.

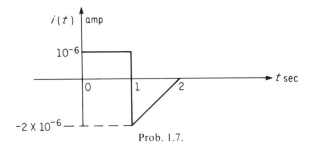

Prob. 1.7.

**1.8.** The triangular pulse shown represents the waveform of the voltage across a 0.5-h inductor. (a) Calculate and plot the current $i_L(t)$ if $i_L(0) = 0$, (b) calculate the energy stored in the inductance at $t = 1$ and at $t = \infty$. (c) Plot the power $p(t)$.

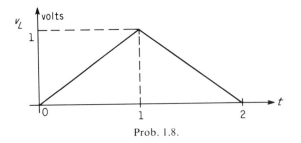

Prob. 1.8.

**1.9.** For the transformer circuit shown, let $i_1 = 10 \sin t$, $i_2 = 0$. Calculate the voltages $v_1$ and $v_2$.

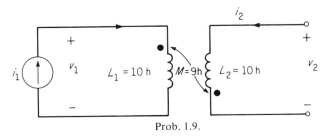

Prob. 1.9.

**1.10.** A voltage source $v(t)$ is connected to a capacitor $C = 2f$. Find the energy stored in the capacitor from $t = 0$ to $t = 10$ sec if

(a) $v(t) = t^2 e^{-2t}$   (b) $v(t) = t \sin t$   (c) $(\sin t)e^{-t}$

Use a computer program.

**1.11.** (a) The current through a linear time-invariant resistor of $2\Omega$ is given by

$i(t) = \cos^2 \pi t$.  Find the energy dissipated in the resistor starting from $t_0 = 0$ to $t_1 = 5$ sec, using a computer program.

(b) Repeat the above for $t_1 = 1, 2, 3, 4, 6$ sec.  Use a DO loop for varying the upper limit.

**1.12.** Consider the gyrator shown.  Let the gyration constant $\alpha = 2$.

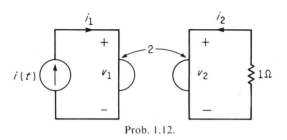

Prob. 1.12.

Assume that $i(t) = 10 \sin \omega t$.  Find $v_2, i_2$, and $v_1$.

**1.13.** The $v$-$i$ relation of a nonlinear resistor is given by

$$v(t) = \frac{1}{2} i^2(t)$$

Is this resistor voltage-controlled?  Current-controlled?

**1.14.** Consider the tunnel diode and its $i$-$v$ characteristics as shown.

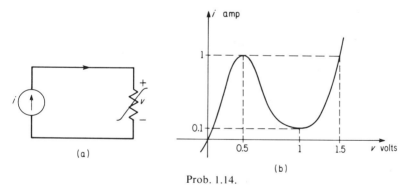

Prob. 1.14.

The current source $i(t)$ is given by

$$i(t) = 0.5 + 0.4 \sin \omega t$$

Plot the voltage $v(t)$ graphically.

**1.15.** The $i$-$v$ relation of a $pn$-junction diode is given by

$$i(t) = 0.1(e^{0.2v(t)} - 1)$$

Let

$$v(t) = \sin 3t$$

(a) Find the instantaneous power.  (b) Use a computer program to compute the energy dissipated in this diode from $t_0 = 0$ to $t_1 = 10$ sec.

**1.16.** The voltage across a nonlinear inductor is given by

$$v = \tanh i$$

Show that this resistor is both voltage-controlled and current controlled. Find $i$ in terms of $v$.

**1.17.** The nonlinear characteristic of a capacitor is given by

$$q(t) = 0.5v^2(t)$$

The voltage across this capacitor is given by

$$v(t) = 1 + 0.5 \sin t$$

Find the current through this capacitor.

**1.18.** Repeat Prob. 1.17 for a capacitor whose $q$-$v$ equation is given by

$$q(t) = v(t) + \tanh [v(t)]$$

**1.19.** Find the energy stored in the nonlinear capacitor of Prob. 1.17 from $t = 0$ to $t = 1$ sec.

**1.20.** Consider a charge-controlled capacitor whose $v$-$q$ relation is given by

$$v = \frac{10^4 q}{10^4 - q^2}$$

Use a computer program to compute the energy required for placing 10 coulombs of electric charge on this capacitor when (a) initial charge on the capacitor is zero, (b) initial charge on the capacitor is 5 coulombs.

**1.21.** The flux through a nonlinear inductor is given in terms of current through it by

$$\phi(t) = \frac{2i(t)}{1 + |i(t)|}$$

Show that this inductor is both flux controlled and current controlled. Find the current $i(t)$ in terms of $\phi(t)$.

**1.22.** Repeat Prob. 1.21 for the nonlinear inductor whose $\phi$-$i$ characteristic is given by

$$\phi(t) = e^{0.2i(t)}$$

**1.23.** Find the energy stored in an inductor from $t = 0$ to $t = 1$ whose $\phi$-$i$ characteristic is given by

$$\phi(t) = \frac{1}{3} i^3(t)$$

and the current through it is given by

$$i(t) = 2 \sin t$$

**1.24.** The capacitance of a linear time-varying capacitor is given by

$$C(t) = C_0(1 + te^{-t^2})$$

and the voltage across this capacitor is given by

$$v(t) = e^{-t} \sin t$$

Find the current through it.

**1.25.** The inductance of a linear time-varying inductor is given by

$$L(t) = L_0(t + \tanh t)$$

and the current through it is given by

$$i(t) = \cos \omega t$$

Find the voltage across this inductor.

## CHAPTER 2

# Kirchhoff's Laws and Basic Concepts of Linearity and Superposition

### 2.1. INTRODUCTION

We have studied the behavior of basic circuit elements in Chapter 1. These are the elements which are primarily encountered in electrical networks. In each case we discussed the element voltage-current relationships. Although we talked briefly about elements other than the resistor, inductor, capacitor and transformer, our main interest was the properties of these four basic elements. In this chapter we will be concerned primarily with the behavior of these elements when connected into various configurations to form what is called a *network* or a *circuit*. Once the configuration of the network is known, we are interested in what happens at the terminals of each element or a combination of elements when the circuit is connected to voltage or current sources.

### Some Basic Definitions

Let us consider a simple interconnection of elements, $R$, $L$, $C$ to form a network of the form shown in Fig. 2.1.1. We have two resistors $R_1$ and $R_2$, an inductor $L$ and a capacitor $C$. The voltage source is denoted by $v$.

We now define a few terms which are commonly used in network analysis.

*BRANCH.* A branch of a network usually represents a two-terminal element of the network. This branch can be a resistor, a capacitor, an inductor or a source element.

In the network of Fig. 2.1.1, points 1 and 2 are connected together

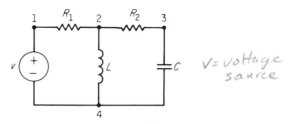

Fig. 2.1.1. Simple network.

through a resistive branch. Points 3 and 4 are connected together by a capacitive branch, points 2 and 4 are connected together by an inductive branch and so on.

*NODE.* A node is defined as the end point of a branch or where two or more branches meet.

In Fig. 2.1.1, all points 1, 2, 3, and 4 can be thought of as nodes. The point where only two branches meet is called a *simple node*. Nodes 1 and 3 of Fig. 2.1.1 are simple nodes.

*LOOP.* A loop is an interconnection of branches which form a closed path.

In Fig. 2.1.1 branches $L$, $R_2$ and $C$ form a loop; branches $v$, $R_1$, and $L$ also form a loop.

The terms branch, node and loop play a fundamental role in developing the basic network equations. We will use these terms throughout the rest of this book. Next we state two of the most important laws in network analysis.

## 2.2. KIRCHHOFF'S LAWS

In Chapter 1 we developed the basic element voltage-current relationships for some of the most common network elements. In this section we introduce two basic laws concerning the voltages and currents of these elements *after* they are connected together to form a network. These are called Kirchhoff's laws. These laws apply to any network configuration whether or not the elements of that network are linear, nonlinear, time-varying or time-invariant.

### Kirchhoff's Current Law (KCL)

Before stating Kirchhoff's current law we make the following sign convention. For a given network, we assign an arbitrary direction to the currents in each branch and designate this direction by an arrow. We assign a positive sign to the currents whose direction points *toward* a node and a negative sign to the currents whose direction points *away from* a node. Then we have

KCL:   *The algebraic sum of all the currents entering or leaving a node is zero.*

or equivalently: the sum of the currents entering a node is equal to the sum of the currents leaving that node.   Consider Fig. 2.2.1.   Let the

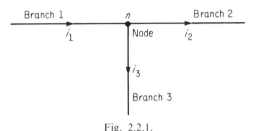

Fig. 2.2.1.

current in branches 1, 2, 3 be $i_1$, $i_2$, and $i_3$ respectively and let these be in the directions shown.   According to KCL, the current flowing into the node $n$: i.e., $i_1$ must equal the current flowing out of the node: i.e., $i_2 + i_3$. Therefore

$$i_1 = i_2 + i_3 \tag{2.2.1}$$

We can also formulate the above by saying that the current flow *into* the node from the branches 1, 2, 3 is $i_1$, $-i_2$, and $-i_3$ respectively.   The minus sign is due to the fact that we have reversed the direction of $i_2$ and $i_3$. Therefore, by the above sign convention and KCL, we have

$$i_1 - i_2 - i_3 = 0 \tag{2.2.2}$$

which is, of course, the same as Eq. 2.2.1 except written differently.

### Kirchhoff's Voltage Law (KVL)

Consider a simple loop shown in Fig. 2.2.2.   Let the voltage source be $v$ and let us denote the rest of the branches by $a$, $b$, and $c$ as shown.

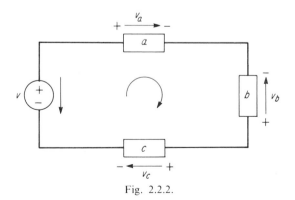

Fig. 2.2.2.

Choose an arbitrary orientation for this loop (say, clockwise, as shown) and denote the voltage drops on branches $a$, $b$, and $c$ by $v_a$, $v_b$, and $v_c$ respectively. These voltage drops are indicated by arrows in the figure.

As a general rule, throughout the rest of this book we assume that the voltage drop in each branch is from + polarity to − polarity. If the voltage drop across a branch is in the same direction as the loop direction, we assign a positive sign to the voltage drop; otherwise we assign a negative sign. For example, in the loop shown in Fig. 2.2.2, the voltage drops across branches $a$ and $c$ are positive and the voltage drops across the branch $b$ and the source are negative.

With the above sign convention we can now state Kirchhoff's voltage law.

KVL: *The algebraic sum of all the voltage drops in any loop is equal to zero.*

This law is completely general and applies to any circuit whether elements of that circuit are linear, nonlinear, time-varying or time-invariant. Applying KVL to the loop shown in Fig. 2.2.2, we get

$$v_a - v_b + v_c - v = 0 \qquad (2.2.3)$$

*Example 2.2.1*

Consider the network shown in Fig. 2.2.3. Write all the KCL and KVL equations for this network.

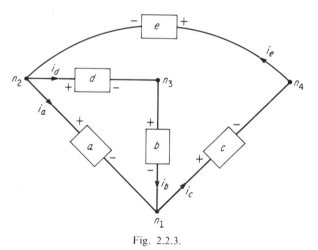

Fig. 2.2.3.

*Solution*

There are four nodes in this network: $n_1$, $n_2$, $n_3$, and $n_4$; hence we have four KCL equations. Adopting the reference directions given in Fig. 2.2.3, we can write these as

$$\text{node } n_1: \quad + i_a + i_b - i_c = 0$$

*[handwritten: $-i_a - i_b + i_c$   $n_2 = -n_1$]*

$$\text{node } n_2: \quad -i_a - i_d + i_e = 0$$
$$\text{node } n_3: \quad \quad +i_d - i_b = 0 \qquad\qquad (2.2.4)$$
$$\text{node } n_4: \quad \quad +i_c - i_e = 0$$

These are all the KCL equations we can write for this network. A quick look at Eq. 2.2.4 reveals that not all the equations are *linearly independent*. Since the first equation can be obtained by adding the last three equations together, it is linearly dependent on the last three. In other words, the first KCL equation does not convey any new information in lieu of the last three. In the next section we give a rule by which we can write the linear independent KCL equations by inspection. Let us now turn to the KVL equations. There are three loops in the network under consideration. We assume that all these loops are clockwise oriented. Then the corresponding KVL equations are

$$\text{loop } dba: \qquad v_d + v_b - v_a = 0$$
$$\text{loop } ecbd: \quad -v_e - v_c - v_b - v_d = 0 \qquad (2.2.5)$$
$$\text{loop } eca: \qquad -v_e - v_c - v_a = 0$$

Again, a careful examination of these equations shows that only two out of these three equations are linearly independent. For example, we can obtain the last equation by adding the first two equations together. That is, the last equation is a consequence of the first two; hence it does not convey any new information about the network. In the next section we introduce a systematic method of writing linearly independent KVL equations.

## 2.3. LINEARLY INDEPENDENT KCL AND KVL EQUATIONS

One of the basic objectives of circuit analysis is to obtain a set of linearly independent equations that can be solved for the voltages and the currents of a given circuit. For instance, for the network shown in Fig. 2.2.3 it is desirable to write a set of equations that can be solved for the currents $i_a, i_b, i_c, i_d, i_e$ and the voltages $v_a, v_b, v_c, v_d,$ and $v_e$. To do this we need ten linearly independent equations. Three of these equations can be obtained by writing linearly independent KCL equations and two can be obtained by writing linearly independent KVL equations. The remaining five can be obtained from the voltage-current relations (VCR) of the five branches $a, b, c, d,$ and $e$.

Writing linearly independent KVL and KCL equations, therefore, plays an extremely important role in the solution of network problems. Before we introduce a method for writing such KCL and KVL equations we need to discuss some elementary notions in network topology.

### Elementary Network Topology

Consider a network $\mathfrak{N}$ consisting of resistors, inductors, capacitors, transformers and sources. Replace each branch of this network by a line segment and each node by a dot. The resulting figure is called the *graph* of $\mathfrak{N}$ and is denoted by $G$. As an example, consider the network shown in Fig. 2.3.1a. The corresponding graph is drawn in Fig. 2.3.1b.

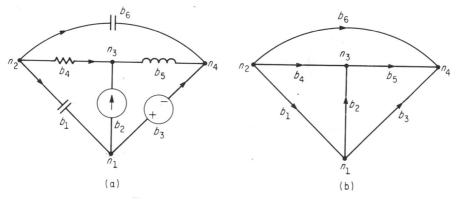

Fig. 2.3.1. (a) Network $\mathfrak{N}$. (b) Graph $G$.

There are six branches and four nodes in $\mathfrak{N}$. The branches are numbered $b_1$ through $b_6$ and the nodes are numbered $n_1$ through $n_4$. Each branch is terminated in exactly two nodes. In general, a graph $G$ of a network $\mathfrak{N}$ is a collection of line segments and nodes indicating how the branches of the corresponding network are connected to one another.

If the direction of the currents in the network are specified, then the branches of the corresponding graph are oriented and the orientation is designated by arrows. Such a graph is called an *oriented graph*.

A graph is called a *planar* graph if it can be drawn on a plane in such a way that no two branches intersect except at the nodes. Graph $G$ of Fig. 2.3.1b is a planar graph whereas the graph shown in Fig. 2.3.2 is

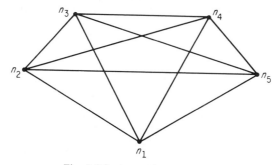

Fig. 2.3.2. A nonplanar graph.

nonplanar. The branches of this graph intersect at points which are not nodes. In this chapter we concern ourselves only with the planar networks. We postpone the discussion of the nonplanar networks until Chapter 14.

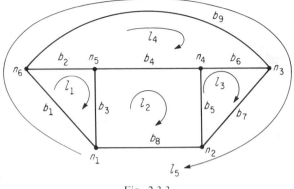

Fig. 2.3.3.

Among all the loops in a planar graph those that contain no branches in their interior are called *meshes*. For example in Fig. 2.3.3 loops $l_1$, $l_2$, $l_3$, and $l_4$ are meshes but $l_5$ is not a mesh, since it contains branches $b_2$ through $b_6$ in its interior.

A *cutset* of a graph is a set of minimum number of branches whose removal will separate the graph into two disjointed parts. For example, in Fig. 2.3.3 branches $(b_1, b_3, b_5, b_7)$, $(b_1, b_2, b_9)$ and $(b_7, b_6, b_9)$ are cutsets. The removal of the first set of branches will break the network into two disjoint subnetworks; the branch $b_8$ is one part and branches $b_2$, $b_4$, $b_6$, and $b_9$ comprise the second part. The removal of the second set will also break the network into two parts, the node $n_6$ and branches $b_3, b_4$, $b_5, b_6, b_7$, and $b_8$. (Notice that the removal of these branches has left the node $n_6$ intact.) Similarly, the last set of branches is a cutset since their removal will break the network into $n_3$ and $b_1, b_2, b_3, b_4, b_5$ and $b_8$. With this background in network topology, we are now ready to discuss the procedures for writing linearly independent KCL and KVL equations for planar networks.

### Independent KCL Equations

For the network of Fig. 2.2.3 with four nodes we showed that we can write only three linearly independent KCL equations. We now state the following general rule for a network containing $N + 1$ nodes:

*For a network with $N + 1$ nodes we can write at most $N$ linearly independent KCL (or node) equations.*

In implementing this rule, we can apply KCL equations to any $N$ nodes of the network under consideration; the remaining node is called the *reference* or *datum*. Hence in a given network we first choose a datum and then write KCL equations for the rest of the nodes. The resulting KCL equations are all linearly independent.

### Independent KVL Equations

We can state the following fact:

*For a network with* $N + 1$ *nodes and* B *branches there are exactly* B − N *linearly independent KVL (or loop) equations.*

For example, the network of Fig. 2.2.3 has 4 nodes and 5 branches; therefore $N = 3$ and $B = 5$, then the number of the linearly independent loop equations is

$$B - N = 5 - 3 = 2$$

A rigorous proof of the above fact can be given using network topology. At this stage, however, we shall concentrate on its application and refer the interested student to the literature cited at the end of the book.

To choose the linearly independent node equations, we can easily take any $N$ nodes out of $N + 1$ possible nodes and apply the KCL equations. In the case of loop equations, however, it is not that simple. In the remainder of this section we outline two of the commonly used techniques for writing the independent loop equations of a network.

*METHOD 1.* For a planar network with $N + 1$ nodes and $B$ branches, we draw the graph of the network so that we can indicate all the *meshes* of the network by inspection. It can be shown that the total number of these meshes is $B - N$. This can always be done. Now if we write the KVL equations for these meshes the resulting equations will be linearly independent. This rule can be rigorously proved. However, at this stage we are interested only in its application.

*Example 2.3.1*

Consider a network shown in Fig. 2.3.4. This network has 4 nodes and 6 branches; therefore $N = 3$ and $B = 6$. Taking $n_1$ as the datum

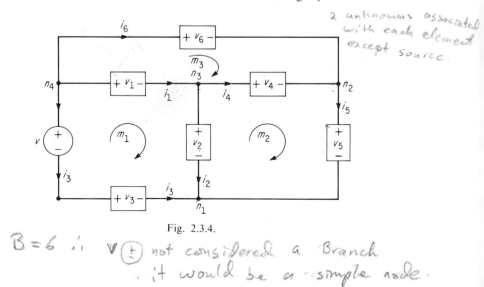

2 unknowns associated with each element except source.

Fig. 2.3.4.

$B = 6$ ∴ $V(\pm)$ not considered a Branch. it would be a simple node.

(reference node) we can write the three linearly independent KCL equations for the remaining nodes.

$$
\begin{aligned}
n_2: &\quad i_4 - i_5 + i_6 = 0 \\
n_3: &\quad i_1 - i_2 - i_4 = 0 \\
n_4: &\quad -i_3 - i_1 - i_6 = 0
\end{aligned}
\tag{2.3.1}
$$

There are also $B - N = 6 - 3 = 3$ linearly independent KVL equations. This network is planar; hence the meshes are $m_1, m_2$, and $m_3$ as shown. Writing KVL for these meshes we get

$$
\begin{aligned}
m_1: &\quad -v + v_1 + v_2 - v_3 = 0 \\
m_2: &\quad + v_4 + v_5 - v_2 = 0 \\
m_3: &\quad + v_6 - v_4 - v_1 = 0
\end{aligned}
\tag{2.3.2}
$$

Equations 2.3.1 together with Eq. 2.3.2 give *six* linearly independent equations. However, there are twelve unknowns in this circuit. The remaining six linearly independent equations can be obtained from the branch voltage current relations (VCR). For example, if branch 1 is a linear resistor with resistance $R_1$, then $v_1$ and $i_1$ would be related through

$$
v_1 = R_1 i_1
$$

or if branch 2 is a linear time-invariant capacitor with capacitance $C_2$ we would have

$$
i_2 = C_2 \frac{dv_2}{dt}
$$

and so on.

*METHOD 2.* In this method we choose the loops that yield linearly independent KVL equations by inspection. In choosing these loops we must satisfy two conditions:

(i) For a network with $N + 1$ nodes and $B$ branches we must choose $N - B$ loops.

(ii) Each new loop that we choose must contain at least one branch that is not considered in the previous loops.

In satisfying condition (ii) we must be careful not to exhaust the branches of the network before satisfying condition (i).

*Example 2.3.2*

Consider the network shown in Fig. 2.3.5. This network has 4 nodes and 6 branches; therefore, $N = 3$ and $B = 6$. Consequently, we can write 3 independent node (KCL) equations and $B - N = 6 - 3 = 3$ independent loop (KVL) equations. Taking $n_1$ as the reference node (datum) the node equations are

$$
\begin{aligned}
n_2: &\quad \qquad\qquad + i_6 - i_1 = 0 \\
n_3: &\quad + i_1 - i_2 - i_3 - i_4 = 0 \\
n_4: &\quad \qquad\quad + i_4 + i_3 - i_5 = 0
\end{aligned}
\tag{2.3.3}
$$

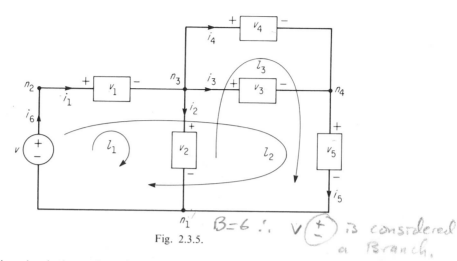

Fig. 2.3.5.

*B=6 ∴  V(±) is considered a Branch.*

To write the independent loop equations, we use method 2 discussed above. We need to choose three loops—these can be chosen as $l_1, l_2,$ and $l_3$ shown in the figure. Notice that in each of these loops there is at least one branch which is not in the other loops. KVL equations for these loops are

$$
\begin{aligned}
l_1: &\quad + v_1 + v_2 - v = 0 \\
l_2: &\quad v_1 + v_3 + v_5 - v = 0 \\
l_3: &\quad + v_4 + v_5 - v_2 = 0
\end{aligned}
\qquad (2.3.4)
$$

Now KVL equations for any other loop of Fig. 2.3.5 will be a linear combination of the equations in Eq. 2.3.4. These two sets of equations provide six linearly independent equations for the network under consideration. There are, however, eleven unknowns ($v_1$ through $v_5$ and $i_1$ through $i_6$). The remaining five independent equations can be obtained by writing the branch voltage-current relations (VCR). A more systematic method of writing linearly independent KVL equations will be introduced in Chapter 14. In the next section we shall discuss the implementation of VCR.

*REMARK.* Consider the network of Fig. 2.3.5. The KCL equation for the node $n_2$ is

$$ + i_6 - i_1 = 0 $$

or

$$ i_1 = i_6 $$

That is, we can eliminate node $n_2$ altogether and replace $i_6$ by $i_1$ (one less unknown and one less equation). Therefore, we can write the KCL equations only for the nodes that are the intersection of *three or more* branches. In other words, we can ignore the *simple nodes* by observing

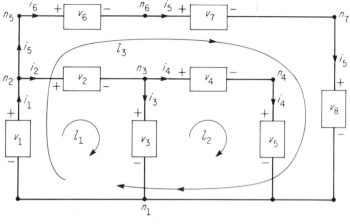

Fig. 2.3.6.

that the current entering a simple node is equal to the current leaving it. The following example illustrates this point. Consider the network shown in Fig. 2.3.6. For this network we write the KCL equations only for two nodes, $n_2$ and $n_3$ ($n_1$ is taken as the datum). KCL equations for the rest of the nodes ($n_4, n_5, n_6$, and $n_7$) are trivially satisfied; for example, at node $n_4$ it will give $i_4 - i_4 = 0$.

Let us now write the independent loop and node equations for the network of Fig. 2.3.6.

KCL

$$n_2: \quad + i_1 - i_2 - i_5 = 0$$
$$n_3: \quad + i_2 - i_3 - i_4 = 0 \tag{2.3.5}$$

KVL

$$l_1: \qquad v_2 + v_3 - v_1 = 0$$
$$l_2: \qquad v_4 + v_5 - v_3 = 0 \tag{2.3.6}$$
$$l_3: v_6 + v_7 + v_8 - v_1 = 0$$

These five equations together with eight branch current-voltage relations form thirteen linearly independent equations in thirteen unknowns ($v_1$ through $v_8$ and $i_1$ through $i_5$) that can be solved for the voltages and the currents of the network. In the next section we discuss various methods of applying KCL, KVL, and VCR to networks which consist of resistors, inductors, capacitors and transformers.

## 2.4. METHODS OF ANALYSIS

Consider the simple circuit shown in Fig. 2.4.1. There are four nodes and six branches in this network, i.e., $N = 3$ and $B = 6$. Hence we can

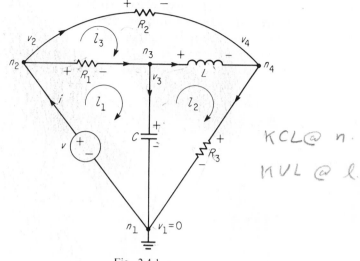

Fig. 2.4.1.

write three independent node equations and $B - N = 3$ independent loop equations. Take $n_1$ as the datum and write KCL and KVL equations:

KCL

$$
\begin{aligned}
n_2: & \quad i - i_{R_1} - i_{R_2} = 0 \\
n_3: & \quad i_{R_1} - i_C - i_L = 0 \\
n_4: & \quad i_L + i_{R_2} - i_{R_3} = 0
\end{aligned}
\tag{2.4.1}
$$

KVL

$$
\begin{aligned}
l_1: & \quad v_{R_1} + v_C - v = 0 \\
l_2: & \quad v_L + v_{R_3} - v_C = 0 \\
l_3: & \quad v_{R_2} - v_L - v_{R_1} = 0
\end{aligned}
\tag{2.4.2}
$$

We can also write the branch voltage-current relations (VCR) for all the branches except the voltage source. These are

VCR

$$
\begin{aligned}
R_1: & \quad v_{R_1} = R_1 i_{R_1} \\
R_2: & \quad v_{R_2} = R_2 i_{R_2} \\
R_3: & \quad v_{R_3} = R_3 i_{R_3} \\
C: & \quad i_C = C \frac{dv_C}{dt} \quad \text{or} \quad v_C = \frac{1}{C} \int_0^t i_C(t')\,dt' + v_C(0) \\
L: & \quad v_L = L \frac{di_L}{dt} \quad \text{or} \quad i_L = \frac{1}{L} \int_0^t v_L(t')\,dt' + i_L(0)
\end{aligned}
\tag{2.4.3}
$$

Equations 2.4.1, 2.4.2, and 2.4.3 give eleven linearly independent equations in eleven unknowns ($v_{R_1}$, $v_{R_2}$, $v_{R_3}$, $i_{R_1}$, $i_{R_2}$, $i_{R_3}$, $v_C$, $i_C$, $v_L$, $i_L$, and $i$)

that can be solved for these unknowns. However, in most practical applications we are only interested in some but not all the unknowns, say, the voltage across the inductor and the current through the resistor $R_1$. In this case, to avoid solving eleven integrodifferential equations in eleven unknowns (which could be quite costly and time consuming), we resort to the two special techniques discussed below, namely, *nodal analysis* and *loop analysis*. In these methods we introduce some auxiliary variables (such as the node voltages $v_2, v_3$, and $v_4$) to reduce the number of the equations and unknowns.

## Nodal Analysis

Consider the network shown in Fig. 2.4.1. Let us denote the voltages at nodes $n_1, n_2, n_3, n_4$, by $v_1, v_2, v_3$, and $v_4$ respectively. Next assume that $v_1 = 0$ and write the KCL equations for nodes $n_2, n_3$, and $n_4$ using the voltage current relations given by Eq. 2.4.3. Note that the currents in the resistors are given by

$i = \dfrac{V}{R}$

$$i_{R_1} = \frac{v_2 - v_3}{R_1}, \quad i_{R_2} = \frac{v_2 - v_4}{R_2}, \quad i_{R_3} = \frac{v_4 - v_1}{R_3}$$

Also from Chapter 1, we recall that the current through the linear time-invariant capacitor $C$ is given by

$i_C = C \dfrac{dv}{dt}$

$$i_C = C \frac{d}{dt}(v_3 - v_1) \quad = C \frac{d}{dt} v_3$$

and the current through the linear time-invariant inductor $L$ is given by

$$i_L = \frac{1}{L} \int_0^t [v_3(t') - v_4(t')] \, dt' + i_L(0)$$

For simplicity assume that $i_L(0) = 0$; then, using these voltage-current relations we can rewrite Eq. 2.4.1 in the form

$$n_2: \quad i - \frac{v_2 - v_3}{R_1} - \frac{v_2 - v_4}{R_2} = 0$$

$$n_3: \quad \frac{v_2 - v_3}{R_1} - C\frac{d}{dt}(v_3 - v_1) - \frac{1}{L}\int_0^t [v_3(t') - v_4(t')]\, dt' = 0$$

$$n_4: \quad \frac{1}{L}\int_0^t [v_3(t') - v_4(t')]\, dt' + \frac{v_2 - v_4}{R_2} - \frac{v_4 - v_1}{R_3} = 0$$

Also from Fig. 2.4.1 it is easy to see that

$$v_2 = v \quad \text{and} \quad v_1 = 0 \tag{2.4.4}$$

Then the above equations can be written as

$$i - \frac{1}{R_1}(v - v_3) - \frac{1}{R_2}(v - v_4) = 0$$

$$\frac{1}{R_1}(v - v_3) - C\frac{dv_3}{dt} - \frac{1}{L}\int_0^t [v_3(t') - v_4(t')]\, dt' = 0 \qquad (2.4.5)$$

$$\frac{1}{L}\int_0^t [v_3(t') - v_4(t')]dt' + \frac{1}{R_2}(v - v_4) - \frac{1}{R_3}v_4 = 0$$

Equations 2.4.5 represent three linearly independent integrodifferential equations that can be solved for $i$, $v_3$, and $v_4$. Then, every branch voltage and current in the network can be found using node voltages $v_2$, $v_3$ and $v_4$. For example, the current through the inductor $i_L$ is given by

$$i_L = \frac{1}{L}\int_0^t [v_3(t') - v_4(t')]\, dt' \qquad (2.4.6)$$

and so on. Hence we have reduced a set of eleven equations in eleven unknowns to a set of three equations in three unknowns by introducing the node voltages $v_2$, $v_3$, and $v_4$ as auxiliary variables. This procedure is known as *nodal analysis*. Procedure outlined above can be extended to take into account the circuits that have mutual inductances. For the sake of simplicity, however, we omit this extension.

Nodal analysis is especially useful for circuits that have many branches and very few nodes. One such network is considered in the following example.

*Example 2.4.1*

Consider the resistive network shown in Fig. 2.4.2. Take $n_1$ as the datum and denote the voltages at nodes $n_2$ and $n_3$ with respect to $n_1$ as $v_2$

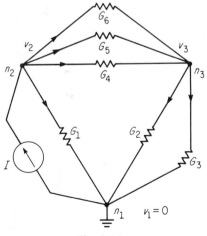

Fig. 2.4.2.

$$G = \frac{1}{R} \quad i(t) = G\,v(t)$$

and $v_3$ respectively. Also denote the conductance of branches $b_1$ through $b_6$ by $G_1$ through $G_6$. In this network we can write two linearly independent node equations:

$$n_2: \quad I - G_1 v_2 - G_4(v_2 - v_3) - G_5(v_2 - v_3) - G_6(v_2 - v_3) = 0$$
$$n_3: \quad G_4(v_2 - v_3) + G_5(v_2 - v_3) + G_6(v_2 - v_3) - G_2 v_3 - G_3 v_3 = 0$$

or after rearranging these equations we have

$$I - (G_1 + G_4 + G_5 + G_6)v_2 + (G_4 + G_5 + G_6)v_3 = 0$$
$$(G_4 + G_5 + G_6)v_2 - (G_4 + G_5 + G_6 + G_2 + G_3)v_3 = 0 \qquad (2.4.7)$$

Equations 2.4.7 represent a set of two equations and two unknowns that can be solved for $v_2$ and $v_3$. Having found $v_2$ and $v_3$ it is quite easy to find the current in any of the branches. We discuss the solution of such sets of equations in Chapter 4. Notice that if we use the previous method we would have thirteen simultaneous equations in thirteen unknowns to solve. Hence nodal analysis in this case has a clear advantage over the previous method.

### Loop Analysis

This method of analysis is especially useful for circuits that have many nodes and very few meshes or loops. In this method we define a *loop current* for each of the meshes and write the independent KVL equations in terms of these loop currents. Let us consider the network shown in Fig. 2.4.3. There are three meshes in this network. Denote the *loop*

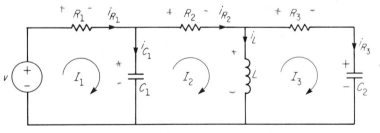

Fig. 2.4.3.

*currents* by $I_1$, $I_2$, and $I_3$, these are *hypothetical* currents circulating the loops. The branch currents are therefore given by

$$i_{R_1} = I_1, \quad i_{C_1} = I_1 - I_2, \quad i_{R_2} = I_2$$
$$i_L = I_2 - I_3, \quad i_{R_3} = I_3 \qquad (2.4.8)$$

The linear independent KVL equations are

$$-v + R_1 I_1 + \frac{1}{C_1} \int_0^t (I_1 - I_2)\, dt = 0$$

$$-\frac{1}{C_1} \int_0^t (I_1 - I_2)\, dt + R_2 I_2 + L \frac{d}{dt}(I_2 - I_3) = 0 \qquad (2.4.9)$$

$$- L \frac{d}{dt}(I_2 - I_3) + R_3 I_3 + \frac{1}{C_2} \int_0^t I_3\, dt = 0$$

These are three integrodifferential equations in three unknowns that can solved for the loop currents $I_1$, $I_2$, and $I_3$. Having solved Eq. 2.4.9 for $I_1, I_2$, and $I_3$, it is easy to find the currents in each branch and the voltages across the resistors, capacitors or inductors.

In conclusion of this section, notice that the loop currents are not the actual currents that we can measure in the lab. These are auxiliary variables that we choose to reduce the number of the integrodifferential equations that we must solve. Of course, actual branch currents (the currents that can be measured in the lab by simply connecting an ammeter in series to the branch) can be expressed in terms of these currents. More discussion of nodal analysis and loop analysis will be given in Chapters 9 and 10.

## 2.5. SERIES AND PARALLEL CONNECTIONS

Consider the two networks connected to terminals 1 and 2 in Fig. 2.5.1. We say that the two networks are *equivalent* with respect to

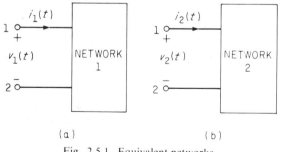

(a)                            (b)

Fig. 2.5.1. Equivalent networks.

terminals 1,2 provided their terminal voltage-current characteristics are identical. Equivalent networks can be used to reduce the amount of effort required to establish circuit performance. We now investigate methods of establishing simple equivalent networks.

## Series Combination

Two or more two-terminal network elements are said to be connected in *series* if the current through them is the same.   Consider the network of Fig. 2.5.2.   Here we say that $R$, $L$, and $C$ are in series, for when a

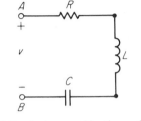

Fig. 2.5.2.   Series combination of $R$, $L$ and $C$.

voltage $v$ is connected across the terminal $AB$, the same current will flow through each of them.

If there are two or more elements of the same type in series, they can be combined together to simplify the network representation.   Next, we explore this in more detail.

### Resistors in Series

Let $R_1$ and $R_2$ be two linear resistors in series as shown in Fig. 2.5.3a. If we apply a voltage source $v$ to the terminals, the same current say, $i$, will flow through each of them.   So we have by KVL that

$$v = iR_1 + iR_2 = i(R_1 + R_2) \equiv iR \qquad (2.5.1)$$

We see that $R_1$ and $R_2$ can be replaced by a single resistor $R = R_1 + R_2$. This will be true even when we have more than two resistors in series.   In general, the linear resistors in series can be replaced by a single resistor whose resistance is equal to the sum of the resistances in series.

### Inductors in Series

Let $L_1$ and $L_2$ be two linear time-invariant inductors in series as shown in Fig. 2.5.3b.   If we apply a voltage $v$ and assuming a current $i$, we have by KVL

$$v = L_1 \frac{di}{dt} + L_2 \frac{di}{dt} = (L_1 + L_2) \frac{di}{dt} \equiv L \frac{di}{dt} \qquad (2.5.2)$$

Hence we note that inductors in a series can be added to form a single equivalent inductor.   This would naturally be true if we have more than two inductors in series.

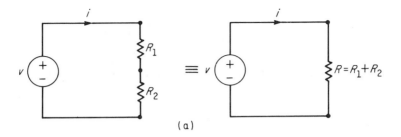

(a)

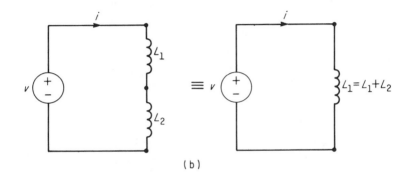

(b)

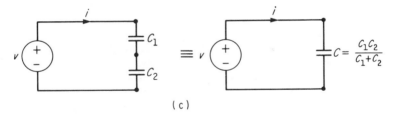

(c)

Fig. 2.5.3. (a) Resistors in series.  (b) inductors in series.  (c) capacitors in series.

### Capacitors in Series

Let $C_1$ and $C_2$ be two linear time-invariant capacitors in series as shown in Fig. 2.5.3c. If we apply a voltage $v$, then we can apply KVL to obtain

$$v(t) = \frac{1}{C_1} \int_{t_0}^{t} i(t')\, dt' + \frac{1}{C_2} \int_{t_0}^{t} i(t')\, dt'$$

$$= \left[ \frac{1}{C_1} + \frac{1}{C_2} \right] \int_{t_0}^{t} i(t')\, dt' \equiv \frac{1}{C} \int_{t_0}^{t} i(t')\, dt' \qquad (2.5.3)$$

where

$$\frac{1}{C} = \frac{1}{C_1} + \frac{1}{C_2} \tag{2.5.4}$$

Thus we can replace the capacitors $C_1$ and $C_2$ by a single capacitor $C$ such that

$$C = \frac{C_1 C_2}{C_1 + C_2} \tag{2.5.5}$$

Now if we had three capacitors $C_1$, $C_2$, $C_3$ in series we could write

$$\frac{1}{C} = \frac{1}{C_1} + \frac{1}{C_2} + \frac{1}{C_3} \tag{2.5.6}$$

This discussion gives us the rule for combining capacitors when they are in series.

### Parallel Combination

A set of elements are said to be in *parallel* if they are connected to the same pair of nodes. A simple example of a parallel combination can be seen in Fig. 2.5.4. In this circuit we note that across nodes 1 and 2 the resistor $R_2$ is in parallel with inductor $L$. Similarly across nodes 2 and 3,

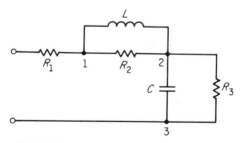

Fig. 2.5.4.   Network having parallel branches.

$R_3$ and $C$ are in parallel. As in the case of series combination we can combine parallel branches to reduce the number of the elements in a network. This procedure is especially convenient if the elements in parallel are of the same nature. In the following we consider some of these cases.

### Resistors in Parallel

Let us consider two resistors in parallel as shown in Fig. 2.5.5a. If we apply a voltage $v$ to the combination, we can write from the figure

$$v = i_1 R_1 = i_2 R_2 \tag{2.5.7}$$

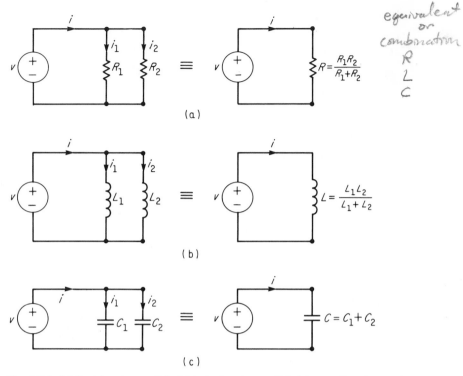

equivalent
or
combination
$R$
$L$
$C$

Fig. 2.5.5. (a) Resistors in parallel, (b) inductors in parallel, (c) capacitors in parallel.

where $i_1 + i_2 = i$. We can combine these equations to read $V\left(\dfrac{1}{R_1} + \dfrac{1}{R_2}\right) = i$

$$\frac{v}{R_1} + \frac{v}{R_2} = i \quad \text{or} \quad v = \frac{R_1 R_2}{R_1 + R_2} i \equiv Ri \qquad (2.5.8)$$

$V\left(\dfrac{R_1 + R_2}{R_1 R_2}\right) = i$

This implies that two resistors $R_1$ and $R_2$ in parallel can be replaced by a combination resistor $R$ such that

$$R = \frac{R_1 R_2}{R_1 + R_2} \qquad (2.5.9)$$

Alternately,

$$\frac{1}{R} = \frac{1}{R_1} + \frac{1}{R_2} \qquad (2.5.10)$$

Now if we had three resistors $R_1$, $R_2$, and $R_3$ in parallel, then the combination resistor $R$ will be given by

$$\frac{1}{R} = \frac{1}{R_1} + \frac{1}{R_2} + \frac{1}{R_3} \qquad (2.5.11)$$

and so on.

### Inductors in Parallel

We can use an argument similar to resistors in parallel to develop the relationship between two inductors in parallel. From Fig. 2.5.5b,

$$v = L_1 \frac{di_1}{dt} = L_2 \frac{di_2}{dt} \qquad (2.5.12)$$

where

$$i = i_1 + i_2 \quad \text{or} \quad \frac{di}{dt} = \frac{di_1}{dt} + \frac{di_2}{dt}$$

Simplifying these equations as above we get

$$v = \frac{L_1 L_2}{L_1 + L_2} \frac{di}{dt} \equiv L \frac{di}{dt} \qquad (2.5.13)$$

which implies that if we had two inductors $L_1$ and $L_2$ in parallel, they can be replaced by a combined inductor $L$, such that

$$\frac{1}{L} = \frac{1}{L_1} + \frac{1}{L_2}$$

or

$$L = \frac{L_1 L_2}{L_1 + L_2} \qquad (2.5.14)$$

This procedure can be easily extended to the case where there are several inductors in parallel.

### Capacitors in Parallel

Consider two capacitors having capacitances $C_1$ and $C_2$ in parallel as shown in Fig. 2.5.5c. Voltage across each capacitor will be $v$, if such a voltage is applied to the combination as shown. We shall have

$$i_1 = C_1 \frac{dv}{dt} \quad \text{and} \quad i_2 = C_2 \frac{dv}{dt}$$

where

$$i_1 + i_2 = i \qquad (2.5.15)$$

Hence

$$i = (C_1 + C_2) \frac{dv}{dt} \equiv C \frac{dv}{dt} \qquad (2.5.16)$$

or

$$C = C_1 + C_2 \qquad (2.5.17)$$

Hence capacitors in parallel can be replaced by a single capacitor whose capacitance is the sum of all the capacitances.

*REMARK.* Although we have not mentioned it explicitly, throughout Sec. 2.5 we have assumed that all the initial conditions in the energy-storing elements are zero.

## 2.6. APPLICATIONS

We have developed some of the basic laws which govern electrical networks. In order to have a better appreciation and understanding, we implement these laws to work out a number of specific examples.

*Example 2.6.1*

For the network shown in Fig. 2.6.1, perform the loop analysis.

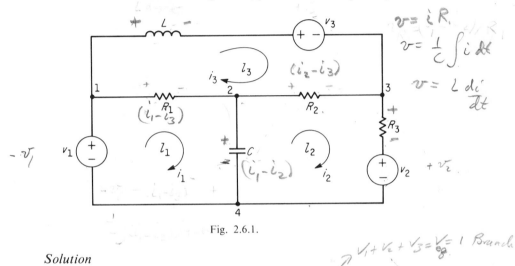

Fig. 2.6.1.

*Solution*

If we examine Fig. 2.6.1, we note that $N = 3$ and $B = 6$ and therefore the number of independent loops is $B - N = 3$. In this simple planar network these independent loops can be taken to be $l_1, l_2,$ and $l_3$ as shown. Let us denote the corresponding loop currents by $i_1, i_2,$ and $i_3$.

Consider loop $l_1$, the voltage drop across $R_1$ is $(i_1 - i_3)R_1$ and the voltage drop across the capacitor is $\frac{1}{C} \int (i_1 - i_2)\, dt$. Therefore the application of KVL gives

$$v_1 = (i_1 - i_3)R_1 + \frac{1}{C} \int (i_1 - i_2)\, dt$$

For loop $l_2$, taking the clockwise direction, we must have (by application of KVL)

$$-\frac{1}{C} \int (i_1 - i_2)\, dt + (i_2 - i_3)R_2 + i_2 R_3 + v_2 = 0$$

Similarly, for loop $l_3$,

$$-(i_2 - i_3)R_2 - (i_1 - i_3)R_1 + L\frac{di_3}{dt} + v_3 = 0$$

These three equations describe the network and can be solved for $i_1$, $i_2$, and $i_3$. Having found these three variables any branch voltage or current can then be found by simple manipulations.

*Example 2.6.2*

Use the loop-analysis method to develop KVL equations for the network shown in Fig. 2.6.2.

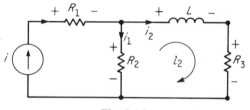

Fig. 2.6.2.

*Solution*

In this network we have a current source, so the current through $R_1$ is $i$. Now denote the current through $R_2$ and $L$ by $i_1$ and $i_2$ respectively. Since $i = i_1 + i_2$, then all we need to do is to write one KVL equation around the loop $l_2$. Choosing a clockwise direction for $l_2$, we get

$$L\frac{di_2}{dt} + i_2 R_3 - i_1 R_2 = 0$$

But

$$i_1 = i - i_2$$

Then

$$L\frac{di_2}{dt} + (R_3 + R_2)i_2 - R_2 i = 0$$

This is a first-order differential equation that can be solved for $i_2$.

*Example 2.6.3*

Consider the network of Fig. 2.6.3. Note that in this case there are three nodes $n_1$, $n_2$, $n_3$ and eight branches. Choosing $n_3$ as the datum we

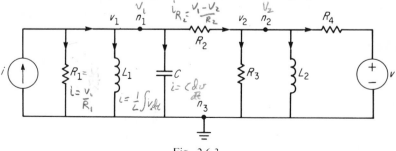

Fig. 2.6.3.

can use the nodal analysis discussed earlier to write a set of linearly independent integrodifferential equations that can be solved for node voltages $v_1$ and $v_2$. These variables will completely describe the network. Consider node $n_1$. We have

$$n_1:\quad i - \frac{v_1}{R_1} - \frac{1}{L_1}\int_{t_0}^{t} v_1(t')\,dt' - C\frac{dv_1}{dt} - \frac{v_1 - v_2}{R_2} = 0$$

Consider node $n_2$. We have

$$n_2:\quad \frac{v_1 - v_2}{R_2} - \frac{v_2}{R_3} - \frac{1}{L_2}\int_{t_0}^{t} v_2(t')\,dt' - \frac{v_2 - v}{R_4} = 0$$

KCL equations for $n_1$ and $n_2$ completely describe the network. All other information can be derived from these equations.

*Example 2.6.4*

Find the equivalent resistor $R$ and equivalent capacitor $C$ as shown in Fig. 2.6.4, where $\mu$f denotes a microfarad, equivalent to $10^{-6}$ farad.

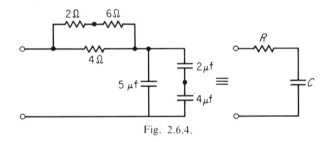

Fig. 2.6.4.

*Solution*

First let us consider the resistors. We note that 2-$\Omega$ and 6-$\Omega$ resistors are in series and can be replaced by a single resistance of $6 + 2 = 8$ $\Omega$. Now 8 $\Omega$ and 4 $\Omega$ are in parallel. Therefore they can be combined together to get a single resistor $R$ where $R$ is given by

$$\frac{1}{R} = \frac{1}{8} + \frac{1}{4} \quad \text{or} \quad R = \frac{8}{3}\,\Omega$$

As for the capacitors, 2 $\mu$f and 4 $\mu$f capacitors are in series. They can be combined to give a capacitor of $\dfrac{2 \times 4}{2 + 4}$ $\mu$f or 4/3 $\mu$f. This will be in parallel with a 5 $\mu$f capacitor. Hence

$$C = 5 + \frac{4}{3} = \frac{19}{3}\,\mu\text{f}$$

## 2.7. EFFECT OF MUTUAL INDUCTANCE ON NETWORK EQUATIONS

We briefly mentioned the mutual inductance between inductor coils in Chapter 1. We will now examine how mutual inductances affect the KVL and KCL equations. Naturally there can be no effect of mutual inductance on KCL equations as it only affects the voltage. However, KVL equations are affected because additional voltages are induced due to mutual inductance. Consider the network of Fig. 2.7.1. This could be thought of as a transformer with applied voltages $v_1$ and $v_2$.

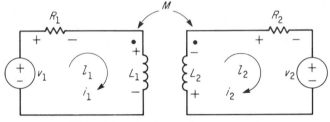

Fig. 2.7.1.   Simple transformer network.

We have two loops $l_1$ and $l_2$. Let the loop currents be $i_1$ and $i_2$. Let $L_1$ and $L_2$ be the self-inductances of the coils and $M$ the mutual inductance. Let us assume further that the coils are wound in such a way that the induced voltage due to mutual inductance opposes the self-induced voltages due to self-inductances. According to the dot convention, this implies that $i_1$ enters the coil $L_1$ at the dot and $i_2$ leaves the coil $L_2$ at the dot. This is also shown in Fig. 2.7.1. Hence, in loop $l_1$ the voltage induced due to $M$ and $i_2$ will be $-M\dfrac{di_2}{dt}$ and if we apply KVL to loop $l_1$, we get

$$-v_1 + i_1 R_1 + L_1 \frac{di_1}{dt} - M \frac{di_2}{dt} = 0 \qquad (2.7.1)$$

In loop $l_2$ the voltage induced due to $i_1$ in $l_1$ is $-M\dfrac{di_1}{dt}$. Now if we apply KVL to loop $l_2$, we get

$$L_2 \frac{di_2}{dt} + i_2 R_2 + v_2 - M \frac{di_1}{dt} = 0 \qquad (2.7.2)$$

Solving Eqs. 2.7.1 and 2.7.2 will give us $i_1$ and $i_2$ and hence the total behavior of the network.

*Example 2.7.1*

Write down the network equations for the network shown in Fig. 2.7.2.

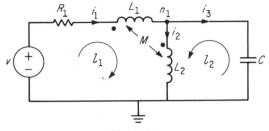

Fig. 2.7.2.

*Solution*

Let us first consider loop $l_1$. Here we have two inductances $L_1$ and $L_2$, with mutual inductance $M$. Since $i_1$ and $i_2$ both enter the dots according to the dot convention, the induced voltage has a positive sign. In loop $l_1$ using VCR and KVL and KCL we get

   VCR

Voltage drop across $R_1$ = $i_1 R_1$

Voltage drop across $L_1$ = voltage drop due $i_1$ + voltage drop due to $i_2$

$$= L_1 \frac{di_1}{dt} + M \frac{di_2}{dt}$$

Voltage drop across $L_2$ = voltage drop due to $i_2$ + voltage drop due to $i_1$

$$= L_2 \frac{di_2}{dt} + M \frac{di_1}{dt}$$

   KVL

Now applying KVL to loop $l_1$, we get

$$- v + i_1 R_1 + L_1 \frac{di_1}{dt} + M \frac{di_2}{dt} + L_2 \frac{di_2}{dt} + M \frac{di_1}{dt} = 0$$

Similarly we apply KVL to loop $l_2$ to obtain

$$L_2 \frac{di_2}{dt} + M \frac{di_1}{dt} - \frac{1}{C} \int_{t_0}^{t} i_3(t') \, dt' = 0$$

   KCL

Applying KCL to $n_1$, we get

$$i_1 = i_2 + i_3$$

The last three equations when solved give us the total solution.

## 2.8. LINEAR AND NONLINEAR NETWORKS: SUPERPOSITION AND HOMOGENEITY

It was mentioned earlier in this chapter that the basic problem in circuit analysis is to determine the branch voltages and currents of a given network which is excited by independent voltage or current sources. We used nodal and loop methods of analysis to obtain a set of integrodifferential equations that can be solved for the node voltages and loop currents. It was then shown that the branch voltages and currents can be found by simple manipulation of these auxiliary variables.   In many practical cases, however, one is interested in the voltage across or current through a particular circuit element due to a particular voltage or current excitation.  For example, consider the network shown in Fig. 2.8.1; this

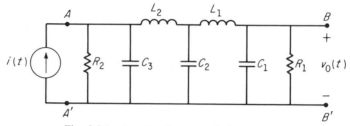

Fig. 2.8.1.   Input and output of a low-pass filter.

network is widely used in communication systems and is known as a *low-pass filter*. The excitation (or the input) is the current source $i(t)$ and the response (or the output) is the voltage across the terminating resistor $v_0(t)$. Given the input $i(t)$, we can use KCL, KVL and the branch voltage current relations (VCR) to obtain the output $v_0(t)$.

In this section we introduce some useful terms and definitions concerning the input-output relation of a network which is comprised of linear resistors, capacitors, inductors and mutual inductances.  To facilitate the discussion we assume that the network under consideration is placed in a *black box* in the sense that only input and output are available for examination.  Schematic representation of such a network is shown in Fig. 2.8.2.

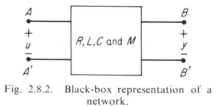

Fig. 2.8.2.   Black-box representation of a network.

Assume that the input is $u$ and the output is $y$. Let us consider two distinct inputs $u_1$ and $u_2$ and denote their corresponding outputs by $y_1$ and $y_2$. Then

$$u_1 \rightarrow y_1 \qquad (2.8.1)$$

and

$$u_2 \rightarrow y_2 \qquad (2.8.2)$$

(i.e., the input $u_1$ gives the output $y_1$ and the input $u_2$ gives the output $y_2$).

Now if *all the network elements are linear* and if *all the initial conditions are equal to zero*, then

$$u_1 + u_2 \rightarrow y_1 + y_2 \qquad (2.8.3)$$

That is, if both the inputs are applied simultaneously, the output will be the sum of the individual outputs corresponding to the inputs applied separately. This property of the network is known as the *superposition* property.

Furthermore, if we multiply the input by a constant $k$, the output will also be multiplied by $k$, i.e.,

$$ku \rightarrow ky \qquad (2.8.4)$$

This property of the network is known as the *homogeneity* property. If a network whose initial conditions are equal to zero satisfies *both* superposition property and homogeneity property, it is called *linear*.

*Example 2.8.1*

Consider the network shown in Fig. 2.8.3. Let the input be the voltage source $v$ and the output to be the current $i$. Show that this network is linear.

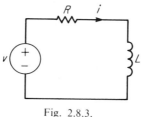

Fig. 2.8.3.

*Solution*

Let us establish superposition and homogeneity to show linearity.

1. Let $v = v_1$, $i = i_1$, and $i(0) = 0$. Then KVL gives

$$v_1 = i_1 R + L\frac{di_1}{dt}$$

2. Let $v = v_2$, $i = i_2$, and $i(0) = 0$. Then KVL gives

$$v_2 = i_2 R + L\frac{di_2}{dt}$$

3. Now let $v = v_1 + v_2$, $i = i_3$, and $i(0) = 0$. Then KVL gives

$$v_1 + v_2 = Ri_3 + L\frac{di_3}{dt}$$

Adding equations given in 1 and 2,

$$v_1 + v_2 = R(i_1 + i_2) + L\frac{d(i_1 + i_2)}{dt}$$

Comparing the above equation with that given in 3, we get,

$$i_3 = i_2 + i_2$$

Hence the response of $v_1 + v_2$ is $i_1 + i_2$. The principle of superposition is satisfied.

4. Let $v = kv_1$, $i = i_4$, and $i(0) = 0$. Then KVL gives

$$kv_1 = i_4 R + L \frac{di_4}{dt}$$

Multiplying the equation given in 1 by $k$ and comparing with the above equation gives $i_4 = ki_1$. Hence the response to $kv_1$ is $ki_1$. The principle of homogeneity is satisfied.

Hence the network is linear. It is intuitively obvious that any combination of linear resistors, capacitors and inductors will result in a linear network.

*A network is said to be nonlinear if it does not satisfy either superposition or homogeneity conditions.* There are two important classes of networks that may be considered as nonlinear networks—first, networks that are comprised of linear resistors, capacitors and inductors but for which some of the initial conditions are nonzero, and second, networks that contain one or more nonlinear elements.

*Example 2.8.2*

Consider the network shown in Fig. 2.8.4. Let the input be the current source $u$ and the output be the voltage $y$. Let the initial voltage on

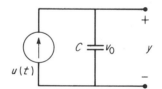

Fig. 2.8.4.    Linear capacitor with nonzero initial condition behaves as a nonlinear circuit.

the capacitor be $v_0 \neq 0$. Since the current through the capacitor is $u(t)$, we can write

$$y(t) = \frac{1}{C} \int_{t_0}^{t} u(t') \, dt' + v_0$$

or in the input-output notations

$$u(t) \rightarrow \frac{1}{C} \int_{t_0}^{t} u(t') \, dt' + v_0$$

Now let us multiply the input by $k$, if the network is linear, the output $y(t)$ must also be multiplied by $k$, but

$$ku(t) \rightarrow \frac{k}{C} \int_{t_0}^{t} u(t') \, dt' + v_0 \neq k \left[ \frac{1}{C} \int_{t_0}^{t} u(t') \, dt' + v_0 \right]$$

Hence the homogeneity is not satisfied, consequently the network is not linear. However, if $v_0 = 0$, then the network would have been considered as linear. For this reason this class of networks is said to be *zero-state linear*. Throughout the rest of this book we delete the words *zero state* and define a linear network as follows.

*DEFINITION.* A network is said to be *linear* if it is comprised of linear elements and independent voltage and current sources.

If the network under consideration contains one or more nonlinear elements, it will fail either the superposition or the homogeneity test. We can then state:

*DEFINITION.* A network is said to be nonlinear if it contains one or more nonlinear elements.

*Example 2.8.3*

Consider the network shown in Fig. 2.8.5. Let the resistor be linear with resistance $R$ and the capacitor be voltage controlled with $q$-$v$ relation

$$q = f(v) = v + \tfrac{1}{3} v^3$$

The problem is to find the voltage $v_1$ at node $n_1$.

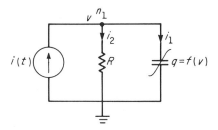

Fig. 2.8.5.   Nonlinear network.

*Solution*

We mentioned earlier that the KVL and KCL equations are independent of the nature of the elements. They hold for any network whether its elements are linear, nonlinear, or time-varying. Applying KCL at node $n_1$ we get

$$i(t) = i_1(t) + i_2(t)$$

But by VCR,

$$i_2 = \frac{v}{R}$$

and

$$i_1 = \frac{d}{dt} q = \left\{ \frac{d}{dv} f(v) \; \frac{dv}{dt} \right\}$$

or

$$i_1 = (1 + v^2)\frac{dv}{dt}$$

Replacing $i_1$ and $i_2$ in the above equation we obtain

$$(1 + v^2)\frac{dv}{dt} + \frac{1}{R}v = i$$

This is a *nonlinear* differential equation that can be solved for the voltage $v$. Several methods of numerical solutions of such equations will be discussed in Chapter 7.

**PROBLEMS**

**2.1.**  Write all the KCL and KVL equations for the networks shown, and choose node voltages and branch currents arbitrarily.

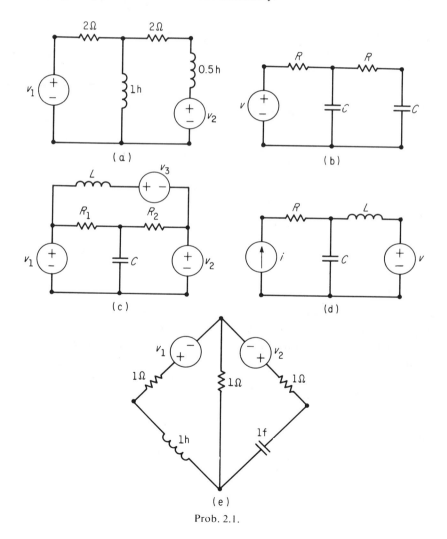

Prob. 2.1.

**2.2.** Draw the graphs of the networks of Prob. 2.1.
**2.3.** Write the *linear independent* KCL equations for the networks of Prob. 2.1.
**2.4.** Indicate all the meshes in the networks of Prob. 2.1.
**2.5.** Write the *linear independent* KVL equations for the networks of Prob. 2.1.
**2.6.** Use the nodal analysis to obtain a set of linearly independent equations that can be solved for the node voltages of the networks in Prob. 2.1.
**2.7.** Use the loop analysis to obtain a set of linearly independent equations that can be solved for the mesh currents of the networks of Prob. 2.1.
**2.8.** Perform the nodal analysis on the network shown.

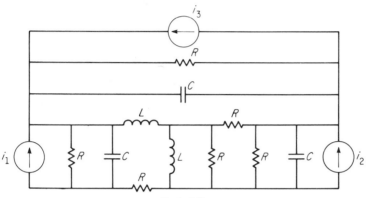

Prob. 2.8.

**2.9.** Perform the mesh analysis on the network shown.

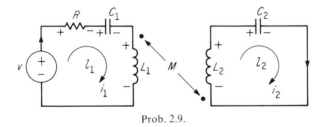

Prob. 2.9.

**2.10.** Find the loop equation for the networks shown.

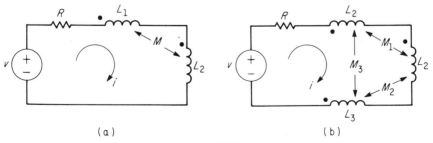

(a)                          (b)

Prob. 2.10.

**2.11.** Find $R$, $L$, and $C$ for the networks shown.

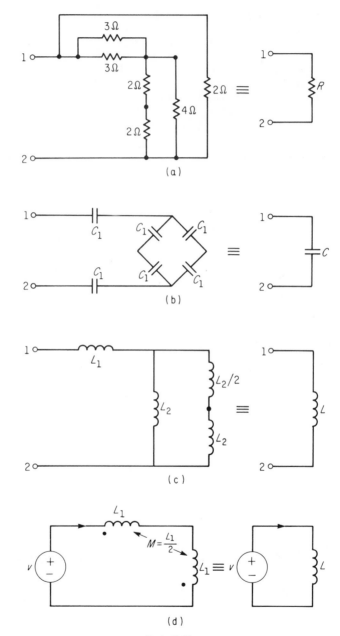

(a)

(b)

(c)

(d)

Prob. 2.11.

## CHAPTER 3

# Representation and Specification of Signals

## 3.1. INTRODUCTION

Up to this point in our discussions of circuit elements and network equations we have not considered specific forms for voltage or current signals which drive our circuit elements and networks. In this chapter we discuss several basic types of input signals that are quite useful in circuit analysis. These signals are useful either because they model physical signals frequently used in the laboratory, or because they are helpful in obtaining analytical results which are fundamental to the mathematical description of networks.

## 3.2. ELEMENTARY SIGNALS

Consider the independent voltage source shown in Fig. 3.2.1. This source consists of a battery in series with a switch that is closed at time

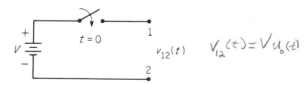

Fig. 3.2.1.   Independent voltage source.

$t = 0$. The terminals marked 1 and 2 are to be connected to a network so that the voltage which is applied to the network is $v_{12}(t)$. How can $v_{12}(t)$ be described in mathematical form? We can consider dividing the time axis, $-\infty < t < \infty$, into two parts, $-\infty < t < 0$ and $0 \le t < \infty$.

For the time interval $-\infty < t < 0$, the switch is open and the voltage $v_{12}(t)$ is 0; that is,

$$v_{12}(t) = 0 \qquad -\infty < t < 0 \qquad (3.2.1)$$

On the interval $0 \le t < \infty$, the switch is closed and the voltage $v_{12}(t)$ is $V$; that is,

$$v_{12}(t) = V \qquad 0 \le t < \infty \qquad (3.2.2)$$

We can rewrite Eqs. 3.2.1 and 3.2.2 in a single relationship describing $v_{12}$ as a function of time:

$$v_{12}(t) = \begin{cases} 0 & -\infty < t < 0 \\ V & 0 \le t < \infty \end{cases} \qquad (3.2.3)$$

A plot of Eq. 3.2.3 is shown in Fig. 3.2.2. Notice the voltage $v_{12}(t)$ takes

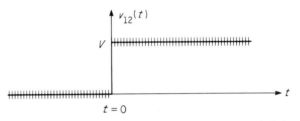

Fig. 3.2.2.   Time signal generated by battery and switch in series.

a *step* of size $V$ at the instant $t = 0$. We can describe this mathematically by defining a function which exhibits this property.

### Unit Step Function

The unit step function $u_0(x)$ is defined by the relationship

$$u_0(x) = \begin{cases} 1 & x \ge 0 \\ 0 & x < 0 \end{cases} \qquad (3.2.4)$$

This function is plotted in Fig. 3.2.3. Notice we have specified the value

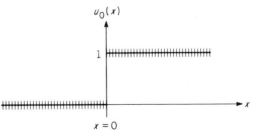

Fig. 3.2.3.   Unit step function.

of $u_0(x)$ at $x = 0$ as being 1. Since the function is discontinuous at the point $x = 0$, the value we assign it at this point is arbitrary. We have defined the value of the function at the discontinuity as the value the function assumes immediately after the discontinuity. Thus we can write the voltage $v_{12}(t)$ of Fig. 3.2.1 as

$$v_{12}(t) = Vu_0(t) \tag{3.2.5}$$

*Example 3.2.1*

Write the voltage which appears as $v_{12}(t)$ in Fig. 3.2.4a as a mathematical function of the time variable $t$.

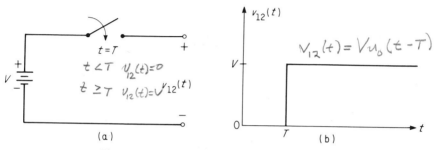

Fig. 3.2.4.   Unit step function applied at $t = T$.

*Solution*

The voltage $v_{12}(t)$ is zero for $t < T$ and equals $V$ volts for $t \geq T$. Thus we write

$$v_{12}(t) = Vu_0(x)$$

where $x < 0$ for $t < T$ and $x > 0$ for $t > T$. Now let $x = t - T$. Then

$$v_{12}(t) = Vu_0(t - T)$$

This is shown in Fig. 3.2.4b.

Other types of signals also arise quite naturally when considering simple network configurations. For example consider the circuit shown in Fig. 3.2.5 containing a capacitor in series with a current source of

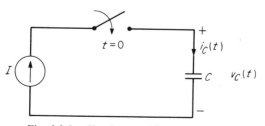

Fig. 3.2.5.   Simple capacitive series circuit.

constant value $I$. At $t = 0$ the switch is closed. The voltage $v_C(t)$ appearing across the capacitor terminals is

$$v_C(t) = \frac{1}{C} \int_{-\infty}^{t} i_C(\sigma)\, d\sigma \tag{3.2.6}$$

However,

$$i_C(t) = I u_0(t) \tag{3.2.7}$$

Hence

$$v_C(t) = \frac{1}{C} \int_{-\infty}^{t} I u_0(\sigma)\, d\sigma \tag{3.2.8}$$

Since

$$u_0(t) = \begin{cases} 0 & t < 0 \\ 1 & t \geq 0 \end{cases} \tag{3.2.9}$$

Then

$$v_C(t) = \begin{cases} \dfrac{1}{C} \displaystyle\int_{-\infty}^{t} 0 \cdot d\sigma & t < 0 \\[2ex] \dfrac{1}{C} \displaystyle\int_{-\infty}^{0} 0 \cdot d\sigma + \dfrac{1}{C} \displaystyle\int_{0}^{t} I\, d\sigma & t \geq 0 \end{cases} \tag{3.2.10}$$

or in terms of the unit step function,

$$v_C(t) = \frac{It}{C} u_0(t) \tag{3.2.11}$$

The function $v_C(t)$ is plotted in Fig. 3.2.6.  The voltage $v_C(t)$ is linearly

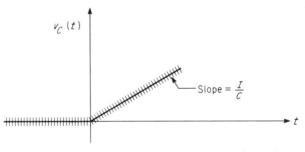

Fig. 3.2.6.   Capacitor voltage for circuit in Fig. 3.2.5.

increasing for $t \geq 0$, forming a *ramp* with slope $I/C$.  We can conveniently describe this behavior mathematically by considering the integral of the step function.

### Unit Ramp Function

The unit ramp function, $u_1(x)$, is defined as the integral of the step function

$$u_1(x) \triangleq \int_{-\infty}^{x} u_0(\sigma)\, d\sigma \qquad (3.2.12)$$

This integral can be evaluated as before, however, it is useful to consider the integral from its basic definition as being the area under the function from $-\infty$ to $x$. As indicated in Fig. 3.2.7, for $x < 0$, this area is zero

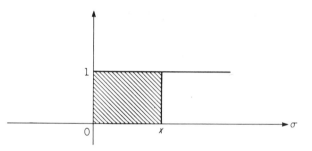

Fig. 3.2.7.   Graphical evaluation of integral in Eq. 3.2.12.

while for $x \geq 0$, it is equal to the area contained in a rectangle of height 1 and base $x$. Hence we have

$$u_1(x) = \begin{cases} 0 & x < 0 \\ x & x \geq 0 \end{cases} \qquad (3.2.13)$$

*Example 3.2.2*

Write the voltage $v_C(t)$ of Eq. 3.2.10 using the unit ramp function.

*Solution*

Since $v_C(t)$ is zero for $t < 0$ and increases linearly for $t \geq 0$ with slope $I/C$ we have

$$v_C(t) = \frac{I}{C} u_1(t)$$

The unit ramp function, $u_1(x)$, is then the indefinite integral of the unit step $u_0(x)$, and has a slope of unity for $x > 0$. Since $u_1(x)$ is the integral of $u_0(x)$, we must have

$$\frac{du_1(x)}{dx} = u_0(x) \qquad (3.2.14)$$

i.e., the unit step function is the derivative of the unit ramp function. We could continue to integrate the unit step function to generate higher order functions of $x$. For example, integrating the unit step function twice and multiplying by a constant 2 we can define $u_2(x)$ as

$$u_2(x) = \begin{cases} 0 & x < 0 \\ x^2 & x \geq 0 \end{cases} \tag{3.2.15}$$

or equivalently

$$u_2(x) = 2 \int_{-\infty}^{x} u_1(\sigma)\, d\sigma \tag{3.2.16}$$

Similarly, we can obtain

$$u_3(x) = \begin{cases} 0 & \text{for } x < 0 \\ x^3 & \text{for } x \geq 0 \end{cases} \tag{3.2.17}$$

or

$$u_3(x) = 3 \int_{-\infty}^{x} u_2(\sigma)\, d\sigma \tag{3.2.18}$$

In general, we define the function $u_n(x)$ as

$$u_n(x) \triangleq n \int_{-\infty}^{x} u_{n-1}(\sigma)\, d\sigma \tag{3.2.19}$$

so that $u_n(x)$ has the property

$$u_n(x) = \begin{cases} 0 & x < 0 \\ x^n & x \geq 0 \end{cases} \tag{3.2.20}$$

Also

$$u_{n-1}(x) = \frac{1}{n} \frac{d}{dx} u_n(x) \tag{3.2.21}$$

*Example 3.2.3*

Write the signal $f(t)$ shown in Fig. 3.2.8 using the functions $u_n(x)$.

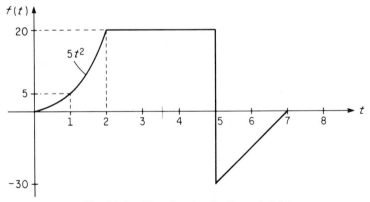

Fig. 3.2.8.   Time function for Example 3.2.3.

*Solution*

From the Fig. 3.2.8 we have

$$f(t) = \begin{cases} 0 & t < 0 \\ 5t^2 & 0 \le t < 2 \\ 20 & 2 \le t < 5 \\ 15(t - 7) & 5 \le t < 7 \\ 0 & 7 \le t \end{cases}$$

This function can be regarded as the sum of the three functions $f_1(t)$, $f_2(t)$ and $f_3(t)$ shown in Fig. 3.2.9. The function $f_1(t)$ is

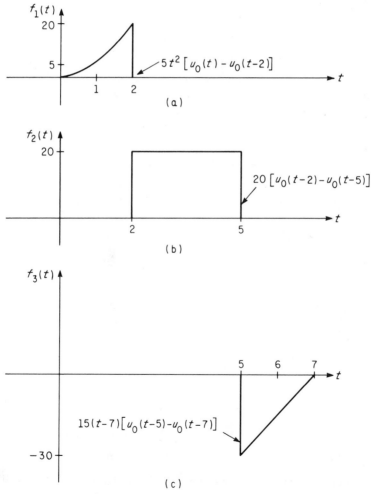

Fig. 3.2.9. Components of function $f(t)$.

$$f_1(t) = 5t^2[u_0(t) - u_0(t - 2)]$$

or

$$f_1(t) = 5u_2(t) - 5u_2(t)u_0(t - 2)$$

The function $f_2(t)$ is

$$f_2(t) = 20[u_0(t - 2) - u_0(t - 5)]$$

and $f_3(t)$ is

$$f_3(t) = 15(t - 7)[u_0(t - 5) - u_0(t - 7)]$$

or equivalently

$$f_3(t) = -[30u_0(t - 5) - 15u_1(t - 5)][u_0(t - 5) - u_0(t - 7)]$$

Now we combine $f_1(t), f_2(t),$ and $f_3(t)$ to obtain

$$\begin{aligned} f(t) &= f_1(t) + f_2(t) + f_3(t) \\ &= 5u_2(t) + [20 - 5u_2(t)]u_0(t - 2) \\ &\quad -[50 - 15u_1(t - 5)]u_0(t - 5) + [30 - 15u_1(t - 5)]u_0(t - 7) \end{aligned}$$

We have seen that the integral of the unit step function occurs quite naturally in circuit analysis. Another signal which occurs is the *derivative of the unit step function*. Consider the circuit shown in Fig. 3.2.10 con-

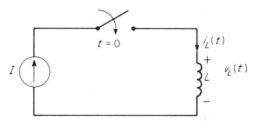

Fig. 3.2.10.   Simple inductive series circuit.

taining an inductor in series with a current source. The inductor voltage $v_L(t)$ is

$$v_L(t) = L\frac{di_L(t)}{dt} \tag{3.2.22}$$

However, $i_L(t) = Iu_0(t)$, hence we have

$$v_L(t) = LI\frac{du_0(t)}{dt} \tag{3.2.23}$$

The function $u_0(t)$ is a constant (0 or 1) for either $t < 0$ or $t > 0$, hence, $\frac{du_0}{dt} = 0$ for $t < 0$ and $t > 0$. At $t = 0$, the function $u_0(t)$ is discontinuous, taking a step of height 1 and having an unbounded slope. We write the derivative of $u_0(t)$ as $\delta(t)$, and require that $\delta(t)$ integrate to the unit step, i.e.,

$$\delta(t) = 0 \qquad \text{for all } t \neq 0 \tag{3.2.24}$$

and

$$\int_{-\infty}^{t} \delta(\sigma)\, d\sigma = u_0(t) \tag{3.2.25}$$

The signal $\delta(t)$ can also be obtained as the limit of the derivative of the waveform shown in Fig. 3.2.11a. As $\epsilon \to 0$, the waveform in Fig. 3.2.11a

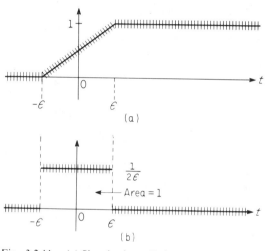

Fig. 3.2.11.   (a) Signal whose limit as $\epsilon \to 0$ is $u_0(t)$,
(b) derivative of (a).

becomes the unit step.  The derivative of this waveform is shown in Fig. 3.2.11b.  As $\epsilon$ approaches zero, the waveform shown in Fig. 3.2.11b approaches zero everywhere except the origin where the amplitude $1/2\epsilon$ becomes unbounded. However, we note that the area contained under the curve remains 1 as $\epsilon \to 0$. Thus in the limit, we can visualize $\delta(t)$ as approaching a very large spike or *impulse* at the origin with unbounded amplitude, zero width, and area equal to 1.

### Unit Impulse

The signal $\delta(t)$ is called the *unit impulse* or delta function. It is defined in Eqs. 3.2.24 and 3.2.25.  A useful property of the unit impulse is its *sampling property*.  If we consider multiplying the unit impulse by a function $f(t)$, we have from Eq. 3.2.24,

$$f(t)\delta(t) = 0 \qquad t < 0, t > 0 \tag{3.2.26}$$

Now, writing $f(t)$ as $f(0) + [f(t) - f(0)]$ and integrating $f(t)\delta(t)$ over the interval $(-\infty, t)$, we have

$$\int_{-\infty}^{t} f(\sigma)\delta(\sigma)\, d\sigma = \int_{-\infty}^{t} f(0)\delta(\sigma)\, d\sigma + \int_{-\infty}^{t} [f(\sigma) - f(0)]\delta(\sigma)\, d\sigma \qquad (3.2.27)$$

The first integral on the right-hand side of Eq. 3.2.27 can be evaluated using Eq. 3.2.25 as

$$\int_{-\infty}^{t} f(0)\delta(\sigma)\, d\sigma = f(0) \int_{-\infty}^{t} \delta(\sigma)\, d\sigma = f(0)u_0(t) \qquad (3.2.28)$$

For the second integral of Eq. 3.2.27 we have from Eq. 3.2.24 that the integrand is zero for $0 < \sigma$, $\sigma > 0$. In addition, $[f(\sigma) - f(0)]$ is zero for $\sigma = 0$, hence the second integral, being an integral whose integrand is zero over the region of integration, is zero. Thus, rewriting Eq. 3.2.27, we have

$$\int_{-\infty}^{t} f(\sigma)\delta(\sigma)\, d\sigma = f(0) \int_{-\infty}^{t} \delta(\sigma)\, d\sigma \qquad (3.2.29)$$

Differentiating both sides of the above equation gives the sampling property of the unit impulse:

$$f(t)\delta(t) = f(0)\delta(t) \qquad (3.2.30)$$

This equality indicates that multiplication of a function by a unit impulse corresponds to sampling the function at the time instant where the impulse is nonzero. We will elaborate more on the impulse function in Chapter 8.

*Example 3.2.4*

Find the first derivative of the function $f(t)$ in Fig. 3.2.8.

*Solution*

We have found in Example 3.2.3

$$f(t) = 5u_2(t) + [20 - 5u_2(t)]u_0(t - 2) - [50 - 15u_1(t - 5)]u_0(t - 5)$$
$$+ [30 - 15u_1(t - 5)]u_0(t - 7)$$

Hence

$$\frac{df(t)}{dt} = 10u_1(t) + [20 - 5u_2(t)]\delta(t - 2) - 10u_1(t)u_0(t - 2)$$

$$-[50 - 15u_1(t - 5)]\delta(t - 5) + 15u_0(t - 5)u_0(t - 5)$$
$$+ [30 - 15u_1(t - 5)]\delta(t - 7) - 15u_0(t - 5)u_0(t - 7)$$

Evaluating coefficients and simplifying gives

$$\frac{df(t)}{dt} = 10u_1(t) - 10u_1(t)u_0(t - 2) - 50\delta(t - 5)$$

$$+ 15u_0(t - 5) - 15u_0(t - 7)$$

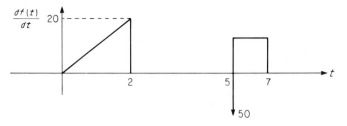

Fig. 3.2.12.   Derivative of $f(t)$ of Fig. 3.2.8.

This function is plotted in Fig. 3.2.12. A negative impulse of strength 50 is indicated at $t = 5$ by a spike with the number 50. By comparing this with Fig. 3.2.8, we see that this impulse occurred because of the discontinuity in $f(t)$ at $t = 5$. The *strength* of the impulse is simply the magnitude of the discontinuity in the function $f(t)$ at $t = 5$.

### The Exponential Function

Another signal which we will encounter frequently is the *exponential function $e^{at}$*. This function has the properties

$$\frac{de^{at}}{dt} = ae^{at} \tag{3.2.31}$$

and

$$\int_{-\infty}^{t} e^{a\sigma}d\sigma = \frac{1}{a} e^{at} \tag{3.2.32}$$

More generally,

$$\frac{d^n}{dt^n} (e^{at}) = a^n e^{at} \tag{3.2.33}$$

and

$$\underbrace{\int \cdots \int}_{n \text{ times}} e^{at}\,dt = \frac{1}{a^n} e^{at} \tag{3.2.34}$$

## 3.3. PERIODIC SIGNALS

The signals which we discussed in the previous section were similar in the respect that they were not repetitive in time. We now take up the description of signals which are repetitive or *periodic*.

### Sinusoidal Waveform

The sinusoidal waveform

$$\sin (2\pi ft)$$

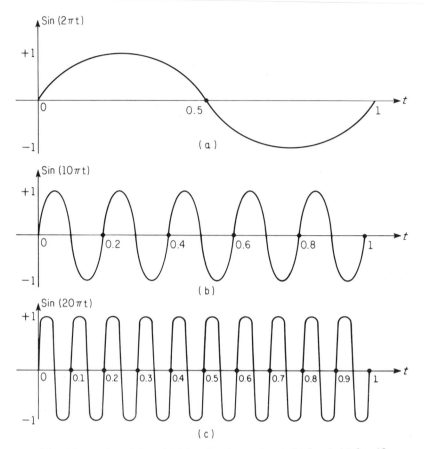

Fig. 3.3.1.  Plot of sinusoidal function for (a) $f = 1$, (b) $f = 5$, (c) $f = 10$.

is plotted in Fig. 3.3.1a, b, and c for three values of the parameter $f$. The parameter $f$ is called the *frequency of the sinusoid* and has units of *Hertz* or *cycles per second*. Notice that no matter which value of $f$ is chosen, the resulting waveforms remain periodic, repeating the same values over each interval of length $1/f$ sec. This interval, the time period associated with one *cycle* of the waveform is called the *period* of the signal and will be denoted by $T$. Notice from the Fig. 3.3.1, the sinusoid with frequency $f = 1$ Hz goes through 1 cycle each second; i.e., 1 cycle per second. The sinusoid with $f = 5$ Hz goes through 5 cycles per second, and the sinusoid with $f = 10$ Hz goes through 10 cycles per second. Hence $f = 1/T$.

The sinusoidal function $\sin(2\pi \overline{ft + \phi})$, where $\overline{t + \phi}$ is the shorthand notation for $(t + \phi)$, is plotted in Fig. 3.3.2 for three values of the *phase parameter* $\phi$. Note from the figure the periodic waveform can be generated by shifting the single cycle of the sinusoid, shown undashed in the

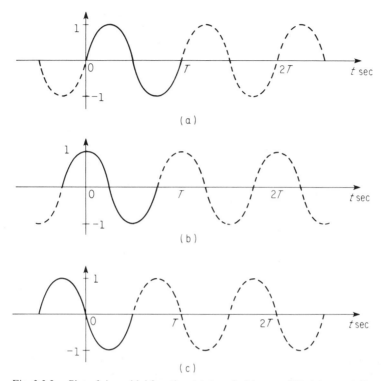

Fig. 3.3.2.   Plot of sinusoidal function (a) $\phi = 0$, (b), $\phi = T/4$, (c) $\phi = T/2$.

figure, through all integer multiples of the period.   The phase parameter determines the portion of the period of that fundamental cycle which lies to the left of the axis $t = 0$.   For any chosen value of $\phi$, the resulting waveform remains periodic.

The periodic sinusoid has the property

$$\sin (2\pi f \overline{t + \phi}) = \sin (2\pi f \overline{t + T + \phi}) \qquad \forall t \qquad (3.3.1)$$

as can easily be shown by expanding the argument of the right hand function and using trigonometric identities.   This property suggests the following definition for a periodic function.

*DEFINITION.*   A function $g(t)$ is said to be periodic with period $T$ provided

$$g(t) = g(t + T), \qquad -\infty < t < \infty \qquad (3.3.2)$$

where $T$ is the smallest number which satisfies the equation.   The *fundamental frequency*, $f_0$, of $g(t)$ is defined by

$$f_0 \triangleq \frac{1}{T} \qquad (3.3.3)$$

and represents the number of repetitive cycles of the waveform which occur in a period of 1 sec.

### Square Wave

A square-wave signal is shown in Fig. 3.3.3. This type of signal occurs quite frequently in computer and communications circuits and is a special

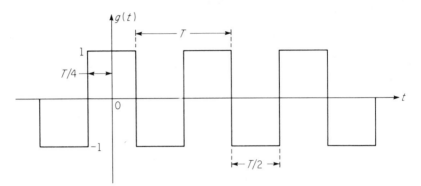

Fig. 3.3.3.  Square-wave signal.

case of a binary (two-level) waveform. This waveform satisfies the definition of a periodic function, the period is $T$ sec, the fundamental frequency $f_0$ is $1/T$ Hz. The square wave can be written in analytical form by noting that it is a repetition of the signal

$$s(t) = u_0(t) - 2u_0\left(t - \frac{T}{2}\right) + u_0(t - T) \qquad (3.3.4)$$

shown in Fig. 3.3.4. Thus using the shifting property of the unit step we have

$$g(t) = \sum_{n=-\infty}^{\infty} s(t + nT + \phi) \qquad (3.3.5)$$

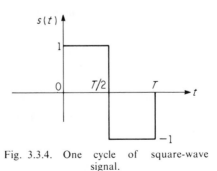

Fig. 3.3.4.  One  cycle  of  square-wave signal.

The phase term $\phi$, as in the case of the sinusoid, determines the portion of period lying to the left of axis $t = 0$. For the signal shown in Fig. 3.3.3, $\phi = T/4$.

$$g(t) = \sum_{n=-\infty}^{\infty} s\left(t + nT + \frac{T}{4}\right) \tag{3.3.6}$$

**Sawtooth Waveform**

The sawtooth waveform shown in Fig. 3.3.5 is one quite often encountered in television and oscilloscope circuits. An analytical expression

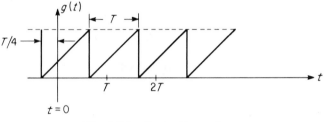

Fig. 3.3.5.   Sawtooth waveform.

for this waveform can be quickly obtained by noting that it is a repetition of the signal

$$s(t) = u_1(t) - u_1(t)u_0(t - T) \tag{3.3.7}$$

Thus the general sawtooth waveform can be written as

$$g(t) = \sum_{n=-\infty}^{\infty} s(t + nT + \phi) \tag{3.3.8}$$

For the waveform shown in Fig. 3.3.5, $\phi = T/4$, hence

$$g(t) = \sum_{n=-\infty}^{\infty} s\left(t + nT + \frac{T}{4}\right) \tag{3.3.9}$$

**Impulse Train**

The signal indicated in Fig. 3.3.6 is called the *unit impulse train*. As will be discussed later, this signal plays a fundamental role in the analysis of steady-state circuit response to a periodic input. Obviously, $g(t)$ in this case is just a repetition of the signal $\delta(t)$, hence, the impulse train can be described analytically as

$$g(t) = \sum_{n=-\infty}^{\infty} \delta(t + nT + \phi) \tag{3.3.10}$$

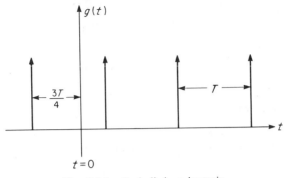

Fig. 3.3.6.  Periodic impulse train.

For the specific case shown in Fig. 3.3.6, $\phi = \sqrt[3]{4}\,T$.  Thus

$$g(t) = \sum_{n=-\infty}^{\infty} \delta\left(t + nT + \frac{3}{4}\,T\right) \qquad (3.3.11)$$

## 3.4.  SIGNAL SPECIFICATION

Signals and waveforms are specified according to those characteristics which affect circuit design.  Because many circuit elements are linear only over specified voltage or current levels, the *peak* value of the waveform is often specified.  This is simply the maximum value which the waveform assumes in an absolute sense.  The *average* value of the waveform over a given time interval is also of frequent interest.  The average or *mean* is defined as the time integral of the waveform over the interval of interest divided by the interval, i.e.,

$$g(t) = \frac{1}{t_1 - t_0} \int_{t_0}^{t_1} g(t)\,dt \qquad (3.4.1)$$

where $t_0$ and $t_1$ denote the beginning and end points of the desired interval.

### Root Mean Square (rms) Values

One of the most widely used signal specifications is the *Root Mean Square* (*rms*) value.  Recall from Chapter 1 that the energy dissipated in a linear resistor $R$ over the interval $(t_0, t_1)$ is

$$E[t_0, t_1] = \frac{1}{R} \int_{t_0}^{t_1} v^2(t)\,dt \qquad (3.4.2)$$

The rms value of the voltage waveform, over the interval $(t_0, t_1)$ is the equivalent constant voltage which would be required to deliver the same energy to the resistor as the waveform of interest, i.e.,

$$E[t_0, t_1] = \frac{V_{rms}^2(t_1 - t_0)}{R} = \frac{1}{R} \int_{t_0}^{t_1} v^2(t)\, dt \qquad (3.4.3)$$

Solving Eq. 3.4.3 for $V_{rms}$ gives

$$V_{rms} \overset{\Delta}{=} \sqrt{\frac{1}{t_1 - t_0} \int_{t_0}^{t_1} v^2(t)\, dt} \qquad (3.4.4)$$

Therefore to find the rms value of a waveform, we take the square root of the mean of the square of the waveform. For periodic signals, $g(t)$, it is easy to show that if the interval $(t_0, t_1)$ contains a large number of cycles, then the rms value is approximately equal to the rms value obtained over one period of the signal, i.e.,

$$G_{rms} = \sqrt{\frac{1}{T} \int_{a}^{a+T} g^2(t)\, dt} \qquad (3.4.5)$$

where $a$ is an arbitrary constant. Quite often it will be convenient to choose $a = -\phi$, when $\phi$ is the phase of the periodic signal.

*Example 3.4.1*

Find the rms value of the periodic signal shown in Fig. 3.3.5.

*Solution*

We use Eq. 3.4.5 choosing $a = -T/4$, hence

$$G_{rms} = \sqrt{\frac{1}{T} \int_{-T/4}^{3T/4} u_1^2(t + T/4)\, dt}$$

Changing variables of integration gives

$$\frac{1}{T} \int_{-T/4}^{3T/4} u_1^2\left(t + \frac{T}{4}\right) dt = \frac{1}{T} \int_{0}^{T} u_1^2(t')\, dt' = \frac{1}{T} \int_{0}^{T} t'^2\, dt'$$

$$= \frac{t'^3}{3T}\Big|_{0}^{T} = \frac{T^2}{3}$$

Hence

$$G_{rms} = \frac{T}{\sqrt{3}}$$

**Evaluation of Average and rms Values by Use of A Digital Computer**

The calculation of the average value and the rms value of a waveform involves the evaluation of a definite integral. We have already developed a computer program in Chapter 1 which evaluates definite integrals using Simpson's Rule of Integration. We will show how this program is used to evaluate the rms value of periodic waveforms.

In general the evaluation of rms value of a periodic waveform $g(t)$

involves the evaluation of an integral of the form

$$\frac{1}{T} \int_{-\phi}^{-\phi+T} g^2(t)\,dt$$

In order to use the integration computer program developed in Chapter 1, we have to note that

$$T0 = -\phi$$
$$T1 = -\phi + T$$
$$f(t) = g^2(t)$$
$$N = \text{to be chosen as an even number}$$

Then

$$\text{VIN} = \int_{-\phi}^{-\phi+T} g^2(t)\,dt$$

Now

$$G_{\text{rms}} = \sqrt{\frac{1}{T} \int_{-\phi}^{-\phi+T} g^2(t)\,dt}$$

$$= \sqrt{\frac{\text{VIN}}{T}} = \sqrt{\frac{\text{VIN}}{T1 - T0}}$$

For evaluating rms value, all we have to do is to introduce a new card in the program after VIN as

$$\text{RMS} = \text{SQRT (VIN}/(T1 - T0))$$

Instead of printing VIN, we now print RMS. We now give two examples evaluating the rms and average values.

*Example 3.4.2*

Use the computer program to evaluate the rms value of the periodic waveform of Fig. 3.3.5. Assume $T = 1$.

*Solution*

Here as shown in Example 3.4.1, we have for $T = 1$

$$G_{\text{rms}} = \sqrt{\int_{-1/4}^{3/4} u_1^2\left(t + \frac{1}{4}\right) dt}$$

$$= \sqrt{\int_{-1/4}^{3/4} \left(t + \frac{1}{4}\right)^2 dt}$$

We note for the computer program $T0 = -1/4$, $T1 = 3/4$, $f(t) = (t + 1/4)^2$. Choosing $N = 16$, we have the computer program and printout of rms value.

```
C       THIS PROGRAM IS FOR EXAMPLE 3.4-2
C       THIS PROGRAM COMPUTES THE RMS VALUE,
C       USING SIMPSON'S RULE OF INTEGRATION,
C       CHOOSE N AS AN EVEN NUMBER,  NOTE THAT N
C       IS RESERVED FOR INTEGER NUMBERS IN FORTRAN
C       SO WE LET N = AN,
C       THIS PART COMPUTES THE VALUE OF THE INTEGRAL(VIN)
        N=16
        AN = N
        T0=-0,25
        T1=0,75
        H = (T1-T0)/AN
        SUM=0,
        TA = T0
        TB = TA+H
        TC = TB+H
C       FTA IS THE GIVEN INTEGRAND F(T),T BEING REPLACED BY TA
C       SIMILARLY FTB AND FTC
C       THE FOLLOWING SECTION IS THE DO LOOP,
        M = N/2
        DO 10 I=1,M
        FTA = (TA+0,25)**2
        FTB = (TB+0,25)**2
        FTC = (TC+0,25)**2
        SUM  = SUM+FTA+4,*FTB+FTC
        TA = TA+2,0*H
        TB = TA+H
        TC = TB+H
   10 CONTINUE
        VIN = SUM*H/3,
C       THIS PART COMPUTES THE RMS VALUE AND PRINTS IT,
        RMS = SQRT(VIN/(T1-T0))
        PRINT 15,RMS
   15 FORMAT (5X,'RMS VALUE IS',F10,6/)
        END
```

```
        RMS VALUE IS   ,577350
```

*Example 3.4.3*

   The voltage across a certain branch of a network can be approximated by a waveform as shown in Fig. 3.4.1.  Find (a) the average value of this voltage, and (b) the rms value of the voltage.

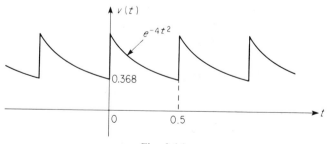

Fig. 3.4.1.

*Solution*

(a) Here

$$V_{avg} = \frac{1}{0.5} \int_0^{0.5} v(t)\,dt$$

$$= \frac{1}{0.5} \int_0^{0.5} e^{-4t^2}\,dt$$

To use the integration computer program we note $T0 = 0$, $T1 = 0.5$, $f(t) = e^{-4t^2}$. We choose $N = 16$. Then

$$AVG = VIN / ((T1 - T0))$$

The computer program and the average value is printed below.

```
C       THIS PROGRAM IS FOR EXAMPLE 3,4-3A
C       THIS PROGRAM COMPUTES THE AVG VALUE,
C       USING SIMPSON'S RULE OF INTEGRATION,
C       CHOOSE N AS AN EVEN NUMBER,  NOTE THAT N
C       IS RESERVED FOR INTEGER NUMBERS IN FORTRAN
C       SO WE LET N = AN,
C       THIS PART COMPUTES THE VALUE OF THE INTEGRAL(VIN)
        N=16
        AN = N
        T0=0,
        T1=0,5
        H = (T1-T0)/AN
        SUM=0,
        TA = T0
        TB = TA+H
        TC = TB+H
C       FTA IS THE GIVEN INTEGRAND F(T),T BEING REPLACED BY TA
C       SIMILARLY FTB AND FTC
C       THE FOLLOWING SECTION IS THE DO LOOP,
        M = N/2
        DO 10 I=1,M
        FTA = EXP(-4,*TA**2)
        FTB = EXP(-4,*TB**2)
        FTC = EXP(-4,*TC**2)
        SUM  = SUM+FTA+4,*FTB+FTC
        TA = TA+2,0*H
        TB = TA+H
        TC = TB+H
     10 CONTINUE
        VIN = SUM*H/3,
C       THIS PART COMPUTES THE AVG VALUE AND PRINTS IT,
        AVG=VIN/(T1-T0)
        PRINT 15,AVG
     15 FORMAT (5X,'AVG VALUE IS',F10,6/)
        END


        AVG VALUE IS   ,746824
```

(b) Here

$$V_{rms} = \sqrt{\frac{1}{0.5} \int_0^{0.5} v^2(t)\,dt}$$

$$= \sqrt{\frac{1}{0.5} \int_0^{0.5} e^{-8t^2}\,dt}$$

To use the integration computer program, we note $T0 = 0$, $T1 = 0.5$, $f(t) = e^{-8t^2}$. We choose $N = 16$. Then

$$RMS = SQRT\,(VIN/T1 - T0)$$

The computer program as well as the rms value is printed below.

```
C       THIS PROGRAM IS FOR EXAMPLE 3,4-3B
C       THIS PROGRAM COMPUTES THE RMS VALUE,
C       USING SIMPSON'S RULE OF INTEGRATION,
C       CHOOSE N AS AN EVEN NUMBER,  NOTE THAT N
C       IS RESERVED FOR INTEGER NUMBERS IN FORTRAN
C       SO WE LET N = AN,
C       THIS PART COMPUTES THE VALUE OF THE INTEGRAL(VIN)
        N=16
        AN = N
        T0=0,
        T1=0,5
        H = (T1-T0)/AN
        SUM=0,
        TA = T0
        TB = TA+H
        TC = TB+H
C       FTA IS THE GIVEN INTEGRAND F(T),T BEING REPLACED BY TA
C       SIMILARLY FTB AND FTC
C       THE FOLLOWING SECTION IS THE DO LOOP,
        M = N/2
        DO 10 I=1,M
        FTA = EXP(-8,*TA**2)
        FTB = EXP(-8,*TB**2)
        FTC = EXP(-8,*TC**2)
        SUM  = SUM+FTA*4,*FTB*FTC
        TA = TA+2,0*H
        TB = TA+H
        TC = TB+H
     10 CONTINUE
        VIN = SUM*H/3,
C       THIS PART COMPUTES THE RMS VALUE AND PRINTS IT,
        RMS = SQRT(VIN/(T1-T0))
        PRINT 15,RMS
     15 FORMAT (5X,'RMS VALUE IS',F10,6/)
        END


        RMS VALUE IS    ,773398
```

**PROBLEMS**

**3.1.** Develop an analytical expression for the signal shown.

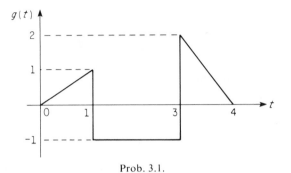

Prob. 3.1.

**3.2.** Develop an analytical expression for the signal shown.

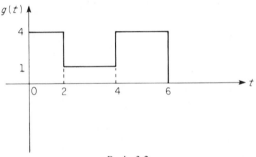

Prob. 3.2.

**3.3.** Write an expression for the derivative of the waveforms of (a) Prob. 3.1, and (b) Prob. 3.2.

**3.4.** Develop an analytical expression for the waveform shown.

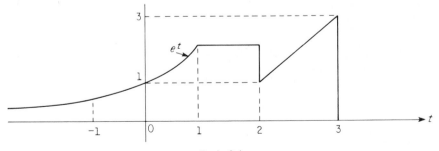

Prob. 3.4.

**3.5.**  Write an expression for the derivative of the waveform of Prob. 3.4.

**3.6.**  (a) Write an expression for the periodic waveform shown. (b) What is the period of this waveform? the fundamental frequency?

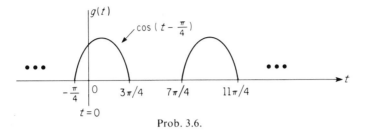

Prob. 3.6.

**3.7.**  (a) Write an expression for the periodic waveform shown. (b) What is the period of the waveform? the fundamental frequency?

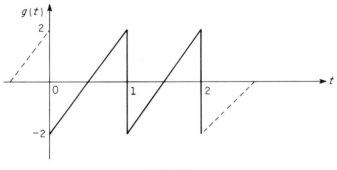

Prob. 3.7.

**3.8.**  (a) Find the rms value of the sinusoidal signal shown in Fig. 3.3.1a with $f = 1$. (b) Does the rms value change if we consider a different value of $f$ and a different value of $\phi$? (c) What is the rms value of the signal $A \sin(2\pi ft + \phi)$?

**3.9.**  Assume the waveform of Prob. 3.1 represents a voltage across a $10\Omega$ resistor. Find the energy delivered to the resistor over the time intervals (a) (0, 1), (b) (0, 2), and (c) (0, 5) seconds.

**3.10.**  Find the rms value of the waveform of Prob. 3.1 over the time intervals (a) (0,5), (b) (0,10).

**3.11.**  (a) Find the rms value of the waveform of Prob. 3.4 over the interval $-1,3$). (b) If the waveform of part (a) represents a current, find the energy delivered to a 5-$\Omega$ resistor by the current over the interval $(-1,3)$.

**3.12.**  Find the rms and average values of the waveform of Prob. 3.6 with and without using the computer program.

**3.13.**  Find the rms and average values of the waveform of Prob. 3.7 with and without using the computer program.

**3.14.**  Using the square wave in Fig. 3.3.3, (a) calculate the rms value over one period, (b) calculate the rms value over the interval $(0,9.5T)$ and compare answer with that for part (a). (c) Does the interval effect the rms value in this case?

**3.15.** Using the sawtooth wave in Fig. 3.3.5, (a) calculate the rms value over one period, (b) calculate the rms value over the interval $(0, 9.5T)$ and compare your answer with part (a). (c) Does the interval affect the rms value in this case? (d) Repeat (a) and (b) using the computer program.

**3.16.** A voltage waveform can be represented as $v(t) = te^{-t^2}$, $0 < t < 5$. Use the computer program to evaluate the average as well as rms value of $v(t)$.

**3.17.** Use the computer program to evaluate average as well as rms values of periodic waveforms shown.

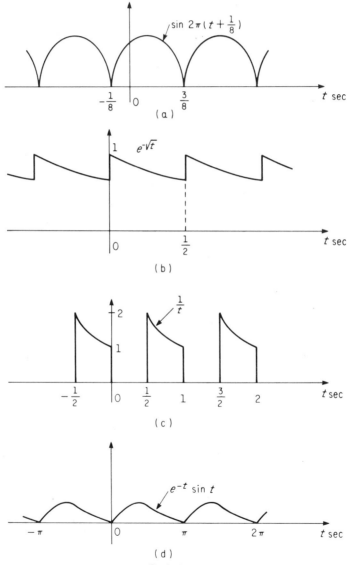

Prob. 3.17.

## CHAPTER 4

# Resistive Networks and Notions in Matrices and Determinants

## 4.1. INTRODUCTION AND SOME BASIC IDEAS ON MATRICES

In this chapter we develop the response in terms of voltages and currents for a given input. However, we will restrict ourselves to resistive networks. This will reduce the network equations to purely algebraic relationships. The primary emphasis in this chapter will be on the solution of these algebraic equations by the use of the digital computer. Before we formulate the solution for actual networks, we start with some ideas on matrices.

### Matrix Notation and Elementary Properties

Let us consider a set of three simultaneous algebraic equations as

$$a_{11}x_1 + a_{12}x_2 + a_{13}x_3 = s_1$$
$$a_{21}x_1 + a_{22}x_2 + a_{23}x_3 = s_2 \qquad (4.1.1)$$
$$a_{31}x_1 + a_{32}x_2 + a_{33}x_3 = s_3$$

We can write these equations as follows

$$\begin{bmatrix} a_{11} & a_{12} & a_{13} \\ a_{21} & a_{22} & a_{23} \\ a_{31} & a_{32} & a_{33} \end{bmatrix} \begin{bmatrix} x_1 \\ x_2 \\ x_3 \end{bmatrix} = \begin{bmatrix} s_1 \\ s_2 \\ s_3 \end{bmatrix} \qquad (4.1.2)$$

If we define

$$\begin{bmatrix} a_{11} & a_{12} & a_{13} \\ a_{21} & a_{22} & a_{23} \\ a_{31} & a_{32} & a_{33} \end{bmatrix} = \mathbf{A}, \begin{bmatrix} x_1 \\ x_2 \\ x_3 \end{bmatrix} = \mathbf{x}, \quad \text{and} \quad \begin{bmatrix} s_1 \\ s_2 \\ s_3 \end{bmatrix} = \mathbf{s} \qquad (4.1.3)$$

Equation (4.1.2) reduces to

$$\mathbf{Ax} = \mathbf{s} \qquad (4.1.4)$$

Equation 4.1.4 means exactly the same as Eq. 4.1.1 and provides a short-hand notation for writing simultaneous algebraic equations. Quantities $\mathbf{A}$, $\mathbf{x}, \mathbf{s}$ are called matrices. In general, we define a *matrix* $\mathbf{A}$ as a rectangular array of numbers arranged in $m$ rows and $n$ columns with $a_{ij}$ denoting an element in the $i$th row and $j$th column.

$$\mathbf{A} = \begin{bmatrix} a_{11} & a_{12} & \cdots & \cdots & a_{1n} \\ a_{21} & a_{22} & \cdots & \cdots & a_{2n} \\ \cdots & \cdots & a_{ij} & \cdots & \cdots \\ a_{m1} & a_{m2} & \cdots & \cdots & a_{mn} \end{bmatrix} \qquad (4.1.5)$$

The *dimension* of the matrix $\mathbf{A}$ is $m \times n$ and it is of *order* $(m,n)$. If $m = n$, then the number of rows is equal to the number of columns and the matrix is called a *square matrix* of order $n$. The matrix $\mathbf{A}$ of Eq. 4.1.3 has 3 rows and 3 columns. It is a $3 \times 3$ square matrix with 9 elements. On the other hand, both $\mathbf{x}$ and $\mathbf{s}$ are $3 \times 1$ nonsquare matrices. If $m = 1$, then the matrix has only one row. This matrix is called a *row vector*. It is

$$[a_{11} \quad a_{12} \quad \cdots \quad a_{1n}] \qquad (4.1.6)$$

If $n = 1$, the matrix has only one column. This matrix is called a *column vector*. It is

$$\begin{bmatrix} a_{11} \\ a_{21} \\ \vdots \\ a_{m1} \end{bmatrix} \qquad (4.1.7)$$

Both $\mathbf{x}$ and $\mathbf{s}$ of Eq. 4.1.3 are column vectors. Notationally, the matrix $\mathbf{A}$ of Eq. 4.1.5 is sometimes written

$$\mathbf{A} = (a_{ij}), \quad i = 1,\ldots,m, \quad j = 1,\ldots,n \qquad (4.1.8)$$

Consider two matrices

$$\mathbf{A} = (a_{ij}), \mathbf{B} = (b_{ij}), \quad i = 1,\ldots,m, \quad j = 1,\ldots,n$$

Now, if

$$a_{ij} = b_{ij}, \forall i,j \text{ then } \mathbf{A} = \mathbf{B} \qquad (4.1.9)$$

The above implies that matrices **A** and **B** are *equal matrices* and they have the same number of rows, columns, and elements.

*ADDITION OF MATRICES.* Two matrices **A** and **B** can be added if they have the same dimensions $m \times n$, and each element of one is added to the corresponding element of the other, i.e., if

$$\mathbf{A} = (a_{ij}) \quad \text{and} \quad \mathbf{B} = (b_{ij})$$

Then

$$\mathbf{A} + \mathbf{B} = (a_{ij} + b_{ij}) \qquad (4.1.10)$$

Similarly, for *subtraction* of matrices

$$\mathbf{A} - \mathbf{B} = (a_{ij} - b_{ij}) \qquad (4.1.11)$$

*Example 4.1.1.* Let

$$\mathbf{A} = \begin{bmatrix} 1 & -1 & 2 \\ 3 & 2 & 3 \end{bmatrix} \quad \text{and} \quad \mathbf{B} = \begin{bmatrix} 2 & 8 & 3 \\ 1 & 5 & 1 \end{bmatrix}$$

Then

$$\mathbf{A} + \mathbf{B} = \begin{bmatrix} 3 & 7 & 5 \\ 4 & 7 & 4 \end{bmatrix} \quad \text{and} \quad \mathbf{A} - \mathbf{B} = \begin{bmatrix} -1 & -9 & -1 \\ 2 & -3 & 2 \end{bmatrix}$$

It can be easily verified that if we have three matrices **A**, **B**, **C**, then

$$(\mathbf{A} + \mathbf{B}) + \mathbf{C} = \mathbf{A} + (\mathbf{B} + \mathbf{C}) \qquad (4.1.12)$$

*MULTIPLICATION OF MATRICES.* Before we define the rules of multiplication formally, we rewrite Eq. 4.1.2 which is a representation of Eq. 4.1.1. The representation is valid only if

$$\begin{bmatrix} a_{11} & a_{12} & a_{13} \\ a_{21} & a_{22} & a_{23} \\ a_{31} & a_{32} & a_{33} \end{bmatrix} \begin{bmatrix} x_1 \\ x_2 \\ x_3 \end{bmatrix} = \begin{bmatrix} a_{11}x_1 + a_{12}x_2 + a_{13}x_3 \\ a_{21}x_1 + a_{22}x_2 + a_{23}x_3 \\ a_{31}x_1 + a_{32}x_2 + a_{33}x_3 \end{bmatrix} \qquad (4.1.13)$$

The left-hand side of Eq. 4.1.13 represents a product of two matrices, **A** and **x**, resulting in the matrix on the right-hand side. The first element is formed by multiplying each element of the first row of **A** by the corresponding positioned element in the first column of matrix **x**, and adding the products. The second row of **A** times the column of **x** give the elements of row 2, respectively. The other elements are similarly obtained. Obviously, this procedure will fail if the number of elements in a row of **A** is not exactly the same as the number of elements in a column of **x**. This is then the primary condition of multiplication of two matrices: The number of columns of any matrix **A** must be equal to the number of rows of matrix **B** in order that there is a product **AB**. Obviously, if **AB** exists, it is not necessary that **BA** exist. Therefore, in general,

$$\mathbf{AB} \neq \mathbf{BA} \qquad (4.1.14)$$

When the number of columns of **A** is the same as the number of rows of **B**, then **A** is said to be *conformable* to **B** for product **AB**. Let

$$\mathbf{A} = (a_{ij})_{m \times r} \quad \text{and} \quad \mathbf{B} = (b_{ij})_{r \times n} \qquad (4.1.15)$$

The product $\mathbf{A} \cdot \mathbf{B} = \mathbf{P}$ is defined as

$$\mathbf{P} = (p_{ij}) = \left( \sum_{k=1}^{r} a_{ik} b_{kj} \right), \qquad i = 1, \dots, m, \quad j = 1, 2, \dots, n \qquad (4.1.16)$$

The dimension of **P** is $m \times n$. The element $p_{ij}$ of the $i$th row and $j$th column of **P** is the inner product of two vectors $\mathbf{a}_i = (a_{i1}, \dots, a_{ir})$ and $\mathbf{b}_j = (b_{1j}, \dots, b_{rj})$ and can be written as $\mathbf{a}_i \cdot \mathbf{b}_j$ or $\mathbf{a}_i \mathbf{b}_j$. If a scalar number $\alpha$ multiplies a matrix **A**, each element of the matrix is multiplied by $\alpha$. If

$$\mathbf{A} = (a_{ij}), \quad \text{then} \quad \alpha \mathbf{A} = (\alpha a_{ij}) \qquad (4.1.17)$$

We can easily verify that

$$(\mathbf{A} + \mathbf{B})\mathbf{C} = \mathbf{AC} + \mathbf{BC}$$
$$\mathbf{C}(\mathbf{A} + \mathbf{B}) = \mathbf{CA} + \mathbf{CB}$$

and

$$(\mathbf{AB})\mathbf{C} = \mathbf{A}(\mathbf{BC}) \qquad (4.1.18)$$

If $\mathbf{AB} = \mathbf{BA}$, then **A** and **B** are called *commutable* matrices.

*Example 4.1.2*

Let

$$\mathbf{A} = \begin{bmatrix} 2 & 2 \\ 1 & 2 \\ 4 & 2 \end{bmatrix}, \quad \mathbf{B} = \begin{bmatrix} 3 & 1 \\ 1 & 2 \end{bmatrix}$$

Here the dimension of **A** is $3 \times 2$. The dimension of **B** is $2 \times 2$. So the product **AB** has dimension $3 \times 2$. (Note that **BA** does not exist.)

$$\mathbf{AB} = \begin{bmatrix} 8 & 6 \\ 5 & 5 \\ 14 & 8 \end{bmatrix}$$

*Example 4.1.3*

Consider the resistive network shown in Fig. 4.1.1. Represent the resulting network equations in the matrix form.

*Solution*

We note that we have three independent loops so we can write the three KVL loop equations as

$$i_1(R_1 + R_2) - i_2 R_2 - i_3 R_1 = v_1$$

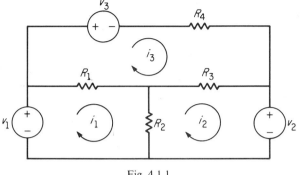

Fig. 4.1.1.

$$i_1 R_2 - i_2(R_2 + R_3) + i_3 R_3 = v_2$$
$$i_1 R_1 + i_2 R_3 - i_3(R_1 + R_3 + R_4) = v_3$$

This is easily written in the matrix form

$$\begin{bmatrix} (R_1 + R_2) & -R_2 & -R_1 \\ R_2 & -(R_2 + R_3) & R_3 \\ R_1 & R_3 & -(R_1 + R_3 + R_4) \end{bmatrix} \begin{bmatrix} i_1 \\ i_2 \\ i_3 \end{bmatrix} = \begin{bmatrix} v_1 \\ v_2 \\ v_3 \end{bmatrix}$$

which can be written as the matrix equation $\mathbf{Ri} = \mathbf{v}$.

Note that by multiplying out the matrices, we obtain the original equations. This equation can then be solved for the unknown vector $\mathbf{i}$ by multiplying both sides of the above equation by the inverse of $\mathbf{R}$. A systematic method of solving such matrix equations will be presented in Sec. 4.2. Let us now discuss the multiplication of matrices by a digital computer.

### Matrix Multiplication by Use of a Digital Computer

We have seen above how the multiplication of matrices enables us to use shorthand notation to represent equations. If we have two matrices $\mathbf{A}$ and $\mathbf{B}$, we can store the elements of $\mathbf{A}$ and $\mathbf{B}$ in a digital computer and generate a simple computer program which will give us the product $\mathbf{AB}$. Such a computer program eliminates hand calculations and will be found useful in later work involving network analysis.

We will assume that the matrix $\mathbf{A}$ is of dimension $m \times r$ and $\mathbf{B}$ is of dimension $r \times n$. Then the product $\mathbf{P}$ is of dimension $m \times n$. A simple flow chart and a computer program for the product of two matrices is given next.

Flow Chart for Multiplication of Matrices

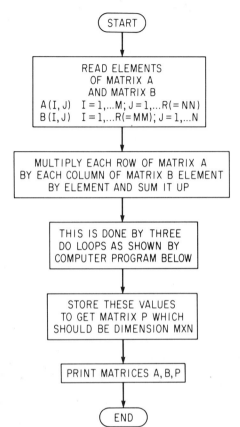

## Computer Program for Multiplication of Matrices

```
C       THIS PROGRAM IS THE GENERAL MATRIX  MULTIPLICATION
C       THIS PROGRAM MULTIPLIES THE TWO MATRICES, A AND B,
C       TO GIVE THE PRODUCT MATRIX P, MAXIMUM ARRAY SIZE IS 10
        DIMENSION A(10,10),B(10,10),P(10,10)
C       THE DIMENSIONS OF MATRICES ARE   A(M,NN),
C       B(MM,N), AND P(M,N)
C       THE ACTUAL VALUES OF THE DIMENSIONS MUST BE READ IN,
        READ 1,M,NN,N,MM
        PRINT 7
C       READ MATRIX ELEMENTS
        DO 19 I=1,M
        READ 5(A(I,J),J=1,NN)
C       WE PRINT MATRIX A AND B TO CHECK
C       THAT WE READ THEM CORRECTLY,
     19 PRINT 55,(A(I,J),J=1,NN)
        PRINT 8
        DO 21 I=1,MM
        READ 5(B(I,J),J=1,N)
```

```
 21 PRINT 55,(B(I,J),J=1,N)
    PRINT 9
C       CALCULATE PRODUCT P =A*B
C       THESE THREE DO LOOPS DO THE MULTIPLYING ELEMENT
C       BY ELEMENT AND SUMMING IN THE PROPER FASHION,
    DO 20 I=1,NN
    DO 25 J=1,MM
    K=M
    P(I,J)=0,
    DO 10 K=1,M
 10 P(I,J)=P(I,J)+A(I,K)*B(K,J)
 25 CONTINUE
    PRINT6    (P(I,JJ),JJ=1,N)
 20 CONTINUE
  1 FORMAT(4I2)
  5 FORMAT(10F8,3)
  6 FORMAT(10F8,3)
  7 FORMAT(1H1//  ,'    THE INPUT  A MATRIX IS'//)
  8 FORMAT(   //  ,'    THE INPUT  B MATRIX IS'//)
  9 FORMAT(///  ,'    THE OUTPUT P MATRIX IS'//)
 55 FORMAT(10F8,3)
    END
```

*Example 4.1.4*

Obtain $\mathbf{P} = \mathbf{AB}$ using the computer program if

$$\mathbf{A} = \begin{bmatrix} 4 & 3 & 2 & 1 \\ 2 & 1 & 1 & 1 \\ 0 & 4 & 2 & 1 \\ 1 & 3 & 2 & 2 \end{bmatrix} \quad \mathbf{B} = \begin{bmatrix} 1 & 1 & 1 & 1 \\ 2 & 2 & 3 & 1 \\ 3 & 1 & 1 & 1 \\ 1 & 1 & 1 & 2 \end{bmatrix}$$

*Solution*

Here $M = 4$, $MM = 4$, $NN = 4$, $N = 4$. So we read in values of $\mathbf{A}$ and $\mathbf{B}$. Substituting values of $M$, $MM$, $NN$, and $N$, we have the printout of the computer program as well as matrices $\mathbf{A}$, $\mathbf{B}$ and the product $\mathbf{P}$. Matrices $\mathbf{A}$ and $\mathbf{B}$ are printed out to check against the given matrices to insure accuracy.

```
C       THIS PROGRAM IS FOR EXAMPLE 4,1=4
C       THIS PROGRAM MULTIPLIES THE TWO MATRICES, A AND B,
C       TO GIVE THE PRODUCT MATRIX P,
        DIMENSION A(10,10),B(10,10),P(10,10)
C       THE DIMENSIONS OF MATRICES ARE,  A(M,NN),
C       B(MM,N), AND P(M,N)
C       THE ACTUAL VALUES OF THE DIMENSIONS MUST BE READ IN,
        READ 1,M,NN,N,MM
        PRINT 7
C       READ MATRIX ELEMENTS
        DO 19 I=1,M
        READ 5(A(I,J),J=1,NN)
C       WE PRINT MATRIX A AND B TO CHECK
C       THAT WE READ THEM CORRECTLY,
     19 PRINT 55,(A(I,J),J=1,NN)
        PRINT 8
```

```
      DO 21 I=1,MM
      READ 5(B(I,J),J=1,N)
   21 PRINT 55,(B(I,J),J=1,N)
      PRINT 9
C     CALCULATE PRODUCT P =A*B
C     THESE THREE DO LOOPS DO THE MULTIPLYING ELEMENT
C     BY ELEMENT AND SUMMING IN THE PROPER FASHION,
      DO 20 I=1,NN
      DO 25 J=1,MM
      K=M
      P(I,J)=0,
      DO 10 K=1,M
   10 P(I,J)=P(I,J)+A(I,K)*B(K,J)
   25 CONTINUE
      PRINT6      (P(I,JJ),JJ=1,N)
   20 CONTINUE
    1 FORMAT(4I2)
    5 FORMAT(10F8,3)
    6 FORMAT(10F8,3)
    7 FORMAT(1H1//  ,'   THE INPUT  A MATRIX IS'//)
    8 FORMAT(   //  ,'   THE INPUT  B MATRIX IS'//)
    9 FORMAT(///  ,'    THE OUTPUT P MATRIX IS'//)
   55 FORMAT(10F8,3)
      END
```

THE INPUT   A MATRIX IS

| | | | |
|---|---|---|---|
| 4,000 | 3,000 | 2,000 | 1,000 |
| 2,000 | 1,000 | 1,000 | 1,000 |
| ,000 | 4,000 | 2,000 | 1,000 |
| 1,000 | 3,000 | 2,000 | 2,000 |

THE INPUT   B MATRIX IS

| | | | |
|---|---|---|---|
| 1,000 | 1,000 | 1,000 | 1,000 |
| 2,000 | 2,000 | 3,000 | 1,000 |
| 3,000 | 1,000 | 1,000 | 1,000 |
| 1,000 | 1,000 | 1,000 | 2,000 |

THE OUTPUT P MATRIX IS

| | | | |
|---|---|---|---|
| 17,000 | 13,000 | 16,000 | 11,000 |
| 8,000 | 6,000 | 7,000 | 6,000 |
| 15,000 | 11,000 | 15,000 | 8,000 |
| 15,000 | 11,000 | 14,000 | 10,000 |

*Example 4.1.5*

Consider the network shown in Fig. 4.1.1.  Given $i_1 = 1.1$ amp, $i_2 = 2.1$ amp, $i_3 = 0.7$ amp, $R_1 = 2.3$ Ω, $R_2 = 3.9$ Ω, $R_3 = 1.8$ Ω, and $R_4 = 0.6$ Ω.  Use the computer program on multiplication of matrices developed above to obtain $v_1, v_2,$ and $v_3$.

*Solution*

Using the result from Example 4.1.3, we have **Ri** = **v**, where

$3 \times 3$                                                    $3 \times 1$

$$\mathbf{R} = \begin{bmatrix} 6.2 & -3.9 & -2.3 \\ 3.9 & -5.7 & 1.8 \\ 2.3 & 1.8 & -4.7 \end{bmatrix}, \qquad \mathbf{i} = \begin{bmatrix} 1.1 \\ 2.1 \\ 0.7 \end{bmatrix} \qquad V = 3 \times 1$$

In order to use the computer program we have $\mathbf{A} = \mathbf{R}$, $\mathbf{B} = \mathbf{i}$, $M = 3$, $NN = 3$, $MM = 3$ and $N = 1$. The elements of $\mathbf{P}$ give $v_1, v_2, v_3$. We read in $\mathbf{A}$ and $\mathbf{B}$. The computer program and the result are given below. We also have printed $\mathbf{A}$ and $\mathbf{B}$ to check their accuracy.

```
C       THIS PROGRAM IS FOR EXAMPLE 4.1-5
C       THIS PROGRAM MULTIPLIES THE TWO MATRICES, A AND B,
C       TO GIVE THE PRODUCT MATRIX P.
        DIMENSION A(10,10),B(10,10),P(10,10)
C       THE DIMENSIONS OF MATRICES ARE    A(M,NN),
C       B(MM,N), AND P(M,N)
C       THE ACTUAL VALUES OF THE DIMENSIONS MUST BE READ IN.
        READ 1,M,NN,N,MM
        PRINT 7
C       READ MATRIX ELEMENTS
        DO 19 I=1,M
        READ 5(A(I,J),J=1,NN)
C       WE PRINT MATRIX A AND B TO CHECK
C       THAT WE READ THEM CORRECTLY.
     19 PRINT 55,(A(I,J),J=1,NN)
        PRINT 8
        DO 21 I=1,MM
        READ 5(B(I,J),J=1,N)
     21 PRINT 55,(B(I,J),J=1,N)
        PRINT 9
C       CALCULATE PRODUCT P =A*B
C       THESE THREE DO LOOPS DO THE MULTIPLYING ELEMENT
C       BY ELEMENT AND SUMMING IN THE PROPER FASHION.
        DO 20 I=1,NN
        DO 25 J=1,MM
        K=M
        P(I,J)=0.
        DO 10 K=1,M
     10 P(I,J)=P(I,J)+A(I,K)*B(K,J)
     25 CONTINUE
        PRINT6     (P(I,JJ),JJ=1,N)
     20 CONTINUE
      1 FORMAT(4I2)
      5 FORMAT(10F8.3)
      6 FORMAT(10F8.3)
      7 FORMAT(1H1//  ,'    THE INPUT  A MATRIX IS'//)
      8 FORMAT(   //  ,'    THE INPUT  B MATRIX IS'//)
      9 FORMAT(///  ,'    THE OUTPUT P MATRIX IS'//)
     55 FORMAT(10F8.3)
        END
```

THE INPUT  A MATRIX IS          THE INPUT  B MATRIX IS

```
6.200  -3.900  -2.300          1.100
3.900  -5.700   1.800          2.100
2.300   1.800  -4.700           .700
```

```
THE OUTPUT P MATRIX IS

-2,980
-6,420
 3,020
```

## More on Matrices

*DIAGONAL MATRIX.* If all the elements of a square matrix except the diagonal elements are zero, the matrix is called a *diagonal matrix.*

$$\mathbf{D} = \begin{bmatrix} a_{11} & & & \bigcirc \\ & a_{22} & & \\ & & \ddots & \\ \bigcirc & & & a_{nn} \end{bmatrix} \qquad (4.1.19)$$

*UNIT OR IDENTITY MATRIX.* The unit or identity matrix is a diagonal matrix with all diagonal elements unity.

$$\mathbf{I} = \begin{bmatrix} 1 & & & \bigcirc \\ & 1 & & \\ & & \ddots & \\ \bigcirc & & & 1 \end{bmatrix} \qquad (4.1.20)$$

We immediately note that

$$\mathbf{AI} = \mathbf{IA} = \mathbf{A} \qquad (4.1.21)$$

*ZERO OR NULL MATRIX.* A matrix having all its elements zero is called a *zero* or *null matrix.*

*SYMMETRIC MATRIX.* A *square* matrix $\mathbf{A}$ is symmetric if $a_{ij} = a_{ji}$ for all $i$ and $j$.

*TRANSPOSE OF A MATRIX.* If matrix $\mathbf{A}$ is of order $(m,n)$, the transpose of $\mathbf{A}$ is $\mathbf{A}^T$ and is obtained by interchanging rows and columns of $\mathbf{A}$ and is of order $(n,m)$. As an example, consider

$$\mathbf{A} = \begin{bmatrix} 3 & 2 & 2 \\ 4 & 5 & 6 \end{bmatrix}, \quad \text{then } \mathbf{A}^T = \begin{bmatrix} 3 & 4 \\ 2 & 5 \\ 2 & 6 \end{bmatrix}$$

Note that if $\mathbf{A}^T = \mathbf{A}$, then the matrix $\mathbf{A}$ is symmetric. We further note

$$(\mathbf{A}^T)^T = \mathbf{A}, \quad (\mathbf{A} + \mathbf{B})^T = \mathbf{A}^T + \mathbf{B}^T, \quad \text{and } (\alpha\mathbf{A})^T = \alpha\mathbf{A}^T \qquad (4.1.22)$$

*TRANSPOSE OF PRODUCT OF TWO MATRICES.* We have seen in Eq. 4.1.16 that

$$(\mathbf{AB})^T = \left(\sum_{k=1}^{n} a_{ik} b_{kj}\right)^T ; \quad i = 1, \ldots, m, \quad j = 1, \ldots, p$$

$$= (p_{ij})^T = (p_{ji}) \text{ by definition of transpose}$$

$$= \left(\sum_{k=1}^{n} b_{jk} a_{ki}\right) = \mathbf{B}^T \mathbf{A}^T \tag{4.1.23}$$

*Example 4.1.6*

Let

$$\mathbf{A} = \begin{bmatrix} 1 & 2 \\ 2 & 3 \end{bmatrix}, \mathbf{B} = \begin{bmatrix} -1 & 1 \\ 3 & 4 \end{bmatrix}$$

Then

$$\mathbf{AB} = \begin{bmatrix} 5 & 9 \\ 7 & 14 \end{bmatrix}$$

and

$$\mathbf{B}^T \mathbf{A}^T = \begin{bmatrix} -1 & 3 \\ 1 & 4 \end{bmatrix}\begin{bmatrix} 1 & 2 \\ 2 & 3 \end{bmatrix} = \begin{bmatrix} 5 & 7 \\ 9 & 14 \end{bmatrix} = (\mathbf{AB})^T$$

*POWER OF A MATRIX.* If we have to find $n$th power of a matrix $\mathbf{A}$, it just means that the matrix has to be multiplied $n$ times:

$$\mathbf{A}^n = \underbrace{\mathbf{A} \cdot \mathbf{A} \cdots \mathbf{A}}_{n \text{ times}}, \tag{4.1.24}$$

It can also be easily verified that

$$\mathbf{I}^n = \mathbf{I} \quad \text{and} \quad \mathbf{D}^n = \begin{bmatrix} a_{11}^n & & \text{\Large O} \\ & \ddots & \\ \text{\Large O} & & a_{mm}^n \end{bmatrix} \tag{4.1.25}$$

## 4.2. MATRIX INVERSION AND DETERMINANTS

To see the need for the inverse of a matrix, let us consider a set of simultaneous equations written in the matrix form as given by Eq. 4.1.2.

$$\mathbf{Ax} = \mathbf{s} \tag{4.2.1}$$

We would like to solve this matrix equation for $\mathbf{x}$. We can obtain $\mathbf{x}$, provided a new matrix $\mathbf{Q}$ can be found such that

$$\mathbf{QA} = \mathbf{I} \qquad (4.2.2)$$

where $\mathbf{I}$ is the unit or identity matrix.

Multiplying both sides of Eq. 4.2.1 by $\mathbf{Q}$, we get

$$\mathbf{QAx} = \mathbf{Qs} \quad \text{or} \quad \mathbf{Ix} = \mathbf{Qs} \quad \text{or} \quad \mathbf{x} = \mathbf{Qs} \qquad (4.2.3)$$

Then in order to get $\mathbf{x}$, we simply multiply $\mathbf{s}$ by $\mathbf{Q}$. Note that this technique eliminates all the work required in the systematic elimination; furthermore, all the unknowns $\mathbf{x}$ are given simultaneously. We define

$$\mathbf{Q} = \mathbf{A}^{-1} \qquad (4.2.4)$$

such that

$$\mathbf{A}^{-1}\mathbf{A} = \mathbf{AA}^{-1} = \mathbf{I} \qquad (4.2.5)$$

The matrix $\mathbf{A}^{-1}$ is called the *inverse of matrix* $\mathbf{A}$. Note that to have $\mathbf{A}^{-1}\mathbf{A} = \mathbf{AA}^{-1} = \mathbf{I}$, $\mathbf{A}$ has to be a square matrix. Hence, we have the very fundamental requirement: a matrix has to be square to have an inverse. We now introduce a formula for inverting a matrix $\mathbf{A}$. The sketch of the proof is also discussed; however, the details of the proof are omitted. Given a matrix $\mathbf{A}$, the inverse of $\mathbf{A}$ is obtained as

$$\mathbf{A}^{-1} = \begin{bmatrix} \dfrac{A_{11}}{\Delta} & \dfrac{A_{21}}{\Delta} & \cdots & \dfrac{A_{n1}}{\Delta} \\ \dfrac{A_{12}}{\Delta} & \cdots & \cdots & \dfrac{A_{n2}}{\Delta} \\ \cdots & \cdots & \cdots & \cdots \\ \dfrac{A_{1n}}{\Delta} & \cdots & \cdots & \dfrac{A_{nn}}{\Delta} \end{bmatrix} \qquad (4.2.6)$$

where

$$\mathbf{A} = \begin{bmatrix} a_{11} & \cdots & \cdots & a_{1n} \\ a_{21} & \cdots & \cdots & a_{2n} \\ \cdots & \cdots & \cdots & \cdots \\ a_{n1} & \cdots & \cdots & a_{nn} \end{bmatrix} \qquad (4.2.7)$$

and $\Delta$ is defined as the *determinant* of matrix to be inverted (in this case $\mathbf{A}$) and is written as

$$\Delta = |\mathbf{A}| = \begin{vmatrix} a_{11} & a_{12} & \cdots & a_{1n} \\ \cdot & \cdot & \cdots & \cdot \\ \cdot & \cdot & \cdots & \cdot \\ \cdot & \cdot & \cdots & \cdot \\ a_{n1} & a_{n2} & \cdots & a_{nn} \end{vmatrix} \qquad (4.2.8)$$

$A_{ij}$ is called the *cofactor* of element $a_{ij}$ of determinant $\Delta$ and is $(-1)^{i+j}$ times the determinant of the submatrix of order $(n-1)$ obtained by deleting the $i$th row and $j$th column from **A**. The technique of obtaining the inverse of **A**, therefore, is:

1. Replace each element $a_{ij}$ with its cofactor $A_{ij}$ in matrix **A**. This new matrix is then $(A_{ij})$.

2. Find the transpose of the new matrix which is $(A_{ij})^T = (A_{ji})$. This is sometimes called the *adjoint matrix* of matrix **A**.

3. Divide each element of this matrix by $\Delta$. The resulting matrix is the inverse of matrix **A**. If $\Delta = 0$, then $\mathbf{A}^{-1}$ does not exist. So we have

$$\mathbf{A}^{-1} = \frac{(A_{ji})}{\Delta}, \quad \text{provided } \Delta \neq 0 \tag{4.2.9}$$

We must have by definition

$$\mathbf{A}\mathbf{A}^{-1} = (a_{ij})\left(\frac{A_{ji}}{\Delta}\right) = \left(\sum_{k=1}^{n} \frac{a_{ik}A_{jk}}{\Delta}\right) = \left(\frac{c_{ij}}{\Delta}\right) = \mathbf{I} \tag{4.2.10}$$

Therefore

$$c_{ii} = \Delta, \quad i = 1,\ldots,n \quad \text{and} \quad c_{ij} = 0 \; \forall \, i \neq j \tag{4.2.11}$$

Before we actually find the inverse, we have still to define a determinant and explain how we evaluate it. The determinant of any square matrix is a scalar number denoted by

$$\Delta = |\mathbf{A}| = \begin{vmatrix} a_{11} & a_{12} & \cdots & a_{1n} \\ \vdots & \vdots & \cdots & \vdots \\ a_{n1} & a_{n2} & \cdots & a_{nn} \end{vmatrix}$$

The determinant given above is evaluated to obtain a scalar which is given by

$$|\mathbf{A}| = \sum_{j=1}^{n} a_{ij}A_{ij} = \sum_{i=1}^{n} a_{ij}A_{ij} \tag{4.2.12}$$

where $A_{ij}$ is the cofactor of $a_{ij}$ as defined above.

The evaluation of $|\mathbf{A}|$ from the first equation of expressions 4.2.12 implies that any row of **A** can be selected. Each element of this selected row is multiplied by its cofactor and the result is summed. This is the value of the determinant. The result is the same for any row. The evaluation of $|\mathbf{A}|$ from the second equation of (4.2.12) permits selection of any column of **A**. Each column element is multiplied by its cofactor and the result is summed. The result is the same for any column. However, the difficulty is that the cofactors are also determinants but of order $n-1$, if **A** is of order $n$. Therefore, we must apply the same rule to evaluate the cofactors as we do the determinants.

The order of the determinants can be systematically reduced by one each time until we have a determinant of order 1. This technique is then used to evaluate all cofactors as ordinary numbers.

*Example 4.2.1*

Consider

$$|\mathbf{A}| = \begin{vmatrix} 2 & 3 \\ 1 & 2 \end{vmatrix}$$

Here $a_{11} = 2, a_{12} = 3, a_{21} = 1, a_{22} = 2$. Therefore

$$A_{11} = (-1)^{1+1}(2) = 2, \qquad A_{21} = (-1)^{2+1}(3) = -3$$
$$A_{12} = (-1)^{1+2}(1) = -1, \qquad A_{22} = (-1)^{2+2}(2) = 2$$

Hence

$$|\mathbf{A}| = a_{11}A_{11} + a_{12}A_{12} = a_{21}A_{21} + a_{22}A_{22}$$
$$= a_{11}A_{11} + a_{21}A_{21} = a_{12}A_{12} + a_{22}A_{22} = 1$$

This is a very simple example because the cofactors themselves are just ordinary numbers. For higher order matrices we will have to evaluate determinants within determinants. The total result can usually be written directly with a little practice.

*Example 4.2.2*

Evaluate the determinant

$$\Delta = \begin{vmatrix} 1 & -4 & -5 \\ 1 & 2 & 3 \\ -3 & 1 & -2 \end{vmatrix}$$

*Solution*

We have

$$\Delta = 1\begin{vmatrix} 2 & 3 \\ 1 & -2 \end{vmatrix} - (-4)\begin{vmatrix} 1 & 3 \\ -3 & -2 \end{vmatrix} + (-5)\begin{vmatrix} 1 & 2 \\ -3 & 1 \end{vmatrix}$$
$$= 1(-4 - 3) + 4(-2 + 9) - 5(1 + 6) = -7 + 28 - 35 = -14$$

*Example 4.2.3*

Invert the matrix

$$\mathbf{A} = \begin{bmatrix} 3 & 4 \\ -1 & 2 \end{bmatrix}$$

*Solution*

Here $a_{11} = 3, a_{12} = 4, a_{21} = -1, a_{22} = 2$. We get cofactors as $A_{11} = 2, A_{12} = 1, A_{21} = -4, A_{22} = 3$. Therefore

$$\Delta = |\mathbf{A}| = 6 + 4 = 10$$

We can therefore obtain

$$
\mathbf{A}^{-1} = \begin{bmatrix} \dfrac{A_{11}}{\Delta} & \dfrac{A_{21}}{\Delta} \\[2ex] \dfrac{A_{12}}{\Delta} & \dfrac{A_{22}}{\Delta} \end{bmatrix} = \begin{bmatrix} \dfrac{2}{10} & \dfrac{-4}{10} \\[2ex] \dfrac{1}{10} & \dfrac{3}{10} \end{bmatrix}
$$

Check:

$$
\mathbf{A}\mathbf{A}^{-1} = \begin{bmatrix} 3 & 4 \\ -1 & 2 \end{bmatrix} \begin{bmatrix} \dfrac{2}{10} & \dfrac{-4}{10} \\[2ex] \dfrac{1}{10} & \dfrac{3}{10} \end{bmatrix} = \begin{bmatrix} 1 & 0 \\ 0 & 1 \end{bmatrix} = \mathbf{I}
$$

We note that the inverse of a matrix exists only if the determinant of the matrix is not zero ($\Delta \neq 0$). If for a matrix $\mathbf{A}$, $|\mathbf{A}| = 0$, $\mathbf{A}$ is called a *singular matrix*.

The evaluation of a determinant can be simplified to a great extent if we use some of the properties of determinants.

**Properties of Determinants**

1. If all the elements of any one column or any one row are zero, the value of the determinant is zero.
2. The value of the determinant of any matrix $\mathbf{A}$ is the same as that of its transpose $\mathbf{A}^{T}$.
3. If any two consecutive columns or rows are interchanged, the determinant changes sign. As an example, we have

$$
\begin{vmatrix} 2 & 3 \\ 2 & 4 \end{vmatrix} = - \begin{vmatrix} 2 & 4 \\ 2 & 3 \end{vmatrix} = \begin{vmatrix} 4 & 2 \\ 3 & 2 \end{vmatrix}
$$

4. If to any row or column any proportion of another row or column is added, the value of the determinant remains unchanged.
5. If all the elements of any column or any one row are exactly or proportionately the same as any other column or any other row respectively, element by element and in the same order, the value of the determinant is zero.
6. If a determinant is multiplied by a constant, then only one row or column is multiplied by that constant. Conversely, if there is a common factor in any row or column, it can be brought out. For example,

$$
\begin{vmatrix} 2 & 6 & 8 \\ 3 & 3 & 5 \\ 4 & 5 & 4 \end{vmatrix} = 2 \begin{vmatrix} 1 & 3 & 4 \\ 3 & 3 & 5 \\ 4 & 5 & 4 \end{vmatrix}
$$

*Note that these properties are useful only to evaluate the determinant; if certain cofactors are required to invert a matrix, they should be obtained without changing the matrix in any way.*

*Example 4.2.4*

Evaluate the determinant

$$\Delta = \begin{vmatrix} 3 & 4 & -3 \\ 1 & 5 & 2 \\ 4 & -4 & 3 \end{vmatrix}$$

*Solution*

We note the following:

1. No common factor in any row or column.

2. If we add row 3 to row 1 we get two zeros.   The determinant becomes

$$\Delta = \begin{vmatrix} 7 & 0 & 0 \\ 1 & 5 & 2 \\ 4 & -4 & 3 \end{vmatrix} = 7 \begin{vmatrix} 5 & 2 \\ -4 & 3 \end{vmatrix} = 7(15 + 8) = 161$$

Hence we notice that we are able to reduce our work considerably by using the simple properties given above.

*Example 4.2.5*

Solve for $x_1, x_2, x_3$.

$$x_1 - x_2 + x_3 = 1$$
$$2x_1 + x_2 + 2x_3 = 5$$
$$-x_1 + 2x_2 + 3x_3 = 7$$

*Solution*

We write the equation in matrix form as

$$\begin{bmatrix} 1 & -1 & 1 \\ 2 & 1 & 2 \\ -1 & 2 & 3 \end{bmatrix} \begin{bmatrix} x_1 \\ x_2 \\ x_3 \end{bmatrix} = \begin{bmatrix} 1 \\ 5 \\ 7 \end{bmatrix}$$

or

$$\mathbf{Ax} = \mathbf{s}$$

We first find the cofactor matrix of **A**, which is

$$\mathbf{A}_c = (A_{ij}) = \begin{bmatrix} -1 & -8 & 5 \\ 5 & 4 & -1 \\ -3 & 0 & 3 \end{bmatrix}$$

The determinant of **A** is then $|\mathbf{A}| = -1 + 8 + 5 = 12$. Hence

$$\mathbf{A}^{-1} = \begin{bmatrix} \dfrac{-1}{12} & \dfrac{5}{12} & \dfrac{-3}{12} \\[2mm] \dfrac{-8}{12} & \dfrac{4}{12} & 0 \\[2mm] \dfrac{5}{12} & \dfrac{-1}{12} & \dfrac{3}{12} \end{bmatrix}$$

Note that $\mathbf{A}^{-1}$ is the transpose of $\mathbf{A}_c$ divided by $|\mathbf{A}|$. Hence

$$\mathbf{x} = \mathbf{A}^{-1}\mathbf{s} = \begin{bmatrix} \dfrac{-1}{12} & \dfrac{5}{12} & \dfrac{-3}{12} \\[2mm] \dfrac{-8}{12} & \dfrac{4}{12} & 0 \\[2mm] \dfrac{5}{12} & \dfrac{-1}{12} & \dfrac{3}{12} \end{bmatrix} \begin{bmatrix} 1 \\ 5 \\ 7 \end{bmatrix} = \begin{bmatrix} \dfrac{1}{4} \\[2mm] 1 \\[2mm] \dfrac{7}{8} \end{bmatrix}$$

*Example 4.2.6*

Consider the network shown in Fig. 4.2.1. Solve for voltages at nodes $n_1$ and $n_2$.

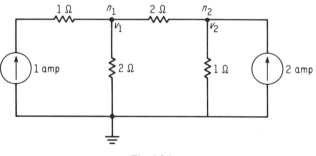

Fig. 4.2.1.

*Solution*

We have two independent nodes here, $n_1$ and $n_2$, so we can choose voltages $v_1$ and $v_2$ with respect to the datum node as shown. In this case we have to write KCL equations for nodes $n_1$ and $n_2$. For node $n_1$ we have

$$\frac{v_1}{2} + \frac{v_1 - v_2}{2} = 1$$

For node $n_2$, we have

$$\frac{v_2}{1} + \frac{v_2 - v_1}{2} = 2$$

We rewrite the above two equations as

$$2v_1 - v_2 = 2$$
$$-v_1 + 3v_2 = 4$$

In the matrix form these are

$$\begin{bmatrix} 2 & -1 \\ -1 & 3 \end{bmatrix}\begin{bmatrix} v_1 \\ v_2 \end{bmatrix} = \begin{bmatrix} 2 \\ 4 \end{bmatrix}$$

or

$$\mathbf{Gv} = \mathbf{i}$$

In order to obtain $\mathbf{v}$, we need $\mathbf{G}^{-1}$, so that

$$\mathbf{v} = \mathbf{G}^{-1}\mathbf{i}$$

Here

$$\mathbf{G}^{-1} = \frac{1}{5}\begin{bmatrix} 3 & 1 \\ 1 & 2 \end{bmatrix}$$

so

$$\mathbf{v} = \frac{1}{5}\begin{bmatrix} 3 & 1 \\ 1 & 2 \end{bmatrix}\begin{bmatrix} 2 \\ 4 \end{bmatrix} = \begin{bmatrix} 2 \\ 2 \end{bmatrix}$$

Hence $v_1 = 2$ volts, $v_2 = 2$ volts.

*Example 4.2.7*

Find the currents $i_1$, $i_2$, and $i_3$ for network shown in Fig. 4.1.1 if $R_1 = R_2 = R_3 = 1\ \Omega$ and $v_1 = v_2 = v_3 = 1$ volt. Assume $R_4$ to be a negative resistance of $-5\ \Omega$.

*Solution*

From example 4.1.3, we have the matrix equation as

$$\begin{bmatrix} 2 & -1 & -1 \\ 1 & -2 & 1 \\ 1 & 1 & 3 \end{bmatrix}\begin{bmatrix} i_1 \\ i_2 \\ i_3 \end{bmatrix} = \begin{bmatrix} 1 \\ 1 \\ 1 \end{bmatrix}$$

or

$$\mathbf{Ri} = \mathbf{v}$$

We need $\mathbf{R}^{-1}$. We first obtain $\mathbf{R}_c$, the cofactor matrix of $\mathbf{R}$, as

$$\mathbf{R}_c = \begin{bmatrix} -7 & -2 & 3 \\ 2 & 7 & -3 \\ -3 & -3 & -3 \end{bmatrix}$$

Also $|\mathbf{R}| = -15$, thus

$$\mathbf{R}^{-1} = \frac{\mathbf{R}_c^T}{|\mathbf{R}|} = \frac{-1}{15} \begin{bmatrix} -7 & 2 & -3 \\ -2 & 7 & -3 \\ 3 & -3 & -3 \end{bmatrix}$$

Hence

$$\mathbf{i} = \mathbf{R}^{-1}\mathbf{v} = \begin{bmatrix} \dfrac{8}{15} \\ \dfrac{-2}{15} \\ \dfrac{3}{15} \end{bmatrix}$$

So $i_1 = \frac{8}{15}$, $i_2 = -\frac{2}{15}$, and $i_3 = \frac{3}{15}$ amp.

### More on Matrices

*RANK OF A MATRIX.* The determinant of a submatrix of order $r$ of a given matrix $\mathbf{A}$ is called the determinant of order $r$ of a matrix. A matrix is said to be of rank $r$ if and only if it has at least one nonzero determinant of order equal to $r$ and higher order determinants are zero, or we can say that the rank of matrix is the order of the largest nonvanishing determinant of the matrix. A matrix is of rank zero if and only if all its elements are zero. A nonsingular square matrix $\mathbf{A}$ of order $n$ is then obviously of rank $n$.

*EIGENVALUE OF A MATRIX.* The eigenvalue $\lambda$ of a square matrix is obtained from the equation

$$|\mathbf{A} - \lambda\mathbf{I}| = 0 \tag{4.2.13}$$

If $\mathbf{A}$ is of order $n$, Eq. 4.2.13 will be a polynomial of degree $n$ in $\lambda$ giving $n$ values of $\lambda$ as the roots. All these roots are called eigenvalues of matrix $\mathbf{A}$. Equation 4.2.13 is defined as the *characteristic equation* of matrix $\mathbf{A}$. The eigenvalues of a matrix $\mathbf{A}$ are extensively used in Chapter 7 for solving a set of simultaneous first-order differential equations.

*Example 4.2.8*

Find the eigenvalues of matrix $\mathbf{A}$ where

$$\mathbf{A} = \begin{bmatrix} 2 & 6 \\ 1 & 1 \end{bmatrix}$$

*Solution*

First we form the matrix

$$\mathbf{A} - \lambda\mathbf{I} = \begin{bmatrix} 2 & 6 \\ 1 & 1 \end{bmatrix} - \lambda\begin{bmatrix} 1 & 0 \\ 0 & 1 \end{bmatrix} = \begin{bmatrix} 2 - \lambda & 6 \\ 1 & 1 - \lambda \end{bmatrix}$$

Now we form the characteristic equation

$$g(\lambda) \equiv |\mathbf{A} - \lambda\mathbf{I}| = \lambda^2 - 3\lambda - 4 = 0$$

The eigenvalues are

$$\lambda = -1, 4$$

## Solving a Set of Simultaneous Equations by the Digital Computer

We have seen above that the computation of the inverse of a matrix enables us to solve a set of equations very rapidly. This is extremely useful for resistive network analysis because here we have only simultaneous equations. However, it is obvious that as the order of network increases the computation will be much more laborious because this involves inverting higher order matrices.

In this section we would like to discuss an alternate method to solve a set of simultaneous equations. This method is called the *Gauss elimination method* and does not involve the invertion of a matrix. This method has also the advantage of being easily programmed on a digital computer. We will first discuss the method and then develop a flow chart for the computer and finally we will give the computer program.

### Solving a Set of Simultaneous Equations by the Gauss Elimination Method

In this case we actually solve a set of equations $\mathbf{Ax} = \mathbf{s}$. The technique is demonstrated here for equations of network in Example 4.2.7. These equations are

$$\begin{aligned} 2i_1 - i_2 - i_3 &= 1 \\ i_1 - 2i_2 + i_3 &= 1 \\ i_1 + i_2 + 3i_3 &= 1 \end{aligned} \qquad (4.2.14)$$

We first normalize the first equation by dividing it out by coefficient of $i_1$. Then we use this new equation to eliminate $i_1$ from equations 2 and 3 which in this case is just subtraction of this new equation from these two equations. We get a set of equations as

$$i_1 - \tfrac{1}{2}i_2 - \tfrac{1}{2}i_3 = \tfrac{1}{2}$$
$$-\tfrac{3}{2}i_2 + \tfrac{3}{2}i_3 = \tfrac{1}{2} \qquad (4.2.15)$$
$$\tfrac{3}{2}i_2 + \tfrac{7}{2}i_3 = \tfrac{1}{2}$$

Now we normalize second equation from expression 4.2.15 and then use it to eliminate $i_2$ from equations 1 and 3 by multiplying the normalized equation ($i_2 - i_3 = -\tfrac{1}{3}$) by $\tfrac{1}{2}$ and $-\tfrac{3}{2}$ and adding to equations 1 and 3 respectively. We get

$$i_1 - i_3 = \tfrac{1}{2} - \tfrac{1}{6}$$
$$i_2 - i_3 = -\tfrac{1}{3} \qquad (4.2.16)$$
$$5i_3 = 1$$

Now we normalize the last equation of expression 4.2.16. Use it to eliminate $i_3$ in equations 1 and 2. In this case the normalized equation ($i_3 = \tfrac{1}{5}$) can just be added to the first two equations to obtain

$$i_1 = \tfrac{1}{2} - \tfrac{1}{6} + \tfrac{1}{5} = \tfrac{8}{15}$$
$$i_2 = -\tfrac{1}{3} + \tfrac{1}{5} = -\tfrac{2}{15} \qquad (4.2.17)$$
$$i_3 = \tfrac{1}{5}$$

This result checks with that of Example 4.2.7. The technique discussed above is the Gauss elimination procedure which gives the solution to a set of simultaneous equations.

Let us now rewrite the original equations 4.2.14 in the matrix equation form

$$\begin{bmatrix} 2 & -1 & -1 \\ 1 & -2 & 1 \\ 1 & 1 & 3 \end{bmatrix} \begin{bmatrix} i_1 \\ i_2 \\ i_3 \end{bmatrix} = \begin{bmatrix} 1 \\ 1 \\ 1 \end{bmatrix} \qquad (4.2.18)$$

or

$$\mathbf{Ri} = \mathbf{v} \qquad (4.2.19)$$

The Gauss elimination method discussed above can also be applied directly to the matrix represented as $\mathbf{R}$. This is done by forming an *augmented matrix* $\mathbf{R}_a$ which is just matrix $\mathbf{R}$ augmented by the additional column vector $\mathbf{v}$. So, in this case, we have

$$\mathbf{R}_a = \begin{bmatrix} 2 & -1 & -1 & 1 \\ 1 & -2 & 1 & 1 \\ 1 & 1 & 3 & 1 \end{bmatrix} \qquad (4.2.20)$$

We now apply Gauss elimination methods to the rows of this augmented matrix. We first multiply the first row by $\frac{1}{2}$ (normalize it) and subtract it from rows 2 and 3 element by element. Our aim is to obtain the first element of row 2 and row 3 to be zero while normalizing the first diagonal element. We get the new matrix as

$$
\begin{bmatrix}
1 & -\dfrac{1}{2} & -\dfrac{1}{2} & \dfrac{1}{2} \\[2ex]
0 & -\dfrac{3}{2} & \dfrac{3}{2} & \dfrac{1}{2} \\[2ex]
0 & \dfrac{3}{2} & \dfrac{7}{2} & \dfrac{1}{2}
\end{bmatrix}
\tag{4.2.21}
$$

Note that the elements of this new matrix correspond exactly to coefficients of the equations 4.2.15 when we eliminate $i_1$ from the last two equations of 4.2.14.

Now we normalize the second diagonal element by dividing the second row by $-\frac{3}{2}$. We get the matrix as

$$
\begin{bmatrix}
1 & -\dfrac{1}{2} & -\dfrac{1}{2} & \dfrac{1}{2} \\[2ex]
0 & 1 & -1 & -\dfrac{1}{3} \\[2ex]
0 & \dfrac{3}{2} & \dfrac{7}{2} & \dfrac{1}{2}
\end{bmatrix}
\tag{4.2.22}
$$

We use the second row to obtain zeros in the second column except in the diagonal element. This is done by multiplying the second row by $\frac{1}{2}$ and $-\frac{3}{2}$ and adding it to the first row and third row respectively. We get

$$
\begin{bmatrix}
1 & 0 & -1 & \dfrac{1}{2} & -\dfrac{1}{6} \\[2ex]
0 & 1 & -1 & -\dfrac{1}{3} \\[2ex]
0 & 0 & 5 & 1
\end{bmatrix}
\tag{4.2.23}
$$

The elements in this matrix check exactly with coefficients of Eq. 4.2.16. We now normalize the third diagonal element by dividing the third row by 5. Using this we can get zeros in the third column except in the third row by just adding the normalized third row to the first two rows. We get

$$
\begin{bmatrix}
1 & 0 & 0 & \dfrac{1}{2} - \dfrac{1}{6} + \dfrac{1}{5} \\[2ex]
0 & 1 & 0 & -\dfrac{1}{3} + \dfrac{1}{5} \\[2ex]
0 & 0 & 1 & \dfrac{1}{5}
\end{bmatrix}
\tag{4.2.24}
$$

The last column gives us the values of $i_1$, $i_2$, and $i_3$ as given in Eq. 4.2.17.

The example considered here clearly suggests that we can use the technique very effectively to solve a set of simultaneous equations without resorting to inverting a matrix. We now proceed to develop a computer program which will accomplish the steps discussed above.

*REMARK.* In the example considered we can see that if we were interested in obtaining the determinant of $\mathbf{R}$, $|\mathbf{R}|$, then all we have to do is to multiply the coefficients which were used to normalize each row. In this case the product of these coefficients is $2 \cdot -\frac{3}{2} \cdot 5$ which gives us $|\mathbf{R}| = -15$. Note further that if any of the diagonal elements becomes zero, we cannot divide it out to normalize that row and in this case $|\mathbf{R}| = 0$ and there is no unique solution to a set of simultaneous equations. Hence we can state that if any diagonal element becomes zero in the Gauss elimination procedure, we stop there, because then there is no solution to the set of simultaneous equations $\mathbf{Ax} = \mathbf{s}$ (it is assumed that $\mathbf{s} \neq \mathbf{0}$).

### Development of Flowchart to Implement Gauss Elimination Procedure on a Digital Computer

Let the set of simultaneous equations we wish to solve be given by

$$
\mathbf{Ax} = \mathbf{s}
\tag{4.2.25}
$$

Let $N$ be the number of simultaneous equations to be solved.

We start by reading in elements of $\mathbf{A}$ and $\mathbf{s}$. Now we augment $\mathbf{A}$ by introducing another column which is made of $\mathbf{s}$. Since we want to have unity in the first diagonal element, we can divide out the first row by the first element of the row. Now we use the normalized first row to obtain zeros in the remaining first column by subtracting suitable multiplications of the first row from remaining rows. Next we normalize the second diagonal element and use it to obtain zeros in the second column except the diagonal element. We keep repeating the procedure until all diagonal elements are unity and off diagonal elements are zero. The last column is then the solution of the set of simultaneous equations. In case any diagonal element becomes zero, we stop and state that there is no unique solution to the set of simultaneous equations and that **A** is singular.

Flow Chart for Solving a Set of Simultaneous Equations AX = S

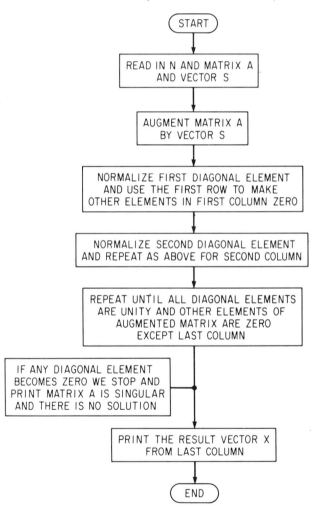

The computer program follows.

**Computer Program for Solving a Set of Linear Equations**

```
C        THIS PROGRAM IS FOR SOLVING LINEAR ALGEBRIC EQUATIONS
C        OF THE TYPE AX=S BY GAUSS=ELIMINATION METHOD, THE
C        MAXIMUM NUMBER OF UNKNOWNS IS 10, THE DATA REQUIRED
C        IS 'N' THE NUMBER OF UNKNOWNS, THE MATRIX 'A' AND THE
C        VECTOR 'S',
         DIMENSION A(10,11),S(10)
C        READ IN N, MATRIX 'A', VECTOR 'S'
         READ 1, N
         READ 2,((A(I,J), J=1,N),I=1,N),
         READ 2, (S(I),I=1,N)
C        WE PRINT MATRIX A AND VECTOR S TO CHECK THAT WE
C        HAVE NOT MADE AN ERROR IN READING IN THEM,
         PRINT 31
         DO 37 I=1,N
         PRINT 39, (A(I,J),J=1,N)
     37  CONTINUE
         PRINT 32
         PRINT 34, (S(K), K=1,N)
C        AUGMENT THE MATRIX 'A' WITH VECTOR 'S'
         M=N+1
         DO 3 I=1,N
      3  A(I,M)=S(I)
C        INDEX VARIABLESS I AND L STANDS FOR ROW AND J
C        STANDS FOR COLUMN , THIS LOOP IS FOR THE ROW,
         DO 6 I=1,N
         D=A(I,I)
C        NOW AN IF STATEMENT IS PUT TO CHECK IF MATRIX A IS
C        SINGULAR, THAT IS IF ONE OF THE DIAGONAL ELEMENTS
C        BECOME ZERO, IN THAT CASE PROGRAM STOPS
C        AND THE FACT THAT MATRIX A IS SINGULAR IS PRINTED OUT,
         IF (D) 19,20,19
C        THIS LOOP PRODUCES ONES ON DIAGONAL AND DIVIDES
C        THE ROW BY THAT DIAGONAL ELEMENT,
     19  DO 7 J=1,M
      7  A(I,J)=A(I,J)/D
C        THE TWO LOOPS PRODUCE ZEROS IN THE
C        COLUMNS CONTAINING ONES IN THE DIAGONAL ELEMENTS,
         DO 8 L=1,N
         IF (L ,EQ, I) GO TO 8
         E=A(L,I)
         DO 9 J=1,M
      9  A(L,J)=A(L,J)=A(I,J)*E
      8  CONTINUE
      6  CONTINUE
C        PRINTING OUT THE RESULT VECTOR X
         PRINT 18
         PRINT 10, (A(I,M), I=1,N)
         GO TO 22
     20  PRINT 21
      1  FORMAT (I2)
      2  FORMAT (7F10,5)
     10  FORMAT (1X, F10,5)
     18  FORMAT (1H0, 'THE SOLUTION VECTOR IS')
     21  FORMAT (1X,'MATRIX  A  SINGULAR ')
     31  FORMAT (1H0, 'THE MATRIX A IS')
     32  FORMAT (1H0, 'THE VECTOR S IS')
     34  FORMAT (1H , 10X, F10,5)
     39  FORMAT (10F8,3/)
     22  STOP
         END
```

*Example 4.2.9*

Given

$$
\begin{bmatrix}
4 & 3 & -2 & -1 \\
-2 & -1 & -1 & -1 \\
0 & -4 & 2 & 1 \\
1 & 3 & 2 & -2
\end{bmatrix}
\mathbf{x} =
\begin{bmatrix}
1 \\
1 \\
1 \\
1
\end{bmatrix}
$$

Solve for **x**.

*Solution*

The computer program given above is used. We just read in $N = 4$ and **A** and **s** from above. The printout of **A**, **s** and solution vector **x** are given below.

```
THE MATRIX A IS
   4.000     3.000    -2.000   -1.000
  -2.000    -1.000    -1.000   -1.000
    .000    -4.000     2.000    1.000
   1.000     3.000     2.000   -2.000

THE VECTOR S IS
                      1.00000
                      1.00000
                      1.00000
                      1.00000

THE SOLUTION VECTOR IS
      .36283
     -.54867
     -.01770
    -1.15929
```

*Example 4.2.10*

A network is shown in Fig. 4.2.2. There are four loops in the network. Find the currents in each loop using the computer program as developed.

*Solution*

There are four loops in the network, so we can write the four loop equations as

$$(1.15 + 3.25 + 0.71)i_1 - 0.71i_2 - 3.25i_4 = 1.5$$
$$-0.71i_1 + (0.71 + 0.23 + 0.92)i_2 - 0.92i_3 - 0.23i_4 = -1.3$$
$$-0.92i_2 + (0.92 + 1.12 + 0.82)i_3 - 1.12i_4 = 1.3 - 8.4$$
$$-3.25i_1 - 0.23i_2 - 1.12i_3 + (0.95 + 1.12 + 0.23 + 3.25)i_4 = -2.1$$

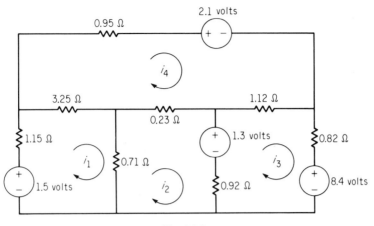

Fig. 4.2.2.

We can represent these equations in the matrix form

$$\begin{bmatrix} 5.11 & -0.71 & 0 & -3.25 \\ -0.71 & 1.86 & -0.92 & -0.23 \\ 0 & -0.92 & 2.86 & -1.12 \\ -3.25 & -0.23 & -1.12 & 5.55 \end{bmatrix} \begin{bmatrix} i_1 \\ i_2 \\ i_3 \\ i_4 \end{bmatrix} = \begin{bmatrix} 1.5 \\ -1.3 \\ -7.1 \\ -2.1 \end{bmatrix}$$

The above is of the form $\mathbf{Ax} = \mathbf{s}$. Here we have $N = 4$. Now we read in values of $\mathbf{A}$ and $\mathbf{s}$ into the computer program given above. The printout of $\mathbf{A}$, $\mathbf{s}$ and the solution vector, in this case loop currents, is given below.

```
THE MATRIX A IS
   5,110    -,710     ,000   -3,250
   -,710    1,860    -,920    -,230
    ,000    -,920    2,860   -1,120
  -3,250    -,230   -1,120    5,550

THE VECTOR S IS
            1,50000
           -1,30000
           -7,10000
           -2,10000

THE SOLUTION VECTOR IS
   -2,04437
   -4,25588
   -4,92696
   -2,74617
```

*Example 4.2.11*

For the network shown in Fig. 4.2.3, find the voltage $v_0$. Also find the power dissipated in the resistor $R$.

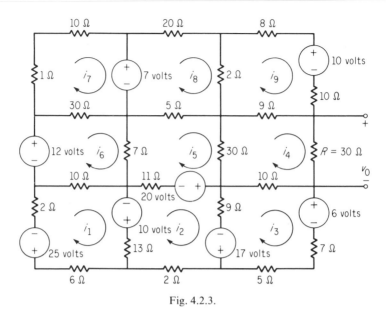

Fig. 4.2.3.

*Solution*

In order to find voltage $v_0$ we need the current in the $R = 30\ \Omega$ resistor. We choose currents in each mesh in a systematic fashion as shown in the Fig. 4.2.3. There are nine meshes so we have to find the nine mesh currents, only then can we find $i_4$. Then

$$v_0 = Ri_4 = 30i_4 \text{ volts}$$

and power in the resistor $R$ is

$$P_R = v_0^2/R = v_0^2/30 \text{ watts}$$

Starting from mesh involving $i$, we write our mesh equations as

$$(6 + 2 + 10 + 13)i_1 - 13i_2 - 10i_6 = -25 + 10$$
$$-13i_1 + (13 + 11 + 9 + 2)i_2 - 9i_3 - 11i_5 = -10 + 17 + 20$$
$$-9i_2 + (9 + 10 + 7 + 5)i_3 - 10i_4 = -17 - 6$$
$$-10i_3 + (10 + 30 + 9 + 30)i_4 - 30i_5 - 9i_9 = 0$$
$$-11i_2 - 30i_4 + (11 + 7 + 5 + 30)i_5 - 7i_6 - 5i_8 = -20$$
$$-10i_1 - 7i_5 + (10 + 30 + 7)i_6 - 30i_7 = 12$$
$$-30i_6 + (30 + 1 + 10)i_7 = -7$$
$$-5i_5 + (5 + 20 + 2)i_8 - 2i_9 = 7$$
$$-9i_4 - 2i_8 + (9 + 2 + 8 + 10)i_9 = -10$$

These equations are written in the matrix form as

$$\mathbf{Ax} = \mathbf{s}$$

where

$$
\mathbf{s} = \begin{bmatrix} -15 \\ 27 \\ -23 \\ 0 \\ -20 \\ 12 \\ -7 \\ 7 \\ -10 \end{bmatrix}
\qquad
\mathbf{A} = \begin{bmatrix}
31 & -13 & 0 & 0 & 0 & -10 & 0 & 0 & 0 \\
-13 & 35 & -9 & 0 & -11 & 0 & 0 & 0 & 0 \\
0 & -9 & 31 & -10 & 0 & 0 & 0 & 0 & 0 \\
0 & 0 & -10 & 79 & -30 & 0 & 0 & 0 & -9 \\
0 & -11 & 0 & -30 & 53 & -7 & 0 & -5 & 0 \\
-10 & 0 & 0 & 0 & -7 & 47 & -30 & 0 & 0 \\
0 & 0 & 0 & 0 & 0 & -30 & 41 & 0 & 0 \\
0 & 0 & 0 & 0 & -5 & 0 & 0 & 27 & -2 \\
0 & 0 & 0 & -9 & 0 & 0 & 0 & -2 & 29
\end{bmatrix}
$$

Now we use the computer program above. We read in $N = 9$ and $\mathbf{A}$ and $\mathbf{s}$ given above. The printout of $\mathbf{A}$, $\mathbf{s}$ and the solution vector, in this case the loop currents, is given below.

```
THE MATRIX A IS
 31.000 -13.000    .000    .000    .000 -10.000    .000    .000    .000
-13.000  35.000  -9.000    .000 -11.000    .000    .000    .080    .000
   .000  -9.000  31.000 -10.000    .000    .000    .000    .000    .000
   .000    .000 -10.000  79.000 -30.000    .000    .000    .000  -9.000
   .000 -11.000    .000 -30.000  53.000  -7.000    .000  -5.000    .000
-10.000    .000    .000    .000  -7.000  47.000 -30.000    .000    .000
   .000    .000    .000    .000    .000 -30.000  41.000    .000    .000
   .000    .000    .000    .000  -5.000    .000    .000  27.000  -2.000
   .000    .000    .000  -9.000    .000    .000    .000  -2.000  29.000

THE VECTOR S IS
        -15.00000
         27.00000
        -23.00000
           .00000
        -20.00000
         12.00000
         -7.00000
          7.00000
        -10.00000

THE SOLUTION VECTOR IS
         -.37137
          .27850
         -.76990
         -.33733
         -.49960
         -.01329
         -.18045
          .13413
         -.44027
```

From the printout,

$$i_4 = -0.33733 \text{ amp}$$

Therefore

$$v_0 = 30i_4 = -10.12 \text{ volts}$$

$$P_R = \frac{v_0^2}{30} = 3.415 \text{ watts}$$

## 4.3. RESISTIVE LADDER NETWORKS

In the previous section we have shown how the network equations can be solved for resistive networks with and without the use of the digital computer. In order to use the digital computer for solving the equation $\mathbf{Ax} = \mathbf{s}$ we have to read in values of $(a_{ij})$ and $(s_i)$. In actual networks we have to first write equations in order to determine $(a_{ij})$. However, it is possible to just read in values of various resistors of the network and let the computer automatically determine $(a_{ij})$. This is possible for any planar network, but here we limit our discussion to a resistive ladder network, a network encountered quite frequently in circuit analysis.

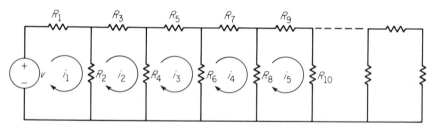

Fig. 4.3.1.

A resistive ladder network is shown in Fig. 4.3.1. We choose the resistances and loop currents as shown. Applying KVL we have

$$(R_1 + R_2)i_1 - R_2 i_2 = v$$
$$-R_2 i_1 + (R_2 + R_3 + R_4)i_2 - R_4 i_3 = 0$$
$$-R_4 i_2 + (R_4 + R_5 + R_6)i_3 - R_6 i_4 = 0 \qquad (4.3.1)$$
$$-R_6 i_3 + (R_6 + R_7 + R_8)i_4 - R_8 i_5 = 0$$
$$\vdots \qquad \vdots \qquad \vdots \quad \vdots$$

In matrix form, these equations can be written as

$$
\begin{bmatrix}
R_1 + R_2 & -R_2 & 0 & 0 & 0 & \cdot \\
-R_2 & R_2 + R_3 + R_4 & -R_4 & 0 & 0 & \cdot \\
0 & -R_4 & R_4 + R_5 + R_6 & -R_6 & 0 & \cdot \\
0 & 0 & -R_6 & R_6 + R_7 + R_8 & -R_8 & \cdot \\
\vdots & \vdots & \vdots & \vdots & \vdots & \vdots
\end{bmatrix} \mathbf{i} = \mathbf{v}
$$

$$(4.3.2)$$

where

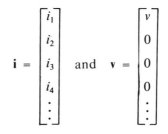

The above equation can be solved whenever the resistance values and $v$ are known.  The solution can be obtained with or without the use of the computer.

*Example 4.3.1*

For the ladder network shown in Fig. 4.3.2, find the power dissipated in resistor $R$.

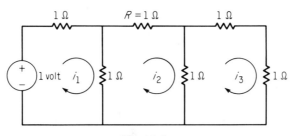

Fig. 4.3.2.

*Solution*

Choosing loop currents as $i_1$, $i_2$, and $i_3$, we can write the KVL equations as

$$2i_1 - i_2 = 1$$
$$-i_1 + 3i_2 - i_3 = 0$$
$$-i_2 + 3i_3 = 0$$

These equations can be rewritten as

$$\begin{bmatrix} 2 & -1 & 0 \\ -1 & 3 & -1 \\ 0 & -1 & 3 \end{bmatrix} \begin{bmatrix} i_1 \\ i_2 \\ i_3 \end{bmatrix} = \begin{bmatrix} 1 \\ 0 \\ 0 \end{bmatrix}$$

Inverting the matrix, we get the loop currents as

$$\begin{bmatrix} i_1 \\ i_2 \\ i_3 \end{bmatrix} = \tfrac{1}{13} \begin{bmatrix} 8 & 3 & 1 \\ 3 & 6 & 2 \\ 1 & 2 & 5 \end{bmatrix} \begin{bmatrix} 1 \\ 0 \\ 0 \end{bmatrix} = \begin{bmatrix} 8/13 \\ 3/13 \\ 1/13 \end{bmatrix} \text{ amp}$$

The power in resistor $R = i_2^2 R = i_2^2 = {}^9\!/_{169}$ watts.

Equation 4.3.2 can be written as

$$\mathbf{A}\mathbf{x} = \mathbf{s} \tag{4.3.3}$$

We can use the digital computer to determine $(a_{ij})$ directly from various resistor values.

### Development of a Computer Program for Determining A from the Resistor Values of a Ladder Network

Let us define general element of $\mathbf{A}$ as $A(I, J)$ and resistance of ladder network as $R(K) = R_k$, $K = 1, 2, \ldots, 2N$. Then from Eq. 4.3.2 we note

$$A(1, 1) = R(1) + R(2)$$
$$A(1, 2) = -R(2)$$
$$A(1, J) = 0, \quad J = 3, \ldots, N$$

Flow Chart for Determining $A(I, J)$ for a Resistive Ladder Network

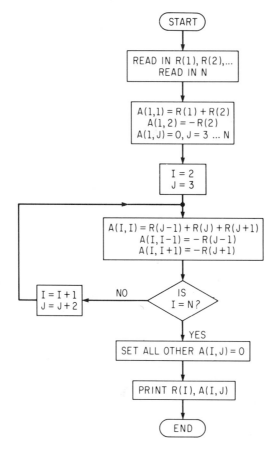

where $N$ is the number of loops in the network. We can now define for $I = 2, \ldots, N$, $J = 3, 5, \ldots, 2N - 1$.

$$A(I, I) = R(J - 1) + R(J) + R(J + 1)$$
$$A(I, I - 1) = -R(J - 1)$$
$$A(I, I + 1) = R(J + 1)$$

All other $A(I, J) = 0$.

Now we can develop a flow chart to write a computer program to determine $A(I, J)$. The flow chart is as shown.

Having the matrix **A** in the computer we can read in **s** and then bring in the Gauss elimination program to calculate **x**. The total program is printed below.

Computer Program for Solution of a Ladder Network

```
C       THIS PROGRAM IS FOR SOLVING RESISTIVE LADDER NETWORK,
C       FIRST MATRIX 'A' IS FORMED FROM THE RESISTANCE VALUES
C       READ AND THEN GAUSS ELIMINATION PROCEDURE
C       IS USED TO SOLVE FOR THE LOOP CURRENTS,
        DIMENSION R(20),A(10,11),S(10)
C       WE READ IN VALUES OF N THE NUMBER OF
C       LOOPS, 2N RESISTANCES R(I), I=1,...,2N, THE VECTOR S,
        READ 1, N
        READ 4, S(1)
C       SINCE OTHER ELEMENTS OF VECTOR S ARE
C       ZERO THEREFORE, WE SET THEM UP BY A DO LOOP,
        DO 14 I=2,N
     14 S(I)=0,0
        N1=2*N
        READ 2, (R(I), I=1,N1)
C       THIS SECTION IS THE SECOND BOX ON THE FLOWCHART,
        A(1,1)=R(1)+R(2)
        A(1,2)=-R(2)
C       THIS SECTION SETS UP THE DO LOOP OF THE FLOWCHART,
        DO 11 I=3,N
     11 A(1,I)=0,0
        J=2
        DO 12 I=2,N
        A(I,I)=R(J)+R(J+1)+R(J+2)
        I1=I-1
        A(I,I1)=-R(J)
        I2=I+1
        A(I,I2)=-R(J+2)
        DO 13 K=1,N
        IF (K ,EQ, I1) GO TO 13
        IF (K ,EQ, I2) GO TO 13
        IF (K ,EQ, I) GO TO 13
        A(I,K)=0,0
     13 CONTINUE
     12 J=J+2
C       WE PRINT RESISTANCES AND THE MATRIX A
C       TO CHECK ANY READING ERRORS,
        PRINT 35
        PRINT 32, (K,R(K), K=1,N1)
```

```
      PRINT 31
      DO 37 I=1,N
      PRINT 39, (A(I,J),J=1,N)
   37 CONTINUE
C     THIS PART OF THE PROGRAM IS FOR SOLVING LINEAR
C     ALGEBRIC EQUATIONS OF THE TYPE AX=S BY GAUSS-
C     ELIMINATION METHOD. THE MAXIMUM NUMBER OF UNKNOWNS
C     IS 10. SINCE MATRIX A IS ALREADY AVAILABLE AND
C     VECTOR S HAS BEEN READ WE CAN PROCEED TO EVALUATE
C     VECTOR X.
C     AUGMENT THE MATRIX 'A' WITH VECTOR 'S'
      M=N+1
      DO 3 I=1,N
    3 A(I,M)=S(I)
C     INDEX VARIABLESS I AND L STANDS FOR ROW AND J
C     STANDS FOR COLUMN , THIS LOOP IS FOR THE ROW,
      DO 6 I=1,N
      D=A(I,I)
C     NOW AN IF STATEMENT IS PUT TO CHECK IF MATRIX A IS
C     SINGULAR, THAT IS IF ONE OF THE DIAGONAL ELEMENTS
C     BECOME ZERO, IN THAT CASE PROGRAM STOPS
C     AND THE FACT THAT MATRIX A IS SINGULAR IS PRINTED OUT.
      IF (D) 19,20,19
C     THIS LOOP PRODUCES ONES ON DIAGONAL AND DIVIDES
C     THE ROW BY THAT DIAGONAL ELEMENT,
   19 DO 7 J=1,M
    7 A(I,J)=A(I,J)/D
C     THE TWO LOOPS PRODUCE ZEROS IN THE
C     COLUMNS CONTAINING ONES IN THE DIAGONAL ELEMENTS,
      DO 8 L=1,N
      IF (L .EQ. I) GO TO 8
      E=A(L,I)
      DO 9 J=1,M
    9 A(L,J)=A(L,J)-A(I,J)*E
    8 CONTINUE
    6 CONTINUE
C     PRINTING OUT THE RESULT VECTOR X
      PRINT 18
      PRINT 10, (A(I,M), I=1,N)
      GO TO 22
   20 PRINT 21
    1 FORMAT (I2)
    2 FORMAT (7F10.5)
    4 FORMAT (F10.5)
   10 FORMAT (1X, F10.5)
   18 FORMAT (1H0, 'THE SOLUTION VECTOR IS')
   21 FORMAT (1X,'MATRIX  A  SINGULAR')
   31 FORMAT (1H0, 'THE MATRIX A IS')
   32 FORMAT (1H ,'R(',I2,')=',1X,F10.5)
   35 FORMAT (1H ,'THE RESISTANCES ARE')
   39 FORMAT (10F8.3/)
   22 STOP
      END
```

*Example 4.3.2*

Use the computer program above to evaluate the loop currents in the network shown in Fig. 4.3.3.

*Solution*

Here $N = 5$. Also $S(1) = 10$, $S(2) = S(3) = S(4) = S(5) = 0$. The

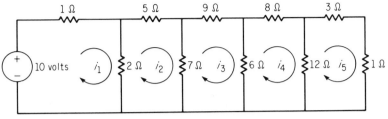

Fig. 4.3.3.

resistance values are $R(1) = 1$, $R(2) = 2$, $R(3) = 5$, $R(4) = 7$, $R(5) = 9$, $R(6) = 6$, $R(7) = 8$, $R(8) = 12$, $R(9) = 3$, $R(10) = 1$.

Now we read in these values in the computer program above. The printout giving $R(I)$, $I = 1,\ldots,10$, **A** and the solution vector, in this case the loop currents, is given below.

```
THE RESISTANCES ARE
R( 1)=    1.00000
R( 2)=    2.00000
R( 3)=    5.00000
R( 4)=    7.00000
R( 5)=    9.00000
R( 6)=    6.00000
R( 7)=    8.00000
R( 8)=   12.00000
R( 9)=    3.00000
R(10)=    1.00000

THE MATRIX A IS
    3.000   -2.000    .000     .000     .000
   -2.000   14.000   -7.000    .000     .000
    .000    -7.000   22.000   -6.000    .000
    .000     .000    -6.000   26.000  -12.000
    .000     .000     .000   -12.000   16.000

THE SOLUTION VECTOR IS
    3.76897
     .65346
     .23006
     .08120
     .06090
```

## 4.4. NETWORKS WITH NONLINEAR RESISTORS

If we have a nonlinear resistor in a resistive network, then the resulting network equations will not be linear. Therefore, the methods discussed in this chapter so far will not be useful in solving such networks. In this section we consider the solution of such networks by inspection.

Consider a simple network of Fig. 4.4.1. By KVL we can write

$$V_1 = iR + v \qquad (4.4.1\text{a})$$

$$i = f(v) \qquad (4.4.1\text{b})$$

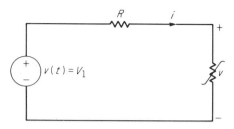

Fig. 4.4.1. Simple network with nonlinear resistor.

where we assume $V_1$ to be a constant voltage source. First we assume that the nonlinear resistor can only be characterized by an $i$-$v$ characteristic as shown in Fig. 4.4.2. How do we solve for $i$? Equation 4.4.1a can be rewritten as

$$i = -\frac{1}{R} v + \frac{1}{R} V_1 \tag{4.4.2}$$

Equation 4.4.2 is a straight line in the ($i$-$v$) plane with slope $-(1/R)$. This line usually is referred to as the *load line*. The point of intersection of the load line and $i$-$v$ characteristic of the nonlinear resistor is the solution of Eq. 4.4.1 because only at this point are both satisfied simultaneously. This point of intersection is called the *operating point*.

The graphical technique presented here will obviously be much more involved if we have a more complicated network or more than one non-linear resistor in the circuit. Let the $i$-$v$ relation of the nonlinear resistor be given analytically, say, by

$$i = \alpha(e^{\beta v} - 1) \tag{4.4.3}$$

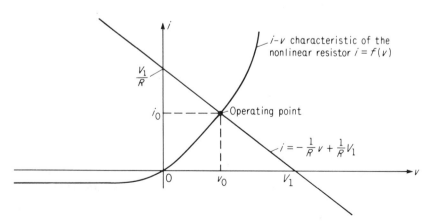

Fig. 4.4.2. Determination of the operating point.

In this case the network equations are

$$V_1 = iR + v$$
$$i = \alpha(e^{\beta v} - 1)$$

(4.4.4)

which must be solved simultaneously to obtain the current $i$ or whatever is desired.

*Example 4.4.1*

Consider the network of Fig. 4.4.1. Let $R = 1\ \Omega$ and for the nonlinear resistor let $i = e^{1.1v} - 1$. Find the current in the resistance if $V_1 = 1$ volt.

*Solution*

We have

$$1 = i + v$$
$$i = e^{1.1v} - 1$$

Substituting $i$ into the second equation from the first we get

$$v + e^{1.1v} = 2$$

We must solve for $v$ from this equation and use this $v$ to obtain $i$. In this simple case we can use a trial-and-error method (starting from $v = 0$ and moving in steps of 0.1) to obtain approximately

$$v = 0.4 \text{ volt}$$

Hence

$$i = e^{1.1v} - 1 = 0.6 \text{ amp}$$

*Example 4.4.2*

Consider the network of Fig. 4.4.3. Find $i$ if the $v$-$i$ relationship of the nonlinear resistor is given by $i = v + 0.13v^2$.

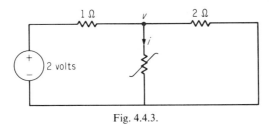

Fig. 4.4.3.

*Solution*

If we apply KCL to node at $v$, we get

$$\frac{v - 2}{1} + i + \frac{v}{2} = 0$$

Now $i = v + 0.13v^2$. Substituting, we get

$$\frac{3v}{2} - 2 + v + 0.13v^2 = 0$$

$$0.13v^2 + 2.5v - 2 = 0$$

or

$$v = \frac{-2.5 \pm \sqrt{6.25 + 1.04}}{0.26}$$

giving us

$$v = {}^{10}\!/_{13}, \quad -20 \text{ volts}$$

This means that we have two possible solutions.

For $v = {}^{10}\!/_{13}$ volts,    $i = {}^{11}\!/_{13}$ amp

For $v = -20$ volts,    $i = 32$ amp

### Diode and Its Application

One of the most useful nonlinear resistors is a diode whose character-istic is very similar to one shown in Fig. 4.4.2, but which can be idealized (approximated) to the one shown in Fig. 4.4.4a. The schematic symbol for a diode is shown in Fig. 4.4.4b. The arrow indicates that current

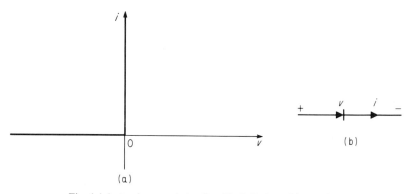

Fig. 4.4.4. *i-v* characteristic of an ideal diode and its symbol.

goes in that direction. From the figure it is seen that an ideal diode has a *zero forward resistance* (for $v > 0$) which is given by the slope of the line ($v/i$) in the first quadrant and the diode has an infinite *backward resistance* (for $v < 0$). So the current can flow only in the way the arrow is shown. The current cannot flow backward into the diode. The bar on the illustration signifies this.

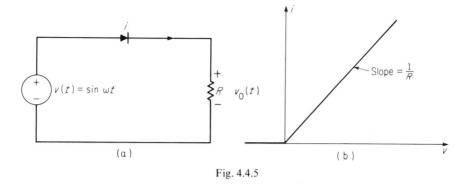

(a)                              (b)

Fig. 4.4.5

A diode has many uses in circuit applications. Consider the network of Fig. 4.4.5a. The $i$-$v$ characteristic of the *combination* of ideal diode and the linear resistor is shown in Fig. 4.4.5b. If we apply a sinusoidal voltage to diode in series with a resistor, then the current $i$ will only exist if $v > 0$ and it will be zero if $v < 0$. In this case $v_0(t)$ will be just $iR$ and will be a rectified sine wave. Both $v(t)$ and $v_0(t)$ are shown in Fig. 4.4.6.

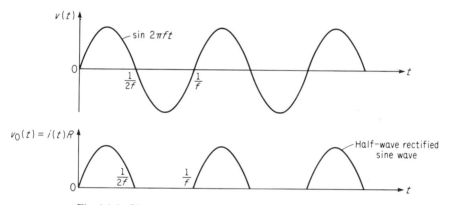

Fig. 4.4.6. Obtaining a rectified sine wave using a diode circuit.

### Diode As a Logic Element

Diodes are also used extensively as logic elements which are the basis of digital computer design. We consider the two basic circuits.

"*OR*" *CIRCUIT*. Consider the network shown in Fig. 4.4.7.

Condition 1

Let $V_1$, $V_2$ be both $> V$; then $i = 0$ and $V_0 = V$. We define

$$V_1 > V \quad \text{as} \quad V_1 = 0$$
$$V_2 > V \quad \text{as} \quad V_2 = 0$$
$$V_0 = V \quad \text{as} \quad V_0 = 0$$

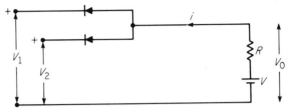

Fig. 4.4.7. "OR" circuit using diodes.

Condition 2

Let $V_1 < V$ or $V_2 < V$ or $V_1$, and $V_2 < V$. In each case $i$ flows and $V_0 < V$. We define

$$V_1 < V \quad \text{as} \quad V_1 = 1$$
$$V_2 < V \quad \text{as} \quad V_2 = 1$$
$$V_0 < V \quad \text{as} \quad V_0 = 1$$

From Conditions 1 and 2 we can build up a table of operation as

"OR" TABLE

| $V_1$ | $V_2$ | $V_0$ |
|---|---|---|
| 0 | 0 | 0 |
| 1 | 0 | 1 |
| 0 | 1 | 1 |
| 1 | 1 | 1 |

This table clearly implies that the output $V_0$ is 1 if either $V_1$ OR $V_2$ is 1. Otherwise, the output is zero. Such a circuit is called an "OR" circuit and is used as an "OR" logic in logic circuits.

*"AND" CIRCUIT.* "AND" circuit is a circuit where the output changes only if both inputs $V_1$ and $V_2 < V$ simultaneously. Such a circuit is shown in Fig. 4.4.8.

Condition 1

Let $V_1 > V$, $V_2 > V$ or $V_1$, and $V_2 > V$. In each case $i$ flows and $V_0 > V$.

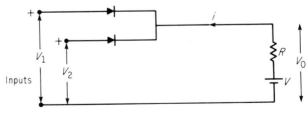

Fig. 4.4.8. "AND" circuit using diodes.

We define

$$V_1 > V \quad \text{as} \quad V_1 = 0$$
$$V_2 > V \quad \text{as} \quad V_2 = 0$$
$$V_0 > V \quad \text{as} \quad V_0 = 0$$

Condition 2

Let $V_1$ and $V_2 < V$. Then $i = 0$ and $V_0 = V$. We define

$$V_1 < V \quad \text{as} \quad V_1 = 1$$
$$V_2 < V \quad \text{as} \quad V_2 = 1$$
$$V_0 = V \quad \text{as} \quad V_0 = 1$$

From Conditions 1 and 2 we again build up the table of operation as

"AND" TABLE

| $V_1$ | $V_2$ | $V_0$ |
|-------|-------|-------|
| 0 | 0 | 0 |
| 1 | 0 | 0 |
| 0 | 1 | 0 |
| 1 | 1 | 1 |

This table clearly indicates the output $V_0$ is 1 only if $V_1$ AND $V_2$ are 1. Otherwise the output is zero.

## PROBLEMS

**4.1.** Obtain the following products and state the dimension of the new matrix. Can the order of multiplication be reversed?

(a)
$$\begin{bmatrix} 2 & 4 & -5 \\ -7 & -1 & -2 \\ -3 & 0 & -1 \end{bmatrix} \begin{bmatrix} 1 & -2 \\ 3 & 3 \\ 1 & 5 \end{bmatrix}$$

(b)
$$\begin{bmatrix} 1 & -3 & -1 \\ 5 & 2 & 7 \end{bmatrix} \begin{bmatrix} 1 \\ 2 \\ 3 \end{bmatrix}$$

(c)
$$\begin{bmatrix} 6 & 1 & -1 \\ -1 & 4 & 7 \\ -3 & 3 & 1 \end{bmatrix} \begin{bmatrix} 2 & -4 & -6 \\ 4 & -1 & 0 \\ 6 & 3 & -2 \end{bmatrix}$$

(d)
$$\begin{bmatrix} 1 & 2 & \frac{1}{2} \\ \frac{3}{2} & -\frac{1}{2} & \frac{5}{2} \\ -1 & -2 & 3 \end{bmatrix} \begin{bmatrix} 1 & 7 & 11 \\ 14 & 3 & 2 \\ -7 & 5 & -6 \end{bmatrix}$$

(e) $\begin{bmatrix} 3 & -3 \\ 1 & 1 \end{bmatrix} \begin{bmatrix} x_1 \\ x_2 \end{bmatrix} + \begin{bmatrix} x_1 & -3 \\ -2 & x_2 \end{bmatrix} \begin{bmatrix} 1 \\ 2 \end{bmatrix}$

**4.2.** Write circuit equations in the matrix form for circuits given in the figure.

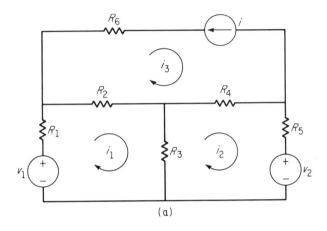

(a)

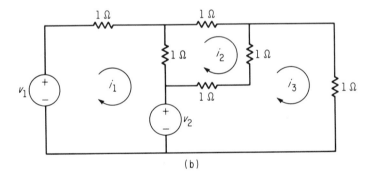

(b)

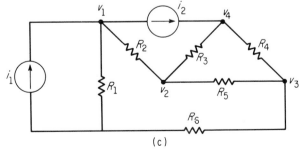

(c)

Prob. 4.2

**4.3.** Solve for $i_1$, $i_2$, $i_3$ if $v_1 = 2$ volts, $v_2 = 3$ volts for the (b) circuit of Prob. 4.2.

**4.4.** If $R_1 = R_2 = R_3 = 1\ \Omega$ and $R_4 = R_5 = R_6 = 3\ \Omega$ in (a) of Prob. 4.2, evaluate $v_1$, $v_2$ and $i$ if $i_1 = 3$, $i_2 = 2$ and $i_3 = 1$ amp.

**4.5.** (a) Use the computer program for (c) and (d) of Prob. 4.1.
   (b) Find the determinant of the matrix of (c) and (d) of Prob. 4.1.

**4.6.** (a) Evaluate the determinants of the following matrices, first by cofactors and then by simplification.

$$A = \begin{bmatrix} 3 & 2 & 3 \\ -2 & 2 & 1 \\ 9 & 7 & -3 \end{bmatrix}, \quad B = \begin{bmatrix} 1 & 5 & -4 \\ -2 & 1 & 0 \\ 1 & 0 & 3 \end{bmatrix}, \quad C = \begin{bmatrix} 2 & 5 & -1 \\ 1 & -1 & 2 \\ 3 & 1 & 4 \end{bmatrix}$$

   (b) Find $A^{-1}$, $B^{-1}$, and $C^{-1}$.
   (c) Show that:

$$(i)\ (AB)^T = B^T A^T$$
$$(ii)\ (AC)^T = C^T A^T$$
$$(iii)\ (BC)^T = C^T B^T$$
$$(iv)\ (AB)^{-1} = B^{-1} A^{-1}$$
$$(v)\ (AC)^{-1} = C^{-1} A^{-1}$$
$$(vi)\ (BC)^{-1} = C^{-1} B^{-1}$$
$$(vii)\ (ABC)^{-1} = C^{-1} B^{-1} A^{-1}$$
$$(viii)\ |AB| = |A||B|$$
$$(ix)\ |ABC| = |A||B||C|$$

   (d) Show that $A(B + C) = AB + AC$.

**4.7.** Evaluate the following determinants with or without using the computer program

$$(a)\ \begin{vmatrix} 1 & -3 & 0 & -1 \\ 2 & 0 & 4 & -1 \\ 2 & -2 & 1 & 0 \\ 4 & 7 & 1 & 3 \end{vmatrix} \qquad (b)\ \begin{vmatrix} 1 & 3 & 2 & -1 \\ 0 & 3 & -3 & 2 \\ -2 & 1 & -1 & 1 \\ 1 & 2 & 0 & -4 \end{vmatrix}$$

**4.8.** Use matrix inversion as well as the Gauss elimination procedure to solve for $x_1$, $x_2$, and $x_3$.

$$(a)\quad x_1 + 2x_2 + 3x_3 = 5$$
$$x_1 - 3x_2 + x_3 = 1$$
$$2x_1 + x_2 + 2x_3 = -4$$

$$(b)\quad x_1 - 2x_2 + 3x_3 = 3$$
$$2x_1 - x_2 - x_3 = 1$$
$$3x_1 + x_2 + x_3 = 5$$

$$(c)\quad x_1 + 3x_3 = 2$$
$$x_1 + x_2 - x_3 = 5$$
$$2x_1 + 3x_2 + 6x_3 = 7$$

**4.9.** Solve for $a$, $b$, $c$, and $d$ using the computer program:

$$a + b + c - d = 5$$
$$2a + 3b + 2c = 1$$
$$a - 2b + 4c + 3d = 4$$
$$a - b + c + d = -1$$

**4.10.** Solve for nodal voltages for networks shown.  Use computer programs where appropriate.

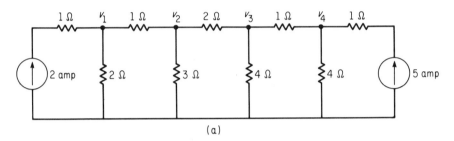

(a)

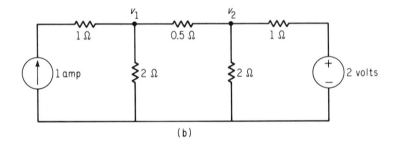

(b)

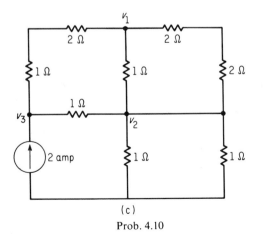

(c)

Prob. 4.10

**4.11.** Solve for loop currents for networks shown. Use computer programs where appropriate.

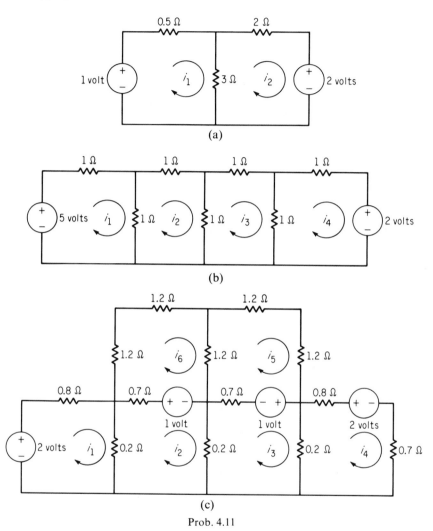

(a)

(b)

(c)

Prob. 4.11

**4.12.** Given a set of homogeneous equations

$$Ax = 0$$

Show that the equation will have a nonzero solution for **x** if and only if **A** is singular.

**4.13.** Find the eigenvalues of matrices

(a) $\begin{bmatrix} 3 & 1 \\ 1 & 3 \end{bmatrix}$    (b) $\begin{bmatrix} 2 & 2 & 1 \\ 1 & 3 & 1 \\ 1 & 2 & 2 \end{bmatrix}$    (c) $\begin{bmatrix} 2 & -1 & 0 \\ 9 & 4 & 6 \\ -8 & 0 & -3 \end{bmatrix}$

**4.14.** Let

$$A = \begin{bmatrix} 3 & 1 \\ 1 & 3 \end{bmatrix}$$

Find the characteristic equation of **A**, say $g(\lambda)$. Then show that if $\lambda$ is replaced in $g(\lambda)$ by the matrix **A**, then the resulting matrix is a null matrix. *This leads to a general result that a square matrix satisfies its own characteristic equation and is called the Cayley-Hamilton theorem.*

**4.15.** Let a matrix **A** be given as

$$A = \begin{bmatrix} -1 & -1 \\ 2 & -4 \end{bmatrix}$$

(a) Find $A^{-1}$.
(b) Find the eigenvalues of **A** as $\lambda_1$ and $\lambda_2$ and substitute them in equation $\lambda^{-1} = \alpha_0 + \alpha_1 \lambda$ to evaluate $\alpha_0$ and $\alpha_1$. Hence show that

$$A^{-1} = \alpha_0 I + \alpha_1 A$$

Actually it can be shown that for any function of the above matrix $f(A)$ can be found from

$$f(A) = \alpha_0 I + \alpha_1 A$$

provided $\alpha_0$ and $\alpha_1$ are found from two equations obtained by putting eigenvalues $\lambda_1$, $\lambda_2$ in equation

$$f(\lambda) = \alpha_0 + \alpha_1 \lambda$$

Hence evaluate the matrices $e^A$ and $e^{At}$. These results can be generalized for higher-order matrices.

**4.16.** Use the computer program to find the voltage across resistor $R = 1\ \Omega$ of the network shown.

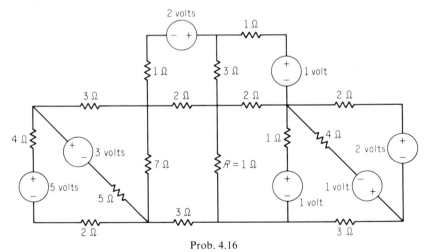

Prob. 4.16

**4.17.** In Example 4.2.11, calculate the power dissipated in each resistor and hence the total dissipated power in the network. Show that this power is equal to $i^T A i$, $i$ being the loop currents, by using the computer program on multiplication of matrices.

**4.18.** Use the resistive ladder network analysis computer program to solve for all the loop currents in the ladder network shown in (a) and (b) of the accompanying diagrams and hence calculate the power dissipated in the network resistors.

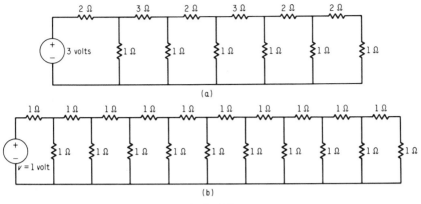

(a)

(b)

Prob. 4.18

**4.19.** Consider the network shown.

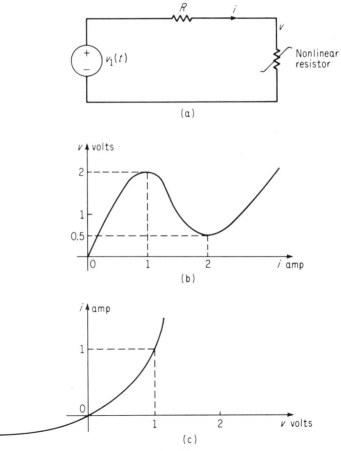

(a)

(b)

(c)

Prob. 4.19

(a) For $R = 1\,\Omega$, use graphical procedure to calculate $i$ if $i$-$v$ characteristic of the nonlinear resistor is given in (b), (c). Assume $v_1(t) = 5$ volts.

(b) If $v_1(t) = 2 \sin t$ and $R = 1\,\Omega$, plot the voltage across the nonlinear resistor as shown in (c).

**4.20.** In Prob. 4.19a let the nonlinear resistor be described by
  (a) $i = \tanh v$
  (b) $i = 2(e^{1.2v} - 1)$
  (c) $i = v + 0.5v^2 + 0.1v^3$
  Find $i$ for the circuit in each case if $R = 1\,\Omega$.

**4.21.** Find $i$ for the network shown.

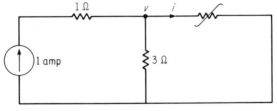

Prob. 4.21

Given $v = i/\sqrt{2 + i^2}$ for the nonlinear resistor.

**4.22.** Consider the network of Prob. 4.19a. Assume that the nonlinear resistor is an ideal diode having a resistance 0 when $v > 0$ and resistance $\infty$ when $v < 0$. If $R = 0.5$ and $v(t) = \cos t$, plot the voltage across the diode for $0 < t < 4\pi$ sec.

**4.23.** Plot $v_0(t)$ for the circuit shown for ideal diodes.

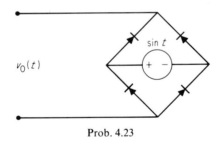

Prob. 4.23

**4.24.** A network with two nonlinear resistors is shown. Find the current $i$ by trial-and-error numerical procedure.

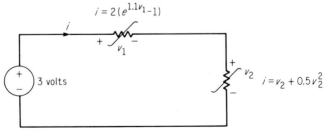

Prob. 4.24

## CHAPTER 5

# Elementary Transient Analysis

## 5.1. INTRODUCTION

In Chapter 2 we used Kirchhoff's voltage law, Kirchhoff's current law, and the branch voltage-current relations to obtain a set of linearly independent equations that can be solved for all the branch voltages and branch currents. In Chapter 4 we solved this problem for circuits comprised of *resistive* elements only. For this reason the circuit equations were a set of *algebraic* equations. However, if the circuit under study contains one or more energy-storing elements (either capacitors, inductors or both) the set of equations that must be solved for the branch voltages or currents is a set of integrodifferential equations.

In this chapter we consider the class of linear time-invariant circuits which contain a single energy-storing element; it turns out that such circuits will result in a single differential equation and a set of algebraic equations. This class of circuits are therefore called *first-order* circuits. It should be mentioned that in some special cases a first-order circuit may contain more than one energy-storing element. Such cases will also be discussed in this chapter.

In order to solve the differential equations describing circuits with energy-storing elements, we must consider the effect of initial currents through the inductors and the initial voltages across the capacitors. We will therefore begin the development of the solution of these differential equations by introducing a method of representing the initial conditions in the form of independent voltage and current sources.

157

## 5.2. REPRESENTATION OF INITIAL CONDITIONS

### Initial Voltage on a Capacitor

As described in Chapter 1, the capacitor is an energy-storage device and, as such, the energy stored in a capacitor at the beginning of an observation interval will influence the voltages and currents of each circuit element throughout the observation. The initial condition of the capacitor is completely characterized by specifying the voltage or the charge of the capacitor at the beginning of the observation interval; that is, if we are attempting to describe circuit performance over a time interval from $t_0$ to $t$, the voltage on the capacitor at time $t_0$, $V_0$, will affect the circuit solution. Of course, for a linear time-invariant capacitor, if the initial charge $q_0$ is given then the initial voltage can be obtained from

$$V_0 = \frac{1}{C} q_0$$

where $C$ represents the capacitance of the capacitor. Consider the linear, time-invariant capacitor shown in Fig. 5.2.1a. The terminal voltage $v_{ab}(t)$ can be written as

$$v_{ab}(t) = v_C(t_0) + \frac{1}{C} \int_{t_0}^{t} i_C(\sigma) \, d\sigma$$

$$= V_0 + \frac{1}{C} \int_{t_0}^{t} i_C(\sigma) \, d\sigma \qquad t \geq t_0 \qquad (5.1.1)$$

Similarly, writing Kirchhoff's voltage law for the circuit in Fig. 5.2.1b we have the terminal voltage $v_{ab}(t)$ is given by

$$v_{ab}(t) = v_C(t_0) + \frac{1}{C} \int_{t_0}^{t} i_C(\sigma) \, d\sigma + V_0 \qquad t \geq t_0 \qquad (5.1.2)$$

Since in this case $v_C(t_0) = 0$, we see that the *terminal* voltage $v_{ab}(t)$ is the same for Fig. 5.2.1a and b. These two circuits are therefore *equivalent*, since their terminal voltage current relationships are identical. In terms of an analysis technique, this relationship tells us that we can, for analysis purposes, *replace a capacitor with an initial condition $V_0$ by a capacitor with zero initial condition in series with a voltage source of value $V_0$.*

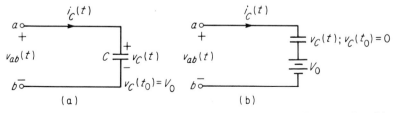

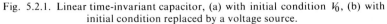

Fig. 5.2.1.  Linear time-invariant capacitor, (a) with initial condition $V_0$, (b) with initial condition replaced by a voltage source.

## Initial Current in an Inductor

The initial condition of an inductive element is specified by the value of the current through the inductor or the flux at the beginning of the observation interval. As in the case of the capacitor, this initial condition will influence the branch voltages and currents of a circuit to which the inductor is connected. We can replace an inductor with initial condition $I_0$ by an inductor with zero initial condition in parallel with a current source $I_0$. To see this, consider the inductor shown in Fig. 5.2.2a. The relationship between the terminal voltage and current in this figure is described by the equation

$$i_{ab}(t) = i_L(t_0) + \frac{1}{L} \int_{t_0}^{t} v_L(\sigma)\, d\sigma$$

$$= I_0 + \frac{1}{L} \int_{t_0}^{t} v_L(\sigma)\, d\sigma \qquad t \geq t_0 \qquad (5.2.3)$$

In Fig. 5.2.2b we have an inductor also of value $L$ but with zero initial condition. In this case, using Kirchhoff's current law at either node gives the terminal current as

$$i_{ab}(t) = i_L(t) + I_0 \qquad (5.2.4)$$

and since $i_L(t)$ can be found from

$$i_L(t) = i_L(t_0) + \frac{1}{L} \int_{t_0}^{t} v_L(\sigma)\, d\sigma$$

$$= \frac{1}{L} \int_{t_0}^{t} v_L(\sigma)\, d\sigma \qquad t \geq t_0 \qquad (5.2.5)$$

we have

$$i_{ab}(t) = \frac{1}{L} \int_{t_0}^{t} v_L(\sigma)\, d\sigma + I_0 \qquad t \geq t_0 \qquad (5.2.6)$$

Equations 5.2.6 and 5.2.3 indicate that the terminal voltage-current relationships for the circuits in Figs. 5.2.2a and b are identical, hence, these two representations of an inductor are equivalent with respect to the

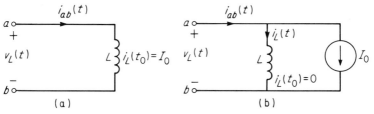

Fig. 5.2.2. Linear, time invariant inductor, (a) with initial condition $I_0$, (b) with initial condition replaced by a current source.

terminals $a$, $b$. Thus *an inductor with initial condition $I_0$ can be replaced by a zero initial condition inductor of the same value in parallel with a current source $I_0$.*

### Behavior of Capacitor Voltages and Inductor Currents

In many practical cases the initial conditions of the circuits under study are not given explicitly. It is then necessary to obtain these initial conditions from the knowledge of the circuit behavior prior to the initial time $t_0$. For this reason, it is important to be able to answer the following two questions:

1. Given the voltage across a capacitor at a time prior to the initial time $t_0$, what is the voltage across this capacitor at the time just after the initial time $t_0$? More precisely, given $v_C(t_0 - \epsilon)$, what is $v_C(t_0 + \epsilon)$? Here $\epsilon$ represents an arbitrary small number.

2. Given the current through an inductor at $(t_0 - \epsilon)$, namely $i_L(t_0 - \epsilon)$, what is $i_L(t_0 + \epsilon)$?

To answer the first question, consider the voltage across a capacitor $C$ at $t_0 + \epsilon$ given by

$$v_C(t_0 + \epsilon) = v_C(t_0) + \frac{1}{C} \int_{t_0}^{t_0+\epsilon} i_C(\sigma)\, d\sigma \tag{5.2.7}$$

At time $t_0$, $v_C(t_0)$ is given by

$$v_C(t_0) = v_C(t_0 - \epsilon) + \frac{1}{C} \int_{t_0-\epsilon}^{t_0} i_C(\sigma)\, d\sigma \tag{5.2.8}$$

Substituting Eq. 5.2.8 into Eq. 5.2.7, we can write

$$v_C(t_0 + \epsilon) = v_C(t_0 - \epsilon) + \frac{1}{C} \int_{t_0-\epsilon}^{t_0} i_C(\sigma)\, d\sigma$$

$$+ \frac{1}{C} \int_{t_0}^{t_0+\epsilon} i_C(\sigma)\, d\sigma \tag{5.2.9}$$

or equivalently

$$v_C(t_0 + \epsilon) - v_C(t_0 - \epsilon) = \frac{1}{C} \int_{t_0-\epsilon}^{t_0+\epsilon} i_C(\sigma)\, d\sigma \tag{5.2.10}$$

If now we let $\epsilon \to 0$, we have

$$\lim_{\epsilon \to 0} [v_C(t_0 + \epsilon) - v_C(t_0 - \epsilon)] = \frac{1}{C} \lim_{\epsilon \to 0} \int_{t_0-\epsilon}^{t_0+\epsilon} i_C(\sigma)\, d\sigma \tag{5.2.11}$$

Now, *if the current through the capacitor is not an impulse function* $\delta(t - t_0)$, the right-hand side of Eq. 5.2.11 will go to zero as $\epsilon \to 0$. Hence, using the following notations,

$$t_0^- \triangleq \lim_{\epsilon \to 0} (t_0 - \epsilon) \tag{5.2.12}$$

and

$$t_0^+ \triangleq \lim_{\epsilon \to 0} (t_0 + \epsilon) \tag{5.2.13}$$

we get

$$v_C(t_0^+) = v_C(t_0^-) \tag{5.2.14}$$

That is, *the voltage across a capacitor is continuous if the current through it is finite* (it is not an impulse function). Quite clearly, if

$$i_C(t) = i_C(t)\, \delta(t - t_0) \tag{5.2.15}$$

then Eq. 5.2.11 yields

$$v_C(t_0^+) = v_C(t_0^-) + \frac{1}{C} i_C(t_0) \tag{5.2.16}$$

In a similar manner we can prove that for an inductor with inductance $L$, if the voltage across the inductor at $t_0$, $v_L(t_0)$, remains finite (it is not an impulse function), we get

$$i_L(t_0^+) = i_L(t_0^-) \tag{5.2.17}$$

That is, *the current through an inductor is continuous if the voltage across it is finite* (it is not an impulse function). If, however,

$$v_L(t) = v_L(t)\, \delta(t - t_0)$$

then

$$i_L(t_0^+) = i_L(t_0^-) + \frac{1}{L} v_L(t_0) \tag{5.2.18}$$

Obviously, the voltage across the resistor follows all variations of the current. If the current is discontinuous at time $t_0$, the voltage will also be discontinuous. If the current is continuous, then the voltage will be continuous. Next, we give an example to illustrate the results obtained above.

### Example 5.2.1

Consider the circuit shown in Fig. 5.2.3. Assume $i_L(0^-) = i_R(0^-) = 0$ and $v_C(0^-) = 2$ volts. Calculate $i_L(0^+)$, $i_R(0^+)$, $v_C(0^+)$, $[dv_C(t)/dt]_{t=0^+}$, and $[di_L(t)/dt]_{t=0^+}$.

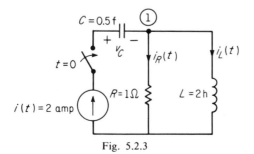

Fig. 5.2.3

*Solution*

The source applied to the circuit is $2u_0(t)$, a discontinuous but finite current over the interval $(0 - \epsilon, 0 + \epsilon)$. Therefore, according to our discussion above, the voltage across the capacitor will remain continuous:

$$v_C(0^+) = v_C(0^-) = 2 \text{ volts}$$

Now, applying KCL at node 1 gives

$$2 = i_R(0^+) + i_L(0^+)$$

Since $i_R(t)$ can be discontinuous, we have

$$i_R(0^-) = 0; \qquad i_R(0^+) = 2$$

The voltage across the inductor is, therefore, discontinuous but finite yielding a continuous current, i.e.,

$$i_L(0^-) = i_L(0^+) = 0$$

To calculate the derivative of the capacitor voltage, we note

$$C \frac{dv_C}{dt} = i_C = i_R + i_L$$

so that

$$0.5 \left. \frac{dv_C}{dt} \right|_{t=0^+} = i_R(0^+) + i_L(0^+) = 2 + 0 = 2$$

or

$$\left. \frac{dv_C}{dt} \right|_{t=0^+} = 4$$

Applying KVL gives

$$v_R(t) = v_L(t) = L \frac{di_L}{dt}$$

but

$$v_R(t) = R i_R(t)$$

Hence

$$\left. \frac{di_L}{dt} \right|_{t=0^+} = \frac{1}{L} v_R(0^+) = \frac{R}{L} i_R(0^+)$$

or

$$\left. \frac{di_L}{dt} \right|_{t=0^+} = \frac{1}{2} \cdot 2 = 1$$

This example illustrates that any initial condition can be derived from our knowledge of circuit and element relationships. It is important to remember that KCL and KVL apply for all instants of time and, in particular, at the instants $t = t_0 \pm \epsilon$.

## 5.3. FIRST-ORDER CIRCUITS

As mentioned earlier, circuits which can be described by a single first-order differential equation are said to be of *first order*. When the circuit elements are linear and time-invariant, the describing equation is of the form

$$a_1 \frac{dx(t)}{dt} + a_0 x(t) = u(t); \qquad x(t_0) = x_0 \qquad (5.3.1)$$

where $a_1$ and $a_0$ are scalar constants, $u(t)$ represents the input sources, and $x(t)$ represents the unknown; the initial condition $x_0$ is assumed to be given. To solve for the branch voltages and currents of the first-order, linear, time-invariant circuits, we must be able to solve equations of the form (5.3.1). Since Eq. 5.3.1 is a linear time-invariant differential equation, its solution can be written as the sum of two solutions; the homogenous solution (or zero-input solution) and a particular solution.

### Homogeneous Solution (Zero-Input Solution)

The homogeneous or zero-input equation associated with Eq. 5.3.1 is found by setting the input function, $u(t)$, equal to zero, i.e.,

$$a_1 \frac{dx(t)}{dt} + a_0 x(t) = 0 \qquad (5.3.2)$$

The solution, $x_h(t)$, to Eq. 5.3.2 is called the homogeneous solution or the zero-input solution of Eq. 5.3.1. This solution can be found by integration; in particular we have

$$\frac{dx(t)}{x(t)} = -\frac{a_0}{a_1} dt \qquad (5.3.3)$$

so that integration gives

$$\ln [x(t)] = -\frac{a_0}{a_1} t + K \qquad (5.3.4)$$

where ln denotes the natural logarithm and $K$ is the constant of integration. Thus we have

$$x(t) = e^{-(a_0/a_1)t + K} = e^K \cdot e^{-(a_0/a_1)t} = ke^{-(a_0/a_1)t}$$

where $k \triangleq e^K$ is a nonzero constant. Hence, the zero input or the homogeneous solution, $x_h(t)$, is given by

$$x_h(t) = ke^{-(a_0/a_1)t} \qquad (5.3.5)$$

where the constant $k$ can be obtained by considering the initial condition $x_0$ and the particular solution of the differential equation. This is made clear when we discuss the "total solution" of Eq. 5.3.1 below.

### Particular Solution

A *particular solution* to a differential equation is *any* solution which satisfies the equation. That is if $x_p(t)$ is a particular solution to Eq. 5.3.1, we must have

$$a_1 \frac{dx_p(t)}{dt} + a_0 x_p(t) = u(t) \qquad (5.3.6)$$

To determine $x_p(t)$ from the above relationship requires that we find a function which when multiplied by $a_0$ and added to $a_1$ times its derivative is equal to the input function $u(t)$. Obviously, the particular solution, $x_p(t)$, depends on the input function $u(t)$. Let us first consider a simple example to illustrate this idea and then give a systematic method of obtaining the particular solution of linear time-invariant first-order differential equations.

*Example 5.3.1*

Consider the first-order differential equation

$$4 \frac{dx(t)}{dt} + 2x(t) = 3e^{-t}$$

Comparing with Eq. 5.3.1, we see that in this case

$$u(t) = 3e^{-t}$$
$$a_0 = 2$$
$$a_1 = 4$$

From Eq. 5.3.5 we find the homogeneous solution is

$$x_h(t) = ke^{-(1/2)t}$$

For the particular solution, we seek some function $x_p(t)$ which when multiplied by 2 and added to 4 times its derivative equals $3e^{-t}$. One method of finding $x_p(t)$ is simply to guess a solution and then check to see if the guess is correct. An alternate method, one step removed from a pure guess, is the method of *undetermined coefficients*. To use this method, we guess at the *form* of the solution and solve for an undetermined coefficient by substitution in the differential equation. The form which is used will depend on the input function. In this example, since the input function is $3e^{-t}$, we guess that the particular solution is of the form

$$x_p(t) = k_1 e^{-t}$$

Substituting this form of $x_p(t)$ into the original differential equation gives

$$-4k_1 e^{-t} + 2k_1 e^{-t} = 3e^{-t}$$

which we can solve for $k_1$ as

$$k_1 = \frac{3e^{-t}}{-2e^{-t}} = -\frac{3}{2}$$

As this example illustrates, the particular solution depends on the driving function, $u(t)$. For different forms of $u(t)$ we must choose different forms of the particular solution. Table 5.3.1 gives the form of the particular solution for the class of input functions which are often used in electric circuit analysis. For input functions which are the sum of several terms in the left-hand side of the table, the appropriate form of the particular solution is the sum of the corresponding terms on the right-hand side of the table.

TABLE 5.3.1. FORM OF PARTICULAR SOLUTION FOR FIRST-ORDER DIFFERENTIAL EQUATION

$$a_1 \frac{dx(t)}{dt} + a_0 x(t) = u(t).$$

| Input Function, $u(t)$ | | Form of Particular Solution $x_p(t)$. |
|---|---|---|
| 1 | $e^{-at}, a \neq a_0/a_1$ | $ke^{-at}$ |
| 2 | $e^{-at}, a = a_0/a_1$ | $kte^{-at}$ |
| 3 | $\left. \begin{array}{l} \sin \omega t \\ \cos \omega t \end{array} \right\}$ | $k_1 \cos \omega t + k_2 \sin \omega t$ |
| 4 | | |
| 5 | 1 | $k$ |
| 6 | $t^n$ | $k_n t^n + k_{n-1} t^{n-1} + \cdots + k_0$ |
| 7 | $\left. \begin{array}{l} e^{-at} \sin \omega t \\ e^{-at} \cos \omega t \end{array} \right\}$ | $k_1 e^{-at} \cos \omega t + k_2 e^{-at} \sin \omega t$ |
| 8 | | |
| 9 | $\left. \begin{array}{l} t^n e^{-at} \sin \omega t \\ t^n e^{-at} \cos \omega t \end{array} \right\}$ | $(k_n t^n + k_{n-1} t^{n-1} + \cdots + k_0) e^{-at} \cos \omega t$ $\quad + (c_n t^n + c_{n-1} t^{n-1} + \cdots + c_0) e^{-at} \sin \omega t$ |
| 10 | | |
| 11 | $\alpha \delta(t)*$ | $(\alpha/a_1) e^{-(a_0/a_1)t} u_0(t)$ |

*The justification of this unintuitive form will be clear when we study the properties of the impulse function in Chapter 8.

## Total Solution

The *total solution* to a linear differential equation is the sum of the homogeneous solution and any particular solution. For the differential equation considered in Example 5.3.1, namely,

$$4 \frac{dx}{dt} + 2x(t) = 3e^{-t}$$

we found the homogeneous solution to be

$$x_h(t) = ke^{-t/2}$$

and the particular solution was given by

$$x_p(t) = -\tfrac{3}{2}e^{-t}$$

Hence the total solution in this case is

$$x(t) = x_h(t) + x_p(t) = ke^{-t/2} - \tfrac{3}{2}e^{-t}$$

The constant $k$ in the total solution is determined by the initial condition, i.e., we solve for $k$ by requiring that $x(t)$ evaluated at time $t_0$ be equal to the given initial condition, $x(t_0) = x_0$. For instance, if in Example 5.3.1, $x(0) = x_0 = 1$, then we get

$$x(0) = ke^{-0} - \tfrac{3}{2}e^{-0} = k - \tfrac{3}{2} = 1$$

then $k = \tfrac{5}{2}$ and replacing this in the equation for $x(t)$ we obtain the total solution as

$$x(t) = \tfrac{5}{2}e^{-t/2} - \tfrac{3}{2}e^{-t}$$

Quite often it is necessary to apply our knowledge of voltage and current relationships within a particular circuit to determine the required value $x(t_0)$. The following example will give an illustration of this case.

*Example 5.3.2*

Consider the circuit shown in Fig. 5.3.1. The switch $S$ has been closed for a long time and is opened at $t = t_0$. Find the voltage $v_C(t)$ for $t \geq t_0$.

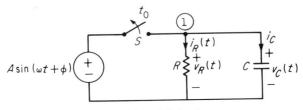

Fig. 5.3.1. *RC* circuit.

*Solution*

Applying KVL to the $RC$ loop we get

$$v_C(t) - v_R(t) = 0$$

and from KCL applied at node 1 we obtain

$$i_R(t) + i_C(t) = 0 \qquad t \geq t_0$$

Branch voltage current relationships (VCR) of the capacitor and resistor yield

$$i_C(t) = C \frac{dv_C}{dt}$$

and

$$i_R(t) = \frac{v_R(t)}{R}$$

Substituting $i_C(t)$ and $i_R(t)$ in the KCL equation and eliminating $v_R(t)$ from the resulting KCL equation and the KVL equation gives the following first-order homogeneous differential equation:

$$RC \frac{dv_C(t)}{dt} + v_C(t) = 0 \qquad t \geq t_0$$

The solution of this equation is in the form of Eq. 5.3.5, namely,

$$v_C(t) = k e^{-t/RC} \qquad t \geq t_0 \tag{5.3.7}$$

where the constant $k$ must be determined from the initial conditions. Note in this case the particular solution is equal to zero, since the input function, $u(t)$, is identically equal to zero for $t \geq t_0$.

To determine the initial condition, we must find the value of $v_C(t)$ at

$t = t_0^-$ and then use Eq. 5.2.14 to obtain $v_C(t_0^+)$. From Fig. 5.3.1 it is obvious that

$$v_C(t) = A \sin (\omega t + \phi) \quad \text{for all } t < t_0$$

where $A$ is a constant representing the amplitude of the sinusoidal voltage source. At the instant just before the switch is opened, say at $t = t_0^-$, the voltage across the capacitor is

$$v_C(t_0^-) = A \sin (\omega t_0^- + \phi)$$

and since $v_C(t)$ is continuous, by Eq. 5.2.14:

$$v_C(t_0^+) = v_C(t_0^-) = v_C(t_0) = A \sin (\omega t_0 + \phi) \tag{5.3.8}$$

From the solution of the differential equation (5.3.7) we must have at $t = t_0$,

$$v_C(t_0) = ke^{-t_0/RC} \tag{5.3.9}$$

Therefore, comparing Eqs. 5.3.8 and 5.3.9, we have

$$A \sin (\omega t_0 + \phi) = ke^{-t_0/RC}$$

or

$$k = A \sin (\omega t_0 + \phi) e^{t_0/RC}$$

Hence, substituting for $k$, we have

$$v_C(t) = A \sin (\omega t_0 + \phi) e^{-(t - t_0)/RC} \qquad t \geq t_0$$

This result is plotted in Fig. 5.3.2 for several values of the phase term $\phi$.

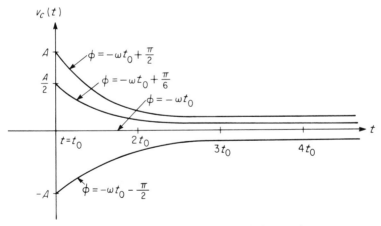

Fig. 5.3.2. Voltage $v_C(t)$ as a function of phase angle $\phi$.

*Example 5.3.3*

Consider the parallel $RL$ circuit shown in Fig. 5.3.3. Assume that the initial current through the inductor is $I$, i.e.,

$$i_L(0^-) = I \text{ amp}$$

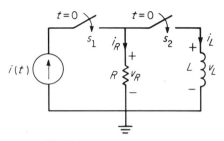

Fig. 5.3.3. *RL* parallel circuit.

Also assume that the current source $i(t)$ is in the form

$$i(t) = A \sin \omega t$$

the problem is to find the current $i_L(t)$ for $t \geq 0$.

*Solution*

Since both switches $s_1$ and $s_2$ are closed at $t = 0$, the circuit of Fig. 5.3.3 can be redrawn as in Fig. 5.3.4. Applying KCL at node 1 we get

$$i_R + i_L = A \sin \omega t \qquad (5.3.10)$$

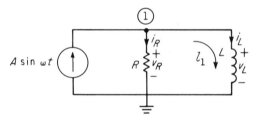

Fig. 5.3.4. This circuit is equivalent to the circuit shown in Fig. 5.3.3. for all $t \geq 0$.

But the branch voltage current relationship of the resistor implies that

$$i_R = \frac{1}{R} v_R$$

Applying KVL in loop $l_1$ and writing the branch voltage current relationship of the inductor we obtain

$$v_R = v_L$$

and

$$v_L = L \frac{di_L}{dt}$$

Hence from the last three equations we can easily write

$$i_R = \frac{L}{R} \frac{di_L}{dt}$$

Replacing $i_R$ from above equation into Eq. 5.3.10 we get

$$\frac{L}{R}\frac{d}{dt}\,i_L(t) + i_L(t) = A\sin\omega t; \qquad i_L(0^-) = I \qquad (5.3.11)$$

But since the current through the inductor remains finite, due to continuity of the inductor current, Eq. 5.2.17 yields

$$i_L(0^+) = i_L(0^-) = i_L(0) = I$$

Hence Eq. 5.3.11 can be written as

$$\frac{L}{R}\frac{d}{dt}\,i_L(t) + i_L(t) = A\sin\omega t; \qquad i_L(0) = I \qquad (5.3.12)$$

This is a first-order linear time-invariant differential equation of the form (5.3.1) where

$$a_1 = \frac{L}{R}$$

$$a_0 = 1$$

$$u(t) = A\sin\omega t$$

Consequently, the homogeneous part of the solution $[i_L(t)]_h$ can be obtained from Eq. 5.3.5; i.e.,

$$[i_L(t)]_h = ke^{-(R/L)t} \qquad (5.3.13)$$

where the constant $k$ can be determined by considering the initial condition $i_L(0)$ in the total solution.

Referring to Table 5.3.1, the form of the particular solution will be

$$[i_L(t)]_p = k_1\cos\omega t + k_2\sin\omega t \qquad (5.3.14)$$

In order to obtain the constants $k_1$ and $k_2$ we must substitute Eq. 5.3.14 into Eq. 5.3.12:

$$\frac{L\omega}{R}\,[-k_1\sin\omega t + k_2\cos\omega t] + k_1\cos\omega t + k_2\sin\omega t = A\sin\omega t$$

or

$$\left(\frac{-L\omega}{R}k_1 + k_2\right)\sin\omega t + \left(k_1 + k_2\frac{L\omega}{R}\right)\cos\omega t = A\sin\omega t$$

This relation must hold for *all* $t \geq 0$, hence we must have

$$k_2 - k_1\frac{L\omega}{R} = A$$

and

$$k_1 + k_2\frac{L\omega}{R} = 0$$

Solving these two equations for $k_1$ and $k_2$ we get

$$k_1 = \frac{-(L\omega/R)\,A}{1 + (L\omega/R)^2} \quad \text{and} \quad k_2 = \frac{A}{1 + (L\omega/R)^2}$$

Replacing these in Eq. 5.3.14 we obtain

$$[i_1(t)]_p = \frac{A}{1 + (L\omega/R)^2}\left[\sin \omega t - \frac{L\omega}{R}\cos \omega t\right] \tag{5.3.15}$$

The total solution of the differential equation, therefore, is the sum of the homogeneous and particular solutions as given by Eqs. 5.3.13 and 5.3.15 respectively. We have

$$i_L(t) = ke^{-(R/L)t} + \frac{A}{1 + (L\omega/R)^2}\left[\sin \omega t - \frac{L\omega}{R}\cos \omega t\right]$$

Now, to obtain the value of the constant $k$ we use the initial condition in Eq. 5.3.12, namely $i_L(0) = I$, i.e.,

$$i_L(0) = I = k + \frac{A}{1 + (L\omega/R)^2}\left[0 - \frac{L\omega}{R} \times 1\right]$$

or

$$k = I + \frac{A(L\omega/R)}{1 + (L\omega/R)^2}$$

And finally $i_L(t)$ becomes

$$i_L(t) = \left(I + \frac{A(L\omega/R)}{1 + (L\omega/R)^2}\right)e^{-(R/L)t} + \frac{A}{1 + (L\omega/R)^2}\left[\sin \omega t - \frac{L\omega}{R}\cos \omega t\right]$$

As a numerical example, let

$$I = 0, \quad L = 1\text{ h}, \quad R = 10^6\ \Omega, \quad A = 1\text{ volt}, \quad \text{and} \quad \omega = 10^6\text{ rad/sec}$$

then

$$i_L(t) = 0.5[e^{-10^6 t} + \sin 10^6 t - \cos 10^6 t]$$

*Example 5.3.4*

Consider the circuit shown in Fig. 5.3.5. Assume that $i_{L_1}(0) = I_1$ and $i_{L_2}(0) = I_2$, the problem is to find $i_R(t)$ for $t \geq 0$.

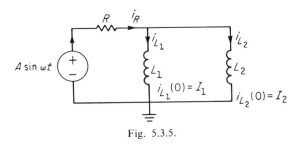

Fig. 5.3.5.

*Solution*

Let us use Eq. 5.2.4 to represent the initial currents through the inductors by independent current sources. The circuit shown in Fig. 5.3.6 is therefore equivalent to that shown in Fig. 5.3.5. Now, writing KCL

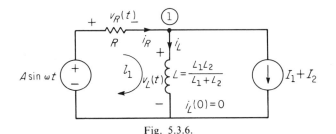

Fig. 5.3.6.

for node 1 and KVL for loop $l_1$, we get

$$i_R(t) = i_L(t) + (I_1 + I_2) \tag{5.3.16}$$

and

$$A \sin \omega t = v_R(t) + v_L(t) \tag{5.3.17}$$

But

$$v_R(t) = Ri_R(t) \tag{5.3.18}$$

and

$$v_L(t) = L \frac{di_L}{dt} \tag{5.3.19}$$

Since $I_1 + I_2$ is constant, differentiating both sides of Eq. 5.3.16, we get

$$\frac{d}{dt} i_R(t) = \frac{d}{dt} i_L(t)$$

Using this relation in Eq. 5.3.19 and using the results together with Eq. 5.3.17 in Eq. 5.3.18 we get

$$A \sin \omega t = Ri_R(t) + L \frac{d}{dt} i_R(t)$$

From Fig. 5.3.6 it is clear that

$$i_R(0) = i_L(0) + I_1 + I_2 = I_1 + I_2$$

Hence the differential equation that must be solved for $i_R(t)$ is given by

$$L \frac{d}{dt} i_R(t) + Ri_R(t) = A \sin \omega t; \qquad i_R(0) = I_1 + I_2 \tag{5.3.20}$$

The solution to this equation can be obtained in a manner similar to the previous example. To avoid repetition, we leave the solution of Eq. 5.3.20 as an exercise for the reader.

## 5.4. EXPONENTIAL RESPONSES

As we have seen in the previous section the homogeneous part of the solution of a first-order circuit usually contains an exponential term of the form $ke^{-(a_0/a_1)t}$. For instance, the homogeneous part of the solution of the circuit considered in Example 5.3.3 was $ke^{-(R/L)t}$. It turns out that for a first-order $RC$ circuit this homogeneous solution will be in the form of $ke^{-t/RC}$. Since it is often desirable to obtain quick sketches of these responses, we discuss in this section a few of the properties of the exponential response.

The product $RC$ is called the *time constant* (denoted by $T$) of a first-order $RC$ network. Similarly, the quotient $L/R$ is called the *time constant* $T$ of a first-order $RL$ network. In either case, the exponential response is written $e^{-t/T}$. When $t$ takes on integer multiples of the time constant, i.e., when $t = nT, n = 1, 2, \dots$, then the exponential response takes on the values $e^{-n}, n = 1, 2, \dots$. Also, on any interval of length $T$, the function $e^{-t/T}$ decays to a value $1/e$ (or approximately 37 percent) times its value at the beginning of the interval. This behaviour is plotted in Fig. 5.4.1. For

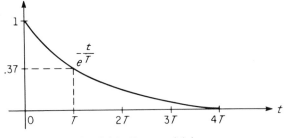

Fig. 5.4.1. Exponential decay.

values of $t \geq 3T$, the exponential function has decayed to less than .05 of its original value; for this reason, three time constants are often considered to be the time required for the exponential response to become negligible in a first-order $RC$ or $RL$ network.

*Example 5.4.1: Unit Step Response with Zero Initial Conditions*

Consider the $RC$ circuit shown in Fig. 5.4.2. It is desired to calculate the voltage across the capacitor, i.e., the desired *response* in this case is $v_C(t)$. We assume the driving function is a unit step in voltage $v(t) = u_0(t)$.

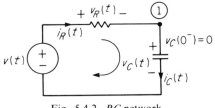

Fig. 5.4.2. $RC$ network.

*Solution*

Writing KVL around the loop gives

$$v_R(t) + v_C(t) = v(t)$$

By the voltage-current relationship VCR of the capacitor and KCL at node 1 we get

$$i_R(t) = i_C(t) = C\frac{dv_C}{dt}$$

Hence, using $v_R(t) = i_R(t)R$ and combining the above two equations, we have the differential equation defining the response $v_C(t)$:

$$RC\frac{dv_C(t)}{dt} + v_C(t) = u_0(t): \qquad v_C(0) = 0$$

For $t \geq 0$, this equation becomes

$$RC\frac{dv_C}{dt} + v_C(t) = 1; \qquad v_C(0) = 0 \tag{5.4.1}$$

The homogeneous part of the solution of this equation is given as in Eq. 5.3.5 by

$$[v_C(t)]_h = ke^{-t/RC} \tag{5.4.2}$$

Also, using Table 5.3.1, the particular solution is given by

$$[v_C(t)]_p = k_1 \tag{5.4.3}$$

where $k_1$ is a constant. To evaluate $k_1$, replace the particular solution given by Eq. 5.4.3 in Eq. 5.4.1; then

$$RC \cdot 0 + k_1 = 1$$

hence $k_1 = 1$. The total solution is therefore given by

$$v_C(t) = [v_C(t)]_h + [v_C(t)]_p = 1 + ke^{-t/RC} \tag{5.4.4}$$

Now, to evaluate the constant $k$ we use the initial condition $v_C(0) = 0$ in Eq. 5.4.4; hence

$$v_C(0) = 1 + k = 0$$

hence $k = -1$. Thus, replacing this value of $k$ in Eq. 5.4.4, the total solution is

$$v_C(t) = (1 - e^{-t/RC}); \qquad t \geq 0$$

For $t < 0$, the input function is zero and therefore

$$v_C(t) = 0; \qquad t < 0$$

Combining the two expressions for $v_C(t)$ gives

$$v_C(t) = (1 - e^{-t/RC})u_0(t) \qquad -\infty < t < \infty$$

The function $v_C(t)$ is called the *unit step response* of the $RC$ circuit under study. This function is plotted in Fig. 5.4.3. Note, that because the time scale has been normalized by the $RC$ time constant, this plot can be used for all values of the product $RC$.

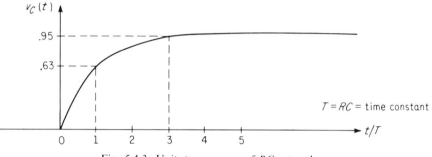

Fig. 5.4.3. Unit step response of $RC$ network.

*Example 5.4.2: Unit Impulse Response*

The *unit impulse response* of a network is the response obtained under zero initial conditions with an applied source $\delta(t)$. Let us consider the circuit shown in Fig. 5.4.2. As in the previous example, we assume the desired response is the voltage $v_C(t)$. The relationship between the response and excitation, as before is

$$RC\frac{dv_C(t)}{dt} + v_C(t) = \delta(t); \qquad v_C(0^-) = 0$$

The homogeneous solution is therefore given by

$$[v_C(t)]_h = ke^{-t/RC}$$

The particular solution is found from Table 5.3.1:

$$[v_C(t)]_p = \frac{1}{RC}e^{-t/RC}u_0(t)$$

Since the initial condition is zero the homogeneous solution will be zero and the total solution is

$$v_C(t) = [v_C(t)]_h + [v_C(t)]_p = [v_C(t)]_p = \frac{1}{RC}e^{-t/RC}u_0(t)$$

Notice the unit impulse response is the derivative of the unit step response and in this case the capacitor voltage is discontinuous at the instant $t = 0$. This indicates the capacitor current has an impulsive component. We can find the capacitor current by differentiating the capacitor voltage

$$i_C(t) = C\frac{dv_C}{dt} = C\left[-\frac{1}{R^2C^2}e^{-t/RC}u_0(t) + \frac{1}{RC}e^{-t/RC}\delta(t)\right]$$

or
$$i_C(t) = -\frac{1}{R^2C} e^{-t/RC} u_0(t) + \frac{1}{R} \delta(t)$$

using the sampling property of the impulse function.

In the conclusion of this chapter it should be emphasized that the class of the circuits considered in this chapter is the class of first order linear time-invariant circuits.   These circuits give rise to a first-order differential equation which is linear and time-invariant.   If the circuit under study contains any nonlinear and/or time-varying elements, the corresponding differential equations are nonlinear and/or time-varying. We postpone the solution of such differential equations until Chapter 7.

## PROBLEMS

**5.1.**  For the circuit shown, set up a first order differential equation that can be solved for the current $i$.   Specify the initial conditions by replacing the initial capacitor voltages by independent voltage sources.

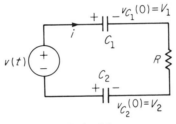

Prob. 5.1

**5.2.**  For the circuit shown, set up a first-order differential equation that can be solved for the current $i(t)$. Assume that $i_{L_1}(0) = 1$ amp and $i_{L_2}(0) = 0$.

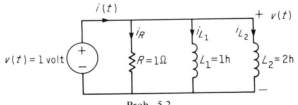

Prob. 5.2

**5.3.**  For the network shown,
    (a) Choose $i(t)$ as the unknown of the circuit and write a first-order differential equation in $i(t)$.
    (b) Give the homogeneous solution to the equation obtained in (a).
    (c) Give the particular solution to the equation obtained in (a).
    (d) Write down the total solution of the equation obtained in (a) and determine the unknown constant using the initial condition.
    (e) Sketch the plot of $i(t)$ versus $t$.

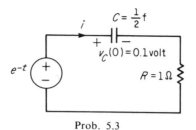

Prob. 5.3

**5.4.** Repeat Prob. 5.3 for the circuit shown, but this time choose $v$ as the unknown of the circuit.

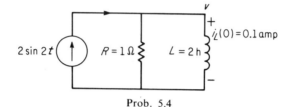

Prob. 5.4

**5.5.** For the following differential equation
(a) Find the homogeneous solution.
(b) Find the particular solution.
(c) Write down the total solution and determine the unknown constant.

$$-2 \frac{dv(t)}{dt} + 2v(t) = t^2 + 2t + 1; \qquad v(0) = 1$$

**5.6.** Repeat Prob. 5.5 for the following differential equation:

$$\frac{di(t)}{dt} + 0.5i(t) = t^2 \sin 2t; \qquad i(0) = 2$$

**5.7.** Repeat Prob. 5.5 for the following differential equation:

$$\frac{dx(t)}{dt} = e^{-t} \sin 2t; \qquad x(0) = 1$$

**5.8.** Calculate the voltage $v_C(t)$ for the circuit shown for $t \geq 0$.

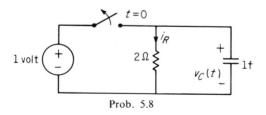

Prob. 5.8

**5.9.** Calculate the response $v_C(t)$ in the RC circuit shown with $v_C(0) = 2$ and $v(t) = u_0(t) - u_0(t - 1)$.

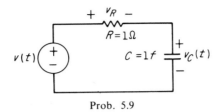

Prob. 5.9

**5.10.** Calculate and plot $i(t)$, of the series $RL$ circuit shown,
   (a) for $v(t) = u_0(t)$
   (b) for $v(t) = \delta(t)$

Assume zero initial conditions.

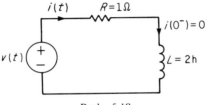

Prob. 5.10

**5.11.** In the circuit shown,
   (a) Use KVL, KCL and the branch voltage current relations to obtain a first-order differential equation in $i_L(t)$.
   (b) Solve the equation obtained in part (a) assuming $i_L(0) = 1$ amp.

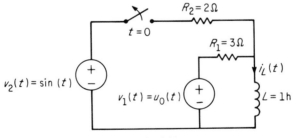

Prob. 5.11

**5.12.** Verify the forms for the particular solutions given in Table 5.3.1 by showing the particular solutions satisfy the equation

$$a_1 \frac{dx(t)}{dt} + a_0 x(t) = u(t)$$

**5.13.** The *zero-state* response of a circuit is the response with zero initial conditions. The *zero-input* response is the response to nonzero initial conditions when the driving function is set equal to zero. It is true in general that the total response of a linear circuit is the sum of the zero-state and zero-input responses. Show that this is true for the circuit shown. Let the input be the current source $i(t)$ and the response be the current through the inductor $i_L(t)$. Assume $i_L(0) = I_0$.

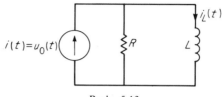

Prob. 5.13

**5.14.** The circuit shown is operating as shown until time $t = 1$ when the switch is thrown to position 2. Calculate $i_R(t)$, assuming zero initial condition on inductors.

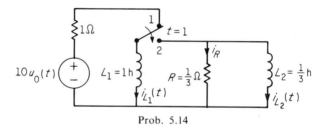

Prob. 5.14

**5.15.** Consider applying a unit ramp voltage source to a series $RL$ circuit as shown. Compute the voltages $v_R(t)$ and $v_L(t)$ with zero initial condition for (a) $L = 0.1$ h, (b) $L = 1$ h, and (c) $L = 10$ h.

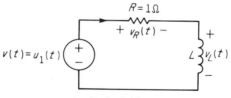

Prob. 5.15

## CHAPTER 6

# More on Transient Analysis

## 6.1. INTRODUCTION

In Chapter 5 we considered the analysis of $RL$ and $RC$ circuits and found these circuits could be described by first-order differential equations. Therefore, finding the response of $RL$ and $RC$ circuits to various inputs reduced to the problem of solving a first-order differential equation with various driving functions. We now take up the broader problem of analyzing more general types of circuits which are described by higher-order differential equations. The first class of circuits which we will consider is the class of second-order circuits, i.e. circuits described by a second-order differential equation.

As in Chapter 5, we develop our solution first using classical methods for solving a second-order differential equation. Our discussion is again limited to linear time-invariant circuits.

## 6.2. SECOND-ORDER CIRCUITS

Consider the series linear time-invariant $RLC$ circuit shown in Fig. 6.2.1. Assume the applied voltage $v(t)$ is known and it is desired to calculate the voltage response $v_C(t)$. Applying KVL around the loop gives

$$v(t) = v_R(t) + v_L(t) + v_C(t) \qquad (6.2.1)$$

Applying KCL at nodes 1, 2 and 3 gives

$$i(t) = i_R(t) = i_L(t) = i_C(t) = C\frac{dv_C}{dt} \qquad (6.2.2)$$

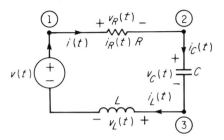

Fig. 6.2.1.    Series *RLC* circuit.

The voltages $v_L$ and $v_R$ are given by

$$v_R(t) = Ri(t) = RC\frac{dv_C}{dt} \tag{6.2.3}$$

and

$$v_L(t) = L\frac{di(t)}{dt} = LC\frac{d^2v_C}{dt^2} \tag{6.2.4}$$

Substituting $v_R(t)$ from Eq. 6.2.3 and $v_L(t)$ from Eq. 6.2.4 into Eq. 6.2.1 gives the desired relationship between the response $v_C(t)$ and the applied voltage $v(t)$:

$$LC\frac{d^2v_C}{dt^2} + RC\frac{dv_C}{dt} + v_C = v(t) \tag{6.2.5}$$

or, dividing through by $LC$,

$$\frac{d^2v_C}{dt^2} + \frac{R}{L}\frac{dv_C}{dt} + \frac{1}{LC}v_C = \frac{1}{LC}v(t) \tag{6.2.6}$$

Thus the response of the series *RLC* circuit shown in Fig. 6.2.1 is described by a linear time-invariant *second-order* differential equation. The circuit is therefore termed a *second-order* circuit. Note that after solving Eq. 6.2.6 for $v_C(t)$, all other unknowns in the circuit, namely, $v_L(t)$, $v_R(t)$, and $i(t)$ can be obtained from Eqs. 6.2.3 and 6.2.4.

### Solution of Second-Order Linear Time-Invariant Differential Equations

As indicated in the previous discussion, a second-order circuit comprised of linear time-invariant elements will give rise to a second-order linear time-invariant differential equation of the form

$$\frac{d^2x}{dt^2} + a_1\frac{dx}{dt} + a_0x = u(t) \tag{6.2.7}$$

where $a_1$ and $a_0$ are scalar constants.

As mentioned earlier, throughout the rest of this chapter we consider only the solution of linear time-invariant networks; hence, assuming that this fact is understood, we omit the words *linear time-invariant* hereafter.

To solve for the response of second-order circuits we must be able to solve equations of the form (6.2.7). As in the case of the first-order differential equation, the solution is developed as the sum of the homogeneous and particular solutions.

### Homogeneous Solution

The homogeneous equation is obtained by setting $u(t)$ to zero in Eq. 6.2.7,

$$\frac{d^2x}{dt^2} + a_1 \frac{dx}{dt} + a_0 x = 0 \qquad (6.2.8)$$

As in the case of first-order differential equations, let us guess the *form* of the solution and then check to see whether it is correct. In this case we choose the form of the homogeneous solution to be

$$x_h(t) = ke^{st} \qquad (6.2.9)$$

where $s$ is a constant which depends on $a_0$ and $a_1$; $k$ is a constant which depends on the initial conditions. Hence, substituting Eq. 6.2.9 into Eq. 6.2.8 gives

$$ke^{st}(s^2 + a_1 s + a_0) = 0 \qquad (6.2.10)$$

Since $k$ is generally nonzero, this relationship is satisfied only if

$$s^2 + a_1 s + a_0 = 0 \qquad (6.2.11)$$

which can be solved for $s$ in terms of $a_1$ and $a_0$. This relationship is called the *characteristic equation* of (6.2.8). We can solve for the roots $s_1$ and $s_2$, using the quadratic formula

$$s_1 = -\left(\frac{a_1}{2}\right) + \sqrt{\left(\frac{a_1}{2}\right)^2 - a_0}$$

$$s_2 = -\left(\frac{a_1}{2}\right) - \sqrt{\left(\frac{a_1}{2}\right)^2 - a_0} \qquad (6.2.12)$$

The homogeneous solution then consists, in general, of two terms; hence, we must revise our original guess in Eq. 6.2.9 to the following:

$$x_h(t) = k_1 e^{s_1 t} + k_2 e^{s_2 t} \qquad (6.2.13)$$

This homogeneous solution can be written in various forms, depending on the relative values of the constants $a_1$ and $a_0$. For example, if

$$\left(\frac{a_1}{2}\right)^2 > a_0 \qquad (6.2.14)$$

the quantity within the radical in Eq. 6.2.12 is positive and $s_1$ and $s_2$ are distinct real numbers. It is convenient to define the following two parameters $\alpha$ and $\beta$,

$$\alpha \triangleq \frac{a_1}{2} \qquad (6.2.15)$$

$$\beta \triangleq \sqrt{\left(\frac{a_1}{2}\right)^2 - a_0}$$

Then

$$s_1 = -\alpha + \beta$$

and

$$s_2 = -\alpha - \beta \qquad (6.2.16)$$

Substituting these relationships into Eq. 6.2.13 gives

$$x_h(t) = k_1 e^{-\alpha t} e^{\beta t} + k_2 e^{-\alpha t} e^{-\beta t} \qquad (6.2.17)$$

A second condition on the radical in Eq. 6.2.12 exists when

$$\left(\frac{a_1}{2}\right)^2 < a_0 \qquad (6.2.18)$$

This condition results in $s_1$ and $s_2$ taking on complex values and we define

$$s_1 = -\alpha + j\omega_d$$

and

$$s_2 = -\alpha - j\omega_d \qquad (6.2.19)$$

where

$$\alpha \triangleq \frac{a_1}{2}, \quad j \triangleq \sqrt{-1}$$

and

$$\omega_d \triangleq \sqrt{a_0 - \left(\frac{a_1}{2}\right)^2} \qquad (6.2.20)$$

where $\omega_d$ is called the *damped natural frequency* of the circuit. Substituting these relationships into Eq. 6.2.13 gives the homogeneous solution

$$x_h(t) = k_1 e^{-\alpha t} e^{j\omega_d t} + k_2 e^{-\alpha t} e^{-j\omega_d t} \qquad (6.2.21)$$

or

$$x_h(t) = e^{-\alpha t}[k_1 e^{j\omega_d t} + k_2 e^{-j\omega_d t}] \qquad (6.2.22)$$

Now, using the Euler relationship

$$e^{j\omega_d t} = \cos \omega_d t + j \sin \omega_d t \text{ and } e^{-j\omega_d t} = \cos \omega_d t - j \sin \omega_d t$$

this homogeneous solution can be written as

$$x_h(t) = k_1' e^{-\alpha t} \cos \omega_d t + k_2' e^{-\alpha t} \sin \omega_d t \qquad (6.2.23)$$

where $k_1'$ and $k_2'$ are again scalar constants.

A third condition on the radical in Eq. 6.2.12 arises when

$$\left(\frac{a_1}{2}\right)^2 = a_0 \qquad (6.2.24)$$

In this case $s_1$ and $s_2$ are identical and Eq. 6.2.13 yields only one portion of the homogeneous solution to the differential equation. To find a complete solution, we try

$$x(t) = kte^{st} \tag{6.2.25}$$

Substituting Eq. 6.2.25 into Eq. 6.2.8 yields

$$kte^{st}(s^2 + a_1 s + a_0) + ke^{st}(2s + a_1) = 0 \tag{6.2.26}$$

This relationship is satisfied for all $t$ if and only if $s$ is the simultaneous solution to the two equations

$$2s + a_1 = 0 \tag{6.2.27}$$

and

$$s^2 + a_1 s + a_0 = 0 \tag{6.2.28}$$

Equations 6.2.24, 6.2.27, and 6.2.28 give

$$s = -\frac{a_1}{2} \tag{6.2.29}$$

The homogeneous solution in this case is therefore of the form

$$x_h(t) = k_1 e^{-(a_1/2)t} + k_2 t e^{-(a_1/2)t} \tag{6.2.30}$$

Thus Eqs. 6.2.17, 6.2.23, and 6.2.30 represent three possible homogeneous solutions to the second-order differential equation (6.2.8). The homogeneous solution in any specific problem depends upon the roots of the characteristic equation. To determine the homogeneous solution it is necessary to solve for the roots of characteristic equation. The solution depends on whether these roots are real and distinct, real and identical, or complex. These results are summarized in Table 6.2.1 given on the next page.

*Example 6.2.1*

In Fig. 6.2.1, assume $R = 4\ \Omega$, $L = 4\ h$, and $C = \frac{1}{2}\ f$. Find the homogeneous solution for the capacitor voltage, $v_C(t)$.

*Solution*

The differential equation describing the circuit is given in (6.2.6). Setting $v(t) = 0$, the homogeneous equation is

$$\frac{d^2 v_C}{dt^2} + \frac{R}{L}\frac{dv_C}{dt} + \frac{1}{LC}v_C = 0$$

Substituting the values for $R$, $L$, and $C$ given above yields

$$\frac{d^2 v_C}{dt^2} + \frac{dv_C}{dt} + \frac{1}{2}v_C = 0$$

Comparing this with Eq. 6.2.8, the coefficients $a_1$ and $a_0$ are found to be

$$a_1 = 1$$

$$a_0 = \frac{1}{2}$$

TABLE 6.2.1. SUMMARY OF HOMOGENEOUS SOLUTION.

Differential equation: $\dfrac{dx^2}{dt^2} + a_1\dfrac{dx}{dt} + a_0 x = 0$

Characteristic equation: $f(s) = s^2 + a_1 s + a_0 = 0$

| Roots of $f(s)$ | Homogeneous Solution |
|---|---|
| 1. $\left(\dfrac{a_1}{2}\right)^2 > a_0$ <br> $s_1 = -\alpha + \beta$ <br> $s_2 = -\alpha - \beta$ <br> $\alpha \triangleq \dfrac{a_1}{2},\ \beta \triangleq \sqrt{\left(\dfrac{a_1}{2}\right)^2 - a_0}$ | $k_1 e^{-\alpha t}e^{\beta t} + k_2 e^{-\alpha t}e^{-\beta t}$ |
| 2. $a_0 > \left(\dfrac{a_1}{2}\right)^2$ <br> $s_1 = -\alpha + j\omega_d$ <br> $s_2 = -\alpha - j\omega_d$ <br> $\alpha \triangleq \dfrac{a_1}{2}\ \ \omega_d \triangleq \sqrt{a_0 - \left(\dfrac{a_1}{2}\right)^2}$ | $k_1 e^{-\alpha t}e^{j\omega_d t} + k_2 e^{-\alpha t}e^{-j\omega_d t}$ <br> or equivalently <br> $k_1' e^{-\alpha t}\cos\omega_d t + k_2' e^{-\alpha t}\sin\omega_d t$ |
| 3. $\left(\dfrac{a_1}{2}\right)^2 = a_0$ <br> $s_1 = s_2 = -\alpha = -\dfrac{a_1}{2}$ | $(k_1 + k_2 t)e^{-\alpha t}$ |

For this case we have $\left(\dfrac{a_1}{2}\right)^2 < a_0$.

Hence from Eq. 6.2.20,

$\alpha = \frac12, \omega_d = \sqrt{\frac12 - (\frac12)^2} = \frac12$

and from Table 6.2.1,

$$v_C(t) = e^{-(1/2)t}\,[k_1'\cos(\tfrac12 t) + k_2'\sin(\tfrac12 t)]$$

*Example 6.2.2*

Consider the *RLC* parallel network shown in Fig. 6.2.2. Find the differential equation and the homogeneous solution for the voltage $v(t)$ with $R = 1\,\Omega, L = 4\,h$, and $C = \frac12\,f$.

*Solution*

Applying KVL around each loop gives

$$v_R(t) = v_L(t) = v_C(t) = v(t)$$

Applying KCL at node 1 gives

$$i(t) = i_R(t) + i_L(t) + i_C(t) \qquad t \ge 0$$

Using the terminal voltage-current relationships for each element together

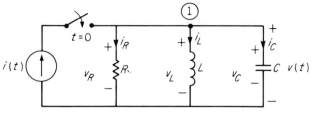

Fig. 6.2.2.   *RLC parallel network.*

with the above relationships gives

$$i(t) = \frac{1}{R} v(t) + i_L(0) + \frac{1}{L} \int_0^t v(\sigma)\, d\sigma + C \frac{dv(t)}{dt}, \qquad t \geq 0$$

This is a first-order integrodifferential equation in $v(t)$. In order to reduce this to a second-order differential equation in the form of (6.2.8) we differentiate both sides of the equation with respect to $t$. Since $i_L(0)$ is constant, we obtain

$$\frac{di(t)}{dt} = \frac{1}{L} v(t) + \frac{1}{R} \frac{dv(t)}{dt} + C \frac{d^2v(t)}{dt^2}, \qquad t \geq 0 \qquad (6.2.31)$$

The associated homogeneous equation is

$$\frac{d^2v(t)}{dt^2} + \frac{1}{RC} \frac{dv(t)}{dt} + \frac{1}{LC} v(t) = 0$$

Comparing this relationship with Eq. 6.2.8, we find

$$a_1 = \frac{1}{RC} = 2$$

and

$$a_0 = \frac{1}{LC} = \frac{1}{2}$$

For this case we have $\left(\dfrac{a_1}{2}\right)^2 - a_0 > 0$. Then from Eq. 6.2.15,

$$\alpha = 1, \quad \beta = \sqrt{\left(\frac{2}{2}\right)^2 - \frac{1}{2}} = \sqrt{\frac{1}{2}}$$

From Table 6.2.1 with the above values for the parameters $a_1$ and $a_0$ the homogeneous solution is found to be

$$v_h(t) = k_1 e^{-[1-(1/\sqrt{2})]t} + k_2 e^{-[1+(1/\sqrt{2})]t}$$

### Particular Solution

Just as in the case of the first-order differential equation we expect that the form of the particular solution will depend on the driving function, $v(t)$. For second-order equations, the method of undetermined coefficients can be employed to find the particular solution. Table 6.2.2 lists

TABLE 6.2.2. FORM OF PARTICULAR SOLUTION OF SECOND-ORDER
DIFFERENTIAL EQUATION WITH CHARACTERISTIC FUNCTION
$$f(s) = s^2 + a_1 s + a_0.$$

| Driving Function, $u(t)$ | Form of Particular Solution |
|---|---|
| 1. $e^{-at}$ ($f(-a) \neq 0$) | 1. $Ke^{-at}$ |
| 2. $e^{-at}$($f(s) = (s + a)(s + b)$) | 2. $Kte^{-at}$ |
| 3. $e^{-at}$($f(s) = (s + a)^2$) | 3. $Kt^2 e^{-at}$ |
| 4. $\sin \omega t$ or $\cos \omega t$ ($f(j\omega) \neq 0$) | 4. $K_1 \sin \omega t + K_2 \cos \omega t$ |
| 5. $\sin \omega t$ or $\cos \omega t$ ($f(j\omega) = 0$) | 5. $K_1 t \sin \omega t + K_2 t \cos \omega t$ |
| 6. $1$ | 6. $K$ |
| 7. $t^n$ | 7. $K_n t^n + K_{n-1} t^{n-1} + \cdots + K_0$ |
| 8. $e^{-at} \sin \omega t$ or $e^{-at} \cos \omega t$, $\quad f(a + j\omega) \neq 0$ | 8. $K_1 e^{-at} \cos \omega t + K_2 e^{-at} \sin \omega t$ |
| 9. $e^{-at} \sin \omega t$ or $e^{-at} \cos \omega t$, $\quad f(a + j\omega) = 0$ | 9. $K_1 te^{-at} \cos \omega t + K_2 te^{-at} \sin \omega t$ |

the form of the particular solution for several common types of driving functions.

*Example 6.2.3*

In the $RLC$ circuit of Fig. 6.2.2, assume $i(t)$ is a sinusoidal source

$$i(t) = \sqrt{2} \sin \frac{3}{\sqrt{2}} t$$

Determine the particular solution to its differential equation which is given in (6.2.31).

*Solution*

From Example 6.2.2, the corresponding differential equation is given by Eq. 6.2.31 as (using the values of $R$, $L$, $C$ as given there)

$$\frac{d^2 v(t)}{dt^2} + 2 \frac{dv(t)}{dt} + \frac{1}{2} v(t) = 6 \cos \frac{3}{\sqrt{2}} t, \qquad t \geq 0$$

From Table 6.2.2 the form of the particular solution for this type of driving function is given by

$$v_p(t) = K_1 \sin \frac{3}{\sqrt{2}} t + K_2 \cos \frac{3}{\sqrt{2}} t$$

where constants $K_1$ and $K_2$ are determined by substituting $v_p(t)$ given above in the original differential equation. Substitution gives

$$-(4K_1 + 3\sqrt{2}K_2) \sin \frac{3}{\sqrt{2}} t + (3\sqrt{2}K_1 - 4K_2) \cos \frac{3}{\sqrt{2}} t = 6 \cos \frac{3}{\sqrt{2}} t$$

Hence we must have

$$4K_1 + 3\sqrt{2}K_2 = 0$$
$$3\sqrt{2}K_1 - 4K_2 = 6$$

Solving these equations, we get

$$K_1 = 0.749 \quad \text{and} \quad K_2 = -0.706$$

Substituting these in $v_p(t)$ gives the particular solution as

$$v_p(t) = 0.749 \sin\left(\frac{3}{\sqrt{2}} t\right) - 0.706 \cos\left(\frac{3}{\sqrt{2}} t\right), \quad t \geq 0$$

### Total Solution

The total solution of a second-order differential equation is found by adding the homogeneous and particular solutions and evaluating the constants using initial conditions. Since the homogeneous solution for a second-order equation has two constants, two initial conditions must be specified to evaluate these constants. These initial conditions are obtained from the initial voltages across capacitors and initial currents through inductors.

*Example 6.2.4*

Find the total solution for the voltage $v(t)$ in the circuit shown in Fig. 6.2.2. Assume a sinusoidal source

$$i(t) = \sqrt{2} \sin \frac{3}{\sqrt{2}} t$$

with initial conditions $i_L(0) = 3.5$ amp, $v_C(0) = 10$ volts.

*Solution*

In Examples 6.2.2 and 6.2.3 the homogeneous and particular solutions have already been calculated. Hence the form of the total solution is

$$v(t) = k_1 e^{-0.293t} + k_2 e^{-1.707t} + 0.749 \sin\left(\frac{3}{\sqrt{2}} t\right) - 0.706 \cos\left(\frac{3}{\sqrt{2}} t\right)$$

Since there are no impulse functions, the initial condition on the capacitor gives

$$v_C(0^+) = v_C(0^-) = v(0) = k_1 + k_2 - 0.706 = 10$$

or

$$k_1 + k_2 = 10.706 \tag{6.2.32}$$

A second relationship between $k_1$ and $k_2$ must be determined by making use of the initial condition on the inductor. From KCL at node 1 evaluated at time $t = 0^+$ we get

$$i(0^+) = i_R(0^+) + i_L(0^+) + i_C(0^+)$$

In our case $i(t) = \sqrt{2} \sin \frac{\sqrt{3}}{2} t$, therefore $i(0^+) = 0$. There are no impulse functions applied, so

$$i_L(0^+) = i_L(0^-) = 3.5$$

Also

$$i_R(0^+) = \frac{v_R(0^+)}{R} = \frac{v_C(0^+)}{R} = 10$$

Substituting the values of $i(0^+)$, $i_L(0^+)$ and $i_R(0^+)$ in the KCL equation at $t = 0^+$ above, we get

$$i_C(0^+) = i(0^+) - i_R(0^+) - i_L(0^+)$$
$$= 0 - 10 - 3.5$$
$$= -13.5$$

Now

$$i_C(t) = C\frac{dv_C}{dt} = C\frac{dv}{dt}$$
$$= \frac{1}{2}\left\{-0.293k_1e^{-0.293t} - 1.707k_2e^{-1.707t}\right.$$
$$\left. + 0.749 \times \frac{3}{\sqrt{2}}\cos\left(\frac{3}{\sqrt{2}}t\right) + 0.706 \times \frac{3}{\sqrt{2}}\sin\left(\frac{3}{\sqrt{2}}t\right)\right\}$$

At $t = 0^+$, we evaluate

$$i_C(0^+) = \frac{1}{2}\left[-0.293k_1 - 1.707k_2 + 0.749 \times \frac{3}{\sqrt{2}}\right]$$

However, we obtained above

$$i_C(0^+) = -13.5$$

Therefore

$$\tfrac{1}{2}[-0.293k_1 - 1.707k_2 + 1.59] = -13.5$$

or

$$-0.293k_1 - 1.707k_2 = -28.59 \qquad (6.2.33)$$

Now we can solve Eqs. 6.2.32 and 6.2.33 to obtain

$$k_1 = -7.28 \quad \text{and} \quad k_2 = 17.98$$

Hence the output voltage is given by

$$v(t) = -7.28e^{-0.293t} + 17.98e^{-1.707t} + 0.749\sin\frac{3}{\sqrt{2}}t$$

$$-0.706\cos\frac{3}{\sqrt{2}}t$$

*Example 6.2.5*

For the circuit shown in Fig. 6.2.1, calculate the total response, assuming *zero initial conditions* [i.e., $v_C(0) = 0$, $i_L(0) = 0$] when $R = 8\Omega$, $L = 4$ h, $C = \frac{1}{2}$ f and $v(t) = v_0e^{-1.707t}$.

*Solution*

In Example 6.2.1, the differential equation describing the circuit was found to be

$$\frac{d^2 v_C}{dt^2} + \frac{R}{L}\frac{dv_C}{dt} + \frac{1}{LC}v_C = \frac{1}{LC}v(t)$$

which in this case becomes

$$\frac{d^2 v_C}{dt^2} + 2\frac{dv_C}{dt} + \frac{1}{2}v_C = \frac{1}{2}v_0 e^{-1.707t}$$

for which the characteristic equation is

$$s^2 + 2s + \tfrac{1}{2} = 0$$

Using Table 6.2.1 with $a_1 = 2$ and $a_0 = \tfrac{1}{2}$, the *homogeneous solution* is

$$v_h(t) = k_1 e^{-1.707t} + k_2 e^{-0.293t}$$

From Table 6.2.2 the form of the *particular solution* is given by

$$v_p(t) = Kte^{-1.707t}$$

Substituting $v_p(t)$ into the differential equation above we can find

$$K = -0.354v_0$$

Hence the form of the total solution is found by adding $v_h(t)$ and $v_p(t)$:

$$v_C(t) = k_1 e^{-1.707t} + k_2 e^{-0.293t} - 0.354v_0 te^{-1.707t}$$

The constants $k_1$ and $k_2$ must be determined from the initial conditions. Since by assumption $v_C(0) = 0$, we can substitute $t = 0$ in $v_C(t)$ above to obtain

$$v_C(0) = k_1 + k_2 = 0 \tag{6.2.34}$$

The second initial condition relates to the inductor current $i_L(t)$. Since the inductor and the capacitor are in series combination, we must have

$$i_L(t) = i_C(t) = C\frac{dv_C}{dt}$$

for all time instants. In particular at $t = 0^+$,

$$i_L(0^+) = C\frac{dv_C}{dt}\bigg|_{t=0^+} = \frac{1}{2}[k_1(-1.707) + k_2(-0.293) - 0.354v_0] = 0$$

$$\tag{6.2.35}$$

Simultaneous solution of Eqs. 6.2.34 and 6.2.35 yields

$$k_1 = -0.25v_0 \quad \text{and} \quad k_2 = 0.25v_0$$

so that the total solution is given by

$$v_C(t) = 0.25v_0 e^{-0.293t} - 0.25v_0 e^{-1.707t} - 0.354v_0 te^{-1.707t}$$

*Example 6.2.6*

Calculate the current $i_L(t)$ and the voltage $v_C(t)$ in the parallel *RLC* network of Fig. 6.2.3. Assume zero input with initial conditions $v_C(t_0) = V; i_L(t_0) = I$.

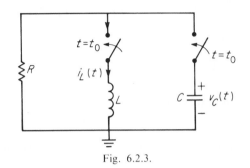

Fig. 6.2.3.

*Solution*

Under zero input conditions, the circuit response for $t > t_0$ is simply due to the initial voltage on the capacitor and current in the inductor. The differential equation governing both the inductor current and the capacitor voltage is of the form (see Example 6.2.2)

$$\frac{d^2x}{dt^2} + \frac{1}{RC}\frac{dx}{dt} + \frac{1}{LC}x = 0$$

The solutions that we seek are therefore simply the homogeneous solution with constants evaluated to fit the initial conditions. This solution is of the form

$$x(t) = k_1 e^{s_1 t} + k_2 e^{s_2 t}$$

Evaluating the constants $k_1$ and $k_2$ under these conditions gives, for the inductor current

$$
\begin{aligned}
i_L(t) = & \frac{1}{s_2 - s_1}\left[-\frac{V}{L} + s_2 I\right] e^{s_1(t-t_0)} \\
& + \frac{1}{s_2 - s_1}\left[\frac{V}{L} - s_1 I\right] e^{s_2(t-t_0)}, \quad t \geq t_0
\end{aligned}
$$

and for the capacitor voltage,

$$
\begin{aligned}
v_C(t) = & \frac{1}{s_2 - s_1}\left[\frac{V}{RC} + \frac{I}{C} + s_2 V\right] e^{s_1(t-t_0)} \\
& - \frac{1}{s_2 - s_1}\left[\frac{V}{RC} + \frac{I}{C} + s_1 V\right] e^{s_2(t-t_0)}, \quad t \geq t_0
\end{aligned}
$$

In both cases above $s_1 \neq s_2$. If the characteristic roots are identical, i.e., $s_1 = s_2$, the solution will be

$$i_L(t) = \left[ I + \left( \frac{V}{L} - s_1 I \right)(t - t_0) \right] e^{-s_1(t-t_0)}, \quad t \geq t_0$$

$$v_C(t) = \left[ V - \left( \frac{I}{C} + \frac{V}{RC} + s_1 V \right)(t - t_0) \right] e^{-s_1(t-t_0)}, \qquad t \geq t_0$$

Using algebraic and trigonometric manipulations, these solutions can be rewritten in various forms depending on whether or not the roots of the characteristic equation $s_1$ and $s_2$ are real or complex. These solutions are summarized in Table 6.2.3 given on the next two pages for both the series and parallel $RLC$ networks.

## Development of the Computer Program for Plotting the Network Response

In a few examples in this section we have shown how the second-order differential equation can be solved to obtain the response of second-order circuits. Once we have the response whether it is a current or a voltage, it is sometimes desirable to plot this response as a function of time. Such a plot gives a visual picture of what is happening to the response. This plot can be obtained by evaluating the response for several values of $t$ over the time interval of interest, and the results can be plotted by hand. This same plot can also be achieved using the digital computer. First the response is calculated for several values of $t$ over the time interval of interest using a DO loop and simultaneously the calculated values are stored in the computer. A computer program called the GRAPHX *subroutine* is then called in which plots these stored values as response versus time. We will not go into great details of the GRAPHX *subroutine*, however, we will show how it is used by specifying the input to this routine.

### The Basic Plot Program

The computer program developed in this section will plot two given functions $f(t)$ and $g(t)$ simultaneously for discrete values of the independent variable $t$ over an interval $[t_0, t_1]$. In order to avoid repeating this program in each case we introduce a *subroutine* called GRAPHX which can be used later on. Let us now work out an example to illustrate the plot program.

*Example 6.2.7*

Consider the functions

$$f(t) = 1 - e^{-0.3t} \cos \pi t \qquad \text{and} \qquad g(t) = 1 - e^{-0.2t}$$

Develop a computer program for plotting these functions over the interval of [0, 10] sec at increments of 0.1 sec.

TABLE 6.2.3. ZERO INPUT RESPONSE FOR SERIES AND
PARALLEL $RLC$ NETWORKS.

*Series RLC Network*

Differential equation: $\dfrac{d^2x}{dt^2} + \dfrac{R}{L}\dfrac{dx}{dt} + \dfrac{1}{LC}x = 0$    $v_C(t_0) = V,$    $i_L(t_0) = I$

Characteristic equation: $s^2 + \dfrac{R}{L}s + \dfrac{1}{LC} = 0$

Network parameters: $\alpha = \dfrac{R}{2L},$    $\beta^2 = \left(\dfrac{R}{2L}\right)^2 - \dfrac{1}{LC},$

$$\omega_d^2 = \dfrac{1}{LC} - \left(\dfrac{R}{2L}\right)^2,\qquad \theta = \tan^{-1}\dfrac{\alpha}{\omega_d}$$

1. $\left(\dfrac{R}{2L}\right)^2 > \dfrac{1}{LC}$

$$i_L(t) = \dfrac{1}{2\beta}\left[\left(-\dfrac{R}{L} + \alpha + \beta\right)I - \dfrac{V}{L}\right]e^{-(\alpha-\beta)(t-t_0)}$$

$$+ \dfrac{1}{2\beta}\left[\left(\dfrac{R}{L} - \alpha + \beta\right)I + \dfrac{V}{L}\right]e^{-(\alpha+\beta)(t-t_0)},\qquad t \geq t_0$$

$$v_C(t) = \dfrac{1}{2\beta}\left[\dfrac{I}{C} + (\alpha + \beta)V\right]e^{-(\alpha-\beta)(t-t_0)}$$

$$+ \dfrac{1}{2\beta}\left[-\dfrac{I}{C} - (\alpha - \beta)V\right]e^{-(\alpha+\beta)(t-t_0)},\qquad t \geq t_0$$

2. $\left(\dfrac{R}{2L}\right)^2 = \dfrac{1}{LC}$

$$i_L(t) = \left[-\dfrac{V}{L} + I[1 + \alpha(t - t_0)]\right]e^{-\alpha(t - t_0)},\quad t \geq t_0$$

$$v_C(t) = \left[\dfrac{I}{C} + [1 + \alpha(t - t_0)]V\right]e^{-\alpha(t-t_0)},\qquad t \geq t_0$$

3. $\left(\dfrac{R}{2L}\right)^2 < \dfrac{1}{LC}$

$$i_L(t) = I\sqrt{1 + \left(\dfrac{\alpha}{\omega_d}\right)^2}\cos[\omega_d(t - t_0) + \theta]e^{-\alpha(t-t_0)}$$

$$+ V\left(-\dfrac{1}{\omega_d L}\sin\omega_d(t - t_0)\right)e^{-\alpha(t-t_0)},\qquad t \geq t_0$$

$$v_C(t) = V\cos[\omega_d(t - t_0) - \theta]e^{-\alpha(t-t_0)}$$

$$+ I\left(\dfrac{1}{\omega_d}\sin\omega_d(t - t_0)\right)e^{-\alpha(t-t_0)},\qquad t \geq t_0$$

TABLE 6.2.3.   (*continued*)
*Parallel RLC Network*

Differential equation: $\dfrac{dx^2}{dt^2} + \dfrac{1}{RC}\dfrac{dx}{dt} + \dfrac{1}{LC}x = 0,$   $v_C(t_0) = V,$   $i_L(t_0) = I$

Characteristic equation: $s^2 + \dfrac{1}{RC}s + \dfrac{1}{LC} = 0$

Network  parameters: $\alpha = \dfrac{1}{2RC},$   $\beta^2 = \left(\dfrac{1}{2RC}\right)^2 - \dfrac{1}{LC},$

$$\omega_d^2 = \dfrac{1}{LC} - \left(\dfrac{1}{2RC}\right)^2,\qquad \theta = \tan^{-1}\dfrac{\alpha}{\omega_d}$$

---

1. $\left(\dfrac{1}{2RC}\right)^2 > \dfrac{1}{LC}$

$$i_L(t) = \dfrac{1}{2\beta}\left[\dfrac{V}{L} + (\alpha + \beta)I\right]e^{-(\alpha-\beta)(t-t_0)}$$

$$+ \dfrac{1}{2\beta}\left[-\dfrac{V}{L} - (\alpha - \beta)I\right]e^{-(\alpha+\beta)(t-t_0)},\qquad t \geq t_0$$

$$v_C(t) = \dfrac{1}{2\beta}\left[\left(-\dfrac{1}{RC} + \alpha + \beta\right)V - \dfrac{I}{C}\right]e^{-(\alpha-\beta)(t-t_0)}$$

$$+ \dfrac{1}{2\beta}\left[\left(\dfrac{1}{RC} - \alpha + \beta\right)V + \dfrac{I}{C}\right]e^{-(\alpha+\beta)(t-t_0)},\qquad t \geq t_0$$

---

2. $\left(\dfrac{1}{2RC}\right)^2 = \dfrac{1}{LC}$

$$i_L(t) = \left[\dfrac{V}{L} + [1 + \alpha(t - t_0)]I\right]e^{-\alpha(t-t_0)},\qquad t \geq t_0$$

$$v_C(t) = \left[-\dfrac{I}{C} + V[1 - \alpha(t - t_0)]\right]e^{-\alpha(t-t_0)},\qquad t \geq t_0$$

---

3. $\left(\dfrac{1}{2RC}\right)^2 < \dfrac{1}{LC}$

$$i_L(t) = I\cos\,[\omega_d(t - t_0) - \theta]e^{-\alpha(t-t_0)}$$

$$+ V\left(\dfrac{1}{\omega_d}\sin \omega_d(t - t_0)\right)e^{-\alpha(t-t_0)},\qquad t \geq t_0$$

$$v_C(t) = V\sqrt{1 + \left(\dfrac{\alpha}{\omega_d}\right)^2}\cos\,[\omega_d(t - t_0) + \theta]e^{-\alpha(t-t_0)}$$

$$+ I\left(-\dfrac{1}{\omega_d C}\sin \omega_d(t - t_0)e^{-\alpha(t-t_0)}\right),\qquad t \geq t_0$$

---

*Solution*

The basic steps consist of breaking $[0, 10]$ into suitable increments and then using a DO loop to evaluate and store $f(t)$ and $g(t)$ for each $t$.  Then the GRAPHX *subroutine* plots these values as $f(t)$ and $g(t)$ versus $t$. The following flow chart gives a summary of the steps involved in this plot.

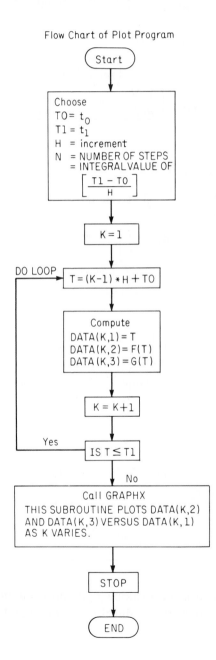

Flow Chart of Plot Program

Computer Program for Plotting Two Functions f(t) and g(t) versus t, an Example

```
C        THIS PROGRAM IS FOR EXAMPLE 6,2=7
C        PLOT PROGRAM
C        THIS PROGRAM PLOTS TWO GIVEN FUNCTIONS F(,) AND G(,)
C        SIMULTANOUSLY, DATA(K,1) CORRESPONDS TO VALUES OF T
C        AND PLOTS THE HORIZONTAL LINE, DATA(K,2) AND DATA(K,3)
C        CORRESPOND TO THE VALUES OF F(,) AND G(,) AT T=K
C        RESPECTIVELY,
         DIMENSION DATA(100,3)
C        DEFINE THE TIME INTERVAL OF INTEREST
C        AND TIME INCREMENT,
         TO=0,
         TI=10,
         H=0,2
C        OBTAIN THE NUMBER OF POINTS TO BE PLOTTED,
C        THEY MUST BE LESS THAN 100,
         N=INT((TI=TO)/ H)+1
C        OBTAIN TNE VALUES OF THE FUNCTIONS AT THESE INCREMENTS
         DO 1 K=1,N
         T=(K=1) * H+TO
         DATA(K,1) = T
         PI= 3,1416
         DATA(K,2)=1,=(EXP(=0,3*T))*COS(PI*T)
      1  DATA(K,3)=1,=EXP(=0,2*T)
C        NEXT, USE THE SUBROUTINE GRAPHX TO PLOT F(K), G(K),
         CALL GRAPHX(DATA,K,1HT,3HF,G)
         END
```

The plot of $f(t)$ and $g(t)$ versus $t$ is given in Fig. 6.2.4.

GRAPHX Subroutine

```
         SUBROUTINE GRAPHX(DATA,N,VINDEP,VARDEP)
         DIMENSION DATA(100,3),B(121)
         DOUBLE PRECISION VINDEP,VARDEP
         PRINT 300,VINDEP
         PRINT 400,VARDEP
         BIGEST=DATA(1,2)
         SMAL=DATA(1,2)
         DO 1 I=2,N
         IF(DATA(I,2),GT,BIGEST)BIGEST=DATA(I,2)
         IF(DATA(I,2),LT,SMAL)SMAL=DATA(I,2)
      1  CONTINUE
         DO 2 I=2,N
         IF(DATA(I,3),GT,BIGEST)BIGEST=DATA(I,3)
         IF(DATA(I,3),LT,SMAL)SMAL=DATA(I,3)
      2  CONTINUE
         PRINT 200,SMAL,BIGEST
C        TO EXTEND THE PLOT TO FULL PAGE WIDTH, WE ONLY
C        NEED TO REPLACE K=61 BY K=121,
C        ALSO IN FORMAT STATEMENT 200 4X
C        MUST BE REPLACED BY 48X, AND 61 BY 121,
         K=61
         BMINS=BIGEST=SMAL
         DO 3 I=1,K
      3  B(I)=1H
         DO 4 I=1,N
         DATA(I,2)=(DATA(I,2)=SMAL)*FLOAT(K)/BMINS+1,0
         DATA(I,3)=(DATA(I,3)=SMAL)*FLOAT(K)/BMINS+1,0
         INDEX=DATA(I,2)
         JNDEX=DATA(I,3)
```

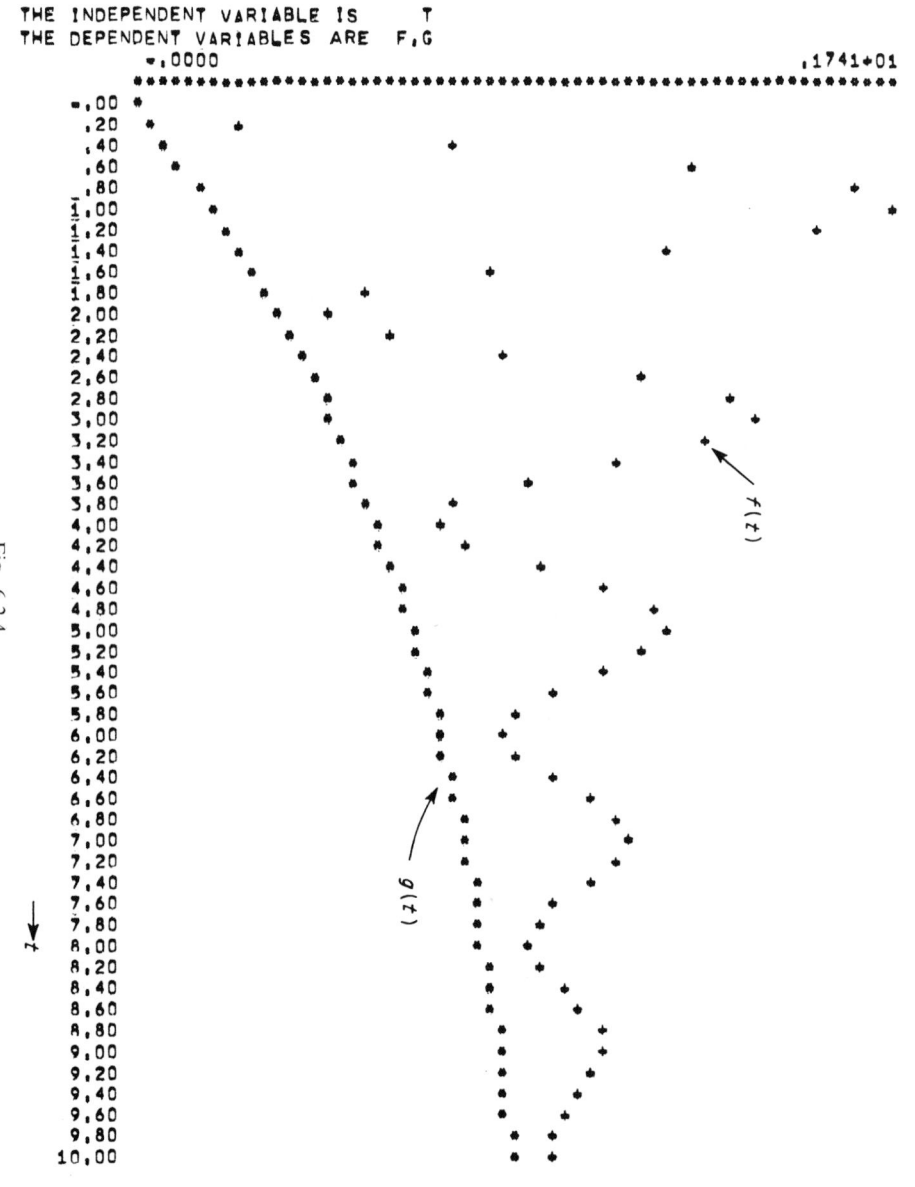

Fig. 6.2.4.

```
      B(INDEX)=1H*
      B(JNDEX)=1H*
      PRINT 100,DATA(I,1),(B (N),N=1,K)
      B(INDEX)=1H
    4 B(JNDEX)=1H
  100 FORMAT(1HZ,F8,2,1X,121A1)
  200 FORMAT(9X,E11,4,35X,1H ,4X,E11,4,/10X,61(1H*))
  300 FORMAT (1H1,'THE INDEPENDENT VARIABLE IS ',2A10)
  400 FORMAT (1X,'THE DEPENDENT VARIABLE IS ',2A10//)
      RETURN
      END
```

*Example 6.2.8:  Plot Program Used to Plot Network Response*

We show the use of the above program for the network response of Example 6.2.4.  Here we had

$$v(t) = -7.28e^{-0.293t} + 17.98e^{-1.707t} + 0.749 \sin \frac{3}{\sqrt{2}}t - 0.706 \cos \frac{3}{\sqrt{2}}t$$

To sketch this we need $T0$, $T1$ and we need to choose $H$.  Note also that here we have only one time function $v(t)$ to plot.  So we make

$$DATA(K, 1) = T$$
$$DATA(K, 2) = V(T)$$
$$DATA(K, 3) = 0$$

If we examine $v(t)$ we can see that $t = 0$ to $t = 10$ with 0.2 step should suffice.  So we let $T0 = 0$, $T1 = 10$ and $H = 0.2$.  The computer program and the plot is given below.   Note that we have just called in the GRAPHX subroutine and we have not listed it again.  $v(t)$ is plotted in Fig. 6.2.5.

```
C     THIS PROGRAM IS FOR EXAMPLE 6,2=8
C     PLOT PROGRAM
C     THIS PROGRAM PLOTS THE FUNCTION
C     F(T)==7,28*EXP(=0,293*T)+17,98*EXP(=1,707*T)+0,749*
C     SIN(3,0*T/SQRT(2,0))=0,706*COS(3,0*T/SQRT(2,0))
      DIMENSION DATA(100,3)
C     DEFINE THE TIME INTERVAL OF INTEREST
C     AND TIME INCREMENT,
      TO=0,
      TI=10,
      H=0,2
C     OBTAIN THE NUMBER OF POINTS TO BE PLOTTED,
C     THEY MUST BE LESS THAN 100,
      N=INT((TI=TO)/ H) +1
C     OBTAIN TNE VALUES OF THE FUNCTIONS AT THESE INCREMENTS
      DO 1 K=1,N
      T=(K=1) * H+TO
      RT= SQRT(2)
      DATA(K,1) = T
      DATA(K,2)==7,28*EXP(=0,293*T) +17,98*EXP(=1,707*T)
     1+0,749*SIN(3,*T/RT) =0,706*COS(3,*T/RT)
    1 DATA(K,3)=0,00
C     NEXT, USE THE SUBROUTINE GRAPHX TO PLOT F(K)=DATA(K,2)
      CALL GRAPHX(DATA,K,1HT,4HF(T))
      END
```

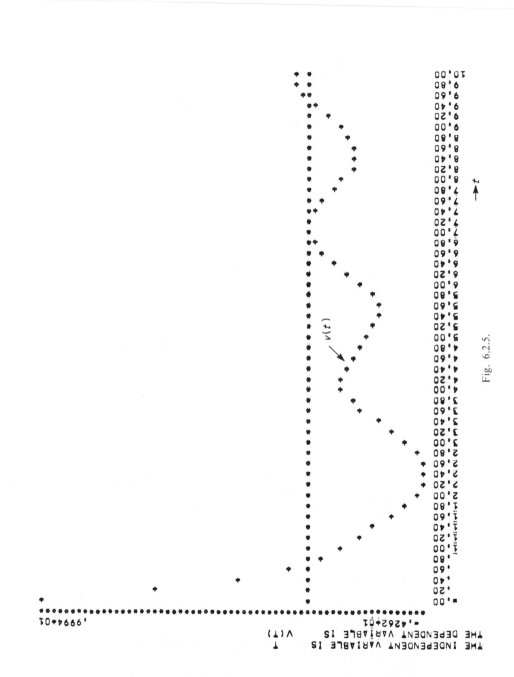

Fig. 6.2.5.

## 6.3. STEP AND IMPULSE RESPONSE OF SECOND-ORDER CIRCUITS

We have seen that the response of second-order circuits can be described by a differential equation of the form

$$\frac{d^2x}{dt^2} + a_1 \frac{dx}{dt} + a_0 x = a_0 u(t) \tag{6.3.1}$$

Let us consider the case when the driving function is the unit step, $u_0(t)$; assume all the initial conditions are zero. The total solution is called the *unit step response*, $s(t)$, and is given by

$$s(t) = \begin{cases} \left[ \left( \frac{\alpha}{2\beta} - \frac{1}{2} \right) e^{-(\alpha+\beta)t} - \left( \frac{\alpha}{2\beta} + \frac{1}{2} \right) e^{-(\alpha-\beta)t} + 1 \right] u_0(t) \\ \qquad\qquad\qquad\qquad \text{for } \left( \frac{a_1}{2} \right)^2 > a_0 \\[2mm] \left[ 1 - \sqrt{1 + \left( \frac{\alpha}{\omega_d} \right)^2}\, e^{-\alpha t} \cos(\omega_d t - \theta) \right] u_0(t) \\ \qquad\qquad \text{for } \left( \frac{a_1}{2} \right)^2 < a_0, \quad \text{where } \theta = \tan^{-1}\left( \frac{\alpha}{\omega_d} \right) \\[2mm] [1 - (\alpha t + 1) e^{-\alpha t}] u_0(t) \qquad \text{for } \left( \frac{a_1}{2} \right)^2 = a_0 \end{cases} \tag{6.3.2}$$

The parameters $\alpha$, $\beta$, and $\omega_d$ are as defined in Table 6.2.1. These solutions of Eq. 6.3.2 represent the unit step response of a second-order network described by Eq. 6.3.1. A plot of these three solutions is shown in Fig. 6.3.1, assuming that in each case $\alpha > 0$. From the figure we can see

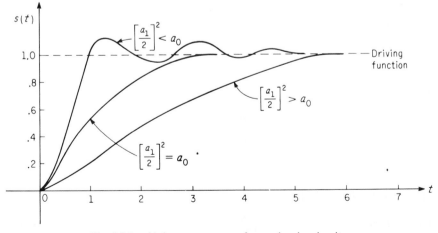

Fig. 6.3.1.   Unit step response of second order circuit.

that all three solutions have an identical response as $t \to \infty$ which is equal to the driving function value. This is called the *steady-state response* of the second-order circuit. However, for small values of $t$, there is a considerable difference in the form of the step response. For $(a_1/2)^2 < a_0$, we see that the response *overshoots* the driving function and then forms a decaying oscillation prior to reaching the steady-state value. Because of this oscillatory behavior about its final value, this solution is said to be *underdamped* and, similarly, a network whose step response behaves in this manner is said to be an *underdamped* network. The parameter $\alpha$ in this solution is called the *damping factor*, while $\omega_d$ is called the *damped natural frequency*. The response for $(a_1/2)^2 > a_0$ does not overshoot but instead builds up slowly to the steady-state value. A circuit with this response is said to be *overdamped*. If we define the *rise time* as being the time required for the response to rise from zero to 95 percent of its steady-state value, we see that the rise time of the underdamped circuit is considerably shorter than that for the overdamped circuit. The minimum rise time to be achieved with zero overshoot occurs for the *critically damped* circuit. Critical damping occurs when

$$\left(\frac{a_1}{2}\right)^2 = a_0$$

The critically damped solution is also shown in Fig. 6.3.1.

We can relate these three solutions to network parameters for particular networks. For the series $RLC$ network shown in Fig. 6.3.2,

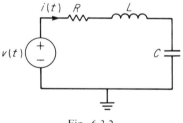

Fig. 6.3.2.

we have

$$a_0 = \frac{1}{LC} \tag{6.3.3}$$

$$a_1 = \frac{R}{L} \tag{6.3.4}$$

Thus a series $RLC$ circuit is

*underdamped if:*
$$\left(\frac{R}{2L}\right)^2 < \frac{1}{LC} \tag{6.3.5}$$

*overdamped if:*
$$\left(\frac{R}{2L}\right)^2 > \frac{1}{LC} \qquad (6.3.6)$$

*critically damped if:*
$$\left(\frac{R}{2L}\right)^2 = \frac{1}{LC} \qquad (6.3.7)$$

The factors $1/\sqrt{LC}$ and $(1/\sqrt{LC})(L/R)$ occur frequently in circuit analysis and are given special names. If we examine the expression for $\omega_d$ in the underdamped solution, we have

$$\omega_d = \sqrt{\frac{1}{LC} - \alpha^2} \qquad (6.3.8)$$

As the damping factor $\alpha$ approaches zero, the *undamped natural frequency of oscillation*, $\omega_0$, is given by

$$\omega_0 \triangleq \omega_d \mid_{\alpha = 0} = \frac{1}{\sqrt{LC}} \qquad (6.3.9)$$

The factor $(1/\sqrt{LC})(L/R)$ can then be written in terms of the natural frequency $\omega_0$ as

$$Q \triangleq \frac{1}{\sqrt{LC}}\frac{L}{R} = \frac{\omega_0 L}{R} \qquad (6.3.10)$$

The parameter $Q$ is called the *quality factor* of the circuit. For $Q \gg \frac{1}{2}$, we have a highly underdamped response, while for $Q < \frac{1}{2}$ we have the overdamped response.

We can investigate other second-order circuits in a manner identical to that which we have used for the series $RLC$ circuit. Another second-order circuit of practical interest is the parallel $RLC$ circuit for which the natural frequency is also given by

$$\omega_0 = \frac{1}{\sqrt{LC}} \qquad (6.3.11)$$

but whose quality factor is

$$Q = \frac{R}{\omega_0 L} \qquad (6.3.12)$$

As with circuits of first order, the *unit impulse response* $h(t)$ can be found in a straightforward manner by differentiating the response due to the unit step. The unit step and unit impulse responses for series and parallel $RLC$ networks are indicated in Table 6.3.1 along with a summary of the results relating the quality factor $Q$ to the various response forms.

Note from the last entry in Table 6.3.1 that as the damping factor $\alpha$ becomes zero, an impulse input to either network will produce sustained oscillations of the form $\omega_0 \sin \omega_0 t$. In addition, if we let the damping factor become negative, an impulse input to the network creates a response which grows larger and larger with time. These two types of re-

TABLE 6.3.1. STEP AND IMPULSE RESPONSE OF $RLC$ CIRCUITS WITH ZERO INITIAL CONDITIONS.

| | |
|---|---|
| $v_C(t)$ = response | $i_L(t)$ = response |
| $\dfrac{d^2 v_C}{dt^2} + 2\alpha \dfrac{dv_C}{dt} + \omega_0^2 v_C = \omega_0^2 v(t)$ | $\dfrac{d^2 i_L}{dt^2} + 2\alpha \dfrac{di_L}{dt} + \omega_0^2 i_L = \omega_0^2 i(t)$ |
| $\alpha = \dfrac{R}{2L} \qquad \omega_0^2 = \dfrac{1}{LC} \qquad Q = \dfrac{\omega_0 L}{R}$ | $\alpha = \dfrac{1}{2RC} \qquad \omega_0^2 = \dfrac{1}{LC} \qquad Q = \dfrac{R}{\omega_0 L}$ |
| $\beta = \sqrt{\alpha^2 - \omega_0^2} \qquad \omega_d = \sqrt{\omega_0^2 - \alpha^2}$ | $\beta = \sqrt{\alpha^2 - \omega_0^2} \qquad \omega_d = \sqrt{\omega_0^2 - \alpha^2}$ |

$Q < \frac{1}{2}$  *Overdamped*

$$s(t) = 1 + \frac{1}{2}\left(\frac{\alpha}{\beta} - 1\right)e^{-(\alpha+\beta)t} - \frac{1}{2}\left(\frac{\alpha}{\beta} + 1\right)e^{-(\alpha-\beta)t}, \qquad t \geq 0$$

$$h(t) = -\frac{\omega_0^2}{2\beta} e^{-(\alpha+\beta)t} + \frac{\omega_0^2}{2\beta} e^{-(\alpha-\beta)t}, \qquad t \geq 0$$

$Q = \frac{1}{2}$  *Critically Damped*

$$s(t) = 1 - (\alpha t + 1)e^{-\alpha t}, \qquad t \geq 0$$
$$h(t) = \alpha^2 t e^{-\alpha t}, \qquad t \geq 0$$

$Q > \frac{1}{2}$  *Underdamped*

$$s(t) = 1 - \sqrt{1 + \left(\frac{\alpha}{\omega_d}\right)^2}\, e^{-\alpha t} \cos(\omega_d t - \theta), \; \theta = \tan^{-1}\left(\frac{\alpha}{\omega_d}\right), t \geq 0$$

$$h(t) = \frac{\omega_0^2}{\omega_d} e^{-\alpha t} \sin \omega_d t$$

sponses are shown in Fig. 6.3.3. A network with the first type of response is said to be *oscillatory* because any input will develop sustained oscillations.

A network with the second type of response is said to be *unstable* because any input will develop sustained and unbounded oscillations. We say that the circuit is *stable* if $\alpha > 0$. We might consider how an unstable condition can arise with a physical circuit. From Table 6.3.1, we see that for the series circuit $\alpha$ can be made nonpositive by making the resistance function nonpositive. Such a situation can be realized approximately by using nonlinear elements, such as the tunnel diode, which exhibit a terminal voltage-current relationship with a negative slope over a limited range of input current values.

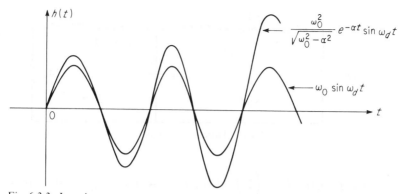

Fig. 6.3.3. Impulse response of an underdamped $RLC$ circuit with $\alpha = 0$ and $\alpha < 0$.

## 6.4. HIGHER-ORDER CIRCUITS

We have developed methods for analyzing the response of first- and second-order circuits, i.e., circuits described by first- or second-order differential equations. Many circuits encountered in practice are described by differential equations of higher order. The analysis procedures which we have used for first- and second-order circuits can be directly extended to higher-order circuits. We can develop analytical solutions by the following procedure.

1. Applying KCL, KVL, and branch voltage-current relations to determine the equation of operation relating the desired response to the driving function.
2. Set the driving function equal to zero to find the homogeneous equation. Find the solution to this differential equation, this is the *homogeneous solution*. The homogeneous solution of an *n*th order differential equation contains *n* arbitrary constants.
3. Using the specified driving function, find a *particular solution* to the equation of operation. The particular solution satisfies the equation of operation exactly and contains no arbitrary constants.
4. Form the *total solution* by summing the homogeneous and particular solutions. Use initial conditions to evaluate the arbitrary constants.

*Example 6.4.1*

Find the current $i_1(t)$ for the circuit shown in Fig. 6.4.1. Assume the initial conditions $v_C(0) = 1$, $i_1(0) = i_2(0) = 0$. Use the plot program to sketch $i_1(t)$.

*Solution*

Applying KVL around loop $l_1$ and loop $l_2$ gives for $t > 0$

$$\left( 2 \int_0^t i_1(\sigma)\, d\sigma + 4i_1(t) + \frac{di_1}{dt} \right) - 2 \int_0^t i_2(\sigma)\, d\sigma = 1 \qquad (6.4.1)$$

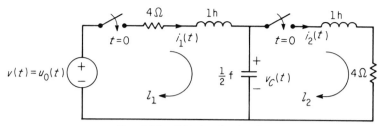

Fig. 6.4.1.   Third-order circuit.

$$-2 \int_0^t i_1(\sigma)\, d\sigma + \left(2 \int_0^t i_2(\sigma)\, d\sigma + 4i_2(t) + \frac{di_2}{dt}\right) = 0 \qquad (6.4.2)$$

Since we want to obtain $i_1(t)$, we must eliminate $i_2$ from Eqs. 6.4.1 and 6.4.2 to obtain a differential equation in $i_1$. Adding Eqs. 6.4.1 and 6.4.2, we get

$$4i_1(t) + 4i_2(t) + \frac{di_1}{dt} + \frac{di_2}{dt} = 1 \qquad (6.4.3)$$

Also differentiating Eq. 6.4.1, we get

$$i_2(t) = i_1(t) + 2\frac{di_1}{dt} + \frac{1}{2}\frac{d^2 i_1}{dt^2} \qquad (6.4.4)$$

We can now substitute $i_2(t)$ and the derivative of $i_2(t)$ using Eq. 6.4.4 into Eq. 6.4.3 to obtain a differential equation only in $i_1$ as

$$\frac{d^3 i_1}{dt^3} + 8\frac{d^2 i_1}{dt^2} + 20\frac{di_1}{dt} + 16i_1 = 2$$

The characteristic equation for this differential equation is

$$s^3 + 8s^2 + 20s + 16 = 0$$

which has roots

$$s_1 = s_2 = -2 \quad \text{and} \quad s_3 = -4$$

The homogeneous solution is therefore

$$i_h(t) = (k_1 + k_2 t)e^{-2t} + k_3 e^{-4t}$$

The particular solution in this case is

$$i_p(t) = \tfrac{1}{8}$$

So the total solution is given by

$$i_1(t) = i_h(t) + i_p(t) = (k_1 + k_2 t)e^{-2t} + k_3 e^{-4t} + \tfrac{1}{8} \qquad (6.4.5)$$

The remaining step is to evaluate the constants $k_1$, $k_2$, and $k_3$ from the initial conditions. The initial conditions are

$$i_1(0) = 0, \qquad i_2(0) = 0, \qquad v_C(0) = 1$$

In order to use these initial conditions we need $i_2(t)$ and $v_C(t)$ in addition to $i_1(t)$. If we substitute Eq. 6.4.5 into Eq. 6.4.4 we get

$$i_2(t) = (k_1 + k_2 t)e^{-2t} + k_3 e^{-4t} + \tfrac{1}{8}$$
$$+ 2[-2k_1 e^{-2t} + k_2 e^{-2t} - 2k_2 t e^{-2t} - 4k_3 e^{-4t}]$$
$$+ \tfrac{1}{2}[4k_1 e^{-2t} - 4k_2 e^{-2t} + 4k_2 t e^{-2t} + 16k_3 e^{-4t}] \qquad (6.4.6)$$

Also, note from Fig. 6.4.1,

$$v_C(t) = 2\left[\int_0^t i_1(\sigma)\,d\sigma - \int_0^t i_2(\sigma)\,d\sigma\right]$$

Therefore, from Eq. 6.4.1, we get

$$\frac{di_1}{dt} + 4i_1 + v_C(t) = 1$$

or substituting for $i_1(t)$ and $di_1/dt$, we have

$$v_C(t) = 1 - 4[(k_1 + k_2 t)e^{-2t} + k_3 e^{-4t} + \tfrac{1}{8}]$$
$$- [-2k_1 e^{-2t} - 2k_2 t e^{-2t} + k_2 e^{-2t} - 4k_3 e^{-4t}] \qquad (6.4.7)$$

Now we let $t = 0$ in Eqs. 6.4.5, 6.4.6, and 6.4.7 and we are given that $i_1(0) = 0$, $i_2(0) = 0$ and $v_C(0) = 1$. Therefore we get

$$0 = k_1 + k_3 + \tfrac{1}{8}$$
$$0 = k_1 + k_3 + \tfrac{1}{8} - 4k_1 + 2k_2 - 8k_3 + 2k_1 - 2k_2 + 8k_3$$
$$1 = 1 - 4[k_1 + k_3 + \tfrac{1}{8}] - [-2k_1 + k_2 - 4k_3]$$

Solving these three equations we obtain

$$k_1 = 0, \qquad k_2 = -\tfrac{1}{2}, \qquad k_3 = -\tfrac{1}{8}$$

Thus the solution $i_1(t)$ is given by

$$i_1(t) = \tfrac{1}{8} - \tfrac{1}{2}t e^{-2t} - \tfrac{1}{8}e^{-4t}$$

*Sketch of $i_1(t)$*

We can plot $i_1(t)$ versus $t$ using the computer program developed earlier. Examining $i_1(t)$, we note that the sketch from $t = 0$ to $t = 5$ will suffice. We can again use 0.1 steps. Hence

$$T0 = 0, \qquad T1 = 5, \qquad H = 0.1$$

Also,

$$DATA(K, 1) = T$$
$$DATA(K, 2) = F(T) = I1(T)$$
$$DATA(K, 3) = 0$$

The computer program and the plot is given below. Note that again we have not listed the GRAPHX subroutine. The cards for GRAPHX subroutine are available from Example 6.2.7. The plot is given in Fig. 6.4.2.

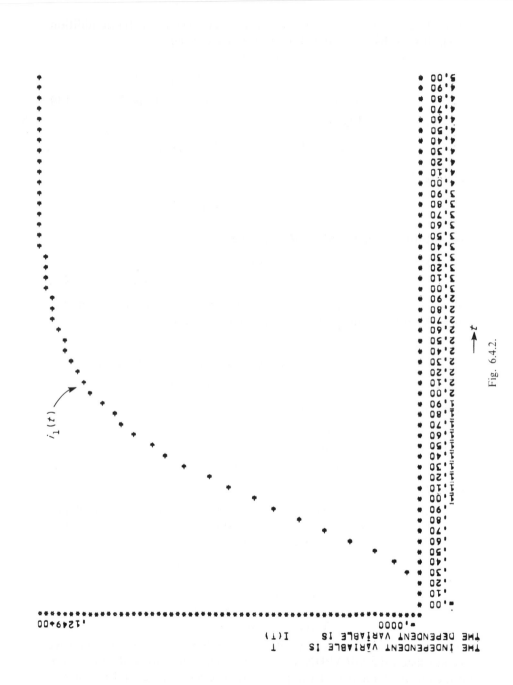

$i_1(t)$

$t$

Fig. 6.4.2.

THE INDEPENDENT VARIABLE IS     T
THE DEPENDENT VARIABLE IS     I(T)

```
C      THIS PROGRAM IS FOR EXAMPLE 6.4-1
C      PLOT PROGRAM
C      THIS PROGRAM PLOTS THE FUNCTION
C      F(T)=1./8.-(1./2.)*T*EXP(-2.*T)-(1./8.)*EXP(4.*T)
       DIMENSION DATA(100,3)
C      DEFINE THE TIME INTERVAL OF INTEREST
C      AND TIME INCREMENT.
       TO=0.
       TI=5.
       H=0.1
C      OBTAIN THE NUMBER OF POINTS TO BE PLOTTED.
C      THEY MUST BE LESS THAN 100.
       N=INT((TI-TO)/ H) +1
C      OBTAIN TNE VALUES OF THE FUNCTIONS AT THESE INCREMENTS
       DO 1 K=1.N
       T=(K-1) * H+TO
       DATA(K,1) = T
       DATA(K,2)=1./8.-(1./2.)*T*EXP(-2.*T)-(1./8.)*EXP(-4.*T)
     1 DATA(K,3)=0.00
C      NEXT. USE THE SUBROUTINE GRAPHX TO PLOT F(K)=DATA(K,2)
       CALL GRAPHX(DATA,K,1HT,4HF(T))
       END
```

It should be observed that as the network order increases, the amount of labor involved in developing an analytical solution also increases. This illustrates the advantage of machine computation. Using matrix methods of formulating network problems, a single computer program can be used to solve networks of arbitrary order with only very minor program changes required. Matrix formulation of network problems is considered in the next chapter.

## PROBLEMS

**6.1.** Calculate the zero input response of the series $RLC$ network shown in Fig. 6.2.1 for nonzero initial conditions. Verify all three of the solutions shown in Table 6.2.3.

**6.2.** (a) Calculate and sketch the voltage response $v_C(t)$ for the network shown. Assume zero initial conditions.

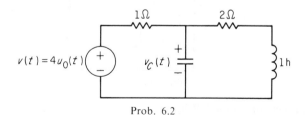

Prob. 6.2

(b) Is the circuit underdamped, critically damped, or overdamped?

**6.3.** For the circuit shown, solve analytically for the capacitor voltage $v_C(t)$. Establish the initial conditions from circuit relationships.

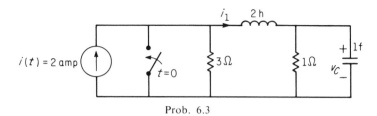

Prob. 6.3

**6.4.** For the circuit shown, solve for currents $i_1$ and $i_2$.

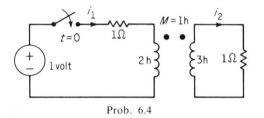

Prob. 6.4

**6.5.** For the $RLC$ circuit shown, find and sketch the voltage $v_C(t)$ and the current $i_L(t)$ with zero initial conditions.

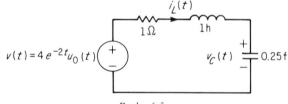

Prob. 6.5

**6.6.** (a) For the $RLC$ network shown, assume initial conditions $v_C(0) = 3$ volts and $i_L(0) = 5$ amp. Find and sketch $i_L$ and $v_C$.

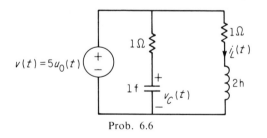

Prob. 6.6

(b) Is this network stable? Why?
(c) Is the network underdamped, overdamped, or critically damped?

**6.7.** For the network shown, let $v_C(0) = 5$ volts and $i_L(0) = 1$ amp. Find the voltage $v(t)$. Using the computer graph routine developed in Sec. 6.2, sketch $v(t)$ for $0 \le t \le 10$.

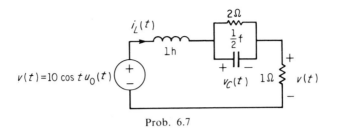

Prob. 6.7

**6.8.** All the initial conditions on the circuit shown are zero. Find and sketch the response $v_C(t)$.

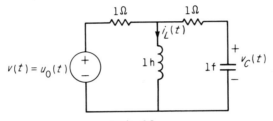

Prob. 6.8

**6.9.** Part (a) of the drawing shows a tunnel diode transistor oscillator. The linear model of this circuit is shown in Part (b).
  (a) Using the linear model, develop a differential equation which describes circuit performance.
  (b) Assuming initial conditions $v_{C_1}(0) = v_{C_2}(0) = 0$ and $i_L(0) = 1$ amp, find and sketch the network output of $v_{R_3}(t)$ for $0 \le t \le 2$.
  (c) Is this circuit stable?

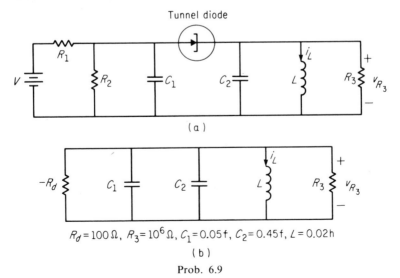

Prob. 6.9

**6.10.** In the circuit shown, calculate and sketch the current through the inductor for $0 \leq t \leq 10$ when $v(t)$ is the waveform shown, using the computer graph routine. Assume zero initial conditions.

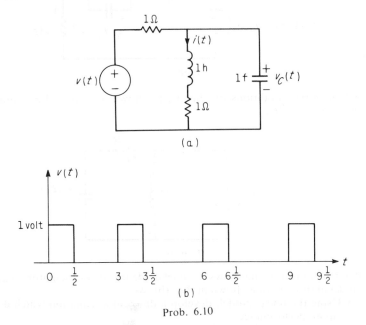

(a)

(b)

Prob. 6.10

**6.11.** The circuit shown has initial conditions $v_C(t_0) = 1$ volt, $i_L(t_0) = 0$, where $t_0 = 1$ sec. Calculate and sketch $i_L(t)$ for $t_0 \leq t \leq 6$ using the computer graph routine.

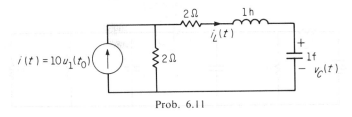

Prob. 6.11

**6.12.** In the circuit shown, assume zero initial conditions. Calculate and sketch $v_C(t)$ for $0 \leq t \leq 5\pi$.

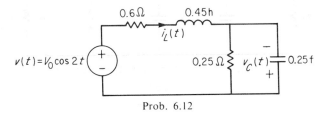

Prob. 6.12

## CHAPTER 7

# State-Variable Method

## 7.1. INTRODUCTION

In previous chapters we showed that circuits containing energy-storing elements, such as capacitors and inductors, give rise to integro-differential equations. If a circuit is of first order, the differential equation describing it is of first order; if a circuit is of second order, the differential equation obtained is of second order and so on. In many practical applications the circuits that we deal with consist of numerous energy-storing elements; differential equations describing such circuits are then generally of high order. To solve efficiently and economically such differential equations of order three and higher, one must resort to digital, analog, or hybrid computers.

An $n$th-order differential equation is not generally suitable for computer solution; it is best to obtain a set of $n$ *first-order* simultaneous differential equations from the given *nth-order* differential equation, using a set of auxiliary variables called the *state variables*. The resulting first-order equations are called *state equations*. For this reason, in the first part of this chapter (Sec. 7.2), we introduce a systematic method for obtaining the state equations from a given $n$th-order differential equation. In the second part (Sec. 7.3), we discuss a method for writing the state equations of a network directly by choosing appropriate state variables. In the third part of this chapter (Sec. 7.4), we present a method of solving state equations of linear time-invariant networks. Finally, we give several numerical methods of solving these equations and develop a computer program to work out a few examples.

## 7.2. FROM $n$TH-ORDER DIFFERENTIAL EQUATIONS TO STATE EQUATIONS

Let us start by considering a second-order circuit such as the one shown in Fig. 7.2.1. This circuit contains two energy-storing elements;

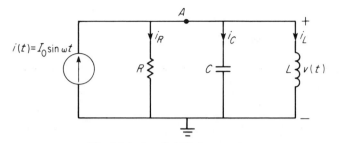

Fig. 7.2.1. Parallel $RLC$ network.

hence we expect the describing differential equation to be of second order. The current source $i(t)$ is the input and the voltage across all three elements, $v(t)$, is the response. Applying KCL at node $A$ we get

$$i = i_R + i_C + i_L \qquad (7.2.1)$$

From the branch voltage-current relations (VCR) we can obtain

$$i_R = \frac{1}{R} v, \qquad i_C = C \frac{dv}{dt}, \qquad i_L = \frac{1}{L} \int_0^t v(\sigma) \, d\sigma \qquad (7.2.2)$$

Then Eq. 7.2.1 can be written

$$C \frac{dv}{dt} + \frac{1}{R} v + \frac{1}{L} \int_0^t v(\sigma) \, d\sigma = I_0 \sin \omega t \qquad (7.2.3)$$

Differentiating both sides of this equation and dividing by $C$, we obtain

$$\frac{d^2v}{dt^2} + \frac{1}{RC} \frac{dv}{dt} + \frac{1}{LC} v = \frac{\omega}{C} I_0 \cos \omega t \qquad (7.2.4)$$

This is the differential equation describing the network shown in Fig. 7.2.1.

As a first step in writing Eq. 7.2.4 in the state form we introduce two new variables $x_1(t)$ and $x_2(t)$ such that

$$x_1(t) = v(t) \qquad (7.2.5a)$$
$$x_2(t) = \dot{v}(t) \qquad (7.2.5b)$$

The next step is to eliminate $v$ among Eqs. 7.2.4, 7.2.5a, and 7.2.5b. Differentiating Eq. 7.2.5a and using Eq. 7.2.5b, we get

$$\dot{x}_1 = x_2 \qquad (7.2.6)$$

Differentiating Eq. 7.2.5b and using Eq. 7.2.4 we obtain

$$\dot{x}_2 = \ddot{v}(t) = -\frac{1}{RC} \dot{v} - \frac{1}{LC} v + \frac{\omega}{C} I_0 \cos \omega t$$

or

$$\dot{x}_2 = -\frac{1}{LC} x_1 - \frac{1}{RC} x_2 + \frac{\omega}{C} I_0 \cos \omega t \qquad (7.2.7)$$

Putting Eqs. 7.2.6 and 7.2.7 in matrix form yields

$$\begin{bmatrix} \dot{x}_1 \\ \dot{x}_2 \end{bmatrix} = \begin{bmatrix} 0 & 1 \\ -(1/LC) & -(1/RC) \end{bmatrix} \begin{bmatrix} x_1 \\ x_2 \end{bmatrix} + \begin{bmatrix} 0 \\ I_0(\omega/C)\cos \omega t \end{bmatrix} \quad (7.2.8)$$

Equation 7.2.8 is the desired state equation; it consists of two simultaneous first-order differential equations. Quite clearly, if we can solve these state equations for $x_1(t)$ and $x_2(t)$, then solving for other variables of the network is an easy task. For example, to find $v(t)$, the voltage across the elements, we use Eq. 7.2.5a. Also the currents through the elements can be found from Eq. 7.2.2, i.e.,

$$i_R = \frac{1}{R} x_1, \qquad i_C = Cx_2 \qquad \text{and} \qquad i_L = \frac{1}{L} \int_0^t x_1(\sigma)\, d\sigma$$

We will discuss the solution of the matrix differential equation (7.2.8) in Sec. 7.4 of this chapter; in fact, we give a systematic method for solving any first-order matrix differential equation of the form

$$\dot{x}(t) = Ax + bu$$

## A Third-Order Example

Let us consider a third-order circuit whose describing differential equation is given by

$$v^{(3)}(t) + a_3 v^{(2)}(t) + a_2 v^{(1)} + a_1 v = u(t) \quad (7.2.9)$$

where $v^{(i)}(t)$ denotes the $i$th derivative of $v(t)$; $a_1, a_2, a_3$ are constants and $u(t)$ is the input. The objective is to transform this third-order differential equation to a set of three first-order simultaneous differential equations.

STEP 1. Define a set of state variables $x_1(t)$, $x_2(t)$ and $x_3(t)$ such that

$$x_1(t) = v(t)$$
$$x_2(t) = v^{(1)}(t) \quad (7.2.10)$$
$$x_3(t) = v^{(2)}(t)$$

STEP 2. Take the derivative of (7.2.10):

$$\dot{x}_1(t) = v^{(1)}(t)$$
$$\dot{x}_2(t) = v^{(2)}(t) \quad (7.2.11)$$
$$\dot{x}_3(t) = v^{(3)}(t)$$

STEP 3. In Eq. 7.2.11 express $v^{(1)}$, $v^{(2)}$, and $v^{(3)}$ in terms of $x_1$, $x_2$, and $x_3$ using Eqs. 7.2.10 and 7.2.9:

$$\dot{x}_1 = x_2$$
$$\dot{x}_2 = x_3 \quad (7.2.12)$$
$$\dot{x}_3 = u(t) - a_1 x_1 - a_2 x_2 - a_3 x_3$$

*STEP 4.*    Put the equations obtained in Step 3 in matrix form.

$$\begin{bmatrix} \dot{x}_1 \\ \dot{x}_2 \\ \dot{x}_3 \end{bmatrix} = \begin{bmatrix} 0 & 1 & 0 \\ 0 & 0 & 1 \\ -a_1 & -a_2 & -a_3 \end{bmatrix} \begin{bmatrix} x_1 \\ x_2 \\ x_3 \end{bmatrix} + \begin{bmatrix} 0 \\ 0 \\ 1 \end{bmatrix} u \qquad (7.2.13)$$

Note that Eq. 7.2.13 is in the form

$$\dot{x}(t) = Ax(t) + bu(t) \qquad (7.2.14)$$

where $x(t) \triangleq [x_1(t) \quad x_2(t) \quad x_3(t)]^T$, $A$ is the $3 \times 3$ constant matrix given in Eq. 7.2.13 and $b \triangleq [0 \quad 0 \quad 1]^T$. Equation 7.2.14 is called the *normal form* of state equations.

## 7.3. DIRECT METHOD FOR WRITING STATE EQUATIONS

In this section we introduce a method by which the state equations of the network can be written directly from the network. In this method the state variables are chosen among the physical variables of the network such as the currents through the inductors and the voltages across the capacitors. For this reason, these state variables are sometimes called *physical variables*. In general, two types of variables in a given network qualify as state variables. First, voltages across the capacitors and currents through the inductors. Second, charges across the capacitors and fluxes through the inductors. The latter class of variables are especially suitable for the state variables of nonlinear and time-varying networks. Before formalizing this method, let us consider some simple examples.

*Examples 7.3.1: A First-Order Circuit*

Consider the first-order circuit shown in Fig. 7.3.1. This circuit contains only one energy-storing element (the capacitor). Therefore, we need

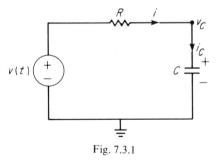

Fig. 7.3.1

to define only one state variable; we can choose the state variable to be the voltage across the capacitor, $v_C$. Furthermore, we expect the state equation to be a first-order differential equation: *KVL* equation gives

$$v(t) = Ri(t) + v_C(t) \tag{7.3.1}$$

but

$$i(t) = i_C(t) = C\frac{dv_C}{dt}$$

Then Eq. 7.3.1 becomes

$$v(t) = RC\frac{dv_C}{dt} + v_C(t)$$

or

$$\frac{dv_C}{dt} = -\frac{1}{RC}v_C(t) + \frac{1}{RC}v(t) \tag{7.3.2}$$

Denoting the state variable $v_C(t)$ by $x(t)$, Eq. 7.3.2 becomes

$$\dot{x}(t) = -\frac{1}{RC}x(t) + \frac{1}{RC}v(t) \tag{7.3.3}$$

Equation 7.3.3 is the desired state equation.

*Example 7.3.2: A Second-Order Circuit*

Consider the series *RLC* circuit shown in Fig. 7.3.2. The voltage $v_C$ and the current $i_L$ are two candidates for the state variables. KVL

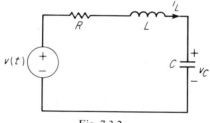

Fig. 7.3.2

equation for this circuit is

$$v(t) = Ri_L + L\frac{di_L}{dt} + v_C \tag{7.3.4}$$

The voltage-current relation (VCR) of the capacitor *C* is

$$i_L = C\frac{dv_C}{dt} \tag{7.3.5}$$

Rearranging Eqs. 7.3.4 and 7.3.5, we get

$$\frac{di_L}{dt} = -\frac{R}{L}i_L - \frac{1}{L}v_C + \frac{1}{L}v(t)$$

and

$$\frac{dv_C}{dt} = \frac{1}{C}i_L$$

These equations can be put in the following matrix form:

$$
\begin{bmatrix} \dfrac{di_L}{dt} \\[2ex] \dfrac{dv_C}{dt} \end{bmatrix} = \begin{bmatrix} -\dfrac{R}{L} & -\dfrac{1}{L} \\[2ex] \dfrac{1}{C} & 0 \end{bmatrix} \begin{bmatrix} i_L \\[2ex] v_C \end{bmatrix} + \begin{bmatrix} \dfrac{1}{L} \\[2ex] 0 \end{bmatrix} v(t) \qquad (7.3.6)
$$

If we now let

$$
x_1(t) = i_L(t), \qquad u(t) = v(t)
$$

and

$$
x_2(t) = v_C(t)
$$

then Eq. 7.3.6 can be written

$$
\begin{bmatrix} \dot{x}_1 \\[2ex] \dot{x}_2 \end{bmatrix} = \begin{bmatrix} -\dfrac{R}{L} & -\dfrac{1}{L} \\[2ex] \dfrac{1}{C} & 0 \end{bmatrix} \begin{bmatrix} x_1 \\[2ex] x_2 \end{bmatrix} + \begin{bmatrix} \dfrac{1}{L} \\[2ex] 0 \end{bmatrix} u(t) \qquad (7.3.7)
$$

or in the more compact form,

$$
\dot{\mathbf{x}}(t) = \mathbf{A}\mathbf{x}(t) + \mathbf{b}u(t) \qquad (7.3.8)
$$

where $\mathbf{x}(t) \triangleq [x_1(t) \quad x_2(t)]^T$, $\mathbf{b} \triangleq [1/L \quad 0]^T$ and $\mathbf{A}$ is the $2 \times 2$ matrix given in Eq. 7.3.7. If Eq. 7.3.7 is solved for the variables $x_1(t)$ and $x_2(t)$, then all voltages and currents in the network can be easily derived:

$$
v_R = Ri_L = Rx_1, \quad v_L = L\frac{di_L}{dt} = L\dot{x}_1 \quad \text{and} \quad i_C = i_L = x_1
$$

*Example 7.3.3: A Third-Order Circuit*

Let us consider the circuit shown in Fig. 7.3.3. There are three energy-storing elements in this circuit; therefore, three state variables

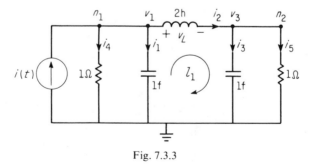

Fig. 7.3.3

should be specified. The steps taken in writing the state equations for this circuit are as follows:

(i) choose $v_1$, $i_2$, and $v_3$ as the state variables

(ii) write the independent node and loop equations:

$$n_1: \qquad i = i_4 + i_1 + i_2$$
$$n_2: \qquad i_2 = i_3 + i_5 \tag{7.3.9}$$
$$l_1: \qquad v_1 = v_L + v_3$$

(iii) Use the branch voltage-current relations (VCR) to express all the variables in terms of the state variables $v_1$, $i_2$, $v_3$ and their derivatives:

$$i_4 = \frac{v_1}{1} = v_1$$

$$i_1 = C\frac{dv_1}{dt} = \frac{dv_1}{dt}$$

$$v_L = L\frac{di_2}{dt} = 2\frac{di_2}{dt} \tag{7.3.10}$$

$$i_3 = C\frac{dv_3}{dt} = \frac{dv_3}{dt}$$

$$i_5 = \frac{v_3}{1} = v_3$$

(iv) Use Eq. 7.3.10 in Eq. 7.3.9 to eliminate all the variables that are not the state variables chosen in step (i). Then Eq. 7.3.9 becomes

$$i = v_1 + \frac{dv_1}{dt} + i_2$$

$$i_2 = \frac{dv_3}{dt} + v_3$$

$$v_1 = 2\frac{di_2}{dt} + v_3$$

or rearranging these equations, we have

$$\frac{dv_1}{dt} = -v_1 - i_2 + i$$

$$\frac{di_2}{dt} = \frac{1}{2}v_1 - \frac{1}{2}v_3$$

$$\frac{dv_3}{dt} = -v_3 + i_2$$

(v) Write the relationships obtained in Step (iv) as a matrix equation to obtain the state equations in the normal form

$$
\begin{bmatrix} \dfrac{dv_1}{dt} \\[3mm] \dfrac{di_2}{dt} \\[3mm] \dfrac{dv_3}{dt} \end{bmatrix} = \begin{bmatrix} -1 & -1 & 0 \\[2mm] \dfrac{1}{2} & 0 & -\dfrac{1}{2} \\[2mm] 0 & 1 & -1 \end{bmatrix} \begin{bmatrix} v_1 \\[3mm] i_2 \\[3mm] v_3 \end{bmatrix} + \begin{bmatrix} 1 \\[3mm] 0 \\[3mm] 0 \end{bmatrix} i \qquad (7.3.11)
$$

Equation 7.3.11 is a set of three first-order differential equations that can be solved either analytically or by a digital computer for the state variables $v_1$, $i_2$, and $v_3$. Having solved Eq. 7.3.11 for the state variables, Eq. 7.3.10 can then be used to solve for the remaining unknown variables in the circuit.

*REMARK 7.3.1.* At this point we should mention that the choice of the state variables is not unique. It is quite possible and sometimes more convenient to choose a different set of variables as the state variables. The following is an example of this alternative procedure:

*Example 7.3.4: Charges and Fluxes as the State Variables*

Consider the network shown in Fig. 7.3.3. Let us write the state equations of this network using the charges on the capacitors and the flux in the inductor as the state variables. The steps taken in this case are parallel to those taken in Example 7.3.3:

   (i) Choose $q_1$, $q_3$ (charges across the capacitors) and $\phi_2$ (the flux through the inductor) as the state variables.

  (ii) Write the independent node and loop equations:

$$
\begin{aligned}
i &= i_4 + i_1 + i_2 \\
i_2 &= i_3 + i_5 \\
v_1 &= v_L + v_3
\end{aligned} \qquad (7.3.12)
$$

 (iii) Use the branch voltage-current relations to express all the variables in terms of the state variables $q_1$, $q_3$, $\phi_2$ and their derivatives:

$$
\begin{aligned}
v_1 &= \frac{q_1}{C_1} = q_1 & i_1 &= \frac{dq_1}{dt} \\[2mm]
i_2 &= \frac{\phi_2}{L} = \frac{1}{2}\phi_2 & i_3 &= \frac{dq_3}{dt} \\[2mm]
v_3 &= \frac{q_3}{C_3} = q_3 & v_L &= \frac{d\phi_2}{dt} \\[2mm]
i_4 &= \frac{v_1}{1} = q_1 & i_5 &= \frac{v_3}{1} = q_3
\end{aligned} \qquad (7.3.13)
$$

(iv) Use equations 7.3.13 in Eq. 7.3.12 to eliminate all the variables other than the state variables $q_1$, $q_2$, $\phi_2$, (i.e., eliminate $i_1$, $i_2$, $i_3$, $i_4$, $i_5$, $v_1$, $v_3$, $v_L$), then Eq. 7.3.12 becomes

$$i = q_1 + \dot{q}_1 + \tfrac{1}{2}\phi_2$$
$$\tfrac{1}{2}\phi_2 = \dot{q}_3 + q_3$$
$$q_1 = \dot{\phi}_2 + q_3$$

By rearranging we get:

$$\dot{q}_1 = -q_1 - \tfrac{1}{2}\phi_2 + i$$
$$\dot{\phi}_2 = q_1 - q_3$$
$$\dot{q}_3 = \tfrac{1}{2}\phi_2 - q_3 \qquad (7.3.14)$$

(v) Put the equations obtained in Step (iv) in matrix form:

$$
\begin{bmatrix} \dot{q}_1 \\ \dot{\phi}_2 \\ \dot{q}_3 \end{bmatrix}
=
\begin{bmatrix} -1 & -\tfrac{1}{2} & 0 \\ 1 & 0 & -1 \\ 0 & \tfrac{1}{2} & -1 \end{bmatrix}
\begin{bmatrix} q_1 \\ \phi_2 \\ q_3 \end{bmatrix}
+
\begin{bmatrix} 1 \\ 0 \\ 0 \end{bmatrix} i \qquad (7.3.15)
$$

Equation 7.3.15 is therefore another form of state representation of the network shown in Fig. 7.3.3. Quite clearly, once we have solved Eq. 7.3.15 for $q_1$, $\phi_2$ and $q_3$, all the other variables can be found using Eq. 7.3.13.

## State Equations For Nonlinear and Time-Varying Circuits

One of the important features of the state-variable method is the fact that circuits containing nonlinear and time-varying elements can be treated just as easily as linear time-invariant circuits. For this class of circuits, however, it is generally best to choose the charges on the capacitors and the fluxes through the inductors as the state variables. The steps followed in writing the state equations of a nonlinear or a time-varying circuit are the same as the steps followed in writing the state equations of a linear time-invariant circuit with the exception of step (iii). In this case the current through a time-varying capacitor should be replaced by the derivative of the charge across it and the voltage across a time-varying inductor should be replaced by the derivative of the flux through it. Typically we assume that all the capacitors are *charge-controlled* and the inductors are *flux-controlled*; i.e., we assume that the nonlinear capacitors and inductors are given by

$$v_C = f_1(q)$$
$$i_L = f_2(\phi) \qquad (7.3.16)$$

where $f_1(\cdot)$ and $f_2(\cdot)$ are nonlinear functions. In this case also, the currents through the capacitors should be replaced by the derivative of the charges and the voltages across the inductors should be replaced by the derivatives of the fluxes, i.e.,

$$i_c = \dot{q}$$

and (7.3.17)

$$v_L = \dot{\phi}$$

These points are illustrated in the following examples.

*Example 7.3.5: A Linear Time-Varying Circuit*

Consider the linear time-varying second-order circuit shown in Fig. 7.3.4. Let us assume that the resistor $R$ is linear time-invariant but the

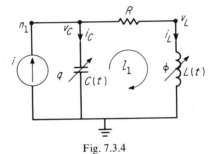

Fig. 7.3.4

energy storing elements are linear time-varying. The steps taken in writing the state equations are as follows:

    (i) Choose $q$ and $\phi$ as the state variables.

    (ii) Write the independent node and loop equations:

$$\begin{aligned} n_1: &\quad i = i_C + i_L \\ l_1: &\quad v_C = Ri_L + v_L \end{aligned} \qquad (7.3.18)$$

    (iii) Write the branch voltage-current relations to express all the variables appearing in Eq. 7.3.18 in terms of the state variables ($q$ and $\phi$) and their derivatives:

$$i_C = \dot{q}(t), \qquad i_L = \frac{1}{L(t)}\phi(t)$$

and (7.3.19)

$$v_C = \frac{1}{C(t)}q(t) \qquad v_L = \dot{\phi}(t)$$

    (iv) Use Eq. 7.3.19 in Eq. 7.3.18 to eliminate all the variables that are not state variables (i.e., eliminate $i_L$, $i_C$, $v_C$, $v_L$); then Eq. 7.3.18 becomes

$$i = \dot{q} + \frac{1}{L(t)}\phi$$

$$\frac{1}{C(t)}q = R\frac{1}{L(t)}\phi + \dot{\phi}$$

Rearranging these equations, we get

$$\dot{q} = -\frac{1}{L(t)}\phi + i$$

$$\dot{\phi} = \frac{1}{C(t)}q - \frac{R}{L(t)}\phi$$

(v) Put the equations obtained in Step (iv) in matrix form:

$$\begin{bmatrix} \dot{q} \\ \dot{\phi} \end{bmatrix} = \begin{bmatrix} 0 & -\dfrac{1}{L(t)} \\ \dfrac{1}{C(t)} & -\dfrac{R}{L(t)} \end{bmatrix} \begin{bmatrix} q \\ \phi \end{bmatrix} + \begin{bmatrix} 1 \\ 0 \end{bmatrix} i \qquad (7.3.20)$$

This equation is the desired state equation. To put this in a more compact form, let

$$\mathbf{x}(t) \triangleq [q(t) \quad \phi(t)]^T$$

$$\mathbf{b} \triangleq [1 \quad 0]^T, \qquad u(t) \triangleq i(t)$$

and

$$\mathbf{A}(t) \triangleq \begin{bmatrix} 0 & -\dfrac{1}{L(t)} \\ \dfrac{1}{C(t)} & -\dfrac{R}{L(t)} \end{bmatrix}$$

Then Eq. 7.3.20 can be rewritten as

$$\dot{\mathbf{x}}(t) = \mathbf{A}(t)\mathbf{x}(t) + \mathbf{b}u(t) \qquad (7.3.21)$$

which is in the *normal form*. In this case, however, the square matrix $\mathbf{A}(t)$ is time-varying. To obtain the network variables $i_C$, $i_L$, $v_C$, and $v_L$ we first solve Eqs. 7.3.20 for $q$ and $\phi$ and then use Eq. 7.3.19. While the analytical solution of matrix differential equations with time-varying coefficients is in general quite complicated, numerical solutions are readily obtained using the digital computer. Several of these methods are discussed in Sec. 7.5.

*Example 7.3.6: A Nonlinear Time-Invariant Circuit*

Consider the network shown in Fig. 7.3.5. Assume that the terminating resistors are linear and time invariant, the inductor is flux controlled and the capacitors are charge-controlled, i.e., we assume that

$$v_1 = f_1(q_1)$$
$$v_3 = f_3(q_3) \qquad (7.3.22)$$

and

$$i_2 = f_2(\phi_2)$$

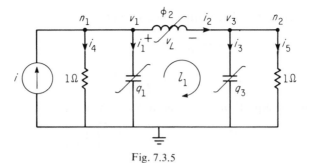

Fig. 7.3.5

The steps taken in writing the state equations of this nonlinear circuit are

(i) Choose $q_1$, $\phi_2$, and $q_3$ as the state variables.

(ii) Write the independent node and loop equations:

$$
\begin{aligned}
n_1: \quad & i = i_4 + i_1 + i_2 \\
n_2: \quad & i_2 = i_3 + i_5 \\
l_1: \quad & v_1 = v_L + v_3
\end{aligned}
\tag{7.3.23}
$$

(iii) Use the branch voltage-current relations to express all the variables appearing in Eq. 7.3.23 in terms of the state variables $q_1$, $\phi_2$, $q_3$ and their derivatives:

$$
\begin{aligned}
i_1 &= \dot{q}_1 & v_1 &= f_1(q_1) & i_4 &= f_1(q_1) \\
i_2 &= f_2(\phi_2) & v_3 &= f_3(q_3) & i_5 &= f_3(q_3) \\
i_3 &= \dot{q}_3 & v_L &= \dot{\phi}_2
\end{aligned}
\tag{7.3.24}
$$

(iv) Use Eq. 7.3.24 in Eq. 7.3.23 to eliminate all the variables that are not the state variables. Then Eq. 7.3.23 becomes

$$
\begin{aligned}
i &= f_1(q_1) + \dot{q}_1 + f_2(\phi_2) \\
f_2(\phi_2) &= \dot{q}_3 + f_3(q_3) \\
f_1(q_1) &= \dot{\phi}_2 + f_3(q_3)
\end{aligned}
$$

or rearranging these equations, we get

$$
\begin{aligned}
\dot{q}_1 &= -f_1(q_1) - f_2(\phi_2) + i \\
\dot{\phi}_2 &= f_1(q_1) - f_3(q_3) \\
\dot{q}_3 &= f_2(\phi_2) - f_3(q_3)
\end{aligned}
$$

(v) Put the equations obtained in Step (iv) in matrix form:

$$
\begin{bmatrix} \dot{q}_1 \\ \dot{\phi}_2 \\ \dot{q}_3 \end{bmatrix} =
\begin{bmatrix} -1 & -1 & 0 \\ 1 & 0 & -1 \\ 0 & 1 & -1 \end{bmatrix}
\begin{bmatrix} f_1(q_1) \\ f_2(\phi_2) \\ f_3(q_3) \end{bmatrix} +
\begin{bmatrix} 1 \\ 0 \\ 0 \end{bmatrix} i
\tag{7.3.25}
$$

Now if we let

$$\mathbf{x}(t) \triangleq [q_1 \quad \phi_2 \quad q_3]^T, \quad u(t) \triangleq i(t)$$

$$\mathbf{f}(\mathbf{x}) \triangleq [f_1(q_1) \quad f_2(\phi_2) \quad f_3(q_3)]^T,$$

$$\mathbf{b} \triangleq [1 \quad 0 \quad 0]^T$$

and

$$\mathbf{A} \triangleq \begin{bmatrix} -1 & -1 & 0 \\ 1 & 0 & -1 \\ 0 & 1 & -1 \end{bmatrix}$$

then Eq. 7.3.25 can be written in normal form as

$$\dot{\mathbf{x}} = \mathbf{A}\mathbf{f}(\mathbf{x}) + \mathbf{b}u \qquad (7.3.26)$$

This single matrix equation represents a set of three simultaneous *non-linear* first order differential equations. Equations of the form (7.3.26) can usually be solved by a digital computer using methods discussed in Sec. 7.5.

### General Case

In this section we consider the formulation of the state equations of a rather general class of networks. The steps followed here are identical to those taken in the previous examples. In order to obtain a set of *linearly independent* state variables for a given network, we assume that the network under consideration *does not have* any loop which is comprised of two or more capacitors and possibly some independent voltage sources only (such loops are called *capacitor-only loops*) or any nodes to which only two or more inductors and possibly some independent current sources are incident (such nodes are called *inductor-only nodes*). Such networks are called *proper* networks. This restriction will be removed in Chapter 14 where we make extensive use of graph theory to treat networks that are not proper. In order to see how the state variables of such a network can be linearly dependent, consider the network shown in Fig. 7.3.6. This network has a capacitor-only loop $(C_1, C_2, C_3)$ and an inductor-only node $(L_4, L_5, L_6)$. There are six energy-storing elements in this network and according to Step (i) of the previous examples, we expect to have six state variables, namely $v_1(t)$, $v_2(t)$, $v_3(t)$, $i_4(t)$, $i_5(t)$ and $i_6(t)$. Or if we choose the charges and fluxes as the state variables, we would have $q_1, q_2, q_3, \phi_4, \phi_5$, and $\phi_6$. However, a careful look at the structure of the network shows that two out of these six state variables are linear combinations of the other four and hence convey no new information

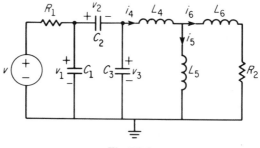

Fig. 7.3.6

regarding the state of the network. To see this dependence, let us write KVL equations for the loop of capacitors and KCL equations for the node of inductors:

$$\text{KVL:} \quad v_1 = v_2 + v_3$$
$$\text{KCL:} \quad i_4 = i_5 + i_6 \tag{7.3.27}$$

Hence we can find only four linearly independent state variables for the network under consideration. If we choose charges and fluxes as the state variables, Eq. 7.3.27 can be written as

$$\frac{q_1}{C_1} = \frac{q_2}{C_2} + \frac{q_3}{C_3}$$

and

$$\frac{\phi_4}{L_4} = \frac{\phi_5}{L_5} + \frac{\phi_6}{L_6}$$

or equivalently

$$q_1 = \frac{C_1}{C_2} q_2 + \frac{C_1}{C_3} q_3$$

and $\tag{7.3.28}$

$$\phi_4 = \frac{L_4}{L_5} \phi_5 + \frac{L_4}{L_6} \phi_6$$

hence $q_1$ and $\phi_4$ are linear combinations of $q_2, q_3, \phi_5,$ and $\phi_6$.

In this simple example it is easy to detect the linear dependency of the state variables by inspection. In more complicated networks, however, this is not generally possible; we postpone treating such networks until Chapter 14.

### State Equations of Proper Networks

Let us now summarize the steps taken in writing the state equations for a linear time-invariant network which does not contain any capacitor-only loop or any inductor-only node.

*STEP 1.* Choose either

(a) the inductor currents and capacitor voltages, or

(b) the inductor fluxes and capacitor charges

as the state variables. The number of the state variables, therefore, is equal to the total number of the inductors and capacitors.

*STEP 2.* Use the techniques discussed in Chapter 2 to write linear independent KVL and KCL equations.

*STEP 3.* Use the branch voltage-current relations (VCR) to express all the network variables that are not the chosen state variables in terms of the state variables chosen in Step 1.

*STEP 4.* Use the equations obtained in Step 3 to eliminate all network variables that are not the chosen state variables in the equations obtained in Step 2. The resulting equations, therefore, contain only the state variables chosen in Step 1 and their derivatives. Transfer all the derivatives to the left-hand side, and

*STEP 5.* Put the equations obtained in Step 4 in the form

$$\mathbf{x}(t) = \mathbf{A}\mathbf{x}(t) + \mathbf{b}u \qquad (7.3.29)$$

where $\mathbf{x}(t)$ is an $n$-column vector whose components are the state variables chosen in Step 1, $\mathbf{A}$ is an $n \times n$ constant matrix, and $\mathbf{b}$ is an $n$-column vector.

*REMARK 7.3.2.* From the foregoing discussions it is clear that the number of the state variables in a "proper" network is equal to the number of the reactive elements (inductors and capacitors) of that network. Furthermore, the choice of the state variables in Step 1 guarantees that the state equations do not contain any of the variables in the integral form—they contain the state variables and their first derivatives only. The result, therefore, is a set of first-order differential equations which can easily be written as a matrix equation in normal form.

## 7.4. ANALYTIC SOLUTION OF THE STATE EQUATIONS

In this section we give an analytic method of solving a set of first-order differential equations. We shall start by solving a single first-order differential equation of the form

$$x(t) = \alpha x(t) + \beta u(t), \qquad x(t_0) = x_0 \qquad (7.4.1)$$

where $\alpha$ and $\beta$ are constant scalars, $x(t)$ and $u(t)$ are scalar functions of $t$; $\dot{x}(t)$ denotes the derivative of $x(t)$ with respect to $t$. The scalar constant $x_0$ is the value of $x$ at the initial time $t_0$. Next we give a precise definition of the solution of Eq. 7.4.1.

*DEFINITION.* A unique continuous scalar function $\tilde{x}(t)$ defined for all $t \geq t_0$ is said to be the solution of Eq. 7.4.1 if

(i) $\tilde{x}(t)$ satisfies the initial condition; $\tilde{x}(t_0) = x_0$ and

(ii) $\tilde{x}(t)$ satisfies the differential equation; $\dot{\tilde{x}}(t) = \alpha\tilde{x}(t) + \beta u(t)$.

Notice that the domain of definition of $\tilde{x}(t)$ is from $t_0$ to $\infty$ (see Fig. 7.4.1).

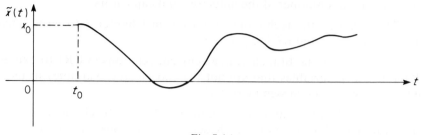

Fig. 7.4.1

We now claim that the solution of Eq. 7.4.1 is given by

$$\tilde{x}(t) = e^{\alpha(t-t_0)}x_0 + \int_{t_0}^{t} e^{\alpha(t-\tau)}\beta u(\tau)\, d\tau \tag{7.4.2}$$

To prove that this is the desired solution we must show that it satisfies conditions (i) and (ii) just stated:

(i) $\quad \tilde{x}(t_0) = e^{\alpha(t_0-t_0)}x_0 + \int_{t_0}^{t_0} e^{\alpha(t_0-\tau)}\beta u(\tau)\, d\tau = x_0$

since $e^0 = 1$ and $\int_{t_0}^{t_0} f(t, \tau)\, d\tau = 0$ for any function $f$.

(ii) Since the integration in Eq. 7.4.2 is with respect to $\tau$, we can pull out $e^{\alpha t}$ and rewrite Eq. 7.4.2 in the following form:

$$\tilde{x}(t) = e^{\alpha(t-t_0)}x_0 + e^{\alpha t}\int_{t_0}^{t} e^{-\alpha\tau}\beta u(\tau)\, d\tau$$

Taking the derivative of this equation with respect to $t$ yields

$$\dot{\tilde{x}}(t) = \alpha e^{\alpha(t-t_0)}x_0 + \frac{d}{dt}\left\{e^{\alpha t}\int_{t_0}^{t} e^{-\alpha\tau}\beta u(\tau)\, d\tau\right\} \tag{7.4.3}$$

or

$$\dot{\tilde{x}}(t) = \alpha e^{\alpha(t-t_0)}x_0 + \alpha e^{\alpha t}\int_{t_0}^{t} e^{-\alpha\tau}\beta u(\tau)\, d\tau + e^{\alpha t}[e^{-\alpha\tau}\beta u(\tau)]\Big|_{\tau=t}$$

i.e., $\tag{7.4.4}$

$$\dot{\tilde{x}}(t) = \alpha\left[e^{\alpha(t-t_0)}x_0 + \int_{t_0}^{t} e^{\alpha(t-\tau)}\beta u(\tau)\, d\tau\right] + e^{\alpha t}e^{-\alpha t}\beta u(t)$$

Hence

$$\dot{\tilde{x}}(t) = \alpha\left[e^{\alpha(t-t_0)}x_0 + \int_{t_0}^{t} e^{\alpha(t-\tau)}\beta u(\tau)\, d\tau\right] + \beta u(t) \tag{7.4.5}$$

Using Eq. 7.4.2 in Eq. 7.4.5 we get

$$\overset{\star}{x}(t) \;=\; \alpha \tilde{x}(t) + \beta u(t)$$

Hence $\tilde{x}(t)$ given by Eq. 7.4.2 satisfies the required conditions and therefore is the solution of Eq. 7.4.1. Throughout the rest of this chapter, for simplicity, we denote the solution of Eq. 7.4.1 by $x(t)$ and rewrite Eq. 7.4.2 as

$$x(t) \;=\; e^{\alpha(t-t_0)}x_0 + e^{\alpha t}\int_{t_0}^{t} e^{-\alpha \tau}\beta u(\tau)\,d\tau \qquad (7.4.6)$$

*Example 7.4.1*

Consider the first-order circuit given in Fig. 7.4.2. KCL at node $n_1$ yields

$$i \;=\; \frac{v_C}{R} + C\dot{v}_C$$

or

$$\dot{v}_C \;=\; -\frac{1}{RC}\,v_C + \frac{1}{C}\,i, \qquad v_C(0) = 1 \qquad (7.4.7)$$

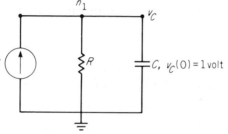

Fig. 7.4.2

Comparing Eqs. 7.4.7 and 7.4.1, we have $\alpha = -(1/RC)$ and $\beta = 1/C$. Therefore, using Eq. 7.4.6, the solution of Eq. 7.4.7 is given by

$$v_C(t) \;=\; e^{-(1/RC)(t-0)}v_C(0) + e^{-(1/RC)t}\int_0^t e^{+(1/RC)\tau}\frac{1}{C}\cdot i(\tau)\,d\tau$$

or

$$v_C(t) \;=\; e^{-(1/RC)t} + \frac{1}{C}e^{-(1/RC)t}\int_0^t e^{(1/RC)\tau}i(\tau)\,d\tau$$

As a numerical example, if we let

$$R = 2\,\Omega, \quad C = \tfrac{1}{2}f, \quad \text{and} \quad i(t) = \text{unit step function}$$

we get

$$v_C(t) \;=\; e^{-t}\left[1 + 2\int_0^t e^{\tau}\cdot 1\cdot d\tau\right]$$

$$v_C(t) \;=\; e^{-t}[1 + 2(e^t - e^0)] \;=\; e^{-t}(2e^t - 1)$$

or finally

$$v_C(t) = 2 - e^{-t} \qquad \text{for } t \geq 0$$

### Solution of Matrix Differential Equations

Let us now assume that the state equations are given in the form

$$\dot{\mathbf{x}}(t) = \mathbf{A}\mathbf{x}(t) + \mathbf{b}u(t) \qquad \mathbf{x}(t_0) = \mathbf{x}_0 \qquad (7.4.8)$$

where

$$\mathbf{x}(t) \triangleq [x_1(t), x_2(t), \ldots, x_n(t)]^T$$
$$\mathbf{A} \triangleq (a_{ij}); \quad \text{an } n \times n \text{ matrix}$$
$$\mathbf{b} \triangleq [b_1, b_2, \ldots, b_n]$$

and $u(t)$ is a scalar function. The constant $n$-column vector $\mathbf{x}_0$ is the value of $\mathbf{x}(t)$ at $t = t_0$. As in the scalar case, a vector function $\mathbf{x}(t)$ is said to be the solution of the matrix differential equation (7.4.8) if (i) $\mathbf{x}(t)$ satisfies the initial conditions and (ii) $\mathbf{x}(t)$ satisfies the differential equation. In order to give an explicit form of the solution of Eq. 7.4.8 we must first define a state transition matrix. Consider an $n \times n$ constant matrix $\mathbf{A}$, then an $n \times n$ matrix $\boldsymbol{\Phi}(t)$ is said to be the *state transition matrix* of the linear time-invariant matrix differential equation (7.4.8) if

$$\boldsymbol{\Phi}(t) \triangleq e^{\mathbf{A}t} = \mathbf{I} + \mathbf{A}t + \frac{1}{2!}\mathbf{A}^2 t^2 + \cdots + \frac{1}{n!}\mathbf{A}^n t^n + \cdots \qquad (7.4.9)$$

where $\mathbf{I}$ denotes the $n \times n$ identity matrix.

If we now differentiate both sides of Eq. 7.4.9, with respect to $t$ we get

$$\dot{\boldsymbol{\Phi}}(t) = \frac{d}{dt} e^{\mathbf{A}t} = 0 + \mathbf{A} \cdot 1 + \mathbf{A}^2 t + \frac{1}{2!}\mathbf{A}^3 t^2 + \cdots + \frac{1}{(n-1)!}\mathbf{A}^n t^{n-1} \cdots$$

or

$$\dot{\boldsymbol{\Phi}}(t) = \frac{d}{dt} e^{\mathbf{A}t} = \mathbf{A}e^{\mathbf{A}t} \qquad (7.4.10)$$

Furthermore,

$$\boldsymbol{\Phi}(0) = e^{\mathbf{A} \cdot 0} = \mathbf{I} + \mathbf{A} \cdot 0 \cdots = \mathbf{I} \qquad (7.4.11)$$

As in the scalar case, we claim that the solution of Eq. 7.4.8 is given by

$$\mathbf{x}(t) = e^{\mathbf{A}(t-t_0)}\mathbf{x}_0 + \int_{t_0}^{t} e^{\mathbf{A}(t-\tau)}\mathbf{b}u(\tau)\, d\tau \qquad (7.4.12)$$

where $\mathbf{x}(t)$ is an $n$-column vector, $e^{\mathbf{A}(t-t_0)}$ is the state transition matrix evaluated at $t - t_0$, and $e^{\mathbf{A}(t-\tau)}\mathbf{b}u(\tau)$ is an $n$-column vector. To prove that Eq. 7.4.12 is indeed the solution of Eq. 7.4.8 we check conditions (i) and (ii) stated below:

(i)

$$\mathbf{x}(t_0) = e^{\mathbf{A}(t_0-t_0)}\mathbf{x}_0 + \int_{t_0}^{t_0} e^{\mathbf{A}(t_0-\tau)}\mathbf{b}u(\tau)\, d\tau \qquad (7.4.13)$$

$$e^{A(t_0-t_0)} = e^{A \cdot 0} = I$$

is the $n \times n$ identity matrix and

$$\int_{t_0}^{t_0} e^{A(t_0-\tau)} bu(\tau) \, d\tau = 0$$

hence

$$x(t_0) = x_0$$

and condition (i) is satisfied.

(ii) Write Eq. 7.4.12 in the form

$$x(t) = e^{A(t-t_0)} x_0 + e^{At} \int_{t_0}^{t} e^{-A\tau} bu(\tau) \, d\tau \qquad (7.4.14)$$

Take the time derivative of both sides of Eq. 7.4.14 and use Eq. 7.4.10 to obtain

$$\dot{x}(t) = A e^{A(t-t_0)} x_0 + A e^{At} \int_{t_0}^{t} e^{-A\tau} bu(\tau) \, d\tau + e^{At} \cdot e^{-At} bu(t)$$

or

$$\dot{x}(t) = A \left[ e^{A(t-t_0)} x_0 + e^{At} \int_{t_0}^{t} e^{-A\tau} bu(\tau) \, d\tau \right] + bu(t) \quad (7.4.15)$$

Comparing Eqs. 7.4.15 and 7.4.14, we get

$$\dot{x}(t) = Ax + bu(t)$$

This completes the proof that $x(t)$ given in Eq. 7.4.12 is the solution of the matrix state equation (7.4.8).

The problem of solving for the solution of Eq. 7.4.8 is then reduced to the problem of computing $e^{At}$ and the integral in Eq. 7.4.12. The integral can be computed using standard integration techniques. There are several methods for computing $e^{At}$, one is the Laplace transform method which we postpone until Chapter 9. In this section we outline a technique which makes use of the characteristic roots (or the eigenvalues) of the matrix $A$.

## Computation of $e^{At}$

Consider the $n \times n$ matrix $A$, by definition, the characteristic roots (or eigenvalues) $\lambda_i$, $i = 1, 2, \ldots, n$ of $A$ are the roots of the $n$th order polynomial:

$$\det [A - \lambda I] = 0 \qquad (7.4.16)$$

The roots of this polynomial are either real or complex numbers. Next we present an important relation which can be used to compute $e^{At}$.

$$e^{At} = \alpha_0(t) I + \alpha_1(t) A + \alpha_2(t) A^2 + \cdots + \alpha_{n-1}(t) A^{n-1} \quad (7.4.17)$$

where $\alpha_0(t)$, $\alpha_1(t), \ldots, \alpha_{n-1}(t)$ are scalar time functions which depend on the eigenvalues of $\mathbf{A}$ and $\mathbf{I}$ is the $n \times n$ identity matrix. Justification of this equation is quite involved and hence is deleted here. In order to determine the factors $\alpha_0(t), \alpha_1(t), \ldots, \alpha_{n-1}(t)$ in Eq. 7.4.17 we consider two cases.

### Case 1: Distinct Eigenvalues

Assume that all the eigenvalues of $\mathbf{A}$, $\lambda_i$, are distinct, i.e., $\lambda_1 \neq \lambda_2 \neq \lambda_3 \neq \cdots \neq \lambda_n$; then $\alpha_0(t), \alpha_1(t), \ldots, \alpha_{n-1}(t)$ can be found from the following $n$-linear algebraic equations:

$$\alpha_0 + \alpha_1 \lambda_1 + \alpha_2 \lambda_1^2 + \cdots + \alpha_{n-1} \lambda_1^{n-1} = e^{\lambda_1 t}$$

$$\alpha_0 + \alpha_1 \lambda_2 + \alpha_2 \lambda_2^2 + \cdots + \alpha_{n-1} \lambda_2^{n-1} = e^{\lambda_2 t}$$

$$\vdots \qquad \vdots \qquad \vdots \qquad \vdots \qquad (7.4.18)$$

$$\alpha_0 + \alpha_1 \lambda_n + \alpha_2 \lambda_n^2 + \cdots + \alpha_{n-1} \lambda_n^{n-1} = e^{\lambda_n t}$$

*Example 7.4.2*

For the matrix

$$\mathbf{A} = \begin{bmatrix} -2 & 1 \\ 0 & -1 \end{bmatrix}$$

compute $e^{\mathbf{A}t}$ for all $t \geq 0$.

*Solution*

Eigenvalues of $\mathbf{A}$ are the solution of

$$\det(\mathbf{A} - \lambda\mathbf{I}) = \det \begin{bmatrix} -\lambda - 2 & 1 \\ 0 & -\lambda - 1 \end{bmatrix} = (\lambda + 1)(\lambda + 2) = 0$$

Therefore

$$\lambda_1 = -1 \quad \text{and} \quad \lambda_2 = -2$$

and from Eq. 7.4.17, we have (since $n = 2$)

$$e^{\mathbf{A}t} = \alpha_0(t)\mathbf{I} + \alpha_1(t)\mathbf{A}$$

where $\alpha_0(t)$ and $\alpha_1(t)$ are yet to be found. From Eq. 7.4.18 we have

$$\alpha_0 + \alpha_1 \cdot (-1) = e^{-t}$$

$$\alpha_0 + \alpha_1 \cdot (-2) = e^{-2t}$$

or after some simple manipulations,

$$\alpha_1(t) = e^{-t} - e^{-2t}$$

and

$$\alpha_0(t) = 2e^{-t} - e^{-2t}$$

Using these values of $\alpha_0(t)$ and $\alpha_1(t)$ we have

$$e^{\mathbf{A}t} = (2e^{-t} - e^{-2t}) \begin{bmatrix} 1 & 0 \\ 0 & 1 \end{bmatrix} + (e^{-t} - e^{-2t}) \begin{bmatrix} -2 & 1 \\ 0 & -1 \end{bmatrix}$$

or

$$e^{\mathbf{A}t} = \begin{bmatrix} e^{-2t} & e^{-t} - e^{-2t} \\ 0 & e^{-t} \end{bmatrix}$$

### Case 2: Multiple Eigenvalues

If the eigenvalues of $\mathbf{A}$ in Eq. 7.4.16 are not distinct, the method of evaluating $\alpha_i(t)$ discussed in Case 1 breaks down. To compute the coefficients $\alpha_i(t)$ in this case we proceed as follows. Without loss of generality assume that the characteristic polynomial of $\mathbf{A}$, defined in Eq. 7.4.16 has a root of multiplicity $m$ and $(n - m)$ distinct roots, i.e., the roots are

$$\lambda_1, \lambda_1, \ldots, \lambda_1, \lambda_{m+1}, \ldots, \lambda_n$$

then $\alpha_i(t)$ can be found by solving the following set of equations:

$$\alpha_0 + \alpha_1 \lambda_1 + \alpha_2 \lambda_1^2 + \cdots + \alpha_{n-1} \lambda_1^{n-1} = e^{\lambda_1 t}$$

$$\frac{d}{d\lambda_1}(\alpha_0' + \alpha_1 \lambda_1 + \alpha_2 \lambda_1^2 + \cdots + \alpha_{n-1} \lambda_1^{n-1}) = \frac{d}{d\lambda_1} e^{\lambda_1 t}$$

$$\frac{d^2}{d\lambda_1^2}(\alpha_0 + \alpha_1 \lambda_1 + \alpha_2 \lambda_1^2 + \cdots + \alpha_{n-1} \lambda_1^{n-1}) = \frac{d^2}{d\lambda_1^2} e^{\lambda_1 t}$$

$$\vdots \qquad \qquad \vdots \qquad \vdots \qquad \qquad \vdots \qquad (7.4.19)$$

$$\frac{d^{m-1}}{d\lambda_1^{m-1}}(\alpha_0 + \alpha_1 \lambda_1 + \alpha_2 \lambda_1^2 + \cdots + \alpha_{n-1} \lambda_1^{n-1}) = \frac{d^{m-1}}{d\lambda_1^{m-1}} e^{\lambda_1 t}$$

$$\alpha_0 + \alpha_1 \lambda_{m+1} + \alpha_2 \lambda_{m+1} + \cdots + \alpha_{n-1} \lambda_{m+1}^{n-1} = e^{\lambda_{m+1} t}$$

$$\vdots \qquad \qquad \vdots \qquad \vdots \qquad \qquad \vdots$$

$$\alpha_0 + \alpha_1 \lambda_n + \alpha_2 \lambda_n^2 + \cdots + \alpha_{n-1} \lambda_n^{n-1} = e^{\lambda_n t}$$

In general, if a root $\lambda_p$ of the characteristic polynomial is of multiplicity $m$, then Eq. 7.4.19 contains up to $(m - 1)$st derivative of Eq. 7.4.17.

*Example 7.4.3*

For the matrix

$$\mathbf{A} = \begin{bmatrix} -1 & 0 \\ 2 & -1 \end{bmatrix}$$

compute $e^{\mathbf{A}t}$

*Solution*

The eigenvalues of **A** are the solution of

$$\det \begin{bmatrix} -\lambda - 1 & 0 \\ 2 & -\lambda - 1 \end{bmatrix} = (\lambda + 1)^2 = 0$$

**A** has multiple eigenvalues and we must use the method discussed in Case 2. Since $n = 2$, Equation 7.4.17 becomes

$$e^{\mathbf{A}t} = \alpha_0(t)\mathbf{I} + \alpha_1(t)\mathbf{A}$$

and by Eq. 7.4.19, $\alpha_0(t)$ and $\alpha_1(t)$ are the solution of

$$\alpha_0 + \alpha_1\lambda_1 = e^{\lambda_1 t}$$

$$\frac{d}{d\lambda_1}(\alpha_0 + \alpha_1\lambda_1) = \frac{d}{d\lambda_1}e^{\lambda_1 t}$$

Then, since $\lambda_1 = -1$

$$\begin{cases} \alpha_0 - \alpha_1 = e^{-t} \\ \alpha_1 = te^{-t} \end{cases}$$

hence

$$\alpha_0(t) = e^{-t} + te^{-t} \quad \text{and} \quad \alpha_1(t) = te^{-t}$$

Using these values of $\alpha_0(t)$ and $\alpha_1(t)$, we have

$$e^{\mathbf{A}t} = \begin{bmatrix} e^{-t} + te^{-t} & 0 \\ 0 & e^{-t} + te^{-t} \end{bmatrix} + \begin{bmatrix} -te^{-t} & 0 \\ 2te^{-t} & -te^{-t} \end{bmatrix} = \begin{bmatrix} e^{-t} & 0 \\ 2te^{-t} & e^{-t} \end{bmatrix}$$

As a final example of this section, let us complete the solution of the circuit discussed in Example 7.3.2.

*Example 7.4.4*

Consider the circuit shown in Fig. 7.3.2; let $R = 1\ \Omega$, $L = \frac{1}{4}$ h, $C = \frac{1}{3}$ f, $v_C(0) = 0.5$ volt and $i_L(0) = 0$. Let the input voltage $v(t)$ be a unit step applied at time $t = 0$, i.e., let

$$v(t) = \begin{cases} 0 & \text{for } t < 0 \\ 1 & \text{for } t \geq 0 \end{cases}$$

The state equations of this circuit are given in Eq. 7.3.6. With the specific element values given above the matrix **A** becomes

$$\mathbf{A} = \begin{bmatrix} -4 & -4 \\ \frac{3}{4} & 0 \end{bmatrix}$$

The eigenvalues are therefore the solution of

$$\det \begin{bmatrix} -4 - \lambda & -4 \\ \frac{3}{4} & -\lambda \end{bmatrix} = \lambda^2 + 4\lambda + 3 = 0,$$

hence

$$\lambda_1 = -1 \quad \text{and} \quad \lambda_2 = -3$$

Since the eigenvalues are distinct, we can use Eqs. 7.4.17 and 7.4.18 to compute $e^{\mathbf{A}t}$.

$$e^{\mathbf{A}t} = \alpha_0(t)\mathbf{I} + \alpha_1(t)\mathbf{A}$$

and

$$\alpha_0(t) - 3\alpha_1(t) = e^{-3t}$$
$$\alpha_0(t) - \alpha_1(t) = e^{-t}$$

Solving the last two equations, we get

$$\alpha_0(t) = \frac{3e^{-t} - e^{-3t}}{2} \quad \text{and} \quad \alpha_1(t) = \frac{e^{-t} - e^{-3t}}{2}$$

Then

$$e^{\mathbf{A}t} = \begin{bmatrix} -\frac{1}{2}e^{-t} + \frac{3}{2}e^{-3t} & -2e^{-t} + 2e^{-3t} \\ \frac{3}{8}e^{-t} - \frac{3}{8}e^{-3t} & \frac{3}{2}e^{-t} - \frac{1}{2}e^{-3t} \end{bmatrix}$$

The state equations of the network under consideration are in the form

$$\dot{\mathbf{x}} = \mathbf{A}\mathbf{x} + \mathbf{b}u \qquad \mathbf{x}(0) = \mathbf{x}_0$$

where $\mathbf{A}$ is given above and $\mathbf{x}_0 = [0 \quad 0.5]^T$. The solution of the state equations are, therefore, given by Eq. 7.4.12 with $t_0 = 0$:

$$\mathbf{x}(t) = e^{\mathbf{A}t}\mathbf{x}(0) + \int_0^t e^{\mathbf{A}(t-\tau)}\mathbf{b}u(\tau)\,d\tau$$

Then

$$e^{\mathbf{A}t}\mathbf{x}(0) = \begin{bmatrix} -\frac{1}{2}e^{-t} + \frac{3}{2}e^{-3t} & -2e^{-t} + 2e^{-3t} \\ \frac{3}{8}e^{-t} - \frac{3}{8}e^{-3t} & \frac{3}{2}e^{-t} - \frac{1}{2}e^{-3t} \end{bmatrix}\begin{bmatrix} 0 \\ \frac{1}{2} \end{bmatrix} = \begin{bmatrix} -e^{-t} + e^{-3t} \\ \frac{3}{4}e^{-t} - \frac{1}{4}e^{-3t} \end{bmatrix}$$

and since $\mathbf{b} = [4 \quad 0]^T$ and $u(t) = v(t) = 1$ for $t \geq 0$, then

$$\int_0^t e^{\mathbf{A}(t-\tau)}\mathbf{b}u(\tau)\,d\tau = \int_0^t \begin{bmatrix} -\frac{1}{2}e^{-(t-\tau)} + \frac{3}{2}e^{-3(t-\tau)} \\ \frac{3}{8}e^{-(t-\tau)} - \frac{3}{8}e^{-3(t-\tau)} \end{bmatrix} \cdot 4 \cdot d\tau$$

$$= 4\begin{bmatrix} -\frac{1}{2}e^{-(t-\tau)} + \frac{1}{2}e^{-3(t-\tau)} \\ \frac{3}{8}e^{-(t-\tau)} - \frac{1}{8}e^{-3(t-\tau)} \end{bmatrix}_0^t = 4\begin{bmatrix} -\frac{1}{2} + \frac{1}{2} \\ \frac{3}{8} - \frac{1}{8} \end{bmatrix} - 4\begin{bmatrix} -\frac{1}{2}e^{-t} + \frac{1}{2}e^{-3t} \\ \frac{3}{8}e^{-t} - \frac{1}{8}e^{-3t} \end{bmatrix}$$

$$= 4\begin{bmatrix} \frac{1}{2}e^{-t} - \frac{1}{2}e^{-3t} \\ \frac{1}{4} - \frac{3}{8}e^{-t} + \frac{1}{8}e^{-3t} \end{bmatrix}$$

Therefore, we have the state vector given by

$$\begin{bmatrix} i_L \\ v_C \end{bmatrix} = \begin{bmatrix} -e^{-t} + e^{-3t} \\ \frac{3}{4}e^{-t} - \frac{1}{4}e^{-3t} \end{bmatrix} + 4\begin{bmatrix} \frac{1}{2}e^{-t} - \frac{1}{2}e^{-3t} \\ \frac{1}{4} - \frac{3}{8}e^{-t} + \frac{1}{8}e^{-3t} \end{bmatrix}$$

$$= \begin{bmatrix} e^{-t} - e^{-3t} \\ 1 - \frac{3}{4}e^{-t} + \frac{1}{4}e^{-3t} \end{bmatrix}$$

or

$$i_L(t) = e^{-t} - e^{-3t} \quad \text{and} \quad v_C(t) = 1 - \tfrac{3}{4}e^{-t} + \tfrac{1}{4}e^{-3t}$$

Other variables of the circuit can be derived using the state variables just found; for instance, the voltage across the inductor is given by

$$v_L(t) = L\frac{di_L}{dt} = -\tfrac{1}{4}e^{-t} + \tfrac{3}{4}e^{-3t}$$

## 7.5. NUMERICAL SOLUTION OF STATE EQUATIONS

In Sec. 7.4 we discussed the analytical solution of linear time invariant state equations. In the present section we introduce several numerical methods of solution that apply to linear time invariant as well as nonlinear and time varying state equations. First, we discuss several methods for solving a scalar nonlinear differential equation of the form

$$\dot{x}(t) = f(x(t), u(t)), \qquad x(t_0) = x_0 \qquad (7.5.1)$$

where $f(\cdot, \cdot)$ is a given function of the state $x$ and the input $u$, and $x_0$ is the initial state at time $t_0$. We will later generalize these methods to develop the solution of a matrix nonlinear differential state equation. Note that since linear state equations are just a special case of the non-linear state equations, the methods discussed below can be used to solve linear state equations as well. These methods are suitable for programming on a digital computer.

### Euler's Method

Consider a scalar differential equation in the form of Eq. 7.5.1. A function $x(t)$ is said to be the "solution" of Eq. 7.5.1 if it satisfies conditions (i) and (ii) of page 226. Let us plot $x(t)$ in Fig. 7.5.1. This solution starts at $t_0$ and continues from there on. Let us denote the values of

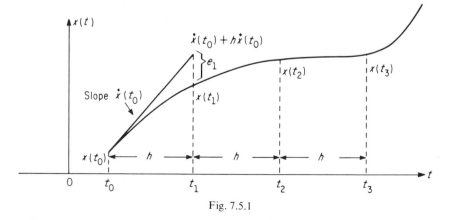

Fig. 7.5.1

$x(t)$ at some discrete points $t_1, t_2, \ldots, t_n$ by $x(t_1)$, $x(t_2), \ldots$, etc.    From Fig. 7.5.1 we can write

$$x(t_1) = x(t_0) + hx(t_0) - e_1 \qquad (7.5.2)$$

Now if $h$ is sufficiently small, the error $e_1$ is very small and we can approximate Eq. 7.5.2 by

$$x(t_1) \simeq x(t_0) + hx(t_0) \qquad (7.5.3)$$

where $\simeq$ means "approximately equal." Replacing $x(t_0)$ from Eq. 7.5.1 we have

$$x(t_1) \simeq x(t_0) + hf(x(t_0), u(t_0)) \qquad (7.5.4)$$

Hence, if we choose $h$ small enough, since $x(t_0)$, $u(t_0)$, and $f(x(t_0), u(t_0))$ are known, we can compute $x(t_1)$ approximately from Eq. 7.5.4. Having computed $x(t_1)$, we can repeat the same process to compute $x(t_2)$, this time taking $x(t_1)$ as the starting point, i.e.,

$$x(t_2) \simeq x(t_1) + hf(x(t_1), u(t_1)) \qquad (7.5.5)$$

In general, having $x(t_k)$, we can compute $x(t_{k+1})$ by

$$x(t_{k+1}) \simeq x(t_k) + hf(x(t_k), u(t_k)) \qquad (7.5.6)$$

In order to write these equations in a more compact form, let us use the following notations:

$$t_k \triangleq t_0 + kh \qquad (7.5.7)$$

$$x_k \triangleq x(t_k) = x(t_0 + kh) \qquad (7.5.8)$$

$$u_k \triangleq u(t_k) = u(t_0 + kh) \qquad (7.5.9)$$

Also, throughout the rest of this chapter we assume that the approximate sign $\simeq$ is understood and we replace it by the usual equality sign. Equation 7.5.5 is therefore written as

$$x_{k+1} = x_k + hf(x_k, u_k) \qquad k = 1, 2, \ldots \qquad (7.5.10)$$

Equation 7.5.10 is known as *Euler's equation*. This equation, however, is rather crude and is seldom used in the actual computation of the solution of differential equations. The reason is that the error $e_1$ in Eq. 7.5.2 will show up in each step of the integration and, in many cases, accumulates in such a way that the computed solution is not a "good" approximation of the true solution. In the rest of this section we discuss several refinements of Euler's equation.

### Trapezoidal Rule

Consider the solution $x(t)$ shown in Fig. 7.5.1. It is clear that the error $e_1$ will be much smaller if we take the *average* of the slopes at $t_0$ and $t_1$, i.e.,

$$x(t_1) = x(t_0) + h\left(\frac{\dot{x}(t_0) + \dot{x}(t_1)}{2}\right) - \tilde{e}_1 \qquad (7.5.11)$$

where $\tilde{e}_1$ is the new error which is much smaller than $e_1$. Again, for a sufficiently small $h$, we can write Eq. 7.5.11 as

$$x(t_1) = x(t_0) + \frac{h}{2}[f(x(t_1), u(t_1)) + f(x(t_0), u(t_0))]$$

or

$$x_1 = x_0 + \frac{h}{2}[f(x_1, u_1) + f(x_0, u_0)] \qquad (7.5.12)$$

One difficulty with this approach is that $x_1$ appears on both sides of Eq. 7.5.12. To resolve this difficulty, we use Euler's equation to approximate $x_1$ in the right-hand side of Eq. 7.5.12:

$$x_1 = x_0 + \frac{h}{2}[f(x_0 + hf(x_0, u_0), u_1) + f(x_0, u_0)] \qquad (7.5.13)$$

Since all the elements in the right-hand side of Eq. 7.5.13 are known we can, therefore, compute $x_1$. Taking $x_1$ as the new starting point and repeating this process we can find $x_2$ and so on. The general equation for trapezoidal rule can then be written as

$$x_{k+1} = x_k + \frac{h}{2}[f(x_k + hf(x_k, u_k), u_{k+1}) + f(x_k, u_k)] \qquad (7.5.14)$$

Equation 7.5.14 can easily be programmed on a digital computer to solve a nonlinear or linear state equation. Next we discuss a more sophisticated routine for solving differential equations.

### Runge-Kutta Method

This is one of the most celebrated methods of numerical solution of differential equations. The advantage of this method over previous ones is a greater accuracy for the same amount of computation. There are several versions of Runge-Kutta methods, the most common one is the fourth order. All the Runge-Kutta methods are based on the Taylor series expansion of a function. In this section we give the formula for a fourth-order Runge-Kutta method. The proof of this formula is rather involved; hence we omit it.

Consider a first-order differential equation of the form (7.5.1). According to the fourth-order Runge-Kutta, given $x_k$ and the input $u_k$ and $u_{(k+1/2)}$ we can compute $x_{k+1}$ from the following relations:

$$x_{k+1} = x_k + \frac{1}{6}(K_1 + 2K_2 + 2K_3 + K_4) \qquad (7.5.15)$$

where $K_1, K_2, K_3$, and $K_4$ are given by

$$K_1 = hf(x_k, u_k) \qquad (7.5.16)$$

$$K_2 = hf[x_k + \tfrac{1}{2}K_1, u_{(k+1/2)}] \qquad (7.5.17)$$

$$K_3 = hf[x_k + \tfrac{1}{2}K_2, u_{(k+1/2)}] \qquad (7.5.18)$$

and

$$K_4 = hf(x_k + K_3, u_{k+1}) \qquad (7.5.19)$$

where

$$u_{(k+1/2)} \triangleq u[t_0 + (k + \tfrac{1}{2})h] \qquad (7.5.20)$$

and $h$ is the step size.

To illustrate this method we work out two examples, one linear and one nonlinear. Let us first introduce a flow chart of a computer program based on the above equations.

FLOW CHART FOR SOLVING DIFFERENTIAL EQUATION
BY RUNGE-KUTTA METHOD

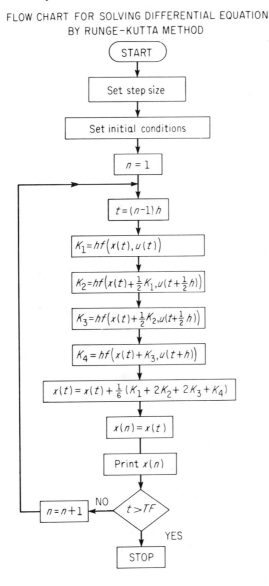

*Example 7.5.1*

Use the Runge-Kutta method to compute the solution of the following linear differential equation.

$$\dot{x} = -2x + \sin t \qquad x(0) = 1 \qquad (7.5.21)$$

for $0 \leq t \leq 10$ sec.

*Solution*

The following FORTRAN program can easily be written using Eqs. 7.5.15 to 7.5.20. We choose the step size $h$ to be 0.01 sec.

```
C         THIS PROGRAM IS FOR EXAMPLE 7.5-1
C         PROGRAM RUNGE-KUTTA
C         SOLUTION OF LINEAR DIFFERENTIAL EQUATION
C         DX=-2.*X+SIN(T), X(0)=1.0
          REAL K1,K2,K3,K4,T
          DIMENSION XT(2000)
          PRINT 13
C         SET THE STEP SIZE
          H=0.01
C         SET THE INITIAL CONDITION
          X=1
          DO 10 N=1,1001
          T=(N-1)*H
C         COMPUTE RUNGE-KUTTA PARAMETERS K1,K2,K3 AND K4
          K1=H*(-2*X+SIN(T))
          K2=H*(-2*(X+K1/2)+SIN(T+H/2))
          K3=H*(-2*(X+K2/2)+SIN(T+H/2))
          K4=H*(-2*(X+K3)+SIN(T+H))
C         USE RUNGE KUTTA FORMULA TO COMPUTE THE SOLUTION
          X=X+(K1+2*K2+2*K3+K4)/6
   10     XT(N)=X
C         PRINT X(T) ONLY AT T=0,0,2,0,4,.....,10 SECOND
          DO 12 K=1,51
          M=20*(K-1)+1
          T=(M-1)*H
   12     PRINT 11,T,XT(M)
   11     FORMAT(1H ,2E16.5)
   13     FORMAT (1H ,8X,'TIME',14X,'X(T)')
          END
```

The printout of $x(t)$ and $t$ and the plot of $x(t)$ versus $t$ are shown in Fig. 7.5.2.

*Example 7.5.2*

Use the Runge-Kutta method to compute the solution to the following nonlinear differential equation.

$$\dot{x} = -x^3 + 0.2 \sin t, \qquad x(0) = 0.707 \qquad (7.5.22)$$

*Solution*

The following FORTRAN program based on Eqs. 7.5.15 to 7.5.20 can be written.

```
C         THIS PROGRAM IS FOR EXAMPLE 7.5-2
C         PROGRAM RUNGE-KUTTA
```

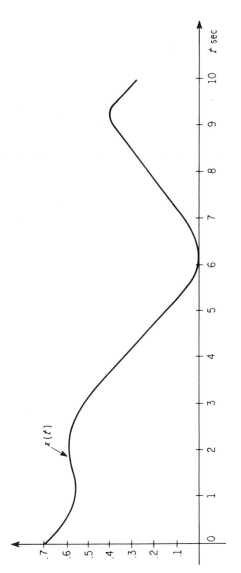

| TIME | X(T) |
|---|---|
| .00000 | .70362-00 |
| .20000-00 | .64696-00 |
| .40000-00 | .60926-00 |
| .60000-00 | .58667-00 |
| .80000-00 | .57387-00 |
| .10000+01 | .56825-00 |
| .12000+01 | .56746-00 |
| .14000+01 | .56934-00 |
| .16000+01 | .57202-00 |
| .18000+01 | .57392-00 |
| .20000+01 | .57375-00 |
| .22000+01 | .57051-00 |
| .24000+01 | .56350-00 |
| .26000+01 | .55250-00 |
| .28000+01 | .53667-00 |
| .30000+01 | .51658-00 |
| .32000+01 | .49214-00 |
| .34000+01 | .46359-00 |
| .36000+01 | .43127-00 |
| .38000+01 | .39562-00 |
| .40000+01 | .35718-00 |
| .42000+01 | .31661-00 |
| .44000+01 | .27469-00 |
| .46000+01 | .23230-00 |
| .48000+01 | .19048-00 |
| .50000+01 | .15032-00 |
| .52000+01 | .11305+00 |
| .54000+01 | .79854-01 |
| .56000+01 | .51906-01 |
| .58000+01 | .30235-01 |
| .60000+01 | .15674-01 |
| .62000+01 | .87923-02 |
| .64000+01 | .98628-02 |
| .66000+01 | .18842-01 |
| .68000+01 | .35369-01 |
| .70000+01 | .58771-01 |
| .72000+01 | .88072-01 |
| .74000+01 | .12200+00 |
| .76000+01 | .15903-00 |
| .78000+01 | .19740-00 |
| .80000+01 | .23522-00 |
| .82000+01 | .27058-00 |
| .84000+01 | .30170-00 |
| .86000+01 | .32707-00 |
| .88000+01 | .34558-00 |
| .90000+01 | .35655-00 |
| .92000+01 | .35946-00 |
| .94000+01 | .35506-00 |
| .96000+01 | .34311-00 |
| .98000+01 | .32441-00 |
| .10000+02 | .29968-00 |

Fig. 7.5.2

```
C       SOLUTION OF NONLINEAR DIFFERENTIAL EQUATION
C       DX=-X**3+0,2*SIN(T), X(0)=0,707
        REAL K1,K2,K3,K4,T
        DIMENSION XT(2000)
        PRINT 13
C       SET THE STEP SIZE
        H=0,01
C       SET THE INITIAL CONDITION
        X=0,5*SQRT(2)
        DO 10 N=1,1001
        T=(N-1)*H
C       COMPUTE RUNGE-KUTTA PARAMETERS K1,K2,K3 AND K4
        K1=H*(-X**3+0,2*SIN(T))
        K2=H*(-(X+K1/2)**3+,2*SIN(T+H/2))
        K3=H*(-(X+K2/2)**3+,2*SIN(T+H/2))
        K4=H*(-(X+2*K3)**3+0,2*SIN(T+H))
C       USE RUNGE KUTTA FORMULA TO COMPUTE THE SOLUTION
        X=X+(K1+2*K2+2*K3+K4)/6
     10 XT(N)=X
C       PRINT X(T) ONLY AT T=0,0,2,0,4,,,,,10 SECOND
        DO 12 K=1,51
        M=20*(K-1)+1
        T=(M-1)*H
     12 PRINT 11,T,XT(M)
     11 FORMAT(1H ,2E16,5)
     13 FORMAT (1H ,8X,'TIME',14X,'X(T)')
        END
```

The printout of $x(t)$ and $t$ and the plot of $x(t)$ versus $t$ are shown in Fig. 7.5.3.

The Runge-Kutta method can also be used to solve a set of first-order simultaneous differential equations of the form

$$\dot{\mathbf{x}}(t) = \mathbf{f}(\mathbf{x}(t), \mathbf{u}(t)); \qquad \mathbf{x}(t_0) = \mathbf{x}_0 \qquad (7.5.23)$$

where $\mathbf{x}(t)$ is an $n$-vector, $\mathbf{u}(t)$ is an $m$-vector, and $\mathbf{f}(\cdot, \cdot)$ is a vector valued function which may be linear or nonlinear. In this case the procedure is similar to the previous case except for each increment of time, all the equations in Eq. 7.5.23 must be solved using Eq. 7.5.15 before going to the next increment. In order to facilitate the use of the Runge-Kutta method for solution of simultaneous differential equations we develop a subroutine called DIFF that can be used for any differential equation of the form (7.5.23). The notations used in this subroutine and the subroutine follow

### Notations

$N$ = the number of the simultaneous differential equations that must be solved.

$X(N)$ = the $N$th component of $\mathbf{x}$

$DX = \dfrac{d}{dt}\mathbf{x}(t)$

$T1$ = Time, $t$

$Y$ = temporary values of $\mathbf{x}$

$Z$ = temporary values of $d\mathbf{x}/dt$

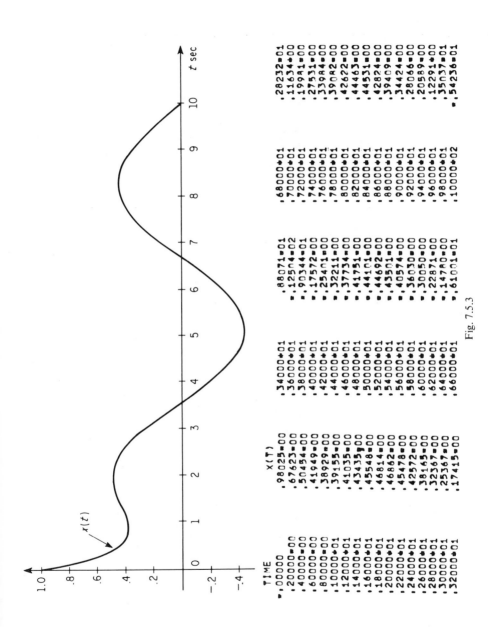

Fig. 7.5.3

K = used to switch to different subprograms

I = 1 or 2

DIFF Subroutine

```
    SUBROUTINE DIFF (N,K,I,X,DX,T1,H)
    DIMENSION Y(1000),Z(1000),X(N),DX(N)
    K=K+1
    GO TO (1,2,3,4,5),K
  2 DO 10 J=1,N
    Z(J)= DX(J)
    Y(J)= X(J)
 10 X(J)= Y(J)+0,5*H*DX(J)
 25 T1=T1+0,5*H
  1 I=1
    RETURN
  3 DO 15 J=1,N
    Z(J)= Z(J)+2,0*DX(J)
 15 X(J)= Y(J)+0,5*H*DX(J)
    I=1
    RETURN
  4 DO 20 J=1,N
    Z(J)= Z(J)+2,0*DX(J)
 20 X(J)= Y(J)+H*DX(J)
    GO TO 25
  5 DO 30 J=1,N
 30 X(J)= Y(J)+(Z(J)+DX(J))*H/6,0
    I=2
    K=0
    RETURN
    END
```

Let us now work out some examples to illustrate the use of subroutine DIFF.

*Example 7.5.3*

Consider the linear time-varying circuit considered in Example 7.3.5. Let

$$C(t) = 1 + 0.2 \sin t, \quad L(t) = 1 + 0.2 \cos t, \quad R = 1 \, \Omega$$

$$i(t) = \text{unit step function}$$

$$\phi(0) = 0 \quad \text{and} \quad q(0) = 0$$

Use the Runge-Kutta method to find $\phi(t)$ and $q(t)$ for $0 \le t \le 10$ sec.

*Solution*

The differential equation describing the circuit is given by Eq. 7.3.20. Let us rewrite this equation as follows:

$$\dot{q} = \frac{-1}{L(t)} \phi + i$$

$$\dot{\phi} = \frac{1}{C(t)} q - \frac{R}{L(t)} \phi$$

if we now let

$$X(1) \triangleq q(t), \quad X(2) \triangleq \phi(t), \quad u = i(t)$$

the following computer program can be written to solve the above equations.

```
C       THIS PROGRAM IS FOR EXAMPLE 7.5-3
C       SOLUTION OF LINEAR TIME-VARYING DIFFERENTIAL EQUATION
C       DX=A(T)X+B(T)U USING RUNGE-KUTTA METHOD.
        DIMENSION X(2),DX(2)
        REAL L
C       SET THE INITIAL CONDITIONS
        X(1)=0.
        X(2)=0.
C       SET INITIAL AND FINAL TIMES
        T=0.0
        TF=10.0
C       SET STEP SIZE
        H=0.2
        PRINT 10
        PRINT 20, T,X(1),X(2)
C       INITIALIZE K
        K=0
C       WRITE THE DIFFERENTIAL EQUATIONS
        U=1.0
      1 C=1.+0.2*SIN(T)
        L=1.+0.2*COS(T)
        DX(1)=-(1.0/L)*X(2)+U
        DX(2)= (1.0/C)*X(1)-(1.0/L)*X(2)
      3 CALL DIFF(2,K,I,X,DX,T,H)
        GO TO (1,2),I
      2 K1=T/H
C       PRINT OUT EVERY 'STEP'.
        NSTEP=1
        STEP=NSTEP
        K2=NSTEP*INT(T/H/STEP)
        IF(K1.EQ.K2) GO TO 4
        GO TO 5
      4 PRINT 20,T,X(1),X(2)
      5 TTF=TF-0.5*H
        IF(T.LT.TTF) GO TO 1
     10 FORMAT (10X,4HTIME,9X,2HX1,11X,2HX2)
     20 FORMAT(6X,F7.3,6X,F7.3,6X,F7.3)
        END
```

The results are printed out below.

| TIME  | X1    | X2   |
|-------|-------|------|
| .000  | .000  | .000 |
| .200  | .199  | .018 |
| .400  | .392  | .067 |
| .600  | .575  | .138 |
| .800  | .744  | .224 |
| 1.000 | .895  | .318 |
| 1.200 | 1.028 | .414 |
| 1.400 | 1.140 | .509 |
| 1.600 | 1.231 | .597 |
| 1.800 | 1.300 | .678 |
| 2.000 | 1.347 | .748 |
| 2.200 | 1.374 | .807 |
| 2.400 | 1.382 | .855 |
| 2.600 | 1.374 | .893 |
| 2.800 | 1.352 | .923 |

| TIME | X1 | X2 |
|------|------|------|
| 3.000 | 1.320 | .946 |
| 3.200 | 1.281 | .965 |
| 3.400 | 1.238 | .983 |
| 3.600 | 1.194 | 1.000 |
| 3.800 | 1.151 | 1.020 |
| 4.000 | 1.110 | 1.041 |
| 4.200 | 1.073 | 1.064 |
| 4.400 | 1.039 | 1.088 |
| 4.600 | 1.009 | 1.113 |
| 4.800 | .983 | 1.136 |
| 5.000 | .962 | 1.157 |
| 5.200 | .945 | 1.174 |
| 5.400 | .933 | 1.187 |
| 5.600 | .924 | 1.194 |
| 5.800 | .919 | 1.196 |
| 6.000 | .918 | 1.193 |
| 6.200 | .919 | 1.185 |
| 6.400 | .922 | 1.172 |
| 6.600 | .928 | 1.154 |
| 6.800 | .934 | 1.133 |
| 7.000 | .941 | 1.108 |
| 7.200 | .949 | 1.081 |
| 7.400 | .956 | 1.051 |
| 7.600 | .962 | 1.019 |
| 7.800 | .968 | .985 |
| 8.000 | .972 | .952 |
| 8.200 | .976 | .918 |
| 8.400 | .978 | .886 |
| 8.600 | .980 | .857 |
| 8.800 | .982 | .832 |
| 9.000 | .983 | .812 |
| 9.200 | .985 | .798 |
| 9.400 | .986 | .793 |
| 9.600 | .988 | .795 |
| 9.800 | .990 | .806 |
| 10.000 | .992 | .826 |

*Example 7.5.4*

Consider the circuit given in Example 7.3.3.   Let $v_1(0) = 0$, $i_2(0) =$ 1 amp, and $v_3(0) = 2$ volts. Assume that the current source $i(t)$ is given by $i(t) = \sin 2t$.  Find $v_1(t)$, $i_2(t)$, and $v_3(t)$ for $0 \le t \le 10$ sec.

*Solution*

The differential equations describing this circuit are given by Eq. 7.3.11 which we repeat here for convenience.

$$\dot{v}_1 = -v_1 - i_2 + i$$

$$\dot{i}_2 = \frac{1}{2}v_1 - \frac{1}{2}v_3$$

$$\dot{v}_3 = i_2 - v_3$$

Now let

$$X(1) = v_1(t), \quad X(2) = i_2(t), \quad X(3) = v_3(t)$$

$$u = i(t) = \sin 2t$$

then the following computer program can be written to solve the above equations and print out the result for increments of 0.2 sec.

```
C       THIS PROGRAM IS FOR EXAMPLE 7.5-4
C       SOLUTION OF LINEAR TIME-INVARIANT DIFFERENTIAL
C       EQUATION DX=AX+BU USING RUNGE-KUTTA METHOD,
        DIMENSION X(3),DX(3)
C       SET THE INITIAL CONDITIONS
        X(1)=0.0
        X(2)=1.0
        X(3)=2.0
C       SET INITIAL AND FINAL TIMES
        T=0.0
        TF=10.0
C       SET STEP SIZE
        H=0.2
        PRINT 20
        PRINT 30, T,X(1),X(2),X(3)
C       INITIALIZE K
        K=0
C       WRITE THE DIFFERENTIAL EQUATIONS
    1   U=SIN(2.0*T)
        DX(1)=-X(1)-X(2)+U
        DX(2)= 0.5*X(1)-0.5*X(3)
        DX(3)= X(2)-X(3)
    3   CALL DIFF(3,K,I,X,DX,T,H)
        GO TO (1,2),I
    2   PRINT 30, T,X(1),X(2),X(3)
        TTF=TF-0.5*H
        IF(T.LT.TTF) GO TO 1
   20   FORMAT (10X,1HT, 12X,2HX1, 10X, 2HX2,12X,2HX3,//)
   30   FORMAT(6X,F7.3,6X,F7.3,6X,F7.3,6X,F7.3)
        END
```

The results of the printout are given below.

| T | X1 | X2 | X3 |
|---|---|---|---|
| .000 | .000 | 1.000 | 2.000 |
| .200 | -.126 | .803 | 1.800 |
| .400 | -.128 | .619 | 1.602 |
| .600 | -.050 | .459 | 1.408 |
| .800 | .066 | .328 | 1.223 |
| 1.000 | .180 | .227 | 1.051 |
| 1.200 | .258 | .152 | .895 |
| 1.400 | .281 | .097 | .755 |
| 1.600 | .241 | .055 | .631 |
| 1.800 | .144 | .017 | .523 |
| 2.000 | .007 | -.023 | .428 |
| 2.200 | -.143 | -.068 | .342 |
| 2.400 | -.279 | -.120 | .263 |
| 2.600 | -.374 | -.175 | .188 |
| 2.800 | -.408 | -.230 | .117 |
| 3.000 | -.370 | -.278 | .050 |
| 3.200 | -.263 | -.312 | -.013 |
| 3.400 | -.100 | -.326 | -.069 |
| 3.600 | .096 | -.317 | -.115 |
| 3.800 | .296 | -.284 | -.149 |
| 4.000 | .469 | -.230 | -.169 |
| 4.200 | .588 | -.159 | -.173 |
| 4.400 | .634 | -.080 | -.164 |
| 4.600 | .600 | -.003 | -.141 |

| T | X1 | X2 | X3 |
|---|---|---|---|
| 4.800 | .488 | .065 | -.109 |
| 5.000 | .316 | .115 | -.073 |
| 5.200 | .108 | .141 | -.036 |
| 5.400 | -.104 | .143 | -.003 |
| 5.600 | -.290 | .122 | .022 |
| 5.800 | -.471 | .083 | .036 |
| 6.000 | -.479 | .034 | .040 |
| 6.200 | -.457 | -.018 | .034 |
| 6.400 | -.359 | -.062 | .021 |
| 6.600 | -.203 | -.092 | .003 |
| 6.800 | -.014 | -.102 | -.016 |
| 7.000 | .176 | -.091 | -.031 |
| 7.200 | .338 | -.062 | -.039 |
| 7.400 | .445 | -.018 | -.039 |
| 7.600 | .479 | .032 | -.031 |
| 7.800 | .435 | .081 | -.015 |
| 8.000 | .320 | .120 | .006 |
| 8.200 | .152 | .142 | .029 |
| 8.400 | -.043 | .143 | .050 |
| 8.600 | -.233 | .124 | .066 |
| 8.800 | -.388 | .085 | .073 |
| 9.000 | -.484 | .034 | .070 |
| 9.200 | -.505 | -.023 | .058 |
| 9.400 | -.448 | -.076 | .039 |
| 9.600 | -.320 | -.118 | .014 |
| 9.800 | -.143 | -.141 | -.013 |
| 10.000 | .056 | -.143 | -.037 |

*Example 7.5.5*

Consider the third-order nonlinear time-invariant circuit shown in Fig. 7.3.5. Let

$$f_1(q_1) = q_1 + q_1^2$$
$$f_2(\phi_2) = \phi_2^3$$
$$f_3(q_3) = q_3 + 2q_3^3$$

Find and plot $q_1(t)$ and $\phi_2(t)$ for $0 \le t \le 6$ sec if $i(t) =$ unit step function and all the initial conditions are zero.

*Solution*

The differential equations describing this circuit are given in Eq. 7.3.25. Let us rewrite these equations in the form

$$\dot{q}_1 = -f_1(q_1) - f_2(\phi_2) + i$$
$$\dot{\phi}_2 = f_1(q_1) - f_3(q_3)$$
$$\dot{q}_3 = f_2(\phi_2) - f_3(q_3)$$

Denoting

$$X(1) \triangleq q_1(t), X(2) \triangleq \phi_2(t), X(3) = q_3(t) \text{ and } u = i(t)$$

the plot of $X(1)$ and $X(2)$ is given in Fig. 7.5.4 using the computer program developed below. This program uses DIFF subroutine and GRAPHX subroutine developed in Chapter 6 to solve and plot the above equations.

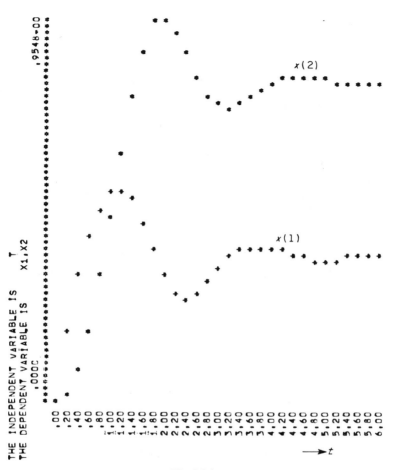

Fig. 7.5.4

```
C       THIS PROGRAM IS FOR EXAMPLE 7.5-5
C       SOLUTION OF THE THIRD-ORDER NONLINEAR
C       TIME-INVARIANT DIFFERENTIAL EQUATION
C       DX=F(X,T) USING RUNGE-KUTTA METHOD.
        DIMENSION X(3),DX(3),DATA(100,3)
C       SET THE INITIAL CONDITIONS
        X(1)=0.0
        X(2)=0.0
        X(3)=0.0
C       SET INITIAL AND FINAL TIMES
        T=0.0
        TF=6.0
C       STORE INITIAL VALUES FOR PLOTTING.
        DATA(1,1)=T
        DATA(1,2)=X(1)
        DATA(1,3)=X(2)
```

```
C      SET STEP SIZE
       H=0.2
       PRINT 20
       PRINT 30, T,X(1),X(2),X(3)
C      INITIALIZE K
       K=0
C      WRITE THE DIFFERENTIAL EQUATIONS
       U=1.0
  1 DX(1)=-X(1)-X(1)**2-X(2)**3+U
    DX(2)= X(1)+X(1)**2-X(3)=2.0*X(3)**3
    DX(3)= X(2)**3-X(3)-2.0*X(3)**3
  3 CALL DIFF(3,K,I,X,DX,T,H)
    GO TO (1,2),I
  2 PRINT 30, T,X(1),X(2),X(3)
    M=(T/H+0.01)+1.0
    DATA(M,1)=T
    DATA(M,2)=X(1)
    DATA(M,3)=X(2)
    TTF=TF=0.5*H
    IF(T.LT.TTF) GO TO 1
C      PLOT X(1) AND X(2)
    CALL GRAPHX(DATA,M,1HT,5HX1,X2)
 20 FORMAT (10X,1HT, 12X,2HX1, 10X, 2HX2,12X,2HX3,//)
 30 FORMAT(6X,F7.3,6X,F7.3,6X,F7.3,6X,F7.3)
    END
```

## PROBLEMS

**7.1.** Write the following integrodifferential equations in the state form.

(a) $\dfrac{d^2v}{dt^2} + a\dfrac{dv}{dt} + bv + C\displaystyle\int_0^t v(t')\,dt' = \sin t$

(b) $\dfrac{dx}{dt} + ax + b\displaystyle\int_0^t x(t')\,dt' + C\int_0^t \int_0^\tau x(t')\,dt'd\tau = 0$

**7.2.** Write the following differential equations in the state form.

(a) $\dfrac{d^4x}{dt^4} + 2\dfrac{d^3x}{dt^3} + 4\dfrac{d^2x}{dt^2} = u(t)$

(b) $x^{(n)} + a_n x^{(n-1)} + a_{n-1}x^{(n-2)} + \cdots + a_1 x = u(t)$

**7.3.** Find the original differential equation for which the state representation is given by

$$\begin{bmatrix} \dot{x}_1 \\ \dot{x}_2 \\ \dot{x}_3 \end{bmatrix} = \begin{bmatrix} 0 & 1 & 0 \\ 0 & 0 & 1 \\ -1 & -2 & -3 \end{bmatrix} \begin{bmatrix} x_1 \\ x_2 \\ x_3 \end{bmatrix} + \begin{bmatrix} 0 \\ 0 \\ 1 \end{bmatrix} u(t)$$

$$y(t) = x_1(t)$$

**7.4.** Write the state equation for the network shown.

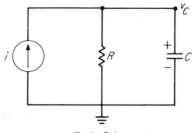

Prob. 7.4

**7.5.** Choose the capacitor voltage and inductor current to write the state equations for the network shown.

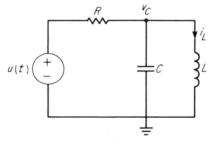

Prob. 7.5

**7.6.** Repeat Prob. 7.5 for the network shown.

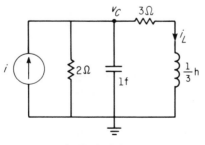

Prob. 7.6

**7.7.** Choose the charges and fluxes to write the state equations for the network of Prob. 7.5.
**7.8.** Repeat Prob. 7.7 for the network of Prob. 7.6.
**7.9.** Repeat Prob. 7.7 for the network of Fig. 7.3.2.
**7.10.** Repeat Prob. 7.5 for the network shown.

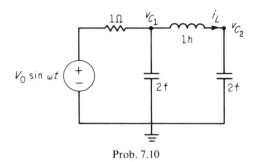

Prob. 7.10

**7.11.** Repeat Prob. 7.7 for the network of Prob. 7.10.

**7.12.** Write the state equations for the time-varying network shown. Choose the charges and the fluxes as the state variables and let $C(t) = 1 + 0.5 \sin 2t$ and $L(t) = 2 + \sin 2t$.

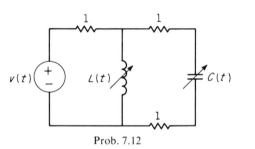

Prob. 7.12

**7.13.** Repeat Prob. 7.12 for the network shown.

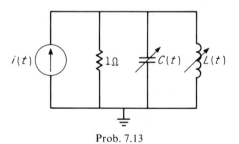

Prob. 7.13

**7.14.** Write the state equations for the nonlinear network shown. Let $v_C = q_C + \frac{1}{3}q_C^3$, $i_L = \phi_L + \frac{1}{2}\phi_L^2$.

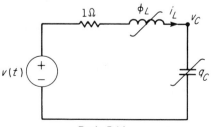

Prob. 7.14

**7.15.** Write the state equations for the nonlinear network shown. Let $v_1 = \tanh(q_1)$, $i_2 = 2\tanh(\phi_2)$, $v_3 = \frac{1}{2}\tanh(q_3)$.

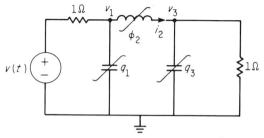

Prob. 7.15

**7.16.** Choose a set of *linearly independent* state variables and write the state equations for the network shown.

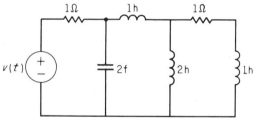

Prob. 7.16

**7.17.** Write the state equations for the network shown.

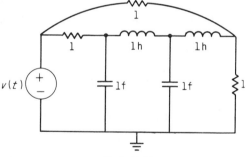

Prob. 7.17

**7.18.** Repeat Prob. 7.17 for the network shown.

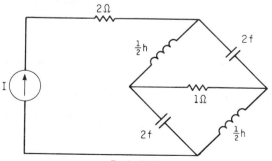

Prob. 7.18

**7.19.** Find the eigenvalues of the following matrices:

$$\mathbf{A}_1 = \begin{bmatrix} 1 & 2 \\ 3 & -1 \end{bmatrix}, \quad \mathbf{A}_2 = \begin{bmatrix} 0 & \alpha \\ -\alpha & 0 \end{bmatrix}, \quad \mathbf{A}_3 = \begin{bmatrix} a & 0 \\ -a & b \end{bmatrix}$$

$$\mathbf{A}_4 = \begin{bmatrix} -1 & 0 & 0 \\ 4 & -2 & 0 \\ -5 & -2 & -3 \end{bmatrix}, \quad \mathbf{A}_5 = \begin{bmatrix} 0 & 1 & 0 \\ 0 & 0 & 1 \\ -6 & -11 & -6 \end{bmatrix}$$

**7.20.** Find $e^{\mathbf{A}t}$, where $\mathbf{A} = \mathbf{A}_2$, given in Prob. 7.19.

**7.21.** Find $e^{\mathbf{A}t}$, where $\mathbf{A} = \mathbf{A}_5$, given in Prob. 7.19.

**7.22.** Find $e^{\mathbf{A}t}$, where $\mathbf{A}$ is given by

$$\mathbf{A} = \begin{bmatrix} -1 & 0 & 0 & 0 \\ 2 & -1 & 0 & 0 \\ 3 & 0 & -2 & 0 \\ -3 & 0 & 2 & -2 \end{bmatrix}$$

**7.23.** Find the solution for the equation $\mathbf{x} = \mathbf{A}\mathbf{x} + \mathbf{b}u; \mathbf{x}(0) = \mathbf{x}_0$ where

$$\mathbf{A} = \begin{bmatrix} 1 & 0 \\ -2 & 2 \end{bmatrix}, \quad \mathbf{b} = \begin{bmatrix} 1 \\ 2 \end{bmatrix}, \quad \mathbf{x}_0 = \begin{bmatrix} -1 \\ 0 \end{bmatrix},$$

$$u(t) = \delta(t) \quad \text{(impulse function)}$$

**7.24.** Repeat Prob. 7.23 but assume that $\mathbf{A} = \mathbf{A}_3$ given in Prob. 7.19.

**7.25.** Repeat Prob. 7.23 but assume that

$$\mathbf{A} = \begin{bmatrix} 0 & -\omega \\ -\omega & 0 \end{bmatrix}, \quad \mathbf{b} = \begin{bmatrix} 0 \\ 1 \end{bmatrix}, \quad \mathbf{x}_0 = \begin{bmatrix} 1 \\ 1 \end{bmatrix}, \quad u(t) = \text{unit step function}$$

**7.26.** Repeat Prob. 7.23 but assume that $\mathbf{A} = \mathbf{A}_5$, given in Prob. 7.19, $\mathbf{b} = [0, \ 0, \ 1]^T, \mathbf{x}(0) = [1 \ 1 \ 0]^T$, and $u(t) = $ unit step function.

**7.27.** Find $v_C$ and $i_L$ for the circuit shown in Prob. 7.6, assume that $v_C(0) = 0$, $i_L(0) = 0$, and $i(t) = $ unit impulse function.

**7.28.** Use the Runge-Kutta method to solve the following differential equation by computer:

$$x = -5x + 2\cos t, \quad x(0) = 2.0$$

**7.29.** Repeat Prob. 7.28 for the differential equation

$$\dot{x} = \sin(x), \quad x(0) = 1.0$$

**7.30.** Find $v_C$ and $i_L$ for the circuit shown in Prob. 7.6, using a computer program. Let $v_C(0) = 1$ volt, $i_L(0) = 0$ and $u(t) = 2\sin 2t$.

**7.31.** Compute and plot the voltage on the terminating resistor of the circuit considered in Prob. 7.15 for $0 \le t \le 10$ sec. Assume that all the initial conditions are zero and the input voltage is a unit step function.

**7.32.** Repeat Prob. 7.31 for the circuit shown in Prob. 7.16.

## CHAPTER 8

# Elementary Time
# Functions and Convolution

## 8.1. INTRODUCTION

When a signal is applied to an electrical network we have to determine the response of the network in terms of some voltage, current, or state. From what we have studied so far, this usually entails solving some sort of differential equation. While this is one method of solving for network response, it is useful to have other methods of obtaining and expressing the solution. There are two types of inputs which we will commonly encounter. One is an *aperiodic* waveform like the step, ramp, exponential, etc., and the other is the *periodic* waveforms like the rectangular pulse train, the sinusoidal waveform, and the like. It would obviously be very useful if we could establish techniques for solving network problems using specific inputs both for the aperiodic and the periodic case and then be able to use these basic results for development of solutions for other types of inputs. Such an approach is even more useful when these specific inputs can be related to experimental measurements. In this chapter we derive the network response for two specific inputs called *elementary time functions* and then we demonstrate the utility of these responses in solving for more general inputs. We will restrict our discussion to linear time-invariant networks.

### Impulse Response

Impulse response of an electrical network is its response in terms of voltages and currents when an impulse function is applied as the excitation. We defined the impulse function in Chapter 3 and the impulse response in Chapter 5. We will further elaborate on these in the present chapter.

253

It is not difficult to generate an approximate impulse function of voltage or current in the laboratory and apply it to an electrical network. The output (response) of the network can be easily measured or recorded. So the impulse response of any network can be directly related to experimental measurements.

Mathematically we can decompose an input function into impulse functions of various strengths which when applied to a network give the same response as the actual input. Therefore, the knowledge of the impulse response of the network enables us to determine the response to any input. We will see that these results are straightforward especially for aperiodic inputs and linear time-invariant networks. For periodic inputs, the impulse function is also useful. We can obtain what is called an *impulse-train response* of a network which serves as a basis for obtaining network response for other periodic inputs. The impulse-train response of a network is its response to an input made up of periodic train of impulse functions. More on this will be developed in Section 8.5.

The impulse function is considered as an elementary time function because a knowledge of its network response enables us to construct the network response of other inputs.

### Sinusoidal Response

If a periodic input is applied to a linear time-invariant network, the network response is also periodic. In particular, if the input is sinusoidal, the response of the network is also sinusoidal. This is an extremely important behavior of electrical networks which we can measure very easily in the laboratory. The response of the network to sinusoids of various frequencies can be recorded to develop what is known as *network-frequency response*. Any periodic waveform which is not a sinusoid can be decomposed into sum of sinusoids of various frequencies. Knowledge of the sinusoidal response of any network then enables us to determine the response to any periodic input.

A sinusoid can therefore be considered as another elementary time function. Usually a sinusoid is expressed as sin $(\omega t)$ or imaginary part of $e^{j\omega t}$. Actually it is sufficient to consider the elementary time signal for sinusoidal decomposition as being $e^{j\omega t}$. We then just consider the real or imaginary part of the result as the case may be. We will discuss this procedure in Section 8.6.

Apart from these two elementary time functions, another which is very useful from a mathematical framework is $e^{st}$ where $s = \sigma + j\omega$. This elementary time function is just a generalization of $e^{j\omega t}$, described above, and is basic to the development of the Laplace transform. We will discuss the Laplace transform in the next chapter. We introduced the impulse function in Chapter 3. Now we define it more formally and develop some of its properties not previously developed.

## 8.2. THE IMPULSE FUNCTION

*DEFINITION.* The impulse function $\delta(t - a)$ is defined to be a function such that

$$\delta(t - a) = 0 \quad \forall t \neq a \tag{8.2.1}$$

and

$$\int_{-\infty}^{\infty} \delta(t - a)\, dt = 1 \tag{8.2.2}$$

The magnitude of $\delta(t - a)$ at $t = a$ can be thought of as being infinite.

The area under the impulse function as shown in Fig. 8.2.1a is called the *strength* of the impulse function. When this area is unity, as in Eq. 8.2.2, the impulse function is a *unit impulse*. Note that an impulse function is not really a mathematical function in the usual sense but is a useful representation. An approximate way of generating an impulse function is shown in Fig. 8.2.1b. It is a pulse of height $1/(b - a)$ and as $b \rightarrow a$,

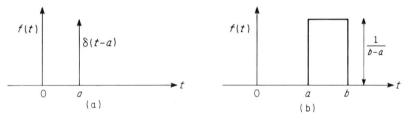

Fig. 8.2.1. (a) Impulse function, (b) an approximation.

we have a unit impulse. Hence we can think of an impulse function as a pulse of high magnitude and very short duration. We can write

$$\delta(t - a) = \lim_{b \rightarrow a} \frac{1}{b - a} [u_0(t - a) - u_0(t - b)] \tag{8.2.3}$$

*HIGHER-ORDER IMPULSE FUNCTION.* An *n*th-order impulse function is defined as the *n*th derivative of the impulse function. We write

$$\delta^{(n)}(t) = \frac{d^n}{dt^n} [\delta(t)] \tag{8.2.4}$$

$\delta^{(1)}(t)$ is called a *doublet*, $\delta^{(2)}(t)$ is called a *triplet*, and so on.

### Properties of the Impulse Function

1. *Impulse function as a derivative of step function.* It was demonstrated in Chapter 3 that

$$\delta(t) = \frac{d}{dt} [u_0(t)] \tag{8.2.5}$$

2. *Sifting property.* Consider the integral

$$\int_a^b f(t) \delta(t - \alpha) \, dt \tag{8.2.6}$$

Let $a < \alpha < b$, then integrating by parts and using Eq. 8.2.5, we obtain

$$\int_a^b f(t) \delta(t - \alpha) \, dt = f(t) u_0(t - \alpha) \Big|_a^b - \int_a^b u_0(t - \alpha) f^{(1)}(t) \, dt \tag{8.2.7}$$

or

$$\int_a^b f(t) \delta(t - \alpha) \, dt = f(b) - \int_\alpha^b f^{(1)}(t) \, dt = f(\alpha) \tag{8.2.8}$$

We can let $a \to -\infty$ and $b \to \infty$, then for any $|\alpha| < \infty$, we have

$$\int_{-\infty}^\infty f(t) \delta(t - \alpha) \, dt = f(\alpha) \tag{8.2.9}$$

This is known as the *sifting property of the impulse function.* The above method can be extended to show that

$$\int_{-\infty}^\infty f(t) \delta^{(n)}(t - \alpha) \, dt = (-1)^n \frac{d^n}{dt^n} \{f(t)\} \Big|_{t = \alpha} \tag{8.2.10}$$

3. *Sampling property.* It was demonstrated in Chapter 3 that

$$f(t) \delta(t) = f(0) \delta(t) \tag{8.2.11}$$

We can easily see from above that we will have

$$f(t) \delta(t - a) = f(a) \delta(t - a) \tag{8.2.12}$$

We can also extend the above to evaluate $f(t) \delta^{(1)}(t - a)$. The result is given by

$$f(t) \delta^{(1)}(t - a) = f(a) \delta^{(1)}(t - a) - f^{(1)}(a) \delta(t - a) \tag{8.2.13}$$

We note that multiplying a function with an impulse function of first order gives a more involved result than multiplication with just an impulse function. We will utilize the above properties of the impulse function in network problems.

*Example 8.2.1*

Evaluate (i) $t\delta(t - 1)$   (ii) $\int_{-\infty}^\infty t\delta(t - 1) \, dt$   (iii) $t\delta^{(1)}(t - 1)$

*Solution*

Here $f(t) = t$ and $\alpha = 1$. Thus

(i) $t\delta(t - 1) = 1.\delta(t - 1) = \delta(t - 1)$

(ii) $\int_{-\infty}^\infty t\delta(t - 1) \, dt = t \Big|_{t = 1} = 1$

(iii)  Using Eq. 8.2.13, we get

$$t\delta^{(1)}(t - 1) = 1.\delta^{(1)}(t - 1) - \frac{d}{dt}\{t\}\bigg|_{t=1} \cdot \delta(t - 1)$$

$$= \delta^{(1)}(t - 1) - \delta(t - 1)$$

## 8.3. IMPULSE RESPONSE

We have discussed the importance of the impulse response of a network. How do we determine it? It can be determined experimentally as well as from network equations. Determination of the impulse response of a first-order network was developed in Chapter 5 using network equations. We discuss the more general case now. Note that the determination of impulse response assumes zero initial conditions in the network. In other words, the network is assumed in the zero state.

For any linear time-invariant single input network we can write the state differential equation as

$$\dot{\mathbf{x}} = \mathbf{A}\mathbf{x} + \mathbf{b}u \qquad (8.3.1)$$

The solution of such an equation was discussed in Chapter 7 and is given by

$$\mathbf{x} = e^{\mathbf{A}t}\mathbf{x}_0 + \int_0^t e^{\mathbf{A}(t-\tau)}\mathbf{b}u(\tau)\,d\tau \qquad (8.3.2)$$

Assuming zero initial condition, i.e., $\mathbf{x}_0 = \mathbf{0}$, and assuming that the input is an impulse function, the state impulse response is given from Eq. 8.3.2

$$\mathbf{x} = \int_0^t e^{\mathbf{A}(t-\tau)}\mathbf{b}\delta(\tau)\,d\tau \qquad (8.3.3)$$

Using the sifting property of the impulse function (8.2.8), we obtain

$$\mathbf{x}(t) = e^{\mathbf{A}t}\mathbf{b}, \qquad t \geq 0$$

$$= e^{\mathbf{A}t}\mathbf{b}u_0(t) \qquad (8.3.4)$$

Equation 8.3.4 gives the state impulse response for any network provided we can find $e^{\mathbf{A}t}$ and $\mathbf{b}$. A method of obtaining $e^{\mathbf{A}t}$ and $\mathbf{b}$ was discussed in Chapter 7. We now proceed with two examples.

*Example 8.3.1*

Determine the impulse response of the $RL$ network of Fig. 8.3.1.

*Solution*

In this case we have only one state, namely, the current $i$. So the state variable equation is

$$L\frac{di}{dt} + Ri = u(t)$$

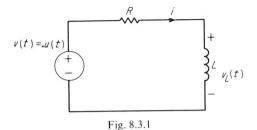

Fig. 8.3.1

or

$$\dot{x} = -\frac{R}{L} x + \frac{1}{L} u, \qquad x \triangleq i$$

Here

$$\mathbf{A} = -\frac{R}{L} \quad \text{and} \quad \mathbf{b} = \frac{1}{L}$$

Therefore the impulse response, which we will denote by $h(t)$, is given by the current $i$:

$$i(t) = h(t) = e^{\mathbf{A}t}\mathbf{b}u_0(t) = \frac{1}{L} e^{-(R/L)t}u_0(t)$$

The result implies that if a voltage impulse function is applied to the $RL$ series network, a current with exponential decay will flow in the network in the direction shown.

Now suppose that the impulse response we want is the voltage across the inductor. All we have to do is evaluate $v_L(t)$. This is given by

$$v_L(t) = L\frac{di}{dt} = L\frac{d}{dt}\left(\frac{1}{L} e^{-(R/L)t}u_0(t)\right) = -\frac{R}{L} e^{-(R/L)t}u_0(t)$$

$$+ e^{-(R/L)t}\delta(t) = -\frac{R}{L} e^{-(R/L)t}u_0(t) + \delta(t)$$

using the sampling property of the impulse function as given by Eq. 8.2.11. This example suggests that to determine the state impulse response, we find $e^{\mathbf{A}t}$ and $\mathbf{b}$. We can then obtain any other impulse response by using network and element relationships.

*Example 8.3.2*

Consider the $RLC$ network shown in Fig. 8.3.2. Find the output voltage $v_C(t)$ for an impulse input. Assume zero initial conditions.

*Solution*

Here we have two energy-storage elements $L$ and $C$, so we have two state variables $i_L(t)$ and $v_C(t)$. If we let

$$x_1(t) = i_L(t)$$
$$x_2(t) = v_C(t)$$

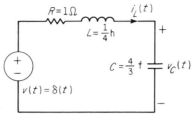

Fig. 8.3.2

we have exactly the same circuit as in Example 7.3.2 for which we have already shown (in that example) that

$$\dot{\mathbf{x}} = \mathbf{A}\mathbf{x} + \mathbf{b}u$$

where

$$\mathbf{A} = \begin{bmatrix} -4 & -4 \\ \tfrac{3}{4} & 0 \end{bmatrix}, \qquad \mathbf{b} = \begin{bmatrix} 4 \\ 0 \end{bmatrix}$$

For this $\mathbf{A}$, $e^{\mathbf{A}t}$ was calculated in Example 7.4.4 as

$$e^{\mathbf{A}t} = \begin{bmatrix} -\tfrac{1}{2}e^{-t} + \tfrac{3}{2}e^{-3t} & -2e^{-t} + 2e^{-3t} \\ \tfrac{3}{8}e^{-t} - \tfrac{3}{8}e^{-3t} & \tfrac{3}{2}e^{-t} - \tfrac{1}{2}e^{-3t} \end{bmatrix}$$

Now, the state impulse response is given by

$$\mathbf{x}(t) = e^{\mathbf{A}t}\mathbf{b}u_0(t)$$

$$= 4 \begin{bmatrix} -\tfrac{1}{2}e^{-t} + \tfrac{3}{2}e^{-3t} \\ \tfrac{3}{8}e^{-t} - \tfrac{3}{8}e^{-3t} \end{bmatrix} u_0(t)$$

Therefore the output-voltage impulse response is given by

$$v_C(t) = x_2(t) = 4(\tfrac{3}{8}e^{-t} - \tfrac{3}{8}e^{-3t})u_0(t)$$

## 8.4. CONVOLUTION

One of the primary reasons of developing the concept of the impulse response is to be able to establish a solution of the network response to any other input through simple manipulations. Let us consider a single-input, single-response network. Let the input be the impulse function $\delta(t)$ and the corresponding impulse response be $h(t)$. Then we can write

$$\delta(t) \xrightarrow{\text{gives}} h(t) \tag{8.4.1}$$

Since the network is assumed to be time-invariant (i.e., no parameters of the network change with time), we have

$$\delta(t - \tau) \xrightarrow{\text{gives}} h(t - \tau) \tag{8.4.2}$$

Now let the input be $u(t)$ and let its value be $u(\tau)$ at $t = \tau$. Then *since the network is linear*, we can write

$$u(\tau)\,\delta(t - \tau) \xrightarrow{\text{gives}} u(\tau)\,h(t - \tau) \tag{8.4.3}$$

Now multiplying both sides of Eq. 8.4.3 by $d\tau$ (a constant) and integrating from $-\infty$ to $\infty$, we get

$$\int_{-\infty}^{\infty} u(\tau)\,\delta(t - \tau)\,d\tau \xrightarrow{\text{gives}} \int_{-\infty}^{\infty} u(\tau)\,h(t - \tau)\,d\tau \tag{8.4.4}$$

Using the sifting property and noting $\delta(t - \tau) = \delta(\tau - t)$ we have that

$$u(t) \xrightarrow{\text{gives}} \int_{-\infty}^{\infty} u(\tau)\,h(t - \tau)\,d\tau \tag{8.4.5}$$

The integral of Eq. 8.4.5 is called the *superposition integral* or the *convolution integral*. The result means that if we know the impulse response of a network, we can determine the response to any input by using this integral.

We have noted also that the state impulse response for a single input case is given by $e^{At}\mathbf{b}$. Therefore if we use Eq. 8.4.5, we can easily say that the state response to any input $u(t)$ will be

$$\mathbf{x}(t) = \int_{-\infty}^{\infty} e^{A(t-\tau)}\mathbf{b}u(\tau)\,d\tau \tag{8.4.6}$$

The evaluation of the convolution integral to obtain the response to any input is quite involved and one has to be very careful. First note that by simple change of variables we can write

$$\int_{-\infty}^{\infty} u(\tau)\,h(t - \tau)\,d\tau = \int_{-\infty}^{\infty} u(t - \tau)\,h(\tau)\,d\tau \tag{8.4.7}$$

We write the convolution operation as given in the above integrals as $u(t)*h(t)$.

### Evaluation of the Convolution Integral

In order to fully understand how to evaluate the convolution it is best that we first develop a graphical evaluation. Let us evaluate, say,

$$\int_{-\infty}^{\infty} u(t - \tau)\,h(\tau)\,d\tau \tag{8.4.8}$$

with the assumption that $h(t)$ is given as in Fig. 8.4.1a and the input given as in Fig. 8.4.1b. We have chosen these arbitrarily in order to demonstrate the procedure. Now we need $h(\tau)$ and $u(t - \tau)$. $u(\tau)$ and $h(\tau)$ are the same as $u(t)$ and $h(t)$ respectively, $t$ being replaced by $\tau$. $u(-\tau)$ is the image of $u(\tau)$ about the ordinate axis. $u(-\tau)$ is shown in Fig. 8.4.2a. In order to obtain $u(t - \tau)$, we just shift $u(-\tau)$ by some quantity $t$.

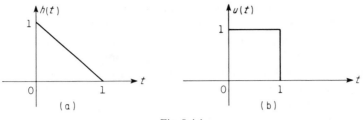

Fig. 8.4.1

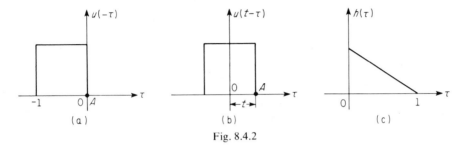

Fig. 8.4.2

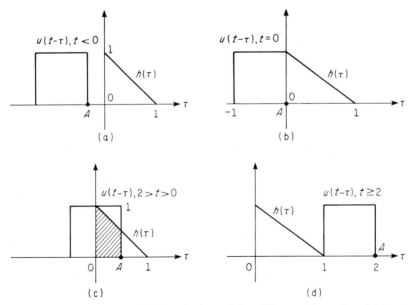

Fig. 8.4.3. Multiplication of $h(\tau)$ and $u(t - \tau)$ for different values of $t$.   (a) Product = 0, $t < 0$, (b) Product = 0, $t = 0$, (c) Product = shaded area, $0 < t < 2$, (d) Product = 0, $t \geq 2$.

$u(t - \tau)$ is shown in Fig. 8.4.2b. To obtain the integral of Eq. 8.4.8 we have to multiply $h(\tau)$ and $u(t - \tau)$, for each value of $t$ and then find the area under this multiplication. This will then be the value of the integral for that value of $t$. The value of $t$ will change from $-\infty$ to $\infty$ as the point $A$ shown in Fig. 8.4.2b is moved from $-\infty$ to $\infty$. Note that $h(\tau)$ is shown in Fig. 8.4.2c.

The product of $u(t - \tau)$ and $h(\tau)$ is shown in Fig. 8.4.3 as $t$ is changed.

We plot the area under the product for each value of $t$ as shown in Fig. 8.4.4.

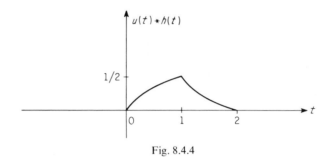

Fig. 8.4.4

### Rules for Evaluating Convolution Integral

1. Reverse $u(t)$, i.e., take mirror image of $u(t)$ about ordinate axis.
2. Move reversed $u(t)$ to left or right until the point originally at the origin of $u(t)$ coincides with the present value of time.
3. Form the graphical plot of the product $u(t - \tau)$ and $h(\tau)$ at the present value of time, $t$.
4. The area under this graph is then the value of the convolution integral at the value of time, $t$.
5. The value of time, $t$, is varied from $-\infty$ to $\infty$.

*Example 8.4.1*

A step input is applied to the $RL$ network as shown in Fig. 8.4.5. Find the current $i(t)$.

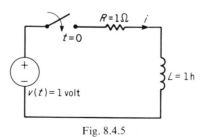

Fig. 8.4.5

*Solution*

We can find the output by use of convolution integral, i.e.,

$$i(t) = \int_{-\infty}^{\infty} u(t - \tau) h(\tau) \, d\tau$$

We already know the impulse response of this network from Example 8.3.1 as $(1/L) e^{-(R/L)t} u_0(t)$. In our case $R = L = 1$, so

$$h(t) = e^{-t} u_0(t)$$

Also we have $u(t) = 1$, $t > 0$, so we construct the convolution as shown in Fig. 8.4.6.

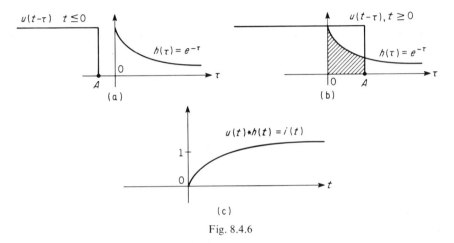

Fig. 8.4.6

From Fig. 8.4.6a we note that the value of the product of $u(t - \tau)$ and $h(\tau)$ is zero for $t \leq 0$. The product has a value for all $t > 0$. In that case $u(t - \tau)$ is always unity. So the area under the product $u(t - \tau)$ is just the area under $e^{-\tau}$ for any $t \geq 0$. Figure 8.4.6c shows $i(t)$. We can also determine $i(t)$ analytically if we examine Figs. 8.4.6a and b carefully. We note

$$i(t) = \int_{-\infty}^{\infty} u(t - \tau) h(\tau) \, d\tau$$
$$= 0, \qquad t \leq 0$$
$$= \int_{0}^{t} e^{-\tau} \, d\tau, \qquad t > 0$$
$$= (1 - e^{-t}), \qquad t > 0$$

The above result when plotted checks with Fig. 8.4.6c.

This simple example shows how the limits of integration can be determined from the graphical procedure to determine the convolution result analytically.

### Evaluation of the Convolution Integral Using a Digital Computer

The evaluation of the convolution integral involves the determination of the area under the product of time functions for each value of time $t$. Let us see how the integration program developed in Chapter 1 can be utilized for this evaluation. First the limits on the integral are determined by using the graphical technique discussed above and then we use the integration program with varying upper limit and print out the integral value as we vary the time $t$. We can also plot the result by using the GRAPHX subroutine of Chapter 6. We show the actual details by an example.

*Example 8.4.2*

Consider the network of Fig. 8.4.7. The output voltage for an impulse input voltage is given by $e^{-t}$. Now an input voltage $u(t) = \sin t, 0 < t < \pi$ and $u(t) = 0$ otherwise, is applied to the network. Use the convolution and computer programs to develop and plot the output voltage.

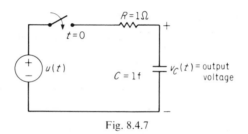

Fig. 8.4.7

*Solution*

The impulse response is given by $e^{-t}$. Then the output voltage is given by the convolution integral

$$v_C(t) = \int_{-\infty}^{\infty} u(t - \tau) e^{-\tau} d\tau$$

In order to determine the limits, we plot the impulse response $e^{-t}$, the input $u(t)$ as shown in Fig. 8.4.8a. Then we plot $e^{-\tau}$ and $u(-\tau)$ as shown in Fig. 8.4.8b. As we trace $\sin(t - \tau)$ from $t = 0$ onward as shown in Fig. 8.4.8c, we note

$$v_C(t) = 0, \qquad t \leq 0$$

$$v_C(t) = \int_0^t \sin(t - \tau) e^{-\tau} d\tau, \qquad 0 < t \leq \pi$$

and

$$v_C(t) = \int_{t-\pi}^t \sin(t - \tau) e^{-\tau} d\tau, \qquad \pi < t < \infty$$

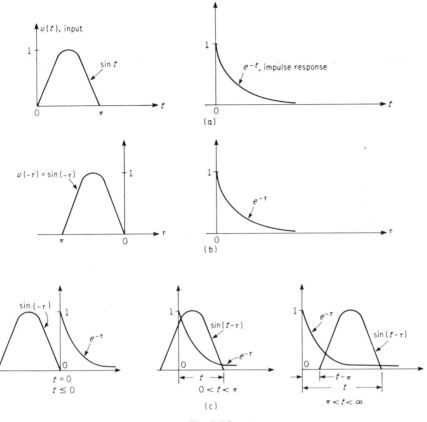

Fig. 8.4.8

We note that the convolution just involves the evaluation of one integral with varying limits. We can use the integration computer program of Chapter 1. In our case the integrand is

$$f(\tau) = \sin(t - \tau)e^{-\tau}$$

where $t$ is the upper limit.

Between $0 < t \leq \pi$, the lower limit is fixed. So $T0 = 0$, $T1 = t$ is varying from 0 to $\pi$—that is, from 0 to 3.1416—so we can change $T1$ in steps. The program we developed in Example 1.3.2 is directly applicable here provided we note that

$$f(T) = \sin(T1 - T)e^{-T}$$

where $T$ has to be replaced by $TA$, $TB$, and $TC$ respectively.

For $\pi < t < \infty$, the lower limit also is variable. So $T0$, the lower limit, is to be changed to $T1 - 3.1416$, that is

$$T0 = T1 - 3.1416$$

The upper limit stays $T1$. How can we modify our computer program as $T1$ goes through the value $\pi = 3.1416$. We must be able to change $T0$ from 0 to $T1 - 3.1416$. This is done by an IF statement in the computer program which states that keep $T0 = 0$ as long as $T1 \leq 3.1416$ but change $T0 = T1 - 3.1416$ when $T1 > 3.1416$.

We have actually calculated the integral as $T1$ is changed from 0 to $2\pi$ in twenty steps. This choice depends of course upon the problem under consideration. In this case this variation of $T1$ suffices. The value of the integral (VIN) and $T1$ are stored for each value as we print them. Then the graph routine of Chapter 6 is called to plot VIN versus $T1$. This in the output voltage. The plot of the output voltage is shown in Fig. 8.4.9. The flowchart, the computer program and the printout are given on pages 267 to 269.

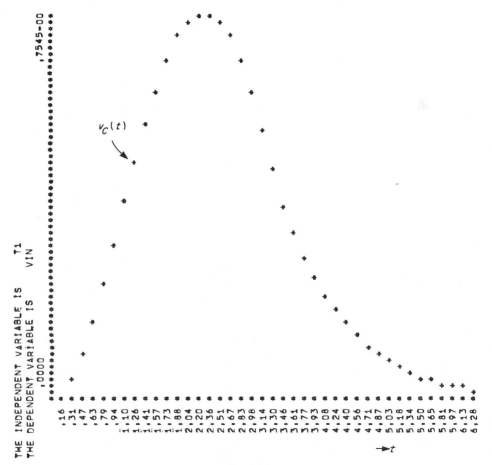

Fig. 8.4.9

FLOW CHART FOR EVALUATION AND PLOTTING OF THE
CONVOLUTION INTEGRAL, EXAMPLE 8.4.2.

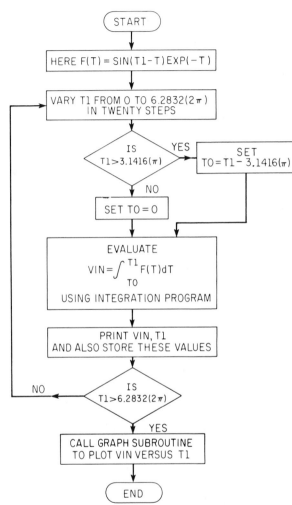

Computer Program for the Evaluation of the Convolution Integral—An Example

```
C       THIS PROGRAM IS FOR EXAMPLE 8.4.2.
C       THIS PROGRAM EVALUATES THE CONVOLUTION INTEGRAL WITH
C       VARYING UPPER LIMITS USING SIMPSON'S RULE OF
C       INTEGRATION. CHOOSE N AS EVEN NUMBER, NOTE THAT N
C       IS RESERVED FOR INTEGER NUMBERS IN FORTRAN
C       SO WE LET N = AN,
        DIMENSION VIN(100),DATA(100,3)
        N=16
        AN=N
C       WE HAVE A DO LOOP FOR VARYING THE UPPER LIMIT,
        DO 14 J=1,40
```

```
      AJ=J
      PI=3.14159
C     THE INCREMENTS OF T1 ARE CHOSEN BASED ON THE
C     TIME CONSTANT OF THE PROBLEM.
      T1=0.05*PI*AJ
C     AN IF STATEMENT IS INTRODUCED TO CHANGE THE LOWER
C     LIMIT FROM 0 TO T1-PI FOR T1 GREATER THAN PI.
      IF(T1-PI)2,2,3
    2 TO=0.
      GO TO 4
    3 TO=T1-PI
    4 H = (T1-TO)/AN
      SUM = 0.
      TA = TO
      TB = TA+H
      TC = TB+H
C     THE FOLLOWING DO LOOP EVALUATES THE CONVOLUTION
C     INTEGRAL FOR EACH T1.
      M = N/2
      DO 10 I=1,M
C     FTA IS THE GIVEN INTEGRAND F(T),T BEING REPLACED BY TA
C     SIMILARLY FTB AND FTC
      FTA=SIN(T1-TA)*EXP(-TA)
      FTB=SIN(T1-TB)*EXP(-TB)
      FTC=SIN(T1-TC)*EXP(-TC)
      SUM  = SUM+FTA+4.*FTB+FTC
      TA = TA+2.0*H
      TB = TA+H
      TC = TB+H
   10 CONTINUE
C     THE FOLLOWING SECTION COMPUTES THE CONVOLUTION
C     INTEGRAL PRINTS IT, AND SAVES THE VALUES IN DATA FOR
C     THE CALL TO THE SUBROUTINE GRAPHX.
      VIN(J) = SUM*H/3.
      PRINT 15,J,T1,J,VIN(J)
      DATA(J,1)=T1
      DATA(J,2)=VIN(J)
      DATA(J,3)=0
   14 CONTINUE
C     WE NOW USE THE GRAPH ROUTINE TO PLOT VIN VERSUS T1
C     USING THE STORED VALUES.
      CALL GRAPHX(DATA,J,2HT1,3HVIN)
   15 FORMAT(5X,'T1 'I2 ' = ',F10.6,'  VIN 'I2 ' = 'F10.6)
      END
      SUBROUTINE GRAPHX(DATA,N,VINDEP,VARDEP)
      DIMENSION DATA(100,3),B(121)
      DOUBLE PRECISION VINDEP,VARDEP
      PRINT 300,VINDEP
      PRINT 400,VARDEP
      BIGEST=DATA(1,2)
      SMAL=DATA(1,2)
      DO 1 I=2,N
      IF(DATA(I,2).GT.BIGEST)BIGEST=DATA(I,2)
      IF(DATA(I,2).LT.SMAL)SMAL=DATA(I,2)
    1 CONTINUE
      DO 2 I=2,N
      IF(DATA(I,3).GT.BIGEST)BIGEST=DATA(I,3)
      IF(DATA(I,3).LT.SMAL)SMAL=DATA(I,3)
    2 CONTINUE
      PRINT 200,SMAL,BIGEST
C     TO EXTEND THE PLOT TO FULL PAGE WIDTH, WE ONLY
C     NEED TO REPLACE K=61 BY K=121.
C     ALSO IN FORMAT STATEMENT 200 4X
C     MUST BE REPLACED BY 48X, AND 61 BY 121.
```

```
      K=61
      BMINS=BIGEST-SMAL
      DO 3 I=1,K
    3 B(I)=1H
      DO 4 I=1,N
      DATA(I,2)=(DATA(I,2)-SMAL)*FLOAT(K)/BMINS+1.0
      DATA(I,3)=(DATA(I,3)-SMAL)*FLOAT(K)/BMINS+1.0
      INDEX=DATA(I,2)
      JNDEX=DATA(I,3)
      B(INDEX)=1H+
      B(JNDEX)=1H*
      PRINT 100,DATA(I,1),(B (N),N=1,K)
      B(INDEX)=1H
    4 B(JNDEX)=1H
  100 FORMAT(1HZ,F8.2,1X,121A1)
  200 FORMAT(9X,E11.4,35X,1H ,4X,E11.4,/10X,61(1H*))
  300 FORMAT (1H1,'THE INDEPENDENT VARIABLE IS ',2A10)
  400 FORMAT (1X,'THE DEPENDENT VARIABLE IS ',2A10//)
      RETURN
      END
```

Printout of $v_C(t)$ versus $t$.

```
        T1  1 =    .157080    VIN  1 =    .011691
        T1  2 =    .314159    VIN  2 =    .044182
        T1  3 =    .471239    VIN  3 =    .093606
        T1  4 =    .628318    VIN  4 =    .156128
        T1  5 =    .785397    VIN  5 =    .227969
        T1  6 =    .942477    VIN  6 =    .305446
        T1  7 =   1.099556    VIN  7 =    .385017
        T1  8 =   1.256636    VIN  8 =    .463324
        T1  9 =   1.413715    VIN  9 =    .537244
        T1 10 =   1.570795    VIN 10 =    .603938
        T1 11 =   1.727874    VIN 11 =    .660890
        T1 12 =   1.884954    VIN 12 =    .705951
        T1 13 =   2.042033    VIN 13 =    .737376
        T1 14 =   2.199113    VIN 14 =    .753846
        T1 15 =   2.356192    VIN 15 =    .754489
        T1 16 =   2.513272    VIN 16 =    .738893
        T1 17 =   2.670351    VIN 17 =    .707101
        T1 18 =   2.827431    VIN 18 =    .659605
        T1 19 =   2.984511    VIN 19 =    .597328
        T1 20 =   3.141590    VIN 20 =    .521591
        T1 21 =   3.298669    VIN 21 =    .445770
        T1 22 =   3.455749    VIN 22 =    .380972
        T1 23 =   3.612828    VIN 23 =    .325592
        T1 24 =   3.769908    VIN 24 =    .278263
        T1 25 =   3.926987    VIN 25 =    .237813
        T1 26 =   4.084067    VIN 26 =    .203244
        T1 27 =   4.241146    VIN 27 =    .173700
        T1 28 =   4.398226    VIN 28 =    .148450
        T1 29 =   4.555305    VIN 29 =    .126871
        T1 30 =   4.712385    VIN 30 =    .108428
        T1 31 =   4.869464    VIN 31 =    .092667
        T1 32 =   5.026544    VIN 32 =    .079196
        T1 33 =   5.183623    VIN 33 =    .067684
        T1 34 =   5.340703    VIN 34 =    .057845
        T1 35 =   5.497782    VIN 35 =    .049437
        T1 36 =   5.654862    VIN 36 =    .042250
        T1 37 =   5.811941    VIN 37 =    .036109
        T1 38 =   5.969021    VIN 38 =    .030860
        T1 39 =   6.126100    VIN 39 =    .026374
        T1 40 =   6.283180    VIN 40 =    .022540
```

### Simplification of the Convolution Integral

*DEFINITION.* A network is said to be a *causal network* if its response to $\delta(t), h(t)$ is zero for $t < 0$.

All of the networks studied in this book are causal networks. This enables us to change the lower limit of the convolution integral of Eq. 8.4.8 from $-\infty$ to 0. We also assume that the input to the network $u(t)$ is also applied for only $t \geq 0$. This implies that $u(t - \tau) = 0$ for $\tau > t$. This enables one to change the upper limit of the convolution integral of Eq. 8.4.8 from $\infty$ to $t$. So under the circumstances the convolution integral simplifies to

$$\int_0^t u(t - \tau) h(\tau) \, d\tau \qquad (8.4.9)$$

### Relationship Between Impulse and Step Responses

Consider a causal network with input $u(t)$, such that $u(t) = 0$ for $t < 0$, and impulse response $h(t)$. Then the output $y(t)$ is given by the integral of Eq. 8.4.9 as

$$y(t) = \int_0^t u(t - \tau) h(\tau) \, d\tau \qquad (8.4.10)$$

When the input is a unit step, then

$$u(t - \tau) = u_0(t - \tau) \qquad (8.4.11)$$

The output of the network is then given by

$$y_{\text{step}}(t) = \int_0^t u_0(t - \tau) h(\tau) \, d\tau \qquad (8.4.12)$$

Now, by definition

$$u_0(t - \tau) = 1, \qquad 0 \leq \tau < t \qquad (8.4.13)$$

Thus, Eq. 8.4.12 reduces to

$$y_{\text{step}}(t) = \int_0^t h(\tau) \, d\tau \qquad (8.4.14)$$

Equation 8.4.14 implies that if we know the impulse response, $h(t)$, of a network, then the step response can be obtained by simple integration. Remember that we came across this relationship in Example 5.4.2.

We can also obtain the impulse response from the step response if we differentiate Eq. 8.4.14. We get

$$h(t) = \frac{d}{dt} \{ y_{\text{step}}(t) \} \qquad (8.4.15)$$

The result of Eq. 8.4.15 is very useful because we can generate a step input to any network by just a simple battery. We can measure the step response on the oscilloscope and then we can obtain the impulse response by just differentiating this measured value.

*Example 8.4.3*

Consider the *RL* network of Example 8.4.1. There we found the response due to a step input as $(1 - e^{-t}) u_0(t)$. We can easily find the impulse response $h(t)$ as

$$h(t) = \frac{d}{dt} \{\text{step response}\}$$

$$= \frac{d}{dt} \{(1 - e^{-t}) u_0(t)\}$$

$$= e^{-t} u_0(t) + (1 - e^{-t}) \delta(t)$$

$$= e^{-t} u_0(t)$$

This result checks with that of Example 8.3.1 where we found the impulse response of this network.

## 8.5.  IMPULSE-TRAIN  RESPONSE

As we have already seen, the impulse response of a network is useful in determining the network output given any driving function. In the case where a driving function is *semiperiodic*, i.e. repetitive for $t > t_0$ and zero for $t \leq t_0$ as shown in Fig. 8.5.1, the network output will be zero for

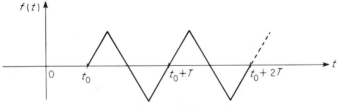

Fig. 8.5.1. Semiperiodic waveform.

$t \leq t_0$ and will be repetitive for sufficiently large $t$. In the immediate time interval following $t_0$, a *transient* in the output will be observed due to the fact that the waveform begins at $t = t_0$. This transient effect becomes negligible as time increases and in the *steady-state* the output waveform becomes repetitive.

Consider the *RL* network shown in Fig. 8.5.2. When the voltage $u(t)$ is the driving function and the current $i(t)$ through the inductor is the desired response, we have found that the impulse response as given in Example 8.3.1 is

$$h(t) = \frac{1}{L} e^{-(R/L)t} u_0(t) \tag{8.5.1}$$

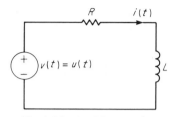

Fig. 8.5.2. An $RL$ network.

Using the convolution integral we can write the response to the semi-periodic function $\sin t \, u_0(t - t_0)$,

$$i(t) = \int_{-\infty}^{\infty} \frac{1}{L} e^{-(R/L)(t - \tau)} u_0(t - \tau) \sin \tau \, u_0(\tau - t_0) \, d\tau \qquad (8.5.2)$$

The function $u_0(\tau - t_0)$ is zero for $\tau < t_0$ and the function $u_0(t - \tau)$ is zero for $\tau > t$; hence the integral in Eq. 8.5.2 reduces to

$$i(t) = \frac{1}{L} e^{-(R/L)t} \int_{t_0}^{t} e^{(R/L)\tau} \sin \tau \, d\tau \qquad (8.5.3)$$

which when evaluated yields

$$i(t) = \begin{cases} K[-e^{-a(t - t_0)} \sin(t_0 - \theta) + \sin(t - \theta)] & t > t_0 \\ 0 & t \le t_0 \end{cases} \qquad (8.5.4)$$

where

$$K = \frac{(1/L)}{\sqrt{1 + (R/L)^2}}; \quad a = \frac{R}{L}; \quad \theta = \tan^{-1}\left(\frac{1}{a}\right)$$

Notice that for $t \le t_0$, the circuit response is zero, whereas for $t - t_0 \gg (1/a)$ the circuit response is approximately sinusoidal. The first term in Eq. 8.5.4 is the *transient component* of the response. This term goes to zero as $t$ increases. The second term is the *steady-state component*. This solution is plotted in Fig. 8.5.3. Note that the steady-state response dominates as the observation time $t$ becomes further and further removed from $t_0$. In particular, if we let $t_0$ approach $-\infty$ then for any finite $t$, only the steady-state component of the solution is observed, i.e., the steady-state component is simply the network response to the strictly periodic applied voltage $u(t) = \sin t$, $-\infty < t < \infty$.

Often, we are not interested in the transient component of the solution but desire instead just the steady-state result. For this purpose, the network impulse-train response is useful.

As discussed in Chapter 3, the impulse train is a periodic repetition of the unit impulse. The period $T$ of the waveform is just the repetition interval as shown in Fig. 8.5.4. Symbolically, we write the unit impulse train as

$$\delta_T(t) \triangleq \sum_{n=-\infty}^{\infty} \delta(t - nT) \qquad (8.5.5)$$

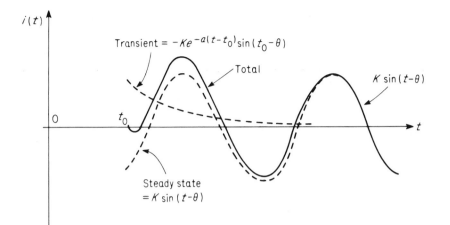

Fig. 8.5.3. Sinusoidal response of an $RL$ network.

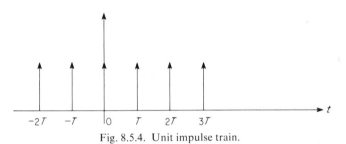

Fig. 8.5.4. Unit impulse train.

Using $\delta_T(t)$ as an input, we can evaluate the *impulse-train response*, $h_T(t)$, of a network having an impulse response $h(t)$ by using the convolution integral as

$$h_T(t) \triangleq \int_{-\infty}^{\infty} \delta_T(t - \tau) h(\tau)\, d\tau \qquad (8.5.6)$$

Substituting Eq. 8.5.5 into Eq. 8.5.6 and interchanging the order of summation and integration as well as using the sifting property of the impulse function, we get

$$h_T(t) = \int_{-\infty}^{\infty} \sum_{n=-\infty}^{\infty} \delta(t - \tau - nT) h(\tau)\, d\tau$$

$$= \sum_{n=-\infty}^{\infty} \int_{-\infty}^{\infty} \delta(t - \tau - nT) h(\tau)\, d\tau = \sum_{n=-\infty}^{\infty} h(t - nT) \quad (8.5.7)$$

which by definition is a strictly periodic time function. Knowing the impulse response $h(t)$, we can, in theory at least, determine the impulse train response by evaluation of the summation. Table 8.5.1 lists a number of commonly occurring responses together with one period of the asso-

TABLE 8.5.1. FREQUENTLY USED IMPULSE-TRAIN RESPONSES.

| Impulse Response, $h(t)$ | One Period of the Periodic Impulse Train Response, $h_T(t)$, $0 - \epsilon \leq t < T$ |
|---|---|
| 1. $\delta(t)$ | 1. $\delta(t)$ |
| 2. $u_0(t) - u_0(t - T_0)$ | 2. $2u_0(t) - u_0(t - T_0 + T) - u_0(t - T)$,    $2T \geq T_0 \geq T$ |
| 3. $e^{-at}u_0(t)$ | 3. $\dfrac{e^{-at}}{1 - e^{-aT}}$ |
| 4. $te^{-at}u_0(t)$ | 4. $\dfrac{te^{-at}(1 - e^{-at}) + Te^{-a(t+T)}}{(1 - e^{-aT})^2}$ |
| 5. $e^{-at}\sin bt\, u_0(t)$ | 5. $\dfrac{b(e^{-at}\sin bt - e^{-a(t+T)}\sin b(t-T))}{1 - 2e^{-aT}\cos bT + e^{-2aT}}$ |
| 6. $e^{-at}\cos bt\, u_0(t)$ | 6. $\dfrac{b(e^{-at}\cos bt - e^{-a(t+T)}\cos b(t-T))}{1 - 2e^{-aT}\cos bT + e^{-2aT}}$ |

ciated impulse-train response. These have been obtained using the summation given in Eq. 8.5.7.

A technique of obtaining the impulse-train response, namely the entries in Table 8.5.1, utilizing the Laplace transform method, will be developed in Sec. 11.3.

## Determination of Steady-State Response

As we have seen in the discussion of the $RL$ network above, the steady-state component can be viewed as the network response to a strictly periodic driving function. To calculate the steady-state response, we can simply insert the strictly periodic driving function $u_T(t)$ into the convolution integral and evaluate the resulting integral, i.e., letting $y_T(t)$ denote the steady-state response

$$y_T(t) = \int_{-\infty}^{\infty} u_T(\tau) h(t - \tau)\, d\tau \qquad (8.5.8)$$

where since $u(t)$ is a strictly periodic function with period $T$,

$$u_T(t) = u_T(t + nT), \qquad -\infty < t < \infty \qquad (8.5.9)$$

We can break up the integral in Eq. 8.5.8 into the summation of an infinite number of finite integrals over a single period:

$$y_T(t) = \sum_{n=-\infty}^{\infty} \int_{b+nT}^{b+(n+1)T} u_T(\tau) h(t - \tau)\, d\tau \qquad (8.5.10)$$

where the constant $b$ is arbitrary. Changing the variable of integration in Eq. 8.5.10 gives

$$y_T(t) = \sum_{n=-\infty}^{\infty} \int_{b}^{b+T} u_T(\tau + nT) h(t - \tau - nT)\, d\tau \qquad (8.5.11)$$

Substituting for $u_T(\tau + nT)$ from Eq. 8.5.9 and changing the order of summation and integration, Eq. 8.5.11 can be written

$$y_T(t) = \int_b^{b+T} u_T(\tau) \left\{ \sum_{n=-\infty}^{\infty} h(t - \tau - nT) \right\} d\tau \qquad (8.5.12)$$

Comparing the definition of the impulse-train response in Eq. 8.5.7 with Eq. 8.5.12, we see that the quantity in brackets is simply the impulse-train response shifted by the $\tau$, i.e.,

$$\sum_{n=-\infty}^{\infty} h(t - \tau - nT) = h_T(t - \tau) \qquad (8.5.13)$$

Substituting this relationship into Eq. 8.5.12 gives the result which we seek:

$$y_T(t) = \int_b^{b+T} u_T(\tau) h_T(t - \tau) d\tau \qquad (8.5.14)$$

which can also be written as

$$y_T(t) = \int_b^{b+T} u_T(t - \tau) h_T(\tau) d\tau \qquad (8.5.15)$$

The integrals in Eqs. 8.5.14 and 8.5.15 are called *finite-convolution* integrals. From these results, we see that finite convolution and the impulse-train response are fundamental to the determination of the steady-state response. Given *any* periodic waveform *of period T*, the finite convolution of that waveform with the impulse-train response $h_T(t)$ gives the steady-state component of the network response.

*Example 8.5.1*

Let us now use the impulse-train response to evaluate the steady-state component in an *RL* network as shown in Fig. 8.5.1. Assume that the input is $u_T(t) = \sin t$.

*Solution*

Our impulse response in this case has been shown to be

$$h(t) = \frac{1}{L} e^{-(R/L)t} u_0(t)$$

Hence from the third entry in Table 8.5.1 we find our impulse-train response as

$$h_T(t) = \frac{(1/L) e^{-(R/L)t}}{1 - e^{-(R/L)T}}, \qquad 0 < t < T$$

The steady-state response is obtained from using Eq. 8.5.15. Note that we can choose $b = 0$ and here $T = 2\pi$. Therefore

$$i_T(t) = \int_0^{2\pi} \left( \frac{1/L}{1 - e^{-(R/L)2\pi}} \right) e^{-(R/L)\tau} \sin(t - \tau) d\tau$$

Evaluation of this integral gives

$$i_T(t) = \frac{1/L}{1 + (R/L)^2} \left\{ \frac{R}{L} \sin t - \cos t \right\}$$

$$= \frac{1}{\sqrt{R^2 + L^2}} \sin (t - \theta)$$

where $\tan \theta = (L/R)$.

One thing to note here is that for the sinusoidal input, the steady-state response is also a sinusoid of the same frequency but with a phase shift and different magnitude, both dependent upon circuit elements.

## 8.6. THE EXPONENTIAL FUNCTION $e^{j\omega t}$

When we apply a sinusoidal driving function to a linear network, the response is also sinusoidal and of the same frequency. This has been seen in previous chapters as well as demonstrated in Example 8.5.2. We note that the response of the $RL$ network is sinusoidal for a sinusoidal input except for an initial transient. In the study of networks, the steady-state response plays a very important role as does the transient response. This is quite obvious, since we must naturally consider whether our networks will function properly when driven by a periodic input.

Networks in general will give different responses when driven by sinusoids of different frequency. This *frequency response* has great significance in the application of networks.

We have shown in the earlier part of this chapter that we can decompose a time function say $u(t)$ into elementary time function $\delta(t)$ such that

$$u(t) = \int_{-\infty}^{\infty} u(\tau) \delta(t - \tau) \, d\tau \qquad (8.6.1)$$

This result enabled us to develop the response of a network to any driving function provided the impulse response is known.

A result of equal significance, which will be discussed in detail in Chapter 11, is that any periodic function (under some conditions) can be expressed as a sum of sinusoidal functions. We can write for a periodic $u(t)$, with period $T$ as

$$u(t) = \sum_{n=-\infty}^{\infty} c_n e^{jn\omega t}, \text{ over any period } T \qquad (8.6.2)$$

where

$$\omega = \frac{2\pi}{T}$$

and $c_n$ is a complex quantity, usually a function of $\omega$. The above equation can also be written

$$u(t) = \sum_{n=0}^{\infty} (a_n \cos n\omega t + b_n \sin n\omega t), \quad \text{for any period} \qquad (8.6.3)$$

Equation 8.6.2 implies that if we can find the response of a network to a general input $e^{j\omega t}$ we can easily construct the response to any periodic input $u(t)$ provided we know $c_n$.

So we note that the determination of the response of a network to a driving function $e^{j\omega t}$ enables us to determine the frequency response of the network as well as the response to any other periodic input. In addition to these two advantages, the response is sinusoidal which eases our work of finding this response. In view of these basic advantages $e^{j\omega t}$ is the second elementary time function which plays as equally an important role as $\delta(t)$.

We have still not shown why it is sufficient to get the response of $e^{j\omega t}$ in order to get the response for $\sin \omega t$ or $\cos \omega t$. We proceed to show this.

Let us consider a linear network. Let the response of the network due to a driving function $\cos \omega t$ be $g_1(t)$ and the response due to a driving function $\sin \omega t$ be $g_2(t)$. Since the network is linear, the response due to $j \sin \omega t$ (note that $j$ is just a constant) will be $jg_2(t)$. Hence we can write

$$\cos \omega t \xrightarrow{\text{gives}} g_1(t) \qquad (8.6.4)$$

$$j \sin \omega t \xrightarrow{\text{gives}} jg_2(t) \qquad (8.6.5)$$

Adding the inputs and outputs (because of superposition) we have

$$\cos \omega t + j \sin \omega t \xrightarrow{\text{gives}} g_1(t) + jg_2(t) \qquad (8.6.6)$$

and since $e^{j\omega t} \triangleq \cos \omega t + j \sin \omega t$, then:

$$e^{j\omega t} \xrightarrow{\text{gives}} g_1(t) + jg_2(t) \qquad (8.6.7)$$

From Eq. 8.6.7 it is quite obvious that if we find the response to $e^{j\omega t}$, then the real part of response, $g_1(t)$ is due to $\cos \omega t$ (real part of $e^{j\omega t}$) and the imaginary part of the response, $g_2(t)$ is due to $\sin \omega t$ (imaginary part of $e^{j\omega t}$).

Hence we conclude that all we need to do is to find the network response due to $e^{j\omega t}$ and then take either the real or imaginary part to find the response due to $\cos \omega t$ or $\sin \omega t$ respectively. We can of course also construct the response to any other periodic input $u(t)$ using Eq. 8.6.2. This is discussed in detail in Chapter 11.

Now we will demonstrate how easily we can evaluate the response of networks to $e^{j\omega t}$ by a simple example.

*Example 8.6.1*

A sinusoidal driving function $V \sin \omega t$ is applied to the $RL$ network shown in Fig. 8.6.1. Find the behavior of current under steady state conditions.

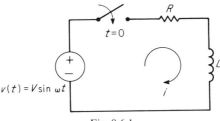

Fig. 8.6.1

*Solution*

We have here

$$L \frac{di}{dt} + iR = V \sin \omega t$$

For steady-state conditions we need only the particular solution. We will replace $V \sin \omega t$ by $Ve^{j\omega t}$ and then find $i$. The imaginary part of the solution will then be the result. We have

$$\frac{di}{dt} + \frac{R}{L} i = \frac{V}{L} e^{j\omega t}$$

The particular solution of this equation is of the form

$$i(t) = ke^{j\omega t}$$

To determine the constant $k$ we must insert $i(t)$ in the above differential equation. Equating the coefficients yields

$$i(t) = \frac{V}{L[(R/L)^2 + \omega^2]} \left\{ \left( \frac{R}{L} - j\omega \right) e^{j\omega t} \right\}$$

or equivalently

$$i(t) = \frac{V}{\sqrt{[R^2 + \omega^2 L^2]}} e^{j[\omega t + \phi]}, \qquad \text{where} \quad \tan \phi = -\frac{\omega L}{R}$$

So the current due to $V \sin \omega t$ is just

$$\frac{V}{\sqrt{R^2 + \omega^2 L^2}} \sin (\omega t + \phi)$$

This is just a sinusoidal response with modified magnitude and shifted phase, both being functions of frequency. We can make a plot of magnitude and phase versus frequency as shown in Fig. 8.6.2.

Suppose now we want to find the response $i(t)$ due to a periodic input $u(t)$, we can use Eq. 8.6.2 to obtain

$$i(t) = \sum_{n=-\infty}^{\infty} c_n \frac{V}{\sqrt{R^2 + n^2\omega^2 L^2}} e^{j(n\omega t + \phi)}, \qquad \text{over each period}$$

This example demonstrates that the finding of response of a network for $e^{j\omega t}$ enables one to know the sinusoidal response, the frequency response as well as the response to any periodic input. Note that the

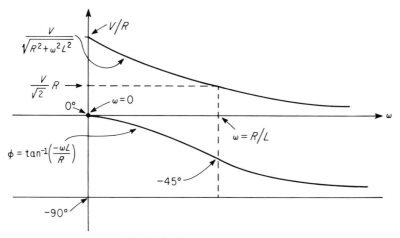

Fig. 8.6.2. Frequency response.

graph of frequency response such as shown in Fig. 8.6.2 enables us to know the magnitude as well as phase shift for any frequency. For example we note that for any $\omega \gg R/L$ we will not see any appreciable output if this network is driven by a sinusoid of this frequency.

We will elaborate further on these points in Chapters 10 and 11.

**PROBLEMS**

**8.1.** Show the following functions $f(t)$ as shown, can be considered as the impulse function in the limit.

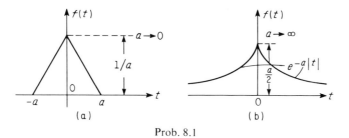

Prob. 8.1

**8.2.** How would you generate an impulse function in laboratory using an $RC$ network. Pick up some suitable values of $R$ and $C$.

**8.3.** Use integration by parts to show that

$$\int_{-\infty}^{\infty} f(t)\, \delta^{(n)}(t)\, dt = (-1)^n \frac{d^n}{dt^n} \left\{ f(t) \right\} \bigg|_{t=0}$$

**8.4.** Show that $f(t)\, \delta^{(1)}(t) = f(0)\, \delta^{(1)}(t) - (df/dt)\,|_{t=0}\, \delta(t)$.

**8.5.** Evaluate
(a) $\sin t\, \delta[t - (\pi/2)]$     (b) $\cos t\, \delta(t - \pi)$     (c) $\sin^2 t\, \delta^{(1)}(t)$.

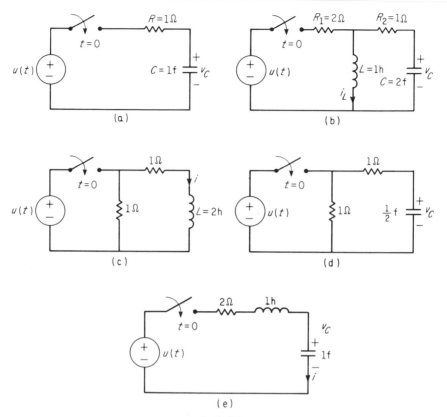

Prob. 8.6

**8.6.** Find the impulse response of networks shown. The response to be found is shown as current and/or voltage on the figure.

**8.7.** Use the impulse responses found in Prob. 8.6 to obtain the step responses.

**8.8.** For the impulse response of networks as obtained in Prob. 8.6, find the response, by convolution, to driving functions $u(t)$:

(a) $e^{-t}$     (b) pulse of height 1 and duration 1 sec.

Repeat the problem using the computer program on convolution.

**8.9.** The impulse response of a network is given by $\sin t$, $0 < t < \pi$, and zero otherwise. Find the response due to (a) step input, (b) $e^{-t}$, (c) pulse of height 1 and duration $\pi$ sec. Repeat the problem using the computer program on convolution.

**8.10.** The impulse response of a *finite-memory integrator* is shown in part (a) of the figure. A periodic signal $u(t)$ shown in part (b) is applied to the finite-memory integrator. Find (a) the impulse-train response of the finite-memory integrator, and (b) the steady-state response of the finite-memory integrator to $u(t)$.

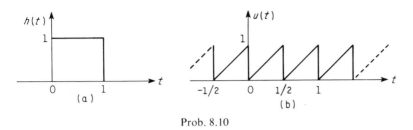

Prob. 8.10

**8.11.** The periodic voltage shown in part (a) of the figure is applied to the $RC$ circuit shown in part (b). Find (a) the impulse-train response of the network, and (b) the steady-state capacitor voltage $v_C(t)$.

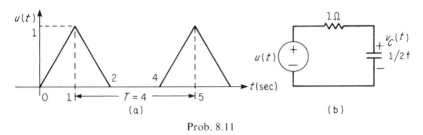

Prob. 8.11

**8.12.** For the networks shown in Prob. 8.6, find the steady-state responses to input $V \cos \omega t$. Plot the magnitude and phase as a function of $\omega$.

# CHAPTER 9

## Analysis of Networks by Laplace Transformation

### 9.1. INTRODUCTION

Chapters 5 and 6 presented analysis procedures for solving linear time-invariant integrodifferential equations which model electric network performance. Chapter 7 presented an analytic method and numerical procedures for solving the state equations of linear and nonlinear networks. These procedures were based on obtaining a direct time domain solution to various order differential equations. We now take up the use of the Laplace transform in solving network equations. The Laplace transform permits us to replace linear time-invariant integrodifferential equations with algebraic equations and therefore in many cases eases their solutions.

### 9.2. DEFINITION AND PROPERTIES OF THE LAPLACE TRANSFORM

In the analysis of electrical networks, we are primarily concerned with the effect of a current or voltage source when switched into a circuit. As we have seen in Chapter 3, if the source is described by some function, $u(t)$, then the effect of switching the source into the network at time $t_0$ is represented by the function

$$u(t)u_0(t - t_0) \tag{9.2.1}$$

where $t_0$ denotes the instant of switching and $u_0(\cdot)$ represents the unit step function. The *one-sided Laplace transform* of a function $f(t)$ starting at some time $t = t_0, t_0 \geq 0$, denoted by $F(s)$, is defined by

$$F(s) = \int_{t_0^-}^{\infty} f(t)e^{-st}\, dt \tag{9.2.2}$$

Note that we are defining the integral to include a vanishingly small interval just to the left of $t_0$. For functions not containing an impulse function, there is no difference between the lower limit being $t_0$ and being $t_0^-$. However, when $f(t)$ involves an impulse function at $t_0$, the lower limit $t_0^-$ implies that we are including the impulse function within the integral. The variable $s$ in Eq. 9.2.2 is a complex variable* conventionally called the *complex frequency* and is written

$$s = \sigma + j\omega \tag{9.2.3}$$

The function $F(s)$, the one-sided Laplace transform of $f(t)$, is sometimes written as $\mathcal{L}[f(t)]$. Equation 9.2.2 has meaning only if the integral converges—that is, if

$$\left| \int_{t_0^-}^{\infty} f(t)e^{-\sigma t}e^{-j\omega t}\, dt \right| < \infty \tag{9.2.4}$$

or, since $|e^{-j\omega t}| = 1$ \hfill (9.2.5)

we get the convergence condition as

$$\left| \int_{t_0^-}^{\infty} f(t)e^{-\sigma t}\, dt \right| < \infty \tag{9.2.6}$$

Time functions of primary interest in engineering are of exponential order. A function $f(t)$ is said to be of *exponential order* if there exists a finite number $\sigma_0$ such that

$$|f(t)| < ke^{\sigma_0 t} \qquad \text{for all } t \geq t_0 \tag{9.2.7}$$

where $k$ is any positive constant. Utilizing this property in Eq. 9.2.6 we obtain

$$\left| \int_{t_0^-}^{\infty} f(t)e^{-\sigma t}\, dt \right| < \left| \int_{t_0^-}^{\infty} ke^{\sigma_0 t}e^{-\sigma t}\, dt \right| \tag{9.2.8}$$

The second integral in Eq. 9.2.8 converges if $\sigma > \sigma_0$. Hence, when $f(t)$ is of exponential order, the Laplace transform of $f(t)$ exists provided

$$\text{Real part of } s \triangleq \text{Re}\,[s] = \sigma > \sigma_0, \tag{9.2.9}$$

where $\sigma_0$ is a finite real number.

In the development which follows, we will assume our functions and any required derivative or integrals of the functions are of exponential order. For simplicity we will assume the initial point of interest occurs at $t_0 = 0$. This second assumption will not restrict the use of the Laplace transform since a *shifting property*, to be developed later, will generalize all our results to the case when $t_0 \neq 0$.

*A review of complex numbers and complex variables is contained in Appendix A.

**Properties of Laplace Transform**

Time Differentiation

The Laplace transform of the derivative can be expressed as

$$\mathcal{L}\left[\frac{d}{dt}(f(t))\right] = sF(s) - f(0^-) \tag{9.2.10}$$

We can develop this relationship quite readily by simply using the definition of the Laplace transform. From Eq. 9.2.2,

$$\mathcal{L}\left[\frac{d}{dt}(f(t))\right] = \int_{0^-}^{\infty} \frac{d}{dt}(f(t))e^{-st}\,dt \tag{9.2.11}$$

Integration by parts gives

$$\mathcal{L}\left[\frac{d}{dt}(f(t))\right] = f(t)e^{-st}\bigg|_{0^-}^{\infty} + s\int_{0^-}^{\infty} f(t)e^{-st}\,dt \tag{9.2.12}$$

Since $f(t)$ is of exponential order

$$\lim_{t\to\infty} |f(t)e^{-st}| < \lim_{t\to\infty} |ke^{-(\sigma-\sigma_0)t}| = 0 \qquad \text{for } \sigma > \sigma_0 \tag{9.2.13}$$

In addition, the integral in Eq. 9.2.12 is simply the Laplace transform of $f(t)$, i.e.,

$$F(s) = \int_{0^-}^{\infty} f(t)e^{-st}\,dt \tag{9.2.14}$$

Combining Eqs. 9.2.13 and 9.2.14 with Eq. 9.2.12 gives the desired result:

$$\mathcal{L}\left[\frac{d}{dt}(f(t))\right] = sF(s) - f(0^-) \tag{9.2.15}$$

We can easily extend this development one step further to obtain the Laplace transform of the second derivative of $f(t)$ with respect to time:

$$\mathcal{L}\left[\frac{d^2f}{dt^2}\right] = s^2F(s) - sf(0^-) - f^{(1)}(0^-) \tag{9.2.16}$$

where $f^{(1)}(0^-)$ is the first derivative of $f(t)$ evaluated at $t = 0^-$. A general relationship can be similarly derived as

$$\mathcal{L}\left[\frac{d^nf}{dt^n}\right] = s^nF(s) - s^{n-1}f(0^-) - s^{n-2}f^{(1)}(0^-) - \cdots - f^{(n-1)}(0^-) \tag{9.2.17}$$

where $f^{(k)}(0^-)$ is the $k$th derivative of $f(t)$ evaluated at $t = 0^-$.

*Example 9.2.1*

Assume initial conditions $y(0^-) = y_0$, $y^{(1)}(0^-) = y_1$, $x(0^-) = 0$ and solve for $Y(s)$ from the relationship

$$\frac{d^2y}{dt^2} + a_1\frac{dy}{dt} + a_0y = b_1\frac{dx}{dt} + b_0x$$

*Solution*

The given differential equation can be viewed as representing the equation of operation for an electrical network. $y(t)$ is then the network response to a known driving function $x(t)$. Since we want to solve for $Y(s)$, the Laplace transform of $y(t)$, we begin by Laplace transforming the differential equation. We obtain

$$\mathcal{L}\left[\frac{d^2y}{dt^2} + a_1\frac{dy}{dt} + a_0y\right] = \mathcal{L}\left[b_1\frac{dx}{dt} + b_0x\right]$$

The Laplace transform is *linear*, hence the above equation reduces to

$$\mathcal{L}\left[\frac{d^2y}{dt^2}\right] + a_1\mathcal{L}\left[\frac{dy}{dt}\right] + a_0\mathcal{L}[y] = b_1\mathcal{L}\left[\frac{dx}{dt}\right] + b_0\,\mathcal{L}\,[x]$$

Applying the differentiation property (9.2.17) gives

$$[s^2 + a_1s + a_0]Y(s) = [b_1s + b_0]X(s) + [s + a_1]y_0 + y_1$$

or solving for $Y(s)$, we obtain

$$Y(s) = \left[\frac{b_1s + b_0}{s^2 + a_1s + a_0}\right]X(s) + \left[\frac{s + a_1}{s^2 + a_1s + a_0}\right]y_0 + \left[\frac{1}{s^2 + a_1s + a_0}\right]y_1$$

This example shows that we can transform differential equations into simple algebraic equations while simultaneously introducing the necessary initial conditions. We will later examine methods for determining $y(t)$ from $Y(s)$.

### Time Integration

The Laplace transform of the integral of the function $f(t)$ with respect to the time variable is given by

$$\mathcal{L}\left[\int_a^t f(\sigma)\,d\sigma\right] = \frac{F(s)}{s} + \frac{f^{(-1)}(0^-)}{s} \qquad (9.2.18)$$

where

$$f^{(-1)}(0^-) = \begin{cases} \displaystyle\int_a^{0^-} f(\sigma)\,d\sigma & \text{when } a < 0^- \\ 0 & \text{otherwise} \end{cases} \qquad (9.2.19)$$

To prove this result we substitute $\displaystyle\int_a^t f(\sigma)\,d\sigma$ into the definition of the Laplace transformation to obtain

$$\mathcal{L}\left[\int_a^t f(\sigma)\,d\sigma\right] = \int_{0^-}^\infty \left\{\int_a^t f(\sigma)\,d\sigma\right\} e^{-st}\,dt \qquad (9.2.20)$$

Using integration by parts gives

$$\mathcal{L}\left[\int_a^t f(\sigma)\,d\sigma\right] = \left\{\int_a^t f(\sigma)\,d\sigma\frac{e^{-st}}{-s}\Big|_{0^-}^{\infty} + \int_{0^-}^{\infty}\frac{e^{-st}}{s}f(t)\,dt \right. \quad (9.2.21)$$

Recalling that $\int_a^t f(\sigma)\,d\sigma$ is of exponential order, evaluating at the upper limit, the first term in Eq. 9.2.21 yields zero and according to Eq. 9.2.19 the lower limit yields $f^{(-1)}(0^-)$. The second term in Eq. 9.2.21 is recognized as being the Laplace transform of $f(t)$ divided by the complex variable $s$. Hence, Eq. 9.2.21 reduces to the desired result:

$$\mathcal{L}\left[\int_a^t f(\sigma)\,d\sigma\right] = \frac{F(s)}{s} + \frac{f^{(-1)}(0^-)}{s} \quad (9.2.22)$$

As in the case of time differentiation, we can easily generalize Eq. 9.2.22 to

$$\mathcal{L}\left[\int_{a_n}^t \int_{a_{n-1}}^t \cdots \int_{a_1}^t f(\sigma)(d\sigma)^n\right] = \frac{F(s)}{s^n} + \sum_{i=1}^n \frac{f^{(-i)}(0^-)}{s^{n-i+1}} \quad (9.2.23)$$

where

$$f^{(-i)}(0^-) = \int_{a_i}^{0^-} \cdots \int_{a_1}^{0^-} f(\sigma)\,(d\sigma)^i \quad (9.2.24)$$

### Translation of the Time Axis

If $f(t)u_0(t)$ is translated on the time axis by an amount $t_0$, the Laplace transform of the translated function can be expressed as

$$\mathcal{L}[f(t - t_0)u_0(t - t_0)] = e^{-st_0}F(s) \quad (9.2.25)$$

where $F(s) = \mathcal{L}[f(t)]$. This relationship is obtained by using the definition of the Laplace transformation

$$\mathcal{L}[f(t - t_0)u_0(t - t_0)] = \int_{t_0^-}^{\infty} f(t - t_0)e^{-st}\,dt \quad (9.2.26)$$

Letting $\tau = t - t_0$ in the right-hand side of Eq. 9.2.26 gives

$$\mathcal{L}[f(t - t_0)u_0(t - t_0)] = e^{-st_0}\int_{0^-}^{\infty} f(\tau)e^{-s\tau}\,d\tau = e^{-st_0}F(s) \quad (9.2.27)$$

### Change of Scale in the Time Domain

Mathematically a change of scale is represented by multiplying the time variable $t$ by a positive scaling factor $b$. Hence the function $f(t)$ after rescaling of the time axis becomes $f(bt)$. To determine the effect of a time-scale change on the Laplace transform we again use the transform definition in Eq. 9.2.2. We have

$$\mathcal{L}[f(bt)] = \int_{0^-}^{\infty} f(bt)e^{-st}\, dt \qquad (9.2.28)$$

Making the change of variable $t = \tau/b$ with $b > 0$,

$$\mathcal{L}[f(bt)] = \frac{1}{b} \int_{0^-}^{\infty} f(\tau)e^{-(s/b)\tau}\, d\tau = \frac{1}{b} F\left(\frac{s}{b}\right) \qquad (9.2.29)$$

Hence scaling by the factor $b$ in the time domain corresponds to scaling the complex variable $s$ by the factor $1/b$.

*Example 9.2.2*

Calculate the Laplace transform of the function (a) $e^{-at}u_0(t)$, (b), $e^{-a(t-1)}u_0(t - 1)$, and (c) $e^{-a(t-1)}u_0(t)$.

*Solution*

We can calculate the transform in each case from definition (9.2.2):

(a)
$$\mathcal{L}[e^{-at}u_0(t)] = \int_{0^-}^{\infty} e^{-at}e^{-st}\, dt = \frac{e^{-(s+a)t}}{-(s + a)}\Big|_{0^-}^{\infty}$$

Now if $\text{Re}[s] = \sigma > -a$, the upper limit will become zero and the lower limit reduces to $\dfrac{1}{s + a}$; hence,

$$\mathcal{L}[e^{-at}u_0(t)] = \frac{1}{s + a}; \qquad \sigma > -a \qquad (9.2.30)$$

(b)
$$\mathcal{L}[e^{-a(t-1)}u_0(t - 1)] = \int_{0^-}^{\infty} e^{-a(t-1)}u_0(t - 1)\, e^{-st}\, dt$$

$$= \int_{1^-}^{\infty} e^{-a(t-1)}u_0(t - 1)\, e^{-st}\, dt$$

Making the change of variable $\tau = t - 1$ in the above integral gives

$$\mathcal{L}[e^{-a(t-1)}u_0(t - 1)] = e^{-s} \int_{0^-}^{\infty} e^{-a\tau}e^{-s\tau}\, d\tau = \frac{e^{-s}}{s + a} \qquad (9.2.31)$$

Comparing (a) and (b), we have an illustration of time axis translation and its effect on the Laplace transform. We could have obtained Eq. 9.2.31 from Eq. 9.2.30 by simply applying the translation property.

(c)
$$\mathcal{L}[e^{-a(t-1)}u_0(t)] = \int_{0^-}^{\infty} e^{-a(t-1)}e^{-st}\, dt = \frac{e^a}{s + a}$$

### Multiplication by Time

We next consider the effect on the Laplace transform of a multiplication in the time domain by the time variable $t$. To determine this effect we multiply a function $f(t)$ by $t$ and calculate the Laplace transform of the product. Using the definition in Eq. 9.2.2, the transform is written as

$$\mathcal{L}[tf(t)] = \int_{0^-}^{\infty} tf(t)e^{-st}\,dt \tag{9.2.32}$$

Notice that

$$te^{-st} = -\frac{d}{ds}(e^{-st}) \tag{9.2.33}$$

Substitution of Eq. 9.2.33 into Eq. 9.2.32 yields

$$\mathcal{L}[tf(t)] = -\int_{0^-}^{\infty} f(t)\frac{d}{ds}(e^{-st})\,dt = -\frac{d}{ds}\int_{0^-}^{\infty} f(t)e^{-st}\,dt \tag{9.2.34}$$

The interchange of differentiation and integration on the right-hand side of Eq. 9.2.34 is valid for most functions, $f(t)$, which are of importance in engineering analysis and for all functions which we will be using in this text. The right-hand side of Eq. 9.2.34 is recognized as being the negative derivative with respect to $s$ of the Laplace transform of $f(t)$. Thus we have the complex differentiation property

$$\mathcal{L}[tf(t)] = -\frac{d}{ds}F(s) \tag{9.2.35}$$

More generally, under similar restrictions on the interchange of differentiation with respect to $s$ and integration with respect to $t$, we can obtain

$$\mathcal{L}[t^n f(t)] = (-1)^n \frac{d^n}{ds^n}F(s) \tag{9.2.36}$$

**Division by Time**

Dividing a time function by the variable $t$ corresponds to an integration operation with respect to the variable $s$. To show this, we again resort to the defining relationship in Eq. 9.2.2. We have

$$\mathcal{L}\left[\frac{f(t)}{t}\right] = \int_{0^-}^{\infty} \frac{f(t)}{t}e^{-st}\,dt \tag{9.2.37}$$

We note that

$$\frac{e^{-st}}{t} = \int_{s}^{\infty} e^{-st}\,ds \tag{9.2.38}$$

Hence, substituting Eq. 9.2.38 into Eq. 9.2.37 and interchanging the order of integration gives

$$\mathcal{L}\left[\frac{f(t)}{t}\right] = \int_{s}^{\infty} ds \int_{0^-}^{\infty} f(t)e^{-st}\,dt = \int_{s}^{\infty} F(s)\,ds \tag{9.2.39}$$

More generally, we can derive the division by time property for any integer power of $t$ to yield

$$\mathcal{L}\left[\frac{f(t)}{t^n}\right] = \underbrace{\int_s^\infty ds \cdots \int_s^\infty}_{n \text{ integrals}} F(s)\, ds \tag{9.2.40}$$

*Example 9.2.3*

Calculate the Laplace transform of $t^n u_0(t)$.

*Solution*

First, we calculate the Laplace transform of $u_0(t)$.

$$\mathcal{L}\left[u_0(t)\right] = \int_{0^-}^\infty e^{-st}\, dt = \left.\frac{e^{-st}}{-s}\right|_{0^-}^\infty = \frac{1}{s}$$

TABLE 9.2.1. USEFUL LAPLACE TRANSFORMS.

|  | $f(t)$ | $F(s)$ |
|---|---|---|
| 1. | $\delta(t)$ | $1$ |
| 2. | $u_0(t)$ | $\dfrac{1}{s}$ |
| 3. | $t^n u_0(t)$ | $\dfrac{n!}{s^{n+1}}$ |
| 4. | $\exp(-at)u_0(t)$ | $\dfrac{1}{s+a}$ |
| 5. | $t^n \exp(-at)u_0(t)$ | $\dfrac{n!}{(s+a)^{n+1}}$ |
| 6. | $\cos(bt)u_0(t)$ | $\dfrac{s}{s^2+b^2}$ |
| 7. | $\sin(bt)u_0(t)$ | $\dfrac{b}{s^2+b^2}$ |
| 8. | $\cosh(bt)u_0(t)$ | $\dfrac{s}{s^2-b^2}$ |
| 9. | $\sinh(bt)u_0(t)$ | $\dfrac{b}{s^2-b^2}$ |
| 10. | $e^{-at}\cos(bt)u_0(t)$ | $\dfrac{s+a}{(s+a)^2+b^2}$ |
| 11. | $e^{-at}\sin(bt)u_0(t)$ | $\dfrac{b}{(s+a)^2+b^2}$ |
| 12. | $[K_1 e^{-at}\cos bt$ $+\left(\dfrac{K_2 - K_1 a}{b}\right)e^{-at}\sin bt]$ $\cdot u_0(t)$ | $\dfrac{K_1 s + K_2}{(s+a)^2+b^2}$ |

Applying multiplication by time property

$$\mathcal{L}\left[t^n u_0(t)\right] = (-1)^n \frac{d^n}{ds^n}\left(\frac{1}{s}\right) = \frac{n!}{s^{n+1}}$$

where $n! \triangleq n(n-1)(n-2)\cdots 3 \times 2 \times 1$. Table 9.2.1 lists a number of additional Laplace transforms which can be calculated using the defining integral (9.2.2) with $t_0 = 0$.

As indicated previously, the Laplace transform is an alternate solution method for the network response. This implies, as in Example 9.2.1, that we first solve for the Laplace transform of the desired response and then solve for time function from this transform. In general, there are two ways in which we can approach this inverse transform problem. The most direct approach is to use the *complex inversion integral*, not developed in this text. A second approach is to rearrange $F(s)$ into a summation of simple factors, similar to those shown in Table 9.2.1, from which the time function can be recognized. This second approach of inverting the transform into a time function is valid because of the uniqueness property of the Laplace transform. A formalized approach to resolving $F(s)$ into a summation of simple factors is called the *method of partial fraction expansion*. This second approach is the one we will follow in this text.

## 9.3. PARTIAL-FRACTION EXPANSION

The method of partial fraction expansion is based on expanding a rational function of $s$ in terms of the factors of the denominator polynomial. By a rational function we mean a function that can be written as a ratio of two polynomials in $s$. Consider the function

$$F(s) = \frac{b_m s^m + b_{m-1} s^{m-1} + \cdots + b_1 s + b_0}{a_n s^n + a_{n-1} s^{n-1} + \cdots + a_1 s + a_0} = \frac{N(s)}{D(s)} \qquad (9.3.1)$$

where $a_k$, $k = 0,1,\ldots,n$ and $b_k$, $k = 0,1,\ldots,m$ are real numbers. Let $N(s)$ denote the numerator polynomial and, likewise, $D(s)$ denote the denominator polynomial. Throughout we assume that $m \leq n$. The roots of the equation

$$N(s) = 0 \qquad (9.3.2)$$

are said to be the *zeros* of $F(s)$. The roots of the equation

$$D(s) = 0 \qquad (9.3.3)$$

are said to be the *poles* of $F(s)$.

Let us rewrite Eq. 9.3.1 after dividing by $a_n$ as

$$F(s) = \frac{\frac{1}{a_n}[b_m s^m + b_{m-1} s^{m-1} + \cdots + b_1 s + b_0]}{s^n + \frac{a_{n-1}}{a_n} s^{n-1} + \cdots + \frac{a_0}{a_n}}$$

$$= \frac{N_1(s)}{s^n + \frac{a_{n-1}}{a_n} s^{n-1} + \cdots + \frac{a_0}{a_n}} \qquad (9.3.4)$$

## Simple Poles

If all the poles of $F(s)$ are of first order, we can factor the denominator in the form

$$F(s) = \frac{N_1(s)}{(s - p_1)\cdots(s - p_k)\cdots(s - p_n)} \qquad (9.3.5)$$

where each of the $p_i$ are distinct. Using the partial-fraction expansion we want to express $F(s)$ as

$$F(s) = \frac{r_1}{(s - p_1)} + \cdots + \frac{r_k}{(s - p_k)} + \cdots + \frac{r_n}{(s - p_n)} \qquad (9.3.6)$$

where $r_1, \ldots, r_k, \ldots, r_n$ are nonzero finite constants. Equations 9.3.5 and 9.3.6 must be equal for such an expansion to be valid. This requires

$$\frac{N_1(s)}{(s - p_1)\cdots(s - p_k)\cdots(s - p_n)}$$

$$= \frac{r_1}{(s - p_1)} + \cdots + \frac{r_k}{(s - p_k)} + \cdots + \frac{r_n}{(s - p_n)} \qquad (9.3.7)$$

To evaluate $r_k$ for any $k$, we multiply both sides by $(s - p_k)$ and let $s \to p_k$. We obtain

$$r_k = \lim_{s \to p_k} (s - p_k)F(s) \qquad (9.3.8)$$

$r_k$ is called the *residue* of $F(s)$ for pole $s = p_k$. Equation 9.3.8 is valid for $k = 1, 2, \ldots, n$.

*Example 9.3.1*

Find the partial-fraction expansion of

$$F(s) = \frac{8s + 2}{(s^2 + 3s + 2)}$$

*Solution*

We have

$$F(s) = \frac{8s + 2}{s^2 + 3s + 2} = \frac{8s + 2}{(s + 1)(s + 2)} = \frac{r_1}{s + 1} + \frac{r_2}{s + 2}$$

Here

$$r_1 = \lim_{s \to -1} (s + 1)F(s) = \lim_{s \to -1} (s + 1) \cdot \frac{8s + 2}{(s + 1)(s + 2)} = -6$$

$$r_2 = \lim_{s \to -2} (s + 2)F(s) = \lim_{s \to -2} (s + 2) \cdot \frac{8s + 2}{(s + 1)(s + 2)} = 14$$

Therefore

$$F(s) = -\frac{6}{s + 1} + \frac{14}{s + 2}$$

It is possible that some of the poles in Eq. 9.3.6 are complex. When this is the case some simplifications occur. Recall the coefficients, $a_k$, $k = 0, 1, \ldots, n$ in the equation

$$D(s) = a_n s^n + a_{n-1} s^{n-1} + \cdots + a_1 s + a_0 = 0$$

are real. Hence, if $p_k$ is a complex root to this equation then, its *complex conjugate*, $p_k^*$, is also a root. The number of complex poles will, therefore, always be even; the complex poles occurring in complex conjugate pairs.

*Example 9.3.2*

Find the partial-fraction expansion of

$$F(s) = \frac{s + 3}{(s + 1)(s^2 + 4s + 8)}$$

*Solution*

We factor the denominator of $F(s)$ and write

$$F(s) = \frac{s + 3}{(s + 1)(s + 2 + 2j)(s + 2 - 2j)} = \frac{r_1}{s + 1} + \frac{r_2}{s + 2 + 2j} + \frac{r_3}{s + 2 - 2j}$$

We obtain

$$r_1 = \lim_{s \to -1} (s + 1)F(s) = \lim_{s \to -1} \frac{s + 3}{s^2 + 4s + 8} = \frac{2}{5}$$

$$r_2 = \lim_{s \to -2 - 2j} (s + 2 + 2j)F(s) = \lim_{s \to -2 - 2j} \frac{s + 3}{(s + 1)(s + 2 - 2j)}$$

$$= \frac{1 - 2j}{(-1 - 2j)(-4j)} = \frac{1 - 2j}{-8 + 4j} = \frac{1 - 2j}{-8 + 4j} \cdot \frac{-8 - 4j}{-8 - 4j}$$

$$= \frac{-16 + 12j}{80} = -\frac{1}{5} + \frac{3}{20} j$$

To obtain $r_3$ we can use the fact that $r_3 = r_2^*$, therefore

$$r_3 = -\frac{1}{5} - \frac{3}{20} j$$

The reader is encouraged to check $r_3$ independently using Eq. 9.3.8. Hence

$$F(s) = \frac{\frac{2}{5}}{s + 1} + \frac{-\frac{1}{5} + \frac{3}{20} j}{s + 2 + 2j} + \frac{-\frac{1}{5} - \frac{3}{20} j}{s + 2 - 2j}$$

In order to avoid the complex representation, the last two terms can be combined. After simplification we obtain

$$F(s) = \frac{2/_5}{s + 1} - \frac{1/_5(2s + 1)}{s^2 + 4s + 8}$$

## Alternate Representation for Complex Poles

We saw in the previous example how complex poles can be combined to yield a quadratic term in the partial fraction expansion. This type of expansion does not involve complex numbers and is sometimes preferable. We can actually obtain it directly without utilizing the intermediate complex representation. Let us illustrate this procedure by considering one real pole and two complex conjugate poles. Consider

$$F(s) = \frac{N(s)}{(s - p_1)(s^2 + as + b)} \tag{9.3.9}$$

We can write

$$F(s) = \frac{N(s)}{(s - p_1)(s^2 + as + b)} = \frac{r_1}{s - p_1} + \frac{r_2 s + r_3}{s^2 + as + b} \tag{9.3.10}$$

Evaluating $r_1$ as before, we have

$$r_1 = \lim_{s \to p_1} (s - p_1)F(s) \tag{9.3.11}$$

To obtain $r_2$ and $r_3$, we note that

$$N(s) = r_1(s^2 + as + b) + (r_2 s + r_3)(s - p_1) \tag{9.3.12}$$

Since the equality must hold for all values of $s$, the coefficients of various powers of $s$ on both sides of the equality must be equal. These equations of equality are solved to obtain $r_2$ and $r_3$.

This procedure is easy to use even if we have many pairs of complex conjugate poles. The partial fraction for each complex conjugate pair will be of the form above.

*Example 9.3.3*

Let us consider the $F(s)$ of Example 9.3.2.

$$F(s) = \frac{s + 3}{(s + 1)(s^2 + 4s + 8)}$$

We write it as

$$F(s) = \frac{s + 3}{(s + 1)(s^2 + 4s + 8)} = \frac{r_1}{s + 1} + \frac{r_2 s + r_3}{s^2 + 4s + 8}$$

Now $r_1$ is found exactly as before and is $2/5$. To find $r_2$ and $r_3$, we note from the above equation that

$$(s + 3) = r_1(s^2 + 4s + 8) + (r_2 s + r_3)(s + 1)$$

Since $r_1$ is known, we need two equations in $r_2$ and $r_3$. We compare coefficients of $s^2$ term and the constant term to get

$$0 = r_1 + r_2$$

and

$$3 = 8r_1 + r_3$$

Therefore

$$r_2 = -r_1 = -\tfrac{2}{5}$$
$$r_3 = 3 - 8r_1 = -\tfrac{1}{5}$$

Hence

$$F(s) = \frac{\tfrac{2}{5}}{s + 1} - \frac{\tfrac{1}{5}(2s + 1)}{s^2 + 4s + 8}$$

which checks with the result obtained in Example 9.3.2.

**Multiple Poles**

In case of multiple poles, obtaining the partial-fraction expansion is more involved. Let us assume that $F(s)$ has all simple poles except say at $s = p_1$ which has a multiplicity $m$. Then we can write

$$F(s) = \frac{N(s)}{(s - p_1)^m(s - p_2)\cdots(s - p_k)\cdots(s - p_n)} \tag{9.3.13}$$

The partial-fraction expansion of $F(s)$ is now given as

$$F(s) = \frac{r_{11}}{(s - p_1)^m} + \frac{r_{12}}{(s - p_1)^{m-1}} + \cdots + \frac{r_{1m}}{(s - p_1)} + \frac{r_2}{(s - p_2)}$$
$$+ \cdots + \frac{r_k}{(s - p_k)} + \cdots + \frac{r_n}{(s - p_n)} \tag{9.3.14}$$

Note that for each simple pole $p_k$ we have just one coefficient $r_k$. However for the multiple pole at $p_1$ we have $m$ coefficients $r_{11}\ldots r_{1m}$.

For simple poles we can proceed as before and obtain

$$r_k = \lim_{s \to p_k} (s - p_k)F(s), \qquad k = 2,\ldots,n \tag{9.3.15}$$

To find $r_{11}\cdots r_{1m}$ we multiply both sides of Eq. 9.3.13 by $(s - p_1)^m$ to obtain

$$(s - p_1)^m F(s) = r_{11} + (s - p_1)r_{12} + \cdots + (s - p_1)^{m-1}r_{1m}$$
$$+ (s - p_1)^m\left\{\frac{r_2}{s - p_2} + \cdots + \frac{r_n}{s - p}\right\} \tag{9.3.16}$$

If we let $s = p_1$ on both sides, we get

$$r_{11} = \lim_{s \to p_1} (s - p_1)^m F(s) \tag{9.3.17}$$

Now we differentiate Eq. 9.3.16 with respect to $s$ and let $s \to p_1$, we have

$$r_{12} = \lim_{s \to p_1} \frac{d}{ds} [(s - p_1)^m F(s)] \tag{9.3.18}$$

We can continue this differentiation process to find the $i$th coefficient $r_{1i}$

$$r_{1i} = \lim_{s \to p_1} \frac{1}{(i - 1)!} \frac{d^{i-1}}{ds^{i-1}} [(s - p_1)^m F(s)] \tag{9.3.19}$$

for

$$i = 1, 2, \ldots, m.$$

We note that $r_2 \cdots r_n$ terms play no role in determining $r_{11}, r_{12} \cdots r_{1m}$ because of the multiplying factor $(s - p_1)^m$ in Eq. 9.3.16.

*Example 9.3.4*

Obtain the partial-fraction expansion of

$$F(s) = \frac{s + 2}{(s + 1)^2 (s + 3)}$$

*Solution*

Note that we have one pole of multiplicity 2. We write

$$F(s) = \frac{r_{11}}{(s + 1)^2} + \frac{r_{12}}{s + 1} + \frac{r_2}{s + 3}$$

where

$$r_2 = \lim_{s \to -3} (s + 3) \cdot \frac{s + 2}{(s + 1)^2 (s + 3)} = -\frac{1}{4}$$

To obtain $r_{11}$ and $r_{12}$, we use Eq. 9.3.19:

$$r_{11} = \lim_{s \to -1} (s + 1)^2 F(s) = \lim_{s \to -1} \frac{s + 2}{s + 3} = \frac{1}{2}$$

$$r_{12} = \lim_{s \to -1} \frac{1}{(2 - 1)!} \frac{d}{ds} [(s + 1)^2 F(s)] = \lim_{s \to -1} \frac{d}{ds} \left[ \frac{s + 2}{s + 3} \right]$$

$$= \lim_{s \to -1} \frac{(s + 3) - (s + 2)}{(s + 3)^2} = \frac{1}{4}$$

Hence

$$F(s) = \frac{\frac{1}{2}}{(s + 1)^2} + \frac{\frac{1}{4}}{(s + 1)} - \frac{\frac{1}{4}}{(s + 3)}$$

*Example 9.3.5*

Obtain the partial-fraction expansion of

$$F(s) = \frac{s^2 + 3s + 1}{(s + 1)^3 (s + 2)^2}$$

*Solution*

In this case we have three poles at $s = -1$ and two poles at $s = -2$. We write

$$F(s) = \frac{r_{11}}{(s + 1)^3} + \frac{r_{12}}{(s + 1)^2} + \frac{r_{13}}{(s + 1)} + \frac{r_{21}}{(s + 2)^2} + \frac{r_{22}}{(s + 2)}$$

We evaluate

$$r_{11} = \lim_{s \to -1} (s + 1)^3 F(s) = \lim_{s \to -1} \frac{s^2 + 3s + 1}{(s + 2)^2} = -1$$

$$r_{12} = \lim_{s \to -1} \frac{d}{ds} \{(s + 1)^3 F(s)\} = \lim_{s \to -1} \frac{d}{ds} \left\{ \frac{s^2 + 3s + 1}{(s + 2)^2} \right\}$$

$$= \lim_{s \to -1} \frac{(s + 2)^2 (2s + 3) - 2(s^2 + 3s + 1) \cdot (s + 2)}{(s + 2)^4}$$

$$= \lim_{s \to -1} \frac{s + 4}{(s + 2)^3} = 3$$

Similarly,

$$r_{13} = \lim_{s \to -1} \frac{1}{2!} \frac{d^2}{ds^2} \{(s + 1)^3 F(s)\} = \lim_{s \to -1} \frac{1}{2} \frac{d}{ds} \left\{ \frac{s + 4}{(s + 2)^3} \right\}$$

$$= \lim_{s \to -1} \frac{-s - 5}{(s + 2)^4} = -4$$

Also

$$r_{21} = \lim_{s \to -2} (s + 2)^2 F(s) = \lim_{s \to -2} \frac{s^2 + 3s + 1}{(s + 1)^3} = 1$$

Similarly,

$$r_{22} = \lim_{s \to -2} \frac{d}{ds} \{(s + 2)^2 F(s)\} = \lim_{s \to -2} \frac{d}{ds} \left\{ \frac{s^2 + 3s + 1}{(s + 1)^3} \right\}$$

$$= \lim_{s \to -2} \frac{-s(s + 4)}{(s + 1)^4} = 4$$

Hence

$$F(s) = \frac{-1}{(s + 1)^3} + \frac{3}{(s + 1)^2} - \frac{4}{s + 1} + \frac{1}{(s + 2)^2} + \frac{4}{s + 2}$$

*Example 9.3.6*

Obtain the time function corresponding to

$$F(s) = \frac{s^2 + 3s + 1}{(s + 1)^3 (s + 2)^2}$$

*Solution*

$F(s)$ as given above was expanded by partial-fraction expansion in Example 9.3.5. We obtained

$$F(s) = \frac{-1}{(s + 1)^3} + \frac{3}{(s + 1)^2} - \frac{4}{s + 1} + \frac{1}{(s + 2)^2} + \frac{4}{s + 2}$$

Using Table 9.2.1 on page 289 we can write the corresponding time function

$$f(t) = -\tfrac{1}{2} t^2 e^{-t} u_0(t) + 3te^{-t} u_0(t) - 4e^{-t} u_0(t) + te^{-2t} u_0(t) + 4e^{-2t} u_0(t)$$

## Use of the Digital Computer to Find the Roots of a Polynomial Equation

We have seen above that if the denominator is known in the factored form we can break the function $F(s)$ into partial fractions without great difficulty. Once the partial fractions are known, the corresponding time function is easily obtained.

In most cases the denominator of $F(s)$ will not be known in the factored form and it will be necessary to find the roots of the denominator polynomial. If the denominator is a quadratic, there is no problem. However, if the denominator is of higher order, finding the roots can be difficult. One should try to find the roots by inspection. If this is not possible, the computer can be of great help.

Computer programs for finding roots of a polynomial equation are available in most computer libraries. Here we will develop a very simple computer program which is sufficient for the work developed in this text.

We will develop a computer program to find the roots of the denominator polynomial. We will assume that it has no more than two complex roots. For the work considered in this text we will not encounter more than one pair of complex roots. We will also limit ourselves up to a fourth-order denominator, which is sufficient for our work. We write the denominator as

$$D(s) = a_4 s^4 + a_3 s^3 + a_2 s^2 + a_1 s + a_0 \qquad (9.3.20)$$

where we will normally have $a_4 = 1$. For a cubic equation we will normally have $a_4 = 0$ and $a_3 = 1$. There are several ways of extracting the roots of an equation. One method which is used extensively and which we will discuss is the Newton-Raphson method. We assume, of course, that there are at least two real roots. Newton-Raphson method is used to extract the real roots. Once we have two real roots say $s_1$ and $s_2$, we can divide these out to obtain

$$D(s) = a_4(s - s_1)(s - s_2)(s^2 + as + b) \qquad (9.3.21)$$

Now the quadratic is easily factored to get the complex roots or the real roots if there are no complex roots.

### Newton-Raphson Method for Extracting Real Roots of an Equation

Consider the equation

$$D(s) = a_4 s^4 + a_3 s^3 + a_2 s^2 + a_1 s + a_0 = 0 \qquad (9.3.22)$$

We want to find a *real value* of $s = \bar{s}$ which makes $D(s) = 0$. Let us assume a plot of $D(s)$ near $s = \bar{s}$ as shown in Fig. 9.3.1.

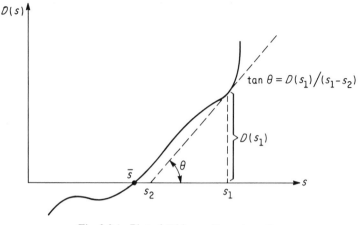

Fig. 9.3.1. Plot of $D(s)$ near its root $s = \bar{s}$.

We make an initial guess $s = s_1$ for the root. This is not difficult and can be done by inspection. Let $s_2$ be a better value of the root obtained from $s_1$ by

$$s_2 = s_1 - \Delta s \qquad (9.3.23)$$

where

$$\Delta s = \frac{D(s_1)}{D'(s_1)}, \quad D'(s_1) = \frac{d}{ds} D(s)\Big|_{s=s_1} \qquad (9.3.24)$$

Or, in general, let $s_{i+1}$ be the $(i + 1)$st iteration of the original guess $s_1$, then

$$s_{i+1} = s_i - \frac{D(s_i)}{D'(s_i)} \qquad (9.3.25)$$

This iteration formula will converge to the root of $s = \bar{s}$ if our initial guess was not too far from the root and if $D(s)$ is well behaved near $s = \bar{s}$. We will assume for our discussion here that such is the case. Whenever $s_{i+1} \cong s_i$ we can stop the iteration and that value of $s_i$ is the root $\bar{s}$. In case $s_{i+1}$ does not converge to $s_i$ we should try a better guess. We want to emphasize that the formula given in (9.3.25) should be used with care and is only useful for some of the simpler polynomials encountered in this text.

Now substituting $D(s)$ from Eq. 9.3.22 into Eq. 9.3.25, the root iteration formula becomes

$$s_{i+1} = s_i - \frac{a_4 s_i^4 + a_3 s_i^3 + a_2 s_i^2 + a_1 s_i + a_0}{4a_4 s_i^3 + 3a_3 s_i^2 + 2a_2 s_i + a_1} \qquad (9.3.26)$$

where $s_1$ (for $i = 1$) is the initial guess of the root and is the starting point. All we have to do is to extract a maximum of two roots, the remaining

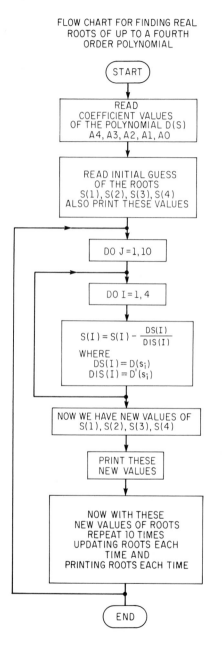

FLOW CHART FOR FINDING REAL
ROOTS OF UP TO A FOURTH
ORDER POLYNOMIAL

quadratic can be easily solved. We can in fact start with a number of initial values, let us assume four.

We then let them iterate simultaneously. If we solve for one root, we can divide it out and begin again with the resulting cubic equation. If we determine more than one root our problem is solved. If we do not determine any roots we begin again with a better guess of the initial values. Note that this program works only if there are no more than two complex roots.

### Development of the Flow Chart for Computer Program for Finding the Real
#### Roots of up to a Fourth-Order Polynomial

Let the initial guess of the roots be $S(1)$, $S(2)$, $S(3)$, and $S(4)$. The initial guess can be made by inspecting $D(s) = 0$ and determining when $D(s)$ changes sign as different values of $s$ are substituted.

The flow chart for the development of the computer program is given on the previous page and the computer program itself is given below.

### Computer Program for Finding the Real Roots of up to Fourth-Order Polynomial

```
C       THIS PROGRAM EXTRACTS THE REAL ROOTS OF UPTO A FOURTH
C       ORDER POLYNOMIAL, KNOWLEDGE OF APPROXIMATE REAL ROOT
C       OR ROOTS IS ASSUMED, FURTHER IT IS ASSUMED THAT THERE
C       IS NO MORE THAN ONE PAIR OF COMPLEX ROOTS,
        DIMENSION S(4),DS(4),DIS(4)
C       READ IN THE VALUES OF THE COEFFICIENTS
C       OF THE POLYNOMIAL,
        A0=
        A1=
        A2=
        A3=
        A4=
C       READ IN THE INITIAL VALUES OF THE ROOTS - JUST A GUESS
        S(1)=
        S(2)=
        S(3)=
        S(4)=
C       NOTE THAT EVEN IF WE FIND ONE REAL ROOT WE CAN DIVIDE
C       IT OUT TO GET A THIRD ORDER POLYNOMIAL AND START AGAIN,
C       ONCE WE REACH A QUADRATIC WE NEED NOT GO ANY FURTHER,
C       HOWEVER IN CASE OF ALL REAL ROOTS THE GUESSED ROOTS
C       MAY CONVERGE TO THE ALL ACTUAL ROOTS, IN THIS CASE WE
C       WILL NOT HAVE A QUADRATIC LEFT,
        DO 9 J=1,10
C       WE PRINT S(I), I=1,2,3,4 AS S(I) CHANGES,
        PRINT 30 (S(I),I=1,4)
C       THIS DO LOOP CALCULATES NEW S(1),S(2),S(3),S(4)
C       STARTING FROM PREVIOUS VALUES,
        DO 11 I=1,4
        DS(I)=(A4*(S(I)**4))+(A3*(S(I)**3))+(A2*(S(I)**2))
       1+(A1*S(I))+A0
        DIS(I)=(4,*A4*(S(I)**3))+(3,*A3*(S(I)**2))
       1+(2,*A2*S(I))+A1
C       NEXT IS THE ITERATING FORMULA,
        S(I)=S(I)-DS(I)/DIS(I)
       11 CONTINUE
        9 CONTINUE
       30 FORMAT (4(F7,3,5X))
        END
```

*Example 9.3.7*

Obtain the partial fractions of

$$F(s) = \frac{s^3 + 2s^2 + 3s + 7}{s^4 + 5s^3 + 11s^2 + 12s + 4.5}$$

Hence, obtain $f(t)$ using Table 9.2.1.

*Solution*

Before we can find partial fractions of $F(s)$, we need to know the denominator of $F(s)$ in the factored form. Here we have

$$D(s) = s^4 + 5s^3 + 11s^2 + 12s + 4.5$$

In order to guess initial values of roots, we try to find the region of values of $s$ in which the real roots of $D(s)$ might be. Quite easily we can substitute $s = 0, s = -1, s = -2, s = -3$ in $D(s)$ to obtain

$$D(0) = 4.5 > 0$$

$$D(-1) = 1 - 5 + 11 - 12 + 4.5 = -0.5 < 0$$

$$D(-2) = 16 - 40 + 44 - 24 + 4.5 = 0.5 > 0$$

$$D(-3) = 81 - 135 + 99 - 36 + 4.5 = 13.5 > 0$$

There is sign change of $D(s)$ between $s = 0$ and $s = -1$ and also between $s = -1$ and $s = -2$. So we can pick the four roots as

$$S(1) = 0, \quad S(2) = -0.5, \quad S(3) = -1, \quad S(4) = -2$$

Here the coefficient values are

$$A4 = 1, \quad A3 = 5, \quad A2 = 11, \quad A1 = 12, \quad A0 = 4.5$$

Now we read in these values. The computer program and the printout of real roots is given below.

```
C       THIS PROGRAM IS FOR EXAMPLE 9.3-7
C       THIS PROGRAM EXTRACTS THE REAL ROOTS OF UPTO A FOURTH
C       ORDER POLYNOMIAL, KNOWLEDGE OF APPROXIMATE REAL ROOT
C       OR ROOTS IS ASSUMED, FURTHER IT IS ASSUMED THAT THERE
C       IS NO MORE THAN ONE PAIR OF COMPLEX ROOTS,
        DIMENSION S(4),DS(4),DIS(4)
C       READ IN THE VALUES OF THE COEFFICIENTS
C       OF THE POLYNOMIAL,
        A0=4.5
        A1=12.0
        A2=11.0
        A3=5.0
        A4=1.0
C       READ IN THE INITIAL VALUES OF THE ROOTS - JUST A GUESS
        S(1)=0.0
        S(2)=-0.5
        S(3)=-1.0
        S(4)=-2.0
C       NOTE THAT EVEN IF WE FIND ONE REAL ROOT WE CAN DIVIDE
C       IT OUT TO GET A THIRD ORDER POLYNOMIAL AND START AGAIN,
C       ONCE WE REACH A QUADRATIC WE NEED NOT GO ANY FURTHER,
C       HOWEVER IN CASE OF ALL REAL ROOTS THE GUESSED ROOTS
C       MAY CONVERGE TO THE ALL ACTUAL ROOTS, IN THIS CASE WE
```

```
C        WILL NOT HAVE A QUADRATIC LEFT,
C        THIS DO LOOP DOES THE ITERATING IN TEN STEPS,
         DO 9 J=1,10
C        WE PRINT S(I), I=1,2,3,4 AS S(I) CHANGES,
         PRINT 30 (S(I),I=1,4)
C        THIS DO LOOP CALCULATES NEW S(1),S(2),S(3),S(4)
C        STARTING FROM PREVIOUS VALUES,
         DO 11 I=1,4
         DS(I)=(A4*(S(I)**4))+(A3*(S(I)**3))+(A2*(S(I)**2))
        1+(A1*S(I))+A0
         DIS(I)=(4.*A4*(S(I)**3))+(3.*A3*(S(I)**2))
        1+(2.*A2*S(I))+A1
C        NEXT IS THE ITERATING FORMULA,
         S(I)=S(I)-DS(I)/DIS(I)
      11 CONTINUE
       9 CONTINUE
      30 FORMAT (4(F7,3,5X))
         END
```

| | | | |
|---|---|---|---|
| .000 | -.500 | -1.000 | -2.000 |
| -.375 | -.662 | -.500 | -1.875 |
| -.606 | -.703 | -.662 | -1.850 |
| -.694 | -.706 | -.703 | -1.849 |
| -.706 | -.706 | -.706 | -1.849 |
| -.706 | -.706 | -.706 | -1.849 |
| -.706 | -.706 | -.706 | -1.849 |
| -.706 | -.706 | -.706 | -1.849 |
| -.706 | -.706 | -.706 | -1.849 |
| -.706 | -.706 | -.706 | -1.849 |

So our real roots are given by $s_1 = -0.706$ and $s_2 = -1.849$. We can factor $D(s)$ to obtain

$$D(s) = (s + 0.706)(s + 1.849)(s^2 + 2.446s + 3.448)$$

The above quadratic is obtained by simple division. $D(s)$ has a pair of complex roots. The partial-fraction expansion is obtained by methods discussed earlier in this section and is given by

$$F(s) = \frac{2.178}{s + 0.706} - \frac{0.734}{s + 1.849} - \frac{0.443(s + 8.8)}{(s + 1.223)^2 + (0.875)^2}$$

Now we use entries in Table 9.2.1 on page 289 and obtain

$$f(t) = [2.178e^{-0.706t} - 0.734e^{-1.849t} - 0.443e^{-1.223t}$$
$$\cdot \{\cos 0.875t + 8.652 \sin 0.875t\}]u_0(t)$$

## 9.4. APPLICATION TO NETWORK ANALYSIS

In applying the Laplace transformation to network analysis problems, we must determine how each of the circuit elements which we have considered in previous chapters is described in transform notation. We should keep in mind that the Laplace transform method applies only to linear

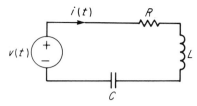

Fig. 9.4.1. Series $RLC$ network.

time-invariant circuits. Before taking up this problem, let us consider the series $RLC$ network shown in Fig. 9.4.1. As we have seen in Chapter 6, the voltage source is related to the current response by

$$v(t) = i(t)R + v_C(0^-) + \frac{1}{C} \int_{0^-}^{t} i(\sigma)\, d\sigma + L\frac{di}{dt}; \quad t \geq 0 \qquad (9.4.1)$$

To solve for the response $i(t)$ we can solve Eq. 9.4.1 directly as in Chapter 6 or, alternately, we can use Laplace transform and solve for $I(s)$ and then take the inverse transform to obtain $i(t)$. We proceed with the second approach, first transforming Eq. 9.4.1 to obtain (we have used Eqs. 9.2.15 and 9.2.22)

$$V(s) = I(s)R + \frac{v_C(0^-)}{s} + \frac{I(s)}{sC} + sLI(s) - Li(0^-) \qquad (9.4.2)$$

Next, from Eq. 9.4.2, we find $I(s)$ as

$$I(s) = \frac{1}{R + \dfrac{1}{sC} + sL}\left[V(s) - \frac{v_C(0^-)}{s} + Li(0^-)\right] \qquad (9.4.3)$$

This represents a solution for the transform of the function we desire. Knowing $V(s)$, we can solve for $i(t)$ from Eq. 9.4.3 and Table 9.2.1 in terms of $R$, $L$, $C$, and the initial conditions. The question arises as to whether we can simplify the solution for $i(t)$ by simply writing Eq. 9.4.3 directly from the circuit diagram without the necessity for writing the integrodifferential equation first. To answer this question we need to examine Kirchhoff's current and voltage law; and $R$, $L$, $C$ voltage-current relationships to determine their representation under Laplace transformation.

### Kirchhoff's Laws

Kirchhoff's voltage and current laws represent linear relationships between voltage variables or current variables within an electrical network. The Laplace transformation preserves these linear relationships. For example, in the network shown in Fig. 9.4.2, application of KVL

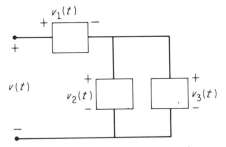

Fig. 9.4.2. Series-parallel network.

gives the linear relationships

$$v(t) = v_1(t) + v_2(t)$$
$$0 = v_2(t) - v_3(t) \tag{9.4.4}$$

Taking the Laplace transform of both sides of Eq. 9.4.4 yields

$$V(s) = V_1(s) + V_2(s)$$
$$0 = V_2(s) - V_3(s) \tag{9.4.5}$$

Next we derive the branch voltage-current relationships (VCR) of *linear time-invariant* resistors, capacitors and inductors in the *s*-domain.

### Resistive Element

A resistive element is specified by its terminal voltage-current relationship

$$v_R(t) = R i_R(t) \tag{9.4.6a}$$

or

$$i_R(t) = G v_R(t) \tag{9.4.6b}$$

which transforms into the equation

$$V_R(s) = R I_R(s) \tag{9.4.7a}$$

or

$$I_R(s) = G V_R(s) \tag{9.4.7b}$$

Comparing Eqs. 9.4.6 and 9.4.7 we see that the constant $R$ completely, describes the relationship between either the resistance terminal voltage

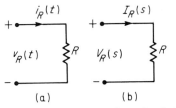

(a)          (b)

Fig. 9.4.3. (a) Time representation of resistive element, (b) transformation of time representation.

and current or the transforms of the terminal voltage and current. This is shown schematically in Fig. 9.4.3. In either the time or transform representation of the circuit, the resistance element is described by the constant $R$.

### Capacitive Element

The capacitive element is described by the time relationship

$$v_C(t) = v_C(0^-) + \frac{1}{C} \int_{0^-}^{t} i_C(\sigma) d\sigma \tag{9.4.8a}$$

or

$$i_C(t) = C \frac{dv_C}{dt} \tag{9.4.8b}$$

Taking the transformation of Eq. 9.4.8 gives

$$V_C(s) = \frac{v_C(0^-)}{s} + \frac{1}{sC} I_C(s) \tag{9.4.9a}$$

and

$$I_C(s) = sCV_C(s) - Cv_C(0^-) \tag{9.4.9b}$$

Thus the capacitive element which is described by either an integral or derivative in the time domain is described by an algebraic relationship after transformation. The parameter $1/sC$ and the initial condition $v_C(0^-)$ completely describe the capacitive element after transformation. Comparing Eq. 9.4.9 with Eq. 9.4.7, we see the parameter $1/sC$ is similar to the resistance parameter $R$ in describing the relationship between voltage and current transforms. For this reason, $1/sC$ is called the *complex capacitive impedance* of the capacitive element. The inverse of this parameter, $sC$, is called the *complex capacitive admittance* of the capacitive element. The relationship expressed in Eq. 9.4.9a indicates that transformation of the capacitive element can be represented by a complex

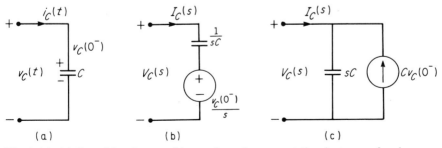

(a)                     (b)                     (c)

Fig. 9.4.4. (a) Capacitive element; (b) transformed representation in terms of series reactance and voltage source; (c) transformed representation in terms of parallel susceptance and current source.

reactance of value $1/sC$ in series with a voltage source of value $\dfrac{v_C(0^-)}{s}$.
Similarly, Eq. 9.4.9b indicates an equivalent representation using a parallel combination of complex susceptance, $sC$, and current source, $Cv_C(0^-)$. These two transformed representations of the capacitance element are shown schematically in Fig. 9.4.4b and c. The use of either representation (b) or (c) will depend upon personal preference and the particular problem to be solved.

### Inductive Element

An inductive element is described by the terminal voltage-current relationship

$$v_L(t) = L \frac{di_L}{dt} \tag{9.4.10a}$$

or

$$i_L(t) = i_L(0^-) + \frac{1}{L} \int_{0^-}^{t} v_L(\sigma)\, d\sigma \tag{9.4.10b}$$

which upon transformation yields

$$V_L(s) = sLI_L(s) - Li_L(0^-) \tag{9.4.11a}$$

and

$$I_L(s) = \frac{i_L(0^-)}{s} + \frac{1}{sL} V_L(s) \tag{9.4.11b}$$

Comparing Eqs. 9.4.11 and 9.4.9, we see that the parameter $sL$ for the inductive element is equivalent to the parameter $1/sC$ for the capacitive element. Hence $sL$ is termed *complex inductive impedance* while $1/sL$ is called the *complex inductive admittance*. The transformed schematic representation of the inductive element are determined from Eq. 9.4.11. These are shown in Fig. 9.4.5b and c.

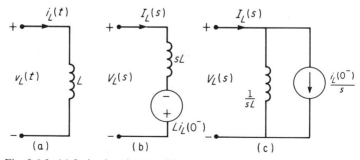

Fig. 9.4.5. (a) Inductive element; (b) transformed representation in terms of series reactance and voltage source; (c) transformed representation in terms of parallel susceptance and current source.

## Other Elements

The transformed schematic representation of other network elements follows in an analogous manner. For example, consider the two-port voltage-current terminal relationships describing the linear transformer shown in Fig. 9.4.6a. We have

$$v_1(t) = L_1 \frac{di_1}{dt} + M \frac{di_2}{dt}$$

$$v_2(t) = M \frac{di_1}{dt} + L_2 \frac{di_2}{dt}$$

(9.4.12)

Using the Laplace transformation on Eq. 9.4.12 gives

$$V_1(s) = sL_1 I_1(s) - L_1 i_1(0^-) + sM I_2(s) - M i_2(0^-)$$

$$V_2(s) = sM I_1(s) - M i_1(0^-) + sL_2 I_2(s) - L_2 i_2(0^-)$$

(9.4.13)

These relationships are shown schematically in Fig. 9.4.6b.

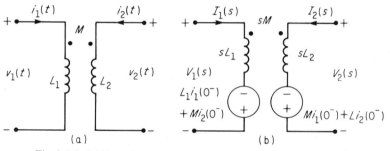

Fig. 9.4.6. (a) Transformer element, (b) transformed representation.

*Example 9.4.2*

Transform the series $RLC$ network shown in Fig. 9.4.7a and derive an expression for the transform of $i(t)$.

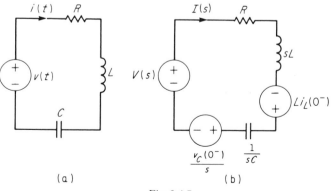

Fig. 9.4.7

*Solution*

Replacing each element in the network by its transformed representation gives the result shown in Fig. 9.4.7b. Note that the initial conditions have been replaced by voltage sources. Applying KVL to the transformed network gives

$$V(s) = I(s)R + I(s)sL - Li_L(0^-) + I(s)\frac{1}{sC} + \frac{v_C(0^-)}{s}$$

or solving for $I(s)$, we obtain

$$I(s) = \frac{1}{R + sL + \dfrac{1}{sC}}\left[V(s) + Li(0^-) - \frac{v_C(0^-)}{s}\right]$$

This is the same result obtained in Eq. 9.4.3.

*Example 9.4.3*

Solve for the current response to a unit step in voltage applied to the series RLC network of Fig. 9.4.7a under zero initial conditions.

*Solution*

Using the development for $I(s)$ in the previous example, we set $i_L(0^-) = v_C(0^-) = 0$ and $V(s) = \frac{1}{s}$. After algebraic simplification, this gives

$$I(s) = \frac{\dfrac{1}{L}}{s^2 + s\dfrac{R}{L} + \dfrac{1}{LC}} = \frac{\dfrac{1}{L}}{(s + s_1)(s + s_2)}$$

where $s_1$ and $s_2$ are given by

$$s_{1,2} = -\frac{R}{2L} \pm \sqrt{\left(\frac{R}{2L}\right)^2 - \frac{1}{LC}}$$

For the case when $s_1 \neq s_2$, we use partial fraction expansion to obtain

$$I(s) = \frac{\dfrac{1}{L(s_2 - s_1)}}{s + s_1} + \frac{\dfrac{1}{L(s_1 - s_2)}}{s + s_2}$$

When $s_1 = s_2$, we have

$$I(s) = \frac{\dfrac{1}{L}}{(s + s_1)^2}$$

For either of these cases, the step response is given as the inverse transforms

$$i(t) = \frac{1}{L(s_2 - s_1)}e^{-s_1 t}u_0(t) + \frac{1}{L(s_1 - s_2)}e^{-s_2 t}u_0(t)$$

or

$$i(t) = \frac{1}{L} te^{-s_1 t} u_0(t)$$

As we have seen in Chapter 6, the second case corresponds to critical damping. The first case corresponds to either the underdamped or over-damped situation depending on whether the roots are complex or real, respectively.

*Example 9.4.4*

Consider the network shown in Fig. 9.4.8a. Find the current in resistor $R_2$. Assume that the initial current in the inductor, $i_L(0^-)$, is 1 amp.

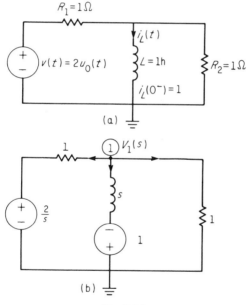

Fig. 9.4.8

*Solution*

We first construct the transformed network as shown in Fig. 9.4.8b. Note that the initial condition in the inductor gives rise to a voltage source = $Li_L(0^-)$ = 1 volt and this is included in the figure with ap-propriate polarity. Applying the KCL to node 1 and using the branch voltage-current relations (VCR) we get

$$\frac{V_1(s) - \frac{2}{s}}{1} + \frac{V_1(s) + 1}{s} + \frac{V_1(s)}{1} = 0$$

or

$$V_1(s) \left[2 + \frac{1}{s}\right] = \frac{2}{s} - \frac{1}{s} = \frac{1}{s}$$

or

$$V_1(s) = \frac{\dfrac{1}{2}}{s + \dfrac{1}{2}}$$

Now the transform of the current in $R_2 = 1\ \Omega$ is given by

$$I_{R_2}(s) = \frac{V_1(s)}{R_2} = \frac{\dfrac{1}{2}}{s + \dfrac{1}{2}}$$

Hence, from Table 9.2.1, we get by inspection $i_{R_2}(t) = \frac{1}{2}e^{-(1/2)t}$ amp.

*Example 9.4.5*

Consider the network of Fig. 9.4.9. Find the current in inductor $L_2$ after the switch is closed at $t = 0$. Assume that the voltage source $v(t)$ is applied at $t = -\infty$.

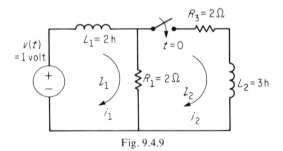

Fig. 9.4.9

*Solution*

Before the switch is closed at $t = 0$, the transients have passed and there are steady-state conditions in loop $l_1$. Hence, at $t = 0^-$, the inductor behaves like a short circuit and the current $i_1$ in loop $l_1$ is simply $v/R_1 = \frac{1}{2}$ amp.

When the switch is closed at $t = 0$, this equilibrium is disturbed. We can now make a transformed network in Fig. 9.4.10. The initial condition in $L_1$ is $i_1(0^-) = \frac{1}{2}$ amp so it can be replaced by voltage source $L_1 i_1(0^-) = 2 \times \frac{1}{2} = 1$ volt. There is no initial current through $L_2$. So we have the transformed network as shown in Fig. 9.4.10. The voltage source $v(t)$ is replaced by $1/s$.

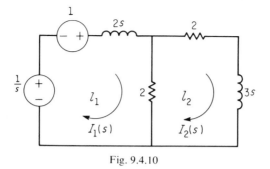

Fig. 9.4.10

In this case we have to find $i_2(t)$. Writing KVL equations for loops $l_1$ and $l_2$ we get from Fig. 9.4.10

$$l_1: \frac{1}{s} + 1 = (2s + 2) I_1(s) - 2I_2(s)$$

$$l_2: \qquad 0 = (4 + 3s) I_2(s) - 2I_1(s)$$

Eliminating $I_1(s)$, which is done by multiplying the second equation by $(s + 1)$ and adding, we get

$$\frac{s + 1}{s} = [(3s + 4)(s + 1) - 2] I_2(s)$$

or

$$I_2(s) = \frac{s + 1}{s(3s^2 + 7s + 2)} = \frac{\frac{1}{3}(s + 1)}{s(s + \frac{1}{3})(s + 2)}$$

Using partial-fraction expansion, we can write

$$I_2(s) = \frac{r_1}{s} + \frac{r_2}{s + \frac{1}{3}} + \frac{r_3}{s + 2}$$

where

$$r_1 = s \cdot \frac{s + 1}{s(3s^2 + 7s + 2)}\bigg|_{s=0} = \frac{1}{2}$$

$$r_2 = \left(s + \frac{1}{3}\right) \cdot \frac{\frac{1}{3}(s + 1)}{s(s + 2)(s + \frac{1}{3})}\bigg|_{s=-(1/3)} = \frac{-2}{5}$$

$$r_3 = (s + 2) \frac{\frac{1}{3}(s + 1)}{s(s + 2)(s + \frac{1}{3})}\bigg|_{s=-2} = \frac{-1}{10}$$

Using entry 4 of Table 9.2.1 on page 289, we obtain $i_2(t)$ from $I_2(s)$ as

$$i_2(t) = (\tfrac{1}{2} - \tfrac{1}{10}e^{-2t} - \tfrac{2}{5}e^{-(1/3)t}) u_0(t)$$

This is the desired current which can be easily plotted by hand or using the GRAPHX subroutine developed in Chapter 6.

*Example 9.4.6*

Calculate $v(t)$ as shown in Fig. 9.4.11 for $t \geq 0$. Use the root solving computer program to factor the denominator of $V(s)$.

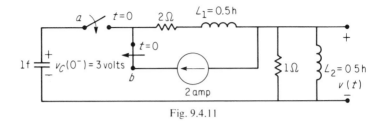

Fig. 9.4.11

*Solution*

At $t = 0$ switch $a$ closes and switch $b$ opens. There is an initial current of 2 amp in the $L_1$ inductor and no initial current in the $L_2$ inductor. So we can make a transformed network as shown in Fig. 9.4.12. The initial current in the $L_1$ inductor has been replaced by a voltage source $L_1 i_{L_1}(0^-) = 0.5 \times 2 = 1$ volt. The initial voltage on the capacitor is replaced by a voltage source $3/s$.

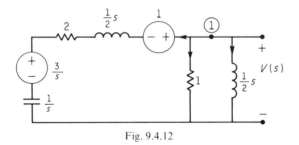

Fig. 9.4.12

Writing KCL equation at node 1 we have

$$\frac{V(s)}{\frac{1}{2}s} + \frac{V(s)}{1} + \frac{V(s) - 1 - (3/s)}{\frac{1}{2}s + 2 + (1/s)} = 0$$

or

$$V(s) = \frac{2s(s + 3)}{s^3 + 8s^2 + 10s + 4} = \frac{N(s)}{D(s)}$$

Before we can invert $V(s)$, we need partial fraction expansion of $V(s)$ which we can obtain if we know $D(s)$ in the factor form. We have

$$D(s) = s^3 + 8s^2 + 10s + 4$$

We use the root-solving computer program developed earlier. In this case we have a cubic equation, so $A4 = 0$, $A3 = 1.0$, $A2 = 8.0$, $A1 = 10.0$ and $A0 = 4.0$. To guess a real root, we start evaluating

$$D(0) = 4 > 0$$
$$D(-1) = -1 + 8 - 10 + 4 = 1 > 0$$
$$D(-5) = -125 + 200 - 50 + 4 = 29 > 0$$
$$D(-10) = -1000 + 800 - 100 + 4 = -296 < 0$$

So at least one real root is between $-5$ and $-10$. We choose the four guesses as

$$S(1) = -5.0$$
$$S(2) = -6.0$$
$$S(3) = -8.0$$
$$S(4) = -10.0$$

We now read in values of $A4$, $A3$, $A2$, $A1$, $A0$, and $S(1)$, $S(2)$, $S(3)$, $S(4)$. The computer program and the printout of the real root is given below.

```
C       THIS PROGRAM IS FOR EXAMPLE 9,4-6
C       THIS PROGRAM EXTRACTS THE REAL ROOTS OF UPTO A FOURTH
C       ORDER POLYNOMIAL, KNOWLEDGE OF APPROXIMATE REAL ROOT
C       OR ROOTS IS ASSUMED, FURTHER IT IS ASSUMED THAT THERE
C       IS NO MORE THAN ONE PAIR OF COMPLEX ROOTS,
        DIMENSION S(4),DS(4),DIS(4)
C       READ IN THE VALUES OF THE COEFFICIENTS
C       OF THE POLYNOMIAL,
        A0=4,0
        A1=10,0
        A2=8,0
        A3=1,0
        A4=0,0
C       READ IN THE INITIAL VALUES OF THE ROOTS - JUST A GUESS
        S(1)=-5,0
        S(2)=-6,0
        S(3)=-8,0
        S(4)=-10,0
C       NOTE THAT EVEN IF WE FIND ONE REAL ROOT WE CAN DIVIDE
C       IT OUT TO GET A THIRD ORDER POLYNOMIAL AND START AGAIN,
C       ONCE WE REACH A QUADRATIC WE NEED NOT GO ANY FURTHER,
C       HOWEVER IN CASE OF ALL REAL ROOTS THE GUESSED ROOTS
C       MAY CONVERGE TO THE ALL ACTUAL ROOTS, IN THIS CASE WE
C       WILL NOT HAVE A QUADRATIC LEFT,
C       THIS DO LOOP DOES THE ITERATING IN TEN STEPS,
        DO 9 J=1,10
C       WE PRINT S(I), I=1,2,3,4 AS S(I) CHANGES,
        PRINT 30 (S(I),I=1,4)
C       THIS DO LOOP CALCULATES NEW S(1),S(2),S(3),S(4)
C       STARTING FROM PREVIOUS VALUES,
        DO 11 I=1,4
        DS(I)=(A4*(S(I)**4))+(A3*(S(I)**3))+(A2*(S(I)**2))
       1+(A1*S(I))+A0
        DIS(I)=(4,*A4*(S(I)**3))+(3,*A3*(S(I)**2))
       1+(2,*A2*S(I))+A1
C       NEXT IS THE ITERATING FORMULA,
        S(I)=S(I)-DS(I)/DIS(I)
     11 CONTINUE
      9 CONTINUE
     30 FORMAT (4(F7,3,5X))
        END
```

| | | | |
|---|---|---|---|
| ▪5,000 | ▪6,000 | ▪8,000 | ▪10,000 |
| 10,800 | ▪6,727 | ▪6,973 | ▪8,027 |
| ▪8,499 | ▪6,578 | ▪6,616 | ▪6,985 |
| ▪7,209 | ▪6,571 | ▪6,571 | ▪6,619 |
| ▪6,675 | ▪6,571 | ▪6,571 | ▪6,572 |
| ▪6,574 | ▪6,571 | ▪6,571 | ▪6,571 |
| ▪6,571 | ▪6,571 | ▪6,571 | ▪6,571 |
| ▪6,571 | ▪6,571 | ▪6,571 | ▪6,571 |
| ▪6,571 | ▪6,571 | ▪6,571 | ▪6,571 |
| ▪6,571 | ▪6,571 | ▪6,571 | ▪6,571 |

Thus one real root is at $s = -6.571$. Now we can obtain

$$D(s) = (s^3 + 8s^2 + 10s + 4)$$
$$= (s + 6.571)(s^2 + 1.429s + 0.608)$$

So we have

$$V(s) = \frac{2s(s + 3)}{(s + 6.571)(s^2 + 1.429s + 0.608)}$$

In order to obtain $v(t)$, we write $V(s)$ in partial-fraction expansion:

$$V(s) = \frac{r_1}{s + 6.571} + \frac{r_2 s + r_3}{s^2 + 1.429s + 0.608}$$

Now

$$r_1 = \frac{2s(s + 3)}{s^2 + 1.429s + 0.608}\Bigg|_{s = -6.571} = 1.362$$

As before we can now compare coefficients of powers of $s$. First we compare constant coefficients; this yields

$$0 = 6.571 r_3 + r_1 \times 0.608 \Rightarrow r_3 = -0.126$$

Similarly comparing coefficients of $s^2$, we get

$$2 = r_1 + r_2 \Rightarrow r_2 = 0.638$$

Using $r_1$, $r_2$, and $r_3$ we can rearrange $V(s)$ in the form

$$V(s) = \frac{1.362}{s + 6.571} + 0.638\left\{\frac{s + 0.715 - 0.912}{(s + 0.715)^2 + (0.315)^2}\right\}$$

This enables us to use entries 4, 10, and 11 of Table 9.2.1 to obtain

$$v(t) = 1.362e^{-6.571t} + 0.638e^{-0.715t}\cos 0.315t - 1.85e^{-0.715t}\sin 0.315t$$

This can be plotted using the GRAPHX subroutine developed in Chapter 6.

### Impedance and Admittance

In Chapter 4 we discussed the solution of resistive networks and found that such networks could be described by algebraic relationships between currents and voltages. Application of the Laplace transformation permits a generalization of resistive network concepts to $RLC$ networks because the transformation establishes algebraic relationships between voltage and current transforms. In Example 9.4.2 the transform of the current response was found from the relationship

$$V(s) + Li_L(0^-) - \frac{v_C(0^-)}{s} = I(s)\left[R + sL + \frac{1}{sC}\right] \qquad (9.4.14)$$

Taking zero initial conditions and defining

$$Z(s) \triangleq \frac{V(s)}{I(s)} = R + sL + \frac{1}{sC} \qquad (9.4.15)$$

we can rewrite Eq. 9.4.14 as

$$V(s) = I(s)Z(s) \qquad (9.4.16)$$

where the analogy to the equation

$$V = IR \qquad (9.4.17)$$

should be apparent. The function $Z(s)$ is called the input or driving point *impedance* of the series $RLC$ network. The impedance is a rational function of $s$ which is the ratio of the transform of the voltage excitation function to the transform of the current response under *zero initial conditions*. Note the impedance of this series network is the summation of the three impedance values which are connected in series. This is not a coincidence; impedance combination follows the same rules as resistance combination. Impedances in series between two terminals are added to find the *equivalent impedance* at the terminals.

*Example 9.4.7*

Find the equivalent impedance of the network shown in Fig. 9.4.13.

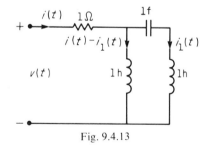

Fig. 9.4.13

*Solution*

The transformed network for calculation of the equivalent impedance is shown in Fig. 9.4.14. Note all initial conditions are zero for calculation of the impedance function. Applying KVL, we have

$$V(s) = I(s) + sI(s) - sI_1(s)$$

$$0 = -sI(s) + 2sI_1(s) + \frac{1}{s}I_1(s)$$

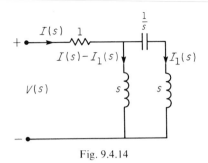

Fig. 9.4.14

Combining these two equations by elimination of $I_1(s)$ gives

$$V(s) = I(s) + sI(s) - \frac{s^3}{2s^2 + 1} I(s)$$

or

$$Z(s) = \frac{V(s)}{I(s)} = \frac{s^3 + 2s^2 + s + 1}{2s^2 + 1}$$

We can also calculate $Z(s)$ by successive combination of series and parallel impedances. The equivalent impedance of the capacitor and inductor in series is

$$Z_{e_1}(s) = \frac{1}{s} + s$$

The equivalent impedance of the remaining inductor in parallel with $Z_{e_1}(s)$ is

$$Z_{e_2}(s) = \frac{1}{[1/Z_{e_1}(s)] + (1/s)} = \frac{s^3 + s}{2s^2 + 1}$$

Finally the series combination of the resistor with $Z_{e_2}(s)$ gives

$$Z(s) = 1 + Z_{e_2}(s) = \frac{s^3 + 2s^2 + s + 1}{2s^2 + 1}$$

These combination steps are indicated schematically in Fig. 9.4.15.

The *admittance function* $Y(s)$ is defined as the ratio of the transform of the current response to the transform of the voltage source under zero initial conditions. For example, consider the transformed parallel $RLC$ network with zero initial conditions shown in Fig. 9.4.16. Applying KCL gives

$$I(s) = V(s)G + V(s)\frac{1}{sL} + V(s)sC \tag{9.4.18}$$

The equivalent admittance function of the network is the ratio of current transform to the voltage transform. From Eq. 9.4.18 we have

$$Y(s) \triangleq \frac{I(s)}{V(s)} = G + \frac{1}{sL} + sC \tag{9.4.19}$$

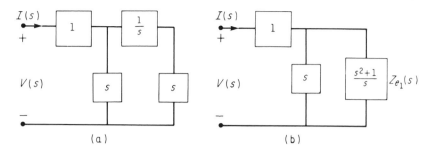

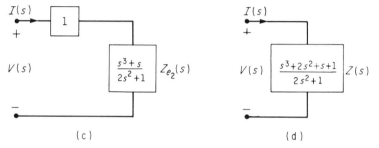

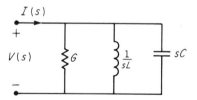

Fig. 9.4.15. Showing steps in using impedance combination rules to obtain impedance $Z(s)$ for network in Fig. 9.4.14.

Fig. 9.4.16. Parallel $RLC$ network.

Note the equivalent admittance is found by taking the summation of the three admittance values which are connected in parallel. In analogy to the case of impedance combination in series; admittance combination follows the same rules as conductance combination in parallel. Admittances in parallel are added to find the equivalent admittance.

### Network Transfer Functions

In addition to the equivalent impedance and admittance functions, the ratio of the transform of the output voltage to the transform of the input voltage under zero initial conditions is often of interest in network analysis. This ratio is called the network *voltage transfer function* and is generally denoted by $H_V(s)$. Similarly, the ratio of output current to input current transforms is called (under zero initial conditions) the *current transfer function* and is denoted by $H_I(s)$.

As an example of a voltage transfer function, let us calculate the ratio of the output voltage $V_2(s)$ to the input voltage $V_1(s)$ in the network

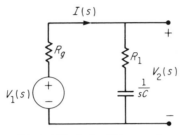

Fig. 9.4.17. Series *RC* network.

shown in Fig. 9.4.17. The current $I(s)$ is given by

$$I(s) = \frac{V_1(s)}{R_1 + R_g + (1/sC)} \qquad (9.4.20)$$

and the voltage $V_2(s)$ is

$$V_2(s) = \left(R_1 + \frac{1}{sC}\right)I(s) = \frac{R_1 + (1/sC)}{R_1 + R_g + (1/sC)} V_1(s) \qquad (9.4.21)$$

The network voltage transfer function is

$$H_V(s) = \frac{V_2(s)}{V_1(s)} = \frac{R_1 + (1/sC)}{R_1 + R_g + (1/sC)} \qquad (9.4.22)$$

The importance of the network transfer function lies in the fact that the voltage response to any voltage source can be found very simply from the relationship

$$V_2(s) = H_V(s) V_1(s) \qquad (9.4.23)$$

If we consider the case when $v_1(t)$ is a unit impulse source, i.e., when

$$v_1(t) = \delta(t) \qquad (9.4.24)$$

then $v_2(t)$ will equal the network impulse response. From Table 9.2.1 we have

$$\mathcal{L}[v_1(t)] = V_1(s) = 1, \qquad \text{when } v_1(t) = \delta(t) \qquad (9.4.25)$$

Substituting Eq. 9.4.25 into Eq. 9.4.23 gives

$$V_2(s)\big|_{v_1(t) = \delta(t)} = H_V(s) \qquad (9.4.26)$$

Since under the hypothesized input, $v_2(t)$ is the unit impulse response, then Eq. 9.4.26 indicates the network transfer function is the Laplace transform of the unit impulse response.

## Relationship to State Variable Methods

The Laplace transform is a useful tool for the formulation and solution of linear network problems, particularly in the case of time-invariant networks. The method of calculating the Laplace transform and its inverse is, however, a logical operation which is poorly suited to machine computation. Hence a direct calculation of network time response from the equation of operation is often preferred, particularly when a digital computation facility is available. However, even in this case the Laplace transformation can be a useful tool in establishing the equation of operation from the network schematic. We will now discuss such techniques and the relationship of the Laplace transform to the state variable method of network analysis.

As we have seen in Chapter 7, the state variable description of a time-invariant network is

$$\dot{\mathbf{x}}(t) = \mathbf{A}\mathbf{x}(t) + \mathbf{B}\mathbf{u}(t) \tag{9.4.27}$$

where $\mathbf{x}(t)$ is an $n$-vector, $\mathbf{u}(t)$ an $m$-vector, $\mathbf{A}$ is an $n \times n$ matrix and $\mathbf{B}$ is an $n \times m$ matrix.

Taking the Laplace transform of this equation gives

$$s\mathbf{X}(s) - \mathbf{x}(0) = \mathbf{A}\mathbf{X}(s) + \mathbf{B}\mathbf{U}(s) \tag{9.4.28}$$

where the Laplace transform of a vector is simply the transform of each component of the vector. Solving for $\mathbf{X}(s)$,

$$\mathbf{X}(s) = [s\mathbf{I} - \mathbf{A}]^{-1}\mathbf{x}(0) + [s\mathbf{I} - \mathbf{A}]^{-1}\mathbf{B}\mathbf{U}(s) \tag{9.4.29}$$

We have seen in Chapter 7, the solution to Eq. 9.4.27 is given by

$$\mathbf{x}(t) = e^{\mathbf{A}t}\mathbf{x}(0) + \int_0^t e^{\mathbf{A}(t-\tau)}\mathbf{B}\mathbf{u}(\tau)\,d\tau \tag{9.4.30}$$

Both Eqs. 9.4.29 and 9.4.30 must hold for all values of $\mathbf{u}(t)$, in particular it must hold for $\mathbf{u}(t) \triangleq \mathbf{0}$. Hence under zero input conditions we have from Eq. 9.4.29

$$\mathbf{X}(s) = [s\mathbf{I} - \mathbf{A}]^{-1}\mathbf{x}(0) \tag{9.4.31}$$

and from Eq. 9.4.30,

$$\mathbf{x}(t) = e^{\mathbf{A}t}\mathbf{x}(0) \tag{9.4.32}$$

From Eq. 9.4.31, after taking the inverse transform of both sides of the equation, we obtain

$$\mathbf{x}(t) = \mathcal{L}^{-1}\{[s\mathbf{I} - \mathbf{A}]^{-1}\}\mathbf{x}(0) \tag{9.4.33}$$

Since Eqs. 9.4.32 and 9.4.33 are valid for all values of the initial condition vector, $\mathbf{x}(0)$, we must have

$$e^{\mathbf{A}t} = \mathcal{L}^{-1}\{[s\mathbf{I} - \mathbf{A}]^{-1}\} \tag{9.4.34}$$

Hence, the Laplace transform provides us an alternate method of calculating the matrix $e^{At}$.

*Example 9.4.8*

Consider the network shown in Fig. 9.4.18. Applying the method of state variables, we choose $i_L(t)$ and $v_C(t)$ as the state variables. Apply-

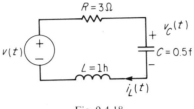

Fig. 9.4.18

ing KCL and KVL gives

$$v(t) = i_L(t) R + v_C(t) + L \frac{di_L}{dt}$$

$$i_L(t) = C \frac{dv_C}{dt}$$

which in matrix form becomes

$$\frac{d}{dt} \begin{bmatrix} i_L(t) \\ v_C(t) \end{bmatrix} = \begin{bmatrix} -(R/L) & -(1/L) \\ 1/C & 0 \end{bmatrix} \begin{bmatrix} i_L(t) \\ v_C(t) \end{bmatrix} + \begin{bmatrix} 1/L \\ 0 \end{bmatrix} v(t)$$

The matrix **A** is

$$\mathbf{A} = \begin{bmatrix} -(R/L) & -(1/L) \\ 1/C & 0 \end{bmatrix} = \begin{bmatrix} -3 & -1 \\ 2 & 0 \end{bmatrix}$$

We will use the Laplace transform to find $e^{At}$. First we calculate

$$[s\mathbf{I} - \mathbf{A}] = \begin{bmatrix} s+3 & 1 \\ -2 & s \end{bmatrix}$$

Calculating the inverse of the matrix $[s\mathbf{I} - \mathbf{A}]$ we get

$$[s\mathbf{I} - \mathbf{A}]^{-1} = \frac{1}{s^2 + 3s + 2} \begin{bmatrix} s & -1 \\ 2 & s+3 \end{bmatrix}$$

$$= \begin{bmatrix} \dfrac{s}{(s+1)(s+2)} & \dfrac{-1}{(s+1)(s+2)} \\ \dfrac{2}{(s+1)(s+2)} & \dfrac{s+3}{(s+1)(s+2)} \end{bmatrix}$$

Hence, calculating the inverse Laplace transform for each term gives

$$e^{\mathbf{A}t} = \mathcal{L}^{-1}[(s\mathbf{I} - \mathbf{A})^{-1}] = \begin{bmatrix} -e^{-t} + 2e^{-2t} & -e^{-t} + e^{-2t} \\ 2e^{-t} - 2e^{-2t} & 2e^{-t} - e^{-2t} \end{bmatrix}$$

Hence, we can use Eq. 9.4.30 to obtain the solution for $i_L(t)$ and $v_C(t)$.

Note that calculating $e^{\mathbf{A}t}$ by means of the Laplace transform involves calculating a matrix inverse together with computing the Laplace inverse. The amount of labor involved can become quite tedious when $\mathbf{A}$ is of order 4 or larger.

## 9.5. MESH AND NODAL ANALYSIS

The Laplace transform permits an extension of the concepts developed for matrix representation of resistive networks to more general $RLC$ networks. We will see in this section that the concept of complex impedance and admittance permit us to develop a formalized method of quickly writing the equations which describe network performance. To illustrate, consider the network shown in Fig. 9.5.1a and its transform representation in Fig. 9.5.1b. Note the three mesh currents have each been defined in the clockwise direction and all initial conditions have been represented by voltage sources.

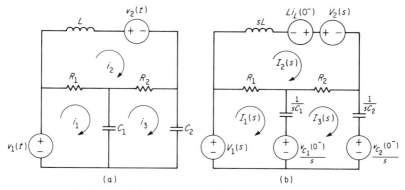

Fig. 9.5.1. (a) $RLC$ network for mesh analysis illustration, (b) transform equivalent network.

Writing KVL around the three meshes in Fig. 9.5.1b gives

$$0 = -V_1(s) + R_1(I_1(s) - I_2(s)) + \frac{1}{sC_1}\left[I_1(s) - I_3(s)\right] + \frac{v_{C_1}(0^-)}{s}$$

$$0 = V_2(s) + R_2(I_2(s) - I_3(s)) + R_1(I_2(s) - I_1(s))$$

$$+ sLI_2(s) - Li_L(0^-) \qquad (9.5.1)$$

$$0 = \frac{v_{C_2}(0^-)}{s} - \frac{v_{C_1}(0^-)}{s} + \frac{1}{sC_1}(I_3(s) - I_1(s))$$

$$+ R_2(I_3(s) - I_2(s)) + \frac{1}{sC_2}I_3(s)$$

Rewriting Eq. 9.5.1 in matrix form,

$$\begin{bmatrix} V_1(s) - \dfrac{v_{C_1}(0^-)}{s} \\[2ex] -V_2(s) + Li_L(0^-) \\[2ex] \dfrac{-v_{C_2}(0^-)}{s} + \dfrac{v_{C_1}(0^-)}{s} \end{bmatrix}$$

$$= \begin{bmatrix} R_1 + \dfrac{1}{sC_1} & -R_1 & -\dfrac{1}{sC_1} \\[2ex] -R_1 & R_1 + R_2 + sL & -R_2 \\[2ex] -\dfrac{1}{sC_1} & -R_2 & R_2 + \dfrac{1}{sC_1} + \dfrac{1}{sC_2} \end{bmatrix} \begin{bmatrix} I_1(s) \\[1ex] I_2(s) \\[1ex] I_3(s) \end{bmatrix} \qquad (9.5.2)$$

or

$$\mathbf{V}(s) = \mathbf{Z}(s)\mathbf{I}(s) \qquad (9.5.3)$$

where the matrix identifications in Eq. 9.5.3 follow from Eq. 9.5.2. Examining the impedance matrix $\mathbf{Z}(s)$ Eq. 9.5.2, we find the elements along the diagonal represent the *self-impedance* of the respective mesh; i.e., the element in row 1, column 1 is the self-impedance of mesh 1; the element in row 2, column 2 is the self-impedance of mesh 2, and so forth. The mesh self-impedance is defined as the summation of impedance around the respective mesh.    The matrix elements in the off diagonal positions are, in absolute value, the *mutual impedances* between meshes; that is the impedances common to each pair of meshes.  For example, the absolute value of the element in row 1, column 2 is $R_1$, the impedance common to meshes 1 and 2.  The algebraic sign of the off diagonal elements is determined by the relative directions of the mesh currents in the respective element. If the mesh currents are in opposing directions in the mutual impedance, the algebraic sign assigned to that element in the matrix is negative.  If the mesh currents are in the same direction through the mutual impedance, the algebraic sign assigned to the matrix element is positive.  Examining the voltage vector $\mathbf{V}(s)$, we see the first component is the algebraic summation of voltage sources in mesh 1; the second component is the algebraic summation of voltage sources in mesh 2; and so on.  To determine the sign on the respective voltage source in the algebraic summation, the source position in the network is examined. If the mesh current flows from the negative to positive terminal of the voltage source, the algebraic sign on the source is positive. Otherwise, the algebraic sign is negative. As can be seen from Eq. 9.5.3, once $\mathbf{Z}(s)$ and $\mathbf{V}(s)$ are known the current vector $\mathbf{I}(s)$ is found from

$$\mathbf{I}(s) = \mathbf{Z}^{-1}(s)\mathbf{V}(s) \tag{9.5.4}$$

To generalize, a formalized procedure of *mesh analysis* can be stated as follows:

1. Represent all sources and initial conditions as voltage sources.
2. Assign mesh currents. To simplify analysis, it is prefereable to assign all currents in the same direction, i.e., either clockwise or counterclockwise.
3. From the network schematic, write the impedance matrix $\mathbf{Z}(s)$. The diagonal element, $Z_{ii}(s)$ of the matrix is the self-impedance of mesh $i$. The magnitude of the diagonal element, $Z_{ij}(s)$ is the mutual impedance between mesh $i$ and mesh $j$. The algebraic sign is determined by the relative direction of the mesh currents flowing through $Z_{ij}(s)$. When all mesh currents are chosen either clockwise or counterclockwise, the algebraic sign is negative.
4. From the network schematic, write the voltage vector $\mathbf{V}(s)$. The element $V_i(s)$ is simply the algebraic sum of the voltage sources in mesh $i$. If the mesh current flows from the negative to positive terminal of the source, the algebraic sign is positive. Otherwise, it is negative.

*Nodal analysis* is a procedure similar to the formalized mesh analysis described above, except the solution is in terms of node voltages rather than mesh currents. To illustrate, we consider the network shown in Fig. 9.5.2. Note all sources and initial conditions have been represented as current sources. The node voltages $v_1$, $v_2$, and $v_3$ are chosen as positive with

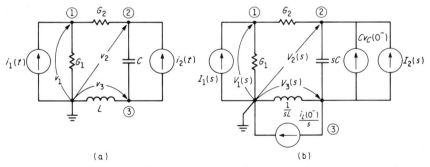

Fig. 9.5.2. (a) *RLC* network for nodal analysis illustration, (b) transform equivalent network.

respect of the reference node. Writing KCL at each node, we obtain

$$0 = -I_1(s) + G_1 V_1(s) + G_2(V_1(s) - V_2(s))$$
$$0 = G_2(V_2(s) - V_1(s)) + sC(V_2(s) - V_3(s)) - Cv_C(0^-) - I_2(s) \qquad (9.5.5)$$
$$0 = sC(V_3(s) - V_2(s)) + \frac{1}{sL} V_3(s) + \frac{i_L(0^-)}{s} + Cv_C(0^-) + I_2(s)$$

where we have defined currents flowing away from each node as being positive. Rewriting Eq. 9.5.5 in matrix form gives

$$\mathbf{I}(s) = \mathbf{Y}(s)\mathbf{V}(s) \qquad (9.5.6)$$

where

$$\mathbf{V}(s) = \begin{bmatrix} V_1(s) \\ V_2(s) \\ V_3(s) \end{bmatrix} \qquad (9.5.7a)$$

$$\mathbf{Y}(s) = \begin{bmatrix} G_1 + G_2 & -G_2 & 0 \\ -G_2 & sC + G_2 & -sC \\ 0 & -sC & sC + \frac{1}{sL} \end{bmatrix} \qquad (9.5.7b)$$

and

$$\mathbf{I}(s) = \begin{bmatrix} I_1(s) \\ I_2(s) + Cv_c(0^-) \\ -I_2(s) - Cv_c(0^-) - \frac{i_L(0^-)}{s} \end{bmatrix} \qquad (9.5.7c)$$

From a knowledge of the admittance matrix, $\mathbf{Y}(s)$ and the equivalent source vector, $\mathbf{I}(s)$, we find the node voltage vector from

$$\mathbf{V}(s) = \mathbf{Y}^{-1}(s)\mathbf{I}(s) \qquad (9.5.8)$$

Examination of Eq. 9.5.7 shows the matrix diagonal terms to be the *self-admittance* of each node, i.e., the summation of all admittances connected to the node. The absolute value of the off diagonal terms represent the admittances common to two nodes. The element in the $i$th row and $j$th column is the negative of the *mutual admittance* between nodes $i$ and $j$. The negative sign arises due to the fact that we have chosen the currents in KCL as being positive when leaving the node.

To generalize a formalized procedure of *nodal analysis* can be stated as follows:

1. Represent all sources and initial conditions as current sources.
2. Assign node voltages to each node except the datum.
3. From the network schematic, write the admittance matrix $\mathbf{Y}(s)$. The diagonal element, $Y_{ii}(s)$, of the matrix is the self-admittance

of the node $i$. The diagonal element, $Y_{ij}(s)$, is the negative of the summation of all admittances connected between $i$ and $j$.

4. From the network schematic, write the current vector $\mathbf{I}(s)$. The element $I_i$ is the algebraic summation of all equivalent source currents flowing into node $i$.

## Equivalent Sources

A requirement for performing the formalized nodal or mesh analysis procedures is the representation of all network sources in either current or voltage form. The conversion of voltage to current source or vice versa is made simple by the Laplace transform representation of the source and network elements. For example, consider the network shown in Fig. 9.5.3a. We desire to convert the voltage source as seen at the terminals

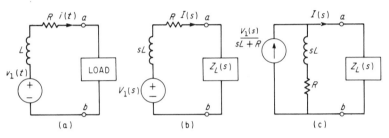

Fig. 9.5.3. Derivation of equivalent source.

$a, b$ to an equivalent current source. The transform representation of the source is shown in Fig. 9.5.3b. Note the initial condition on the inductor is taken to be zero. If this is not the case, then the initial condition is easily included as part of $v_1(t)$. At the terminals $a$, $b$ we have from Fig. 9.5.3b

$$V_{ab}(s) = V_1(s) - I(s)(sL + R) \qquad (9.5.9)$$

This can be seen to be equivalent at the terminal $a$, $b$ to the source in Fig. 9.5.3c where we have

$$V_{ab}(s) = \left\{ \frac{V_1(s)}{sL + R} - I(s) \right\}(sL + R) = V_1(s) - I(s)(sL + R) \qquad (9.5.10)$$

To generalize, we consider a voltage source in series with any impedance $Z(s)$ as shown in Fig. 9.5.4a. The equivalent current source is shown in Fig. 9.5.4b. Similarly, the equivalence between current and voltage sources indicated in Fig. 9.5.5a and b can be established.

*Example 9.5.1*

Using mesh analysis, calculate the impedance matrix $\mathbf{Z}(s)$ for the network shown in Fig. 9.5.6. Assume zero initial conditions.

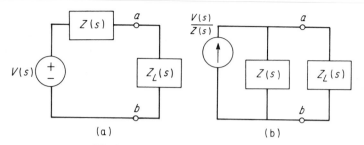

Fig. 9.5.4. Voltage source conversion.

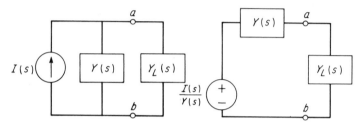

Fig. 9.5.5. Current source conversion.

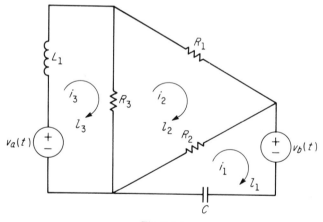

Fig. 9.5.6

*Solution*

Assume clockwise direction for the currents in the loops shown in Fig. 9.5.6. Now we construct the transformed equivalent network as shown in Fig. 9.5.7. From Fig. 9.5.7, the self-impedance of each loop is

$$l_1: \quad Z_{11}(s) = \frac{1}{sC} + R_2$$

$$l_2: \quad Z_{22}(s) = R_1 + R_2 + R_3$$

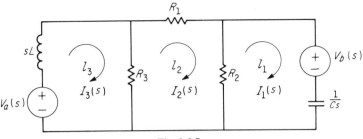

Fig. 9.5.7

$$l_3: \quad Z_{33}(s) = sL_1 + R_3$$

The mutual impedances are

$$Z_{12}(s) = Z_{21}(s) = -R_2$$
$$Z_{13}(s) = Z_{31}(s) = 0$$
$$Z_{23}(s) = Z_{32}(s) = -R_3$$

Hence the impedance matrix is

$$\mathbf{Z}(s) = \begin{bmatrix} \dfrac{1}{sC} + R_2 & -R_2 & 0 \\[2mm] -R_2 & R_1 + R_2 + R_3 & -R_3 \\[2mm] 0 & -R_3 & sL_1 + R_3 \end{bmatrix}$$

The network equation is therefore

$$\begin{bmatrix} -V_b(s) \\ 0 \\ V_a(s) \end{bmatrix} = \mathbf{Z}(s) \begin{bmatrix} I_1(s) \\ I_2(s) \\ I_3(s) \end{bmatrix}$$

*Example 9.5.2*

Using the same network as in the previous example, use nodal analysis to calculate the admittance matrix $\mathbf{Y}(s)$. Assume zero initial conditions.

*Solution*

To perform a nodal analysis, we convert the voltage sources to current sources. The equivalent transform network with sources converted is redrawn from Fig. 9.5.7 and is shown in Fig. 9.5.8. The self-admittance of nodes 1 and 2 is respectively

$$Y_{11}(s) = sC + G_1 + G_2$$
$$Y_{22}(s) = \frac{1}{sL} + G_3 + G_1$$

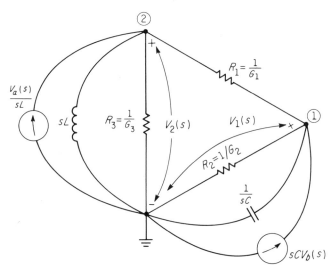

Fig. 9.5.8. Transform equivalent network for Example 9.5.2 with voltage sources replaced by current sources.

The mutual admittance is

$$Y_{12}(s) = Y_{21}(s) = -G_1$$

Thus the matrix $\mathbf{Y}(s)$ and the network equations are

$$\mathbf{Y}(s) = \begin{bmatrix} sC + G_1 + G_2 & -G_1 \\ -G_1 & \dfrac{1}{sL} + G_1 + G_3 \end{bmatrix}$$

$$\begin{bmatrix} sCV_b(s) \\ \dfrac{V_a(s)}{sL} \end{bmatrix} = \mathbf{Y}(s) \begin{bmatrix} V_1(s) \\ V_2(s) \end{bmatrix}$$

*Example 9.5.3*

Calculate $v_1(t)$ and $v_2(t)$ as defined in Example 9.5.2, assuming zero initial conditions and $R_1 = R_2 = R_3 = 1\ \Omega$, $C = 2$ f, and $L = 1$ h. Assume $v_a(t) = v_b(t) = u_0(t)$.

*Solution*

We can just substitute the given values in the equations of the previous example. Note that $G_1 = G_2 = G_3 = 1$. We have

$$\mathbf{Y}(s) = \begin{bmatrix} 2s + 2 & -1 \\ -1 & \dfrac{1}{s} + 2 \end{bmatrix}$$

Also,

$$V_a(s) = V_b(s) = \frac{1}{s}$$

Therefore we have

$$\begin{bmatrix} 2s \cdot \dfrac{1}{s} \\[2ex] \dfrac{1}{s} \cdot \dfrac{1}{s} \end{bmatrix} = \mathbf{Y}(s) \begin{bmatrix} V_1(s) \\[2ex] V_2(s) \end{bmatrix}$$

We need $\mathbf{Y}^{-1}(s)$. This is given by

$$\mathbf{Y}^{-1}(s) = \frac{s}{4s^2 + 5s + 2} \begin{bmatrix} \dfrac{2s + 1}{s} & 1 \\[2ex] 1 & 2s + 2 \end{bmatrix} \begin{bmatrix} 2 \\[2ex] \dfrac{1}{s^2} \end{bmatrix}$$

$$= \begin{bmatrix} \dfrac{4s^2 + 2s + 1}{s(4s^2 + 5s + 2)} \\[3ex] \dfrac{2s^2 + 2s + 2}{s(4s^2 + 5s + 2)} \end{bmatrix}$$

Using partial fraction expansion for each term we can show

$$\begin{bmatrix} V_1(s) \\[2ex] V_2(s) \end{bmatrix} = \begin{bmatrix} \dfrac{\frac{1}{2}}{s} + \dfrac{2s - \frac{1}{2}}{4s^2 + 5s + 2} \\[3ex] \dfrac{1}{s} - \dfrac{2s + 3}{4s^2 + 5s + 2} \end{bmatrix}$$

or

$$\begin{bmatrix} V_1(s) \\[2ex] V_2(s) \end{bmatrix} = \begin{bmatrix} \dfrac{1}{2}\left\{ \dfrac{1}{s} + \dfrac{(s - \frac{1}{4})}{(s + \frac{5}{8})^2 + (\sqrt{7}/8)^2} \right\} \\[3ex] \left\{ \dfrac{1}{s} - \dfrac{\frac{1}{2}(s + \frac{3}{2})}{(s + \frac{5}{8})^2 + (\sqrt{7}/8)^2} \right\} \end{bmatrix}$$

Now we use Table 9.2.1 for inversion into the time domain, especially entry 12, to obtain

$$\begin{bmatrix} v_1(t) \\[2ex] v_2(t) \end{bmatrix} = \begin{bmatrix} \dfrac{1}{2}\left\{ 1 + e^{-(5/8)t}\left( \cos\dfrac{\sqrt{7}}{8}t - \sqrt{7}\sin\dfrac{\sqrt{7}}{8}t \right) \right\} u_0(t) \\[3ex] \left\{ 1 - \dfrac{1}{2}e^{-(5/8)t}\left( \cos\dfrac{\sqrt{7}}{8}t + \sqrt{7}\sin\dfrac{\sqrt{7}}{8}t \right) \right\} u_0(t) \end{bmatrix}$$

**PROBLEMS**

**9.1.** Find the residues of all the poles in the following functions.

(i) $\dfrac{s + 3}{(s + 1)(s + 2)}$

(ii) $\dfrac{s(s + 1)^2}{(s^2 + s + 1)(s + 3)}$

(iii) $\dfrac{s + 1}{(s^3 + 6s^2 + 11s + 6)}$

(*Hint:* The denominator has a root at $-1$.)

**9.2.** Use Table 9.2.1 to find the time functions corresponding to the functions given in Prob. 9.1.

**9.3.** Find the Laplace transform of the following functions. You may use Table 9.2.1.

(i)    $e^{-2t} \sin (t + 2)$
(ii)   $(t^2 + 2t + 1)e^{-2t} \cos t$
(iii)  $\tanh (t)$

**9.4.** Find the partial-fraction expansion of the following functions $F(s)$.

(i) $\dfrac{s^3 + 2s + 2}{(s + 1)(s + 2)^2}$

(ii) $\dfrac{s^2 + 2s + 2}{(s + 1)^2(s + 2)}$

(iii) $\dfrac{s^2 + 2s + 3}{s^3 + 4s^2 + 3s}$

(iv) $\dfrac{s^2 + 2s + 3}{(s + 1)^2(s + 2)(s^2 + 3s + 4)}$

(v) $\dfrac{s + 3}{(s^2 + 2s + 2)^2}$

(vi) $\dfrac{s^2 + s + 2}{(s + 1)(s + 2)(s + 3)}$

**9.5.** Use a computer routine to find the real roots of the following polynomials.

(i)    $s^3 + 3s^2 + 2s + 7 = 0$
(ii)   $s^4 + 3s^3 + 2s^2 + 2s + 1 = 0$
(iii)  $s^3 + 4s^2 + 5s + 2 = 0$

**9.6.** Using Laplace transform techniques, calculate the current $i(t)$ in the circuit shown for (a) $v(t) = 10u_0(t)$, (b) $v(t) = 10 \sin (3t)u_0(t)$, with $v_C(0) = 5$ volts.

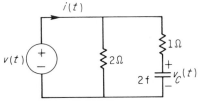

Prob. 9.6

**9.7.**  Calculate the current in the inductor shown.  Assume $v_C(0^-) = 2$ volts, $i_L(0^-) = 1$ amp.  Plot the current $i_L(t)$ using the computer plot routine.

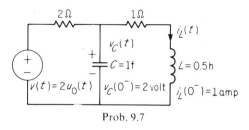

Prob. 9.7

**9.8.**  For the circuit shown, calculate

(a)  The admittance $Y(s) = \dfrac{I(s)}{V(s)}$.

(b)  The transfer function $H_V(s)$ relating $V(s)$ and $V_C(s)$.

(c)  The current $i(t)$, assuming zero initial conditions.

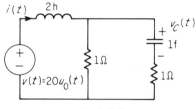

Prob. 9.8

**9.9.**  For the series $RLC$ network shown calculate (a) input impedance, $Z(s)$, (b) current $i(t)$.

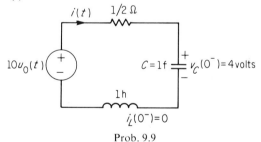

Prob. 9.9

**9.10.**  For the $RL$ circuit shown, calculate the current $i_L(t)$.  The initial condition is $i_L(0^-) = -1$ amp.

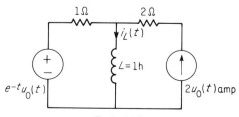

Prob. 9.10

**9.11.** For the *RLC* circuit shown, calculate (a) input impedance, $Z(s)$, (b) transfer function, $H_V(s) = \dfrac{V_C(s)}{V(s)}$, and (c) current, $i_2(t)$ (assume zero initial conditions). Also (d) plot $i_2(t)$ using the GRAPHX subroutine.

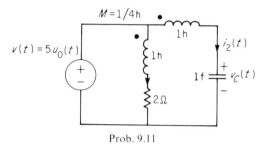

Prob. 9.11

**9.12.** Using the state variable method of describing network response, (a) write the state equation $\dot{x} = \mathbf{A}x + \mathbf{B}u$ for the network shown and (b) using the Laplace transform, calculate the matrix $e^{\mathbf{A}t}$.

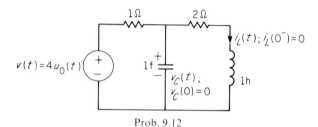

Prob. 9.12

**9.13.** Repeat Prob. 9.12 for the network shown here. The initial condition on the inductor is zero.

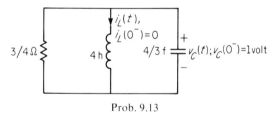

Prob. 9.13

**9.14.** Repeat Prob. 9.12 for the network shown. All initial conditions are zero.

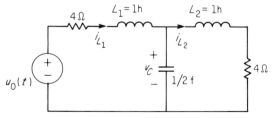

Prob. 9.14

**9.15.** Calculate the admittance $Y(s) = \dfrac{I(s)}{V_1(s)}$ for the network shown.

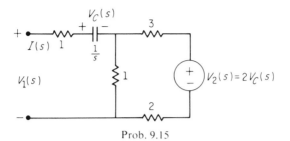

Prob. 9.15

**9.16.** Calculate $i(t)$ for network of Prob. 9.15 if $V_1(s) = 1/s$ and initial conditions are zero.

**9.17.** For the network shown (assume zero initial conditions),
   (i)    Use mesh analysis to solve for the mesh currents.
   (ii)   Use node analysis to solve for the node voltages.
   (iii)  Since either the node voltages or mesh currents fully describe the network, which method of analysis is preferable for this problem? Why?

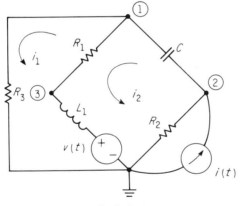

Prob. 9.17

**9.18.** Use the mesh analysis to obtain $i_1(t)$ and $i_2(t)$ for network shown, assuming zero initial conditions.

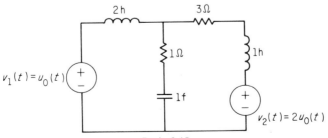

Prob. 9.18

CHAPTER **10**

# Sinusoidal
# Steady-State Analysis

## 10.1. INTRODUCTION

Sinusoidal functions are quite commonly used in network analysis because of their convenient mathematical properties. In addition, as we will see in the next chapter, most functions of practical interest can be represented as a summation of sinusoidal components of different amplitudes, phases, and frequencies. Hence, because of the superposition property of linear networks, we can calculate the response of a network to an arbitrary input by calculating the response to each of its sinusoidal components. In this chapter we develop techniques for obtaining the network response to sinusoidal driving functions. As we will see, these techniques are based on analysis procedures developed in earlier chapters which when applied to sinusoidal driving functions yield particularly simple results. Our analysis is limited to linear time-invariant networks.

## 10.2. NETWORK RESPONSE TO SINUSOIDAL DRIVING FUNCTIONS

Consider the network shown in Fig. 10.2.1. Let us calculate the voltage response $v(t)$ of this network to sinusoidal current source $i(t) = \sin\left(t + \dfrac{\pi}{8}\right)u_0(t)$. The equation of operation is

$$\frac{dv(t)}{dt} + v(t) = \sin\left(t + \frac{\pi}{8}\right) \qquad t \geq 0 \qquad (10.2.1)$$

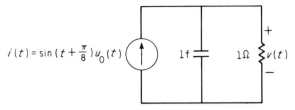

Fig. 10.2.1. *RC* network.

We can evaluate the response $v(t)$ by solving the differential equation to obtain

$$v(t) = \frac{1}{\sqrt{2}} \left[ \sin\left(t - \frac{\pi}{8}\right) + \left\{ \sin\left(\frac{\pi}{8}\right) + \sqrt{2} \, V_0 \right\} e^{-t} \right] \quad t \geq 0 \quad (10.2.2)$$

where $V_0$ is the initial capacitor voltage. Note that the steady state component of the solution is a sinusoid with the same frequency as the driving function but with different phase and amplitude. We also note that the steady-state component is just the particular solution to the differential equation. Hence, if we are solely interested in the steady-state component we need to calculate only the particular solution. Another simplification arises due to the linearity property of the network. Instead of considering the driving function $\sin \omega t$, we can work with the driving function $\cos \omega t + j \sin \omega t = e^{j\omega t}$. Because of the superposition property, we know that our solution will be a summation of two components. The real component will be the response due to $\cos \omega t$. The imaginary component will be the response due to $\sin \omega t$. Hence, in considering sinusoidal steady-state problems, we can calculate the particular solution to the driving function $e^{j\omega t}$. The imaginary part of this solution is the steady-state response to $\sin \omega t$; the real part is the steady-state response to $\cos \omega t$.

*Example 10.2.1*

Calculate the steady-state voltage response of the network shown in Fig. 10.2.1.

*Solution*

We consider the driving function $e^{j\left(t + \frac{\pi}{8}\right)}$. Our particular solution is of the form $Ke^{j\left(t + \frac{\pi}{8}\right)}$. Substituting this into the equation of operation (10.2.1) gives

$$jKe^{j\left(t + \frac{\pi}{8}\right)} + Ke^{j\left(t + \frac{\pi}{8}\right)} = e^{j\left(t + \frac{\pi}{8}\right)}$$

or

$$K = \frac{1}{1 + j} = \frac{1 - j}{2}$$

Since the steady-state response is given by the particular solution itself, the steady-state response to $\sin\left(t + \dfrac{\pi}{8}\right)$ is then given by

$$v(t) = \operatorname{Im}\left[\frac{1-j}{2} e^{j\left(t + \frac{\pi}{8}\right)}\right] = \frac{1}{\sqrt{2}} \sin\left(t - \frac{\pi}{8}\right)$$

which is the same steady-state solution as given in Eq. 10.2.2.

To generalize these results, we need to consider the response of an arbitrary network made up of $RLC$ elements. We have seen in the previous chapters that the response of such networks can be described by a differential equation of the form

$$\left(a_n \frac{d^n}{dt^n} + a_{n-1} \frac{d^{n-1}}{dt^{n-1}} + \cdots + a_1 \frac{d}{dt} + a_0\right) y(t)$$

$$= \left(b_m \frac{d^m}{dt^m} + b_{m-1} \frac{d^{m-1}}{dt^{m-1}} + \cdots + b_1 \frac{d}{dt} + b_0\right) u(t) \qquad (10.2.3)$$

where $u(t)$ is the network driving function and $y(t)$ is the network response. As we have seen for the special case in Example 10.2.1, we can find the steady-state response to the driving function $\sin(\omega t + \phi)$ by calculating the particular solution to the differential equation with driving function $e^{j(\omega t + \phi)}$. Hence, in Eq. 10.2.3 we replace the sinusoidal driving function $u(t)$ with the complex exponential driving function $e^{j(\omega t + \phi)}$ and assume a complex exponential solution* $Y(t) = Ke^{j(\omega t + \phi)}$. This gives

$$K[a_n(j\omega)^n + a_{n-1}(j\omega)^{n-1} + \cdots + a_1(j\omega) + a_0] e^{j(\omega t + \phi)}$$
$$= [b_m(j\omega)^m + b_{m-1}(j\omega)^{m-1} + \cdots + b_1(j\omega) + b_0] e^{j(\omega t + \phi)} \qquad (10.2.4)$$

which when solved for $K$ gives

$$K = \frac{b_m(j\omega)^m + b_{m-1}(j\omega)^{m-1} + \cdots + b_1(j\omega) + b_0}{a_n(j\omega)^n + a_{n-1}(j\omega)^{n-1} + \cdots + a_1(j\omega) + a_0} \qquad (10.2.5)$$

Note that $K$ is a constant with respect to the variable $t$ but is variable with the frequency of the driving function; hence, we will define $K$ as function of $j\omega$:

$$K \triangleq H(j\omega)$$

where $H(j\omega)$ is called the *sinusoidal steady-state transfer characteristic* of the network described by the differential equation (10.2.3). Note that $H(j\omega)$ is identical in form to the transfer function $H(s)$ defined in Chapter 9 when $s$ is replaced by $j\omega$.

Using the sinusoidal steady-state transfer characteristic notation, the particular solution to the differential equation can be written

$$Y(t) = H(j\omega) e^{j(\omega t + \phi)} \qquad (10.2.6)$$

---

*To differentiate between a complex exponential time function and a sinusoidal time function, we will write the former in capital letters, i.e., if $y(t) = \sin(\omega t + \phi)$, then $Y(t) = e^{j(\omega t + \phi)}$.

The function $H(j\omega)$ is in general complex and can be represented in complex exponential form as

$$H(j\omega) = |H(j\omega)|\, e^{j\theta(\omega)} \qquad (10.2.7)$$

where $|H(j\omega)| = \sqrt{H(j\omega)H^*(j\omega)}$

and

$$\theta(\omega) = \tan^{-1}\left(\frac{\mathrm{Im}[H(j\omega)]}{\mathrm{Re}[H(j\omega)]}\right)$$

Hence (10.2.6) can be rewritten

$$Y(t) = |H(j\omega)|\, e^{j(\omega t + \phi + \theta(\omega))} \qquad (10.2.8)$$

Taking the imaginary part of Eq. 10.2.8 yields the response to the driving function $\sin(\omega t + \phi)$,

$$y(t) = \mathrm{Im}[Y(t)] = |H(j\omega)|\sin(\omega t + \phi + \theta(\omega)) \qquad (10.2.9)$$

Thus the steady-state effect of the network on a sinusoidal input is described by an amplitude and phase change through the terms $|H(j\omega)|$ and $\theta(\omega)$ respectively. The computation of these terms can be easily developed using the digital computer as we will see later in this chapter.

*Example 10.2.2*

Calculate the steady-state current response of the network shown in Fig. 10.2.2.

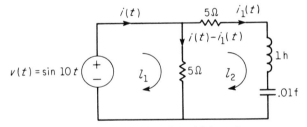

Fig. 10.2.2. *RCL circuit in sinusoidal steady state.*

*Solution*

Writing the KVL equation for loops $l_1$ and $l_2$, we have

$l_1$:  $v(t) = 5i(t) - 5i_1(t)$

$l_2$:  $0 = -5i(t) + 5i_1(t) + 5i_1(t) + \dfrac{di_1}{dt} + 100 \int i_1(t)\, dt$

Eliminating $i_1(t)$, we obtain the equation of operation as

$$\frac{d^2 i}{dt^2} + 5\frac{di}{dt} + 100i = \frac{1}{5}\frac{d^2 v}{dt^2} + 2\frac{dv}{dt} + 20v$$

Using the complex exponential driving function $V(t) = e^{j10t}$ and $I(t) =$

$Ke^{j10t}$, we get

$$K[-100 + j50 + 100]e^{j10t} = \left[-\frac{100}{5} + j20 + 20\right]e^{j10t}$$

Hence we have

$$K \triangleq H(j10) = \frac{j20}{j50} = \frac{2}{5}$$

therefore $\theta(\omega) = \theta(10) = 0$ and $|H(j\omega)| = |H(j10)| = \frac{2}{5}$. Then

$$I(t) = \frac{2}{5}e^{j10t}$$

The steady-state response is found by taking the imaginary part of $I(t)$ and is given by

$$i(t) = \text{Im}[I(t)] = (2/5)\sin 10t$$

*Example 10.2.3*

Calculate the steady-state voltage, $v_C(t)$, for the network shown in Fig. 10.2.3.

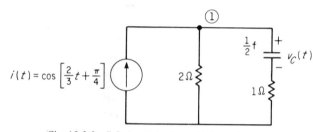

Fig. 10.2.3. *RC* circuit in sinusoidal steady state.

*Solution*

The equation of operation for this circuit is obtained by applying KCL to node 1 and simplyfying as

$$\frac{3}{4} \cdot \frac{dv_c}{dt} + \frac{1}{2}v_C \doteq i(t)$$

In this case, our driving function is $\cos\left(\frac{2}{3}t + \frac{\pi}{4}\right)$. We can take our driving function as

$$i(t) = \text{Re}\left[e^{j\left(\frac{2}{3}t + \frac{\pi}{4}\right)}\right] = \text{Re}[I(t)]$$

We then solve for the response of the network to $I(t)$ and take the real part to find the response due to $i(t)$. Thus our complex exponential response is

$$V_C(t) = \frac{1}{\frac{3}{4} \times j\frac{2}{3} + \frac{1}{2}}e^{j\left(\frac{2}{3}t + \frac{\pi}{4}\right)}$$

Hence, we have in this case

$$\left| H\left( j\frac{2}{3} \right) \right| = \sqrt{2}$$

$$\theta\left( \frac{2}{3} \right) = \tan^{-1}(-1) = -\frac{\pi}{4}$$

This gives

$$V_C(t) = \sqrt{2}\, e^{j\frac{2}{3}t} \tag{10.2.10}$$

Taking the real part of $V_C(t)$, we obtain the solution

$$v_C(t) = \sqrt{2}\cos\left(\tfrac{2}{3}t\right)$$

## 10.3. COMPLEX IMPEDANCE AND ADMITTANCE FUNCTIONS

Comparing Eqs. 10.2.3 and 10.2.4, we can see that the net result of studying the sinusoidal steady state by means of the complex exponential function is to replace the differential operator $\dfrac{d^n}{dt^n}$ by $(j\omega)^n$ wherever it appears in the equation of operation. A natural question which develops from this observation is whether or not it is essential to develop the differential equation when dealing with the sinusoidal steady state; i.e. is it possible to develop the sinusoidal steady-state performance directly from the circuit without writing the differential equation of operation as an intermediate step? The answer to this question is obtained by considering the voltage-current relationships for individual elements under sinusoidal steady state conditions. Assuming an inductor current of the form $I_L(t) = e^{j(\omega t + \phi)}$, the inductor voltage will be

$$V_L(t) = L\frac{dI_L(t)}{dt} = (j\omega L)\, I_L(t) \tag{10.3.1}$$

Similarly, a resistance current of the same form will give a resistance voltage

$$V_R(t) = RI_R(t) \tag{10.3.2}$$

A voltage $V_C(t) = e^{j(\omega t + \phi)}$ applied to the terminals of a capacitor gives rise to a current

$$I_C(t) = C\frac{dV_C(t)}{dt} = (j\omega C)\, V_C(t) \tag{10.3.3}$$

Using these three relationships, we have an algebraic description of the terminal voltage-current relationships for $L$, $R$, and $C$ elements under sinusoidal steady-state conditions as

$$V_L(t) = (j\omega L)I_L(t) \tag{10.3.4}$$

$$V_R(t) = RI_R(t) \qquad (10.3.5)$$

$$V_C(t) = \left(\frac{1}{j\omega C}\right)I_C(t) \qquad (10.3.6)$$

Or, writing the current in terms of the voltage

$$I_L(t) = \frac{1}{j\omega L} V_L(t) \qquad (10.3.7)$$

$$I_R(t) = \frac{1}{R} V_R(t) \qquad (10.3.8)$$

$$I_C(t) = j\omega C V_C(t) \qquad (10.3.9)$$

Note that studying the sinusoidal steady state by means of the complex exponential function permits us to reduce voltage-current terminal relationships for $L$ and $C$ elements to simple multiplicative operations which bear close analogy to the resistor terminal voltage-current relationship. To fully exploit these analogies, we define inductive and capacitive *reactance*, respectively, by

$$X_L = j\omega L$$

$$X_C = \frac{1}{j\omega C} = -\frac{j}{\omega C} \qquad (10.3.10)$$

In studying the sinusoidal steady state, we can replace $L$ and $C$ circuit elements by their reactance values and use the voltage-current terminal relationships indicated in Eqs. 10.3.4 to 10.3.9.

*Example 10.3.1*

Evaluate the sinusoidal steady-state current for the circuit shown in Fig. 10.3.1 (a) by deriving the differential equation and (b) by replacing the circuit by its sinusoidal steady state equivalent.

*Solution*

(a) The differential equation describing the current response is ob-

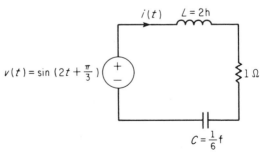

Fig. 10.3.1. *RLC* series circuit in sinusoidal steady state.

tained as

$$2\frac{d^2i}{dt^2} + \frac{di}{dt} + 6i = \frac{dv}{dt}$$

Taking the driving function to be the complex exponential

$$V(t) = e^{j\left(2t + \frac{\pi}{3}\right)}$$

the current response is

$$I(t) = \frac{2j}{-2 + 2j} e^{j\left(2t + \frac{\pi}{3}\right)}$$

or

$$I(t) = \frac{1}{2}(1 - j)e^{j\left(2t + \frac{\pi}{3}\right)}$$

$$= \frac{1}{\sqrt{2}} e^{-j\frac{\pi}{4}} e^{j\left(2t + \frac{\pi}{3}\right)} = \frac{1}{\sqrt{2}} e^{j\left(2t + \frac{\pi}{12}\right)}$$

(b) To obtain the steady-state equivalent of the network, we replace $L$ by $j\omega L$ and $C$ by $\frac{1}{j\omega C}$. The equivalent circuit is shown in Fig. 10.3.2.

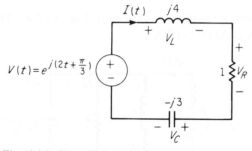

Fig. 10.3.2. Sinusoidal steady-state equivalent of $RLC$ network.

Applying KVL around the loop gives

$$V_L(t) + V_R(t) + V_C(t) = e^{j\left(2t + \frac{\pi}{3}\right)}$$

Applying the sinusoidal steady-state voltage-current terminal relationships for each element yields

$$V_L(t) = j4I(t), \quad V_R(t) = I(t), \quad V_C(t) = -j3I(t)$$

Substituting these in the KVL equation yields

$$I(t)[j4 + 1 - j3] = e^{j\left(2t + \frac{\pi}{3}\right)}$$

or

$$I(t) = \frac{1}{1 + j} e^{j\left(2t + \frac{\pi}{3}\right)} = \frac{1}{\sqrt{2}} e^{j\left(2t + \frac{\pi}{12}\right)}$$

which is the same result obtained using the system differential equation. The steady-state current is then found from

$$i(t) = \text{Im}[I(t)] = \frac{1}{\sqrt{2}} \sin\left(2t + \frac{\pi}{12}\right)$$

*Example 10.3.2*

Find the sinusoidal steady-state voltage $v_C(t)$ for the circuit shown in Fig. 10.3.3 by using the sinusoidal steady-state equivalent network. Let

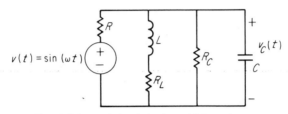

Fig. 10.3.3. *RLC* circuit in sinusoidal steady-state.

$\omega = 10 \text{ rad/sec}, R = R_L = 1\,\Omega, R_C = 2\,\Omega, L = 0.1 \text{ h, and } C = 0.025 \text{ f.}$

*Solution*

The equivalent network is indicated in Fig. 10.3.4. Here $X_L = j\omega L$ and $X_C = 1/j\omega C$. Applying KCL

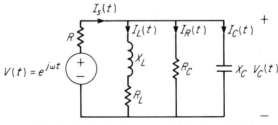

Fig. 10.3.4. Equivalent network for Fig. 10.3.3.

and KVL, we obtain

$$I_s = I_L + I_R + I_C$$
$$V = V_C + I_s R$$
$$V_C = I_C X_C = I_R R_C = I_L(X_L + R_L)$$

Solving the above equations for $V_C(t)$ gives

$$V_C(t) = \left(1 + j\omega CR + \frac{R}{R_C} + \frac{R}{j\omega L + R_L}\right)^{-1} V(t)$$

Substituting for $\omega$, $R$, $R_C$, $R_L$, $L$, and $C$ gives

$$V_C(t) = \frac{V(t)}{2 - j0.25} = 0.496e^{j(10t + 7.1°)}$$

Taking the imaginary part of $V_C(t)$ gives the desired sinusoidal steady state voltage

$$v_C(t) = 0.496 \sin (10t + 7.1°)$$

These examples illustrate the use of inductive and capacitive reactance terms in sinusoidal steady state analysis. Even further analytical simplification can be obtained by considering equivalent two-terminal networks in the steady state. For example, in Fig. 10.3.5a, we seek a single "ele-

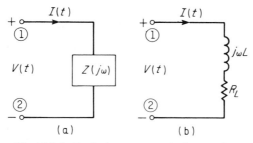

Fig. 10.3.5. Equivalent two-terminal networks.

ment," $Z(j\omega)$, which has the same terminal voltage-current relationship as the circuit in Fig. 10.3.5b. In Fig. 10.3.5b the voltage $V(t)$ is related to the current $I(t)$ by

$$V(t) = I(t)(j\omega L) + I(t)R_L = I(t)[R_L + j\omega L] \qquad (10.3.11)$$

The relationship in Fig. 10.3.5a is

$$V(t) = I(t)Z(j\omega) \qquad (10.3.12)$$

A comparison of Eqs. 10.3.11 and 10.3.12 shows that two networks are equivalent (in steady state) from the terminal pair ①, ② if we make

$$Z(j\omega) = R_L + j\omega L \qquad (10.3.13)$$

The term $Z(j\omega)$ is called the *complex impedance* of the series combination of the resistor and inductor. The complex impedance has combination properties quite similar to those of the resistance function, i.e., the equivalent of two impedances in series is the sum of the individual impedances. Combination rules for impedance functions are readily derived by considering terminal voltage-current relationships. For $n$ impedances in series, the equivalent impedance is simply the summation of the individual impedances as shown in Fig. 10.3.6a and Fig. 10.3.6b.

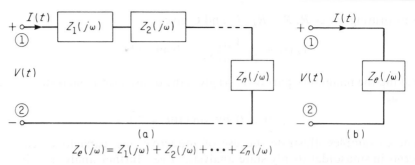

$$Z_e(j\omega) = Z_1(j\omega) + Z_2(j\omega) + \cdots + Z_n(j\omega)$$

Fig. 10.3.6. Equivalent network for impedances in series.

Parallel combinations of elements are analyzed in a similar manner by utilizing the *complex admittance* function, $Y(j\omega)$, which is the reciprocal of the complex impedance. For illustration, we consider deriving the equivalent admittance of the two parallel elements in Fig. 10.3.7a. The

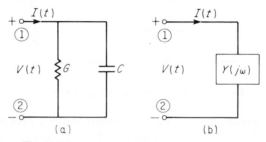

Fig. 10.3.7. Equivalent two-terminal networks.

terminal voltage-current relationship is

$$I(t) = V(t)[G + j\omega C] \tag{10.3.14}$$

For the network shown in Fig. 10.3.7b, we have

$$I(t) = V(t)Y(j\omega) \tag{10.3.15}$$

Comparing Eqs. 10.3.14 and 10.3.15 we see the two networks are equivalent from the terminal pair ①, ② provided

$$Y(j\omega) = G + j\omega C \tag{10.3.16}$$

More generally, the equivalent admittance of $n$ elements in parallel is simply the summation of the individual admittances as indicated in Fig. 10.3.8a and b.

*Example 10.3.3. Voltage Division*

Find the steady state voltage across the capacitor for the circuit

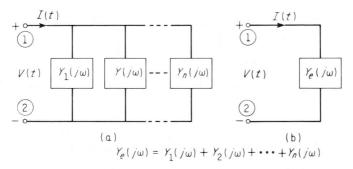

$$Y_e(j\omega) = Y_1(j\omega) + Y_2(j\omega) + \cdots + Y_n(j\omega)$$

Fig. 10.3.8.  Equivalent network for $n$ admittances in parallel.

shown in Fig. 10.3.9a by combining series impedances and parallel admittances to form an equivalent network.

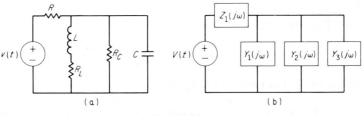

Fig. 10.3.9

*Solution*

The equivalent sinusoidal steady state network can be represented as three parallel admittances in series with an impedance and voltage source as in Fig. 10.3.9b, where

$$Z_1(j\omega) = R$$

$$Y_1(j\omega) = \frac{1}{R_L + j\omega L}$$

$$Y_2(j\omega) = \frac{1}{R_C}$$

$$Y_3(j\omega) = j\omega C$$

This network can be reduced to the circuit shown in Fig. 10.3.10a by combining the parallel admittances and then to the network shown in Fig. 10.3.10b by combining the two series impedances. In Fig. 10.3.10a

$$Z_2(j\omega) = \frac{1}{Y_e(j\omega)}; \quad Y_e(j\omega) = Y_1(j\omega) + Y_2(j\omega) + Y_3(j\omega)$$

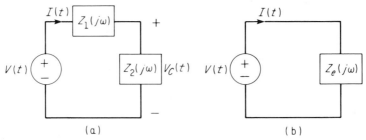

Fig. 10.3.10. Equivalent networks for Fig. 10.3.9.

and, in Fig. 10.3.10b,

$$Z_e(j\omega) = Z_1(j\omega) + Z_2(j\omega)$$

From Fig. 10.3.10b, we have

$$I(t) = \frac{V(t)}{Z_e(j\omega)}$$

while from Fig. 10.3.10a

$$V_C(t) = I(t)Z_2(j\omega) = V(t)\left[\frac{Z_2(j\omega)}{Z_1(j\omega) + Z_2(j\omega)}\right] \qquad (10.3.17)$$

Substituting for $Z_1(j\omega)$ and $Z_2(j\omega)$ gives

$$V_C(t) = \left\{1 + \frac{R}{R_C} + j\omega CR + \frac{R}{R_L + j\omega L}\right\}^{-1} V(t) \qquad (10.3.18)$$

The relationship between $V_C(t)$ and $V(t)$ as given above in Eq. 10.3.17 describes *voltage division*. In any series combination of impedances, the voltage across any particular element is the ratio of the impedance of the element to the total impedance in the series combination multiplied by the applied voltage. Once this relationship is recognized, one can write down expression 10.3.18 immediately.

*Example 10.3.4: Current Division*

Find the steady-state current through the *RL* branch in the circuit shown in Fig. 10.3.11.

*Solution*

The network can be viewed as a current source in parallel with four

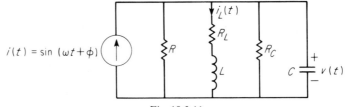

Fig. 10.3.11

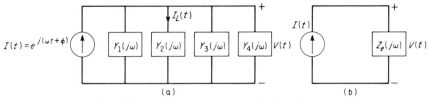

Fig. 10.3.12.  Equivalent networks for Fig. 10.3.11.

admittance elements as shown in Fig. 10.3.12a where

$$Y_1(j\omega) = G$$

$$Y_2(j\omega) = \frac{1}{Z_2(j\omega)}, \qquad Z_2(j\omega) = R_L + j\omega L$$

$$Y_3(j\omega) = \frac{1}{R_C} = G_C$$

$$Y_4(j\omega) = j\omega C$$

The network in Fig. 10.3.12a can be further reduced to the equivalent circuit shown in Fig. 10.3.12b, where

$$Z_e(j\omega) = \frac{1}{Y_e(j\omega)}$$

$$Y_e(j\omega) = Y_1(j\omega) + Y_2(j\omega) + Y_3(j\omega) + Y_4(j\omega)$$

The voltage $V(t)$ is related to the driving current by

$$V(t) = I(t)Z_e(j\omega)$$

and the current $I_L(t)$ is related to the voltage $V(t)$ by

$$I_L(t) = V(t)Y_2(j\omega) = I(t)\left[\frac{Y_2(j\omega)}{Y_1(j\omega) + Y_2(j\omega) + Y_3(j\omega) + Y_4(j\omega)}\right] \quad (10.3.19)$$

Substituting for the admittance functions gives

$$I_L(t) = \frac{1}{(R_L G + 1 + R_L G_C - \omega^2 LC) + j(\omega GL + \omega G_C L + R_L \omega C)} I(t)$$

Finally, we obtain the steady-state current $i_L(t)$ by finding the imaginary part of $I_L(t)$ as

$$i_L(t) = \frac{\sin(\omega t + \phi - \theta(\omega))}{\sqrt{(R_L G + 1 + R_L G_C - \omega^2 LC)^2 + (\omega GL + \omega G_C L + R_L \omega C)^2}}$$

where

$$\theta(\omega) = \tan^{-1}\left(\frac{\omega GL + \omega G_C L + R_L \omega C}{1 + R_L G + R_L G_C - \omega^2 LC}\right)$$

The relationship in Eq. 10.3.19 describes a *current division*.  The current in any particular branch is the total current multiplied by the ratio of the admittance of the particular branch to the total admittance in the parallel combination.

*Example 10.3.5: Equivalent Sources*

The complex impedance and admittance functions can be used to derive equivalent voltage and current sources in the sinusoidal steady state. The terminal voltage for the network shown in Fig. 10.3.13a can

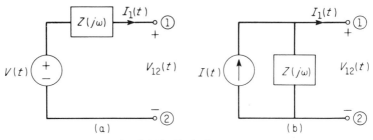

Fig. 10.3.13. Equivalent sources.

be written as

$$V_{12}(t) = V(t) - I_1(t)Z(j\omega)$$

whereas the terminal voltage for the network shown in Fig. 10.3.13b is

$$V_{12}(t) = I(t)Z(j\omega) - I_1(t)Z(j\omega)$$

Obviously the terminal voltages are equal if we make

$$I(t) = \frac{V(t)}{Z(j\omega)}$$

Hence in the steady state a voltage source in series with an impedance can be replaced by a current source in parallel with the impedance. The value of the current source is given by the above equation. Similarly, a current source in parallel with an impedance can be replaced by a voltage source in series with an impedance.

## 10.4. PHASORS

We have seen in the previous sections that time variation of circuit voltages and currents in the sinusoidal steady state can be represented in complex exponential form, $e^{j\omega t}$. Since we know the time variable $t$ will enter into our solution in this manner, quite often it is convenient to suppress the time variation and simply develop a "time invariant" solution in terms of a complex driving function and the complex impedance. After the time invariant solution is obtained, the time variation can be reinserted into the solution by simply multiplying by $e^{j\omega t}$. For example,

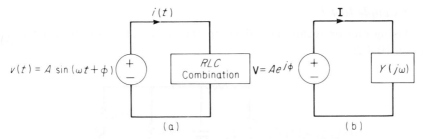

Fig. 10.4.1. Development of time-invariant network solution.

in Fig. 10.4.1a, it is desired to calculate the steady-state current $i(t)$. As we have seen, we can calculate $i(t)$ by calculating the complex exponential response $I(t)$ to the driving function $Ae^{j(\omega t + \phi)}$ and taking the imaginary part of $I(t)$, i.e.,

$$i(t) = \text{Im } [Ae^{j(\omega t + \phi)} Y(j\omega)] \qquad (10.4.1)$$

where $Y(j\omega)$ is the equivalent admittance function of the *RLC* combination. Note that Eq. 10.4.1 can be written as the imaginary part of the time-invariant solution

$$\mathbf{I} = Ae^{j\phi} Y(j\omega) \qquad (10.4.2)$$

multiplied by $e^{j\omega t}$, that is

$$i(t) = \text{Im } [\mathbf{I}e^{j\omega t}] \qquad (10.4.3)$$

To develop the time invariant part of the solution we can use the network shown in Fig. 10.4.1b in which the time variation $e^{j\omega t}$ has been suppressed. The voltage driving function is

$$\mathbf{V} = Ae^{j\phi} \qquad (10.4.4)$$

and the current response becomes

$$\mathbf{I} = \mathbf{V} Y(j\omega) \qquad (10.4.5)$$

To obtain the actual time solution, we multiply Eq. 10.4.5 by $e^{j\omega t}$ and take the imaginary part as indicated in Eq. 10.4.3. The quantities $\mathbf{I}$ and $\mathbf{V}$ are termed *phasors*. We will use boldface letters to denote a phasor quantity. In working with phasors, it is necessary to establish a convention relating the phasor and time solution. Since we have defined the time solution corresponding to the phasor to be the imaginary part of the product of the phasor and the time function $e^{j\omega t}$, our convention is to represent all sinusoidal variations in terms of the sine function. This requires that any driving function of the form $\cos(\omega t + \phi)$ be written in the equivalent form $\sin\left(\omega t + \phi + \dfrac{\pi}{2}\right)$ prior to development of the phasor model.

*Example 10.4.1*

Using phasor techniques, develop the steady-state solution for $v_L(t)$ in Fig. 10.4.2a.

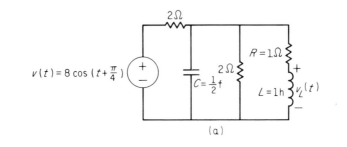

(a)

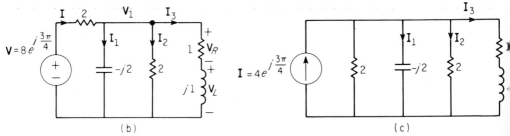

(b)    (c)

Fig. 10.4.2. (a) Circuit in sinusoidal steady state, (b) the phasor model, and (c) equivalent phasor model.

*Solution*

The driving function in this case is

$$v(t) = 8 \cos \left( t + \frac{\pi}{4} \right)$$

Following our phasor convention, we rewrite $v(t)$ as a sine function

$$v(t) = 8 \cos \left( t + \frac{\pi}{4} \right) = 8 \sin \left( t + \frac{3\pi}{4} \right)$$

The phasor driving function corresponding to this $v(t)$ is

$$\mathbf{V} = 8e^{j\frac{3\pi}{4}}$$

The phasor model is now constructed in Fig. 10.4.2b. The phasor response $\mathbf{V}_L$ is given by

$$\mathbf{V}_L = j\mathbf{I}_3$$

In order to evaluate $\mathbf{I}_3$, we convert the voltage source in Fig. 10.4.2b to the current source and equivalent phasor model as shown in Fig. 10.4.2c. Now we use the current division relationship of (10.3.19) to obtain $I_3$ as

$$I_3 = 4e^{j\left(\frac{3\pi}{4}\right)} \left[ \frac{\frac{1}{1+j}}{\frac{1}{2} + j\frac{1}{2} + \frac{1}{2} + \frac{1}{1+j}} \right]$$

$$= \frac{4}{3(1+j)} e^{j\frac{3\pi}{4}} = \frac{2\sqrt{2}}{3} e^{-j\frac{\pi}{4}} e^{j\frac{3\pi}{4}} = \frac{2\sqrt{2}}{3} e^{j\frac{\pi}{2}}$$

Hence

$$V_L = jI_3 = e^{j\frac{\pi}{2}} I_3 = \frac{2\sqrt{2}}{3} e^{j\pi}$$

Therefore

$$v_L(t) = \text{Im} \left[ \frac{2\sqrt{2}}{3} e^{j\pi} e^{j\omega t} \right] = 0.943 \sin(\omega t + \pi)$$

The use of phasor notation permits us to represent voltages and currents as vectors in the complex plane. From this representation, we can use vector manipulations to solve voltage and current relationships. We use an example to illustrate the procedure.

*Example 10.4.2*

Using the complex plane, plot all voltages and currents for the circuit shown in Fig. 10.4.2b.

*Solution*

The voltage $V$ is shown plotted in Fig. 10.4.3a. The length of the vector represents the magnitude of $V$ (in this case 8 volts) and the orientation of the vector denotes the phase angle of the complex exponential function. The voltage $V_L = \frac{2\sqrt{2}}{3} e^{j\pi}$ as derived in the above example is plotted in Fig. 10.4.3b. The current $I_3 = \frac{2\sqrt{2}}{3} e^{j\frac{\pi}{2}}$ as derived in the above example is plotted in Fig. 10.4.3c. The total voltage across the $RL$ series combination is

$$V_1 = V_R + V_L = I_3(1 + j) = \sqrt{2} e^{j\frac{\pi}{4}} I_3 = \frac{4}{3} e^{j\frac{3\pi}{4}}$$

Hence the currents $I_1$ and $I_2$ are

$$I_1 = \left( j\frac{1}{2} \right) V_1 = \frac{1}{2} e^{j\frac{\pi}{2}} V_1 = \frac{2}{3} e^{j\frac{5\pi}{4}}$$

and

$$I_2 = \frac{1}{2} V_1 = \frac{2}{3} e^{j\frac{3\pi}{4}}$$

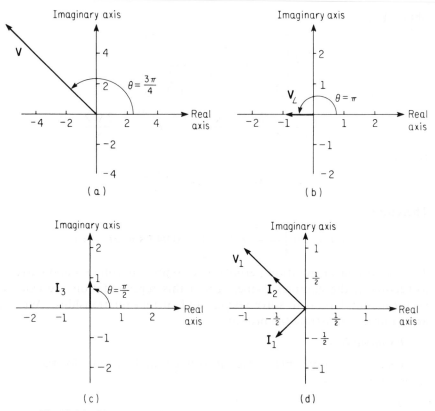

Fig. 10.4.3. Phasor plot of voltages and currents for network of Fig. 10.4.2b.

The voltages $V_1$ and currents $I_1$ and $I_2$ are shown graphically in Fig. 10.4.3d. To facilitate comparison between the various elements, the voltages and currents for each element are shown on the same plot in Fig. 10.4.4a, b, and c. In Fig. 10.4.4a the current through and the voltage across the 1-ohm resistance are shown. Both current and voltage have the same vector position (phase angle) and are therefore said to be *in phase*.

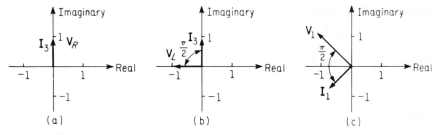

Fig. 10.4.4. Voltage-current relationship for (a) $R$, (b) $L$, (c) $C$ elements.

The inductor voltage-current relationship is shown in Fig. 10.4.4b. In this case, there is a phase angle of $\pi/2$ between current and voltage, that is, the current must be rotated in the positive (counterclockwise) direction by $\pi/2$ to coincide with voltage vector. For this reason, the voltage and current in the inductor are said to be *out of phase* and current is said to *lag* the voltage by $\pi/2$. Similarly, the voltage and current in the capacitor are also out of phase as shown in Fig. 10.4.4c. However, for the capacitor, the current is said to *lead* the voltage by $\pi/2$.

*Example 10.4.3*

Using graphical techniques, calculate the voltage $v_C(t)$ in Fig. 10.4.5a.

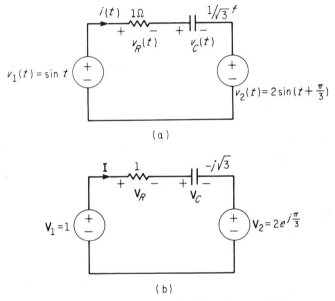

Fig. 10.4.5. (a) An $RC$ circuit, (b) its phasor equivalent.

*Solution*

The time-invariant phasor equivalent circuit is shown in Fig. 10.4.5b. The current **I** satisfies the relationship

$$\mathbf{I}(1 - j\sqrt{3}) = \mathbf{V}_1 - \mathbf{V}_2$$

The voltage $\mathbf{V}_1 - \mathbf{V}_2 = (1 - 2e^{j\frac{\pi}{3}})$ is plotted in Fig. 10.4.6. The current vector **I** can also be plotted, since

$$\mathbf{I} = \frac{1}{1 - j\sqrt{3}}(\mathbf{V}_1 - \mathbf{V}_2)$$

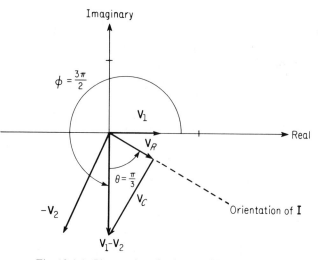

Fig. 10.4.6. Phasor plot of voltages of Fig. 10.4.5b.

From this equation it is clear that $\mathbf{I}$ leads $\mathbf{V}_1 - \mathbf{V}_2$ vector by $\theta = \tan^{-1}\sqrt{3} = \pi/3$ as shown in the figure. The voltage across the resistance is in phase with the current $\mathbf{I}$ as indicated, whereas the voltage across the capacitance lags the current by $\pi/2$. The sum of $\mathbf{V}_R$ and $\mathbf{V}_C$ equals $\mathbf{V}_1 - \mathbf{V}_2$. Hence, from the figure

$$|\mathbf{V}_C| = |\mathbf{V}_1 - \mathbf{V}_2|\sin\theta$$

and

$$\angle\mathbf{V}_C = \phi + \theta - \frac{\pi}{2}$$

Now,

$$\mathbf{V}_1 - \mathbf{V}_2 = \left(1 - 2e^{j\frac{\pi}{3}}\right) = \sqrt{3}e^{j\frac{3\pi}{2}}$$

Since $\theta = \frac{\pi}{3}$, by simple complex algebra we have

$$|\mathbf{V}_C| = \left|\sqrt{3}e^{j\frac{3\pi}{2}}\right|\sin\frac{\pi}{3} = \sqrt{3}\sin\frac{\pi}{3} = \frac{3}{2}$$

$$\angle\mathbf{V}_C = \frac{3\pi}{2} + \frac{\pi}{3} - \frac{\pi}{2} = \frac{4\pi}{3}$$

or

$$\mathbf{V}_C = \frac{3}{2}e^{j\frac{4\pi}{3}}$$

Hence our time solution is

$$v_C(t) = \text{Im}\left[\frac{3}{2} e^{j\left(t + \frac{4\pi}{3}\right)}\right] = \frac{3}{2} \sin\left(t + \frac{4\pi}{3}\right)$$

## 10.5. NETWORK FREQUENCY RESPONSE AND BODE PLOTS

As we have seen in Sec. 10.2, the relationship between driving function and response in the sinusoidal steady state is described by sinusoidal steady state transfer characteristic function $H(j\omega)$. This function is the ratio of two polynomials in $\omega$:

$$H(j\omega) = \frac{B(j\omega)}{A(j\omega)} = \frac{b_m(j\omega)^m + b_{m-1}(j\omega)^{m-1} + \cdots + b_1(j\omega) + b_0}{a_n(j\omega)^n + a_{n-1}(j\omega)^{n-1} + \cdots + a_1(j\omega) + a_0} \quad (10.5.1)$$

As noted previously, $H(j\omega)$ is in general a complex function which can be represented as a magnitude multiplied by a complex exponential

$$H(j\omega) = |H(j\omega)| e^{j\theta(\omega)} \quad (10.5.2)$$

where

$$|H(j\omega)| = \sqrt{H(j\omega)H^*(j\omega)} \quad (10.5.3)$$

and

$$\theta(\omega) = \tan^{-1}\left[\frac{\text{Im}[H(j\omega)]}{\text{Re}[H(j\omega)]}\right] \quad (10.5.4)$$

If $H(j\omega)$ is known for all values of $\omega$, the response to any sinusoidal driving function can be obtained simply by multiplying $H(j\omega)$ by the exponential driving function, i.e., if the driving function is $\sin(\omega_1 t + \phi)$, the response is found from

$$y(t) = \text{Im}[H(j\omega_1)e^{j(\omega_1 t + \phi)}] \quad (10.5.5)$$

Hence it is useful to consider $H(j\omega)$ as a function of a variable $\omega$ until the driving function frequency is specified. To obtain a description of the system response to sinusoids of various frequencies, $H(j\omega)$ can be plotted as a function of the frequency $\omega$. Two curves are necessary to completely specify $H(j\omega)$, normally these are taken as the magnitude $|H(j\omega)|$ and phase $\theta(\omega)$. $|H(j\omega)|$ is called the network *amplitude response* because it specifies the effect of the network on the sinusoidal amplitude as a function of frequency. Similarly, $\theta(\omega)$ is called the network *phase response* since it specifies the effect of the network on the sinusoidal phase as a function of frequency. $|H(j\omega)|$ and $\theta(\omega)$ can be computed using Eqs. 10.5.3 and 10.5.4 as a function of frequency. This can be done conveniently using the digital computer as we will show in the later part of this section. It has become conventional to plot 20 times the logarithm of the magnitude function, rather than the magnitude function itself. This, of course, permits a wide variation in the function $|H(j\omega)|$ to be plotted on a compact graph. Further, there are several shortcuts which can be used to quickly sketch $20 \log_{10} |H(\omega)|$ without resorting to the computer. We will examine these first and we will show how we use these short cuts to plot both $|H(j\omega)|$ and $\theta(\omega)$. These plots are called *Bode plots*.

We first define the *units* of the function

$$20 \log_{10} |H(j\omega)| = 10 \log_{10} |H(j\omega)|^2 \qquad (10.5.6)$$

The units are called *decibels* and are written in abbreviated form as db.

### Bode Plots Amplitude Response

There are several useful shortcuts which can be used to quickly sketch the approximate amplitude function of a network. Recall from Chapter 9 that the types of terms appearing in the transfer function $H(s)$ were of the form

$$\begin{aligned} P_1(s) &= s^n \\ P_2(s) &= (s + a)^n \\ P_3(s) &= s^2 + 2\zeta\omega_n s + \omega_n^2 \end{aligned} \qquad (10.5.7)$$

This implies the polynomials $A(j\omega)$ and $B(j\omega)$ in Eq. 10.5.1 can be written as products of a scalar and factors of the form

$$\begin{aligned} P_1(j\omega) &= (j\omega)^n \\ P_2(j\omega) &= (j\omega + a)^n \\ P_3(j\omega) &= (\omega_n^2 - \omega^2) + j2\zeta\omega_n\omega \end{aligned} \qquad (10.5.8)$$

Since the magnitude function can be written

$$|H(j\omega)| = \left| \frac{B(j\omega)}{A(j\omega)} \right| \qquad (10.5.9)$$

then (note that throughout we write $\log_{10}$ as "log")

$$20 \log |H(j\omega)| = 20 \log |B(j\omega)| - 20 \log |A(j\omega)| \qquad (10.5.10)$$

In addition, the magnitude of each one of the polynomial terms is simply the product of the magnitudes of each of its factors; i.e.,

$$\begin{aligned} 20 \log |H(j\omega)| = {}&20 \log |B_1(j\omega)| + \cdots + 20 \log |B_m(j\omega)| \\ &- 20 \log |A_1(j\omega)| - \cdots - 20 \log |A_n(j\omega)| \end{aligned}$$
$$(10.5.11)$$

where we have assumed

$$B(j\omega) = B_1(j\omega)B_2(j\omega)\cdots B_m(j\omega)$$

$$(10.5.12)$$

$$A(j\omega) = A_1(j\omega)A_2(j\omega)\cdots A_n(j\omega)$$

and each $B_i(j\omega)$, $A_i(j\omega)$ is given by one of the polynomials in Eq. 10.5.8.

Thus a plot of the function $20 \log |H(j\omega)|$ consists of the addition and subtraction of plots corresponding to the magnitude of terms of the form given in (10.5.8).

**The Term $P_1(j\omega) = (j\omega)^n$**

The magnitude of the term $(j\omega)^n$ is simply

$$| P_1(j\omega) | = \omega^n \qquad (10.5.13)$$

Thus, the term to be considered is

$$20 \log | H(j\omega) | = 20 \log \omega^n \qquad (10.5.14)$$

For $\omega = 0.1$ this term is $-20n$ db, for $\omega = 1$ its value is 0 db. For $\omega = 10$ its value is $+20n$ db, etc. A plot of this function on a semilog scale is shown in Fig. 10.5.1. Note that the function increases $20n$ db per decade

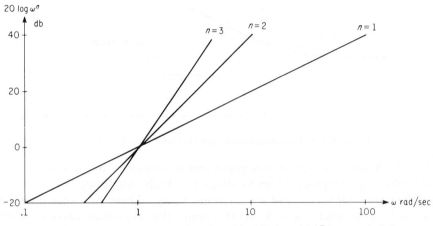

Fig. 10.5.1. Plot of magnitude function with $H(j\omega) = (j\omega)^n$ for $n = 1, 2, 3$.

(a factor of 10 frequency change) or $6n$ db per octave (a factor of 2 frequency change).

**The Term $P_2(j\omega) = (j\omega + a)^n$**

The magnitude of this term is

$$| P_2(j\omega) | = (\omega^2 + a^2)^{\frac{n}{2}} \qquad (10.5.15)$$

Hence the function to be considered is

$$20 \log | H(j\omega) | = 10n \log (\omega^2 + a^2) \qquad (10.5.16)$$

It is convenient to normalize the argument of this function by the parameter $a^2$ to yield a function of the normalized frequency variable $u$

$$u \triangleq \left(\frac{\omega}{a}\right) \qquad (10.5.17)$$

The function to be plotted can then be written

$$20 \log |H(ju)| = 10n \log (1 + u^2) - 10n \log a^2 \qquad (10.5.18)$$

Consider the term $10n \log (1 + u^2)$. For $u \ll 1$, this term is approximately $10n \log (1)$ or zero db. For $u \gg 1$, this term becomes approximately $10n \log (u^2)$ which is the same form studied above. The value $u = 1$ is called the *break point* and at this value of $u$, the magnitude is $10n \log (2)$ or $3n$ db. The magnitude curve is plotted in Fig. 10.5.2 for

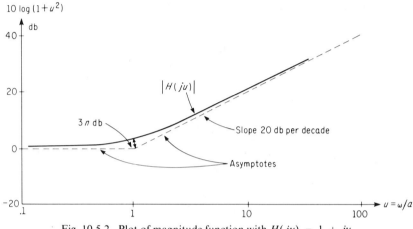

Fig. 10.5.2. Plot of magnitude function with $H(ju) = 1 + ju$.

$n = 1$. A quick sketch of this curve can be obtained by drawing in the straight line asymptotes given by $10 \log 1 = 0$ db and $10 \log u^2$, as shown in the figure, for $u \ll 1$ and $u \gg 1$ respectively. These two lines intersect at the *break frequency* $u = 1$. At this point, the magnitude curve is $3n$ db above the asymptote plot. Two other points on the magnitude curve are easily calculated at an octave below and an octave above the break frequency. At these points, the magnitude curve is $n$ db above the asymptote. The second term in Eq. 10.5.18 is simply a scaling term which shifts the ordinate scale by $10n \log a^2$.

### The Term $P_3(j\omega) = (\omega_n^2 - \omega^2) + j2\zeta\omega_n\omega$

The magnitude of this term is

$$|P_3(j\omega)| = \sqrt{(\omega_n^2 - \omega^2)^2 + 4\zeta^2\omega_n^2\omega^2} \qquad (10.5.19)$$

Hence the function to be considered is

$$20 \log |H(j\omega)| = 10 \log [(\omega_n^2 - \omega^2)^2 + 4\zeta^2\omega_n^2\omega^2] \qquad (10.5.20)$$

Again, it is convenient to normalize the argument, dividing by the parameter $\omega_n^4$ to yield a function of the normalized frequency variable $u$

$$u \triangleq (\omega/\omega_n) \qquad (10.5.21)$$

The function to be plotted can then be written as

$$20 \log | H(ju) | = 10 \log [1 + 2(2\zeta^2 - 1)u^2 + u^4] - 10 \log \omega_n^4$$
$$(10.5.22)$$

Consider the term $10 \log [1 + 2(2\zeta^2 - 1)u^2 + u^4]$.  For $u^2 \ll 1$, this term is approximately $10 \log (1) = 0$ db.  When $u^2 \gg 1$, this function is approximately $10 \log u^4$ which plots as a straight line increasing at 40 db per decade.  Using these two straight lines as asymptotes to the magnitude curve, the asymptotes intersect at the break frequency $u = 1$.  The exact behavior of the magnitude curve for $u$ in the region of the break frequency depends on the value of $\zeta$, called the *damping coefficient*.  A plot of Eq. 10.5.22 is shown in Fig. 10.5.3 for several values of the parameter $\zeta$.  The second term in Eq. 10.5.22 is a constant which simply shifts the ordinate scale by $10 \log \omega_n^4$.

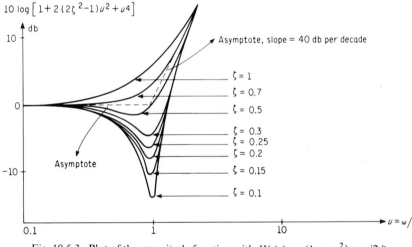

Fig. 10.5.3. Plot of the magnitude function with $H(ju) = (1 - u^2) + j2\zeta u$.

*Example 10.5.1*

Plot the amplitude response for the network shown in Fig. 10.5.4a. Let $v(t)$ be the input and $v_R(t)$ the response.

*Solution*

Utilizing the steady-state impedance functions, the network is redrawn as shown in Fig. 10.5.4b.  The network equations are

$$V(t) = \left( j\omega + 1 - \frac{j4}{\omega} \right) I(t)$$

and

$$V_R(t) = I(t)$$

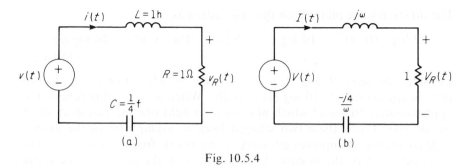

Fig. 10.5.4

Therefore

$$V_R(t) = \frac{V(t)}{\left(j\omega + 1 - \frac{j4}{\omega}\right)} = H(j\omega)V(t)$$

where

$$H(j\omega) = \frac{1}{\left(j\omega + 1 - \frac{j4}{\omega}\right)} = \frac{j\omega}{(4 - \omega^2) + j\omega}$$

Hence the amplitude response for this network is

$$20 \log |H(j\omega)| = 10 \log \frac{\omega^2}{(4 - \omega^2)^2 + \omega^2}$$

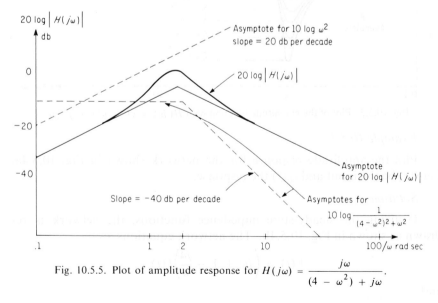

Fig. 10.5.5. Plot of amplitude response for $H(j\omega) = \dfrac{j\omega}{(4 - \omega^2) + j\omega}$.

Simplifying this expression we have

$$20 \log |H(j\omega)| = 10 \log \omega^2 - 10 \log [(4 - \omega^2)^2 + \omega^2]$$

The first term is the magnitude of the polynominal $P_1(j\omega) = j\omega$. The second term is the magnitude of the polynomial $P_3(j\omega) = (\omega_n^2 - \omega^2) + j2\zeta\omega_n\omega$ with the break frequency $\omega_n = 2$ and the damping coefficient $\zeta = 0.25$. Note, however, that we have to plot $-10 \log |P_3(j\omega)|$ rather than $10 \log |P_3(j\omega)|$ as shown in Fig. 10.5.3. The negative sign just inverts the second asymptote, it comes down by 40 db per decade as shown in Fig. 10.5.5. The total asymptote plot is just the sum of the asymptotes of the individual terms as shown in Fig. 10.5.5. The overall response curve is the sum of the two individual response terms where the response $P_3(j\omega)$ has been obtained graphically from Fig. 10.5.3.

## Bode Plots Phase Response

As discussed previously, the phase characteristic

$$\theta(\omega) = \tan^{-1}\left[\frac{\text{Im } [H(j\omega)]}{\text{Re } [H(j\omega)]}\right] \tag{10.5.23}$$

describes the phase of the network sinusoidal steady state response relative to the phase of the sinusoidal driving function. As we have seen, the numerator and denominator polynomials of $H(j\omega)$, $B(j\omega)$ and $A(j\omega)$, are products of factors of the type in Eq. 10.5.8. Writing $A(j\omega)$ and $B(j\omega)$ as the product of these type terms

$$A(j\omega) = A_1(j\omega)A_2(j\omega)\cdots A_n(j\omega) \tag{10.5.24}$$

and

$$B(j\omega) = B_1(j\omega)B_2(j\omega)\cdots B_m(j\omega) \tag{10.5.25}$$

we see that

$$|H(j\omega)| e^{j\theta(\omega)} = \frac{|B_1(j\omega)| |B_2(j\omega)| \cdots |B_m(j\omega)|}{|A_1(j\omega)| |A_2(j\omega)| \cdots |A_n(j\omega)|}$$
$$\exp\left[j\theta_1(\omega) + \cdots + j\theta_m(\omega) - j\phi_1(\omega) - \cdots - j\phi_n(\omega)\right] \tag{10.5.26}$$

where

$$\theta_i(\omega) = \tan^{-1}\left[\frac{\text{Im}[B_i(j\omega)]}{\text{Re}[B_i(j\omega)]}\right] \qquad i = 1, 2, \ldots, m \tag{10.5.27}$$

and

$$\phi_k(\omega) = \tan^{-1}\left[\frac{\text{Im}[A_k(j\omega)]}{\text{Re}[A_k(j\omega)]}\right] \qquad k = 1, 2, \ldots, n \tag{10.5.28}$$

Hence, the total phase response $\theta(\omega)$ is given by

$$\theta(\omega) = \sum_{i=1}^{m} \theta_i(\omega) - \sum_{k=1}^{n} \phi_k(\omega) \tag{10.5.29}$$

To calculate $\theta(\omega)$, we calculate each one of the phase terms due to the individual factors and use the relationship indicated in (10.5.29).

### The Term $P_1(j\omega) = (j\omega)^n$

The phase shift associated with the term $(j\omega)^n$ is easily evaluated by writing it as a complex exponential:

$$(j\omega)^n = \left(\omega e^{j\frac{\pi}{2}}\right)^n = \omega^n e^{j\frac{n\pi}{2}} \tag{10.5.30}$$

Hence for this term

$$\theta(\omega) = \frac{n\pi}{2} \tag{10.5.31}$$

That is, the phase shift is a constant $n\pi/2$ for all frequencies.

### The Term $P(j\omega) = (j\omega + a)^n$

The term $(j\omega + a)^n$ can be written in complex exponential form as

$$a^n(1 + ju)^n = (a\sqrt{1 + u^2} e^{j\phi(u)})^n = a^n(1 + u^2)^{\frac{n}{2}} e^{jn\phi(u)} \tag{10.5.32}$$

where $\phi(u) = \tan^{-1}(u)$; $u = \omega/a$. Hence the total phase shift associated with this factor is

$$\theta(u) = n \tan^{-1}(u) \tag{10.5.33}$$

We have the following asymptotic relationships on $\theta(u)$:

$$\lim_{u \to 0} \theta(u) = \lim_{u \to 0} n \tan^{-1}(u) = 0 \tag{10.5.34}$$

$$\lim_{u \to \infty} \theta(u) = \lim_{u \to \infty} n \tan^{-1}(u) = n\frac{\pi}{2} \tag{10.5.35}$$

At the break frequency $\omega = a$, we have $u = 1$ and

$$\theta(1) = n \tan^{-1}(1) = n\frac{\pi}{4} \tag{10.5.36}$$

These relationships give us two asymptotes and a midpoint for the phase curve. A plot of the phase response for $n = 1$ and $n = 2$ in Fig. 10.5.6.

### The Term $P_3(j\omega) = (\omega_n^2 - \omega^2) + j2\zeta\omega_n\omega$

The phase shift associated with the term $P_3(j\omega) = (\omega_n^2 - \omega^2) + j2\zeta\omega_n\omega$ is

$$\theta(u) = \tan^{-1}\left(\frac{2\zeta u}{1 - u^2}\right) \tag{10.5.37}$$

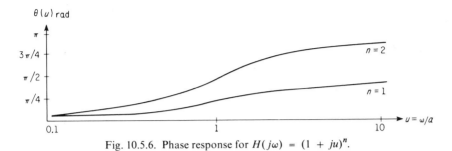

Fig. 10.5.6. Phase response for $H(j\omega) = (1 + ju)^n$.

where $u = \dfrac{\omega}{\omega_n}$. We have two asymptotic relationships on $\theta(u)$:

$$\lim_{u \to 0} \theta(u) = \lim_{u \to 0} \tan^{-1}\left(\frac{2\zeta u}{1 - u^2}\right) = 0 \qquad (10.5.38)$$

$$\lim_{u \to \infty} \theta(u) = \lim_{u \to \infty} \tan^{-1}\left(\frac{2\zeta u}{1 - u^2}\right) = \pi \qquad (10.5.39)$$

At the break frequency $\omega = \omega_n$, we have $u = 1$ and

$$\theta(1) = \lim_{u \to 1} \tan^{-1}\left(\frac{2\zeta u}{1 - u^2}\right) = \frac{\pi}{2} \qquad (10.5.40)$$

Hence the phase shift associated with this quadratic or second-order term goes through values 0 to $\pi$ as $u$ increases from zero and approaches infinity. At $u = 1$, the phase shift is exactly $\pi/2$ and at other points $\theta(u)$ depends on the values of the damping coefficient $\zeta$. A plot of $\theta(u)$ for several values of the damping coefficient is shown in Fig. 10.5.7.

*Example 10.5.2*

Plot the phase response for the network of Example 10.5.1.

*Solution*

As obtained in Example 10.5.1, the transfer function for the network is

$$H(j\omega) = \frac{j\omega}{(4 - \omega^2) + j\omega}$$

The transfer function has one factor in the numerator:

$$B_1(j\omega) = j\omega$$

and a quadratic factor in the denominator:

$$A_1(j\omega) = (4 - \omega^2) + j\omega$$

The total phase shift is given by

$$\theta(\omega) = \theta_1(\omega) - \phi_1(\omega)$$

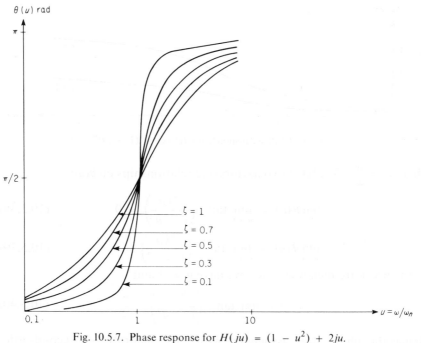

Fig. 10.5.7. Phase response for $H(ju) = (1 - u^2) + 2ju$.

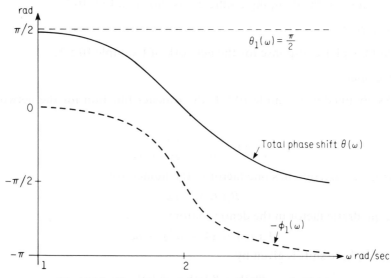

Fig. 10.5.8. Phase response for network of Example 10.5.1.

where

$$\theta_1(\omega) = \frac{\pi}{2}$$

and

$$\phi_1(\omega) = \tan^{-1} \frac{\omega}{4 - \omega^2}$$

The second term can be obtained from Fig. 10.5.7 with $u = \omega/2$ and $\zeta = 0.25$. A plot of the two terms $\theta_1(\omega)$ and $-\phi_1(\omega)$ together with the overall phase shift $\theta(\omega) = \theta_1(\omega) - \phi_1(\omega)$ is shown in Fig. 10.5.8.

## Evaluation of Network Frequency Response Using the Digital Computer

In the last few pages we have shown how the amplitude response and phase response of a network can be sketched approximately as a function of frequency using Bode plots. However, the transfer function numerator and denominator must be known in the standard factored form to apply the Bode plots. In order to obtain the exact plot (especially when the transfer function is only known as a ratio of two polynomials not in the factored form) we must calculate the amplitude and phase response for each frequency. Here the digital computer is of immense value for rapid calculation of $|H(j\omega)|$ and $\theta(\omega)$ for large number of frequencies. We can then use the GRAPHX routine developed in Chapter 6 to plot both $|H(j\omega)|$ and $\theta(\omega)$ using the computed values.

Consider Eq. 10.5.1 again. We can write

$$H(j\omega) = \frac{b_m(j\omega)^m + b_{m-1}(j\omega)^{m-1} + \cdots + b_0}{a_n(j\omega)^n + a_{n-1}(j\omega)^{n-1} + \cdots + a_0} \qquad (10.5.41)$$

or

$$H(j\omega) = |H(j\omega)| e^{j\theta(\omega)}$$
$$= \frac{(b_0 - b_2\omega^2 + b_4\omega^4 - \cdots) + j(b_1\omega - b_3\omega^3 + \cdots)}{(a_0 - a_2\omega^2 + a_4\omega^4 - \cdots) + j(a_1\omega - a_3\omega^3 + \cdots)} \qquad (10.5.42)$$

Now if we examine $H(j\omega)$ from Eq. 10.5.42 we can write

$$H(j\omega) = |H(j\omega)| e^{j\theta(\omega)} = \frac{\text{RENU} + j\text{EMNU}}{\text{REDE} + j\text{EMDE}}$$

where RENU and EMNU are the real and imaginary parts of the numerator of $H(j\omega)$ respectively and REDE and EMDE are real and imaginary parts of the denominator of $H(j\omega)$ respectively. In order to evaluate $|H(j\omega)|$ and $\theta(\omega)$ we need to know the magnitude and phase of RENU + jEMNU and REDE + jEMDE for each $\omega$. Both are just complex numbers for each $\omega$. Hence it would be very worthwhile if we first generate a computer program which just gives the magnitude and phase of this complex number. We will then show how this program is used to obtain amplitude and phase response of a network for a specific example.

### Development of Flow Chart for Determining the Magnitude and Phase of a Complex Number

Let the complex number be $X + jY$. Then in the polar form we write

$$X + jY = R = RMe^{jRA}$$

Where we define

$$RM = \text{magnitude of } R$$

and

$$RA = \text{angle or phase of } R$$

The flow chart to develop the computer program is given below.

Flow Chart for Determining Magnitude and Phase of Complex Number $X + jY$

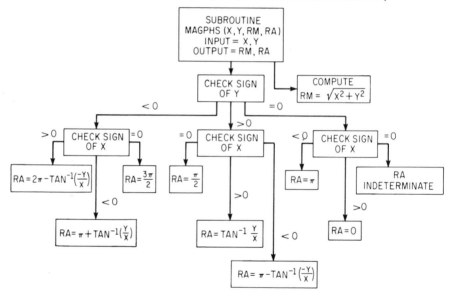

The input to the program will be $X$ and $Y$ and the output will be $RM$ and $RA$. The computer program based on the above flowchart is called MAGPHS subroutine and can be called as MAGPHS $(X, Y, RM, RA)$ in any program. The subroutine is given below.

### Computer Program for Magnitude and Phase of a Complex Number—MAGPHS Subroutine

```
        SUBROUTINE MAGPHS(X,Y,RM,RA)
    C   THIS SUBROUTINE CONVERTS A GIVEN COMPLEX NUMBER IN
```

```
C        CARTESIAN FORM (X+JY) TO POLOR FORM RM,RA THE
C        MAGNITUDE AND PHASE FORM,
C        THE FOLLOWING FOUR IF STATEMENTS DETERMINE THE
C        QUADRANT IN WHICH THE GIVEN VECTOR LIES AND DIRECT
C        THE PROGRAM TO GO TO THE STATEMENT WHICH GIVES THE
C        ANGLE IN THAT QUADRANT,
C        IN CASE BOTH X AND Y ARE ZERO THE ANGLE IS
C        INDETERMINATE AND THAT IS PRINTED AND SUBROUTINE
C        TERMINATES,
C        THIS PART COMPUTES THE ANGLE,
         PI=3,14159
         IF (Y) 61,62,63
      61 IF (X) 64,65,66
      62 IF (X) 67,99,68
      63 IF (X) 69,70,71
      64 RA= PI+ATAN(Y/X)
         GO TO 72
      65 RA=3,0*PI/2,0
         GO TO 72
      66 RA=2,0*PI-ATAN(-Y/X)
         GO TO 72
      67 RA=PI
         GO TO 72
      68 RA=0,0
         GO TO 72
      69 RA=PI-ATAN(-Y/X)
         GO TO 72
      70 RA=PI/2,0
         GO TO 72
      71 RA=ATAN(Y/X)
         GO TO 72
      99 PRINT 98
         GO TO 73
C        THIS PART COMPUTES THE MAGNITUDE,
      72 RM=SQRT(X*X+Y*Y)
      98 FORMAT (1H ,'ANGLE INDETERMINATE')
      73 RETURN
         END
```

Now we can use the above MAGPHS subroutine to develop the computer program to calculate $|H(j\omega)|$ and $\theta(\omega)$. First let us define the following.

$M = m$, order of the numerator of $H(j\omega)$

$N = n$, order of the denominator of $H(j\omega)$

$B(I) \quad I = 1, (M + 1) \quad$ coefficients $b_0, b_1, -b_2, -b_3, b_4 \cdots$

$A(I) \quad I = 1, (N + 1) \quad$ coefficients $a_0, a_1, -a_2, -a_3, a_4 \cdots$

$W = $ omega, $\omega$

RENU = real part of the numerator = $b_0 - b_2\omega^2 + b_4\omega^4 - \cdots$

REDE = real part of the denominator = $a_0 - a_2\omega^2 + a_4\omega^4 - \cdots$

EMNU = imaginary part of the numerator = $b_1\omega - b_3\omega^3 + \cdots$

EMDE = imaginary part of the denominator = $a_1\omega - a_3\omega^3 + \cdots$

AMAG = magnitude of the numerator = $\sqrt{(\text{RENU})^2 + (\text{EMNU})^2}$

BMAG = magnitude of the denominator = $\sqrt{(\text{REDE})^2 + (\text{EMDE})^2}$

APHS = phase of the numerator

BPHS = phase of the denominator

FMAG = amplitude response = $\dfrac{\text{AMAG}}{\text{BMAG}}$

FPHS = phase response = APHS − BPHS

Now we develop the flow chart and the computer program for a specific example.

*Example 10.5.3*

Consider the network shown in Fig. 10.5.9. Find network amplitude and phase frequency response $H(j\omega) = \left[\dfrac{V_0(t)}{V(t)}\right]$. Make use of the digital computer to compute and plot quantities $|H(j\omega)|$ and $\theta(j\omega)$ from $\omega = 0$ to 5 rad/sec in steps of 0.1 rad/sec.

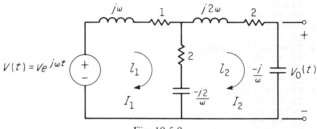

Fig. 10.5.9

*Solution*

We choose loop currents $I_1$ and $I_2$. Now the loop equations are

$$I_1:\quad V(t) = \left(j\omega + 3 - \frac{j2}{\omega}\right)I_1 - \left(2 - \frac{j2}{\omega}\right)I_2$$

$$I_2:\quad 0 = -\left(2 - \frac{j2}{\omega}\right)I_1 + \left(4 + 2j\omega - \frac{j3}{\omega}\right)I_2$$

Also

$$V_0(t) = \frac{-jI_2}{\omega}$$

From $I_1$ and $I_2$ equations, we eliminate $I_1$ to obtain $I_2$ as

$$I_2 = \frac{\left(2 - \frac{j2}{\omega}\right)V(t)}{\left(j\omega + 3 - \frac{j2}{\omega}\right)\left(4 + 2j\omega - \frac{j3}{\omega}\right) - \left(2 - \frac{j2}{\omega}\right)^2}$$

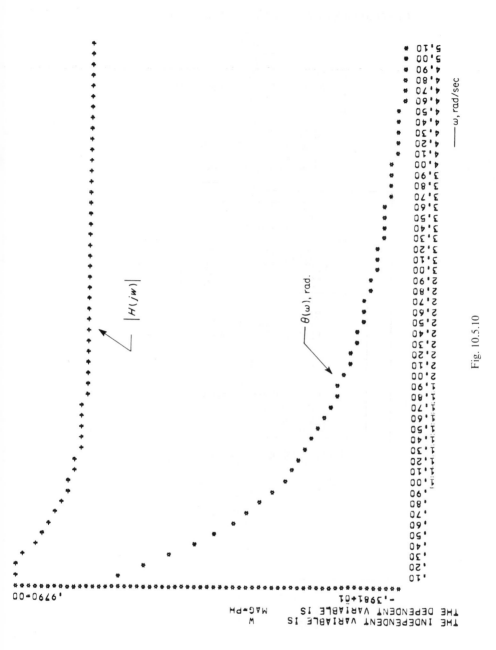

Fig. 10.5.10

Flow Chart for Evaluation of $\left|H(j\omega)\right|$ and $\theta(\omega)$ of Example 10. 5. 3.

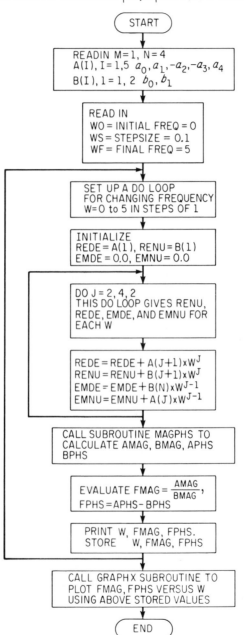

Substituting $I_2$ in $V_0(t)$ equation, we obtain

$$H(j\omega) = \frac{V_0(t)}{V(t)} = \frac{\left(-\dfrac{j}{\omega}\right)\left(2 - j\,\dfrac{2}{\omega}\right)}{\left(j\omega + 3 - j\,\dfrac{2}{\omega}\right)\left(4 + 2j\omega - j\,\dfrac{3}{\omega}\right) - \left(2 - j\,\dfrac{2}{\omega}\right)^2}$$

$$= \frac{2 + j2\,\omega}{2 - 15\omega^2 + 2\omega^4 + j(9\omega - 10\omega^3)}$$

Here $b_0 = 2$, $b_1 = 2$, $a_0 = 2$, $a_1 = 9$, $a_2 = 15$, $a_3 = 10$, and $a_4 = 2$. Also $m = 1$ and $n = 4$.

In order to write a computer program for evaluation of $|H(j\omega)|$ and $\theta(\omega)$, we develop the flow chart on page 370. Note that we use GRAPHX subroutine from Chapter 6 and the MAGPHS subroutine developed above. The computer printout of results is also given. The $|H(j\omega)|$ and $\theta(\omega)$ are shown in Fig. 10.5.10 on page 369.

**Computer Program for Evaluation of $|H(j\omega)|$ and $\theta(j\omega)$, Example 10.5.3**

```
C       THIS PROGRAM IS FOR EXAMPLE 10.5-3
C       THIS PROGRAM COMPUTES THE MAGNITUDE AND PHASE RESPONSE
C       OF A NETWORK AS A FUNCTION OF FREQUENCY,
        DIMENSION A(10),B(10),DATA(100,3)
C       READ IN THE ORDER OF NUMERATOR AND
C       DENOMINATOR POLYNOMIALS,
        READ 1, M
        READ 1, N
        M1=M+1
        N1=N+1
C       READ IN B'S AND A'S,
        READ 2, (B(I), I=1,M1)
        READ 2, (A(I), I=1,N1)
C       READ IN INIATIAL VALUE OF OMEGA, STEP SIZE IN WHICH
C       IT IS TO BE VARIED, AND FINAL VALUE,
        READ 3, WO,WS,WF
C       CONVERTING FLOTING POINT W TO FIXED POINT IW,
        JW=IFIX(W)
        W=WO-WS
        PRINT 7
        DO 10 IW=JW,100
        W=W+WS
C       THIS PART COMPUTES REAL AND IMAGINARY PART OF
C       NUMERATOR AND DENOMINATOR, INITIALIZE THE DO LOOP,
        REDE=A(1)
        RENU=B(1)
        EMDE=0.0
        EMNU=0.0
        DO 11 J=2,9,2
        REDE=REDE+A(J+1)*(W**J)
        RENU=RENU+B(J+1)*(W**J)
        EMDE=EMDE+A(J)*(W**(J-1))
     11 EMNU=EMNU+B(J)*(W**(J-1))
C       WE CALL THE SUBROUTINE MAGPHS TO GET THE MAGNITUDE
C       AND PHASE OF NUMERATOR, AND DENOMINATOR,
        CALL MAGPHS(REDE,EMDE,AMAG,APHS)
        CALL MAGPHS(RENU,EMNU,BMAG,BPHS)
```

```
      FMAG=BMAG/AMAG
      FPHS=BPHS-APHS
      PRINT 30, W,FMAG,FPHS
C     THIS PART GETS DATA READY FOR THE GRAPH ROUTINE
C     TO PLOT FMAG, FPHS VERSUS W.
      DATA(IW,1)=W
      DATA(IW,2)=FMAG
      DATA(IW,3)=FPHS
      IF (WF-W) 20,10,10
   10 CONTINUE
C     NOW WE USE GRAPH ROUTINE TO PLOT FMAG,FPHS VERSUS
C     W USING THE STORED VALUES.
   20 CALL GRAPHX(DATA,IW,1HW,6HMAG=PH)
    1 FORMAT (I2)
    2 FORMAT (7F10,5)
    3 FORMAT (3F10,5)
    7 FORMAT (1H ,3X,'OMEGA',9X,'MAG',8X,'PHASE(RAD)')
   30 FORMAT (1H ,F7,2,5X,2(F10,5,5X))
      END



      SUBROUTINE GRAPHX(DATA,N,VINDEP,VARDEP)
      DIMENSION DATA(100,3),B(121)
      DOUBLE PRECISION VINDEP,VARDEP
      PRINT 300,VINDEP
      PRINT 400,VARDEP
      BIGEST=DATA(1,2)
      SMAL=DATA(1,2)
      DO 1 I=2,N
      IF(DATA(I,2),GT,BIGEST)BIGEST=DATA(I,2)
      IF(DATA(I,2),LT,SMAL)SMAL=DATA(I,2)
    1 CONTINUE
      DO 2 I=2,N
      IF(DATA(I,3),GT,BIGEST)BIGEST=DATA(I,3)
      IF(DATA(I,3),LT,SMAL)SMAL=DATA(I,3)
    2 CONTINUE
      PRINT 200,SMAL,BIGEST
C     TO EXTEND THE PLOT TO FULL PAGE WIDTH, WE ONLY
C     NEED TO REPLACE K=61 BY K=121,
C     ALSO IN FORMAT STATEMENT 200 4X
C     MUST BE REPLACED BY 48X, AND 61 BY 121,
      K=61
      BMINS=BIGEST=SMAL
      DO 3 I=1,K
    3 B(I)=1H
      DO 4 I=1,N
      DATA(I,2)=(DATA(I,2)-SMAL)*FLOAT(K)/BMINS+1,0
      DATA(I,3)=(DATA(I,3)-SMAL)*FLOAT(K)/BMINS+1,0
      INDEX=DATA(I,2)
      JNDEX=DATA(I,3)
      B(INDEX)=1H+
      B(JNDEX)=1H*
      PRINT 100,DATA(I,1),(B (N),N=1,K)
      B(INDEX)=1H
    4 B(JNDEX)=1H
  100 FORMAT(1HZ,F8,2,1X,121A1)
  200 FORMAT(9X,E11,4,35X,1H ,4X,E11,4,/10X,61(1H*))
  300 FORMAT (1H1,'THE INDEPENDENT VARIABLE IS ',2A10)
  400 FORMAT (1X,'THE DEPENDENT VARIABLE IS ',2A10//)
      RETURN
      END
```

| OMEGA | MAG | PHASE(RAD) |
|---|---|---|
| .00 | 1.00000 | .00000 |
| .10 | .97898 | -.34869 |
| .20 | .91884 | -.68909 |
| .30 | .82871 | -1.01176 |
| .40 | .72272 | -1.30758 |
| .50 | .61538 | -1.57079 |
| .60 | .51688 | -1.80023 |
| .70 | .43189 | -1.99831 |
| .80 | .36111 | -2.16921 |
| .90 | .30319 | -2.31738 |
| 1.00 | .25607 | -2.44685 |
| 1.10 | .21775 | -2.56102 |
| 1.20 | .18644 | -2.66260 |
| 1.30 | .16072 | -2.75377 |
| 1.40 | .13944 | -2.83624 |
| 1.50 | .12170 | -2.91137 |
| 1.60 | .10682 | -2.98023 |
| 1.70 | .09424 | -3.04370 |
| 1.80 | .08355 | -3.10248 |
| 1.90 | .07440 | -3.15714 |
| 2.00 | .06652 | -3.20816 |
| 2.10 | .05970 | -3.25593 |
| 2.20 | .05378 | -3.30080 |
| 2.30 | .04860 | -3.34304 |
| 2.40 | .04406 | -3.38289 |
| 2.50 | .04006 | -3.42058 |
| 2.60 | .03652 | -3.45627 |
| 2.70 | .03338 | -3.49014 |
| 2.80 | .03058 | -3.52232 |
| 2.90 | .02808 | -3.55294 |
| 3.00 | .02584 | -3.58212 |
| 3.10 | .02383 | -3.60995 |
| 3.20 | .02202 | -3.63652 |
| 3.30 | .02039 | -3.66192 |
| 3.40 | .01891 | -3.68622 |
| 3.50 | .01756 | -3.70950 |
| 3.60 | .01634 | -3.73180 |
| 3.70 | .01523 | -3.75320 |
| 3.80 | .01421 | -3.77374 |
| 3.90 | .01328 | -3.79347 |
| 4.00 | .01243 | -3.81244 |
| 4.10 | .01165 | -3.83070 |
| 4.20 | .01093 | -3.84826 |
| 4.30 | .01027 | -3.86519 |
| 4.40 | .00966 | -3.88150 |
| 4.50 | .00910 | -3.89723 |
| 4.60 | .00858 | -3.91241 |
| 4.70 | .00809 | -3.92706 |
| 4.80 | .00765 | -3.94122 |
| 4.90 | .00723 | -3.95490 |
| 5.00 | .00684 | -3.96812 |
| 5.10 | .00648 | -3.98092 |

## 10.6. POWER CONSIDERATIONS

Many simplifications in power and energy analysis occur when circuits are operating in the sinusoidal steady state. Consider the network shown in Fig. 10.6.1. A sinusoidal source drives a circuit made up of $R$,

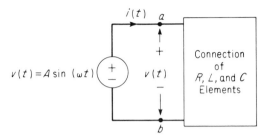

Fig. 10.6.1. Network driven by sinusoidal source.

$L$, and $C$ elements. In the steady state, each current and voltage in the circuit is sinusoidal with the same frequency as the driving function but generally of different phase. Hence the current $i(t)$ can be written in the form

$$i(t) = B \sin(\omega t - \phi) \qquad (10.6.1)$$

where the amplitude $B$ and the phase $\phi$ generally depend on $\omega$ and are determined by the network characteristics. As discussed in Chapter 1, the energy flow over the interval $(t_0, t_1)$ into the $R, L, C$ connection in Fig. 10.6.1 is

$$E(t_0, t_1) = \int_{t_0}^{t_1} p(t) \, dt \qquad (10.6.2)$$

where $p(t)$ is the instantaneous power and is given by

$$p(t) = v(t)i(t) = AB \sin(\omega t) \sin(\omega t - \phi) \qquad (10.6.3)$$

Over one period, the energy delivered to the $R, L, C$ connection is

$$
\begin{aligned}
E(0, T) &= \int_0^T p(t)\, dt = \int_0^T AB \sin(\omega t) \sin(\omega t - \phi)\, dt \\
&= \int_0^T \left[ \frac{AB}{2} \cos\phi - \frac{AB}{2} \cos(2\omega t - \phi) \right] dt \qquad (10.6.4) \\
&= \frac{AB}{2} \cos\phi \; T \text{ watt-sec}
\end{aligned}
$$

Hence the average power over one period is

$$P = \frac{E(0, T)}{T} = \frac{AB}{2} \cos\phi \text{ watts} \qquad (10.6.5)$$

Note, the rms value of the voltage is

$$V_{\text{rms}} = \frac{A}{\sqrt{2}} \qquad (10.6.6)$$

and the rms value of the current is

$$I_{\text{rms}} = \frac{B}{\sqrt{2}} \qquad (10.6.7)$$

From Eq. 10.6.5 we have, therefore, that the average power is related to the rms values of the current and voltage by

$$P = V_{rms} I_{rms} \cos \phi \text{ watts} \qquad (10.6.8)$$

The angle $\phi$ represents the phase difference between the voltage and current and is called the *power angle*, while $\cos \phi$ is termed the *power factor*.

The average power is plotted as a function of the power angle in Fig. 10.6.2. Note the maximum value of the average power is obtained when

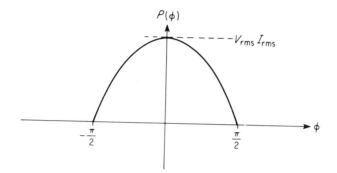

Fig. 10.6.2. Average power as a function of the power angle.

the current and voltage are in phase ($\phi = 0$) corresponding to a purely resistive circuit. When $\phi$ is $-\pi/2$ or $+\pi/2$ corresponding, respectively, to purely capacitive or inductive circuits, the power factor and the average power is zero. We might suspect that since a resistance element dissipates energy, the net energy flow over any one period will always be into the $R, L, C$ combination so that the average power should remain non-negative. This condition implies that the phase angle between the terminal current and voltage in an $R, L, C$ combination should always satisfy

$$-\frac{\pi}{2} \le \phi \le \frac{\pi}{2} \qquad (10.6.9)$$

## Complex Power

Let us examine the power relationships in more detail by reconsidering Fig. 10.6.1. The phasor model of this circuit is shown in Fig. 10.6.3. The connection of $R, L, C$ elements to the right of terminals $a, b$, has been reduced to an equivalent impedance by combination of parallel and series elements.

Rewriting $Z(j\omega)$ in complex exponential form,

$$Z(j\omega) = |Z(j\omega)| e^{j\theta} \qquad (10.6.10)$$

we can solve for $\mathbf{I}$ in terms of $\mathbf{V}$ and $Z(j\omega)$

$$\mathbf{I} = \mathbf{V}/Z(j\omega) = (A/|Z(j\omega)|)e^{-j\theta} = Be^{-j\phi} \qquad (10.6.11)$$

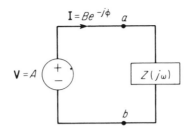

Fig. 10.6.3. Sinusoidal steady state equivalent of
network driven by a single source.

Therefore we must have

$$B = A / |Z(j\omega)|$$

and

$$\phi = \theta = \tan^{-1} \frac{\text{Im}[Z(j\omega)]}{\text{Re}[Z(j\omega)]} \qquad (10.6.12)$$

Hence the power angle is simply the impedance angle of the equivalent
network impedance which is driven by the source. This impedance function is termed the *driving-point impedance* of the network.

We define the *complex power* as

$$\mathbf{P} = \frac{1}{2} \mathbf{V} \mathbf{I}^* = \left|\frac{\mathbf{V}}{\sqrt{2}}\right| \left|\frac{\mathbf{I}}{\sqrt{2}}\right| \cos\phi + j \left|\frac{\mathbf{V}}{\sqrt{2}}\right| \left|\frac{\mathbf{I}}{\sqrt{2}}\right| \sin\phi \quad (10.6.13)$$

Comparing Eqs. 10.6.8 and 10.6.13 we have the average power is given by

$$P = \text{Re}[\mathbf{P}] = \tfrac{1}{2} |\mathbf{V}| |\mathbf{I}| \cos\phi, \text{ watts} \qquad (10.6.14)$$

The imaginary part of the complex power, called the *reactive power*, is
defined as

$$Q = \text{Im}[\mathbf{P}] = \tfrac{1}{2} |\mathbf{V}| |\mathbf{I}| \sin\phi, \text{ vars} \qquad (10.6.15)$$

The units of $Q$ are defined as vars which stands for volt-amperes reactive.
By convention the reactive power is taken as being positive in an inductive circuit ($\phi \geq 0$). The relationship between the average, instantaneous
and reactive power can be made physically meaningful if we consider the
expression for instantaneous power in Eq. 10.6.3 which can be written

$$p(t) = \frac{AB}{2} \cos\phi [1 - \cos 2\omega t] + \frac{AB}{2} \sin\phi \sin 2\omega t \quad (10.6.16)$$

These two terms are plotted in Fig. 10.6.4. The first term is oscillatory
with frequency $2\omega$ about $P$, the average power. The second term is
oscillatory with frequency $2\omega$ about zero and with magnitude $Q$, the
reactive power. The sum of the curves represents the instantaneous
power.

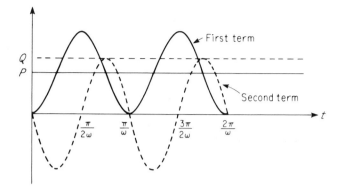

Fig. 10.6.4. Plot of two terms of instantaneous power $p(t)$ of Eq. 10.6.16.

*Example 10.6.1*

(a) Find the average and reactive power for the circuit shown in Fig. 10.6.5. (b) Find the energy dissipated in the resistors over the interval $(0, 10\pi)$.

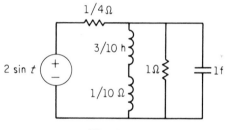

Fig. 10.6.5

*Solution*

For this circuit, the equivalent impedance in series with the voltage source is

$$Z(j\omega) = \cfrac{1}{(1 + j) + \cfrac{1}{\cfrac{1}{10} + j\cfrac{3}{10}}} + \frac{1}{4}$$

noting that $\omega = 1$. This simplifies to

$$Z(j\omega) = \frac{1}{2} + j\frac{1}{4}$$

The average power is given by Eq. 10.6.14 as

$$P = \frac{1}{2} |\mathbf{V}| |\mathbf{I}| \cos \phi$$

where

$$\mathbf{I} = \frac{\mathbf{V}}{Z(j\omega)}$$

and

$$\tan \phi = \frac{\mathrm{Im}\,[Z(j\omega)]}{\mathrm{Re}\,[Z(j\omega)]}$$

Therefore

$$P = \frac{\frac{1}{2}|\mathbf{V}|^2}{|Z(j\omega)|} \frac{\mathrm{Re}\,[Z(j\omega)]}{[\{\mathrm{Re}\,[Z(j\omega)]\}^2 + \{\mathrm{Im}\,[Z(j\omega)]\}^2]^{1/2}}$$

$$= \frac{\frac{1}{2} \cdot 4 \cdot \frac{1}{2}}{\sqrt{\frac{1}{4} + \frac{1}{16}} \sqrt{\frac{1}{4} + \frac{1}{16}}} = \frac{16}{5} \text{ watts}$$

Similarly the reactive power from Eq. 10.6.15 is

$$Q = \frac{1}{2} |\mathbf{V}| |\mathbf{I}| \sin \phi = \left(\frac{8}{5}\right) \text{vars}$$

The energy dissipated in the resistors is simply the energy absorbed by the equivalent impedance. For the interval $(0, 10\pi)$ we have

$$E[0, 10\pi] = 10\pi \times \frac{16}{5} = 32\pi \text{ joules}$$

### Maximum Power Transfer

In some instances, we may be interested in conditions which maximize the energy transfer between the driving source and a load. Consider the network shown in Fig. 10.6.6 in which a source voltage, **V**, is connected

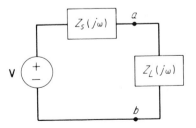

Fig. 10.6.6. Circuit for maximum power-transfer analysis.

to a load impedance, $Z_L(j\omega)$, through the source impedance $Z_s(j\omega)$. We consider the source impedance fixed and seek a load impedance which will maximize the average power in the load impedance. The average power in the load impedance is

$$P = \frac{1}{2} \text{Re} \left[ |\mathbf{V}|^2 \frac{Z_L(j\omega)}{|Z_s(j\omega) + Z_L(\omega)|^2} \right] \tag{10.6.17}$$

Simplifying Eq. 10.6.17, we have

$$P = \frac{1}{2} |\mathbf{V}|^2$$

$$\frac{\text{Re}[Z_L(j\omega)]}{\{\text{Re}[Z_s(j\omega)] + \text{Re}[Z_L(j\omega)]\}^2 + \{\text{Im}[Z_s(j\omega)] + \text{Im}[Z_L(j\omega)]\}^2} \tag{10.6.18}$$

To maximize $P$ with respect to $Z_L(j\omega)$ we take the derivative of $P$ with respect to both the real and imaginary part of $Z_L(j\omega)$ and set them equal to zero. That is,

$$\frac{\partial P}{\partial \text{Im}[Z_L(j\omega)]} = 0$$

$$\frac{\partial P}{\partial \text{Re}[Z_L(j\omega)]} = 0 \tag{10.6.19}$$

The simultaneous solution to these equations is

$$\text{Im}[Z_L(j\omega)] = -\text{Im}[Z_s(j\omega)]$$
$$\text{Re}[Z_L(j\omega)] = \text{Re}[Z_s(j\omega)] \tag{10.6.20}$$

It can be verified that Eq. 10.6.20 represents a maximum in Eq. 10.6.18 rather than a minimum. Thus for maximum energy transfer we must choose

$$Z_L(j\omega) = Z_s^*(j\omega) \tag{10.6.21}$$

The maximum average power in the load impedance is then found by substituting Eq. 10.6.21 into Eq. 10.6.18 and it is given by

$$P_{\max} = \frac{|\mathbf{V}|^2}{8 \text{Re}[Z_s(j\omega)]} \tag{10.6.22}$$

This discussion is called the *maximum power transfer theorem*. A load which satisfies the maximum power transfer relationship is said to be *matched* to the source.

*Example 10.6.2*

For the circuit shown in Fig. 10.6.7, assume the reactive portion of the load can be adjusted. Find $\text{Im}[Z_L(j\omega)]$ for maximum power transfer under the constraint $R_L = 40 \, \Omega$.

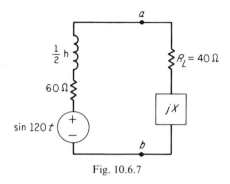

Fig. 10.6.7

*Solution*

In this case we cannot adjust the load resistance to match the source impedance. We note that $Z_s = 60 + j\frac{1}{2} \times 120 = 60 + j60$ and $Z_L(j\omega) = 40 + jX$. Therefore, we have from Eq. 10.6.18

$$P = \frac{1}{2} |V|^2 \frac{40}{(100)^2 + (60 + X)^2}$$

Obviously, to maximize $P$ as a function of $X$ we must have $X = -60$. Hence, as before, the load reactance is chosen as the conjugate of the source reactance. The average load power in this case is

$$P = \frac{1}{2} |V|^2 \frac{40}{100^2} = \frac{160 \times 60}{100^2} \frac{V^2}{8 \times 60} = 0.96 P_{max}$$

using Eq. 10.6.22. Here the average load power is 96 percent of the maximum amount that could be transfered if we were permitted to vary the load resistance to exactly match the source impedance.

## 10.7. TUNED CIRCUITS

Tuned or *resonant* circuits are employed in many applications where it is desired to separate signal components on the basis of their frequency content. A network is said to be *resonant at* or *tuned to* those frequencies which make the driving point impedance (or admittance) angle, $\phi$, equal to zero, or the power factor, $\cos \phi$, equal to unity. Since

$$\phi = \tan^{-1}\left[\frac{\text{Im}[Z(j\omega)]}{\text{Re}[Z(j\omega)]}\right],$$

resonance is achieved when

$$\text{Im}[Z(j\omega)] = 0 \qquad (10.7.1)$$

The quality factor, $Q_0$, of a resonant circuit at the resonant frequency is defined as $2\pi$ times the ratio of the stored energy at any instant to the dissipated energy over the resonant frequency period.

$$Q_0 = 2\pi \frac{\text{stored energy at any instant}}{\text{dissipated energy over one period}} \qquad (10.7.2)$$

To relate this definition to the network parameters, consider the circuit in Fig. 10.7.1b which is the equivalent of the circuit in Fig. 10.7.1a at the

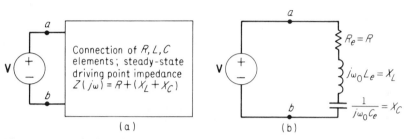

Fig. 10.7.1. Equivalent circuits at resonant frequency (a) arbitrary connection of $R, L, C$ elements, (b) equivalent driving point impedance at resonance.

resonant frequency $\omega_0$. By definition, at resonance we have $|X_L| = |X_C|$. The average power associated with the network is

$$P = \frac{1}{2} \frac{|V|^2}{R_e} \qquad (10.7.3)$$

Hence the dissipated energy over one period is

$$E_R[0, T] = \frac{|V|^2}{2R_e} \left(\frac{2\pi}{\omega_0}\right) \qquad (10.7.4)$$

where $T = \dfrac{2\pi}{\omega_0}$ and $\omega_0$ is the resonant frequency. The calculation of the stored energy is slightly more difficult. The energy stored in the equivalent inductive element as any instant is

$$E_L = \frac{1}{2} L_e i_L^2(t) \qquad (10.7.5)$$

and in the equivalent capacitive element, the energy is

$$E_C = \frac{1}{2} C_e v_C^2(t) \qquad (10.7.6)$$

With $v(t) = |V| \sin \omega_0 t$, we have

$$i_{R_e}(t) = i_L(t) = \frac{|V|}{R_e} \sin \omega_0 t \qquad (10.7.7)$$

and

$$v_C(t) = \frac{-|\mathbf{V}|}{\omega_0 C_e R_e} \cos \omega_0 t \qquad (10.7.8)$$

Hence the total energy stored at any instant is obtained from Eqs. 10.7.5 and 10.7.6:

$$E_s = E_L + E_C = \frac{|\mathbf{V}|^2}{2R_e^2}\left[L_e \sin^2 \omega_0 t + \frac{1}{\omega_0^2 C_e} \cos^2 \omega_0 t\right] \qquad (10.7.9)$$

Now at resonance $\omega_0 L_e = \dfrac{1}{\omega_0 C_e}$ \qquad (10.7.10)

Therefore

$$E_s = \frac{|\mathbf{V}|^2 L_e}{2R_e^2} \qquad (10.7.11)$$

This relationship together with Eq. 10.7.4 gives

$$Q_0 = \frac{2\pi E_s}{E_R(0, T)} = \frac{\omega_0 L_e}{R_e} = \frac{1}{\omega_0 C_e R_e} \qquad (10.7.12)$$

If we define the inductive reactive power as

$$Q_L \triangleq \tfrac{1}{2}|\mathbf{I}|^2 \omega_0 L_e \qquad (10.7.13)$$

and the capacitive reactive power as

$$Q_C \triangleq -\tfrac{1}{2}|\mathbf{I}|^2 \frac{1}{\omega_0 C_e} \qquad (10.7.14)$$

then the resonant circuit quality factor can also be written

$$Q_0 = \frac{\text{magnitude of either capacitive or inductive reactive power}}{\text{average power}}$$

$$(10.7.15)$$

### Parallel RLC Tuned Circuit

To obtain some idea of how the above definitions can be applied to a specific resonant circuit, consider the parallel $RLC$ circuit in Fig. 10.7.2.

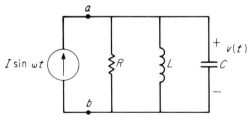

Fig. 10.7.2. Parallel $RLC$ circuit.

The *driving-point admittance* of this network is

$$Y_{ab}(j\omega) = \frac{1}{R} + j\left(\omega C - \frac{1}{\omega L}\right) \qquad (10.7.16)$$

Thus the resonant frequency is given by

$$\omega C - \frac{1}{\omega L} = 0 \quad \text{or} \quad \omega = \omega_0 = \frac{1}{\sqrt{LC}} \qquad (10.7.17)$$

The equivalent driving-point impedance of this circuit at resonance is

$$Z_{ab}(j\omega_0) = R + j\left(\frac{R^2}{\omega_0 L} - R^2\omega_0 C\right) = R_e + j\left(\omega_0 L_e - \frac{1}{\omega_0 C_e}\right)$$

$$(10.7.18)$$

where $R_e = R$, $L_e = \dfrac{R^2}{\omega_0^2 L}$ and $C_e = \dfrac{1}{R^2}\omega_0^2 C$. From Eq. 10.7.12 the quality factor of this circuit is

$$Q_0 = R\omega_0 C = \frac{R}{\omega_0 L} \qquad (10.7.19)$$

which is the same factor $Q$ discussed in Chapter 6 in relationship to the network transient performance. To investigate the effect of $Q_0$ on the steady-state network performance we rewrite the input admittance function as

$$Y_{ab}(j\omega) = \left[1 + jQ_0\left(\frac{\omega}{\omega_0} - \frac{\omega_0}{\omega}\right)\right]\frac{1}{R} \qquad (10.7.20)$$

We can plot Eq. 10.7.20 on the complex plane as a function of $\omega$ as shown in Fig. 10.7.3. At any point on the straight line, a vector drawn from the origin to the line represents the admittance function. The length of the vector represents the magnitude $|Y_{ab}(j\omega)|$ and the angle which the vector makes with the real axis is the complex admittance angle. When the

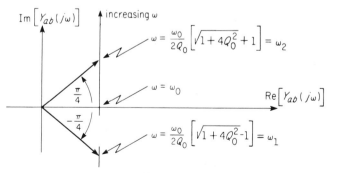

Fig. 10.7.3. Plot of input admittance function for parallel *RLC* network.

angle is $\pm \dfrac{\pi}{4}$, $|Y_{ab}(j\omega)| = \dfrac{\sqrt{2}}{R}$. The difference between the frequencies $\omega_2$ and $\omega_1$ is

$$\omega_2 - \omega_1 = \frac{\omega_0}{Q_0} \tag{10.7.21}$$

which decreases with increasing $Q_0$. This effect is further illustrated by considering the sinusoidal steady-state transfer function.    Letting $v(t)$

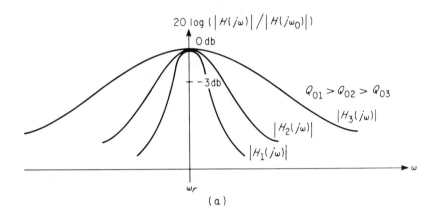

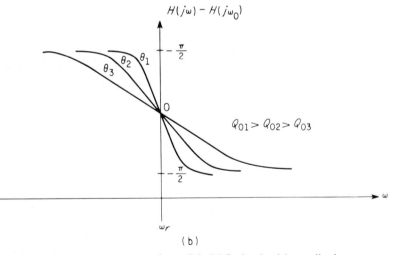

Fig. 10.7.4. Frequency response of parallel $RLC$ circuit: (a) amplitude response, (b) phase response.

in Fig. 10.7.2 be the desired output gives the transfer function as

$$H(j\omega) = Z_{ab}(j\omega) \qquad (10.7.22)$$

and

$$|H(j\omega)|^2 = \frac{1}{|Y_{ab}(j\omega)|^2} = \frac{R^2}{\left[1 + Q_0^2\left(\dfrac{\omega}{\omega_0} - \dfrac{\omega_0}{\omega}\right)^2\right]} \qquad (10.7.23)$$

Normalizing to the value of $|H(j\omega)|^2$ at $\omega = \omega_0$, the transfer function decreases 3 db at the points $\omega = \omega_1$ and $\omega = \omega_2$ as defined in Fig. 10.7.3. Let us define the bandwidth of the filter as $\omega_2 - \omega_1$, the difference in the 3 db frequencies. Equation 10.7.21 then indicates the bandwidth of the filter is inversely proportional to $Q_0$ of the circuit. This is shown graphically in Fig. 10.7.4 where $20\log|H(j\omega)|$ is plotted for several values of the quality factor. Notice that the higher $Q_0$ circuits give better frequency selectivity, i.e., higher rejection of signal components not in the immediate range of the resonant frequency.

**PROBLEMS**

**10.1.**   Find the steady-state current $i(t)$ in the circuit shown. Assume:

$$v(t) = 4\sin\left(2t + \frac{\pi}{4}\right).$$

Prob. 10.1

**10.2.**   Find the equivalent impedance of the network to the right of the terminals $a, b$ in Prob. 10.1.

**10.3.**   Using a phasor diagram, plot each of the voltages $\mathbf{V}$, $\mathbf{V}_R$, and $\mathbf{V}_L$, and $\mathbf{V}_C$ indicated in Prob. 10.1.

**10.4.**   Denoting $v_c(t)$ as the desired response, find the sinusoidal steady-state transfer function $H(j\omega)$ for the circuit of Prob. 10.1.

**10.5.**   (a) A *three-phase* electrical network is shown. Find the steady-state currents $i_1(t)$, $i_2(t)$, and $i_3(t)$. (b) Draw a phasor diagram indicating the driving voltages and the currents $\mathbf{I}_1$, $\mathbf{I}_2$, and $\mathbf{I}_3$.

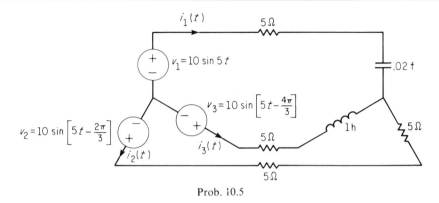

Prob. 10.5

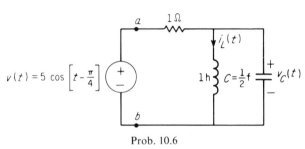

Prob. 10.6

**10.6.**   Solve for the steady-state current $i_L(t)$ in the circuit shown.

**10.7.**   (a) For the circuit shown in Prob. 10.6, find the driving-point impedance function $Z_{ab}(j\omega)$. (b) Assuming $v_C(t)$ is the desired response, solve for the steady state transfer function $H(j\omega)$. Plot as a function of $\omega$ the phase and amplitude response of the network with and without using the computer program.

**10.8.**   The drawing shows a simple low-pass filter. (a) Calculate the steady-state response $v_R(t)$. (b) Determine the steady-state transfer function of the network, $H(j\omega)$, and sketch the amplitude and phase response with and without using the computer program.

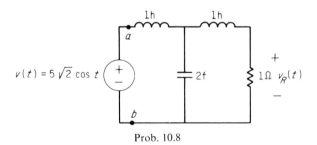

Prob. 10.8

**10.9.**   For the network of Prob. 10.8, find the instantaneous power, the average power, and the reactive power at the terminals $a$, $b$. What is the energy dissipated in the network over a time interval of length 5 sec?

**10.10.** (a) For the network shown, find the steady-state voltage $v_R(t)$.
(b) With $v_R(t)$ as the response, sketch the phase and amplitude transfer characteristics of the network.

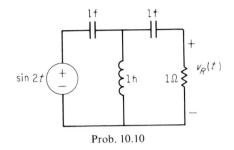

Prob. 10.10

**10.11.** For the circuit shown,
(a) Draw a phasor diagram indicating all voltages and currents.
(b) Using the diagram, calculate the average and reactive powers.

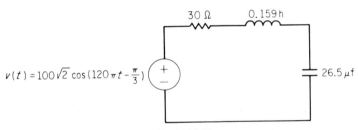

Prob. 10.11

**10.12.** A variable capacitance is connected in series with an inductor and resistor as shown.
(a) The power is observed to be 360 watts.   Find the value of $C$ and the power factor.
(b) The capacitor is readjusted and the power is observed to be 200 watts. Find the new value of $C$ and the new power factor.

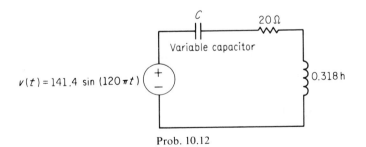

Prob. 10.12

**10.13.** From the definition of the quality factor, find $Q_0$ for the circuits shown in (a) and (b).

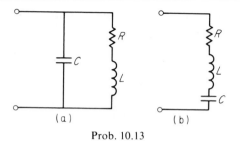

(a)          (b)

Prob. 10.13

**10.14.** The impedances $Z_1 = 20 + j10$ and $Z_2 = 10 - j30$ are connected in parallel as shown. Find the value $Z_3$ which will produce resonance at the terminal $a, b$.

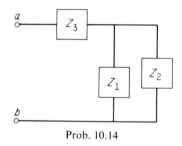

Prob. 10.14

**10.15.** In the circuit shown, $I_1 = 2e^{-j\pi/3}$, $I_2 = 5e^{j\pi/3}$, $I_3 = 1$.

(a) Draw a phasor diagram indicating all voltages and currents in the circuit.

(b) Is the circuit inductive, capacitive, or resonant?

(c) Find the average and reactive power in the circuit.

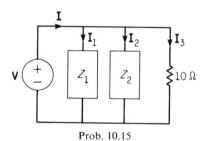

Prob. 10.15

**10.16.** In the circuit shown, the steady-state sinusoidal current $i_C(t)$ is measured to be $i_C(t) = \sin t$.

(a) Calculate $i(t)$ and $v(t)$ using phasor relationships.

(b) From (a), calculate the driving-point impedance $Z_{ab}(j\omega)$ for $\omega = 1$.

(c) Plot $|Z_{ab}(j\omega)|$ and $(\angle Z_{ab})(j\omega)$ as a function of $\omega, 0 \le \omega \le 100$ using the computer program.

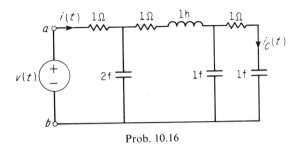

Prob. 10.16

**10.17.** For the circuit shown,
   (a) Find the resonant frequency of the circuit.
   (b) Find the quality factor $Q_0$.
   (c) With $i_R(t)$ as the desired circuit response, find and sketch the phase and amplitude transfer characteristics of the network.

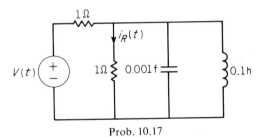

Prob. 10.17

**10.18.** For the circuit shown, find the value of $C$ in terms of the other circuit elements which will yield a unity power factor.

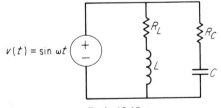

Prob. 10.18

**10.19.** Plot input admittance of network shown as a function of frequency using the computer program.

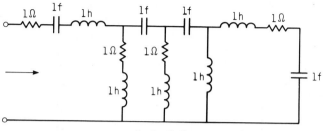

Prob. 10.19

## CHAPTER 11

# Circuit Analysis for Nonsinusoidal Periodic Waveforms

Periodic waveforms play an extremely important role in the analytical study of electrical circuits. The most common is the sinusoidal alternating voltage supply, which gives rise to periodic voltages and currents throughout the circuit as we have seen in the preceding chapter. Combinations of inductors and capacitors when excited also lead to sinusoidal sustained oscillations, the frequency at which the oscillation repeats being dependent upon the parameter values of the inductors and capacitors. Circuits excited by nonsinusoidal periodic inputs also lead to various types of periodic behavior of the currents and voltages. The most common type of nonsinusoidal periodic oscillations encountered in electronic circuits are (i) sawtooth waveforms, (ii) triangular waveforms, (iii) rectangular waveforms, and (iv) exponentially rising or exponentially falling waveforms, etc. Analysis of circuits by analytical means to such different types of periodic waveforms becomes of paramount importance. We have seen that the analysis of circuits for sinusoidal inputs of any frequency is very straightforward and requires only an elementary knowledge of complex numbers. If the input is given, the voltage or current at any other point can be easily determined in *magnitude* and *phase*, these being dependent upon the nature of the input and component values $R$, $L$, $C$ of the circuit.

For other types of periodic inputs, there is no such straightforward method of analysis. In Chapter 8 we developed impulse train response of a network which enables us to obtain response of a periodic input by the use of the convolution integral. However, this method was found to be quite tedious. In this chapter we develop the method of Fourier series which breaks any periodic function as an infinite sum of sines and cosines of various frequencies. Because of the principle of superposition for linear networks, we can find the response for each sinusoidal term of the Fourier series and then just sum up the individual responses to get the total response. In most of our work, the magnitudes of higher-frequency components of periodic waveforms attenuate very rapidly. Hence it is sufficient most of the time to consider only a few terms of the series to get the approximate response which is usually good enough for engineering applications. This procedure is also helpful in generating periodic waveforms by a series connection of sinusoidal generators of various voltages and frequencies in a series.

The response of networks to nonsinusoidal periodic inputs can also be obtained using Laplace transform as well as state variable techniques. We will discuss these in the latter part of this chapter.

We start by developing techniques for finding the Fourier series representation of periodic waveforms, the conditions of existence and convergence of infinite series as well as its application in circuit analysis.

## 11.2. FOURIER SERIES AND ITS USE IN CIRCUIT ANALYSIS

Consider a periodic function $f(t)$ such that

$$f(t + T) = f(t), \qquad T = \frac{2\pi}{\omega} \tag{11.2.1}$$

The French mathematician Jean Baptiste Fourier proved that a periodic waveform $f(t)$, with period $T$, can be represented (under certain conditions to be stated below) as

$$f(t) = \sum_{n=0}^{\infty} (a_n \cos n\omega t + b_n \sin n\omega t)$$

$$\text{over each period } t_0 < t < T + t_0 \tag{11.2.2}$$

There is no loss of generality if we choose $t_0 = 0$. However, some times it is convenient if $t_0$ is chosen as $-T/2$. Once the coefficients $a_n$ and $b_n$ are defined, $f(t)$ is completely known over the period as a sum of sines and cosines, and since it is repetitive, defining the waveform over one period is equivalent to defining the waveform for all time.

### Evaluation of $a_n$ and $b_n$

We multiply both sides of Eq. 11.2.2 by $\cos m\omega t$ and integrate over the period $T$ to get

$$\int_0^T f(t) \cos m\omega t \, dt = \int_0^T \left[ \sum_{n=0}^{\infty} (a_n \cos n\omega t + b_n \sin n\omega t) \right] \cos m\omega t \, dt$$

$$= \sum_{n=0}^{\infty} \left\{ a_n \int_0^T \cos m\omega t \cos n\omega t \, dt \right.$$

$$\left. + b_n \int_0^T \cos m\omega t \sin n\omega t \, dt \right\} \qquad (11.2.3)$$

The integrals appearing on the right-hand side of Eq. 11.2.3 are very easily evaluated because of the *orthogonal properties* of the sine and cosine functions. These can be stated in terms of the following integrals.

1. $\displaystyle\int_0^T \cos m\omega t \cos n\omega t \, dt = 0 \qquad m \neq n$

$$= \frac{T}{2} \qquad m = n \neq 0 \qquad (11.2.4)$$

$$= T \qquad m = n = 0$$

2. $\displaystyle\int_0^T \cos m\omega t \sin n\omega t \, dt = 0 \qquad\qquad\qquad (11.2.5)$

3. $\displaystyle\int_0^T \sin m\omega t \sin n\omega t \, dt = 0 \qquad m \neq n$

$$= \frac{T}{2} \qquad m = n \neq 0 \qquad (11.2.6)$$

$$= 0 \qquad m \text{ or } n = 0$$

Using Eqs. 11.2.4 and 11.2.5 in Eq. 11.2.3 we get

$$a_n = \frac{2}{T} \int_0^T f(t) \cos n\omega t \, dt, \quad n \neq 0 \qquad (11.2.7)$$

Similarly we can get $b_n$ by multiplying Eq. 11.2.2 by $\sin m\omega t$ and integrating over the period $T$, as

$$b_n = \frac{2}{T} \int_0^T f(t) \sin n\omega t \, dt, \qquad n \neq 0 \qquad (11.2.8)$$

Note that

$$b_0 = 0 \qquad (11.2.9)$$

and

$$a_0 = \frac{1}{T} \int_0^T f(t) \, dt \qquad (11.2.10)$$

In summary, we can write

$$f(t) = a_0 + \sum_{n=1}^{\infty} (a_n \cos n\omega t + b_n \sin \omega t), \qquad 0 < t < T \quad (11.2.11)$$

where

$$a_0 = \frac{1}{T} \int_0^T f(t)\, dt \qquad (11.2.12)$$

$$a_n = \frac{2}{T} \int_0^T f(t) \cos n\omega t\, dt \qquad (11.2.13)$$

$$b_n = \frac{2}{T} \int_0^T f(t) \sin n\omega t\, dt \qquad (11.2.14)$$

The representation of $f(t)$ by Eq. 11.2.11 is convergent only if the following conditions (called the Dirichlet conditions) are satisfied within each period.

(i) There are only a finite number of discontinuities of $f(t)$.

(ii) There are only a finite number of maxima and minima of $f(t)$.

These conditions are almost always satisfied in most engineering applications.

It is seen that the procedure of expanding $f(t)$ and finding the coefficients $a_n$ and $b_n$ is quite straightforward, but the number of steps in obtaining them can be reduced by using simple properties of sine and cosine functions.

**Simplifications**

A. $f(t)$ *Even or Odd.* We first note that $f(t)$ in the series expansion is made of three components.

(i) $a_0$, which is just a constant and can be considered an *even function.*

(ii) $a_n \cos n\omega t$, which is an *even function* irrespective of the value of $n$.

(iii) $b_n \sin n\omega t$, which is an *odd function* irrespective of the values of $n$.

We further note that any function can be broken into an even plus an odd function. An even function is made up of even functions only, and an odd function is made up of odd functions only.

This immediately gives us the following rules.

1. If $f(t)$ is even, i.e.,

$$f(t) = f(-t) \qquad (11.2.15)$$

then $b_n = 0$ because $b_n \sin n\omega t$ is odd. Therefore

$$f(t) = a_0 + \sum_{n=1}^{\infty} a_n \cos n\omega t \qquad (11.2.16)$$

2. If $f(t)$ is odd, i.e.,

$$f(t) = -f(-t) \qquad (11.2.17)$$

then $a_n = 0$, for all $n$ because $a_n \cos n\omega t$ is even. Therefore in this case

$$f(t) = \sum_{n=1}^{\infty} b_n \sin n\omega t \qquad (11.2.18)$$

This shows that if $f(t)$ is even or odd, the labor of finding coefficients is reduced to half because half of the coefficients are just zero.

B. *Choice of Origin.* When a waveform is periodic, one can choose the origin at whatever point one wishes; however, in view of the above simplification due to the even or odd nature of $f(t)$, it is worthwhile to choose the origin and therefore the vertical axis in such a manner that the function is odd or even if it is possible to do so.

Sometimes the origin is specified. In this case, the effort spent in finding the Fourier series expansion can still be reduced by choosing an origin which will result in $f(t)$ being even or odd; and after the representation is found, shifting the origin to the required point.

C. *Half Wave Symmetry.* A further simplification is possible if we consider the half wave symmetry of the periodic waveform $f(t)$. Mathematically this is stated as

$$f(t) = -f\left(t + \frac{T}{2}\right)$$

This means that for every positive value of $f(t)$ in a period, there is a corresponding negative value of $f(t)$, the same magnitude and half a period distant. This means that the area under $f(t)$ over the period is zero. This implies that $a_0 = 0$, because $a_0$ is the average area under $f(t)$. Hence we can state that if

$$f(t) = -f\left(t + \frac{T}{2}\right) \qquad (11.2.19)$$

then

$$a_0 = 0 \qquad (11.2.20)$$

Note that it is also possible to have the average value zero, i.e., $a_0 = 0$ without having the half-wave symmetry.

These are the three principal simplifications possible. It is also possible to simplify the integrations necessary for calculating the remaining coefficients. This will become clear as we consider examples and the reader gains experience.

*Example 11.2.1*

Find the Fourier series representation of the periodic waveform shown in Fig. 11.2.1.

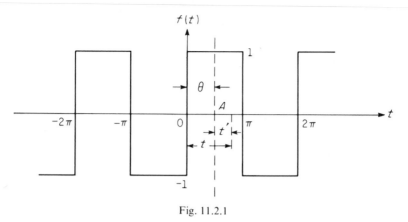

Fig. 11.2.1

*Solution*

Here we note that the origin could be chosen such that the function is even or odd. We choose the origin, as shown, such that the function is odd, i.e.,

$$f(t) = -f(-t)$$

Therefore

$$a_n = 0$$

Also, there is half-wave symmetry

$$f(t) = -f(t + \pi), \quad 2\pi \text{ being the period}$$

Therefore

$$a_0 = 0$$

However, this fact of half-wave symmetry did not help us get any additional information. Because $f(t)$ is odd we already knew that $a_0 = 0$. Hence, the half-wave symmetry test is not necessary if $f(t)$ is odd. So we have only to calculate $b_n$. We have

$$b_n = \frac{2}{T} \int_0^T f(t) \sin n\omega t \, dt = \frac{1}{\pi} \int_0^{2\pi} f(t) \sin nt \, dt$$

since

$$\omega = \frac{2\pi}{T} = 1$$

This gives

$$b_n = \frac{1}{\pi} \left\{ \int_0^{\pi} \sin nt \, dt - \int_{\pi}^{2\pi} \sin nt \, dt \right\}$$

$$= \frac{4}{n\pi}, \quad n \text{ odd}$$

$$= 0, \quad n \text{ even}$$

Therefore

$$f(t') = \sum_{n \text{ odd}} \frac{4}{n\pi} \sin nt = \frac{4}{\pi}\left[\sin t + \frac{1}{3}\sin 3t + \frac{1}{5}\sin 5t + \cdots\right]$$

This shows that if we connect sinusoidal generators of various frequencies in series as shown in Fig. 11.2.2 we can generate $f(t)$.

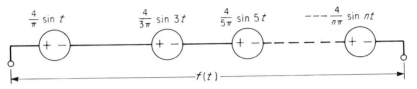

Fig. 11.2.2. Series connection of sinusoidal generators of various frequencies.

Note that the magnitude of sinusoidal terms of higher frequencies decreases rapidly as $n$ increases, hence from an engineering viewpoint only the first few terms of the series are necessary.

The construction of $f(t)$ from the first three terms of the series is shown in Fig. 11.2.3 over a half-period. It is obvious that as more terms are taken, a better approximation results.

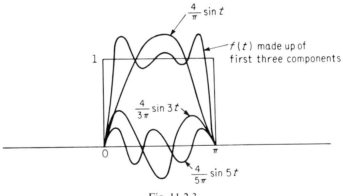

Fig. 11.2.3

We can now very easily deduce the results if we had selected the origin at some other point, say $A$ as shown in Fig. 11.2.1 such that the distance $0A = \theta$. Then

$$t = t' + \theta$$

Hence, in terms of the new time variable $t'$, $f(t)$ above becomes

$$f(t') = \sum_{n \text{ odd}} \frac{4}{n\pi} \sin n(t' + \theta)$$

For $\theta = \pi/2$, we have

$$f(t) = \frac{4}{\pi}\left[\cos t' - \frac{1}{3}\cos 3t' + \frac{1}{5}\cos 5t' \cdots\right]$$

This demonstrates the fact that the origin can be chosen at the most convenient point for Fourier series expansion and later shifted if there is a requirement for choosing the origin at a particular point.

*Example 11.2.2.*

Represent the triangular waveform shown in Fig. 11.2.4 as a Fourier series.

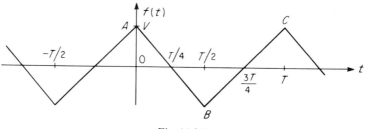

Fig. 11.2.4

*Solution*

We choose the origin to make the function even. Therefore

$$b_n = 0$$

Also the function has half-wave symmetry. Therefore

$$a_0 = 0$$

So we write

$$f(t) = \sum_{n=1}^{\infty} a_n \cos n\omega t, \qquad \omega = \frac{2\pi}{T}$$

where

$$a_n = \frac{2}{T} \int_0^T f(t) \cos n\omega t \, dt$$

As mentioned earlier, we can choose the periodic interval $[t_0, t_0 + T]$ rather than $[0, T]$. In this case it is more convenient to choose it as $\left[-\frac{T}{2}, \frac{T}{2}\right]$ because of the form of $f(t)$. Hence we can write the alternate form of $a_n$ as

$$a_n = \frac{2}{T} \int_{-T/2}^{T/2} f(t) \cos n\omega t \, dt$$

Now both $f(t)$ and $\cos n\omega t$ are even functions. Therefore, the integral must have the same value between $-\dfrac{T}{2}$ to 0 and between 0 and $\dfrac{T}{2}$. We then have

$$a_n = \frac{4}{T} \int_0^{T/2} f(t) \cos n\omega t \, dt$$

This reduces the work in half again because we have to consider $f(t)$ only over half a cycle.

Now over $\left[0, \dfrac{T}{2}\right]$,

$$f(t) = V\left[1 - \frac{4t}{T}\right]$$

Therefore

$$a_n = \frac{4V}{T} \int_0^{T/2} \left(1 - \frac{4t}{T}\right) \cos n\omega t \, dt = \frac{4}{n^2\pi^2}, \quad n \text{ odd}$$

$$= 0, \quad n \text{ even}$$

Substituting $a_n$ in the Fourier series expansion, we have

$$f(t) = \sum_{n \text{ odd}} \frac{4}{n^2\pi^2} \cos n\omega t$$

These simplifications in integrations can be stated as follows:
1. If $f(t)$ is even or odd, integration is required over only half a cycle using twice the value of the resulting integral.
2. If there is half-wave symmetry, the integration is over only half a cycle and there are *no* even harmonic terms, where $\cos \omega t$ or $\sin \omega t$ is defined as the *fundamental frequency* component of $f(t)$ while $\cos n\omega t$ or $\sin n\omega t$ is the *nth harmonic*. All of the harmonics are referred to as components of $f(t)$.

*Example 11.2.3*

The rectangular waveform of Fig. 11.2.1 is applied to an $RC$ network as shown in Fig. 11.2.5. Find the steady-state value of the current.

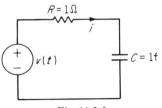

Fig. 11.2.5

*Solution*

If $v(t)$ were sinusoidal, say $V \sin \omega t$, we can find the current $i$ by simply evaluating the impedance $Z$ for frequency $\omega$. We have

$$Z = 1 + \frac{1}{j\omega} = \sqrt{1 + \frac{1}{\omega^2}} \angle \phi$$

where

$$\phi = -\tan^{-1}\left(\frac{1}{\omega}\right)$$

Then

$$i = \text{Im}\left[\frac{Ve^{j\omega t}}{Z(j\omega)}\right] = \frac{V}{\sqrt{1 + 1/\omega^2}} \sin(\omega t - \phi)$$

In our case $v(t)$ is not sinusoidal but rectangular, however we have shown in Example 11.2.1 that

$$v(t) = f(t) = \sum_{n \text{ odd}} \frac{4}{n\pi} \sin nt$$

which is the sum of sinusoids. All we have to do is to find $i$ for the $n$th term. For this we note $V = \frac{4}{n\pi}$ and $\omega = n$. Then the current $i_n$ due to the $n$th voltage term is found (using the above result) as

$$i_n = \frac{\frac{4}{n\pi}}{\sqrt{1 + \frac{1}{n^2}}} \sin(nt - \phi_n) \qquad \text{where } \phi_n = -\tan^{-1}\left(\frac{1}{n}\right)$$

The total steady-state current is then

$$i = \sum_{n \text{ odd}} i_n = \sum_{n \text{ odd}} \frac{\frac{4}{\pi}}{\sqrt{1 + n^2}} \sin\left[nt + \tan^{-1}\left(\frac{1}{n}\right)\right]$$

$$= \sum_{n \text{ odd}} I_n \sin(nt - \phi_n)$$

Suppose now we want to find the rms value of the current. We know

$$I_{\text{rms}}^2 = \frac{1}{T} \int_0^T i^2 dt = \frac{1}{T} \int_0^T \left\{\sum_{n \text{ odd}} I_n \sin(nt - \phi_n)\right\}^2 dt$$

$$= \frac{1}{T} \sum_{n \text{ odd}} \int_0^T I_n^2 \sin^2(nt - \phi_n) \, dt$$

$$+ \frac{1}{T} \sum_{\substack{n \text{ odd} \\ n \neq m}} \sum_{m \text{ odd}} \int_0^T I_n I_m \sin(nt - \phi_n) \\ \sin(mt - \phi_m) \, dt$$

Using the orthogonal properties of sine functions (See Eq. 11.2.6), the second integral in the above expression is zero. Hence we obtain

$$I_{rms} = \sqrt{\frac{1}{2} \sum_{n \text{ odd}} I_n^2} = \sqrt{\sum_{n \text{ odd}} I_{n \text{ rms}}^2}$$

This is a very interesting result, the total rms value can be obtained from the sum of squares of the rms value of the components. In our case

$$\frac{I_n^2}{2} = I_{n \text{ rms}}^2 = \frac{8}{\pi^2(1 + n^2)}$$

Therefore

$$I_{rms} = \sqrt{\frac{8}{\pi^2} \left[ \frac{1}{1 + 1^2} + \frac{1}{1 + 3^2} + \frac{1}{1 + 5^2} + \cdots \right]}$$

### Exponential Form Representation of Fourier Series

In general, $f(t)$ may not be even or odd or have half-wave symmetry. In this case all coefficients must be evaluated. This procedure can be simplified by combining the $a_n$ and $b_n$ coefficients into a single coefficient which can be evaluated by the use of complex numbers. This representation of Fourier series is referred to as *exponential Fourier series*. Consider

$$f(t) = a_0 + \sum_{n=1}^{\infty} (a_n \cos n\omega t + b_n \sin n\omega t) \qquad (11.2.21)$$

This can be written as

$$f(t) = a_0 + \sum_{n=1}^{\infty} \left( a_n \frac{(e^{jn\omega t} + e^{-jn\omega t})}{2} + b_n \frac{(e^{jn\omega t} - e^{-jn\omega t})}{2j} \right)$$

$$= a_0 + \sum_{n=1}^{\infty} \left( \frac{a_n - jb_n}{2} e^{jn\omega t} + \frac{a_n + jb_n}{2} e^{-jn\omega t} \right) \qquad (11.2.22)$$

Let

$$d_n(j) = \frac{a_n - jb_n}{2} \quad \text{and} \quad d_0 = \frac{a_0}{2} \qquad (11.2.23)$$

Then we can write

$$f(t) = 2d_0 + \sum_{n=1}^{\infty} d_n(j) e^{jn\omega t} + \sum_{n=1}^{\infty} d_n(-j) e^{-jn\omega t}$$

$$= 2d_0 + \sum_{n=1}^{\infty} d_n(j) e^{jn\omega t} + \sum_{n=-1}^{-\infty} d_{-n}(-j) e^{jn\omega t}$$

or

$$f(t) = \sum_{n=-\infty}^{\infty} c_n e^{jn\omega t} \qquad (11.2.24)$$

where

$$c_n = d_n(j) \quad \text{from } n = 1 \text{ to } \infty$$
$$= d_{-n}(-j) \quad \text{from } n = -\infty \text{ to } -1 \tag{11.2.25a}$$

and

$$c_0 = 2d_0 \tag{11.2.25b}$$

The representation

$$f(t) = \sum_{n=-\infty}^{\infty} c_n e^{jn\omega t} \tag{11.2.26}$$

is the *exponential Fourier series.* In order to evaluate $c_n$, we multiply both sides of Eq. 11.2.26 by $e^{-jn\omega t}$ and then integrate over one period to obtain

$$c_n = \frac{1}{T} \int_0^T f(t) e^{-jn\omega t} \, dt \tag{11.2.27}$$

This result is due to the fact that all terms except the $n$th term on the right-hand side when integrated over a complete period are zero due to the orthogonal properties of sine and cosine function as explained previously.

The representation of Eq. 11.2.26 is very convenient and only involves one integration given by Eq. 11.2.27. We can always get the trigonometric form by evaluating $a_n$ and $b_n$ from $c_n$ utilizing the relationships given by Eqs. 11.2.23 and 11.2.25. Note that $c_n$ is in general complex and therefore has magnitude and phase.

*Example 11.2.4*

Find the exponential Fourier series of the half-wave rectified sinusoid as shown in Fig. 11.2.6.

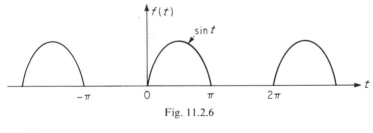

Fig. 11.2.6

*Solution*

Let

$$f(t) = \sum_{n=-\infty}^{\infty} c_n e^{jn\omega t}$$

where

$$c_n = \frac{1}{T} \int_0^T f(t) e^{-jn\omega t} \, dt$$

Here

$$T = 2\pi, \qquad \omega = \frac{2\pi}{T} = 1$$

Therefore

$$c_n = \frac{1}{2\pi} \int_0^\pi \sin t \, e^{-jnt} \, dt$$

$$= \frac{1 + e^{-jn\pi}}{2\pi(1 - n^2)}$$

or

$$c_n = \begin{cases} \dfrac{1}{\pi(1 - n^2)}, & n \text{ even and zero} \\[2mm] \mp j/4, & n = \pm 1 \\[2mm] 0, \, n \text{ odd}, \, n \neq \pm 1 \end{cases}$$

The magnitude of $c_n$ and the phase of $c_n$ for various values of $n$ is plotted in Fig. 11.2.7. The information given by Fig. 11.2.7 completely defines the

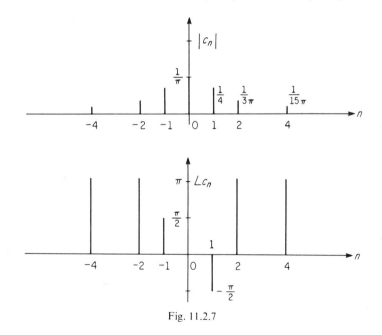

Fig. 11.2.7

frequency components of $f(t)$. This plot is referred to as the *magnitude and angular frequency spectrum* of $f(t)$ and is widely used in network and communication theory. Since $n$ is discrete, these plots are referred to as *line spectra*.

A view of the spectrum usually enables us to determine the number of terms sufficient to approximate a given waveform. The various frequencies required to generate $f(t)$ are sometimes referred to as *frequency content* of $f(t)$.

*Example 11.2.5*

The half-wave rectified sinusoidal voltage of Fig. 11.2.6 is applied to the $RL$ network shown in Fig. 11.2.8. Find the steady state value of the current.

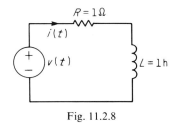

Fig. 11.2.8

*Solution*

From the previous example we have evaluated the Fourier series expansion of the half-wave rectified sinusoidal waveform as

$$v(t) = \sum_{n=-\infty}^{\infty} c_n e^{jn\omega t}$$

$$= \frac{1}{\pi} + \sum_{n \text{ even}} \frac{1}{\pi(1 - n^2)} e^{jnt} - \frac{j}{4} e^{jt} + \frac{j}{4} e^{-jt}$$

$$= V_0 + \sum_{n \text{ even}} V_n e^{jnt} - \frac{j}{4} e^{jt} + \frac{j}{4} e^{-jt}$$

where

$$V_0 = \frac{1}{\pi} \quad \text{and} \quad V_n = \frac{1}{\pi(1 - n^2)}$$

For the network of Fig. 11.2.8, we have the current due to complex exponential input voltage function of frequency $\omega$ as

$$i = \frac{Ve^{j\omega t}}{Z(j\omega)} = \frac{Ve^{j\omega t}}{1 + j\omega}$$

Hence for our case

$$i = V_0 + \sum_{n \text{ even}} \frac{V_n}{1 + jn} e^{jnt} - \frac{je^{jt}}{4(1 + j)} + \frac{je^{-jt}}{4(1 - j)}$$

$$= V_0 + \sum_{n \text{ even}} \frac{V_n}{\sqrt{1 + n^2}} e^{j(nt - \phi_n)} + \frac{1}{\sqrt{8}} \sin(t - 45°)$$

where $\phi_n = \tan^{-1} n$.

Substituting for $V_0$ and $V_n$, the steady-state value of the current is given below:

$$i = \frac{1}{\pi} + \sum_{n \text{ even}} \frac{1}{\pi} \frac{1}{(1 - n^2)\sqrt{1 + n^2}} e^{j(nt - \tan^{-1} n)} + \frac{1}{\sqrt{8}} \sin(t - 45°)$$

It can be shown, using a procedure similar to the one demonstrated in Example 11.2.3, that

$$I_{rms} = \sqrt{\frac{1}{\pi^2} + \sum_{n \text{ even}} \left\{ \frac{1}{\pi(1 - n^2)\sqrt{1 + n^2}} \right\}^2 + \frac{1}{16}}$$

## Numerical Evaluation of Fourier Coefficients

We have mentioned some approximations which can be made in the Fourier series representation of any periodic function in network analysis. The number of terms which are enough to represent any periodic $f(t)$ depends upon the rate of convergence, and there is no rule of thumb except experience. This is the case both for analysis and generation of any periodic waveform.

In actual electronic circuits most of the waveforms actually have no exact mathematical representation because of various *rise times* and other factors associated with electrical components. Hence it is not really possible to perform the integrations analytically because $f(t)$ is not known as a mathematical function; however, a measured waveform can be expanded in a Fourier series, thus enabling one to develop an approximate mathematical representation.

One method of obtaining the Fourier coefficients is to evaluate the integrals numerically. This can be easily programmed on the digital computer. Consider one period of a periodic waveform $f(t)$ as shown in Fig. 11.2.9. This could be a waveform observed with an oscilloscope

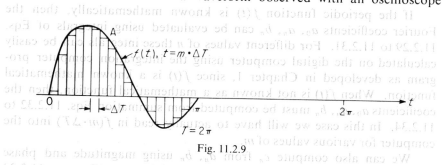

Fig. 11.2.9

which we would like to represent in a Fourier series expansion as

$$f(t) = a_0 + \sum_{n=1}^{\infty} (a_n \cos n\omega t + b_n \sin n\omega t) \qquad (11.2.28)$$

where

$$a_0 = \frac{1}{T} \int_0^T f(t)\, dt \tag{11.2.29}$$

$$a_n = \frac{2}{T} \int_0^T f(t) \cos n\omega t\, dt \tag{11.2.30}$$

$$b_n = \frac{2}{T} \int_0^T f(t) \sin n\omega t\, dt \tag{11.2.31}$$

Since $f(t)$ is not known as a mathematical function, we cannot evaluate the above integrals analytically. However, we can divide $f(t)$ into small pulses of width $\Delta T$ (The more pulses we use, the better the approximation) as shown in Fig. 11.2.9. Then at the start of the $m$th pulse, we have $t = m\Delta T$. The integrations indicated in Eqs. 11.2.29 through 11.2.31 can be replaced by summations

$$a_0 = \frac{1}{T} \sum_m f(m \cdot \Delta T)\, \Delta T \tag{11.2.32}$$

$$a_n = \frac{2}{T} \sum_m f(m \cdot \Delta T) \cos\left\{ n \cdot \frac{2\pi}{T} (m \cdot \Delta T) \right\} \Delta T \tag{11.2.33}$$

$$b_n = \frac{2}{T} \sum_m f(m \cdot \Delta T) \sin\left\{ n \cdot \frac{2\pi}{T} (m \cdot \Delta T) \right\} \Delta T \tag{11.2.34}$$

Equations 11.2.33 and 11.2.34 must be evaluated for each value of $n$. Note that we still can use any symmetrical conditions to reduce our work. We can also use the exponential form which will involve only one complex coefficient.

### Evaluation of Fourier Coefficients Using the Digital Computer

If the periodic function $f(t)$ is known mathematically, then the Fourier coefficients $a_0$, $a_n$, $b_n$ can be evaluated using integrals of Eqs. 11.2.29 to 11.2.31. For different values of $n$ these integrals can be easily calculated on the digital computer using the integration computer program as developed in Chapter 1, since $f(t)$ is a known mathematical function. When $f(t)$ is not known as a mathematical function, then the coefficients $a_0$, $a_n$, $b_n$ must be computed from summation Eqs. 11.2.32 to 11.2.34. In this case we will have to actually read in $f(m \cdot \Delta T)$ into the computer for various values of $m$.

We can also compute $c_n$ from $a_n$, $b_n$ using magnitude and phase computer program as developed in Chapter 10 because (Eqs. see 11.2.23 and 11.2.25)

$$c_n = \frac{a_n - jb_n}{2} \qquad n = 1, \text{ to } \infty$$

and

$$c_{-n} = \frac{a_n + jb_n}{2} \qquad n = 1 \text{ to } \infty \qquad (11.2.35)$$

and

$$c_0 = a_0$$

### Development of the Computer Programs for Evaluating Fourier Coefficients

1. $f(t)$ known mathematically.
Here we have to compute

$$a_0 = \frac{1}{T} \int_0^T f(t)\, dt \qquad (11.2.36)$$

$$a_n = \frac{2}{T} \int_0^T f(t) \cos n\omega t\, dt \qquad (11.2.37)$$

$$b_n = \frac{2}{T} \int_0^T f(t) \sin n\omega t\, dt \qquad (11.2.38)$$

In case we want to obtain $c_n$, we must compute $c_n$ as obtained from Eq. 11.2.35. The magnitude and phase of $c_n$ to be computed are given by
Magnitude of $c_n$:

$$|c_n| = |c_{-n}| = \frac{\sqrt{a_n^2 + b_n^2}}{2}, \qquad n = 1 \text{ to } \infty \qquad (11.2.39)$$

Phase of $c_n$:

$\angle c_n$ is obtained from $\dfrac{a_n - jb_n}{2}$ and is $= \tan^{-1}\left(\dfrac{-b_n}{a_n}\right), \qquad n = 1 \text{ to } \infty$

$$(11.2.40)$$

$\angle c_{-n}$ is obtained from $\dfrac{a_n + jb_n}{2}$ and is $= \tan^{-1}\left(\dfrac{b_n}{a_n}\right), \qquad n = 1 \text{ to } \infty$

$$(11.2.41)$$

We define two functions:

$$\text{SIRPC(T0, T1, WN)} = \int_{T_0}^{T_1} f(t) \cos n\omega t\, dt \qquad (11.2.42)$$

$$\text{SIRPS(T0, T1, WN)} = \int_{T_0}^{T_1} f(t) \sin n\omega t\, dt \qquad (11.2.43)$$

where

$$T0 = T_0,\ T1 = T_1,\ W = \omega, \quad \text{and} \quad N = n$$

Let us examine Eq. 11.2.42 first. If $f(t)$, $T_0$, $T_1$, $n$, $\omega$ are specified, the integral is easily computed using the computer integration program of Chapter 1. For a given $f(t)$, we can just write SIRPC(T0, T1, WN)

Flow Chart for Computer Program Development for Evaluating Fourier
Coefficients, f(t) Known As a Mathematical Function

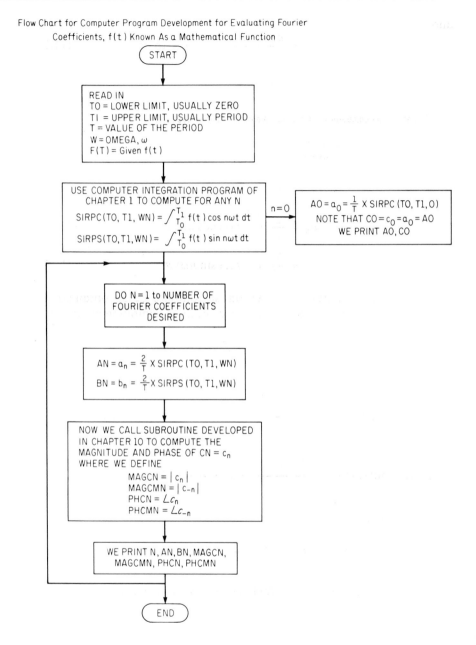

whenever we want to compute integrals of Eq. 11.2.42. Similarly, SIRPS(T0, T1, WN) can be written whenever we want to compute integral of Eq. 11.2.43. Also note that if $n = 0$, we can write

$$SIRPC(T0, T1, 0) = \int_{T_0}^{T_1} f(t)\, dt \qquad (11.2.44)$$

Note that Eqs. 11.2.42 through 11.2.44 cover the integrations needed in Eqs. 11.2.36 through 11.2.38. We must also realize that $f(t)$ may not be continuous over the total period ($T_1 - T_0$); in that case we will have to break up the limits of integration to evaluate the integral.

We will use SIRPC and SIRPS to evaluate $a_0$, $a_n$, and $b_n$ and we will then use these values to obtain magnitude and phase of $c_n$ using the subroutine given in Chapter 10 for obtaining magnitude and phase of a complex number. The flow chart to evaluate the coefficients is given on page 408.

*Example 11.2.6*

Use a computer program to obtain the Fourier coefficients for a periodic waveform $f(t)$ of Fig. 11.2.6, Example 11.2.4.

*Solution*

From Fig. 11.2.6 we note that

$$f(t) = \sin t, \quad T_0 = 0, \quad T_1 = \pi, \quad T = 2\pi, \quad \omega = \frac{2\pi}{T} = 1$$

The computer program based on the above flow chart is given below. Note that both SIRPC(T0, T1, WN), SIRPS(T0, T1, WN) are given separately at the end of the program as they act as FUNCTION statements. The final printout of the Fourier coefficients is also given.

```
C      THIS PROGRAM IS FOR EXAMPLE 11.2-6
C      THIS PROGRAM COMPUTES FOURIER COEFFICIENTS WHEN THE
C      PERIODIC FUNCTION CAN BE EXPRESSED MATHEMATICALLY
C      THIS PROGRAM COMPUTES AO,CO,AN,BN, MAGCN,MAGCMN,PHCN,
C      PHCMN AS A FUNCTION OF N, N=1 TO NUMBER OF FOURIER
C      COEFFICIENTS DESIRED,
       REAL MAGCN,MAGCMN
C      SET TO TO THE LOWER LIMIT
       TO = 0,
C      SET T1,THE UPPER LIMIT
       PI=3,14159
       T1=PI
C      SET PERIOD
       T=2.0*PI
C      SET OMEGA,
       W=1,0
C      COMPUTE AO AND CO,
       AO = SIRPC(TO,T1,0,)/T
       CO = AO
       PRINT 5, AO,CO
       PRINT 33
```

```
C       THIS PART IS DO LOOP TO EVALUATE FOURIER COEFFICIENTS
C       FROM N=1, TO DESIRED NUMBER,
        DO 35 N= 1,10
        WN = W*N
C       THIS PART COMPUTES AN,BN
        AN = SIRPC(T0,T1,WN)*2,/T
        BN = SIRPS(T0,T1,WN)*2,/T
C       THIS PART COMPUTES THE PHASE AND MAGNITUDE USING
C       SIMILAR TECHNIQUES AS GIVEN IN CHAPTER 10,
        IBN=IFIX(BN*10000,0)
        IAN=IFIX(AN*10000,0)
        IF (IAN ,EQ, 0 ,AND, IBN ,EQ, 0) GO TO 34
        GO TO 36
     34 MAGCN=0,0
        MAGCMN=0,0
        PHCN=0,0
        PHCMN=0,0
        GO TO 37
     36 CNR=AN/2,0
        CNI=-BN/2,0
        CMNR=AN/2,0
        CMNI=BN/2,0
        CALL MAGPHS(CNR,CNI,MAGCN,PHCN)
        CALL MAGPHS(CMNR,CMNI,MAGCMN,PHCMN)
C       NOW WE PRINT AN,BN,MAGCN,MAGCMN,PHCN,PHCMN,
     37 PRINT 32, N,AN,BN,MAGCN,MAGCMN,PHCN,PHCMN
     35 CONTINUE
      5 FORMAT (1H ,'A0=',F 8,5,5X,'C0=',F 8,5)
     32 FORMAT(1H ,13,6F10,5)
     33 FORMAT(/1H ,2X,'N',6X,'AN',8X,'BN',6X,'MAGCN',5X,
      1'MAGCMN',2X,'PHCN(RAD',2X,'PHCMN(RAD)'/)
        END



        FUNCTION SIRPC(T0,T1,WN)
C       THIS PROGRAM COMPUTES A DEFINITE INTEGRAL
C       SIRPC(T0,T1,WN) USING SIMPSON'S RULE OF
C       INTEGRATION, SEE CHAPTER 1,
C       CHOOSE K AS AN EVEN NUMBER
        K = 16
        AN = K
C       FTA IS THE GIVEN INTEGRAND F(T),T BEING REPLACED BY TA
C       SIMILARLY FTB AND FTC
        H = (T1-T0)/AN
        SUM = 0,
        TA = T0
        TB = TA+H
        TC = TB+H
        M = K/2
        DO 10 I=1,M
        FTA = SIN(TA) * COS(WN*TA)
        FTB = SIN(TB) * COS(WN*TB)
        FTC = SIN(TC) * COS(WN*TC)
        SUM  = SUM+FTA+4,*FTB+FTC
        TA = TA+2,0*H
        TB = TA+H
        TC = TB+H
     10 CONTINUE
        SIRPC=SUM*H/3,
        END
```

```
      FUNCTION SIRPS(T0,T1,WN)
C     THIS PROGRAM COMPUTES A DEFINITE INTEGRAL
C     SIRPS(T0,T1,WN) USING SIMPSON'S RULE OF
C     INTEGRATION, SEE CHAPTER 1,
C     CHOOSE K AS AN EVEN NUMBER
      K = 16
      AN = K
C     FTA IS THE GIVEN INTEGRAND F(T),T BEING REPLACED BY TA
C     SIMILARLY FTB AND FTC
      H = (T1-T0)/AN
      SUM = 0,
      TA = T0
      TB = TA+H
      TC = TB+H
      M = K/2
      DO 10 I=1,M
      FTA = SIN(TA) * SIN(WN*TA)
      FTB = SIN(TB) * SIN(WN*TB)
      FTC = SIN(TC) * SIN(WN*TC)
      SUM = SUM+FTA+4,*FTB+FTC
      TA = TA+2,0*H
      TB = TA+H
      TC = TB+H
   10 CONTINUE
      SIRPS=SUM*H/3,
      END

      SUBROUTINE MAGPHS(X,Y,RM,RA)
C     THIS SUBROUTINE CONVERTS A GIVEN COMPLEX NUMBER IN
C     CARTESIAN FORM (X+JY) TO POLOR FORM RM,RA THE
C     MAGNITUDE AND PHASE FORM,
C     THE FOLLOWING FOUR IF STATEMENTS DETERMINE THE
C     QUADRANT IN WHICH THE GIVEN VECTOR LIES AND DIRECT
C     THE PROGRAM TO GO TO THE STATEMENT WHICH GIVES THE
C     ANGLE IN THAT QUADRANT,
C     IN CASE BOTH X AND Y ARE ZERO THE ANGLE IS
C     INDETERMINATE AND THAT IS PRINTED AND SUBROUTINE
C     TERMINATES,
C     THIS PART COMPUTES THE ANGLE,
      PI=3,14159
      IF (Y) 61,62,63
   61 IF (X) 64,65,66
   62 IF (X) 67,99,68
   63 IF (X) 69,70,71
   64 RA= PI+ATAN(Y/X)
      GO TO 72
   65 RA=3,0*PI/2,0
      GO TO 72
   66 RA=2,0*PI-ATAN(-Y/X)
      GO TO 72
   67 RA=PI
      GO TO 72
   68 RA=0,0
      GO TO 72
   69 RA=PI-ATAN(-Y/X)
      GO TO 72
   70 RA=PI/2,0
      GO TO 72
   71 RA=ATAN(Y/X)
      GO TO 72
   99 PRINT 98
      GO TO 73
C     THIS PART COMPUTES THE MAGNITUDE,
   72 RM=SQRT(X*X+Y*Y)
   98 FORMAT (1H ,'ANGLE INDETERMINATE')
   73 RETURN
      END
```

*Printout of Fourier Coefficients*

```
AO=  ,31831       CO=  ,31831

  N       AN          BN        MAGCN      MAGCMN    PHCN(RAD   PHCMN(RAD)

  1    -,00000     ,50000      ,25000     ,25000     4,71239    1,57079
  2    -,21214    -,00000      ,10607     ,10607     3,14159    3,14159
  3     ,00000    -,00000      ,00000     ,00000      ,00000     ,00000
  4    -,04214    -,00000      ,02107     ,02107     3,14159    3,14159
  5     ,00000     ,00000      ,00000     ,00000      ,00000     ,00000
  6    -,01741    -,00000      ,00870     ,00870     3,14159    3,14159
  7    -,00000     ,00000      ,00000     ,00000      ,00000     ,00000
  8    -,00829    -,00000      ,00414     ,00414     3,14159    3,14159
  9    -,00000     ,00000      ,00000     ,00000      ,00000     ,00000
 10    -,00215    -,00000      ,00107     ,00107     3,14156    3,14162
```

2. $f(t)$ not known analytically but only graphically.

In this case we first break the period $T$ into $(K - 1)$ parts such that $(K - 1)\,\Delta T = T$. Then we record values of $f(m\Delta T)$, $m = 1$ to $K$. Now from Eqs. 11.2.32 through 11.2.34 we can write

$$a_0 = \frac{1}{T}\sum_{m=1}^{K} f(m\Delta T)\cdot\Delta T \tag{11.2.45}$$

$$a_n = \frac{2}{T}\sum_{m=1}^{K} f(m\Delta T)\cos\left(n\cdot\frac{2\pi}{T}\cdot(m\Delta T)\right)\Delta T \tag{11.2.46}$$

$$b_n = \frac{2}{T}\sum_{m=1}^{K} f(m\Delta T)\sin\left(n\cdot\frac{2\pi}{T}\cdot(m\Delta T)\right)\Delta T \tag{11.2.47}$$

The flow chart to compute the coefficients based on Eqs. 11.2.45 through 11.2.47 is given on the next page.

*Example 11.2.7*

A periodic waveform taken from an oscilloscope is shown in Fig. 11.2.10. Use the computer program to evaluate $a_0$, $a_n$ and $b_n$ from $n = 1$ to 20. Hence, also compute magnitude and phase of $c_n$.

*Solution*

We can break the time period each to 0.05 sec, i.e., $\Delta T = 0.05$ sec., so that $K = 20$.

From the figure we pick up values of $f(I)$, $I = 1,20; f(1) = 0; f(2) = 0.25;$ $f(3) = 0.3;$ $f(4) = 0.5;$ $f(5) = f(6) = f(7) = 1.0;$ $f(8) = 0.55;$ $f(9) = 0.3;$ $f(10) = 0;$ $f(11) = -0.25;$ $f(12) = -0.3;$ $f(13) = -0.3;$ $f(14) = -0.2;$ $f(15) = -0.1;$ $f(16) = f(17) = f(18) = f(19) = f(20) = 0.$ Also $T = 1.$

Now we develop a computer program based on the flow chart given on the next page to obtain a printout of Fourier coefficients.

Flow Chart for Developing Computer Program for Evaluating
Fourier Coefficients When $f(t)$ Is Not Known Analytically

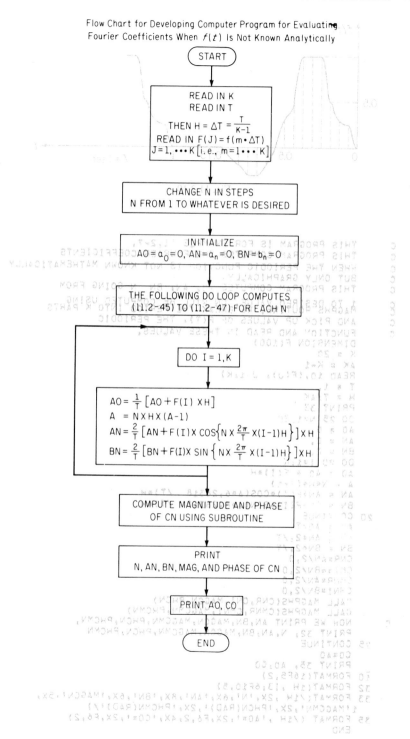

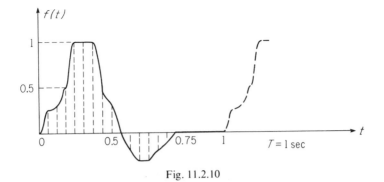

Fig. 11.2.10

```
C          THIS PROGRAM IS FOR EXAMPLE 11.2-7.
C          THIS PROGRAM COMPUTES THE FOURIER COEFFICIENTS
C          WHEN THE PERIODIC FUNCTION IS NOT KNOWN MATHEMATICALLY
C          BUT ONLY GRAPHICALLY.
C          THIS PROGRAM COMPUTES AO, AN, BN  N GOING FROM
C          1 TO DESIRED VALUE. CN WILL BE COMPUTED USING
C          MAGPHS ROUTINE. WE BREAK THE PERIOD INTO K PARTS
C          AND PICK UP VALUES OF F(T), THE PERIODIC
C          FUNCTION AND READ IN THESE VALUES.
           DIMENSION F(100)
           K = 20
           AK = K-1
           READ 10,(F(J), J=1,K)
           T = 1.
           H = T/AK
           PRINT 33
           DO 25 N=1,20
           AO = 0.
           AN = 0.
           BN = 0.
           DO 20 I=1,K
           AO = AO + F(I)*H
           A = N*H*(I-1)
           AN = AN+F(I)*COS(A*6.28318   /T)*H
           BN = BN+F(I)*SIN(A*6.28318   /T)*H
        20 CONTINUE
           AO = AO/T
           AN = AN*2./T
           BN = BN*2./T
           CNR=AN/2.0
           CNI=-BN/2.0
           CMNR=AN/2.0
           CMNI=BN/2.0
           CALL MAGPHS(CNR,CNI,MAGCN,PHCN)
           CALL MAGPHS(CMNR,CMNI,MAGCMN,PHCMN)
C          NOW WE PRINT AN,BN,MAGCN,MAGCMN,PHCN,PHCMN.
           PRINT 32, N,AN,BN,MAGCN,MAGCMN,PHCN,PHCMN
        25 CONTINUE
           CO=AO
           PRINT 35, AO,CO
        10 FORMAT(16F5.2)
        32 FORMAT(1H ,I3,6F10.5)
        33 FORMAT(/1H ,2X,'N',6X,'AN',8X,'BN',6X,'MAGCN',5X,
          1'MAGCMN',2X,'PHCN(RAD)',2X,'PHCMN(RAD)'/)
        35 FORMAT (/1H ,'AO=',2X,F6.2,4X,'CO=',2X,F6.2)
           END
```

```
      SUBROUTINE MAGPHS(X,Y,RM,RA)
   C  THIS SUBROUTINE CONVERTS A GIVEN COMPLEX NUMBER IN
   C  CARTESIAN FORM (X+JY) TO POLOR FORM RM,RA THE
   C  MAGNITUDE AND PHASE FORM,
   C  THE FOLLOWING FOUR IF STATEMENTS DETERMINE THE
   C  QUADRANT IN WHICH THE GIVEN VECTOR LIES AND DIRECT
   C  THE PROGRAM TO GO TO THE STATEMENT WHICH GIVES THE
   C  ANGLE IN THAT QUADRANT,
   C  IN CASE BOTH X AND Y ARE ZERO THE ANGLE IS
   C  INDETERMINATE AND THAT IS PRINTED AND SUBROUTINE
   C  TERMINATES,
   C  THIS PART COMPUTES THE ANGLE,
      PI=3,14159
      IF (Y) 61,62,63
   61 IF (X) 64,65,66
   62 IF (X) 67,99,68
   63 IF (X) 69,70,71
   64 RA= PI+ATAN(Y/X)
      GO TO 72
   65 RA=3,0*PI/2,0
      GO TO 72
   66 RA=2,0*PI=ATAN(=Y/X)
      GO TO 72
   67 RA=PI
      GO TO 72
   68 RA=0,0
      GO TO 72
   69 RA=PI=ATAN(=Y/X)
      GO TO 72
   70 RA=PI/2,0
      GO TO 72
   71 RA=ATAN(Y/X)
      GO TO 72
   99 PRINT 98
      GO TO 73
   C  THIS PART COMPUTES THE MAGNITUDE,
   72 RM=SQRT(X*X+Y*Y)
   98 FORMAT (1H ,'ANGLE INDETERMINATE')
   73 RETURN
      END
```

*Printout of Fourier Coefficients*

| N | AN | BN | MAGCN | MAGCMN | PHCN(RAD) | PHCMN(RAD) |
|---|------|------|------|------|------|------|
| 1 | ,07092 | ,50533 | ,25514 | ,25514 | 4,85182 | 1,43136 |
| 2 | =,26274 | =,11750 | ,14391 | ,14391 | 2,72105 | 3,56213 |
| 3 | ,02532 | =,04067 | ,02395 | ,02395 | 1,01400 | 5,26918 |
| 4 | ,03654 | ,01790 | ,02034 | ,02034 | 5,82764 | ,45554 |
| 5 | =,00074 | ,03335 | ,01668 | ,01668 | 4,69017 | 1,59301 |
| 6 | =,01567 | ,01030 | ,00937 | ,00937 | 3,72289 | 2,56029 |
| 7 | =,02281 | ,02407 | ,01658 | ,01658 | 3,95379 | 2,32939 |
| 8 | =,04237 | =,01562 | ,02258 | ,02258 | 2,78833 | 3,49485 |
| 9 | ,01419 | =,01915 | ,01192 | ,01192 | ,93308 | 5,35010 |
| 10 | ,01419 | ,01915 | ,01191 | ,01191 | 5,35013 | ,93305 |
| 11 | =,04237 | ,01563 | ,02258 | ,02258 | 3,49487 | 2,78831 |
| 12 | =,02281 | =,02407 | ,01658 | ,01658 | 2,32941 | 3,95377 |
| 13 | =,01567 | =,01030 | ,00937 | ,00937 | 2,56028 | 3,72290 |
| 14 | =,00074 | =,03335 | ,01668 | ,01668 | 1,59302 | 4,69016 |
| 15 | ,03654 | =,01790 | ,02034 | ,02034 | ,45557 | 5,82761 |
| 16 | ,02532 | ,04067 | ,02395 | ,02395 | 5,26919 | 1,01399 |
| 17 | =,26273 | ,11751 | ,14391 | ,14391 | 3,56216 | 2,72104 |
| 18 | ,07091 | =,50534 | ,25514 | ,25514 | 1,43139 | 4,85179 |
| 19 | ,39474 | =,00001 | ,19737 | ,19737 | ,00001 | 6,28317 |
| 20 | ,07094 | ,50533 | ,25514 | ,25514 | 4,85185 | 1,43133 |

AO=    ,20    CN=    ,20

## 11.3. NONSINUSOIDAL PERIODIC ANALYSIS BY USE OF LAPLACE TRANSFORMS

In the previous section we used the Fourier series to analyze networks for periodic inputs. The resulting currents and voltages are represented in the form of an infinite series. The method works out very well because the sinusoidal response of networks is easily obtained. The Fourier series method also has merit because of the practical significance. The only disadvantage is that the results are approximate because of infinite-series representation. The Laplace transform technique remedies this drawback and also provides an alternative way of evaluating the periodic response.

### Laplace Transform of a Periodic Waveform

Let us consider a causal periodic waveform (this means it starts at $t = 0$). We can write the Laplace transform as

$$F(s) = \int_0^\infty f(t)e^{-st}\,dt \tag{11.3.1}$$

We rewrite this as

$$F(s) = \int_0^T f(t)e^{-st}\,dt + \int_T^{2T} f(t)e^{-st}\,dt$$

$$+ \cdots + \int_{nT}^{(n+1)T} f(t)e^{-st}\,dt + \cdots$$

$$= \sum_{n=0}^\infty \int_{nT}^{(n+1)T} f(t)e^{-st}\,dt \tag{11.3.2}$$

We now let $t = \tau + nT$ in Eq. 11.3.2; we get

$$F(s) = \sum_{n=0}^\infty \int_0^T f(\tau)e^{-s(\tau+nT)}\,d\tau$$

$$= \int_0^T f(\tau)e^{-s\tau}d\tau[1 + e^{-sT} + e^{-2sT} + \cdots]$$

$$= \frac{\displaystyle\int_0^T f(t)e^{-st}\,dt}{1 - e^{-sT}} \qquad (\text{Replacing } \tau \text{ with } t)$$

$$= \frac{F_T(s)}{1 - e^{-sT}} \tag{11.3.3}$$

where

$$F_T(s) = \int_0^T f(t)e^{-st}\,dt \tag{11.3.4}$$

If we define

$$f_T(t) = f(t) \qquad 0 < t < T$$
$$= 0 \qquad \text{otherwise} \tag{11.3.5}$$

we immediately note that

$$\int_0^T f(t)e^{-st}\,dt = \int_0^T f_T(t)e^{-st}\,dt$$

$$= \int_0^{\infty} f_T(t)e^{-st}\,dt \tag{11.3.6}$$

$$= F_T(s)$$

Equation 11.3.6 implies that if we just take the first period of $f(t)$ and form $f_T(t)$ which is zero outside the first period, then we can take the Laplace transform of this new function $f_T(t)$ to get $F_T(s)$. The Laplace transform of the periodic function is then easily obtained.

*Example 11.3.1*

Find the Laplace transform of the periodic waveform shown in Fig. 11.3.1.

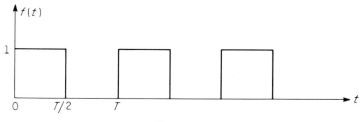

Fig. 11.3.1

*Solution*

We have

$$f(t) = 1 \qquad 0 < t \leq T/2$$
$$= 0 \qquad T/2 < t \leq T$$

Therefore

$$F_T(s) = \int_0^{T/2} 1 \cdot e^{-st}\,dt + \int_{\frac{T}{2}}^{T} 0 \cdot e^{-st}\,dt$$

$$= \frac{1 - e^{-\frac{sT}{2}}}{s}$$

Hence

$$F(s) = \frac{1 - e^{-\frac{sT}{2}}}{s(1 - e^{-sT})}$$

**Evaluating the Periodic Response**

The current or voltage behavior at any point within a network for a periodic excitation can be obtained utilizing the Laplace transform. Let us say that we want to find the current $i$ for a network with input impedance $Z(s)$ and excited by a periodic voltage $v(t)$ as shown in Fig. 11.3.2.

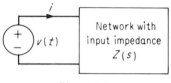

Fig. 11.3.2

We can write

$$I(s) = \frac{V(s)}{Z(s)} \tag{11.3.7}$$

Now for a periodic input, period $T$, we can represent

$$V(s) = \frac{V_T(s)}{1 - e^{-sT}} \tag{11.3.8}$$

Furthermore, the input impedance $Z(s)$ can be represented as

$$Z(s) = \frac{N(s)}{D(s)} = \frac{N(s)}{(s - p_1) \cdots (s - p_n)} \tag{11.3.9}$$

Hence we can write

$$I(s) = \frac{V_T(s)\,N(s)}{(1 - e^{-sT})(s - p_1) \cdots (s - p_n)} \tag{11.3.10}$$

Using partial-fraction expansion, we obtain

$$I(s) = \frac{K_1}{(s - p_1)} + \cdots + \frac{K_n}{(s - p_n)} + \frac{I_T(s)}{(1 - e^{-sT})}$$
$$= I_t(s) + I_p(s) \tag{11.3.11}$$

We have separated $I(s)$ into two components, $I_t(s)$ and $I_p(s)$. $I_t(s)$ depends upon the network poles and is therefore the transient part. $I_p(s)$ has a denominator $(1 - e^{-Ts})$ implying periodicity, and therefore gives the periodic or steady-state component. The periodic component over each period is obtained by finding $i_T(t) = \mathcal{L}^{-1}[I_T(s)]$ which has only values during the period and is zero outside the period. This periodic component is repeated over each interval of $T$ and therefore gives us the steady-state behavior.

*Example 11.3.2*

A voltage waveform represented in Fig. 11.3.1 is applied to the *RC* network of Fig. 11.3.3. Find the transient as well as steady-state current.

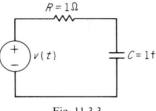

Fig. 11.3.3

*Solution*

We have

$$I(s) = \frac{V(s)}{1 + \dfrac{1}{s}}$$

where we have, from Example 11.3.1,

$$V(s) = \frac{1 - e^{-sT/2}}{s(1 - e^{-sT})}$$

Therefore

$$I(s) = \frac{1 - e^{-sT/2}}{(1 - e^{-sT})(s + 1)} = \frac{K_1}{s + 1} + \frac{I_T(s)}{1 - e^{-sT}}$$

We have

$$1 - e^{-sT/2} = K_1(1 - e^{-sT}) + I_T(s)(s + 1)$$

Let $s = -1$; this yields

$$K_1 = \frac{1 - e^{T/2}}{1 - e^T}$$

Also

$$I_T(s) = \frac{(1 - e^{-sT/2})}{s + 1} - \frac{1 - e^{T/2}}{1 - e^T} \cdot \frac{(1 - e^{-sT})}{s + 1}$$

Now

$$I_t(s) = \frac{K_1}{s + 1} = \frac{1 - e^{T/2}}{1 - e^T} \cdot \frac{1}{s + 1}$$

Therefore

$$i_t(t) = \frac{1 - e^{T/2}}{1 - e^T} e^{-t} u_0(t)$$

This is the *transient current*. To obtain the steady-state or periodic component we must find $i_T(t)$. We have

$$i_T(t) = \mathcal{L}^{-1}\left[\frac{1 - e^{-sT/2}}{s + 1} - \frac{1 - e^{T/2}}{1 - e^T}\frac{(1 - e^{-sT})}{s + 1}\right]$$

$$= \mathcal{L}^{-1}\left[\frac{1}{s + 1} - e^{-sT/2}\frac{1}{s + 1} - \frac{1 - e^{T/2}}{1 - e^{T_i}}\left\{\frac{1}{s + 1} - \frac{e^{-sT}}{s + 1}\right\}\right]$$

$$= e^{-t}u_0(t) - e^{-(t - T/2)}u_0(t - T/2)$$

$$- \frac{1 - e^{T/2}}{1 - e^T}\{e^{-t}u_0(t) - e^{-(t - T)}u_0(t - T)\} \cdot$$

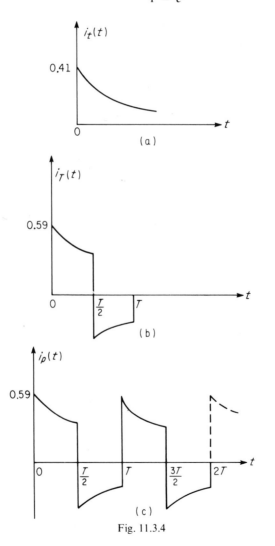

(a)

(b)

(c)

Fig. 11.3.4

Knowing $i_T(t)$, we know the periodic behavior. In order to really appreciate what we have obtained, we pick $T = \log_e 2$ sec. Then

$$i_t(t) = 0.41e^{-t}u_0(t)$$
$$i_T(t) = 0.59e^{-t}u_0(t) - e^{-(t-T/2)}u_0(t - T/2) + 0.41e^{-(t-T)}u_0(t - T)$$

We plot these results in Fig. 11.3.4.

Note that $i_T(t)$ is zero outside the interval $0 < t < T$. We can now build the periodic or steady-state current $i_p(t)$ by just repeating $i_T(t)$ in each period shown.

We note that the Laplace transform method gives the transient and steady state parts very conveniently and exactly rather than as a series. It is clear, however, that the technique is very cumbersome for more involved waveforms or networks and does not have the same practical significance as the Fourier series method.

### Evaluation of Impulse-Train Response

In Chapter 8 we saw that the impulse train response $h_T(t)$ could be used in the finite convolution integral to find the steady state response of a network to any periodic source of period $T$. The impulse train response can be evaluated in closed form using the techniques developed in this section. The impulse-train response is simply the periodic part of the waveform which results when a network is driven by the function described in Fig. 11.3.5. The transform of the first period of this periodic

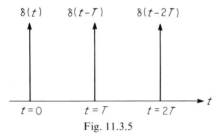

Fig. 11.3.5

waveform is just

$$F_T(s) = 1$$

Hence the transform of the periodic function is

$$F(s) = \frac{1}{1 - e^{-sT}} \tag{11.3.12}$$

If a network has a transfer function

$$H(s) = \frac{N(s)}{(s - p_1)(s - p_2) \cdots (s - p_n)} \tag{11.3.13}$$

then the transform of the total response due to the impulse train is

$$H'(s) = \frac{N(s)}{(s - p_1)(s - p_2) \cdots (s - p_n)(1 - e^{-sT})} \tag{11.3.14}$$

Using a partial-fraction expansion, we can write this response as

$$H'(s) = \frac{K_1}{s - p_1} + \frac{K_2}{s - p_2} + \cdots + \frac{K_n}{s - p_n} + \frac{H_T(s)}{(1 - e^{-sT})} = H_t(s) + H_p(s)$$

where $H_p(s) = \dfrac{H_T(s)}{1 - e^{-sT}}$ is the transform of the periodic function $h_T(t)$

defined in Chapter 8. An example will illustrate the analysis method for determining $h_T(t)$.

*Example 11.3.3*

Determine the current impulse-train response $h_T(t)$ of the network shown in Fig. 11.3.6.

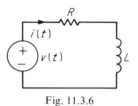

Fig. 11.3.6

*Solution*

For this example, the current is the desired response. Hence the transfer function is

$$H(s) = \frac{I(s)}{V(s)} = \frac{\dfrac{1}{L}}{s + \dfrac{R}{L}}$$

From Eq. 11.3.14 we have

$$H'(s) = \frac{\dfrac{1}{L}}{\left( s + \dfrac{R}{L} \right)(1 - e^{-sT})}$$

This can be written as

$$H'(s) = \frac{\dfrac{1}{L\left(1 - e^{\frac{R}{L}T}\right)}}{s + \dfrac{R}{L}} + \frac{\dfrac{1}{L} - \dfrac{1 - e^{-sT}}{L\left(1 - e^{\frac{R}{L}T}\right)}}{(1 - e^{-sT})\left(s + \dfrac{R}{L}\right)}$$

Over the period, the function we seek is defined as

$$h_T(t) = \mathcal{L}^{-1} \left[ \frac{\dfrac{1}{L} - \dfrac{1 - e^{-sT}}{L\left(1 - e^{\frac{R}{L}T}\right)}}{s + \dfrac{R}{L}} \right] \qquad 0 < t < T$$

or

$$h_T(t) = \mathcal{L}^{-1} \left[ \frac{\dfrac{-e^{\frac{R}{L}T}}{L\left(1 - e^{\frac{R}{L}T}\right)}}{s + \dfrac{R}{L}} + e^{-sT} \frac{\dfrac{1}{L\left(1 - e^{\frac{R}{L}T}\right)}}{s + \dfrac{R}{L}} \right] \qquad 0 < t < T$$

Hence

$$h_T(t) = \frac{-e^{-\frac{R}{L}(t-T)}}{L\left(1 - e^{\frac{R}{L}T}\right)} u_0(t) + \frac{e^{-\frac{R}{L}(t-T)}}{L\left(1 - e^{\frac{R}{L}T}\right)} u_0(t - T) \qquad 0 < t < T$$

Simplifying we obtain

$$h_T(t) = \frac{e^{-\frac{R}{L}t}}{L\left(1 - e^{-\frac{R}{L}T}\right)} \qquad 0 < t < T$$

which is the result listed in Table 8.5.1. Similarly other entries of Table 8.5.1 can be evaluated.

## 11.4. NONSINUSOIDAL PERIODIC ANALYSIS BY STATE-VARIABLE REPRESENTATION

We have already seen how we can do network analysis in terms of state variables. In all cases the input was easily represented mathematically in the time domain. With periodic inputs the representation is not that simple. Let us say that the network is described by

$$\dot{\mathbf{x}} = \mathbf{A}\mathbf{x} + \mathbf{b}u \qquad (11.4.1)$$

where $u$ is now a periodic waveform. How do we proceed and obtain $\mathbf{x}(t)$.

### Using the Laplace Transform

Taking the Laplace transform of Eq. 11.4.1, we have

$$[s\mathbf{I} - \mathbf{A}]\mathbf{X}(s) = \mathbf{b}U(s) \qquad (11.4.2)$$

Now $u(t)$ is periodic, therefore

$$U(s) = \frac{U_T(s)}{1 - e^{-sT}} \tag{11.4.3}$$

Hence

$$X(s) = [sI - A]^{-1}b \frac{U_T(s)}{1 - e^{-sT}} \tag{11.4.4}$$

We can now use the technique of partial fractions developed in Sec. 11.3 to obtain the transient and steady-state behavior of $x(t)$. Note however that we will have to use partial-fraction expansion for every component of state vector $x(t)$.

### Time-Domain Approach

The time-domain solution of (11.4.1) is given by

$$x(t) = e^{At}x(0) + \int_0^t e^{A(t-\tau)}bu(\tau)\,d\tau \tag{11.4.5}$$

Since $u(t)$ is periodic, let us consider the first period $0 < t < T$. If we can represent $u(t)$ analytically Eq. 11.4.5 can be solved either by algebraic manipulation or using the digital computer as shown in Chapter 7. We obtain $x(t)$ for $0 < t < T$ starting from $x(0)$. We can easily obtain a plot for $x(t)$, $0 < t < T$. We can now find $x(T)$ and start the second period. In this second period $u(t)$ is the same as first period, all we have to do is to shift the origin from start of first period to the start of the second period. Equation 11.4.5 changes to

$$x_1(t) = e^{At}x(T) + \int_0^t e^{A(t-\tau)}bu(\tau)\,d\tau \tag{11.4.6}$$

where $x_1(t)$ from $0 < t < T$ is actually $x(t)$ from $T < t < 2T$ because in Eq. 11.4.6 we started from $x(T)$. Now we obtain $x(2T) = x_1(T)$. Having this and shifting the origin to the start of the second period we can obtain

$$x_2(t) = e^{At}x(2T) + \int_0^t e^{A(t-\tau)}bu(\tau)\,d\tau \tag{11.4.7}$$

where $x_2(t)$, $0 < t < T$ is actually $x(t)$ between $2T < t < 3T$.

The above process can be easily programmed on the digital computer and $x(t)$ can be evaluated and plotted. As $t$ increases we will essentially have the steady state response. This approach is very well suited to more complex networks.

### Example 11.4.1

A periodic waveform shown in Fig. 11.3.1 is applied as a voltage source to the *RLC* network shown in Fig. 11.4.1. Find the state vector $x(t)$.

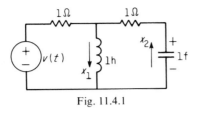

Fig. 11.4.1

*Solution*

For the network, we have the two-loop equation as

$$\dot{x}_1 + (x_1 + \dot{x}_2) = v(t)$$
$$-\dot{x}_1 + \dot{x}_2 + x_2 = 0$$

or

$$\dot{x}_1 = -\tfrac{1}{2}x_1 + \tfrac{1}{2}x_2 + \tfrac{1}{2}v(t)$$
$$\dot{x}_2 = -\tfrac{1}{2}x_1 - \tfrac{1}{2}x_2 + \tfrac{1}{2}v(t)$$

That is,

$$\dot{\mathbf{x}} = \begin{bmatrix} -\tfrac{1}{2} & \tfrac{1}{2} \\ -\tfrac{1}{2} & -\tfrac{1}{2} \end{bmatrix} \mathbf{x} + \begin{bmatrix} \tfrac{1}{2} \\ \tfrac{1}{2} \end{bmatrix} u$$

where $u = v(t)$ is given in Fig. 11.3.1.

The solution of $\dot{\mathbf{x}}(t)$ can be obtained by simple manipulations because the matrix is only of second order. In this case $e^{At}$ is easily obtained. We will, however, use the computer program developed in Chapter 7 to solve $\dot{\mathbf{x}} = \mathbf{A}\mathbf{x} + \mathbf{b}u$. In this case $u$ can be written mathematically as given below in the program. We have assumed $T = 1$ sec. The values of $\mathbf{A}$ and $\mathbf{b}$ are read in. The DIFF subroutine used is from Chapter 7. The computer program for this problem is given below. The printout is $t$, $x_1(t)$, and $x_2(t)$. We have taken $t'$ from 0 sec to 5 sec. We give the printout also from 0 to 5 sec. The GRAPHX subroutine has been used to plot $x_1(t)$ and $x_2(t)$ versus $t$ as shown in Fig. 11.4.2.

```
C       THIS PROGRAM IS FOR EXAMPLE 11.4-1
C       SOLUTION OF THE LINEAR TIME-INVARIANT DIFFERENTIAL
C       EQUATION DX=AX+BU USING RUNGE-KUTTA METHOD,
        DIMENSION X(2),DX(2),DATA(100,3)
C       SET THE INITIAL CONDITIONS
        X(1)=0,0
        X(2)=0,0
C       SET INITIAL AND FINAL TIMES
        T=0,0
        TF=5,0
C       STORE INITIAL VALUES FOR PLOTTING,
        DATA(1,1)=T
        DATA(1,2)=X(1)
        DATA(1,3)=X(2)
C       SET STEP SIZE
        H=0,1
        PRINT 20
        PRINT 30, T,X(1),X(2)
```

```
C       INITIALIZE K
        K=0
C       WRITE THE DIFFERENTIAL EQUATIONS
        PI=3.1416
C       THE INPUT U IS A PERIODIC SQUARE WAVE DEFINED BY
      1 U=0.5*(1.+1.*SIGN(1,SIN(2.*PI*T)))
        DX(1)=-(1./2.)*X(1)+(1./2.)*X(2)+(1./2.)*U
        DX(2)=-(1./2.)*X(1)-(1./2.)*X(2)+(1./2.)*U
      3 CALL DIFF(2,K,I,X,DX,T,H)
        GO TO (1,2),I
      2 PRINT 30, T,X(1),X(2)
C       ADD SMALL VALUE,0.01,TO EXTRACT THE
C       CORRECT INTEGER FOR M,
        M=(T/H+0.01)+1.0
        DATA(M,1)=T
        DATA(M,2)=X(1)
        DATA(M,3)=X(2)
        TTF=TF-0.01
        IF(T.LT.TTF) GO TO 1
C       PLOT X(1) AND X(2)
        CALL GRAPHX(DATA,M,1HT,5HX1,X2)
     20 FORMAT (10X,1HT, 12X,2HX1, 10X, 2HX2,//)
     30 FORMAT(6X,F7.3,6X,F7.3,6X,F7.3)
        END


                SUBROUTINE DIFF (N,K,I,X,DX,T1,H)
        C       N    NO. OF DIFFERENTIAL EQUATOONS
        C       N    NO. OF DIFFERENTIAL EQUATIONS
        C       K     INITIALIZE K=0 IN THE MAIN PROGRAM,
        C       H    STEP SIZE,
                DIMENSION Y(1000),Z(1000),X(N),DX(N)
                K=K+1
                GO TO (1,2,3,4,5),K
              2 DO 10 J=1,N
                Z(J)= DX(J)
                Y(J)= X(J)
             10 X(J)= Y(J)+0.5*H*DX(J)
             25 T1=T1+0.5*H
              1 I=1
                RETURN
              3 DO 15 J=1,N
                Z(J)= Z(J)+2.0*DX(J)
             15 X(J)= Y(J)+0.5*H*DX(J)
                I=1
                RETURN
              4 DO 20 J=1,N
                Z(J)= Z(J)+2.0*DX(J)
             20 X(J)= Y(J)+H*DX(J)
                GO TO 25
              5 DO 30 J=1,N
             30 X(J)= Y(J)+(Z(J)+DX(J))*H/6.0
                I=2
                K=0
                RETURN
                END


        SUBROUTINE GRAPHX(DATA,N,VINDEP,VARDEP)
        DIMENSION DATA(100,3),B(121)
        DOUBLE PRECISION VINDEP,VARDEP
        PRINT 300,VINDEP
        PRINT 400,VARDEP
        BIGEST=DATA(1,2)
        SMAL=DATA(1,2)
        DO 1 I=2,N
        IF(DATA(I,2).GT.BIGEST)BIGEST=DATA(I,2)
```

```
      IF(DATA(I,2).LT.SMAL)SMAL=DATA(I,2)
   1 CONTINUE
      DO 2 I=2,N
      IF(DATA(I,3).GT.BIGEST)BIGEST=DATA(I,3)
      IF(DATA(I,3).LT.SMAL)SMAL=DATA(I,3)
   2 CONTINUE
      PRINT 200,SMAL,BIGEST
C     TO EXTEND THE PLOT TO FULL PAGE WIDTH, WE ONLY
C     NEED TO REPLACE K=61 BY K=121,
C     ALSO IN FORMAT STATEMENT 200 4X
C     MUST BE REPLACED BY 48X, AND 61 BY 121,
      K=61
      BMINS=BIGEST-SMAL
      DO 3 I=1,K
   3 B(I)=1H
      DO 4 I=1,N
      DATA(I,2)=(DATA(I,2)-SMAL)*FLOAT(K)/BMINS+1.0
      DATA(I,3)=(DATA(I,3)-SMAL)*FLOAT(K)/BMINS+1.0
      INDEX=DATA(I,2)
      JNDEX=DATA(I,3)
      B(INDEX)=1H+
      B(JNDEX)=1H*
      PRINT 100,DATA(I,1),(B (N),N=1,K)
      B(INDEX)=1H
   4 B(JNDEX)=1H
 100 FORMAT(1HZ,F8.2,1X,121A1)
 200 FORMAT(9X,E11.4,35X,1H ,4X,E11.4,/10X,61(1H*))
 300 FORMAT (1H1,'THE INDEPENDENT VARIABLE IS ',2A10)
 400 FORMAT (1X,'THE DEPENDENT VARIABLE IS ',2A10//)
      RETURN
      END
```

| T | X1 | X2 |
|---|---|---|
| .000 | .000 | .000 |
| .100 | .050 | .048 |
| .200 | .100 | .090 |
| .300 | .149 | .129 |
| .400 | .198 | .163 |
| .500 | .237 | .184 |
| .600 | .234 | .164 |
| .700 | .230 | .145 |
| .800 | .225 | .126 |
| .900 | .220 | .109 |
| 1.000 | .223 | .102 |
| 1.100 | .266 | .134 |
| 1.200 | .309 | .162 |
| 1.300 | .352 | .187 |
| 1.400 | .393 | .208 |
| 1.500 | .425 | .218 |
| 1.600 | .414 | .187 |
| 1.700 | .402 | .158 |
| 1.800 | .390 | .131 |
| 1.900 | .376 | .106 |
| 2.000 | .371 | .091 |
| 2.100 | .407 | .117 |
| 2.200 | .442 | .139 |
| 2.300 | .476 | .158 |
| 2.400 | .510 | .175 |
| 2.500 | .535 | .182 |
| 2.600 | .516 | .147 |
| 2.700 | .498 | .115 |
| 2.800 | .478 | .086 |
| 2.900 | .458 | .059 |

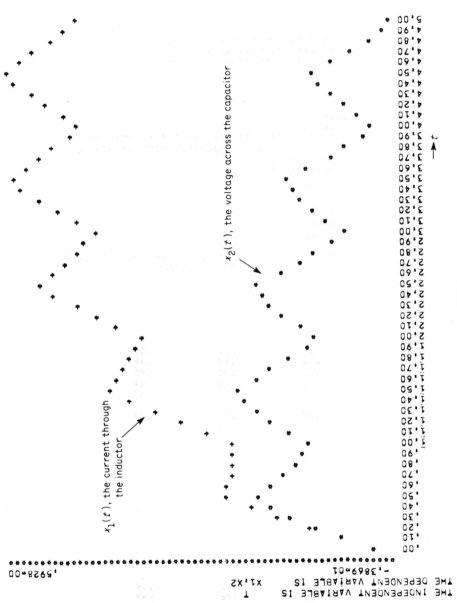

Fig. 11.4.2

| T | X1 | X2 |
|---|---|---|
| 3.000 | .447 | .042 |
| 3.100 | .476 | .067 |
| 3.200 | .506 | .088 |
| 3.300 | .535 | .107 |
| 3.400 | .563 | .124 |
| 3.500 | .592 | .130 |
| 3.600 | .559 | .096 |
| 3.700 | .536 | .065 |
| 3.800 | .512 | .036 |
| 3.900 | .488 | .010 |
| 4.000 | .473 | .006 |
| 4.100 | .499 | .020 |
| 4.200 | .525 | .043 |
| 4.300 | .551 | .063 |
| 4.400 | .576 | .081 |
| 4.500 | .593 | .089 |
| 4.600 | .567 | .056 |
| 4.700 | .542 | .027 |
| 4.800 | .516 | -.000 |
| 4.900 | .490 | -.025 |
| 5.000 | .473 | -.039 |

## PROBLEMS

**11.1.** Show the orthogonal property of the cosine function as $(T = 2\pi/\omega)$

$$\frac{2}{T} \int_0^T \cos m\omega t \cos n\omega t \, dt = 0 \qquad m \neq n$$
$$= 1 \qquad m = n \neq 0$$

**11.2.** Find the Fourier Series representation of the waveforms shown. Use the computer program also. Let $V = 1$ volt and $T = 1$ sec.

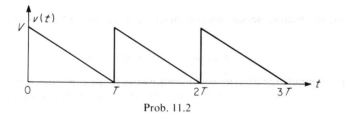

Prob. 11.2

**11.3.** The circuit shown is excited by $v(t)$ of Prob. 11.2. Find the steady-state output voltage and plot it approximately. Also find its root mean square value. Use the computer programs where appropriate.

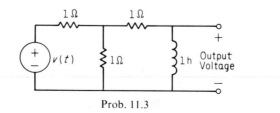

Prob. 11.3

**11.4.** (a) Find the Fourier series representation of the waveform, shown.   Do
this problem by using the computer program also.

(b) If the above waveforms are applied as a voltage source to a series $RC$
network ($R = C = 1$), find the steady state value of the current and its
rms value.

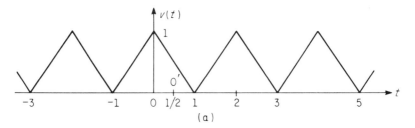

(a)

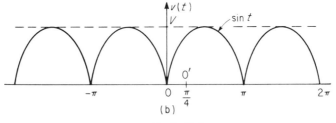

(b)

Prob. 11.4

**11.5.** Modify the Fourier series representation of waveforms of Prob. 11.4 if the
origin is shifted to $0'$.

**11.6.** Find the Fourier series representation of a periodic function with period
$2\pi$, such that

$$f(t) = t^2 \qquad -\pi \le t \le \pi$$

Also compute the Fourier coefficients by use of the computer program.

**11.7.** Find the exponential Fourier series of periodic waveform of Prob. 11.2
and plot the magnitude and angular frequency spectrum.

**11.8.** Consider a periodic waveform shown.  Find the effect of $T$ on $c_n$ by letting
$T = 2\pi$ and then $T = 4\pi$.  What do you think is the effect of continuously
increasing $T$?

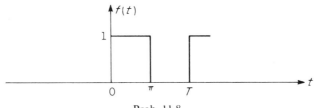

Prob. 11.8

**11.9.** A waveform having half-wave symmetry is given as shown.

(a) Determine the first four coefficients of Fourier series, taking the 30°
steps shown.
(b) Draw the frequency spectrum.
(c) Do you feel that results can be considerably improved if 15° steps
are taken?
(d) Use the computer program for steps (a) and (c).

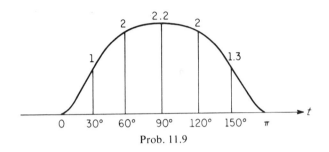

Prob. 11.9

**11.10.** A voltage periodic waveform applied to an electrical network yields a current in a certain branch which can be represented as

(a) $I = I_0 + \sum_{n=1}^{\infty} (I_{n1} \cos n\omega t + I_{n2} \sin n\omega t)$

(b) $I = \sum_{n=-\infty}^{\infty} I_n e^{jn\omega t}$

Find $I_{rms}$.

**11.11.** The periodic waveform of Fig. 11.3.1 is applied to a series $RL$ network
($R = L = 1$). Find the transient and steady-state current, using the
Laplace transform.

**11.12.** Find the Laplace transform of
(i) Waveform of Prob. 11.2.
(ii) Waveforms of Prob. 11.4.

**11.13.** Find the transient and steady-state current if the waveforms of Prob. 11.4
are applied to
(i) series $RC$ network ($R = C = 1$).
(ii) series $RL$ network ($R = L = 1$).

**11.14.** Repeat Prob. 11.3 using the Laplace transform method.

**11.15.** Utilizing the method presented in Example 11.3.3, verify the impulse train
responses listed in Table 8.5.1.

**11.16.** A periodic waveform of Prob. 11.2 is applied to the network of Fig. 11.4.1.
Obtain $x(t)$, using the digital computer.

**11.17.** Repeat Prob. 11.16 with periodic waveforms of Prob. 11.4.

**11.18.** A rectangular waveform shown in part (a) is applied to an $RLC$ of part (b).
Obtain $x(t)$. Use the computer program.

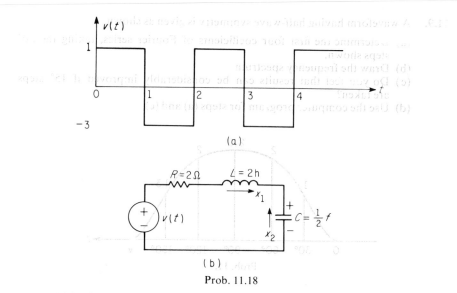

(a)

(b)

Prob. 11.18

**11.19.** A *low-pass filter* is shown in part (a). The input voltage is given in part (b). Find the value of $C$ such that the peak value of the largest a-c component of $v_0(t)$ is $1/25$ of the d-c component.

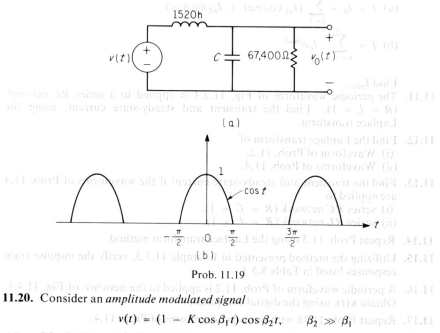

(a)

(b)

Prob. 11.19

**11.20.** Consider an *amplitude modulated signal*

$$v(t) = (1 - K \cos \beta_1 t) \cos \beta_2 t, \qquad \beta_2 \gg \beta_1$$

Determine the bandwidth required of the receiver of this signal such that the entire $v(t)$ passes through it.

## CHAPTER 12

# Two-Port Networks

In the analysis of electrical networks very often we are interested in the input-output behavior of the network rather than the response of a specific element. In such a case the entire network can be considered as a "black box" with a set of terminals that correspond to the input and the output of the network. In a large class of networks, these terminals appear as pairs in such a way that, for each pair of terminals, the current in one terminal is equal and in the opposite direction of the current in the other terminal. We say that such a pair of terminals forms a *port*.

In general, consider the network with $2n$ terminals shown in Fig. 12.1.1. If each pair of these terminals form a port, then the network is

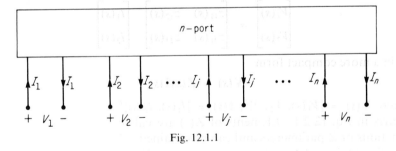

Fig. 12.1.1

called an $n$-port network. For linear time-invariant $n$-port networks, we can use Laplace transform to find a relation between the port voltages and port currents. By analogy to the one port networks discussed in Chapter 9, we define the impedance matrix of an $n$-port network $\mathbf{Z}(s)$ by

$$\mathbf{V}(s) = \mathbf{Z}(s)\mathbf{I}(s) \qquad (12.1.1)$$

where $\mathbf{V}(s) = [V_1(s), V_2(s), \ldots, V_n(s)]^T$, $\mathbf{I}(s) = [I_1(s), I_2(s), \ldots, I_n(s)]^T$ and $\mathbf{Z}(s)$ is an $n \times n$ matrix whose $ij$th element, $z_{ij}(s)$, is a function of $s$.

Similarly, the admittance matrix $\mathbf{Y}(s)$ of an $n$-port network is given by

$$\mathbf{I}(s) = \mathbf{Y}(s)\mathbf{V}(s) \qquad (12.1.2)$$

In this chapter we study the characterization and properties of a simple class of $n$-port networks, namely, two-port networks. In Sec. 12.2 we discuss the short-circuit impedance parameters, open-circuit admittance parameters, transmission parameters and hybrid parameters. In Sec. 12.3 we discuss the relationship among these parameters. Finally, in Sec. 12.4, various interconnections of two-port networks are taken up.

## 12.2. CHARACTERIZATION OF LINEAR TIME-INVARIANT TWO-PORTS

### Z Parameters

As in the case of $n$-port networks, a linear time-invariant two-port network can be characterized by its impedance or admittance matrix.

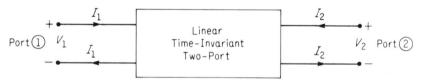

Fig. 12.2.1

Consider the two-port network shown in Fig. 12.2.1. We can write

$$\begin{bmatrix} V_1(s) \\ V_2(s) \end{bmatrix} = \begin{bmatrix} z_{11}(s) & z_{12}(s) \\ z_{21}(s) & z_{22}(s) \end{bmatrix} \begin{bmatrix} I_1(s) \\ I_2(s) \end{bmatrix} \qquad (12.2.1)$$

or in a more compact form

$$\mathbf{V}(s) = \mathbf{Z}(s)\mathbf{I}(s) \qquad (12.2.2)$$

where $\mathbf{V}(s) = [V_1(s),\ V_2(s)]^T$, $\mathbf{I}(s) = [I_1(s),\ I_2(s)]^T$ and $\mathbf{Z}(s)$ is the $2 \times 2$ matrix in Eq. 12.2.1. Elements of $\mathbf{Z}(s)$ are called *open-circuit impedance functions* or $Z$ parameters and can be obtained in the following manner.

To obtain $z_{11}(s)$ apply a voltage source $V_1(s)$ at port ①, open-circuit the port ② (i.e., put $I_2(s) = 0$) and measure the current in port ①; then

$$z_{11}(s) = \left.\frac{V_1(s)}{I_1(s)}\right|_{I_2(s)=0} \qquad (12.2.3)$$

$z_{11}(s)$ is called the *driving-point impedance* of port ①.

To obtain $z_{12}(x)$, apply a current source $I_2(s)$ at port ②, open-circuit port ① (i.e., put $I_1(s) = 0$) and measure the voltage across port ①; then

then

$$z_{12}(s) = \frac{V_1(s)}{I_2(s)}\bigg|_{I_1(s)=0}$$

In a similar manner we can obtain

$$z_{21}(s) = \frac{V_2(s)}{I_1(s)}\bigg|_{I_2(s)=0}$$

and

$$z_{22}(s) = \frac{V_2(s)}{I_2(s)}\bigg|_{I_1(s)=0} \tag{12.2.4}$$

The $Z$ parameters are sometimes called the *open-circuit* parameters since they are obtained with a port open-circuited.

*Example 12.2.1*

Find the $Z$ parameters for the two-port network shown in Fig. 12.2.2.

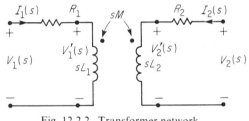

Fig. 12.2.2.  Transformer network.

*Solution*

The operation of the transformer is described by

$$V_1'(s) = sL_1 I_1(s) + sM I_2(s)$$
$$V_2'(s) = sM I_1(s) + sL_2 I_2(s)$$

Hence the terminal voltage-current relationships are

$$V_1(s) = (R_1 + sL_1)I_1(s) + sM I_2(s) \tag{12.2.5}$$
$$V_2(s) = sM I_1(s) + (R_2 + sL_2)I_2(s) \tag{12.2.6}$$

The $Z$ parameters for the two-port network are then

$$z_{11}(s) = \frac{V_1(s)}{I_1(s)}\bigg|_{I_2(s)=0} = R_1 + sL_1$$

$$z_{12}(s) = \frac{V_1(s)}{I_2(s)}\bigg|_{I_1(s)=0} = sM$$

$$z_{21}(s) = \frac{V_2(s)}{I_1(s)}\bigg|_{I_2(s)=0} = sM$$

$$z_{22}(s) = \left.\frac{V_2(s)}{I_2(s)}\right|_{I_1(s)=0} = R_2 + sL_2$$

Note that, in this case, $z_{12}(s) = z_{21}(s) = sM$. In general, two-port networks satisfying the condition

$$z_{12}(s) = z_{21}(s)$$

are called *reciprocal* two-ports.

*Example 12.2.2*

Figure 12.2.3 shows a common-emitter linear equivalent circuit of a transistor amplifier. Find the $Z$ parameters for this two-port network.

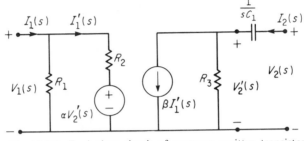

Fig. 12.2.3. Equivalent circuit of common emitter transistor amplifier.

*Solution*

From the figure we obtain the following relationships between terminal voltages and terminal currents:

$$V_1(s) = I_1'(s)R_2 + \alpha V_2'(s)$$

$$I_1(s) = \frac{V_1(s)}{R_1} + I_1'(s)$$

$$V_2(s) = \frac{I_2(s)}{sC_1} + V_2'(s)$$

$$I_2(s) = \beta I_1'(s) + \frac{V_2'(s)}{R_3}$$

Eliminating $I_1'(s)$ and $V_2'(s)$ from the above equations leaves

$$V_1(s) = \left(\frac{R_2 - \alpha\beta R_3}{1 + G_1R_2 - \alpha R_3\beta G_1}\right)I_1(s) + \left(\frac{\alpha R_3}{1 + G_1R_2 - \alpha\beta G_1R_3}\right)I_2(s)$$

$$V_2(s) = \left(\frac{R_3\beta G_1(G_2 - \alpha\beta R_3)}{1 + G_1R_2 - \alpha\beta R_3G_1} - \beta R_3\right)I_1(s)$$

$$+ \left(\frac{\alpha R_3^2\beta G_1}{1 + G_1R_2 - \alpha\beta R_3G_1} + R_3 + \frac{1}{sC_1}\right)I_2(s)$$

where we have used the notation $G_1 \triangleq \dfrac{1}{R_1}$. Thus

$$z_{11}(s) = \frac{R_2 - \alpha\beta R_3}{1 + G_1 R_2 - \alpha\beta R_3 G_1}$$

$$z_{12}(s) = \frac{\alpha R_3}{1 + G_1 R_2 - \alpha\beta G_1 R_3}$$

$$z_{21}(s) = \frac{R_3\beta G_1(G_2 - \alpha\beta R_3)}{1 + G_1 R_2 - \alpha\beta R_3 G_1} - \beta R_3$$

$$z_{22}(s) = \frac{\alpha R_3^2 \beta G_1}{1 + G_1 R_2 - \alpha\beta R_3 G_1} + R_3 + \frac{1}{sC_1}$$

Note, in contrast to the previous example, $z_{12}(s) \neq z_{21}(s)$. This is due to the presence of dependent sources $\alpha V_2'(s)$ and $\beta I_1'(s)$. This network, therefore, is *nonreciprocal*.

## Y Parameters

Another set of parameters of a two-port network that are of considerable importance are the *short circuit admittance parameters* or *Y* parameters defined by

$$\begin{bmatrix} I_1(s) \\ I_2(s) \end{bmatrix} = \begin{bmatrix} y_{11}(s) & y_{12}(s) \\ y_{21}(s) & y_{22}(s) \end{bmatrix} \begin{bmatrix} V_1(s) \\ V_2(s) \end{bmatrix} \qquad (12.2.7)$$

or simply

$$\mathbf{I}(s) = \mathbf{Y}(s)\mathbf{V}(s) \qquad (12.2.8)$$

To obtain $y_{11}(s)$ we apply a current source $I_1(s)$ at port ①, short-circuit the port ② (i.e., set $V_2(s) = 0$) and measure the voltage $V_1(s)$ in port ①; then

$$y_{11}(s) = \left.\frac{I_1(s)}{V_1(s)}\right|_{V_2(s)=0} \qquad (12.2.9)$$

similarly,

$$y_{12}(s) = \left.\frac{I_1(s)}{V_2(s)}\right|_{V_1(s)=0} \qquad (12.2.10)$$

$$y_{21}(s) = \left.\frac{I_2(s)}{V_1(s)}\right|_{V_2(s)=0} \qquad (12.2.11)$$

and

$$y_{22}(s) = \left.\frac{I_2(s)}{V_2(s)}\right|_{V_1(s)=0} \qquad (12.2.12)$$

The *Y* parameters are sometimes called the *short-circuit* parameters since they are obtained with a port short-circuited.

*Example 12.2.3*

Calculate the short-circuit admittance parameters for the transformer circuit considered in Example 12.2.1

*Solution*

The admittance parameters can be calculated in a manner analogous to the method employed in calculating the open-circuit impedance parameters in Example 12.2.1. In fact, putting $V_2(s) = 0$ in Eq. 12.2.6 we get

$$I_2(s) = \frac{-sM}{R_2 + sL_2} I_1(s)$$

Then Eq. 12.2.5 can be written

$$V_1(s) = \frac{(R_1 + sL_1)(R_2 + sL_2) - s^2 M^2}{R_2 + sL_2} I_1(s)$$

Consequently from Eq. 12.2.9 we get:

$$y_{11}(s) = \frac{R_2 + sL_2}{(R_1 + sL_1)(R_2 + sL_2) - s^2 M^2}$$

Similarly, using Eqs. 12.2.5 and 12.2.6 and the definition of the $Y$ parameters we obtain

$$y_{21}(s) = \frac{-sM}{(R_1 + sL_1)(R_2 + sL_2) - s^2 M^2}$$

$$y_{22}(s) = \frac{R_1 + sL_1}{(R_1 + sL_1)(R_2 + sL_2) - s^2 M^2}$$

and

$$y_{12}(s) = \frac{-sM}{(R_1 + sL_1)(R_2 + sL_2) - s^2 M^2}$$

or in the matrix notation

$$\mathbf{Y}(s) = \frac{1}{\Delta} \begin{bmatrix} R_2 + sL_2 & -sM \\ -sM & R_1 + sL_1 \end{bmatrix}$$

where $\Delta = (R_1 + sL_1)(R_2 + sL_2) - s^2 M^2$

*REMARK.*   Comparing Eq. 12.2.1 with Eqs. 12.2.5 and 12.2.6 it is easy to see that if det $\mathbf{Z}(s) \neq 0$, then

$$\mathbf{Y}(s) = \frac{1}{\det \mathbf{Z}(s)} \begin{bmatrix} z_{22}(s) & -z_{12}(s) \\ -z_{21}(s) & z_{11}(s) \end{bmatrix} \qquad (12.2.13)$$

and if det $\mathbf{Y}(s) \neq 0$ then,

$$\mathbf{Z}(s) = \frac{1}{\det \mathbf{Y}(s)} \begin{bmatrix} y_{22}(s) & -y_{12}(s) \\ -y_{21}(s) & y_{11}(s) \end{bmatrix} \qquad (12.2.14)$$

This fact can be verified for the example discussed above. In this case we have

$$\det \mathbf{Y}(s) = \frac{(R_1 + sL_1)(R_2 + sL_2) - s^2 M^2}{\Delta} = 1 \neq 0$$

hence the inverse of $\mathbf{Y}(s)$ given above is

$$\mathbf{Z}(s) = \mathbf{Y}^{-1}(s) = \begin{bmatrix} R_1 + sL_1 & sM \\ sM & R_2 + sL_2 \end{bmatrix}$$

which obviously agrees with the result of Example 12.2.1. For some networks, however, it is possible that either $\det \mathbf{Z}(s) = 0$ or $\det \mathbf{Y}(s) = 0$. For example, consider the simple two-port network shown in Fig. 12.2.4.

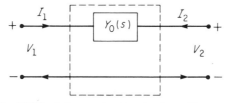

Fig. 12.2.4. A two port network whose $Z$ parameters do not exist.

For this network,

$$y_{11}(s) = \frac{I_1}{V_1}\bigg|_{V_2=0} = Y_0(s) \qquad y_{21}(s) = \frac{I_2}{V_1}\bigg|_{V_2=0} = -Y_0(s)$$

and

$$y_{22}(s) = \frac{I_2}{V_2}\bigg|_{V_1=0} = Y_0(s) \qquad y_{12}(s) = \frac{I_1}{V_2}\bigg|_{V_1=0} = -Y_0(s)$$

Hence $\det \mathbf{Y}(s) = y_{11} y_{22} - y_{21} y_{12} = Y_0^2 - Y_0^2 = 0$. Similarly, for the net-

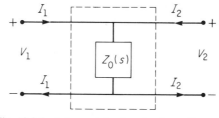

Fig. 12.2.5. A two port network whose $Y$ parameters do not exist.

work shown in Fig. 12.2.5 we have

$$z_{11}(s) = \frac{V_1}{I_1}\bigg|_{I_2=0} = Z_0(s) \qquad z_{21}(s) = \frac{V_2}{I_1}\bigg|_{I_2=0} = -Z_0(s)$$

$$z_{22}(s) = \left.\frac{V_2}{I_2}\right|_{I_1=0} = Z_0(s) \qquad z_{12}(s) = \left.\frac{V_1}{I_2}\right|_{I_1=0} = -Z_0(s)$$

then $\det \mathbf{Z}(s) = 0$.

For a two-port network $N$, if $\det \mathbf{Y}(s) = 0$ then $\mathbf{Z}(s)$ is not defined and if $\det \mathbf{Z}(s) = 0$ then $\mathbf{Y}(s)$ is not defined. In a two-port network, $Y$ and $Z$ parameters express the currents in terms of the voltages and voltages in terms of currents respectively. Another set of parameters which are useful in tandem connection of two-port networks are *transmission parameters* or *ABCD* parameters which we discuss next.

**ABCD Parameters**

For a two-port network, *ABCD* parameters express the voltage and the current of port ① in terms of the voltage and the current of port ②. Namely,

$$\begin{bmatrix} V_1(s) \\ I_1(s) \end{bmatrix} = \begin{bmatrix} A(s) & B(s) \\ C(s) & D(s) \end{bmatrix} \begin{bmatrix} V_2(s) \\ -I_2(s) \end{bmatrix} \tag{12.2.15}$$

To obtain $A(s)$, apply a voltage source $V_1(s)$ to port ① open-circuit port ② (i.e., set $I_2(s) = 0$); then

$$A(s) = \left.\frac{V_1(s)}{V_2(s)}\right|_{I_2(s)=0} \tag{12.2.16}$$

In a similar manner we can obtain

$$B(s) = \left.\frac{V_1(s)}{-I_2(s)}\right|_{V_2(s)=0}, \quad C(s) = \left.\frac{I_1(s)}{V_2(s)}\right|_{I_2(s)=0}, \quad D(s) = \left.\frac{I_1(s)}{-I_2(s)}\right|_{V_2(s)=0}$$
$$\tag{12.2.17}$$

The $2 \times 2$ matrix in Eq. 12.2.15 sometimes is called *transmission parameter* matrix and is denoted by $\mathbf{T}(s)$ i.e.,

$$\mathbf{T}(s) \triangleq \begin{bmatrix} A(s) & B(s) \\ C(s) & D(s) \end{bmatrix} \tag{12.2.18}$$

A useful property of the transmission parameter matrix $\mathbf{T}(s)$ is illustrated in the following example.

*Example 12.2.4*

Consider two networks $N$ and $N'$ with transmission parameter matrices $\mathbf{T}(s)$ and $\mathbf{T}'(s)$. Find the transmission parameter matrix of the tandem connection of these two networks, $\mathbf{T}_d(s)$. (See Fig. 12.2.6).

*Solution*

Let

$$\mathbf{T}(s) \triangleq \begin{bmatrix} A(s) & B(s) \\ C(s) & D(s) \end{bmatrix} \quad \text{and} \quad \mathbf{T}'(s) \triangleq \begin{bmatrix} A'(s) & B'(s) \\ C'(s) & D'(s) \end{bmatrix}$$

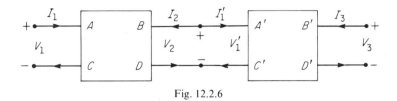

Fig. 12.2.6

Then, since $V_2 = V_1'$ and $-I_2 = I_1'$, we can connect the networks as in Fig. 12.2.7.

$$\begin{bmatrix} V_1 \\ I_1 \end{bmatrix} = \mathbf{T}(s) \begin{bmatrix} V_2 \\ -I_2 \end{bmatrix} \quad \text{and} \quad \begin{bmatrix} V_2 \\ -I_2 \end{bmatrix} = \begin{bmatrix} V_1' \\ I_1' \end{bmatrix} = \mathbf{T}'(s) \begin{bmatrix} V_3 \\ -I_3 \end{bmatrix}$$

Hence

$$\begin{bmatrix} V_1 \\ I_1 \end{bmatrix} = \mathbf{T}(s)\mathbf{T}'(s) \begin{bmatrix} V_3 \\ -I_3 \end{bmatrix} \qquad \text{i.e., } \mathbf{T}_d(s) = \mathbf{T}(s)\mathbf{T}'(s)$$

That is, the transmission parameter of the tandem connection of the circuits is equal to the product of their transmission parameters.

*Example 12.2.5*

Find the $ABCD$ parameters of the network shown in Fig. 12.2.7.

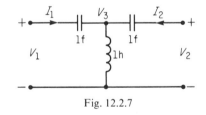

Fig. 12.2.7

*Solution*

From this figure if $I_2 = 0$, then

$$V_1 = I_1\left(\frac{1}{s} + s\right) \quad \text{and} \quad V_2 = V_3 = I_1 s$$

Therefore

$$A(s) = \frac{V_1}{V_2}\bigg|_{I_2=0} = \frac{\frac{1}{s} + s}{s} = 1 + \frac{1}{s^2}$$

Also, if $V_2 = 0$,

$$-I_2 = V_3 s \quad \text{and} \quad V_3 = V_1 - \frac{\frac{1}{s} V_1}{\frac{1}{s} + \frac{s}{s^2 + 1}} = \frac{s^2 V_1}{2s^2 + 1}$$

or simply

$$B(s) = \frac{V_1}{-I_2}\bigg|_{V_2=0} = \frac{2s^2 + 1}{s^3}$$

In a similar manner, $C(s) = \dfrac{1}{s}$ and $D(s) = \dfrac{1 + s^2}{s^2}$.

## Hybrid Parameters

Another set of useful two-port parameters are hybrid or $H$ parameters. These are defined by

$$\begin{bmatrix} V_1(s) \\ I_2(s) \end{bmatrix} = \begin{bmatrix} h_{11}(s) & h_{12}(s) \\ h_{21}(s) & h_{22}(s) \end{bmatrix} \begin{bmatrix} I_1(s) \\ V_2(s) \end{bmatrix} \qquad (12.2.19)$$

To obtain $h_{11}(s)$ we apply a voltage source to port ①, short circuit port ② (i.e., set $V_2 = 0$) and measure the current $I_1$; then

$$h_{11}(s) = \frac{V_1}{I_1}\bigg|_{V_2=0}$$

In a similar manner we get

$$h_{12}(s) = \frac{V_1}{V_2}\bigg|_{I_1=0}, \quad h_{21}(s) = \frac{I_2}{I_1}\bigg|_{V_2=0} \quad \text{and} \quad h_{22}(s) = \frac{I_2}{V_2}\bigg|_{I_1=0}$$

*Example 12.2.6*

Find the hybrid parameters for the network shown in Fig. 12.2.7.

*Solution*

$$h_{11}(s) = \frac{V_1}{I_1}\bigg|_{V_2=0} = \frac{1}{s} + \frac{1}{s + \dfrac{1}{s}} = \frac{2s^2 + 1}{s(s^2 + 1)}$$

and

$$h_{12} = \frac{V_1}{V_2}\bigg|_{I_1=0} \quad \text{where} \quad V_1 = sI_2, \quad V_2 = \left(s + \frac{1}{s}\right)I_2$$

Then

$$h_{12}(s) = \frac{s^2}{s^2 + 1}$$

Similarly,

$$h_{21}(s) = \frac{-s^2}{s^2 + 1} \quad \text{and} \quad h_{22}(s) = \frac{2s^2 + 1}{s(s^2 + 1)}$$

or

$$\mathbf{H}(s) = \frac{1}{s(s^2 + 1)} \begin{bmatrix} 2s^2 + 1 & s^3 \\ -s^3 & 2s^2 + 1 \end{bmatrix} \qquad (12.2.20)$$

In a similar manner we can define the $G$ parameters as

$$\begin{bmatrix} I_1(s) \\ V_2(s) \end{bmatrix} = \begin{bmatrix} g_{11}(s) & g_{12}(s) \\ g_{21}(s) & g_{22}(s) \end{bmatrix} \begin{bmatrix} V_1(s) \\ I_2(s) \end{bmatrix}$$

where

$$g_{11}(s) = \left. \frac{I_1}{V_1} \right|_{I_2 = 0}, \quad g_{12}(s) = \left. \frac{I_1(s)}{I_2(s)} \right|_{V_1 = 0}$$

$$g_{21}(s) = \left. \frac{V_2(s)}{V_1(s)} \right|_{I_2 = 0}, \quad g_{22}(s) = \left. \frac{V_2(s)}{I_2(s)} \right|_{V_1 = 0}$$

Quite clearly if

$$\det \mathbf{G}(s) \triangleq g_{11}(s)g_{22}(s) - g_{21}(s)g_{12}(s) \neq 0$$

then

$$\mathbf{G}(s) = \mathbf{H}^{-1}(s)$$

For instance, the $G$ parameters of the network shown in Fig. 12.2.7 can be obtained by inverting $\mathbf{H}(s)$ given in Eq. 12.2.20.

$$\mathbf{G}(s) = \frac{s(s^2 + 1)}{s^6 + (2s^2 + 1)^2} \begin{bmatrix} 2s^2 + 1 & -s^3 \\ s^3 & 2s^2 + 1 \end{bmatrix}$$

## 12.3  RELATIONSHIPS AMONG DIFFERENT TWO-PORT PARAMETERS

In the previous section we briefly mentioned the relation between $Z$ and $Y$ parameters and showed that under certain conditions we can obtain $Z$ parameters from $Y$ parameters and vice versa. In a similar manner we can express each of the previously mentioned two-port parameters in terms of any of the remaining parameters. For example, let us express the $Z$ parameters in terms of the transmission parameters. For convenience let us rewrite Eqs. 12.2.1 and 12.2.15 here:

$$\begin{bmatrix} V_1 \\ V_2 \end{bmatrix} = \begin{bmatrix} z_{11} & z_{12} \\ z_{21} & z_{22} \end{bmatrix} \begin{bmatrix} I_1 \\ I_2 \end{bmatrix} \tag{12.3.1}$$

$$\begin{bmatrix} V_1 \\ I_1 \end{bmatrix} = \begin{bmatrix} A & B \\ C & D \end{bmatrix} \begin{bmatrix} V_2 \\ -I_2 \end{bmatrix} \tag{12.3.2}$$

We also had $z_{11} = \left. \dfrac{V_1}{I_1} \right|_{I_2 = 0}$. If we put $I_2 = 0$ in Eq. 12.3.2, we get

$$V_1 = A V_2 \quad \text{and} \quad I_1 = C V_2$$

or

$$z_{11} = \frac{V_1}{I_1}\bigg|_{I_2=0} = \frac{A V_2}{C V_2} = \frac{A}{C}$$

Similarly we had,

$$z_{12} = \frac{V_1}{I_2}\bigg|_{I_1=0}$$

Now if we put $I_1 = 0$ in Eq. 12.3.2 we obtain

$$V_1 = A V_2 - B I_2 \quad \text{and} \quad 0 = C V_2 - D I_2$$

Solving these two equations yields:

$$V_2 = \frac{D}{C} I_2$$

and

$$V_1 = \frac{AD - BC}{C} I_2$$

TABLE 12.3.1. CONVERSION CHART FOR TWO-PORT PARAMETERS.

|   | Z | | Y | | T | | H | | G | |
|---|---|---|---|---|---|---|---|---|---|---|
| Z | $z_{11}$ | $z_{12}$ | $\dfrac{y_{22}}{\Delta Y}$ | $\dfrac{-y_{12}}{\Delta Y}$ | $\dfrac{A}{C}$ | $\dfrac{\Delta T}{C}$ | $\dfrac{\Delta H}{h_{22}}$ | $\dfrac{h_{12}}{h_{22}}$ | $\dfrac{1}{g_{11}}$ | $\dfrac{-g_{12}}{g_{11}}$ |
|   | $z_{21}$ | $z_{22}$ | $\dfrac{-y_{21}}{\Delta Y}$ | $\dfrac{y_{11}}{\Delta Y}$ | $\dfrac{1}{C}$ | $\dfrac{D}{C}$ | $\dfrac{-h_{21}}{h_{22}}$ | $\dfrac{1_{22}}{h_{11}}$ | $\dfrac{g_{21}}{g_{11}}$ | $\dfrac{\Delta G}{g_{11}}$ |
| Y | $\dfrac{z_{22}}{\Delta Z}$ | $\dfrac{-z_{12}}{\Delta Z}$ | $y_{11}$ | $y_{12}$ | $\dfrac{D}{B}$ | $\dfrac{-\Delta T}{B}$ | $\dfrac{1}{h_{11}}$ | $\dfrac{-h_{12}}{h_{11}}$ | $\dfrac{\Delta G}{g_{22}}$ | $\dfrac{g_{12}}{g_{22}}$ |
|   | $\dfrac{-z_{21}}{\Delta Z}$ | $\dfrac{z_{11}}{\Delta Z}$ | $y_{21}$ | $y_{11}$ | $\dfrac{-1}{B}$ | $\dfrac{A}{B}$ | $\dfrac{h_{21}}{h_{11}}$ | $\dfrac{\Delta H}{h_{11}}$ | $\dfrac{-g_{21}}{g_{22}}$ | $\dfrac{1}{g_{22}}$ |
| T | $\dfrac{z_{11}}{z_{21}}$ | $\dfrac{\Delta Z}{z_{21}}$ | $\dfrac{-y_{22}}{y_{21}}$ | $\dfrac{1}{-y_{21}}$ | $A$ | $B$ | $\dfrac{-\Delta H}{h_{21}}$ | $\dfrac{h_{11}}{h_{21}}$ | $\dfrac{1}{g_{21}}$ | $\dfrac{g_{22}}{g_{21}}$ |
|   | $\dfrac{1}{z_{21}}$ | $\dfrac{z_{22}}{z_{21}}$ | $\dfrac{-\Delta Y}{y_{21}}$ | $\dfrac{-y_{11}}{y_{21}}$ | $C$ | $D$ | $\dfrac{-h_{22}}{h_{21}}$ | $\dfrac{-1}{h_{21}}$ | $\dfrac{g_{11}}{g_{21}}$ | $\dfrac{\Delta G}{g_{21}}$ |
| H | $\dfrac{\Delta Z}{z_{22}}$ | $\dfrac{z_{12}}{z_{22}}$ | $\dfrac{1}{y_{11}}$ | $\dfrac{-y_{12}}{y_{11}}$ | $\dfrac{B}{D}$ | $\dfrac{\Delta T}{D}$ | $h_{11}$ | $h_{12}$ | $\dfrac{g_{22}}{\Delta G}$ | $\dfrac{-g_{12}}{\Delta G}$ |
|   | $\dfrac{-z_{21}}{z_{22}}$ | $\dfrac{1}{z_{22}}$ | $\dfrac{y_{21}}{y_{11}}$ | $\dfrac{\Delta Y}{y_{11}}$ | $\dfrac{-1}{D}$ | $\dfrac{C}{D}$ | $h_{21}$ | $h_{22}$ | $\dfrac{-g_{21}}{\Delta G}$ | $\dfrac{g_{11}}{\Delta G}$ |
| G | $\dfrac{1}{z_{11}}$ | $\dfrac{-z_{12}}{z_{11}}$ | $\dfrac{\Delta Y}{y_{22}}$ | $\dfrac{y_{12}}{y_{22}}$ | $\dfrac{C}{A}$ | $\dfrac{-\Delta T}{A}$ | $\dfrac{h_{22}}{\Delta H}$ | $\dfrac{-h_{12}}{\Delta H}$ | $g_{11}$ | $g_{12}$ |
|   | $\dfrac{z_{21}}{z_{11}}$ | $\dfrac{\Delta Z}{z_{11}}$ | $\dfrac{-y_{21}}{y_{22}}$ | $\dfrac{1}{y_{22}}$ | $\dfrac{1}{A}$ | $\dfrac{B}{A}$ | $\dfrac{-h_{21}}{\Delta H}$ | $\dfrac{h_{11}}{\Delta H}$ | $g_{21}$ | $g_{22}$ |

Hence

$$z_{12} = \left.\frac{V_1}{I_2}\right|_{I_1=0} = \frac{\Delta T}{C}$$

where $\Delta T$ denotes the determinant of the transmission matrix $\mathbf{T}$;

$$\Delta T \triangleq AD - BC$$

The rest of the elements in the $\mathbf{Z}$ matrix can be expressed in terms of $ABCD$ parameters in a similar manner. In fact, it is an easy exercise to show that each two-port parameter discussed in the last section can be expressed in terms of the other parameters. The result of such relations are tabulated in Table 12.3.1. In this table $\Delta Z = \det \mathbf{Z}$, $\Delta Y = \det \mathbf{Y}$, etc.

### 12.4. INTERCONNECTION OF TWO PORTS

In Example 12.2.4 we mentioned how $ABCD$ parameters of the tandem or cascade connection of two networks can be obtained in terms of $ABCD$ parameters of the individual networks. In this section we extend this idea to other types of interconnections. We shall consider series connection, parallel connection, and series-parallel connection of two-port networks.

#### Series Connection

Figure 12.4.1 shows the series connection of two two-port networks. For the two-port $N$ we have

$$\begin{bmatrix} V_1 \\ V_2 \end{bmatrix} = \begin{bmatrix} z_{11} & z_{12} \\ z_{21} & z_{22} \end{bmatrix} \begin{bmatrix} I_1 \\ I_2 \end{bmatrix} \quad \text{or} \quad \mathbf{V} = \mathbf{ZI} \qquad (12.4.1)$$

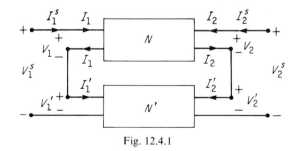

Fig. 12.4.1

and for the two-port $N'$ we have

$$\begin{bmatrix} V_1' \\ V_2' \end{bmatrix} = \begin{bmatrix} z_{11}' & z_{12}' \\ z_{21}' & z_{22}' \end{bmatrix} \begin{bmatrix} I_1' \\ I_2' \end{bmatrix} \quad \text{or} \quad \mathbf{V}' = \mathbf{Z}'\mathbf{I}' \qquad (12.4.2)$$

The objective is to find the $Z$ parameters for the series connection of $N$ and $N'$, i.e., find $\mathbf{Z}^s$ defined by

$$\begin{bmatrix} V_1^s \\ V_2^s \end{bmatrix} = \begin{bmatrix} z_{11}^s & z_{12}^s \\ z_{21}^s & z_{22}^s \end{bmatrix} \begin{bmatrix} I_1^s \\ I_2^s \end{bmatrix} \quad \text{or} \quad \mathbf{V}^s = \mathbf{Z}^s \mathbf{I}^s \qquad (12.4.3)$$

From Fig. 12.4.1 it is clear that

$$\begin{bmatrix} V_1^s \\ V_2^s \end{bmatrix} = \begin{bmatrix} V_1 + V_1' \\ V_2 + V_2' \end{bmatrix} \quad \text{or} \quad \mathbf{V}^s = \mathbf{V} + \mathbf{V}' \qquad (12.4.4)$$

and

$$\begin{bmatrix} I_1^s \\ I_2^s \end{bmatrix} = \begin{bmatrix} I_1 \\ I_2 \end{bmatrix} = \begin{bmatrix} I_1' \\ I_2' \end{bmatrix} \quad \text{or} \quad \mathbf{I}^s = \mathbf{I} = \mathbf{I}' \qquad (12.4.5)$$

Hence, Eqs. 12.4.1 and 12.4.2 together with Eqs. 12.4.4 and 12.4.5 yield

$$\mathbf{V}^s = \mathbf{Z}\mathbf{I} + \mathbf{Z}'\mathbf{I}' = (\mathbf{Z} + \mathbf{Z}')\mathbf{I}^s \qquad (12.4.6)$$

comparing Eq. 12.4.6 with Eq. 12.4.3 we obtain

$$\mathbf{Z}^s = \mathbf{Z} + \mathbf{Z}' \qquad (12.4.7)$$

or

$$\begin{bmatrix} z_{11}^s & z_{12}^s \\ z_{21}^s & z_{22}^s \end{bmatrix} = \begin{bmatrix} z_{11} + z_{11}' & z_{12} + z_{12}' \\ z_{21} + z_{21}' & z_{22} + z_{22}' \end{bmatrix} \qquad (12.4.8)$$

*Example 12.4.1*

Consider the simple networks $N$ and $N'$ shown in Fig. 12.4.2a and b. Find the $Z$ parameters of their series connection.

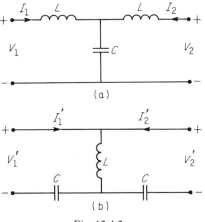

Fig. 12.4.2

*Solution*

Using Eqs. 12.2.2 through 12.2.4, the corresponding $Z$ parameters can be found to be:

$$\mathbf{Z}(s) = \begin{bmatrix} sL + \dfrac{1}{Cs} & \dfrac{1}{Cs} \\[2ex] \dfrac{1}{Cs} & sL + \dfrac{1}{Cs} \end{bmatrix}$$

and

$$\mathbf{Z}'(s) = \begin{bmatrix} sL + \dfrac{1}{Cs} & sL \\[2ex] sL & sL + \dfrac{1}{Cs} \end{bmatrix}$$

Series connection of $N$ and $N'$ is shown in Fig. 12.4.3.

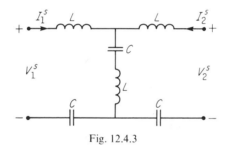

Fig. 12.4.3

From Eq. 12.4.7 and the matrices $\mathbf{Z}(s)$ and $\mathbf{Z}'(s)$ given above we get

$$\mathbf{Z}^s(s) = \left( sL + \frac{1}{Cs} \right) \begin{bmatrix} 2 & 1 \\ 1 & 2 \end{bmatrix}$$

which is obviously the $\mathbf{Z}$ matrix of the network shown in Fig. 12.4.3.

*REMARK.* It should be mentioned that the interconnection of two port networks can only be achieved if certain conditions are satisfied. To see this, consider the two port networks $N$ and $N'$ shown in Fig. 12.4.4. If $V_0$ in Fig. 12.4.4 is equal to zero, the networks $N$ and $N'$ can be connected in series. If $V_0 \neq 0$, by connecting ports ② and ②′ there will be a "circulating current" in the loop $l$ and this will violate the port property of the individual networks. More precisely, the current entering one terminal of port ② will not be equal to the current leaving the other terminal.

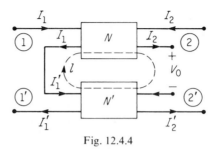

Fig. 12.4.4

For this reason, before connecting two-port networks in series this condition must be checked. This is usually done by inspection.

### Parallel Connection

Consider the parallel connection of two networks $N$ and $N'$ as shown in Fig. 12.4.5.

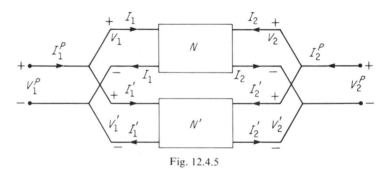

Fig. 12.4.5

In this case we have

$$\begin{bmatrix} I_1^P \\ I_2^P \end{bmatrix} = \begin{bmatrix} I_1 + I_1' \\ I_2 + I_2' \end{bmatrix} \quad \text{or} \quad \mathbf{I}^P = \mathbf{I} + \mathbf{I}' \qquad (12.4.9)$$

and

$$\begin{bmatrix} V_1^P \\ V_2^P \end{bmatrix} = \begin{bmatrix} V_1 \\ V_2 \end{bmatrix} = \begin{bmatrix} V_1' \\ V_2' \end{bmatrix} \quad \text{or} \quad \mathbf{V}^P = \mathbf{V} = \mathbf{V}' \qquad (12.4.10)$$

These equations together with Eqs. 12.2.7 and 12.2.8 yield

$$\mathbf{I}^P = \mathbf{Y}\mathbf{V} + \mathbf{Y}'\mathbf{V}' = (\mathbf{Y} + \mathbf{Y}')\,\mathbf{V}^P \qquad (12.4.11)$$

Now if we denote the $Y$ parameters of the resulting network by $\mathbf{Y}^P$, we can write

$$\begin{bmatrix} I_1^P \\ I_2^P \end{bmatrix} = \begin{bmatrix} y_{11}^P & y_{12}^P \\ y_{21}^P & y_{22}^P \end{bmatrix} \begin{bmatrix} V_1^P \\ V_2^P \end{bmatrix} \quad \text{or} \quad \mathbf{I}^P = \mathbf{Y}^P\mathbf{V}^P \qquad (12.4.12)$$

Comparing Eqs. 12.4.11 and 12.4.12, we obtain

$$\begin{bmatrix} y_{11}^P & y_{12}^P \\ y_{21}^P & y_{22}^P \end{bmatrix} = \begin{bmatrix} y_{11} + y_{11}' & y_{12} + y_{12}' \\ y_{21} + y_{21}' & y_{22} + y_{22}' \end{bmatrix}$$

or

$$\mathbf{Y}^P = \mathbf{Y} + \mathbf{Y}' \qquad (12.4.13)$$

As in the previous case, in order to connect two networks $N$ and $N'$ in parallel they must satisfy a certain condition. Let ports ① and ①' be connected together and let ports ② and ②' be short circuited individually (see Fig. 12.4.6). Then the condition under which two networks can be connected in parallel is that $V_0 = 0$.

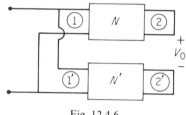

Fig. 12.4.6

*Example 12.4.2*

Consider the networks $N$ and $N'$ shown in Fig. 12.4.7.

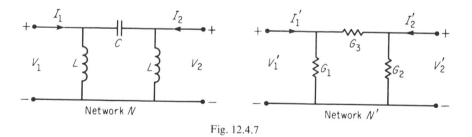

Fig. 12.4.7

The $Y$ parameters for these networks are

$$\mathbf{Y} = \begin{bmatrix} \dfrac{1}{Ls} + Cs & -Cs \\ -Cs & \dfrac{1}{Ls} + Cs \end{bmatrix} \quad \text{and} \quad \mathbf{Y}' = \begin{bmatrix} G_1 + G_3 & -G_3 \\ -G_3 & G_2 + G_3 \end{bmatrix}$$

Parallel connection of $N$ and $N'$ is shown in Fig. 12.4.8.

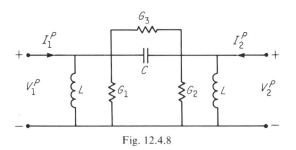

Fig. 12.4.8

Hence the overall admittance matrix of the parallel connection of $N$ and $N'$ is

$$\mathbf{Y}^P = \begin{bmatrix} Cs + \dfrac{1}{Ls} + G_1 + G_3 & -(Cs + G_3) \\ \\ -(Cs + G_3) & Cs + \dfrac{1}{Ls} + G_2 + G_3 \end{bmatrix}$$

(Check this conclusion by finding $\mathbf{Y}^P$ directly from Fig. 12.4.8.)

### Series-Parallel Connection

Figure 12.4.9 shows the series-parallel connection of two networks $N$ and $N'$. Hybrid parameters of $N$ are denoted by $H$ and those of $N'$ are denoted by $H'$.

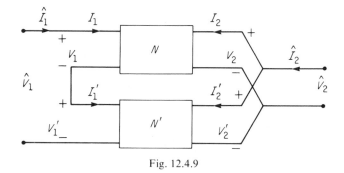

Fig. 12.4.9

From Fig. 12.4.9 it is clear that

$$\begin{bmatrix} \hat{V}_1 \\ \hat{I}_2 \end{bmatrix} = \begin{bmatrix} V_1 \\ I_2 \end{bmatrix} + \begin{bmatrix} V_1' \\ I_2' \end{bmatrix} \qquad (12.4.14)$$

and

$$\begin{bmatrix} \hat{I}_1 \\ \hat{V}_2 \end{bmatrix} = \begin{bmatrix} I_1 \\ V_2 \end{bmatrix} = \begin{bmatrix} I_1' \\ V_2' \end{bmatrix} \qquad (12.4.15)$$

But we have

$$\begin{bmatrix} V_1 \\ I_2 \end{bmatrix} = \begin{bmatrix} h_{11} & h_{12} \\ h_{21} & h_{22} \end{bmatrix} \begin{bmatrix} I_1 \\ V_2 \end{bmatrix} \qquad (12.4.16)$$

and

$$\begin{bmatrix} V_1' \\ I_2' \end{bmatrix} = \begin{bmatrix} h_{11}' & h_{12}' \\ h_{21}' & h_{22}' \end{bmatrix} \begin{bmatrix} I_1' \\ V_2' \end{bmatrix} \qquad (12.4.17)$$

Comparing Eqs. 12.4.14 through 12.4.17 we obtain

$$\begin{bmatrix} \hat{V}_1 \\ \hat{I}_2 \end{bmatrix} = \begin{bmatrix} h_{11} + h_{11}' & h_{12} + h_{12}' \\ h_{21} + h_{21}' & h_{22} + h_{22}' \end{bmatrix} \begin{bmatrix} \hat{I}_1 \\ \hat{V}_2 \end{bmatrix} \qquad (12.4.18)$$

That is, the hybrid parameter of the resulting network is the sum of the hybrid parameters of $N$ and $N'$.

### PROBLEMS

**12.1.** Find the open-circuit impedance parameters for the network shown.

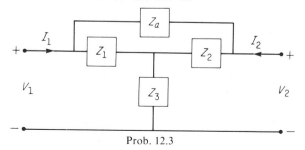

Prob. 12.1

**12.2.** Repeat Prob. 12.1 for the network shown.

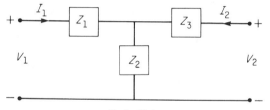

Prob. 12.2

**12.3.** Repeat Prob. 12.1 for the network shown.

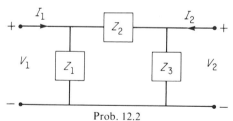

Prob. 12.3

**12.4.** Repeat Prob. 12.1 for the network shown.

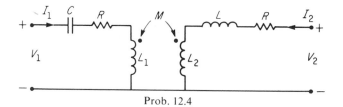

Prob. 12.4

**12.5.** Find the short-circuit admittance parameters for the network of Prob. 12.1.
**12.6.** Repeat Prob. 12.5 for the network of Prob. 12.2.
**12.7.** Repeat Prob. 12.5 for the network of Prob. 12.3.
**12.8.** Repeat Prob. 12.5 for the network of Prob. 12.4.
**12.9.** Obtain the $Y$ parameters of the network of Prob. 12.1 from its $Z$ parameters obtained in Prob. 12.1; check your answer with the result of Prob. 12.5.
**12.10.** Obtain the $Y$ parameters of the network of Prob. 12.2 from its $Z$ parameters obtained in Prob. 12.2; check your answer with the result of Prob. 12.6.
**12.11.** Find the transmission parameters for the network of Prob. 12.1.
**12.12.** Repeat Prob. 12.11 for the network of Prob. 12.2.
**12.13.** Repeat Prob. 12.11 for the network of Prob. 12.3.
**12.14.** Repeat Prob. 12.11 for the network of Prob. 12.4.
**12.15.** Find the transmission parameters of the network shown.

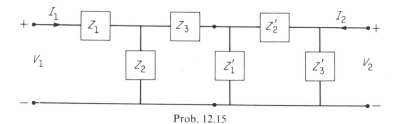

Prob. 12.15

**12.16.** Repeat Prob. 12.15 for the network shown.

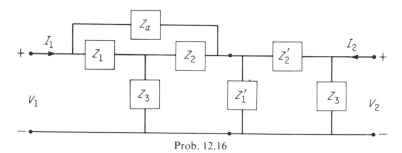

Prob. 12.16

**12.17.** Find the hybrid parameters for the network of Prob. 12.1.
**12.18.** Repeat Prob. 12.17 for the network of Prob. 12.2.
**12.19.** Repeat Prob. 12.17 for the network of Prob. 12.3.
**12.20.** Repeat Prob. 12.17 for the network of Prob. 12.4.

**12.21.** Use Table 12.3.1 to find the $ABCD$ parameters of the network of Prob. 12.1 from its $Z$ parameters.

**12.22.** Repeat Prob. 12.21 for the network of Prob. 12.2.

**12.23.** Repeat Prob. 12.21 for the network of Prob. 12.3.

**12.24.** Use Table 12.3.1 to find the $H$ parameters of the network of Prob. 12.1 from its $Y$ parameters.

**12.25.** Repeat Prob. 12.24 for the network of Prob. 12.2.

**12.26.** Repeat Prob. 12.24 for the network of Prob. 12.3.

**12.27.** Verify the last row of Table 12.3.1.

**12.28.** Find the $Z$ parameters of the network shown.

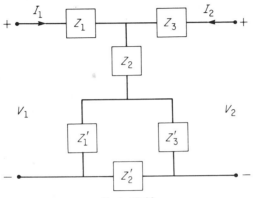

Prob. 12.28

**12.29.** Repeat Prob. 12.28 for the network shown (all values in ohm, henry, and farad).

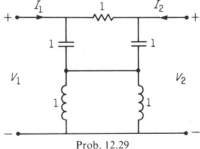

Prob. 12.29

**12.30.** Find the $Y$ parameters for the network shown.

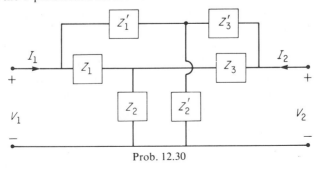

Prob. 12.30

## CHAPTER 13

# Network Theorems

## 13.1. INTRODUCTION

Up to this point in our development of network concepts we have concentrated on the study of specific solution methods as applied to specific network problems. We now wish to take a broader viewpoint in order to illustrate general properties of network response. We will see that these properties, which are common to many networks, can be used to simplify and gain insight into network problems.

## 13.2. LINEAR NETWORKS—SUPERPOSITION THEOREM

In Chapter 2 and again in Chapter 8 we have utilized the principle of superposition in arriving at network response. Recall that the principle of superposition states that if sources $u_1$ and $u_2$ are applied to a linear network with zero initial conditions and if $u_1 \xrightarrow{\text{gives}} x_1$ and $u_2 \xrightarrow{\text{gives}} x_2$ then $(u_1 + u_2) \xrightarrow{\text{gives}} (x_1 + x_2)$. This result formed the basis for developing our network solutions. The superposition theorem is a formal statement of this property for any linear network and any number of sources.

### Superposition Theorem

Given any linear network (time-varying or time-invariant) with zero initial conditions, the network response can be obtained by calculating the response to each independent source, with all other independent sources set equal to zero and then summing to obtain the total response.

As a specific illustration of the superposition property, consider the network shown in Fig. 13.2.1. Applying KVL to loops $l_1$ and $l_2$ we get:

$$v = v_{R_1} + v_C$$
$$0 = v_L - v_C \qquad (13.2.1)$$

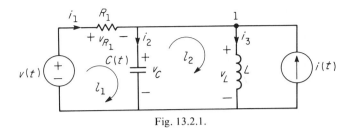

Fig. 13.2.1.

and applying KCL to node 1 we obtain

$$i = -i_1 + i_2 + i_3 \tag{13.2.2}$$

Now let us define the branch voltage $v_C$ as the network response to the sources $v(t)$ and $i(t)$. Applying VCR to Eqs. 13.2.1 and 13.2.2 and combining these equations give

$$R_1 \frac{d}{dt}(C(t)v_C(t)) + v_C(t) + \frac{R_1}{L}\int_0^t v_C(\sigma)\,d\sigma = v(t) + R_1 i(t) \tag{13.2.3}$$

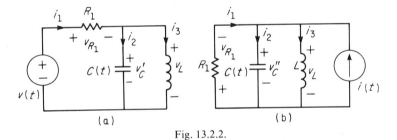

Fig. 13.2.2.

Next, consider the network shown in Fig. 13.2.2a. This is the network formed by replacing the current source in Fig. 13.2.1 by an open circuit (i.e., $i(t) = 0$). Denote the voltage across the capacitor $C(t)$ due to $v(t)$ by $v'_C$. Applying KVL and KCL to this circuit gives

$$v = v_{R_1} + v'_C \tag{13.2.4}$$
$$0 = v_L - v'_C$$

and

$$0 = -i_1 + i_2 + i_3 \tag{13.2.5}$$

Combining Eqs. 13.2.4 and 13.2.5 with the utilization of VCR gives

$$R_1 \frac{d}{dt}(C(t)v'_C(t)) + v'_C(t) + \frac{R_1}{L}\int_0^t v'_C(\sigma)\,d\sigma = v(t) \tag{13.2.6}$$

The network in Fig. 13.2.2b is obtained from Fig. 13.2.1 by shorting the voltage source (i.e., $v(t) = 0$). Denote the voltage across $C(t)$ due to

$i(t)$ by $v_C''$. The equation governing the response $v_C''(t)$ is

$$R_1 \frac{d}{dt}\left(C(t)\, v_C''(t)\right) + v_C''(t) + \frac{R_1}{L}\int_0^t v_C''(\sigma)\, d\sigma = R_1 i(t) \quad (13.2.7)$$

If we solve Eq. 13.2.6 for $v_C'(t)$ and Eq. 13.2.7 for $v_C''(t)$, we can obtain the solution, $v_C(t)$, to the original network in Fig. 13.2.1 as

$$v_C(t) = v_C'(t) + v_C''(t) \quad (13.2.8)$$

This solution can be easily demonstrated by substituting Eq. 13.2.8 for $v_C(t)$ in Eq. 13.2.3 and using conditions (13.2.6) and (13.2.7).

This example illustrates the essential idea of the superposition theorem. To calculate the response of a network to several sources, we calculate the response to each source individually and then take the sum of the individual response. We can illustrate the superposition theorem in a more general manner by considering the solution for network state variables developed in Chapter 7. Recall that if $\mathbf{x}(t)$ is the state variable vector, then

$$\mathbf{x}(t) = e^{\mathbf{A}t}\mathbf{x}(0) + \int_0^t e^{\mathbf{A}(t-\tau)}\mathbf{B}\mathbf{u}(\tau)\, d\tau \quad (13.2.9)$$

where $\mathbf{u}(\tau)$ is an $m \times 1$ *source* vector. We write

$$\mathbf{u}(\tau) = [u_1(\tau)\ \ u_2(\tau)\ \cdots\ u_m(\tau)]^T \quad (13.2.10)$$

Let $\mathbf{b}_1$ be a vector containing the elements in the first column of the matrix $\mathbf{B}$. Similarly, let $\mathbf{b}_2$ be defined by the elements in the second column, and so on for $\mathbf{b}_3, \mathbf{b}_4, \ldots, \mathbf{b}_m$. Then we can write

$$\mathbf{B}\mathbf{u}(\tau) = [\mathbf{b}_1\ \mathbf{b}_2\ \cdots\ \mathbf{b}_m]\mathbf{u}(\tau) = \mathbf{b}_1 u_1(\tau) + \cdots + \mathbf{b}_m u_m(\tau)$$

The state-variable solution (13.2.9) can then be rewritten as

$$\mathbf{x}(t) = e^{\mathbf{A}t}\mathbf{x}(0) + \int_0^t e^{\mathbf{A}(t-\tau)}\mathbf{b}_1 u_1(\tau)\, d\tau + \cdots + \int_0^t e^{\mathbf{A}(t-\tau)}\mathbf{b}_m u_m(\tau)\, d\tau$$

$$(13.2.11)$$

Let

$$\mathbf{x}^j(t) \triangleq \int_0^t e^{\mathbf{A}(t-\tau)}\mathbf{b}_j u_j(\tau)\, d\tau \qquad j = 1, 2, \ldots, m \quad (13.2.12)$$

We note that $\mathbf{x}^j(t)$ is simply the network response to source $u_j(t)$ with all other sources set equal to zero. From Eq. 13.2.11 we have the total network response as

$$\mathbf{x}(t) = e^{\mathbf{A}t}\mathbf{x}(0) + \mathbf{x}^1(t) + \cdots + \mathbf{x}^m(t) \quad (13.2.13)$$

If we have zero initial conditions, i.e., $\mathbf{x}(0) = \mathbf{0}$, Eq. 13.2.13 indicates that the total network response is simply the sum of the responses due to each individual source calculated by setting all other independent sources within the network equal to zero. This illustrates the superposition theorem for all *linear, time-invariant* networks. A similar development can be used to illustrate the superposition principle for linear, time-varying networks.

*Example 13.2.1*

Using the superposition theorem, calculate the voltage $v_C(t)$ in Fig. 13.2.3a.

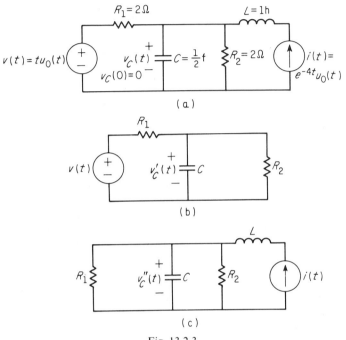

Fig. 13.2.3.

*Solution*

First we calculate the response due to the source $v(t)$ by setting $i(t)$ equal to zero. The equivalent circuit for this case is shown in Fig. 13.2.3b. Applying voltage division, the transform of voltage $v'_C(t)$ is found to be

$$V'_C(s) = \left( \frac{\dfrac{1}{G_2 + sC}}{\dfrac{1}{G_2 + sC} + R_1} \right) V(s) = \frac{1}{(s+2)s^2}$$

Obtaining the inverse Laplace transform we get

$$v'_C(t) = (\tfrac{1}{2}t + \tfrac{1}{4}e^{-2t} - \tfrac{1}{4})u_0(t)$$

Next, we set $v(t)$ equal to zero and calculate the response to $i(t)$. The equivalent circuit is shown in Fig. 13.2.3c. The current $i(t)$ flows through the parallel combination of $R_1$, $C$, and $R_2$. Hence, the transform of voltage $v''_C(t)$ is

$$V''_C(s) = \left(\frac{1}{G_1 + G_2 + sC}\right) I(s) = \left(\frac{2}{s+2}\right)\left(\frac{1}{s+4}\right)$$

Inverting into the time domain, we obtain

$$v''_C(t) = (e^{-2t} - e^{-4t}) u_0(t)$$

The total response due to both sources is found using the superposition theorem

$$v_C(t) = v'_C(t) + v''_C(t) = (\tfrac{5}{4}e^{-2t} - e^{-4t} + \tfrac{1}{2}t - \tfrac{1}{4}) u_0(t)$$

*Example 13.2.2*

Using superposition, calculate the voltage $v_2(t)$ in Fig. 13.2.4a. Assume $R_1 = 1\,\Omega$, $R_2 = 1\,\Omega$, $R_3 = \tfrac{1}{2}\,\Omega$, $C_1 = 2\text{ f}$, $\beta = 2$, $\alpha = 1$, $i(t) = \sin t\, u_0(t)$, and $v(t) = t\, u_0(t)$.

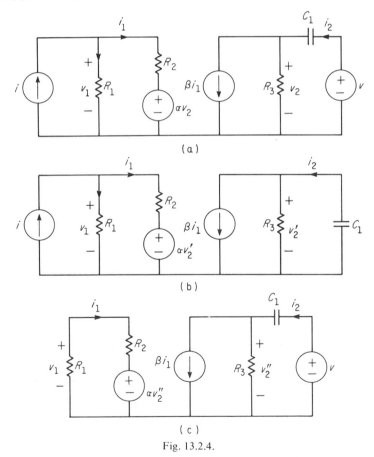

(a)

(b)

(c)

Fig. 13.2.4.

*Solution*

We recognize this network as the equivalent circuit of the common emitter transistor amplifier for which we developed the $Z$ parameters in Chapter 12 (see Example 12.2.2).

Setting the source $v(t)$ equal to zero results in the network shown in Fig. 13.2.4b. We have the current and voltage relationships

$$I(s) = \frac{V_1(s)}{R_1} + I_1(s)$$

$$V_1(s) = I_1(s) R_2 + \alpha V_2'(s)$$

$$V_2'(s) = -\beta I_1(s) \frac{1}{G_3 + sC_1}$$

Eliminating $I_1(s)$ and $V_1(s)$ and substituting for the parameter values give

$$V_2'(s) = -\frac{1}{2}\left(\frac{1}{s + \frac{1}{2}}\right)\left(\frac{1}{s^2 + 1}\right)$$

After Laplace inversion we obtain

$$v_2'(t) = \left[-\frac{2}{5} e^{-(1/2)t} - \frac{1}{\sqrt{5}} \sin(t - 63.5°)\right] u_0(t)$$

Setting $i(t)$ equal to zero gives the circuit shown in Fig. 13.2.4c. For this circuit we have the voltage-current relations

$$V(s) = \frac{1}{sC_1} I_2(s) + V_2''(s)$$

$$\frac{V_2''(s)}{R_3} = I_2(s) - \beta I_1(s)$$

$$I_1(s) = -\frac{\alpha V_2''(s)}{R_1 + R_2}$$

Eliminating $I_1(s)$ and $I_2(s)$ while substituting for the element values gives

$$V_2''(s) = \left(\frac{s}{s + 2}\right)\left(\frac{1}{s^3}\right)$$

Again, inverting to the time domain, we obtain

$$v_2''(t) = \left(\frac{1}{4} e^{-2t} + \frac{t}{2} - \frac{1}{4}\right) u_0(t)$$

Our total solution is therefore found using the superposition theorem, that is

$$v_2(t) = v_2'(t) + v_2''(t)$$

$$v_2(t) = \left[-\frac{2}{5} e^{-(1/2)t} + \frac{1}{4} e^{-2t} - \frac{1}{4} - \frac{1}{\sqrt{5}} \sin(t - 63.5°) + \frac{t}{2}\right] u_0(t)$$

The statement of the superposition theorem requires initial conditions be equal to zero. If initial conditions are not zero, we can represent the initial conditions as equivalent sources and then apply superposition. This procedure is illustrated in the following example.

*Example 13.2.3*

Calculate the driving-point current for the network in Fig. 13.2.5a by converting all initial conditions into equivalent sources and applying the superposition theorem. Assume $R_1 = 3\,\Omega$, $R_2 = 1\,\Omega$, $L = 2$h, $C = \frac{1}{2}$f, $V_0 = -1$ volt, $I_0 = 1$ amp and $v(t) = u_0(t)$.

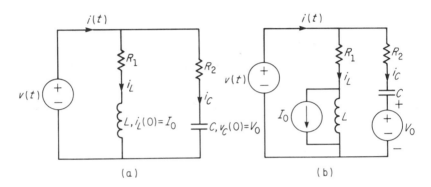

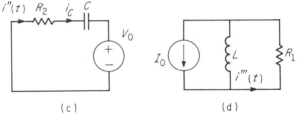

Fig. 13.2.5.

*Solution*

The initial conditions are shown converted into equivalent sources in Fig. 13.2.5b. With $I_0$ and $V_0$ set equal to zero we let $i(t) = i'(t)$, we then have the Laplace transform of $i(t)$ given by

$$I'(s) = V(s)\left\{\frac{1}{R_1 + sL} + \frac{1}{R_2 + \dfrac{1}{sC}}\right\}$$

Substituting for the parameter values gives

$$I'(s) = \frac{1}{s} \cdot \frac{s^2 + 2s + 1}{(s + \frac{3}{2})(s + 2)}$$

or, after inverting to the time domain, we obtain

$$i'(t) = (\tfrac{1}{3} + e^{-2t} - \tfrac{1}{3}e^{-(3/2)t})u_0(t)$$

Setting $v(t)$ and $I_0$ equal to zero gives the equivalent circuit shown in Fig. 13.2.5c. For this case we have

$$I''(s) = -\frac{V_0}{s\left(R_2 + \dfrac{1}{sC}\right)} = \frac{3}{s+2}$$

or inverting to the time domain, we have

$$i''(t) = 3e^{-2t}u_0(t)$$

Setting $v(t)$ and $V_0$ equal to zero gives the equivalent circuit shown in Fig. 13.2.5d. Using current division, the Laplace transform of the current $i'''(t)$ is given by

$$I'''(s) = \frac{I_0}{s} \cdot \frac{G_1}{G_1 + \dfrac{1}{sL}} = \frac{1}{s + \tfrac{3}{2}}$$

or inverting to the time domain, we have

$$i'''(t) = e^{-(3/2)t}u_0(t)$$

Using the superposition theorem, the current $i(t)$ is found from

$$i(t) = i'(t) + i''(t) + i'''(t)$$

Substituting these from above gives

$$i(t) = (\tfrac{1}{3} + 4e^{-2t} + \tfrac{2}{3}e^{-(3/2)t})u_0(t)$$

### 13.3.  RECIPROCITY

In this section we discuss an important property of linear time-invariant two port networks, namely, the reciprocity property. The implications of reciprocity can be used to simplify the analysis and design of this restricted class of networks. Let us first give a definition of reciprocal networks and then proceed with a discussion of their properties.

Consider the two terminal network shown in Fig. 13.3.1 and assume that this network is comprised of linear time-invariant elements. Let the voltage and current of ports 1 and 2 be denoted by $v_1$, $i_1$ and $v_2$, $i_2$ respectively. Since the network is linear time-invariant we can use Laplace transform to define its open-circuit impedance matrix $Z(s)$ through the

Fig. 13.3.1.

relationship

$$\begin{bmatrix} V_1(s) \\ V_2(s) \end{bmatrix} = \begin{bmatrix} z_{11}(s) & z_{12}(s) \\ z_{21}(s) & z_{22}(s) \end{bmatrix} \begin{bmatrix} I_1(s) \\ I_2(s) \end{bmatrix} \tag{13.3.1}$$

or

$$\mathbf{V}(s) = \mathbf{Z}(s)\mathbf{I}(s) \tag{13.3.2}$$

*DEFINITION.* A linear time-invariant two-port network is called *reciprocal* if its open-circuit impedance matrix, $\mathbf{Z}(s)$, is symmetric. This definition can be stated in terms of the short-circuit admittance matrix, $\mathbf{Y}(s)$. That is, a linear time-invariant two-port network is said to be reciprocal if its $\mathbf{Y}(s)$ matrix is symmetric.

*Example 13.3.1*

Consider the network shown in Fig. 13.3.2. Determine whether this network is reciprocal.

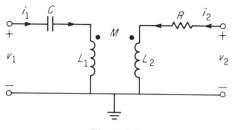

Fig. 13.3.2.

*Solution*

For this network we have

$$V_1(s) = \left( \frac{1}{sC} + sL_1 \right) I_1(s) + sMI_2(s)$$

$$V_2(s) = (R + sL_2) I_2(s) + sMI_1(s)$$

Then

$$\mathbf{Z}(s) = \begin{bmatrix} (1/sC) + sL_1 & sM \\ sM & R + sL_2 \end{bmatrix}$$

Hence the network under consideration is reciprocal.

*Example 13.3.2*

Consider the gyrator shown in Fig. 13.3.3. Show that the gyrator is not a reciprocal network.

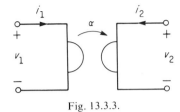

Fig. 13.3.3.

*Solution*

The *v-i* relation of this two-port network is given by

$$\begin{bmatrix} V_1 \\ V_2 \end{bmatrix} = \begin{bmatrix} 0 & \alpha \\ -\alpha & 0 \end{bmatrix} \begin{bmatrix} I_1 \\ I_2 \end{bmatrix}$$

Since, in general, $\alpha \neq -\alpha$, the gyrator is nonreciprocal.

*Example 13.3.3*

Consider the small-signal equivalent circuit of the common-emitter transistor shown in Fig. 13.3.4. Show that this network is nonreciprocal.

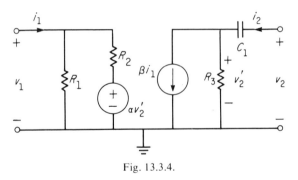

Fig. 13.3.4.

*Solution*

The $z_{12}$ and $z_{21}$ parameters for this network were found in Example 12.2.2 to be

$$z_{12} = \frac{\alpha R_3}{1 + G_1 R_2 - \alpha \beta G_1 R_3}$$

and

$$z_{21} = \frac{R_3 \beta G_1 (G_2 - \alpha \beta R_3)}{1 + G_1 R_2 - \alpha \beta R_3 G_1} - \beta R_3$$

Quite clearly, $z_{12} \neq z_{21}$, and hence the network under study is non-reciprocal.

Notice that the nonreciprocity of the network shown in Fig. 13.3.4 is due to the dependent voltage and current sources. Networks containing dependent sources are, generally, nonreciprocal, although it is quite easy to construct networks composed of linear time-invariant elements and dependent sources that are reciprocal. There is, however, a certain class of networks that are always reciprocal. This class of networks is described in the following theorem.

*THEOREM.* A two-port network comprised of linear time-invariant resistors, capacitors and inductors (coupled or uncoupled) is always reciprocal.

This result is quite general; regardless of the manner by which the *RLC* elements are interconnected, the resulting two-port network is reciprocal. A rigorous proof of this theorem can be given using Tellegen's theorem given in Chapter 14. At this stage, however, we concern ourselves only with the implication of the reciprocity principle. Next we state some of the properties of reciprocal networks.

**Properties of Reciprocal Networks**

1. Consider the two-port network $N$ shown in Fig. 13.3.5. In Fig. 13.3.5a, port 2 is excited with a current source $I_2$ and port 1 is open-circuited; the voltage across port 1 is denoted by $V_1$. In Fig. 13.3.5b, port 1 is excited with a current source $\hat{I}_1$ and port 2 is open-circuited; the voltage across port 2 is denoted by $\hat{V}_2$.

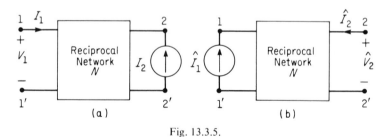

Fig. 13.3.5.

Now assume that the network $N$ is reciprocal and all the initial conditions are zero; then the reciprocity implies that

$$\text{if } \hat{I}_1 = I_2 \quad \text{then} \quad V_1 = \hat{V}_2 \tag{13.3.3}$$

*Proof.* To show this let us use the open-circuit impedance parameters. From Fig. 13.3.5a, since $I_1 = 0$, we get

$$V_1(s) = z_{12}(s) I_2(s) \tag{13.3.4}$$

and from Fig. 13.3.5b, since $\hat{I}_2 = 0$, we get

$$\hat{V}_2(s) = z_{21}(s) \hat{I}_1(s) \tag{13.3.5}$$

Now, since the network is reciprocal, $z_{12}(s) = z_{21}(s)$. Hence, from Eqs. 13.3.4 and 13.3.5, if $\hat{I}_1(s) = I_2(s)$, it follows that $V_1(s) = \hat{V}_2(s)$.

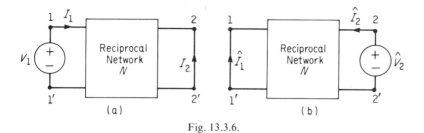

Fig. 13.3.6.

2. Consider the two-port network $N$ shown in Fig. 13.3.6. Assume that $N$ is a linear time-invariant $RLC$ reciprocal network and all the initial conditions are zero, then

$$\text{if } V_1 = \hat{V}_2 \quad \text{then} \quad I_2 = \hat{I}_1 \qquad (13.3.6)$$

*Proof.* In order to prove this result consider the short-circuit admittance parameters. Figure 13.3.6a yields

$$I_2(s) = y_{21}(s) V_1(s) \qquad (13.3.7)$$

and from Fig. 13.3.6b we obtain

$$\hat{I}_1(s) = y_{12}(s) \hat{V}_2(s) \qquad (13.3.8)$$

consequently if $V_1 = \hat{V}_2$ then $I_2 = \hat{I}_1$ since by assumption $y_{12} = y_{21}$.

Notice that in order to check the properties stated above the network must be either under current-excitation voltage response or voltage-excitation current response. In other words, it is not possible to test reciprocity of a network by voltage-excitation voltage response, or by current-excitation current response. Hence, for example we cannot classify the ideal transformer given in Fig. 13.3.7 as a reciprocal two-port.

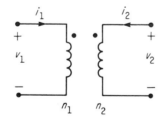

Fig. 13.3.7. Ideal transformer;

$$\frac{v_1}{v_2} = \frac{n_1}{n_2} \quad \text{and} \quad \frac{i_1}{i_2} = -\frac{n_2}{n_1}.$$

## 13.4. OTHER NETWORK THEOREMS—EQUIVALENT NETWORKS

We have seen in earlier chapters that two networks can be viewed as equivalent if their terminal voltage-current relationships are identical. We have used this concept to develop relationships for interchanging cur-

rent and voltage sources, and for representing initial conditions as independent sources. We now wish to generalize on this concept to develop
equivalence relationships which can be used to simplify some network
analysis problems.

### Thevenin's Equivalent Network

Consider the network of Fig. 13.4.1. A portion of the network has
been isolated and designated as the load. It is desired to calculate the
voltage $v_L$ and current $i_L$ which together describe the load terminal charac-

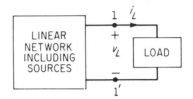

Fig. 13.4.1. Calculating the load response.

teristics. General cut-set and loop-analysis methods can be applied to
solve this problem. However, the solution can possibly be simplified by
representing the linear network to the left of terminals 1, 1' by an equivalent linear element in series with an equivalent voltage source as indicated
in Fig. 13.4.2. The problem is to develop a procedure for calculating

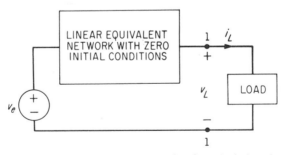

Fig. 13.4.2. Equivalent representation for calculating the
load response.

$v_e$ and determining the equivalent linear network. We will assume, for
convenience, the load and linear network are time invariant so that the
Laplace transform can be employed. Consider first the effect of changing
the load impedance function $Z_L(s)$. As shown in Fig. 13.4.3a and b, if
the load impedance is increased by $\Delta R$, the net change as seen at terminals
1, 1' is zero provided the current source

$$I(s) = \frac{\Delta R}{Z_L(s) + \Delta R} I_L(s) \tag{13.4.1}$$

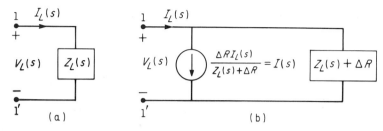

Fig. 13.4.3. (a) Load network, (b) equivalent load network after changing load impedance.

is added in parallel to the load. In either case, the terminal current is $I_L(s)$ and the terminal voltage is

$$V_L(s) = \left[ I_L(s) - \frac{\Delta R}{Z_L(s) + \Delta R} I_L(s) \right] (Z_L(s) + \Delta R) = I_L(s) Z_L(s)$$

$$(13.4.2)$$

With the equivalent load network connected at terminals 1, 1' in the network of Fig. 13.4.1, we obtain the network shown in Fig. 13.4.4a. Letting $\Delta R \to \infty$, the resulting equivalent network is illustrated in Fig. 13.4.4b,

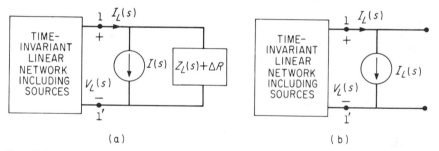

Fig. 13.4.4. (a) Equivalent network with $\Delta R$ change in $Z_L(s)$; (b) equivalent with $\Delta R \to \infty$.

the net result being that $Z_L(s)$ is replaced by a current generator of value $I_L(s)$. At the terminals 1, 1' the two circuits are equivalent. The voltage $V_L(s)$ can now be calculated as the sum of two parts using the superposition theorem. To calculate the first part, we set all independent sources to the left of terminals 1, 1' equal to zero (recall that any initial conditions are represented by independent sources in applying superposition). This gives the network shown in Fig. 13.4.5a. Obviously for this case we have

$$V'_L(s) = -I_L(s) Z_e(s) \qquad (13.4.3)$$

where $Z_e(s)$ is the equivalent impedance function looking into the network from terminals 1, 1' with all independent sources set equal to zero. To

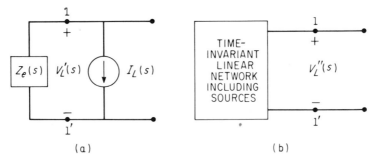

Fig. 13.4.5. (a) Calculating $V'_L(s)$, (b) calculating $V''_L(s)$.

calculate the second part of the solution, we set $I_L(s)$ to zero and calculate the resultant voltage $V''_L(s)$. Obviously, from Fig. 13.4.5b this is just the voltage at terminals 1, 1' when the terminals are open-circuited. Let us define this voltage as $V_{oc}(s)$, then

$$V''_L(s) = V_{oc}(s) \tag{13.4.4}$$

These two solutions together give

$$V_L(s) = V_{oc}(s) - I_L(s) Z_e(s) \tag{13.4.5}$$

Comparing this result with the form of the network shown in Fig. 13.4.2, we see that Eq. 13.4.5 represents the network shown in Fig. 13.4.6. The

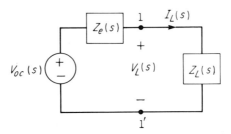

Fig. 13.4.6. Network equivalent of Eq. 13.4.5.

network to the left of 1, 1' is called *Thevenin's equivalent network*. In summary, we have three steps in calculating Thevenin's equivalent network:

1. Represent all initial conditions by independent sources.
2. Disconnect $Z_L(s)$ from the network, set all independent sources equal to zero, and solve for the network impedance function as viewed from terminals 1, 1' to obtain $Z_e(s)$.
3. Calculate the voltage which appears at the open circuited terminals 1, 1' to obtain $V_{oc}(s)$.

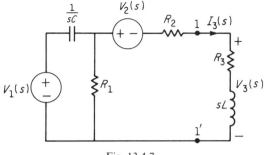

Fig. 13.4.7.

*Example 13.4.1*

Use Thevenin's equivalent network to calculate the voltage $V_3(s)$ in Fig. 13.4.7. Assume zero initial conditions.

*Solution*

To calculate $V_{oc}(s)$ and $Z_e(s)$ we use the networks shown in Fig. 13.4.8a and Fig. 13.4.8b respectively. These calculations yield

$$V_{oc}(s) = \frac{sR_1C}{sR_1C + 1} V_1(s) - V_2(s)$$

and

$$Z_e(s) = R_2 + \frac{R_1}{sR_1C + 1}$$

The solution is then

$$V_3(s) = \frac{Z_3(s)}{Z_3(s) + Z_e(s)} V_{oc}(s)$$

where $Z_3(s) = R_3 + sL$. Substituting, we get

$$V_3(s) = \frac{R_3 + sL}{R_3 + sL + R_2 + \dfrac{R_1}{sR_1C + 1}} \left( \frac{sR_1C}{sR_1C + 1} V_1(s) - V_2(s) \right)$$

which is the required result.

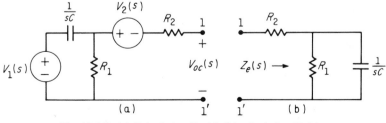

Fig. 13.4.8.  (a) Calculating $V_{oc}(s)$, (b) calculating $Z_e(s)$.

## Norton's Equivalent Network

In Thevenin's equivalent network, the result is a voltage source in series with an impedance. From previous work we might suspect a network representation in terms of a current source in parallel with an admittance. Such a representation is shown in Fig. 13.4.9. The network

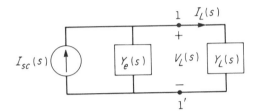

Fig. 13.4.9. Norton's equivalent circuit.

to the left of terminals 1, 1' is known as *Norton's equivalent network*. This representation can be derived in a manner similar to that just used for deriving Thevenin's equivalent network (see Prob. 13.7). Again, three steps are taken in calculating the network:

1.  Represent all initial conditions by independent sources.
2.  Disconnect $Y_L(s)$ from the network, set all independent sources equal to zero, and solve for the network admittance function as viewed from terminals 1, 1' to obtain $Y_e(s)$.
3.  Calculate the current which appears at the short-circuited terminals 1, 1' to obtain $I_{sc}(s)$.

It should be noted (see Prob. 13.8), the results known as Thevenin's and Norton's theorems can be obtained under more general conditions. In particular, the load need not be linear and the remaining network need not be time-invariant. Of course, in this situation, the impedance and admittance functions are not useful. To prove and utilize the more general result a time domain analysis is required.

*Example 13.4.2*

Use Norton's equivalent network to calculate the current $I_3(s)$ in Fig. 13.4.7.

*Solution*

We use the networks in Fig. 13.4.10a and Fig. 13.4.10b to calculate $I_{sc}(s)$ and $Y_e(s)$ respectively. These give

$$I_{sc}(s) = \frac{sR_1C}{R_1 + sR_1R_2C + R_2} V_1(s) - \frac{(sR_1C + 1)}{sCR_1R_2 + R_2 + R_1} V_2(s)$$

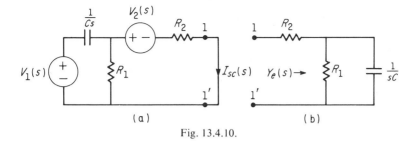

Fig. 13.4.10.

and

$$Y_e(s) = \frac{sR_1C + 1}{sR_1R_2C + R_1 + R_2}$$

The solution for $I_3(s)$ is

$$I_3(s) = I_{sc}(s)\,\frac{Y_3(s)}{Y_3(s) + Y_e(s)}$$

where

$$Y_3(s) = \frac{1}{R_3 + sL}$$

## T-π Equivalent Networks

Network simplification is sometimes possible by use of $T$-$\pi$ (or $Y$-$\Delta$) conversion. This concept is illustrated in Fig. 13.4.11. Recall that two-port networks are equivalent at their ports provided either the open-

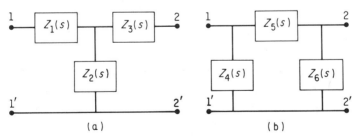

Fig. 13.4.11. (a) $T$ network, (b) $\pi$ network.

circuit impedance parameters or the short-circuit admittance parameters are equal in each case. For Fig. 13.4.11a we have

$$z_{11}(s) = Z_1(s) + Z_2(s)$$
$$z_{22}(s) = Z_2(s) + Z_3(s)$$
$$z_{12}(s) = z_{21}(s) = Z_2(s) \tag{13.4.6}$$

Similarly, for Fig. 13.4.11b, we have

$$z_{11}(s) = \frac{Z_4(s)[Z_5(s) + Z_6(s)]}{Z_4(s) + Z_5(s) + Z_6(s)}$$

$$z_{22}(s) = \frac{Z_6(s)[Z_4(s) + Z_5(s)]}{Z_4(s) + Z_5(s) + Z_6(s)}$$

$$z_{21}(s) = z_{12}(s) = \frac{Z_4(s) Z_6(s)}{Z_4(s) + Z_5(s) + Z_6(s)} \tag{13.4.7}$$

Equating identical terms in Eq. 13.4.6 with Eq. 13.4.7, the $T$ and $\pi$ networks are made equivalent by requiring

$$Z_1(s) = \frac{Z_4(s) Z_5(s)}{Z_4(s) + Z_5(s) + Z_6(s)}$$

$$Z_2(s) = \frac{Z_4(s) Z_6(s)}{Z_4(s) + Z_5(s) + Z_6(s)}$$

$$Z_3(s) = \frac{Z_5(s) Z_6(s)}{Z_4(s) + Z_5(s) + Z_6(s)} \tag{13.4.8}$$

or equivalently, by requiring

$$Z_4(s) = \frac{Z_1(s) Z_2(s) + Z_2(s) Z_3(s) + Z_3(s) Z_1(s)}{Z_3(s)}$$

$$Z_5(s) = \frac{Z_1(s) Z_2(s) + Z_2(s) Z_3(s) + Z_3(s) Z_1(s)}{Z_2(s)}$$

$$Z_6(s) = \frac{Z_1(s) Z_2(s) + Z_2(s) Z_3(s) + Z_3(s) Z_1(s)}{Z_1(s)} \tag{13.4.9}$$

Equations 13.4.8 and 13.4.9 represent the conversion relationship between equivalent $T$ and $\pi$ networks.

*Example 13.4.3*

Derive a $T$ and equivalent $\pi$ network for a transformer with self-inductance values $L$, mutual inductance $M$ and resistance $R$ as shown in Fig. 13.4.12.

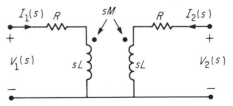

Fig. 13.4.12. Transformer network.

*Solution*

As we have seen previously, for this network

$$z_{11}(s) = R + sL$$
$$z_{12}(s) = z_{21}(s) = sM$$
$$z_{22}(s) = R + sL$$

Using Eq. 13.4.6, we have

$$R + sL = Z_1(s) + Z_2(s)$$
$$sM = Z_2(s)$$
$$R + sL = Z_2(s) + Z_3(s)$$

Hence

$$Z_1(s) = Z_3(s) = R + s(L - M)$$
$$Z_2(s) = sM$$

This network is shown in Fig. 13.4.13.

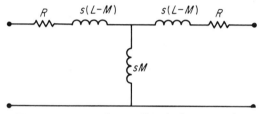

Fig. 13.4.13.  Transformer $T$ equivalent network.

Using $Z_1(s)$, $Z_2(s)$, and $Z_3(s)$ obtained above in Eq. 13.4.9, we obtain

$$Z_4(s) = Z_6(s) = s(L + M) + R$$
$$Z_5(s) = s\left(\frac{L^2}{M} - M\right) + \frac{2RL}{M} + \frac{R^2}{sM}$$

The equivalent $\pi$ network is shown in Fig. 13.4.14.

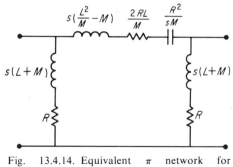

Fig.    13.4.14.  Equivalent    $\pi$    network    for transformer.

**PROBLEMS**

**13.1.** For the circuit shown, show that the response, $v_R(t)$ is *not* the super-position of responses due to the two sources. Why is superposition not valid in this case? Draw an equivalent network such that the superposition theorem can be applied.

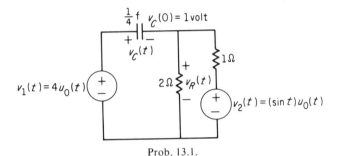

Prob. 13.1.

**13.2.** For the network shown verify the superposition theorem by calculating the current $i_{R_1}(t)$. All initial conditions are zero.

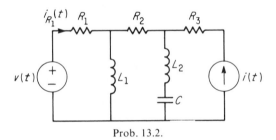

Prob. 13.2.

**13.3.** Show that the network shown in Prob. 13.2 is reciprocal.
**13.4.** For the network shown, verify the reciprocity property by (a) calculating the response with a load connected across terminals 3,4 and a matched source connected across terminals 1, 2, and (b) interchanging load and matched source position and recalculating the response. Take $Z_L = 5\,\Omega$, $v(t) = tu_0(t)$.

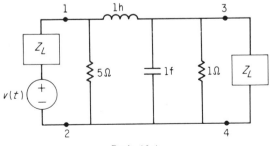

Prob. 13.4.

**13.5.** Using the network shown in Part (*a*) derive Norton's equivalent network shown in Fig. 13.4.9. [*Hint:* Show that the networks in Parts (b) and (c) are equivalent.]

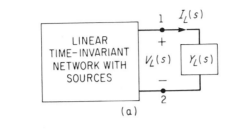

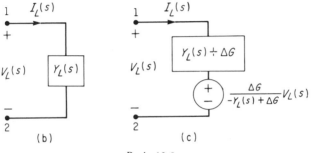

Prob. 13.5.

**13.6.** It can be shown that any network branch element with branch voltage $v(t)$ and branch current $i(t)$ can be replaced by (1) a current source $i(t)$ without affecting the branch voltage $v(t)$, or (2) a voltage source $v(t)$ without affecting the branch current $i(t)$. This result is known as the *substitution theorem.* Using the substitution theorem, derive (a) Thevenin's equivalent network, (b) Norton's equivalent network, for the network shown.

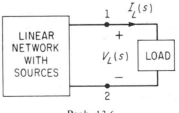

Prob. 13.6.

**13.7.** For the network shown,
   (1) Calculate Thévenin's equivalent network.
   (2) Calculate Norton's equivalent network.

(3) Convert Thevenin's equivalent to a current generator in parallel with an admittance function. Is this the same as Norton's equivalent network? Will this result generally hold true? Explain.

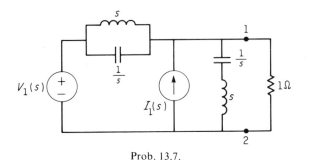

Prob. 13.7.

**13.8.** Develop Norton's equivalent network and Thevenin's equivalent network for the network shown. For each case find $I_L(s)$.

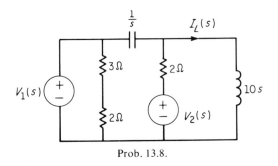

Prob. 13.8.

**13.9.** Derive the equivalent $T$ and $\pi$ networks for the transformer shown.

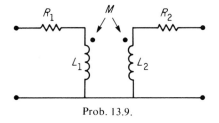

Prob. 13.9.

**13.10.** Using $\pi$-$T$ conversion, put the network shown in (a) into the form in (b) and thus solve for the current $i(t)$.

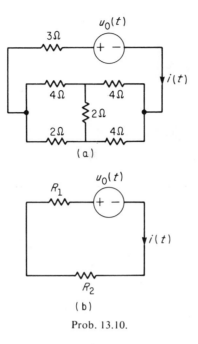

Prob. 13.10.

**13.11.** Show that for a reciprocal two-port network

$$h_{12}(s) = -h_{21}(s)$$

## CHAPTER 14

# Large-Scale Networks

## 14.1. INTRODUCTION

In Chapter 2 some elementary network topology was introduced, and it was shown that using the basic concepts of graph theory we can write a set of linearly independent integrodifferential equations which can be solved for the desired currents or voltages of the network under consideration. These sets of independent equations could have been written by inspection, since the networks under consideration were rather simple and the examples considered involved only a few elements. In today's electronic circuits, however, it is not difficult to find circuits that contain hundreds of elements, particularly with the advent of integrated circuits and microcircuits. For this class of "large-scale" networks it is almost impossible to write a set of linearly independent equations by inspection or by mere intuition. A systematic and step-by-step method is therefore required to deal with such networks.

In this chapter we use the graph-theory approach to write a set of linearly independent loop and node equations that can be solved for the voltages and the currents in a large-scale network. The emphasis of course will be on representing these equations in a form that is suitable for computer solution. In this chapter we first introduce some basic concepts of graph theory (Sec. 14.2) and then present a systematic method for obtaining the incidence matrix, fundamental loop matrix, and the solution of node and loop equations (Sec. 14.3). In Sec. 14.4 we define the normal tree and outline a method for writing the state equations for networks containing loops of capacitors and cutsets of inductors.

## 14.2. BASIC DEFINITIONS AND NOTATIONS

In this section we introduce the basic definitions that are instrumental in the study of graph theory. Consider a network $\mathfrak{N}$ consisting of resistors, inductors, capacitors and ideal sources. Let us represent each element of this network, regardless of its nature, with a line segment called a *branch* (or an edge) and represent the end points of each element by a dot called a *node* (or a vertex). The collection of these branches and nodes is called the *graph* of the network $\mathfrak{N}$ and is denoted by $G$. The following example illustrates these concepts.

*Example 14.2.1*

Consider the network shown in Fig. 14.2.1a. Let us label the elements of this network arbitrarily $b_1, b_2, \ldots, b_9$ and the end points $n_1, n_2, \ldots, n_6$. The corresponding graph $G$ is then given in Fig. 14.2.1b.

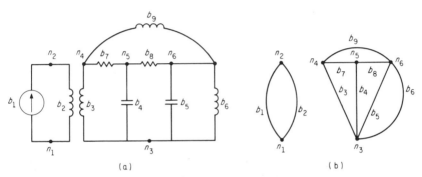

Fig. 14.2.1. (a) Network $\mathfrak{N}$, (b) the graph $G$ of the network.

In this example each branch is associated with two nodes; for instance, the branch $b_1$ is associated with the nodes $n_1$ and $n_2$ and the branch $b_9$ is associated with nodes $n_4$ and $n_6$. In general we can say that the branch $b_k$ is associated with the nodes $n_i$ and $n_j$ where $i$, $j$, $k$ are integers. With this background we can now give a precise definition of a node, a branch, and a graph.

*NODE.*    A node is defined to be an end point of a line segment or an isolated point.

*BRANCH.*    A branch $b_k$ is a line segment associated with two nodes $n_i$ and $n_j$. The branch $b_k$ is said to be *incident* to the nodes $n_i$ and $n_j$.

*GRAPH.*    A graph is a collection of nodes and branches such that the branches intersect each other only at the nodes.

The set of all the branches in a graph is usually denoted by $E = (b_1, \ldots, b_B)$ and the set of all the nodes is denoted by $V = (n_1\, n_2, \ldots, n_{N+1})$; the graph $G$ is then denoted by $G(V, E)$. $B$ is the number of branches and $N + 1$ is the number of nodes.

If we assign a direction to each branch of a graph then the resulting graph is called an *oriented* graph or a *directed* graph. As an example consider the simple circuit shown in Fig. 14.2.2a. Arrows in this circuit

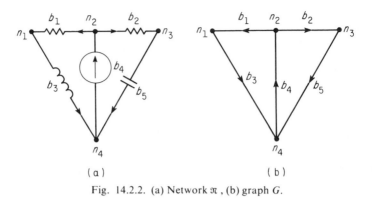

Fig. 14.2.2. (a) Network $\pi$, (b) graph $G$.

indicate the direction of the currents.  The oriented graph corresponding to this circuit is given in Fig. 14.2.2b.

The branch $b_1$, for instance, is said to leave the node $n_2$ and to enter the node $n_1$.

*DEGREE OF A NODE.*    The degree of a node $n_i$ of a graph $G$ is the number of the branches incident to $n_i$. For example in Fig. 14.2.2b, the degree of $n_1$ and $n_3$ is two and the degree of $n_2$ and $n_4$ is three.

*SUBGRAPH.*    A graph $G_1(V_1, E_1)$ is said to be a subgraph of a graph $G(V, E)$ if $V_1$ is a subset of $V$ and if $E_1$ is a subset of $E$.  That is, every node of $G_1$ is a node of $G$ and every branch of $G_1$ is a branch of $G$. Some subgraphs of the graph of Fig. 14.2.2b are shown in Fig. 14.2.3.

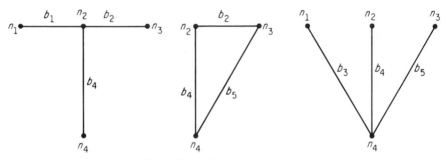

Fig. 14.2.3. Three subgraphs of $G$.

*PATH.*    For a given graph $G$, a path is a set of nodes and branches with the property that exactly two branches of this set are incident to each node of the set with the exception of the initial and terminal nodes.

In Fig. 14.2.2b, for instance, branches $b_5, b_4, b_1$ together with nodes $n_3, n_4, n_2$ and $n_1$ form a path.  Also branches $b_4$ and $b_2$ together with nodes $n_4, n_2,$ and $n_3$ form a path.  These paths are redrawn in Fig. 14.2.4.

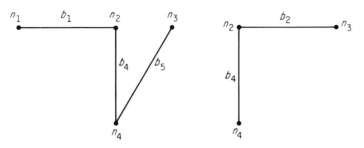

Fig. 14.2.4. Two paths of G.

*LOOP.*   For a graph $G$, if the initial and terminal nodes of a path coincide, the resulting *closed path* is called a *loop*. For example in graph $G$ of Fig. 14.2.2b the following paths are loops:

| | |
|---|---|
| branches $b_5, b_4, b_2$ | and nodes $n_3, n_4, n_2$ |
| branches $b_3, b_1, b_4$ | and nodes $n_4, n_1, n_2$ |
| branches $b_1, b_2, b_5, b_3$ | and nodes $n_1, n_2, n_3, n_4$ |

*CONNECTED GRAPH.*   A graph $G(V,E)$ is said to be connected if there is at least one path between any two nodes of the graph. The graph of Fig. 14.2.2b is a connected graph; given any two nodes in this graph we can find at least one path connecting these nodes. The graph of Fig. 12.2.1b is not connected since there is no path connecting nodes $n_1$ and $n_2$ with the rest of the nodes. Separate subgraphs of a nonconnected graph are called *disjoint graphs*. More precisely; two graphs are said to be disjoint if they have no node in common. Next we define the concepts of a tree and a cotree. These concepts and related topics play an important role in the study of large-scale networks.

*TREE.*   A tree $T$ of a connected graph $G$ is a connected subgraph of $G$ with the following properties:

(i)   $T$ contains all the nodes of $G$
(ii)   $T$ does not contain any loop.

The branches of a tree are called *tree branches*.

*COTREE.*   A cotree of a tree $T$ with respect to a graph $G$ is that part of $G$ which is not in $T$. The branches of the cotree of $T$ are called *chords* of $T$.

*Example 14.2.2*

Consider the network $\mathfrak{N}$ and its corresponding graph $G$ shown in Fig. 14.2.5a. Two typical trees of this graph are shown in Fig. 14.2.5b and 14.2.5c. Tree branches are drawn with solid lines and chords are drawn with broken lines. In Fig. 14.2.5b branches $b_2, b_4, b_7, b_8, b_9$ form a tree and the remaining branches (chords) form the corresponding cotree.

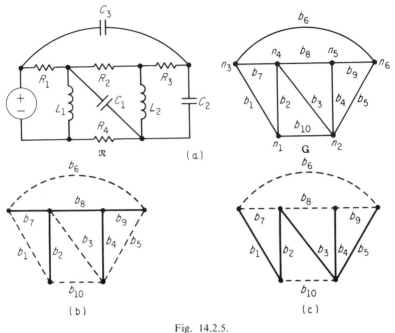

Fig. 14.2.5.

In Fig. 14.2.5c branches $b_1$, $b_2$, $b_3$, $b_4$, $b_5$ form a tree and chords $b_6$, $b_7$, $b_8$, $b_9$, $b_{10}$ form the corresponding cotree.

*CUTSET.* A cutset of a connected graph $G$ is a set of the minimum number of branches whose removal will separate the graph into two disjoint subgraphs.

As an example of cutsets consider the following sets of branches in the graph $G$ of Fig. 14.2.5a: $(b_1, b_7, b_6)$, $(b_1, b_2, b_3, b_4, b_5)$, $(b_1, b_7, b_9, b_5)$ and $(b_6, b_8, b_3, b_{10})$. The removal of each of these sets of branches will cause the connected graph $G$ to be broken into two disjoint subgraphs.

The concept of tree, cotree and cutset will be used extensively in the remainder of this chapter; we use these concepts to write a set of linearly independent loop or node equations. In the next section we show how a graph $G$ can be represented as a matrix.

## 14.3 MATRIX REPRESENTATION OF A GRAPH

In this section we introduce a method of representing a directed graph by a matrix. This form of representation of a graph is extremely important in the analytical studies of a graph, particularly in the computer-aided analysis and synthesis of large scale networks. To a given oriented graph we can associate several matrices; we begin by defining the augmented incidence matrix.

Suppose that a given oriented graph consists of $N + 1$ nodes and $B$ branches. Let us label the branches of this graph arbitrarily $b_1, b_2, \ldots, b_B$ also let us label the nodes arbitrarily by $n_1, n_2, \ldots, n_{N+1}$. Then we have the following definition:

*AUGMENTED INCIDENCE MATRIX.* An $(N + 1) \times B$ matrix:

$$\mathbf{A}_a = (a_{ij})$$

is said to be the augmented incidence matrix of a directed graph $G$ if:

$a_{ij} = 1$ when the branch $b_j$ is incident to the node $n_i$ and is directed *away from it.*

$a_{ij} = -1$ when the branch $b_j$ is incident to the node $n_i$ and is directed toward it.

$a_{ij} = 0$ when the branch $b_j$ is not incident to the node $n_i$.

*Example 14.3.1*

Consider the network $\mathfrak{N}$ and its corresponding graph shown in Fig. 14.3.1. The branches of this graph are numbered $b_1$ through $b_7$ and the

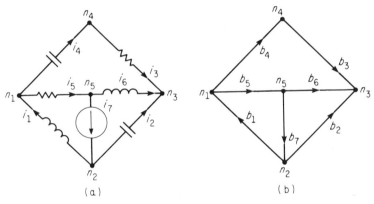

Fig. 14.3.1.

nodes are numbered $n_1$ through $n_5$. The augmented incidence matrix of this graph, therefore, has five rows and seven columns; let us label these rows and columns by $n_1, n_2, \ldots, n_5$ and $b_1, b_2, \ldots, b_7$ respectively.

The corresponding augmented incidence matrix is:

$$\mathbf{A}_a = \begin{array}{c} \\ n_1 \\ n_2 \\ n_3 \\ n_4 \\ n_5 \end{array} \begin{array}{c} \begin{array}{ccccccc} b_1 & b_2 & b_3 & b_4 & b_5 & b_6 & b_7 \end{array} \\ \left[ \begin{array}{ccccccc} -1 & 0 & 0 & 1 & 1 & 0 & 0 \\ 1 & 1 & 0 & 0 & 0 & 0 & -1 \\ 0 & -1 & -1 & 0 & 0 & -1 & 0 \\ 0 & 0 & 1 & -1 & 0 & 0 & 0 \\ 0 & 0 & 0 & 0 & -1 & 1 & 1 \end{array} \right] \end{array} \qquad (14.3.1)$$

It is interesting to notice that each column of $\mathbf{A}_a$ has exactly two nonzero elements, one of which is $+1$ and the other $-1$. This is because each branch of the graph $G$ is incident to exactly two nodes of $G$.

### Node Equations

In order to see the basic properties of the augmented incidence matrix $\mathbf{A}_a$ let us first focus our attention on writing Kirchhoff's current law (KCL) for the nodes of the network $\mathfrak{N}$ discussed in Example 14.3.1. The KCL equations for the network shown in Fig. 14.3.1a are:

$$
\begin{aligned}
\text{node } n_1: && -i_1 + i_4 + i_5 &= 0 \\
\text{node } n_2: && i_1 + i_2 - i_7 &= 0 \\
\text{node } n_3: && -i_2 - i_3 - i_6 &= 0 \\
\text{node } n_4: && i_3 - i_4 &= 0 \\
\text{node } n_5: && -i_5 + i_6 + i_7 &= 0
\end{aligned}
\tag{14.3.2}
$$

We can represent these equations in the following matrix form

$$
\begin{bmatrix}
-1 & 0 & 0 & 1 & 1 & 0 & 0 \\
1 & 1 & 0 & 0 & 0 & 0 & -1 \\
0 & -1 & -1 & 0 & 0 & -1 & 0 \\
0 & 0 & 1 & -1 & 0 & 0 & 0 \\
0 & 0 & 0 & 0 & -1 & 1 & 1
\end{bmatrix}
\begin{bmatrix}
i_1 \\ i_2 \\ i_3 \\ i_4 \\ i_5 \\ i_6 \\ i_7
\end{bmatrix}
= \mathbf{0}
\tag{14.3.3}
$$

If we now denote

$$\mathbf{i}_b \triangleq [i_1 \quad i_2 \quad i_3 \quad i_4 \quad i_5 \quad i_6 \quad i_7]^T$$

and compare Eqs. 14.3.3 and 14.3.1, we immediately recognize that the matrix in the left-hand side of equation (14.3.3) is identical to $\mathbf{A}_a$. Equation 14.3.3 then can be written

$$\mathbf{A}_a \mathbf{i}_b = 0 \tag{14.3.4}$$

Although this equation was derived for the specific network of Fig. 14.3.1, the result is completely general and is true for any network.

A quick look at Eqs. 14.3.2 reveals that these equations are not linearly independent, for example equation $n_5$ can be obtained by adding equations $n_1$ through $n_4$. Therefore the rows of $\mathbf{A}_a$ are not linearly independent. This implies that the rank of $\mathbf{A}_a$ is less than $N + 1$; by adding the first $N$ rows of $\mathbf{A}_a$ to the last row we obtain a row of zeros in $\mathbf{A}_a$. Consequently, the rank of $\mathbf{A}_a$ is at most $N$. In fact it can be shown that the rank of $\mathbf{A}_a$ is exactly $N$. Then we can draw the following conclusion:

*The rank of the augmented incidence matrix $\mathbf{A}_a$ of a connected graph with N + 1 nodes and B branches is N.*

Now let us make use of this property of $\mathbf{A}_a$ and define another matrix whose rank is the same as $\mathbf{A}_a$ and is obtained from $\mathbf{A}_a$ by deleting any one row. This matrix is called the *incidence matrix* of the network $\mathfrak{N}$ and is denoted by $\mathbf{A}$. Equation 14.3.4 therefore, can be written

$$\mathbf{A}\mathbf{i}_b = 0 \tag{14.3.5}$$

This equation represents a set of *linearly independent* equations. The node corresponding to the deleted row of $\mathbf{A}_a$ is called the reference node or *datum*. In Example 14.3.1, if we take the node $n_2$ as the reference node, the matrix $\mathbf{A}$ is obtained from $\mathbf{A}_a$ by deleting the second row:

$$\mathbf{A} = \begin{bmatrix} -1 & 0 & 0 & 1 & 1 & 0 & 0 \\ 0 & -1 & -1 & 0 & 0 & -1 & 0 \\ 0 & 0 & 1 & -1 & 0 & 0 & 0 \\ 0 & 0 & 0 & 0 & -1 & 1 & 1 \end{bmatrix}$$

In summary: a network $\mathfrak{N}$ with $N + 1$ nodes and $B$ branches has $N$ linearly independent node equations. To obtain these independent node equations we first form the augmented incidence matrix $\mathbf{A}_a$ then we obtain the incidence matrix $\mathbf{A}$ by deleting any one row of $\mathbf{A}_a$. The linearly independent node equations (KCL equations) are then given by Eq. 14.3.5, where $\mathbf{A}$ is an $N \times B$ matrix with rank $N$.

It should be emphasized at this point that the number of the components of the vector $\mathbf{i}_b$ is equal to the number of the branches of $\mathfrak{N}$.

Another important matrix of a graph $G$ is the loop matrix. This matrix specifies the relation among the branches and the loops of a graph. Suppose that a given oriented graph consists of $B$ branches and $L$ loops. Let us label the branches arbitrarily $b_1$, $b_2, \ldots, b_B$ and the loops $l_1$, $l_2, \ldots, l_L$. Assume an arbitrary orientation for each loop, then we have the following definition:

*AUGMENTED LOOP MATRIX.*   An $L \times B$ matrix

$$\mathbf{B}_a = (b_{ij})$$

is said to be the *augumented loop matrix* of a directed graph $G$ with $B$ branches and $L$ loops if

$b_{ij} = 1$ when the branch $b_j$ is in the loop $l_i$ and is oriented in the same direction.

$b_{ij} = -1$ when the branch $b_j$ is in the loop $l_i$ and is oriented in the opposite direction.

$b_{ij} = 0$ when the branch $b_j$ is not in loop $l_i$.

*Example 14.3.2*

Consider the network $\mathfrak{N}$ and its corresponding graph shown in Fig. 14.3.2. There are six branches and three loops in graph $G$ shown in

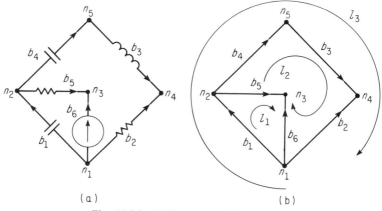

Fig. 14.3.2. (a) Network $\mathfrak{n}$, (b) graph $G$.

Fig. 14.3.2b:

$$l_1: \quad (b_1, b_5, b_6)$$
$$l_2: \quad (b_5, b_4, b_3, b_2, b_6)$$
$$l_3: \quad (b_4, b_3, b_2, b_1)$$

Let us assume that all these three loops are clockwise-oriented. Then the augmented loop matrix of this graph is

$$\mathbf{B}_a = \begin{array}{c} \\ l_1 \\ l_2 \\ l_3 \end{array} \begin{array}{cccccc} b_1 & b_2 & b_3 & b_4 & b_5 & b_6 \\ \left[\begin{array}{cccccc} 1 & 0 & 0 & 0 & 1 & -1 \\ 0 & -1 & 1 & 1 & -1 & 1 \\ 1 & -1 & 1 & 1 & 0 & 0 \end{array}\right] \end{array} \qquad (14.3.6)$$

**Loop Equations**

In order to see the role of the augmented loop matrix in the formulation of loop equations we write the Kirchhoff's voltage law (KVL) equations for each loop of the network shown in Fig. 14.3.2. Let us assume that the arrows in the graph G of Fig. 14.3.2b indicate the direction of the voltage drop in each branch. Let us also assume that the voltage drop in branch $b_j$ is $v_j$, i.e., the voltage drop in branch $b_1$ is $v_1$ and in branch $b_2$ is $v_2$, etc. Then the KVL equations for the network under consideration are

$$\begin{array}{ll} \text{loop } l_1: & v_1 + v_5 - v_6 = 0 \\ \text{loop } l_2: & -v_2 + v_3 + v_4 - v_5 + v_6 = 0 \\ \text{loop } l_3: & v_1 - v_2 + v_3 + v_4 = 0 \end{array} \qquad (14.3.7)$$

Putting these equations in matrix form we get

$$
\begin{bmatrix}
1 & 0 & 0 & 0 & 1 & -1 \\
0 & -1 & 1 & 1 & -1 & 1 \\
1 & -1 & 1 & 1 & 0 & 0
\end{bmatrix}
\begin{bmatrix}
v_1 \\ v_2 \\ v_3 \\ v_4 \\ v_5 \\ v_6
\end{bmatrix} = 0
\qquad (14.3.8)
$$

The $3 \times 6$ matrix in the left-hand side of Eq. 14.3.8 is then seen to be identical to $\mathbf{B}_a$ given in Eq. 14.3.6. Now if we denote

$$
\mathbf{v}_b \triangleq [v_1 \quad v_2 \quad v_3 \quad v_4 \quad v_5 \quad v_6]^T
$$

we can write Eq. 14.3.8 in the more compact form:

$$
\mathbf{B}_a \mathbf{v}_b = 0 \qquad (14.3.9)
$$

This equation represents the Kirchhoff's voltage law equations for all the loops of the network $\mathfrak{N}$. As in the case of node equations, these equations are not all linearly independent. For example, in Eq. 14.3.7 the third equation can be obtained by adding the first two. This implies that only two out of these three equations are linearly independent in the sense that they will provide useful information concerning the network under consideration. This means that the augmented loop matrix $\mathbf{B}_a$ given in Eq. 14.3.6 has rank two.

Next we give a precise statement concerning the rank of the augmented loop matrix of a network $\mathfrak{N}$ and then present a simple method for obtaining a fundamental loop matrix which represents the set of all linearly independent loop equations of a network. Consider a network $\mathfrak{N}$ with $N + 1$ nodes and $B$ branches; then *the rank of $\mathfrak{N}$ is $B - N$*. The proof of this statement is beyond the scope of this book and hence we omit it.

According to the above discussion the augmented loop matrix $\mathbf{B}_a$ has $L$ rows, but only $B - N$ of these are linearly independent. In order to save time and effort it is desirable to obtain a method by which we can write down a set of linearly independent loop equations without obtaining $\mathbf{B}_a$ first. For this reason we first define the concept of fundamental loops of a graph $G$.

*FUNDAMENTAL LOOP.* Consider a graph $G$ with $B$ branches and $N + 1$ nodes. Choose a tree $T$ of this graph; then each chord together with a unique set of tree branches form a fundamental loop (i.e., each fundamental loop contains exactly one chord).

*Example 14.3.3*

Consider a graph $G$ shown in Fig. 14.3.3a, a tree $T$ of this graph is given in Fig. 14.3.3b. There are five nodes and eight branches in this graph, therefore $N = 4$ and $B = 8$, the number of the chords correspond-

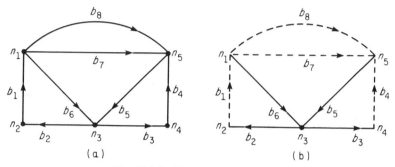

Fig. 14.3.3. (a) Graph $G$, (b) tree $T$.

ing to tree $T$ is $B - N = 4$, this number also represents the number of the fundamental loops of $G$. The tree $T$ consists of branches ($b_2$, $b_3$, $b_5$, $b_6$), the fundamental loops are therefore

$$(b_1, b_2, b_6), (b_4, b_5, b_3), (b_7, b_6, b_5), \text{ and } (b_8, b_6, b_5)$$

Notice that $b_7$ and $b_8$ do not form a fundamental loop since there is more than one chord in this loop; for the same reason $(b_1, b_7, b_4, b_3, b_2)$ and $(b_1, b_8, b_4, b_3, b_2)$ are not fundamental loops either.

We are now in a position to define a fundamental loop matrix. Consider a graph $G$ of $N + 1$ nodes and $B$ branches; choose an arbitrary tree $T$ for this graph, denote the fundamental loops of $G$ corresponding to $T$ by $l_1, l_2, \ldots, l_{B-N}$ and choose an arbitrary orientation for each of them. Then we have the following definition:

*FUNDAMENTAL LOOP MATRIX.* A $(B - N) \times B$ matrix

$$\mathbf{B}_f = (b_{ij})$$

is said to be the fundamental loop matrix of a connected graph with respect to a tree $T$ if

> $b_{ij} = 1$ when the branch (or chord) $b_j$ is in the fundamental loop $l_i$ and is directed in the same direction.
>
> $b_{ij} = -1$ when the branch (or chord) $b_j$ is in the fundamental loop $l_i$ and is directed in the opposite direction.
>
> $b_{ij} = 0$ when the branch (or chord) $b_j$ is not in the fundamental loop $l_i$.

*Example 14.3.4*

Let us find the fundamental loop matrix for the graph $G$ of Example 14.3.3. The fundamental loops of $G$ with respect to tree $T$ are shown in Fig. 14.3.4. An arbitrary direction is also assigned to each loop. The corresponding $\mathbf{B}_f$ matrix is

$$
\mathbf{B}_f =
\begin{array}{c}
\\
l_1 \\
l_2 \\
l_3 \\
l_4
\end{array}
\begin{array}{cccccccc}
b_1 & b_2 & b_3 & b_4 & b_5 & b_6 & b_7 & b_8 \\
\left[\begin{array}{cccccccc}
1 & 1 & 0 & 0 & 0 & 1 & 0 & 0 \\
0 & 0 & 1 & 1 & 1 & 0 & 0 & 0 \\
0 & 0 & 0 & 0 & 1 & -1 & 1 & 0 \\
0 & 0 & 0 & 0 & 1 & -1 & 0 & 1
\end{array}\right]
\end{array}
\tag{14.3.10}
$$

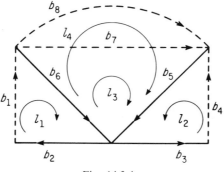

Fig. 14.3.4.

### Independent Loop Equations

With the help of fundamental loop matrix we can now introduce a systematic method for writing down a set of linearly independent loop equations for any network $\mathfrak{N}$ which has a connected graph. This method is rather straightforward and is suitable for computer application. Let us first describe this method for the specific network of Example 14.3.4 and then for a general network. Consider a network whose graph is given in Fig. 14.3.4. Take the voltage drop in each branch in the direction of the arrows and denote the voltage drop in branch $b_j$ by $v_j$. Now write the KVL equations for each fundamental loops:

$$
\begin{aligned}
\text{loop } l_1: & \quad v_1 + v_6 + v_2 = 0 \\
\text{loop } l_2: & \quad v_3 + v_4 + v_5 = 0 \\
\text{loop } l_3: & \quad v_5 - v_6 + v_7 = 0 \\
\text{loop } l_4: & \quad v_5 - v_6 + v_8 = 0
\end{aligned}
\tag{14.3.11}
$$

or equivalently,

$$
\begin{bmatrix}
1 & 1 & 0 & 0 & 0 & 1 & 0 & 0 \\
0 & 0 & 1 & 1 & 1 & 0 & 0 & 0 \\
0 & 0 & 0 & 0 & 1 & -1 & 1 & 0 \\
0 & 0 & 0 & 0 & 1 & -1 & 0 & 1
\end{bmatrix}
\begin{bmatrix}
v_1 \\ v_2 \\ v_3 \\ v_4 \\ v_5 \\ v_6 \\ v_7 \\ v_8
\end{bmatrix}
= \mathbf{0}
\qquad (14.3.12)
$$

Let us denote

$$
\mathbf{v}_b \triangleq [v_1 \quad v_2 \quad v_3 \quad v_4 \quad v_5 \quad v_6 \quad v_7 \quad v_8]^T \qquad (14.3.13)
$$

then comparing Eqs. 14.3.12 and 14.3.11 we see that the $4 \times 8$ matrix in the left-hand side of Eq. 14.3.12 is the same as $\mathbf{B}_f$ given in Eq. 14.3.10. Then we can write

$$
\mathbf{B}_f \mathbf{v}_b = 0 \qquad (14.3.14)
$$

This equation represents *all* the linearly independent loop equations in the network. To check the validity of this statement notice that the graph of Fig. 14.3.4 has 5 nodes and 8 branches; therefore $N = 4$ and $B = 8$. Further, the number of linearly independent loop equations

$$
B - N = 8 - 4 = 4
$$

which is the same as the number of equations in (14.3.12).

We now summarize the steps required for writing a set of linearly independent loop equations for a given network. Let us consider a network $\mathfrak{N}$ with $N + 1$ nodes and $B$ branches;

Step 1. Draw the graph $G$ of $\mathfrak{N}$ and choose a tree $T$ of this graph (There are precisely $N$ branches and $B - N$ chords corresponding to $T$).

Step 2. Each chord together with a unique set of tree branches form a fundamental loop; assign an arbitrary direction to each of these loops. (There are exactly $B - N$ of such loops.)

Step 3. Write KVL equations for each one of the $B - N$ fundamental loops obtained in Step 2.

These equations are linearly independent and are the desired loop equations.

### Analysis of General Linear Time-Invariant Networks

So far in this chapter we have talked about formulation of loop and node equations; the main objective has been to obtain a set of linearly independent equations to be solved for the branch currents and branch voltages of a given network. We have partially fulfilled this objective by obtaining a set of node equations and a set of loop equations; these are

$$\text{KCL:} \quad \mathbf{Ai}_b = 0 \qquad (14.3.15)$$

and

$$\text{KVL:} \quad \mathbf{B}_f\mathbf{v}_b = 0 \qquad (14.3.16)$$

Equation 14.3.15 consists of $N$ linearly independent equations in $B$ unknowns and Eq. 14.3.16 consists of $B - N$ equations in $B$ unknowns. Therefore these equations together provide $B$ equations in $2B$ unknowns. In order to solve for these $2B$ unknowns we need to obtain another set of $B$ linearly independent equations. These equations can be obtained from branch voltage-current relations (VCR); the voltage across each branch is related to the current through that branch via the branch impedance. To discuss these relations in detail we first assume that the network under consideration does not contain any voltage or current source. The general case will then be a simple extension of this special case.

Consider a branch $b_j$ of the *linear time invariant* network $\mathfrak{N}$; since we assumed that there are no sources present, a general form of $b_j$ is shown in Fig. 14.3.5, where $M_{j,k}$ represents the mutual inductance between

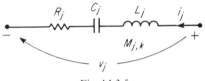

Fig. 14.3.5.

the inductor $L_j$ and the inductor $L_k$ in branch $b_k$. The current through this branch is $i_j$ and the voltage across it is $v_j$. Let the initial voltage on the capacitor be $v_{C_j}(0)$ and the initial current through the inductor be $i_{L_j}(0)$. Then using the Laplace transform (Chapter 9) we can write the voltage-current relation for $b_j$ as:

$$V_j(s) = R_jI_j(s) + \frac{1}{C_js}I_j(s) + \frac{1}{s}v_{C_j}(0) + L_jsI_j(s) - L_ji_j(0)$$

$$+ \sum_{\substack{k=1 \\ k \neq j}}^{B} M_{j,k}[sI_k(s) - i_k(0)] \qquad (14.3.17)$$

where $M_{j,k}$ represents the mutual inductance between branches $b_j$ and $b_k$. Rearranging this equation, we get

$$V_j(s) = \left(R_j + \frac{1}{C_js} + sL_j\right)I_j(s) + s\sum_{\substack{k=1 \\ k \neq j}}^{B} M_{j,k}I_k(s) + \frac{1}{s}v_{C_j}(0)$$

$$- L_ji_j(0) - \sum_{\substack{k=1 \\ k \neq j}}^{B} M_{j,k}i_k(0) \qquad (14.3.18)$$

Since there are $B$ equations of type (14.3.18), we can use matrix notation to represent these equations in a compact form; let $\mathbf{Z}_b(s)$ represent a $B \times B$ matrix whose $j$th diagonal element is $R_j + (1/C_j s) + sL_j$ and whose $j$-$k$th off-diagonal element is $sM_{j,k}$ i.e.:

$$
\mathbf{Z}_b(s) \triangleq
\begin{bmatrix}
R_1 + \dfrac{1}{C_1 s} + sL_1 & sM_{1,2} & \cdots & sM_{1,B} \\
sM_{2,1} & R_2 + \dfrac{1}{C_2 s} + sL_2 & \cdots & \cdots \\
\cdots & \cdots & \cdots & \cdots \\
s\dot{M}_{B,1} & \cdots & \cdots & R_B + \dfrac{1}{C_B s} + sL_B
\end{bmatrix}
$$

Let us also denote

$$
\mathbf{v}_C(0) \triangleq [v_{C_1}(0) \quad \cdots \quad v_{C_B}(0)]^T
$$

and

$$
\mathbf{M} \triangleq
\begin{bmatrix}
L_1 & M_{1,2} & \cdots & M_{1,B} \\
M_{2,1} & L_2 & \cdots & M_{2,B} \\
\vdots & & & \\
M_{B,1} & \cdots & \cdots & L_B
\end{bmatrix}
$$

Then equations of the form (14.3.18) can be written

$$
\mathbf{V}_b(s) = \mathbf{Z}_b(s)\mathbf{I}_b(s) + \frac{1}{s}\,\mathbf{v}_C(0) - \mathbf{M}i_L(0) \qquad (14.3.19)
$$

Equation 14.3.22 is the desired relation between $\mathbf{V}_b$ and $\mathbf{I}_b$. Let us now rewrite the equations that are necessary and sufficient for a unique solution of branch voltages and branch currents of the linear time-invariant network $\mathfrak{N}$. Taking the Laplace transform of Eqs. 14.13.15 and 14.13.16 and rewriting Eq. 14.13.19, we have [note that we will use $\mathbf{Z}_b \triangleq \mathbf{Z}_b(s)$]

$$
\mathbf{A}\mathbf{I}_b(s) = \mathbf{0} \qquad (14.3.20)
$$

$$
\mathbf{B}_f \mathbf{V}_b(s) = \mathbf{0} \qquad (14.3.21)
$$

$$
\mathbf{V}_b(s) = \mathbf{Z}_b\mathbf{I}_b(s) + \frac{1}{s}\,\mathbf{v}_C(0) - \mathbf{M}i_L(0) \qquad (14.3.22)
$$

Replacing $\mathbf{V}_b(s)$ from Eq. 14.3.22 into Eq. 14.3.21 we get

$$
\mathbf{B}_f \mathbf{Z}_b\mathbf{I}_b(s) = -\frac{1}{s}\,\mathbf{B}_f\mathbf{v}_C(0) + \mathbf{B}_f\mathbf{M}i_L(0)
$$

This equation together with Eq. 14.3.20 provide a set of $B$ linearly independent equations in $B$ unknowns; we can combine these equations to get

$$
\begin{bmatrix} \mathbf{B}_f\mathbf{Z}_b \\ \hline \mathbf{A} \end{bmatrix} \mathbf{I}_b(s) =
\begin{bmatrix} -\dfrac{1}{s}\,\mathbf{B}_f\mathbf{v}_C(0) + \mathbf{B}_f\mathbf{M}i_L(0) \\ \hline \mathbf{0} \end{bmatrix} \qquad (14.3.23)
$$

Assuming that $\left[\dfrac{\mathbf{B}_f \mathbf{Z}_b}{\mathbf{A}}\right]$ is nonsingular, and premultiplying both sides of

Eq. 14.3.23 by the inverse of $\left[\dfrac{\mathbf{B}_f \mathbf{Z}_b}{\mathbf{A}}\right]$, we get

$$\mathbf{I}_b(s) = \left[\frac{\mathbf{B}_f \mathbf{Z}_b}{\mathbf{A}}\right]^{-1}\left[\begin{array}{c} -\dfrac{1}{s}\,\mathbf{B}_f \mathbf{v}_C(0) + \mathbf{B}_f \mathbf{M} i_L(0) \\ \hline 0 \end{array}\right] \qquad (14.3.24)$$

This equation gives the solution for all the branch currents in the network $\mathfrak{N}$. To obtain the branch voltages we use Eq. 14.3.24 together with Eq. 14.3.22; every element in the right-hand side of Eq. 14.3.22 is then known and hence $\mathbf{V}_b(s)$ can be calculated. The following example gives an illustration of the technique discussed above.

*Example 14.3.5*

Consider the network shown in Fig. 14.3.6. Let

$C_1 = C_3 = \tfrac{1}{2}\text{f}, \qquad R_2 = 1\ \Omega, \qquad R_5 = 2\ \Omega, \qquad L_4 = 1\ \text{h}, \qquad L_6 = 2\ \text{h}$

$v_{C_1}(0) = 1\ \text{volt}, \qquad v_{C_3}(0) = 0, \qquad i_{L_4}(0) = 1\ \text{amp} \qquad \text{and} \qquad i_{L_6}(0) = 0$

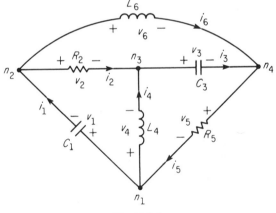

Fig. 14.3.6.

The problem is to find

and

$$\mathbf{i}_b = [i_1\, i_2\, i_3\, i_4\, i_5\, i_6]^T$$

$$\mathbf{v}_b = [v_1\, v_2\, v_3\, v_4\, v_5\, v_6]^T$$

*Solution*

Take $n_1$ as the reference node (datum) and write three independent node equations:

$$n_2: \quad -i_1 + i_2 + i_6 = 0$$
$$n_3: \quad -i_2 + i_3 - i_4 = 0$$

$$n_4: \quad -i_3 + i_5 - i_6 = 0$$

putting these in matrix form we get the incidence matrix **A**.

$$\begin{bmatrix} -1 & 1 & 0 & 0 & 0 & 1 \\ 0 & -1 & 1 & -1 & 0 & 0 \\ 0 & 0 & -1 & 0 & 1 & -1 \end{bmatrix}\underbrace{\phantom{xxxxx}}_{\textstyle \mathbf{A}} \begin{bmatrix} i_1 \\ i_2 \\ i_3 \\ i_4 \\ i_5 \\ i_6 \end{bmatrix} = \mathbf{0} \qquad (14.3.25)$$

Now take a tree of this network such as the one shown in Fig. 14.3.7. Arrows indicate the direction of the voltage drop in the branches and

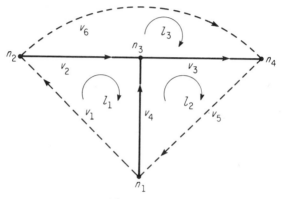

Fig. 14.3.7.

chords. There are three fundamental loops; these are indicated by $l_1$, $l_2$, and $l_3$. Writing KVL equations for each fundamental loop yields

$$l_1: \quad v_1 + v_2 - v_4 = 0$$
$$l_2: \quad v_4 + v_3 + v_5 = 0$$
$$l_3: \quad -v_2 + v_6 - v_3 = 0$$

Putting these in matrix form we get the fundamental loop matrix $\mathbf{B}_f$:

$$\begin{bmatrix} 1 & 1 & 0 & -1 & 0 & 0 \\ 0 & 0 & 1 & 1 & 1 & 0 \\ 0 & -1 & -1 & 0 & 0 & 1 \end{bmatrix}\underbrace{\phantom{xxxxx}}_{\textstyle \mathbf{B}_f} \begin{bmatrix} v_1 \\ v_2 \\ v_3 \\ v_4 \\ v_5 \\ v_6 \end{bmatrix} = \mathbf{0} \qquad (14.3.26)$$

So far we have twelve unknowns and six equations. We can get the other six equations from the branch voltage-current relations. In the $s$-domain, these are

$$\text{branch 1} \quad V_1(s) = \frac{1}{C_1 s} I_1(s) + \frac{1}{s} v_{C_1}(0)$$

$$\text{branch 2} \quad V_2(s) = R_2 I_2(s)$$

$$\text{branch 3} \quad V_3(s) = \frac{1}{C_3 s} I_3(s) + \frac{1}{s} v_{C_3}(0) \qquad (14.3.27)$$

$$\text{branch 4} \quad V_4(s) = L_4 s I_4(s) - L_4 i_4(0)$$

$$\text{branch 5} \quad V_5(s) = R_5 I_5(s)$$

$$\text{branch 6} \quad V_6(s) = L_6 s I_6(s) - L_6 i_6(0)$$

Using the given initial conditions and the element values, Eq. 14.3.27 can be written

$$V_1(s) = \frac{2}{s} I_1(s) + \frac{1}{s}$$

$$V_2(s) = I_2(s)$$

$$V_3(s) = \frac{2}{s} I_3(s)$$

$$V_4(s) = s I_4(s) - 1$$

$$V_5(s) = 2 I_5(s)$$

$$V_6(s) = 2s I_6(s)$$

Therefore the matrix $\mathbf{Z}_b(s)$ is given as

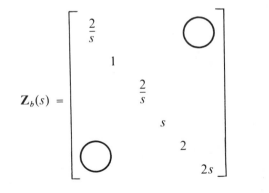

$$\mathbf{Z}_b(s) = \qquad (14.3.28)$$

Also $v_C(0)$, $\mathbf{M}$ and $i_L(0)$ are

$$v_C(0) = \begin{bmatrix} 1 & 0 & 0 & 0 & 0 & 0 \end{bmatrix}^T \qquad (14.3.29)$$

and

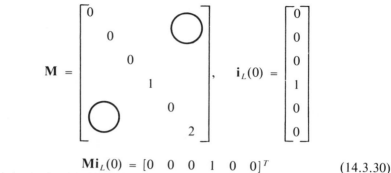

$$\mathbf{M} = \begin{bmatrix} 0 & & & & & \\ & 0 & & & & \\ & & 0 & & & \\ & & & 1 & & \\ & & & & 0 & \\ & & & & & 2 \end{bmatrix}, \quad \mathbf{i}_L(0) = \begin{bmatrix} 0 \\ 0 \\ 0 \\ 1 \\ 0 \\ 0 \end{bmatrix}$$

Hence

$$\mathbf{Mi}_L(0) = [0 \quad 0 \quad 0 \quad 1 \quad 0 \quad 0]^T \tag{14.3.30}$$

Now, from Eqs. 14.2.28 and 14.3.26 we obtain $\mathbf{B}_f \mathbf{Z}_b$ as

$$\mathbf{B}_f \mathbf{Z}_b = \begin{bmatrix} \dfrac{2}{s} & 1 & 0 & -s & 0 & 0 \\ 0 & 0 & \dfrac{2}{s} & s & 2 & 0 \\ 0 & -1 & -\dfrac{2}{s} & 0 & 0 & 2s \end{bmatrix} \tag{14.3.31}$$

From Eqs. 14.3.31 and 14.3.25 we obtain

$$\left[ \begin{array}{c} \mathbf{B}_f \mathbf{Z}_b \\ \hline \mathbf{A} \end{array} \right] = \begin{bmatrix} \dfrac{2}{s} & 1 & 0 & -s & 0 & 0 \\ 0 & 0 & \dfrac{2}{s} & s & 2 & 0 \\ 0 & -1 & -\dfrac{2}{s} & 0 & 0 & 2s \\ \hline -1 & 1 & 0 & 0 & 0 & 1 \\ 0 & -1 & 1 & -1 & 0 & 0 \\ 0 & 0 & -1 & 0 & 1 & -1 \end{bmatrix} \tag{14.3.32}$$

Also from Eq. 14.3.23 we have

$$\left[ \begin{array}{c} -\dfrac{1}{s}\mathbf{B}_f \mathbf{v}_C(0) + \mathbf{B}_f \mathbf{Mi}_L(0) \\ \hline \mathbf{0} \end{array} \right] = \begin{bmatrix} -1 - \dfrac{1}{s} \\ 1 \\ 0 \\ \hline 0 \\ 0 \\ 0 \end{bmatrix} \tag{14.3.33}$$

Finally, from Eq. 14.3.24 we have

$$
\mathbf{I}_b(s) =
\begin{bmatrix}
\dfrac{2}{s} & 1 & 0 & -s & 0 & 0 \\[2mm]
0 & 0 & \dfrac{2}{s} & s & 2 & 0 \\[2mm]
0 & -1 & -\dfrac{2}{s} & 0 & 0 & 2s \\[2mm]
-1 & 1 & 0 & 0 & 0 & 1 \\[2mm]
0 & -1 & 1 & -1 & 0 & 0 \\[2mm]
0 & 0 & -1 & 0 & 1 & -1
\end{bmatrix}^{-1}
\begin{bmatrix}
-1 - \dfrac{1}{s} \\[2mm]
1 \\[2mm]
0 \\[2mm]
0 \\[2mm]
0 \\[2mm]
0
\end{bmatrix}
\qquad (14.3.34)
$$

This equation gives the Laplace transform of the branch currents: the branch voltages can then be calculated using Eq. 14.3.22. Computing $i_b(t)$ from Eq. 14.3.34 is straightforward and we leave it as an exercise for the reader.

### Networks Containing Independent Voltage and Current Sources

In the previous case we assumed that the network under consideration does not contain any voltage or current source; in this section we relax this condition and assume that there are $p$ independent current sources and $q$ independent voltage sources in the network. Therefore the number of the unknown branch currents is $B - p$ and the number of the unknown branch voltages is $B - q$. Since the network has $N + 1$ nodes and $B$ branches,

$$\mathbf{A}\mathbf{i}_b = \mathbf{0} \Longrightarrow N \text{ equations in } B - p \text{ unknowns}$$
$$\mathbf{B}_f\mathbf{v}_b = \mathbf{0} \Longrightarrow B - N \text{ equations in } B - q \text{ unknowns}$$

This means that there are $B$ equations and $2B - (p + q)$ unknowns; we can also write $B - (p + q)$ equations for the branches not containing sources. Hence we have $2B - (p + q)$ equations and $2B - (p + q)$ unknowns.

Rather than going through the general formulation of the solution of these equations let us consider an example of a network containing both voltage sources and current sources: for simplicity let us assume that all the initial conditions are equal to zero.

### Example 14.3.6

Consider the network shown in Fig. 14.3.8, let the resistors be 1 ohm, the capacitor 1 farad and the inductor 1 henry. The problem is to find

$$\mathbf{i}_b = [i_1 \quad i_2 \quad i_3 \quad i_4 \quad i_5]^T$$

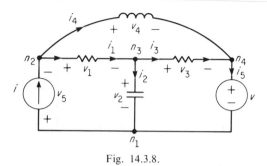

Fig. 14.3.8.

and

$$\mathbf{v}_b = [v_1 \quad v_2 \quad v_3 \quad v_4 \quad v_5]^T$$

*Solution*

Take $n_1$ as the reference node and write three independent node equations (KCL):

$$n_2: \quad -i + i_1 + i_4 = 0$$
$$n_3: \quad -i_1 + i_2 + i_3 = 0$$
$$n_4: \quad -i_3 - i_4 + i_5 = 0$$

Rearranging these equations and putting them in matrix form we get

$$\underbrace{\begin{bmatrix} 1 & 0 & 0 & 1 & 0 \\ -1 & 1 & 1 & 0 & 0 \\ 0 & 0 & -1 & -1 & 1 \end{bmatrix}}_{\mathbf{A}} \begin{bmatrix} i_1 \\ i_2 \\ i_3 \\ i_4 \\ i_5 \end{bmatrix} = \begin{bmatrix} i \\ 0 \\ 0 \end{bmatrix} \qquad (14.3.35)$$

Taking a tree as in Fig. 14.3.9 and writing KVL equations for each fundamental loop we get

$$l_1: \quad v_1 + v_2 + v_5 = 0$$
$$l_2: \quad -v_2 + v_3 + v = 0$$
$$l_3: \quad -v_1 - v_3 + v_4 = 0$$

or

$$\underbrace{\begin{bmatrix} 1 & 1 & 0 & 0 & 1 \\ 0 & -1 & 1 & 0 & 0 \\ -1 & 0 & -1 & 1 & 0 \end{bmatrix}}_{\mathbf{B}_f} \begin{bmatrix} v_1 \\ v_2 \\ v_3 \\ v_4 \\ v_5 \end{bmatrix} = \begin{bmatrix} 0 \\ -v \\ 0 \end{bmatrix} \qquad (14.3.36)$$

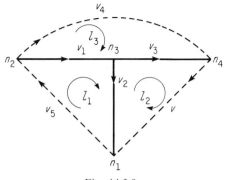

Fig. 14.3.9.

There are also four branch voltage-current relations. In the $s$-domain, these are

$$V_1(s) = I_1(s)$$

$$V_2(s) = \frac{1}{s} I_2(s)$$

$$V_3(s) = I_3(s)$$

$$V_4(s) = sI_4(s)$$

or

$$
\begin{bmatrix} V_1 \\ V_2 \\ V_3 \\ V_4 \end{bmatrix} =
\begin{bmatrix} 1 & & & \\ & \frac{1}{s} & & \\ & & 1 & \\ & & & s \end{bmatrix}
\begin{bmatrix} I_1 \\ I_2 \\ I_3 \\ I_4 \end{bmatrix}
\tag{14.3.37}
$$

We can now write Eq. 14.3.36 in the form

$$
\begin{bmatrix} 1 & 1 & 0 & 0 \\ 0 & -1 & 1 & 0 \\ -1 & 0 & -1 & 1 \end{bmatrix}
\begin{bmatrix} v_1 \\ v_2 \\ v_3 \\ v_4 \end{bmatrix}
+ \begin{bmatrix} 1 \\ 0 \\ 0 \end{bmatrix} v_5 =
\begin{bmatrix} 0 \\ -v \\ 0 \end{bmatrix}
\tag{14.3.38}
$$

Now we take the Laplace transform of Eq. 14.3.38 and using Eq. 14.3.37, we obtain

$$
\begin{bmatrix} 1 & \frac{1}{s} & 0 & 0 \\ 0 & -\frac{1}{s} & 1 & 0 \\ -1 & 0 & -1 & s \end{bmatrix}
\begin{bmatrix} I_1 \\ I_2 \\ I_3 \\ I_4 \end{bmatrix}
+ \begin{bmatrix} 1 \\ 0 \\ 0 \end{bmatrix} V_5 =
\begin{bmatrix} 0 \\ -V \\ 0 \end{bmatrix}
$$

or

$$
\begin{bmatrix}
1 & \dfrac{1}{s} & 0 & 0 & 0 & 1 \\
0 & -\dfrac{1}{s} & 1 & 0 & 0 & 0 \\
-1 & 0 & -1 & s & 0 & 0
\end{bmatrix}
\begin{bmatrix}
I_1 \\ I_2 \\ I_3 \\ I_4 \\ I_5 \\ V_5
\end{bmatrix}
=
\begin{bmatrix}
0 \\ -V \\ 0
\end{bmatrix}
\qquad (14.3.39)
$$

Equation 14.3.35 can also be Laplace transformed and modified to read

$$
\begin{bmatrix}
1 & 0 & 0 & 1 & 0 & 0 \\
-1 & 1 & 1 & 0 & 0 & 0 \\
0 & 0 & -1 & -1 & 1 & 0
\end{bmatrix}
\begin{bmatrix}
I_1 \\ I_2 \\ I_3 \\ I_4 \\ I_5 \\ V_5
\end{bmatrix}
=
\begin{bmatrix}
I \\ 0 \\ 0
\end{bmatrix}
\qquad (14.3.40)
$$

Then combining Eqs. 14.3.39 and 14.3.40 we obtain

$$
\begin{bmatrix}
1 & \dfrac{1}{s} & 0 & 0 & 0 & 1 \\
0 & -\dfrac{1}{s} & 1 & 0 & 0 & 0 \\
-1 & 0 & -1 & s & 0 & 0 \\
1 & 0 & 0 & 1 & 0 & 0 \\
-1 & 1 & 1 & 0 & 0 & 0 \\
0 & 0 & -1 & -1 & 1 & 0
\end{bmatrix}
\begin{bmatrix}
I_1 \\ I_2 \\ I_3 \\ I_4 \\ I_5 \\ V_5
\end{bmatrix}
=
\begin{bmatrix}
0 \\ -V \\ 0 \\ I \\ 0 \\ 0
\end{bmatrix}
\qquad (14.3.41)
$$

or equivalently

$$
\begin{bmatrix}
I_1 \\ I_2 \\ I_3 \\ I_4 \\ I_5 \\ V_5
\end{bmatrix}
=
\begin{bmatrix}
1 & \dfrac{1}{s} & 0 & 0 & 0 & 1 \\
0 & -\dfrac{1}{s} & 1 & 0 & 0 & 0 \\
-1 & 0 & -1 & s & 0 & 0 \\
1 & 0 & 0 & 1 & 0 & 0 \\
-1 & 1 & 1 & 0 & 0 & 0 \\
0 & 0 & -1 & -1 & 1 & 0
\end{bmatrix}^{-1}
\begin{bmatrix}
0 \\ -V \\ 0 \\ I \\ 0 \\ 0
\end{bmatrix}
\qquad (14.3.42)
$$

Now we can use the inverse Laplace transform to obtain

$$[i_1 i_2 i_3 i_4 i_5 v_5]$$

The four remaining unknowns, $[v_1 v_2 v_3 v_4]$ can then be calculated from Eq. 14.3.36.

### Relation Between Branch Voltages and Node Voltages

In Chapter 2 we used the node to datum voltages in the nodal analysis of networks. In this section we show that the branch voltage vector $\mathbf{v}_b$ and the node to datum voltage vector $\mathbf{v}_n$ are related together through a simple relation.

Consider a network with $N + 1$ nodes and $B$ branches. Choose an arbitrary node as the datum and assign voltages $v_{n_1}, v_{n_2}, \ldots, v_{n_N}$ to the remaining $N$ nodes. Also assign voltages $v_{b_1}, v_{b_2}, \ldots, v_{b_B}$ to branches $b_1, b_2, \ldots, b_B$ with arbitrary orientation. Let

$$\mathbf{v}_b \triangleq [v_{b_1} v_{b_2} \cdots v_{b_B}]^T \tag{14.3.43}$$

and

$$\mathbf{v}_n = [v_{n_1} v_{n_2} \cdots v_{n_N}]^T \tag{14.3.44}$$

We will show that $\mathbf{v}_b$ and $\mathbf{v}_n$ are related by

$$\mathbf{v}_b = \mathbf{P}\mathbf{v}_n \tag{14.3.45}$$

where $\mathbf{P}$ is a $B \times N$ constant matrix. In fact we will prove that

$$\mathbf{v}_b = \mathbf{A}^T \mathbf{v}_n \tag{14.3.46}$$

where $\mathbf{A}$ is the $N \times B$ incidence matrix defined in Eq. 14.3.5. To show Eq. 14.4.45, consider an arbitrary branch $b_j$ and two arbitrary nodes $n_i$ and $n_k$ of the network under consideration (see Fig. 14.3.10). Choose an

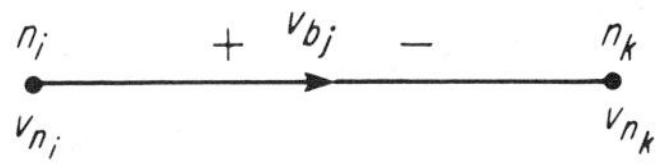

Fig. 14.3.10.

arbitrary orientation for the polarity of the branch voltage $v_{b_j}$. Quite clearly,

$$v_{b_j} = v_{n_i} - v_{n_k}$$

That is, each branch voltage can be written as a linear combination of the node voltages. Or equivalently

$$v_{b_j} = \sum_{i=1}^{B} p_{ji} v_{n_i} \tag{14.3.47}$$

where $p_{ji}$ is either $+1$, $-1$ or zero. More precisely, we have

$p_{ji} = 1$ when the branch $b_j$ is incident to the node $i$ and is directed away from it.

$p_{ji}$ = $-1$ when the branch $b_j$ is incident to the node $i$ and is directed toward it.

$p_{ji}$ = $0$ when the branch $b_j$ is not incident to the node $i$.

Comparing the definition of $p_{ji}$ and that of $a_{ij}$ given on page 483, we obtain

$$p_{ji} = a_{ij} \quad \text{for all } i \text{ and } j \qquad (14.3.48)$$

This means that $\mathbf{P} = \mathbf{A}^T$ and hence Eq. 14.4.46 follows.

We use Eqs. 14.3.5 and 14.3.46 to prove the following important result.

### Tellegen's Theorem

Consider a lumped network $\mathfrak{N}$ with $N + 1$ nodes and $B$ branches. Let $\mathbf{v}_b$ and $\mathbf{i}_b$ denote column vectors whose elements are branch voltages and branch currents of $\mathfrak{N}$ respectively. Then

$$\mathbf{v}_b^T \mathbf{i}_b = 0 \qquad (14.3.49)$$

*Proof.* From Eq. 14.3.46 we get

$$\mathbf{v}_b^T = \mathbf{v}_n^T \mathbf{A} \qquad (14.3.50)$$

Postmultiplying (14.3.50) by $\mathbf{i}_b$ we obtain

$$\mathbf{v}_b^T \mathbf{i}_b = \mathbf{v}_n^T \mathbf{A} \mathbf{i}_b \qquad (14.3.51)$$

But from Eq. 14.3.5,

$$\mathbf{A} \mathbf{i}_b = 0$$

Hence Eq. 14.3.51 becomes

$$\mathbf{v}_b^T \mathbf{i}_b = 0$$

This proves the theorem.

Note that this result is quite general in the sense that Eq. 14.3.47 is true for *any* linear, nonlinear, time-varying and time-invariant network.

### 14.4. STATE SPACE REPRESENTATION

In Chapter 7 we discussed the state space representation of linear and nonlinear networks. The networks considered in Chapter 7 were assumed to have no loops of capacitors only and no cutsets of inductors only. This restriction will be removed in this section and a systematic procedure will be outlined for obtaining state equations for a general class of networks.

Consider a linear time-invariant passive *RLC* network $\mathfrak{N}$ containing independent voltage sources, independent current sources, and possibly some capacitor-only loops and some inductor-only cutsets. By a *capacitor-only loop* we mean a loop which is comprised of two or more capacitors and possibly some independent voltage sources. By an *inductor-only cutset* we mean a cutset which is comprised of two or more inductors and possibly some independent current sources. The objective is to choose a *minimal* set of state variables and a set of first order differential equations in the form

$$\dot{\mathbf{x}}(t) = \mathbf{A}\mathbf{x}(t) + \mathbf{B}\mathbf{u}(t) \tag{14.4.1}$$

where $\mathbf{x}(t) = [x_1(t), \ldots, x_n(t)]^T$ is the state vector, $\mathbf{A}$ is an $n \times n$ constant matrix, $\mathbf{B}$ is an $n \times m$ constant matrix and $\mathbf{u}(t) = [u_1(t), \ldots, u_m(t)]^T$ is a column vector whose elements are either the independent sources or their derivatives. In order to proceed with the formulation of the state equations we must first define a specific tree of $\mathfrak{N}$ called the *normal tree*.

*NORMAL TREE.* A normal tree of a network $\mathfrak{N}$ is a tree that contains all the independent voltage sources, no independent current source, the maximum possible number of capacitances and the minimum possible number of inductances.

If we can find a normal tree for a network $\mathfrak{N}$ we can always represent its state equations in the form of Eq. 14.4.1. Next we indicate the steps that should be taken in choosing the state variables and writing the differential state equations of a network that may have capacitor-only loops or inductor-only cutsets.

### Procedure for Writing the State Equations

Step 1. Choose a normal tree for the network under consideration.

Step 2. Take either the voltages or the charges across the tree-branch capacitors and either the currents or the fluxes through the cotree-chord inductors as the state variables.

Step 3. Write the independent KCL equations, fundamental loop equations and branch voltage current relations.

Step 4. Eliminate all the network variables except the state variables chosen in Step 2 from the equations obtained in Step 3.

Step 5. Rearrange the equations obtained in Step 4 and put them in the form of Eq. 14.4.1.

There are well-established techniques for partitioning the matrices of a graph to facilitate a systematic method of eliminating the variables that are not state variables (Step 4). In this section, rather than discussing this general procedure, we will consider a specific example and refer the interested students to the literature (See Ref. 3 at the end of book).

*Example 14.4.1*

Consider the network shown in Fig. 14.4.1. We wish to obtain a *minimal* set of differential state equations for this network.

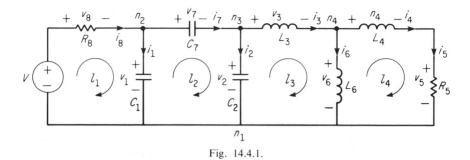

Fig. 14.4.1.

## Solution

It is possible to take the voltages across all the capacitors and the currents through all the inductors as the state variables and follow Steps 3 through 5 to obtain the state equations. The resulting equations however, will not be the minimal set of equations describing the network since capacitors $C_1$, $C_2$, and $C_7$ form a loop and inductors $L_3$, $L_4$, and $L_6$ form a cutset. To obtain the minimal set of state equations we proceed as follows.

### Step 1

To obtain the minimal set of differential equations we first choose a normal tree. This tree is shown in Fig. 14.4.2.

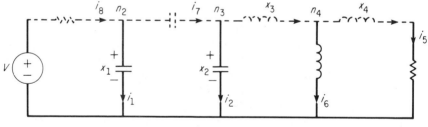

Fig. 14.4.2.

### Step 2

From Fig. 14.4.2 it is clear that the desired state variables are the voltages across the tree branch capacitors ($v_1$ and $v_2$) and the currents through the cotree chords ($i_3$ and $i_4$). Therefore the state vector $\mathbf{x}$ is given by

$$\mathbf{x}(t) = [x_1(t) \quad x_2(t) \quad x_3(t) \quad x_4(t)]^T$$

### Step 3

In this step we write the independent KCL and KVL equations for the network. In order to simplify the algebraic manipulation involved in Step 4 let us incorporate some of the branch voltage-current relationships in the KCL and KVL equations. For example the current through $C_1$ is

$C_1\dot{x}_1$, the voltage across $L_4$ is $L_4\dot{x}_4$, and so on; then

KCL

$$n_2: \quad i_8 = i_7 + C_1\dot{x}_1$$

$$n_3: \quad i_7 = C_2\dot{x}_2 + x_3$$

$$n_4: \quad x_3 = i_6 + x_4$$

KVL

$$l_1: \quad v = v_8 + x_1$$

$$l_2: \quad x_1 = v_7 + x_2$$

$$l_3: \quad x_2 = L_3\dot{x}_3 + v_6$$

$$l_4: \quad v_6 = L_4\dot{x}_4 + R_5x_4$$

VCR

$$r_1: \quad i_7 = C_7\dot{v}_7$$

$$r_2: \quad v_6 = L_6\dot{i}_6$$

$$r_3: \quad v_8 = R_8i_8$$

*Step 4*

In this step we eliminate all the nonstate variables from the relations derived in the previous step. More precisely we eliminate $i_8$, $i_7$, $i_6$, $v_8$, $v_7$, and $v_6$ from KCL, KVL, and VCR developed above. From equations $l_2$, $r_1$, and $n_3$, after eliminating $i_7$ and $v_7$, we get

$$C_7(\dot{x}_1 - \dot{x}_2) = C_2\dot{x}_2 + x_3 \tag{14.4.2}$$

From equations $n_2$, $r_1$, $l_1$, $l_2$, and $r_3$, after eliminating $i_7$, $v_7$, $v_8$, and $i_8$, we obtain

$$C_7(\dot{x}_1 - \dot{x}_2) + C_1\dot{x}_1 = \frac{1}{R_8}(v - x_1) \tag{14.4.3}$$

From equations $l_3$, $r_2$, and $n_4$, after eliminating $v_6$ and $i_6$, we get

$$x_2 = L_3\dot{x}_3 + L_6\dot{x}_3 - L_6\dot{x}_4 \tag{14.4.4}$$

From $l_4$, $r_2$, and $n_4$, after eliminating $v_6$ and $i_6$, we get

$$L_6(\dot{x}_3 - \dot{x}_4) = L_4\dot{x}_4 + R_5x_4 \tag{14.4.5}$$

Equations 14.4.2 through 14.4.5 are the state equations. However, in order to put them in the form of (14.4.1) we must proceed one step further.

*Step 5*

Rearranging Eqs. 14.4.2 through 14.4.5 we obtain

$$C_7\dot{x}_1 - (C_7 + C_2)\dot{x}_2 = x_3$$

$$(C_7 + C_1)\dot{x}_1 - C_7\dot{x}_2 = -\frac{1}{R_8}x_1 + \frac{1}{R_8}v$$

$$(L_6 + L_3)\dot{x}_3 - L_6\dot{x}_4 = x_2$$

$$L_6\dot{x}_3 - (L_4 + L_6)\dot{x}_4 = R_5x_4$$

or

$$
\begin{bmatrix}
C_7 & -(C_7 + C_2) & 0 & 0 \\
(C_7 + C_1) & -C_7 & 0 & 0 \\
0 & 0 & (L_3 + L_6) & -L_6 \\
0 & 0 & L_6 & -(L_6 + L_4)
\end{bmatrix}
\begin{bmatrix}
\dot{x}_1 \\ \dot{x}_2 \\ \dot{x}_3 \\ \dot{x}_4
\end{bmatrix}
$$

$$
=
\begin{bmatrix}
0 & 0 & 1 & 0 \\
-1/R_8 & 0 & 0 & 0 \\
0 & 1 & 0 & 0 \\
0 & 0 & 0 & R_5
\end{bmatrix}
\begin{bmatrix}
x_1 \\ x_2 \\ x_3 \\ x_4
\end{bmatrix}
+
\begin{bmatrix}
0 \\ 1/R_8 \\ 0 \\ 0
\end{bmatrix}
V
$$

Premultiplying both sides of this equation by the inverse of the matrix in the left-hand side of the equation we get

$$
\begin{bmatrix}
\dot{x}_1 \\ \dot{x}_2 \\ \dot{x}_3 \\ \dot{x}_4
\end{bmatrix}
=
\begin{bmatrix}
\dfrac{-(C_2 + C_7)}{\Delta_1 R_8} & 0 & \dfrac{-C_7}{\Delta_1} & 0 \\[2ex]
\dfrac{-C_7}{\Delta_1 R_8} & 0 & \dfrac{-(C_1 + C_7)}{\Delta_1} & 0 \\[2ex]
0 & \dfrac{-(L_6 + L_4)}{\Delta_2} & 0 & \dfrac{R_5 L_6}{\Delta_2} \\[2ex]
0 & \dfrac{-L_6}{\Delta_2} & 0 & \dfrac{R_5(L_3 + L_4)}{\Delta_2}
\end{bmatrix}
$$

$$
\times
\begin{bmatrix}
x_1 \\ x_2 \\ x_3 \\ x_4
\end{bmatrix}
+
\begin{bmatrix}
\dfrac{C_2 + C_7}{\Delta_1} \\[2ex]
\dfrac{C_7}{\Delta_1} \\[2ex]
0 \\[1ex]
0
\end{bmatrix}
V
\qquad (14.4.6)
$$

where

$$
\Delta_1 = C_1 C_2 + C_2 C_7 + C_1 C_7
$$

and

$$
\Delta_2 = -(L_3 L_4 + L_3 L_6 + L_4 L_6)
$$

Using the notation of Eq. 14.4.1 we have as final result

$$\dot{x} = Ax + Bu$$

where **A** and **B** matrices are given in Eq. 14.4.6.

**PROBLEMS**

**14.1.** Consider the network shown.
 (a) Draw a graph of this network and number the branches and nodes arbitrarily.
 (b) Indicate the degree of each node.
 (c) Indicate as many loops of this graph as you can.
 (d) Draw as many trees of this graph as you can.
 (e) What is the number of the branches in each of the trees you found in (d).

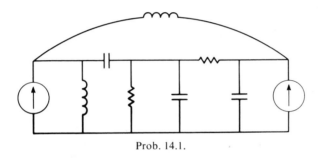

Prob. 14.1.

**14.2.** Repeat Prob. 14.1 for the figure given here.

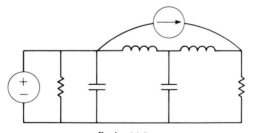

Prob. 14.2.

**14.3.** Find all the cutsets for an arbitrary tree of the network of Prob. 14.2.
**14.4.** For the network given,
 (a) Write down the augmented incidence matrix.
 (b) Indicate the number of the loops.

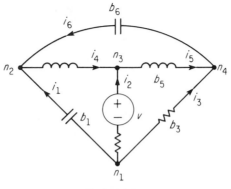

Prob. 14.4.

**14.5.** The augmented incidence matrix of a graph $G$ is given by

$$\mathbf{A}_a = \begin{bmatrix} 1 & 0 & -1 & 1 & -1 & 0 \\ -1 & 1 & 0 & 0 & 1 & -1 \\ 0 & -1 & 1 & -1 & 0 & 1 \end{bmatrix}$$

Draw the graph $G$.

**14.6.** For the network of Prob. 14.4 take $n_1$ as the datum and write down the incidence matrix.

**14.7.** For the network of Prob. 14.4 write down the independent node equations in matrix form.

**14.8.** Repeat Prob. 14.4 for the network shown.

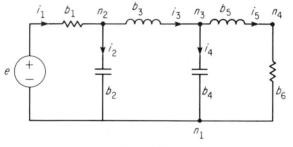

Prob. 14.8

**14.9.** Repeat Prob. 14.6 for the network of Prob. 14.8.

**14.10.** Repeat Prob. 14.7 for the network of Prob. 14.8.

**14.11.** For the network of Prob. 14.4,
(a) Specify all the loops.
(b) Choose arbitrary orientations for the loops and write down the augmented loop matrix.

**14.12.** Repeat Prob. 14.11 for the network of Prob. 14.8.

**14.13.** Choose a tree for the network of Prob. 14.4 and indicate all the corresponding fundamental loops.

**14.14.** Repeat Prob. 14.13 for the network of Prob. 14.8.

**14.15.** Choose a tree for the network of Prob. 14.4 and write down the corresponding fundamental loop matrix.

**14.16.** Repeat Prob. 14.15 for the network of Prob. 14.8.

**14.17.** Consider the network of Prob. 14.4, denote the voltage drop in branch $b_j$ by $v_j$, and write down a set of linearly independent loop equations in matrix form.

**14.18.** Repeat Prob. 14.17 for the network of Prob. 14.8.

**14.19.** For the network shown, let $v_2(0) = 1$ volt, $i_3(0) = 0$ and $v_4(0) = 0$.
   (a) Write down the incidence matrix and the fundamental loop matrix.
   (b) Write down the branch voltage current relations in matrix form.
   (c) Use the matrices found in parts (a) and (b) to set up matrix equations that can be solved for all the branch currents and branch voltages.
   (d) Solve the equation obtained in part (c).

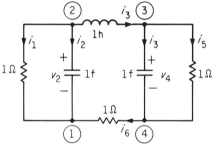

Prob. 14.19.

**14.20.** Repeat Prob. 14.19 for the network of Prob. 14.4. Assume that all the capacitors are 1 farad, all the inductors are 1 henry, the resistor is 1 $\Omega$, all the initial conditions are zero and the input $v_2$ is a unit step function.

**14.21.** Consider the network shown.
   (a) Draw as many *normal* trees as you can for this network.
   (b) Write the minimal state variable representation of this network.

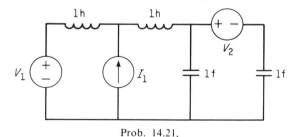

Prob. 14.21.

# Complex Numbers and Complex Variables

## A.1. COMPLEX NUMBERS

### Definitions

A *real number* is thought of as a point on a line with reference to a starting point and a measuring system.

A *complex number* is similarly defined as a point but in a plane and is made up of two real numbers $a$ and $b$ such that $a$ is represented on one line and $b$ is represented on the other line which is taken as perpendicular to the first line. The measurements are, of course, with respect to some origin. The complex number, $c$, is written as

$$c = a + jb \qquad\qquad (A.1.1.)$$

where $j$ can be thought of as a counterclockwise rotation of 90° from the line on which $a$ is chosen. We represent (A.1.1) as shown in Fig. A.1.1. It is quite clear that any complex number can be put as a point in the

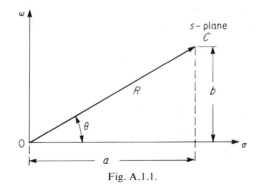

Fig. A.1.1.

defined plane.  We will define this plane as the *complex plane* (or the *s-plane*).  The line on which $a$ is chosen is called the *real axis* or $\sigma$-axis. The line on which $b$ is chosen is called the *imaginary axis* or $\omega$-axis. Note that we have given the names $s$, $\sigma$, and $\omega$ arbitrarily however, we use these letters for the presentation here and throughout the text.  $a$ and $b$ are called the *real part* and *imaginary part* respectively of the complex number $c$.  We can write

$$a = \text{Real } \{c\} = \text{Re } [c]$$
$$b = \text{Imaginary } \{c\} = \text{Im } [c]$$

(A.1.2)

## Some Fundamental Operations

If $c_1 = a_1 + jb_1$   and   $c_2 = a_2 + jb_2$
then

1.  $c_1 + c_2 = (a_1 + a_2) + j(b_1 + b_2)$                 (A.1.3)
2.  $c_1 - c_2 = (a_1 - a_2) + j(b_1 - b_2)$                 (A.1.4)
3.  $c_1 = c_2$ only if $a_1 = a_2$ and $b_1 = b_2$           (A.1.5)
4.  If $c_1 = 0$ then $a_1 = 0$ and $b_1 = 0$                 (A.1.6)
5.  Take a number $a_1$.  This can be plotted on $\sigma$-axis.  Then $ja_1$ would be the quantity $a_1$ on the $\omega$-axis.  What would be $j \cdot ja_1$.  This means, according to our definition of $j$, another counterclockwise 90° rotation of $ja_1$ which will bring the quantity $a_1$ back to the $\sigma$-axis but lying exactly 180° in the opposite direction from original num- $a_1$.  This implies that

$$j^2 a_1 = -a_1$$

(A.1.7)

or

$$j^2 = -1$$

(A.1.8)

or

$$j \triangleq \sqrt{-1}$$

(A.1.9)

This is the *mathematical definition* of $j$.

6.  $c_1 \cdot c_2 = (a_1 + jb_1)(a_2 + jb_2)$
    $= a_1 a_2 + ja_1 b_2 + jb_1 a_2 + j^2 b_1 b_2$
    $= (a_1 a_2 - b_1 b_2) + j(a_1 b_2 + b_1 a_2)$           (A.1.10)
    using Eq. A.1.8.
    Note that by using $j^2 = -1$, we can represent the multiplication of complex numbers as a complex number.

7.  We define the *conjugate* of a complex number $c = a + jb$ as $c^* = a - jb$.  All we do to obtain the conjugate of a complex number is replace $j$ by $-j$ in the original complex number.  Also

$$c \cdot c^* = (a + jb)(a - jb) = a^2 + b^2$$

(A.1.11)

*The multiplication of a complex number by its conjugate is a real number.*

8.  Simplification of

$$\frac{c_1}{c_2} = \frac{a_1 + jb_1}{a_2 + jb_2} \tag{A1.12}$$

In order to simplify Eq. A.1.12 we note that if we multiply the denominator by its conjugate we will just have a real number. So the procedure is that we multiply and divide by the conjugate of the denominator whenever we have the form of (A.1.12). Thus

$$\frac{c_1}{c_2} = \frac{a_1 + jb_1}{a_2 + jb_2} \cdot \frac{a_2 - jb_2}{a_2 - jb_2} = \frac{(a_1 a_2 + b_1 b_2) + j(a_2 b_1 - b_2 a_1)}{a_2^2 + b_2^2}$$

$$\tag{A.1.13}$$

using the fact that $j^2 = -1$.

Hence the division of two complex numbers lead to a complex number. The process of changing the division of two complex numbers to one complex number through the use of the conjugate is called *rationalization*.

*Example A.1.1*

If $c_1 = 2 - j$ and $c_2 = 1 + 3j$, find $c_1 c_2, \dfrac{c_1}{c_2}, c_1^* c_2^*, (c_1 c_2)^*, \left(\dfrac{c_1}{c_2}\right)^*$.

*Solution*

1.  $c_1 c_2 = (2 - j)(1 + 3j) = 2 - 3j^2 + 5j = 5 + 5j$

2.  $\dfrac{c_1}{c_2} = \dfrac{2 - j}{1 + 3j} = \dfrac{2 - j}{1 + 3j} \cdot \dfrac{1 - 3j}{1 - 3j} = \dfrac{-1 - 7j}{1 + 9} = -\dfrac{1}{10} - \dfrac{7}{10}j$

3.  $c_1^* c_2^* = (2 + j)(1 - 3j) = 2 - 3j^2 - 5j = 5 - 5j$

4.  Note that $(c_1 c_2)^* = c_1^* c_2^* = 5 - 5j$.

5.  $\dfrac{c_1^*}{c_2^*} = \dfrac{2 + j}{1 - 3j} = \dfrac{2 + j}{1 - 3j} \cdot \dfrac{1 + 3j}{1 + 3j} = \dfrac{-1 + 7j}{10} = -\dfrac{1}{10} + \dfrac{7}{10}j$

    Note that $\left(\dfrac{c_1}{c_2}\right)^* = \dfrac{c_1^*}{c_2^*} = -\dfrac{1}{10} + \dfrac{7}{10}j$.

*Example A.1.2*

Simplify

$$c = \frac{(1 + j)(1 - 2j) - j(2 + 3j)(1 - j)}{2 - j}$$

*Solution*

We obtain

$$c = \frac{1 + j - 2j - 2j^2 - j\{2 - 2j + 3j - 3j^2\}}{2 - j}$$

$$= \frac{3 - j - j\{5 + j\}}{2 - j} = \frac{4 - 6j}{2 - j} = \frac{4 - 6j}{2 - j} \cdot \frac{2 + j}{2 + j}$$

$$= \frac{8 + 4j - 12j - 6j^2}{5} = \frac{14}{5} - \frac{8}{5}j$$

We note that a combination of complex numbers can be simplified to a single complex number.

## Polar Representation

Let us reexamine Fig. A.1.1. We note that a complex number $c = a + jb$ is a point $C$ in the $s$-plane. We can also represent the point $C$ by the line $OC$ at angle $\theta$ to the $\sigma$-axis. We know that these are the polar coordinates and as a matter of fact any complex number can be represented by a line joining the point to the origin and its angle with the real axis (i.e., the $\sigma$-axis). Let $OC = R$. Then

$$a = R \cos \theta \tag{A.1.14}$$

$$b = R \sin \theta \tag{A.1.15}$$

Therefore

$$c = R \cos \theta + jR \sin \theta \tag{A.1.16}$$

This is called the *polar form* of the complex number while $c = a + jb$ is called the *rectangular form* of $c$. $R$ is called the *absolute value* or *magnitude* or *modulus* of $c$ and $\theta$ is called the *argument*, or *angle* or *phase* of $c$. From Fig. A.1.1 we note that

$$R = \sqrt{a^2 + b^2} \tag{A.1.17}$$

and

$$\theta = \tan^{-1}\left(\frac{b}{a}\right) \tag{A.1.18}$$

We also write

$$R = |c| \tag{A.1.19}$$

and

$$\theta = \arg c = \angle c \tag{A.1.20}$$

### Euler's Theorem

Consider the Taylor expansion of $e^{j\theta}$. It is given by

$$e^{j\theta} = 1 + j\theta + \frac{j^2\theta^2}{2!} + \cdots + \frac{j^n\theta^n}{n!} + \cdots \tag{A.1.21}$$

Now using the fact that $j^2 = -1$, we simplify Eq. A.1.21 and separate into real and imaginary parts to obtain

$$e^{j\theta} = \left[1 - \frac{\theta^2}{2!} + \frac{\theta^4}{4!} - \cdots\right] + j\left[\theta - \frac{\theta^3}{3!} + \frac{\theta^5}{5!} - \cdots\right] \tag{A.1.22}$$

From Taylor series expansions it is known that

$$\cos \theta = 1 - \frac{\theta^2}{2!} + \frac{\theta^4}{4!} - \cdots \qquad (A.1.23)$$

$$\sin \theta = \theta - \frac{\theta^3}{3!} + \frac{\theta^5}{5!} - \cdots \qquad (A.1.24)$$

Therefore

$$e^{j\theta} = \cos \theta + j \sin \theta \qquad (A.1.25)$$

Hence

$$c = R \cos \theta + jR \sin \theta = Re^{j\theta} = R \angle \theta \qquad (A.1.26)$$

### Sine and Cosine Functions

From Eq. A.1.25 we have

$$e^{j\theta} = \cos \theta + j \sin \theta \qquad (A.1.27)$$

If we replace $j$ by $-j$, we have

$$e^{-j\theta} = \cos \theta - j \sin \theta \qquad (A.1.28)$$

The addition and subtraction of Eqs. A.1.27 and A.1.28 gives

$$\cos \theta = \frac{e^{j\theta} + e^{-j\theta}}{2} \quad \text{and} \quad \sin \theta = \frac{e^{j\theta} - e^{-j\theta}}{2j} \qquad (A.1.29)$$

Also if we want to evaluate $\cos j\theta$ and $\sin j\theta$, we have (note that $j^2 = -1$):

$$\cos j\theta = \frac{e^{j(j\theta)} + e^{-j(j\theta)}}{2} = \frac{e^{-\theta} + e^{\theta}}{2} = \cosh \theta \qquad (A.1.30)$$

and

$$\sin j\theta = \frac{e^{j(j\theta)} - e^{-j(j\theta)}}{2j} = \frac{e^{-\theta} - e^{\theta}}{2j} = j\frac{e^{\theta} - e^{-\theta}}{2} = j \sinh \theta \qquad (A.1.31)$$

where $\cosh \theta$ and $\sinh \theta$ are hyperbolic cosine and sine respectively.

### Some Simple Properties of Complex Numbers Using Polar Representation

If $c_1 = R_1 e^{j\theta_1}$ and $c_2 = R_2 e^{j\theta_2}$, then

1. $c_1 c_2 = R_1 e^{j\theta_1} R_2 e^{j\theta_2} = R_1 R_2 e^{j(\theta_1 + \theta_2)} \qquad (A.1.32)$

    This shows that polar representation is very useful for multiplication of complex numbers because arguments just add.

2. Similarly, $\dfrac{c_1}{c_2} = \dfrac{R_1 e^{j\theta_1}}{R_2 e^{j\theta_2}} = \dfrac{R_1}{R_2} e^{j(\theta_1 - \theta_2)} \qquad (A.1.33)$

    Division is also straightforward compared with rectangular representation.

3. $\dfrac{1}{c_1} = \dfrac{1}{R_1 e^{j\theta_1}} = \dfrac{1}{R_1} e^{-j\theta_1} = \dfrac{1}{R_1} \angle -\theta_1 \qquad (A.1.34)$

So if a complex number is inverted the argument changes sign but has the same value.

4. If $c_1 = R_1 e^{j\theta_1}$ then $c_1^* = R_1 e^{-j\theta_1}$.                    (A.1.35)

## Power of a Complex Number

If $c = a + jb$, find $c^n$, $n$ integer. We can write

$$c = Re^{j\theta}, \quad \text{where} \quad R \cos \theta = a, \quad R \sin \theta = b$$

Now

$$c^n = (Re^{j\theta})^n = R^n e^{jn\theta} = R^n(\cos n\theta + j \sin n\theta) \quad \text{(A.1.36)}$$

where

$$\theta = \tan^{-1}(b/a) \quad \text{and} \quad R = \sqrt{a^2 + b^2}$$

We note that the polar representation is very convenient for evaluating the integral power of a complex number.

## Roots of a Complex Number

Given a complex number $c = Re^{j\theta}$, what is $c^{1/n}$, $n$ integer? We have

$$c^{1/n} = R^{1/n}[e^{j\theta}]^{1/n} \quad \text{(A.1.37)}$$

When we find the square root of a real number, it gives us two values, one positive and one negative. Similarly when the $n$th root is to be found it gives us $n$ values. This is also true for complex numbers. From Fig. A.1.1 we note that for any complex number,

$$\theta = \theta + 2k\pi, \quad k = 0, \pm 1, \pm 2, \dots$$

Then

$$e^{j\theta} = e^{j(\theta + 2k\pi)}, \quad k = 0, \pm 1, \pm 2, \dots \quad \text{(A.1.38)}$$

If we consider $(e^{j\theta})^{1/n}$ we will just have one root. However if we take $(e^{j(\theta + 2k\pi)})^{1/n}$, $K = 0, 1, \dots, n - 1$, we will have all the $n$ roots. In order to obtain the $n$ roots we write

$$c^{1/n} = R^{1/n}[e^{j(\theta + 2k\pi)}]^{1/n}, \quad k = 0, 1, \dots, n - 1 \quad \text{(A.1.39)}$$

whenever $c = Re^{j\theta}$.

This result is due to De Moivre. Equation A.1.37 becomes

$$c^{1/n} = R^{1/n}[e^{j(\theta + 2k\pi)}]^{1/n} = R^{1/n} e^{j\left(\frac{\theta + 2k\pi}{n}\right)}$$

$$= R^{1/n}\left[\cos\left(\frac{\theta + 2k\pi}{n}\right) + j \sin\left(\frac{\theta + 2k\pi}{n}\right)\right], \quad k = 0, 1, \dots, n - 1$$

The solutions above from $k = 0$ to $k = n - 1$ are the $n$ roots of the complex numbers.

## Function of a Complex Number

If $c$ is given we can easily find $f(c)$.

(i)  $c = a + jb$

then

$$\sin c = \sin (a + jb)$$

$$\sin c = \sin a \cos jb + \cos a \sin jb = \sin a \cosh b + j \cos a \sinh b$$
(A.1.40)

(ii)  $c = a + jb$

then

$$e^c = e^{a+jb}$$
$$= e^a e^{jb}$$
(A.1.41)
$$= e^a(\cos b + j \sin b)$$

(iii)  $c = a + jb$

then

$$\log c = \log (a + jb)$$

Now $a + jb = Re^{j\theta}$, therefore

$$\log (a + jb) = \log (Re^{j\theta}) = \log R + j\theta$$
(A.1.42)

which is a complex number.

Similarly other functions.

*Example A.1.3*

Find the polar presentation of (i) $1 + j$, (ii) $-1 + j$, (iii) $-1 - j$.

*Solution*

(i)  $c = 1 + j = Re^{j\theta} = R \cos \theta + jR \sin \theta$ or $R \cos \theta = 1$, $R \sin \theta = 1$. Therefore $R = \sqrt{1 + 1} = \sqrt{2} = 1.414$ and $\theta = \tan^{-1}(1) = 45°$ or $225°$. Note that $a = 1$ and $b = 1$, therefore the point is in the first quadrant of the complex plane, hence $\theta = 45°$ is the correct argument.

(ii)  $c = -1 + j = Re^{j\theta}$

Here

$$-1 = R \cos \theta \quad \text{and} \quad 1 = R \sin \theta$$

Therefore

$$R = \sqrt{2}$$

Now $\tan \theta = -1$, i.e., $\theta = 135°$ or $315°$. We can have $\theta$ in second or fourth quadrant. In order to decide which one it is we must see where the complex number lies. In this case it is in second quadrant. Therefore $\theta = 135° = \dfrac{3\pi}{4}$ rad.

(iii)  $c = -1 - j = Re^{j\theta}$

Therefore $R = \sqrt{2}$. Here $\theta = \tan^{-1}(1) = 45°$ or $225°$. In this case the complex number is in the third quadrant, therefore $\theta = 225° = \dfrac{5\pi}{4}$ rad.

From these three cases we note that finding of $R$ is straightforward, however, finding the correct value of $\theta$ needs the knowledge of the quadrant in which the complex number lies. So, care must be exercised.

*Example A.1.4*

For $c = 1 + j$, find $c^4$ and $c^{1/4}$.

*Solution*

First putting $c$ in the polar form, we have

$$R \cos \theta = 1, \quad R \sin \theta = 1$$

Therefore

$$R = \sqrt{2} \quad \text{and} \quad \theta = 45° = \frac{\pi}{4} \text{ rad}$$

Hence

$$c = \sqrt{2} \, e^{j\pi/4}$$

1. $c^4 = [\sqrt{2} \, e^{j\pi/4}]^4 = 4e^{j\pi} = 4(\cos \pi + j \sin \pi) = -4$.
2. To find $c^{1/4}$ we use De Moivre's theorem. There will be 4 roots given by

$$c^{1/4} = \left[ \sqrt{2} \, e^{j\left(\frac{\pi}{4} + 2k\pi\right)} \right]^{1/4}$$

$$= 2^{1/8} \left[ \cos \left( \frac{\pi + 8k\pi}{16} \right) + j \sin \left( \frac{\pi + 8k\pi}{16} \right) \right], \quad k = 0, 1, 2, 3$$

The four roots are

$$c_1 = 2^{1/8} \left[ \cos \frac{\pi}{16} + j \sin \frac{\pi}{16} \right] = 1.07 + j0.214$$

$$c_2 = 2^{1/8} \left[ \cos \frac{9\pi}{16} + j \sin \frac{9\pi}{16} \right] = -0.214 + j1.07$$

$$c_3 = 2^{1/8} \left[ \cos \frac{17\pi}{16} + j \sin \frac{17\pi}{16} \right] = -1.07 - j0.214$$

$$c_4 = 2^{1/8} \left[ \cos \frac{25\pi}{16} + j \sin \frac{25\pi}{16} \right] = 0.214 - j1.07$$

*Example A.1.5*

If $c = 1 - j$, find $\log c$, $e^c$, and $\cos c$.

*Solution*

Here if $c = Re^{j\theta}$, we have $R = \sqrt{2}$ and $\theta = 315° = \frac{7\pi}{4}$. Hence,

1. $\log c = \log \left\{ \sqrt{2} \, e^{j\frac{7\pi}{4}} \right\} = \log \sqrt{2} + j\frac{7\pi}{4}$
2. $e^c = e^{1-j} = ee^{-j} = e[\cos 1 - j \sin 1]$
3. $\cos c = \cos (1 - j) = \cos 1 \cos j + \sin 1 \sin j$
$$= \cos 1 \cosh 1 + j \sin 1 \sinh 1$$

## A.2. INTRODUCTION TO COMPLEX VARIABLES

We define a *complex variable* as

$$s = \sigma + j\omega \qquad (A.2.1)$$

As $\sigma$ and $\omega$ vary we have a point moving in the $s$-plane. This moving point in the $s$-plane is the complex variable. For a particular $\sigma$ and $\omega$ we just have a complex number.

When we are dealing with a real variable, we move along a line. When we are dealing with a complex variable, we are moving in a plane. We can do most of the things with complex variables which we do with real variables but they can be more involved because of two dimensions rather than one. We will expand on some of the ideas in the following paragraphs.

### Function of a Complex Variable, F(s)

A function of the complex variable $s$ is written as $F(s)$. We can write

$$F(s) = F(\sigma + j\omega) = u(\sigma, \omega) + jv(\sigma, \omega) \qquad (A.2.2)$$

$F(s)$ will have real part and an imaginary part.

*Example 6.2.1*

Express $F(s) = s^2 + 3s + 1$ in the form of Eq. A.2.2.

*Solution*

We have

$$\begin{aligned} F(s) &= (\sigma + j\omega)^2 + 3(\sigma + j\omega) + 1 \\ &= (\sigma^2 - \omega^2 + 3\sigma + 1) + j(2\sigma\omega + 3\omega) \qquad (A.2.3) \\ &= u(\sigma, \omega) + jv(\sigma, \omega) \end{aligned}$$

### Zeros and Poles of F(s)

A *zero* of $F(s)$ is defined as the value of $s$ which makes $F(s) = 0$. A *pole* of $F(s)$ is defined as the value of $s$ which makes the denominator of $F(s)$ approach zero or which makes $F(s)$ approach infinity.

In the work developed in this text we have been primarily concerned only with *rational functions* of the form:

$$F(s) = \frac{b_m s^m + b_{m-1} s^{m-1} + \cdots + b_1 s + b_0}{a_n s^n + a_{n-1} s^{n-1} + \cdots + a_1 s + a_0} \qquad (A.2.4)$$

If we factor the numerator and the denominator we may express $F(s)$ as

$$F(s) = k \frac{(s - z_1) \cdots (s - z_m)}{(s - p_1) \cdots (s - p_n)} \qquad (A.2.5)$$

$z_1, \ldots, z_m$ are defined as zeros and $p_1, \ldots, p_n$ are defined as poles of $F(s)$. If there is only one pole at one location, say $s = p_k$, then the pole is *simple*.

If there is more than one pole at one location, then the pole is *multiple*. As an example if we have a factor $(s - p_i)^r$ in the denominator of $F(s)$. This means that we have a pole at $p_i$ of multiplicity $r$. Similarly for zeros. Consider

$$F(s) = 2 \frac{(s + 1)^3(s + 2)}{\left(s + \dfrac{1}{2}\right)(s + 3)(s + 4)^2(s^2 + 2s + 2)} \tag{A.2.6}$$

Here we have a zero at $s = -2$, and a third order zero at $s = -1$. We have poles at $s = -\frac{1}{2}$ and $s = -3$ and a double pole at $s = -4$. We have also poles where $s^2 + 2s + 2 = 0$, i.e., at $s = -1 + j$ and $s = -1 - j$.

If $F(s)$ has an $n$th-order pole at $s = s_k$ then

$$\lim_{s \to s_k} (s - s_k)^n F(s) = a_k \tag{A.2.7}$$

where $a_k$ is a nonzero finite constant.

It is quite common to represent poles and zeros of a function in the complex plane. It is usually called a *pole-zero plot* and comes in handy in many applications.

A pole-zero plot of $F(s)$ of Eq. A.2.6 is shown in Fig. A.2.1.

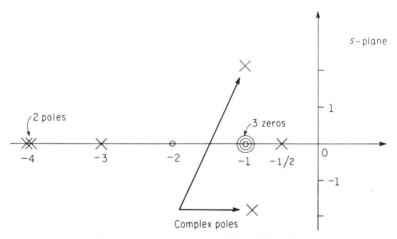

Fig. A.2.1. Pole-zero plot of $F(s)$ of (A.2.6).

A pole-zero plot and the constant multiplier (in our case it is 2) completely specifies $F(s)$. Note also that complex poles and complex zeros always occur in *conjugate pairs*.

## PROBLEMS

**A.1.** Give the rectangular and polar form of the following complex numbers and plot them in the complex plane:

(i)  $2 + j3$    (ii)  $2 \angle 45°$    (iii)  $\dfrac{\sqrt{2} + j4}{1 - j3}$

(iv)  $(1 + j)(-1 + 2j)(3 + j)$    (v)  $\log (\frac{1}{2} + j)$    (vi)  $j^j$

(vii)  $\sin^{-1}(j)$    (viii)  $\log j$

**A.2.**  Express $\tan c$ as a complex number if $c = a + jb$.

**A.3.**  Express the following as $R \cos \theta + jR \sin \theta$:

(i)  $1^j$    (ii)  $(1 - j)^j$    (iii)  $3^{2+j}$    (iv)  $(1 + j)^{1+j}$

**A.4.**  Evaluate:

(i)  $\sqrt[3]{8 + 8j}$    (ii)  $e^{\sqrt{2+3j}}$    (iii)  $\sqrt{1 + j}$

(iv)  $(1 + \sqrt{3}j)^4$    (v)  $\sqrt[5]{1}$

**A.5.**  Find the roots of the quadratic equation

$$x^2 - 3x + 7 = 0$$

and plot them in the complex plane.

**A.6.**  Simplify:

(i)  $\dfrac{(1 + j)(3 - j) - j(1 - j)(2 + j)}{j(j - 2) + (j + 1)(j + 3)}$

(ii)  $\dfrac{(2 + j)^2 - 4e^{j\frac{\pi}{4}} + 2 \cos \dfrac{\pi}{6} + j2 \sin \dfrac{\pi}{6}}{1 \angle 60° + 3 + j}$

**A.7.**  If $c_1 = 5 + j$, $c_2 = 3 - 2j$, and $c_3 = 1 - j$, evaluate

$$\frac{c_1^* c_2 - c_2^* c_3}{c_1^* c_2^* c_3^*}$$

**A.8.**  Find $\log c$, $\sin c$, $\cos c$, and $e^c$ if $c$ is given by

(i)  $\sqrt{3} + 2j$    (ii)  $\dfrac{\sqrt{3} + 2j}{1 + j}$    (iii)  $(1 + j)^2$

**A.9.**  Express the following as $u(\sigma, \omega) + jv(\sigma, \omega)$:

(i)  $e^s$    (ii)  $\dfrac{s + 3}{(s + 1)(s + 2)}$    (iii)  $\dfrac{s}{s^2 + s + 1}$    (iv)  $\log s$

**A.10.**  Make the pole-zero plots of the following functions.  You may have to use the root solving computer program developed in Chapter 9.

(i)  $\dfrac{s + 3}{(s + 1)(s + 2)^2}$

(ii)  $\dfrac{s(s + 1)^2}{(s^2 + s + 1)(s + 3)^3}$

(iii)  $2 \dfrac{s + 1}{s^3 + 3s^2 + 2s + 7}$

(iv)  $3 \dfrac{s^3 + 4s + 5}{s^4 + 2s^3 + 3s^2 + 4s + 1}$

(v)  $\dfrac{1}{2s^3 + 3s^2 - 4s + 2}$

**A.11.**  Find the residues of all the poles of Prob. A.10.

# Answers to Selected Problems

**1.1.** (a) $L = 10$ h    (b) $C = 160$ $\mu$f

**1.2.** (a) $2\pi \times 10^{-5}$ amp.    (b) 0 amp.    (c) $-2\pi \times 10^{-5}$ amp.

(d) 0 amp.    (e) $\sqrt{2}\pi \times 10^{-5}$ amp.    (f) $2\pi \times 10^{-5}$ amp.

**1.3.** (a) $v_{ab} = 0$ volts.    (b) $v_{ab} = 1.59 \times 10^4$ volts

(c) $v_{ab} = 3.18 \times 10^4$ volts    (d) $v_{ab} = 1.59 \times 10^4$ volts

(e) $v_{ab} = 4.66 \times 10^3$ volts    (f) $v_{ab} = 0$ volts

**1.5.** (a) $v_{ab} = 7.5$ volts    (b) $v_{ab} = 7.5$ volts    (c) $v_{ab} = 0$ volts

(d) $v_{ab} = -30$ volts    (e) $v_{ab} = -30$ volts

(f) Undefined; $v_{ab} = -30$ volts at $t = 6-$ or 7.5 volts at $t = 6+$

(g) $v_{ab} = 7.5$ volts    (h) $v_{ab} = 7.5$ volts    (i) $v_{ab} = 7.5$ volts

**1.6.** (a) $1/3$ f    (b) $1/3$ h

**1.7.** a. (i), (ii), and (iii) $v_{ab} = \begin{cases} 0.2t + V_0, & 0 < t < 1 \\ 0.8 - 0.8t + 0.2t^2 + V_0, & 1 < t < 2 \\ V_0, & 2 < t \end{cases}$

c. (i), (ii), and (iii) $E(1) = 2.5 \times 10^{-6}(V_0 + 0.2)^2$

$E(2) = 2.5 \times 10^{-6}V_0^2$

$E(\infty) = 2.5 \times 10^{-6}V_0^2$

**1.9.** $V_1 = 100 \cos t$

$V_2 = -90 \cos t$

**1.10.** a. 0+,    b. 29.5,    c. 0+

**1.11.** a. $E[0, 5] = 7.5$ joules

b. (i) $E[0, 1] = 1.5$ joules

(ii) $E[0, 2] = 3.0$ joules

(iii) $E[0, 3] = 4.5$ joules

(iv) $E[0, 4] = 6.0$ joules

(v) $E[0, 6] = 9.0$ joules

**1.12.** $v_2 = -20 \sin \omega t;\ v_1 = 40 \sin \omega t$

**1.13.** The resistor is current controlled. There is no single-valued function which satisfies $i = f(v)$.

**1.15.** (a) $p(t) = 0.1 \sin 3t(e^{0.2 \sin 3t} - 1)$ watts

(b) $E[0, 10] = 0.1014$ joules

**1.16.** $i = 0.5 \log \dfrac{1 + v}{1 - v},\quad |v| < 1$

**1.17.** $i = [1 + 0.5 \sin t]\,0.5 \cos t$

**1.19.** $E[0, 1] = 0.622$ joules

**1.21.** $i = \dfrac{\phi(t)}{2 - |\phi(t)|},\quad \phi < 2$

**1.23.** $E[0, 1] = 2.03$ joules

**1.25.** $v = L_0(1 + \operatorname{sech}^2 t) \cos \omega t - \omega L_0(t + \tanh t) \sin \omega t$

**CHAPTER 2**

**2.1.** (a)

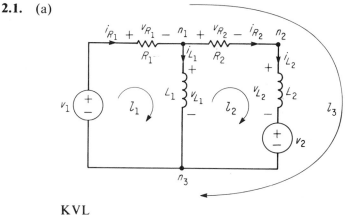

KVL

$l_1:\quad -v_1 + v_{R_1} + v_{L_1} = 0$

$l_2:\quad v_2 - v_{L_1} + v_{R_2} + v_{L_2} = 0$

$l_3:\quad -v_1 + v_2 + v_{R_1} + v_{R_2} + v_{L_2} = 0$

KCL

$n_1:\quad -i_{R_1} + i_{L_1} + i_{R_2} = 0$

$n_2:\quad -i_{R_2} + i_{L_2} = 0$

$n_3:\quad -i_{R_1} + i_{L_1} + i_{L_2} = 0$

(c)

KVL

$l_1:\quad -v_1 + v_{R_1} + v_C = 0$

$l_2:\quad v_2 + v_{R_2} - v_C = 0$

$l_3:\quad v_3 - v_{R_1} - v_{R_2} + v_L = 0$

$l_4:\quad -v_1 + v_2 + v_{R_1} + v_{R_2} = 0$

$l_5$:    $-v_1 + v_3 + v_2 + v_L = 0$
$l_6$:    $-v_1 + v_3 + v_L - v_{R_2} + v_C = 0$
$l_7$:    $-v_2 - v_3 - v_L + v_{R_1} + v_C = 0$
KCL
$n_1$:    $-i_1 + i_{R_1} + i_L = 0$
$n_2$:    $-i_{R_1} + i_{R_2} + i_C = 0$
$n_3$:    $i_2 + i_{R_2} + i_L = 0$
$n_4$:    $-i_C + i_1 + i_2 = 0$

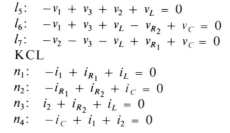

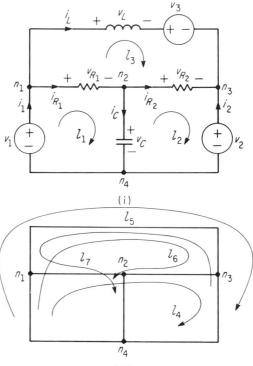

(i)

(ii)

(e)

KVL
$l_1$:    $-v_1 + v_{R_1} + v_L - v_{R_2} = 0$
$l_2$:    $-v_2 + v_{R_3} + v_C - v_{R_2} = 0$
$l_3$:    $-v_1 + v_{R_1} + v_L - v_C - v_{R_3} + v_2 = 0$
KCL
$n_1$:    $i_{R_1} + i_{R_2} + i_{R_3} = 0$
$n_2$:    $i_{R_3} - i_C = 0$
$n_3$:    $i_C + i_{R_2} + i_L = 0$
$n_4$:    $i_{R_1} + i_L = 0$

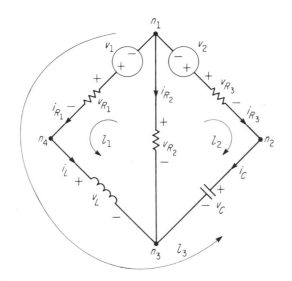

**2.3.** (a) $n_1$:  $-i_{R_1} + i_{L_1} + i_{R_2} = 0$
$\qquad n_2$:  $-i_{R_2} + i_{L_2} = 0$
$\quad$ (c) $n_1$:  $-i_1 + i_{R_1} + i_L = 0$
$\qquad n_2$:  $-i_{R_1} + i_{R_2} + i_C = 0$
$\qquad n_3$:  $i_2 + i_{R_2} + i_L = 0$
$\quad$ (e) $n_1$:  $i_{R_1} + i_{R_2} + i_{R_3} = 0$
$\qquad n_2$:  $i_{R_3} - i_C = 0$
$\qquad n_3$:  $i_C + i_{R_2} + i_L = 0$

**2.5.** (a) $l_1$:  $-v_1 + v_{R_1} + v_{L_1} = 0$
$\qquad l_2$:  $v_2 - v_{L_1} + v_{R_2} + v_{L_2} = 0$
$\quad$ (c) $l_1$:  $-v_1 + v_{R_1} + v_C = 0$
$\qquad l_2$:  $v_2 + v_{R_2} - v_C = 0$
$\qquad l_3$:  $v_3 - v_{R_1} - v_{R_2} + v_L = 0$
$\quad$ (e) $l_1$:  $-v_1 + v_{R_1} + v_L - v_{R_2} = 0$
$\qquad l_2$:  $-v_2 + v_{R_3} + v_C - v_{R_2} = 0$

**2.9.** $l_1$:  $v = v_{R_1} + v_{C_1} + v_{L_1} + v_{M_1}$
$\quad l_2$:  $0 = v_{C_2} + v_{L_2} + v_{M_2}$

$$v_R = i_1 R; \; v_{C_1} = v_{C_1}(0) + \frac{1}{C_1} \int_0^t i_1(\sigma')d\sigma'$$

$$v_{C_2} = v_{C_2}(0) + \frac{1}{C_2} \int_0^t i_2(\sigma')d\sigma'$$

$$v_{L_1} = L_1 \frac{di_1}{dt} \qquad v_{L_2} = L \frac{di_2}{dt} \qquad v_{M_1} = M \frac{di_2}{dt} \qquad v_{M_2} = M \frac{di_1}{dt}$$

**2.10.** $v = Ri + (L_1 + L_2 + 2M) \dfrac{di}{dt}$

**2.11.** (a) $R = 1.271 \; \Omega$    (b) $C_1/3 \; \text{f}$

(c) $L = (L_1 + \tfrac{3}{5} L_2) \; \text{h}$

**2.13.** $-v_1 + v_{R_1} + v_{R_2} + v_{C_1} + v_3 - v_{R_6} = 0$

$v_{C_1} + v_{R_3} + v_{R_4} + v_{R_5} = 0$

$v_{C_3} - v_{R_4} + v_{L_2} - v_2 = 0$

$-v_{L_1} + v_2 + v_{R_7} - v_1 + v_{R_1} = 0$

$-v_{C_3} - v_{R_3} - v_{R_2} - v_{L_1} = 0$

$-v_{R_8} - v_{L_2} + v_{R_5} = 0$

$-v_{R_7} + v_{R_8} - v_{R_6} = 0$

$-v_4 + v_{C_2} + v_{R_5} = 0$

**2.15.** KVL

$-v + v_R + v_{C_{gk}} = 0$

$-v_{C_{gk}} + v_{C_{gp}} + v_{R_L} = 0$

$v_{R_L} - v_{R_P} = 0$

KCL

$i_R - i_{C_{gk}} - i_{C_{gp}} = 0$

$i_{C_{gp}} - g_m v - i_{R_P} - i_{R_L} = 0$

**2.17.** $n_1$:  $i - i_{C_1} - i_{R_1} = 0$

$n_2$:  $i_{C_1} + i_{R_1} - i_{C_2} - i_{R_2} = 0$

$n_3$:  $i_{C_2} + i_{R_2} - i = 0$

$i = \dfrac{kv_1 - v}{R}$   $i_{R_1} = \dfrac{v - v_1}{R_1}$   $i_{C_1} = C_1 \dfrac{d}{dt}(v - v_1)$

$i_{R_2} = \dfrac{v_1 - k^{v_1}}{R_2}$   $i_{C_2} = C_2 \dfrac{d}{dt}(v_1 - k^{v_1})$

**2.19.** $i \cong 2.2, 1.9, 0.3 \; \text{amp.}$    $v_R \cong 0.3, 1.2, 4.0 \; \text{volts.}$

## CHAPTER 3

**3.1.** $t[u_0(t) - u_0(t - 1)] - [u_0(t - 1) - u_0(t - 3)]$

$+ 2(t - 4)[u_0(t - 3) - u_0(t - 4)]$

**3.2.** $4[u_0(t) - u_0(t - 2)] + [u_0(t - 2) - u_0(t - 4)]$

$+ 4[u_0(t - 4) - u_0(t - 6)]$

**3.4.** $e^t u_0 (1 - t) + e[u_0(t - 1) - u_0(t - 2)]$

$+ (2t - 3)[u_0(t - 2) - u_0(t - 3)]$

**3.7.** (a) Take $s(t) = 4t[u_0(t + 1/2) - u_0(t - 1/2)]$

$$g(t) = \sum_{n = -\infty}^{\infty} s(t + n + 1/2)$$

$$= \sum_{n = -\infty}^{\infty} 4(t + n + 1/2)[u_0(t + n + 1) - u_0(t + n)]$$

(b) $T = 1; f_0 = 1$

**3.9.** (a) 1/30 joules    (b) 4/30 joules    (c) 11/30 joules
**3.10.** (a) 0.86    (b) 0.6
**3.11.** (a) 1.96    (b) 76.9 joules
**3.13.** 1.151
**3.15.** (a) 0.576    (b) 0.571
**3.17.** (a) avg = 0.637, rms = 0.707    (c) avg = 0.693, rms = 1.000


**CHAPTER 4**

**4.1.** (a) $\begin{bmatrix} 9 & -17 \\ -12 & 1 \\ -4 & 1 \end{bmatrix}$    (c) $\begin{bmatrix} 10 & -28 & -34 \\ 56 & 21 & -8 \\ 12 & 12 & 16 \end{bmatrix}$    (e) $\begin{bmatrix} 4x_1 - 3x_2 - 6 \\ x_1 + 3x_2 - 2 \end{bmatrix}$

**4.3.** $\begin{bmatrix} i_1 \\ i_2 \\ i_3 \end{bmatrix} = \begin{bmatrix} 1.69 \\ 1.38 \\ 1.92 \end{bmatrix}$ amp.

**4.6.** (a) det $\mathbf{A}$ = $-132$    det $\mathbf{B}$ = 40    det $\mathbf{C}$ = $-10$

**4.8.** (a) $\mathbf{x} = \begin{bmatrix} -40/7 \\ -6/7 \\ 29/7 \end{bmatrix}$    (b) $\mathbf{x} = \begin{bmatrix} 6/5 \\ 2/25 \\ 33/25 \end{bmatrix}$    (c) $\mathbf{x} = \begin{bmatrix} 7/2 \\ 1 \\ -1/2 \end{bmatrix}$

**4.9.** $\begin{bmatrix} a \\ b \\ c \\ d \end{bmatrix} = \begin{bmatrix} -2 \\ -1 \\ 4 \\ -4 \end{bmatrix}$

**4.11.** (a) $i_1$ = $-0.117$ amp, $i_2$ = $-0.470$ amp.
   (b) $i_1$ = 3.19 amp, $i_2$ = 1.38 amp, $i_3$ = 0.93 amp, $i_4$ = 1.47 amp.
**4.13.** (a) $\lambda$ = 2, 4
   (c) $\lambda$ = 1, $-1$, 3

**4.15.** (a) $\mathbf{A}^{-1} = \begin{bmatrix} -0.667 & 0.167 \\ -0.333 & -0.167 \end{bmatrix}$

   (b) $e^{\mathbf{A}t} = \begin{matrix} 2e^{-2t} - e^{-3t} & -e^{-2t} + e^{-3t} \\ 2e^{-2t} - 2e^{-3t} & -e^{-2t} + 2e^{-3t} \end{matrix}$

**4.21.** $i$ = 0.831 (assumed $i_s$ = 1)

**4.23.**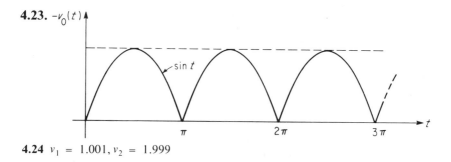

**4.24** $v_1 = 1.001, v_2 = 1.999$

## CHAPTER 5

**5.1.** $\dfrac{di}{dt} + \dfrac{1}{R}\left(\dfrac{1}{C_1} + \dfrac{1}{C_2}\right)i = \dfrac{1}{R}\dfrac{dv_s}{dt}$

**5.2.** $\dfrac{di}{dt} = \dfrac{3}{2}, \qquad i(0+) = 2$

**5.3.** (a) $\dfrac{di}{dt} + 2i = -e^{-t}$

     (b) $i_h = Ke^{-2t}$

     (c) $i_p = -e^{-t}$

     (d) $i = 1.9e^{-2t} - e^{-t}$

**5.5.** (a) $v_h(t) = Ke^t$

     (b) $v_p(t) = \frac{1}{2}t^2 + 2t + \frac{5}{2}$

     (c) $v(t) = \frac{1}{2}t^2 + 2t + \frac{5}{2} - \frac{3}{2}e^t$

**5.7.** (a) $x_h(t) = K$

     (b) $x_p(t) = -0.2e^{-t}\sin 2t - 0.4e^{-t}\cos 2t$

     (c) $x(t) = 1.4 - 0.2e^{-t}\sin 2t - 0.4e^{-t}\cos 2t$

**5.8.** $v(t) = e^{-0.5t}$

**5.9.** $v_c(t) = \begin{cases} 1 + e^{-t} & 1 > t > 0 \\ e^{-(t-1)} + e^{-t} & t > 1 \end{cases}$

**5.10.** (a) $i = [1 - e^{-0.5t}]u_0(t)$     (b) $i = 0.5e^{-0.5t}u_0(t)$

**5.11.** (a) $\dfrac{di_L}{dt} + \dfrac{6}{5}i_L = \dfrac{2}{5} + \dfrac{3}{5}\sin t \qquad t \geq 0; i_L(0) = 1$

     (b) $i_L(t) = \dfrac{167}{183}e^{-(6/5)t} + \dfrac{1}{3}u_0(t) + \dfrac{18}{61}\sin t - \dfrac{15}{61}\cos t$

**5.13.** Zero state response: $i_L(t) = 1 - e^{-\frac{R}{L}t} \qquad t \geq 0$

     Zero input response: $i_L(t) = I_0 e^{-\frac{R}{L}t} \qquad t \geq 0$

     Total response: $i_L(t) = 1 + (I_0 - 1)e^{-\frac{R}{L}t} \qquad t \geq 0$

**5.15.** $v_R(t) = L\left(e^{-\frac{t}{L}} - 1\right) + t$

$v_L(t) = L\left(1 - e^{-\frac{t}{L}}\right)$

**6.2.** $v_C(t) = \dfrac{8}{3}\left[1 - e^{-(3/2)t} \cos \dfrac{\sqrt{3}}{2} t\right]$

**6.3.** $v_C(t) = 1.5e^{-0.5t}[\sqrt{2} \cos(0.5t + 45°) + 2 \sin(0.5t)]$

**6.4.** $i_2(t) = 0.435e^{-0.27t} - 0.435e^{-0.73t}$

**6.5.** $v_C(t) = -2.67e^{-0.5t} \cos 1.93t + 2.07e^{-0.5t} \sin 1.93t + 2.67e^{-2t}$

**6.7.** $i_L(t) = 5 \cos t - 4e^{-t} \cos \sqrt{2}t$

**6.9.** (a) $\dfrac{d^2v}{dt^2} - 0.02 \dfrac{dv}{dt} + 100v = 0$

(b) $-0.2e^{0.01t} \sin 10t$

(c) No

**6.11.** $i_L(t) = 10 + 1.06e^{-3.731(t-1)} - 11.05e^{-0.269(t-1)}$

**7.1.** (a) $\begin{bmatrix} \dot{x}_1 \\ \dot{x}_2 \\ \dot{x}_3 \end{bmatrix} = \begin{bmatrix} 0 & 1 & 0 \\ 0 & 0 & 1 \\ -c & -b & -a \end{bmatrix} \begin{bmatrix} x_1 \\ x_2 \\ x_3 \end{bmatrix} + \begin{bmatrix} 0 \\ 0 \\ 1 \end{bmatrix} \cos t$

**7.3.** $\dfrac{d^3y}{dt^3} + 3 \dfrac{d^2y}{dt^2} + 2 \dfrac{dy}{dt} + y = u(t)$

**7.4.** $\dot{v}_C = -\dfrac{1}{RC} v_C + \dfrac{1}{C} I$

**7.5.** $\begin{bmatrix} \dot{x}_1 \\ \dot{x}_2 \end{bmatrix} = \begin{bmatrix} 0 & \dfrac{1}{L} \\ \dfrac{-1}{C} & \dfrac{-1}{RC} \end{bmatrix} \begin{bmatrix} x_1 \\ x_2 \end{bmatrix} + \begin{bmatrix} 0 \\ \dfrac{1}{RC} \end{bmatrix} u(t); \ x_1 = i_L, \ x_2 = v_C$

**7.7.** $\begin{bmatrix} \dot{x}_1 \\ \dot{x}_2 \end{bmatrix} = \begin{bmatrix} 0 & \dfrac{1}{C} \\ \dfrac{-1}{L} & \dfrac{-1}{RC} \end{bmatrix} \begin{bmatrix} x_1 \\ x_2 \end{bmatrix} + \begin{bmatrix} 0 \\ \dfrac{1}{R} \end{bmatrix} u(t); \ x_1 = \phi_L, \ x_2 = q_C$

**7.9.**
$$\begin{bmatrix} \dot{x}_1 \\ \dot{x}_2 \end{bmatrix} = \begin{bmatrix} \dfrac{-R}{L} & \dfrac{-1}{C} \\ \dfrac{1}{L} & 0 \end{bmatrix} \begin{bmatrix} x_1 \\ x_2 \end{bmatrix} + \begin{bmatrix} 1 \\ 0 \end{bmatrix} v(t); \quad x_1 = \phi_L, \; x_2 = q_C$$

**7.10.**
$$\begin{bmatrix} \dot{x}_1 \\ \dot{x}_2 \\ \dot{x}_3 \end{bmatrix} = \begin{bmatrix} 0 & 1 & -1 \\ \dfrac{-1}{2} & \dfrac{-1}{2} & 0 \\ \dfrac{1}{2} & 0 & 0 \end{bmatrix} \begin{bmatrix} x_1 \\ x_2 \\ x_3 \end{bmatrix} + \begin{bmatrix} 0 \\ \dfrac{1}{2} \\ 0 \end{bmatrix} v_0 \sin \omega t; \quad \begin{aligned} x_1 &= i_L, \; x_2 = v_{C_1}, \\ x_3 &= v_{C_2} \end{aligned}$$

**7.12.**
$$\begin{bmatrix} \dot{q}_C \\ \dot{\phi}_L \end{bmatrix} \begin{bmatrix} \dfrac{-1}{3(1 + 0.5 \sin 2t)} & \dfrac{-1}{3(2 + \sin 2t)} \\ \dfrac{1}{3(1 + 0.5 \sin 2t)} & \dfrac{-2}{3(2 + \sin 2t)} \end{bmatrix} \begin{bmatrix} q_C \\ \phi_L \end{bmatrix} + \begin{bmatrix} \dfrac{1}{3} \\ \dfrac{2}{3} \end{bmatrix} v(t)$$

**7.13.**
$$\begin{bmatrix} \dot{x}_1 \\ \dot{x}_2 \end{bmatrix} = \begin{bmatrix} 0 & \dfrac{1}{C(t)} \\ \dfrac{-1}{L(t)} & \dfrac{-1}{RC(t)} \end{bmatrix} \begin{bmatrix} x_1 \\ x_2 \end{bmatrix} + \begin{bmatrix} 0 \\ 1 \end{bmatrix} i; \quad x_1 = \phi_L, \; x_2 = q_C$$

**7.15.**
$$\begin{bmatrix} \dot{x}_1 \\ \dot{x}_2 \\ \dot{x}_3 \end{bmatrix} = \begin{bmatrix} -1 & -2 & 0 \\ 1 & 0 & -0.5 \\ 0 & 2 & -0.5 \end{bmatrix} \begin{bmatrix} \tanh(x_1) \\ \tanh(x_2) \\ \tanh(x_3) \end{bmatrix} + \begin{bmatrix} 1 \\ 0 \\ 0 \end{bmatrix} v(t)$$
$$x_1 = q_1, \quad x_2 = \phi_2, \quad x_3 = q_3.$$

**7.17.**
$$\begin{bmatrix} \dot{x}_1 \\ \dot{x}_2 \\ \dot{x}_3 \\ \dot{x}_4 \end{bmatrix} = \begin{bmatrix} -1 & -1 & 0 & 0 \\ 1 & 0 & -1 & 0 \\ 0 & 1 & 0 & -1 \\ 0 & 0 & 1 & \dfrac{-1}{2} \end{bmatrix} \begin{bmatrix} x_1 \\ x_2 \\ x_3 \\ x_4 \end{bmatrix} + \begin{bmatrix} 1 \\ 0 \\ 0 \\ \dfrac{-1}{2} \end{bmatrix} v$$
$$x_1 = v_{C_1}, \quad x_2 = i_{L_2}, \quad x_3 = v_{C_3}, \quad x_4 = i_{L_4}.$$

**7.19.** (a) $\lambda_1 = \sqrt{7}, \; \lambda_2 = -\sqrt{7}$
(c) $\lambda_1 = a, \; \lambda_2 = b$
(e) $\lambda_1 = -1, \; \lambda_2 = -2, \; \lambda_3 = -3$

**7.21.** $e^{At} = \begin{bmatrix} 3e^{-t} - 3e^{-2t} + e^{-3t} & \frac{5}{2}e^{-t} - 4e^{-2t} + \frac{3}{2}e^{-3t} & \frac{1}{2}e^{-t} - e^{-2t} + \frac{1}{2}e^{-3t} \\ -3e^{-t} + 6e^{-2t} - 3e^{-3t} & \frac{-5}{2}e^{-t} + 8e^{-2t}\frac{-9}{2}e^{-3t} & \frac{-1}{2}e^{-t} + 2e^{-2t} - \frac{3}{2}e^{-3t} \\ 3e^{-t} - 12e^{-2t} + 9e^{-3t} & \frac{5}{2}e^{-t} - 16e^{-2t} + \frac{27}{2}e^{-3t} & \frac{1}{2}e^{-t} - 4e^{-2t} + \frac{9}{2}e^{-3t} \end{bmatrix}$

**7.23.** $\mathbf{x}(t) = \begin{bmatrix} 0 \\ 2e^{2t} \end{bmatrix}$

**7.25.** $\mathbf{x}(t) = \begin{bmatrix} \dfrac{1}{\omega} + \dfrac{(\omega - 1)}{\omega}\cosh \omega t - \sinh \omega t \\[2mm] \cosh \omega t + \dfrac{(1 - \omega)}{\omega}\sinh \omega t \end{bmatrix}$

**7.27.** $\begin{bmatrix} i_L(t) \\ v_C(t) \end{bmatrix} = \begin{bmatrix} 0.386e^{-0.869t} - 0.386e^{-8.631t} \\ 1.045e^{-0.869t} - 0.0476e^{-8.631t} \end{bmatrix}$

### CHAPTER 8

**8.5.** (a) $\delta(t - \pi/2)$    (b) $-\delta(t - \pi)$    (c) 0

**8.6.** (a) $e^{-t}$    (b) $i_L(t) = \dfrac{1}{3}\left\{ e^{-(5/12)t}\cos\dfrac{\sqrt{23}}{12}t + \dfrac{1}{\sqrt{23}}e^{-(5/12)t}\sin\dfrac{\sqrt{23}}{12}t \right\}$

(e) $te^{-t}$

**8.7.** (c) $(1 - e^{-(1/2)t})$    (e) $v_C(t) = (1 - e^{-t} - te^{-t})$

**8.8.** (i) (d) $2(e^{-t} - e^{-2t})$    (e) $\frac{1}{2}t^2e^{-t}$

(ii) (c) $(1 - e^{-(1/2)t})u_0(t) - (1 - e^{-(1/2)(t-1)})u_0(t - 1)$

**8.9.** (c) $(1 - \cos t)u_0(t) - (1 - \cos(t - 2\pi))u_0(t - 2\pi)$

**8.11.** (b) $v_C(t) = \begin{cases} \dfrac{1}{2}(2t - 1) + \dfrac{e^{-2t}}{2}\left(\dfrac{1 - 2e^{-6} + e^{-4}}{1 - e^{-8}}\right), & 0 < t < 1 \\[3mm] \dfrac{1}{2}(5 - 2t) + \dfrac{e^{-2t}}{2}\left(\dfrac{1 - 2e^2 + e^{-4}}{1 - e^{-8}}\right), & 1 < t < 2 \\[3mm] \dfrac{1}{2}e^{-2t}\left(\dfrac{1 - 2e^2 + e^4}{1 - e^{-8}}\right), & 2 < t < 4 \end{cases}$

### CHAPTER 9

**9.2.** (iii) $e^{-3t} - e^{-2t}$

**9.3.** (i) $\dfrac{\cos 2 + (s + 2)\sin 2}{s^2 + 4s^2 + 5}$

(iii) $\dfrac{1}{s} + 2\displaystyle\sum_{n=1}^{\infty}\dfrac{(-1)^n}{s + 2n}$

**9.5.** (ii) roots: $-0.601$, $-2.449$, $0.025 \pm j0.825$

**9.7.** $i_L(t) = [0.67 + 2.04e^{-1.25t} \sin(1.2t + 9.4°)]$

**9.8.** (c) $20 - 20e^{-(3/8)t}\left[\cos\dfrac{\sqrt{7}}{8}t - \dfrac{1}{\sqrt{7}}\sin\dfrac{\sqrt{7}}{8}t\right]$

**9.9.** (a) $Z(s) = \dfrac{2s^2 + s + 2}{2s}$

(b) $i(t) = 6.2e^{-0.25t}\sin(0.966t)$

**9.10.** $i(t) = 2 + te^{-t} - 3e^{-t}$

**9.13.** (a) $x_1 = i_2$, $x_2 = v_C$, $\dot{\mathbf{x}} = \begin{bmatrix} 0 & 0.25 \\ -0.75 & -1 \end{bmatrix}\mathbf{x}$

(b) $e^{\mathbf{A}t} = \begin{bmatrix} 1.5e^{-0.25t} - 0.5e^{-0.75t} & 0.5e^{-0.25t} - 0.5e^{-0.75t} \\ 1.5e^{-0.75t} - 1.5e^{-0.25t} & 1.5e^{-0.75t} - 0.5e^{-0.25t} \end{bmatrix}$

**9.15.** $Y(s) = 1.834 + 1.333s$

**9.16.** $i(t) = \dfrac{18}{33}e^{-(24/33)t}u_0(t)$

**CHAPTER 10**

**10.1.** $i_{ss}(t) = 4\sin(2t + \pi/4)$

**10.2.** $Z_{ab} = 1$

**10.4.** $H(j\omega) = \dfrac{4}{(j\omega)^2 + j\omega + 4}$

**10.6.** $i_L(t) = 2\sqrt{5}\cos(t - \pi/4 - \tan^{-1}(2))$

**10.8.** (a) $V_R = -5\sqrt{2}\cos t$   (b) $H(j\omega) = \dfrac{0.5}{(j\omega)^3 + (j\omega)^2 + (j\omega) + 0.5}$

**10.9.** $P(t) = 112\cos t\cos(t - 63.4°)$   $P = 25$ watts   $Q = 50$ vars

$E[0, 5] = 86.4$ joules

**10.11.** (a)

(b)  $P = 120$ watts

$\quad\quad Q = -160$ vars

**10.12.** (a)  $C = 25 \times 10^{-6}$f,  $\theta = 32°$

(b)  $C = 36 \times 10^{-6}$f,  $\theta = 51°$

**10.14.**  $Z_3 = (50/13)j$

**10.15.** (b) Capacitive  (c)  $P = 20$ watts  $Q = -19.5$ vars

**10.17.** (a)  $\omega_0 = 100$  (b)  $Q_0 = 50$

(c)  $H(j\omega) = \dfrac{j0.1\omega}{(1 - .0001\omega^2) + j0.0002\omega}$

**10.18.**  $C = \dfrac{R_L^2 + \omega^2 L^2 \pm \sqrt{(R_L^2 + \omega^2 L^2)^2 - 4L^2\omega^2 R_C^2}}{2\omega^2 L R_C^2}$

**10.19.**  $Z_{ab}(j\omega)$

$$= \frac{(3 - 26\omega^2 + 41\omega^4 - 14\omega^6) + j\left(-\dfrac{1}{\omega} + 14\omega - 44\omega^3 + 36\omega^5 - 5\omega^7\right)}{(1 - 10\omega^2 + 16\omega^4 - 4\omega^6) + j(\omega - 7\omega^3 + 7\omega^5)}$$

**CHAPTER 11**

**11.2.**  $v(t) = \dfrac{V}{2} + \dfrac{V}{\pi} \sin \dfrac{2\pi}{T} t + \dfrac{V}{2\pi} \sin \dfrac{4\pi}{T} t + \cdots$

**11.3.**  $v = \displaystyle\sum_{\substack{n=-\infty \\ n \neq 0}}^{\infty} 2\dfrac{V}{\sqrt{(2n\pi)^2 + (1.5)^2}} e^{j(2n\pi t - \tan^{-1}(4n\pi/3))}$

$V_{\mathrm{rms}} = V\sqrt{\displaystyle\sum_{n=1}^{\infty} \dfrac{1}{(2n\pi)^2 + (1.5)^2}}$

**11.4.**  $a_0 = 0.5, a_1 = 0.45289, a_2 = 0.08333, a_3 = 0.12032; b_n = 0$

**11.5.** (a) (i)  $v(t) = \dfrac{1}{2} + \displaystyle\sum_{\substack{n \text{ odd} \\ n>0}} (j)^{m+1} \left(\dfrac{2}{n\pi}\right)^2 \sin(n\pi t)$

**11.6.**  $f(t) = \dfrac{\pi^2}{3} + \displaystyle\sum_{m=1}^{\infty} (-1)^m \dfrac{4}{m^2} \cos mt$

**11.7.**  $v(t) = \dfrac{V}{2} + V \displaystyle\sum_{\substack{n=-\infty \\ m \neq 0}}^{\infty} \left(\dfrac{1}{2n\pi}\right) e^{j(2n\pi t - \pi/2)}$

**11.9.** (a)  $a_0 = 1.42, a_1 = -1.01667, a_2 = 0.31667$

$\quad\quad b_1 = -0.08660, b_2 = -0.08660, b_3 = 0$

**11.11.**  $i_t(t) = -\left(\dfrac{1 - e^{\frac{T}{2}}}{1 - e^T}\right) e^{-t} u_0(t)$

$$i_T(t) = \begin{cases} 1 - e^{-t} + \left(\dfrac{1 - e^{\frac{T}{2}}}{1 - e^T}\right) e^{-t}, & 0 < t < \dfrac{T}{2} \\[4mm] e^{-\left(t - \frac{T}{2}\right)} - e^{-t} + \left(\dfrac{1 - e^{\frac{T}{2}}}{1 - e^T}\right) e^{-t}, & \dfrac{T}{2} < t < T \end{cases}$$

**11.13.** (i) (a) $i_t(t) = 0.538e^{-t}u_0(t)$

$$i_T(t) = \begin{cases} -1 + 1.46e^{-t}, & 0 < t < 1 \\ 1 + 1.46e^{-t} - 2e^{-(t-1)}, & 1 < t < 2 \end{cases}$$

(b) $i_t(t) = 0.545e^{-t}u_0(t)$
$i_T(t) = 0.707 \sin(t + 45°) - 1.045e^{-t}, \quad 0 < t < \pi$

(ii) (a) $i_t(t) = -0.538e^{-t}u_0(t)$

$$i_T(t) = \begin{cases} 2 - t - 1.46e^{-t}, & 0 < t < 1 \\ t - 2 - 1.46e^{-t} + 2e^{-(t-1)}, & 1 < t < 2 \end{cases}$$

(b) $i_t(t) = -0.545e^{-t}u_0(t)$
$i_T(t) = 0.707 \sin(t - 45°) + 1.045e^{-t}, \quad 0 < t < \pi$

**11.19.** $C = 0.0265\text{f}$

**CHAPTER 12**

**12.1.** $z_{11} = Z_1 + Z_2 \qquad z_{22} = Z_2 + Z_3 \qquad z_{12} = z_{21} = Z_2$

**12.3.** $z_{11} = \dfrac{(Z_a Z_1 + Z_a Z_3 + \Delta_1)}{\Delta_2} \qquad z_{22} = \dfrac{(Z_a Z_2 + Z_a Z_3 + \Delta_1)}{\Delta_2}$

$z_{12} = z_{21} = \dfrac{(Z_a Z_3 + \Delta_1)}{\Delta_2}$

$\Delta_1 = Z_1 Z_2 + Z_1 Z_3 + Z_2 Z_3 \qquad \Delta_2 = (Z_a + Z_1 + Z_2)$

**12.4.** $z_{11} = R + \dfrac{1}{Cs} + L_1 s, \qquad z_{22} = R + Ls + L_2 s,$

$z_{12} = Ms = Z_{21}$

**12.8.** $y_{11} = \dfrac{1}{\Delta}(R + Ls + L_2 s), \qquad y_{22} = \dfrac{1}{\Delta}\left(R + \dfrac{1}{Cs} + L_1 s\right),$

$y_{12} = y_{21} = \dfrac{1}{\Delta}(-Ms)$

$\Delta = (R + Ls + L_2 s)\left(R + \dfrac{1}{Cs} + Ls\right) - M^2 s^2$

**12.9.** $y_{11} = \dfrac{Z_2 + Z_3}{\Delta Z} \qquad y_{22} = \dfrac{Z_1 + Z_2}{\Delta Z} \qquad y_{12} = y_{21} = -\dfrac{Z_2}{\Delta Z}$

$\Delta Z = Z_1 Z_2 + Z_2 Z_3 + Z_1 Z_3$

**12.11.** $A = \dfrac{Z_1 + Z_2}{Z_2} \qquad B = \dfrac{Z_1 Z_2 + Z_1 Z_3 + Z_2 Z_3}{Z_2}$

$C = \dfrac{1}{Z_2} \qquad D = \dfrac{Z_2 + Z_3}{Z_2}$

**12.13.** $A = \dfrac{Z_a Z_1 + Z_a Z_3 + \Delta Z}{Z_a Z_3 + \Delta Z}$    $B = \dfrac{Z_a \Delta Z}{Z_a Z_3 + \Delta Z}$

$C = \dfrac{Z_a + Z_1 + Z_2}{Z_a Z_3 + \Delta Z}$    $D = \dfrac{Z_a Z_2 + Z_a Z_3 + \Delta Z}{Z_a Z_3 + \Delta Z}$

$\Delta Z = Z_1 Z_2 + Z_1 Z_3 + Z_2 Z_3$

**12.17.** $h_{11} = \dfrac{-Z_2^2}{Z_2 + Z_3} + Z_1 + Z_2$    $h_{12} = \dfrac{Z_2}{Z_2 + Z_3}$

$h_{21} = -\dfrac{Z_2}{Z_2 + Z_3}$    $h_{22} = \dfrac{1}{Z_2 + Z_3}$

**12.21.** $A = \dfrac{Z_1 + Z_2}{Z_2}$    $B = \dfrac{Z_1 Z_2 + Z_2 Z_3 + Z_1 Z_3}{Z_2}$

$C = \dfrac{1}{Z_2}$    $D = \dfrac{Z_2 + Z_3}{Z_2}$

**12.23.** $A = \dfrac{Z_1 Z_a + Z_3 Z_a + \Delta Z}{Z_3 Z_a + \Delta Z}$    $B = \dfrac{Z_a \Delta Z}{Z_a Z_3 + \Delta Z}$

$C = \dfrac{Z_a + Z_1 + Z_1}{Z_a Z_3 + \Delta Z}$    $D = \dfrac{Z_a Z_s + Z_a Z_2 + \Delta Z}{Z_a Z_3 + \Delta Z}$

$\Delta Z = Z_1 Z_2 + Z_1 Z_3 + Z_2 Z_3$

**12.25.** $h_{11} = \dfrac{Z_1 Z_2}{Z_1 + Z_2}$    $h_{22} = \dfrac{Z_1 + Z_2 + Z_3}{(Z_1 + Z_2) Z_3}$

$h_{12} = -h_{21} = \dfrac{Z_1}{Z_1 + Z_2}$

**12.29.** $z_{11} = z_{22} = \dfrac{s^2 + 1}{s(2 + s^2)} + \dfrac{s}{2}$

$z_{12} = z_{21} = \dfrac{1}{s(2 + s^2)} + \dfrac{s}{2}$

**CHAPTER 13**

**13.3.** $z_{21}(s) = z_{12}(s) = \dfrac{sL_1(s^2 L_2 C + 1)}{s^2 C(L_1 + L_2) + sR_2 C + 1}$

**13.4.** $I_L(s) = \dfrac{1}{10s^2(s^2 + 3.7s + 4)}$

**13.7.** $V_{oc}(s) = I_1(s) Z_e(s) + \left(\dfrac{s^2 + 1}{s}\right) V_1(s) Z_e(S)$

$Z_e(s) = \dfrac{s(s^2 + 1)}{s^4 + 3s^2 + 1}$

**13.8.** $I_L(s) = \dfrac{2s V_1(s) + V_2(s)}{20s^2 + 10s + 2}$

**13.10.** $R_2 = 1.6\,\Omega$,   $R_1 = 0.8\,\Omega$,   $i = 0.157$ amp.

**14.1.**   (a)

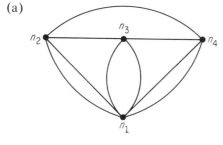

(b) $n_1$:   6
$n_2$:   4
$n_3$:   4
$n_4$:   4

(c) and (d) The possible trees are indicated on page 537.  Some of the loops are formed by completing a path with each chord, other loops can be obtained by inspection.

(e) number of branches $= n - 1 = 3$.

**14.3.**   The tree structure is the same as shown in **14.1**.  When one branch is removed from any of the trees, two disjoint subgraphs are formed.  A cut set consists of the removed tree branch together with those chords which connect the subgraphs.  For tree (v) in **14.1** the cutsets are

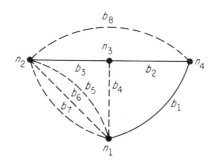

cut set 1:   $\{b_1, b_4, b_5, b_6, b_7\}$
cut set 2:   $\{b_2, b_4, b_5, b_6, b_7, b_8\}$
cut set 3:   $\{b_3, b_5, b_6, b_7, b_8\}$

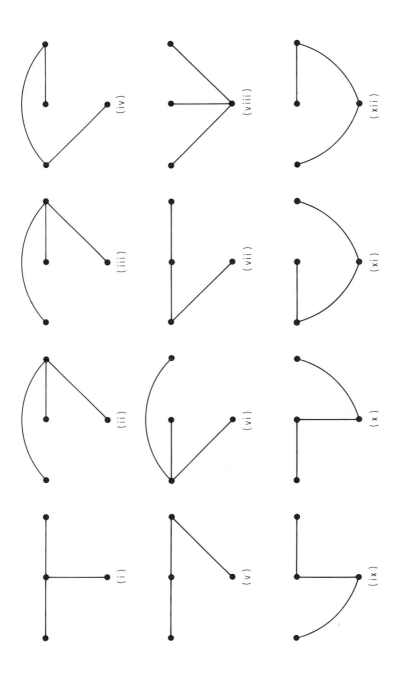

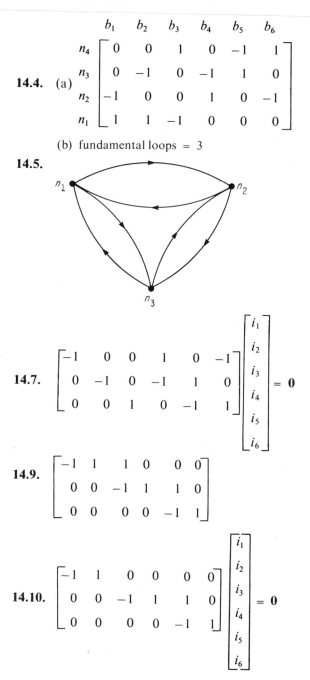

$$
\begin{array}{c}
\phantom{n_4} \quad b_1 \quad b_2 \quad b_3 \quad b_4 \quad b_5 \quad b_6 \\
\textbf{14.4.} \quad (a) \quad
\begin{array}{c} n_4 \\ n_3 \\ n_2 \\ n_1 \end{array}
\begin{bmatrix}
0 & 0 & 1 & 0 & -1 & 1 \\
0 & -1 & 0 & -1 & 1 & 0 \\
-1 & 0 & 0 & 1 & 0 & -1 \\
1 & 1 & -1 & 0 & 0 & 0
\end{bmatrix}
\end{array}
$$

(b) fundamental loops $= 3$

**14.5.**

**14.7.**
$$
\begin{bmatrix}
-1 & 0 & 0 & 1 & 0 & -1 \\
0 & -1 & 0 & -1 & 1 & 0 \\
0 & 0 & 1 & 0 & -1 & 1
\end{bmatrix}
\begin{bmatrix}
i_1 \\ i_2 \\ i_3 \\ i_4 \\ i_5 \\ i_6
\end{bmatrix} = \mathbf{0}
$$

**14.9.**
$$
\begin{bmatrix}
-1 & 1 & 1 & 0 & 0 & 0 \\
0 & 0 & -1 & 1 & 1 & 0 \\
0 & 0 & 0 & 0 & -1 & 1
\end{bmatrix}
$$

**14.10.**
$$
\begin{bmatrix}
-1 & 1 & 0 & 0 & 0 & 0 \\
0 & 0 & -1 & 1 & 1 & 0 \\
0 & 0 & 0 & 0 & -1 & 1
\end{bmatrix}
\begin{bmatrix}
i_1 \\ i_2 \\ i_3 \\ i_4 \\ i_5 \\ i_6
\end{bmatrix} = \mathbf{0}
$$

**14.11.** $\mathbf{B}_a = \begin{bmatrix} 1 & -1 & 0 & 1 & 0 & 0 \\ 0 & 1 & 1 & 0 & 1 & 0 \\ 0 & 0 & 0 & -1 & -1 & -1 \\ 1 & 0 & 1 & 0 & 0 & -1 \\ -1 & 1 & 0 & 0 & 1 & 1 \\ 0 & 1 & 1 & -1 & 0 & -1 \end{bmatrix}$

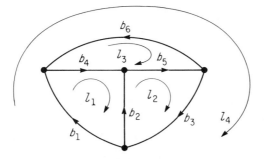

**14.13.** For the tree shown below, the fundamental loops are $l_1$, $l_2$, and $l_3$ shown in **14.11**.

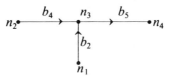

**14.15.** Using the tree of **14.13**, the fundamental loop matrix is

$$\mathbf{B}_f = \begin{bmatrix} 1 & -1 & 0 & 1 & 0 & 0 \\ 0 & 1 & 1 & 0 & 1 & 0 \\ 0 & 0 & 0 & -1 & -1 & -1 \end{bmatrix}$$

**14.17.** $\begin{bmatrix} 1 & -1 & 0 & 1 & 0 & 1 \\ 0 & 1 & 1 & 0 & 1 & 0 \\ 1 & 0 & 1 & 0 & 0 & -1 \end{bmatrix} \begin{bmatrix} v_1 \\ v_2 \\ v_3 \\ v_4 \\ v_5 \\ v_6 \end{bmatrix} = \mathbf{0}$

**14.21.**(a)

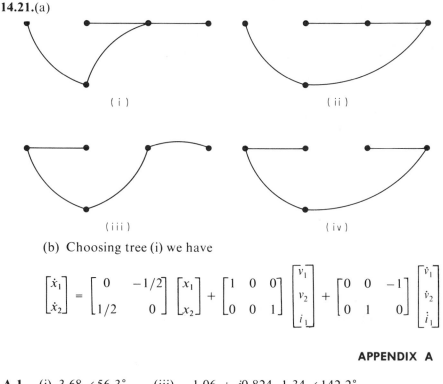

( i )                    ( ii )

( iii )                  ( iv )

(b)  Choosing tree (i) we have

$$\begin{bmatrix} \dot{x}_1 \\ \dot{x}_2 \end{bmatrix} = \begin{bmatrix} 0 & -1/2 \\ 1/2 & 0 \end{bmatrix} \begin{bmatrix} x_1 \\ x_2 \end{bmatrix} + \begin{bmatrix} 1 & 0 & 0 \\ 0 & 0 & 1 \end{bmatrix} \begin{bmatrix} v_1 \\ v_2 \\ i_1 \end{bmatrix} + \begin{bmatrix} 0 & 0 & -1 \\ 0 & 1 & 0 \end{bmatrix} \begin{bmatrix} \dot{v}_1 \\ \dot{v}_2 \\ \dot{i}_1 \end{bmatrix}$$

### APPENDIX  A

**A.1.** (i) $3.68 \angle 56.3°$      (iii) $-1.06 + j0.824,\ 1.34 \angle 142.2°$
(iv) $-10$      (v) $1.12 + j1.11$      (vii) $j0.881$
(viii) $j\dfrac{\pi}{2}$

**A.3.** (ii) $e^{\pi/4} \cos(0.346) + je^{\pi/4} \sin(0.346)$

**A.5.** $1.5 \pm j2.18$

**A.6.** (i) $\dfrac{3 - j}{1 + 2j}$

**A.7.** $-0.308 - j0.462$

**A.8.** (iii) $\log c = \log 2 + \dfrac{j\pi}{2},\quad e^c = \cos 2 + j\sin 2$

**A.9.** (i) $e^\sigma \cos \omega + je^\sigma \sin \omega$      (iv) $\dfrac{1}{2} \log(\sigma^2 + \omega^2) + j\tan^{-1}\!\left(\dfrac{\omega}{\sigma}\right)$

# Suggested Further
# Readings

[1]   C. A. Desoer and E. S. Kuh, *Basic Circuit Theory*. New York: McGraw-Hill, 1969.
[2]   P. M. Chirlian, *Basic Network Theory*. New York: McGraw-Hill, 1969.
[3]   R. A. Rohrer, *Circuit Theory: An Introduction to the State Variable Approach*. New York: McGraw-Hill, 1970.
[4]   L. O. Chua, *Introduction to Nonlinear Network Theory*. New York: McGraw-Hill, 1970.
[5]   C. M. Close, *The Analysis of Linear Circuits*. New York: Harcourt, 1969.
[6]   S. C. Gupta, *Transform and State Variable Methods in Linear Systems*, New York: Wiley, 1966. 1971 reprint, Huntington, N.Y.: Krieger Publishing Co.
[7]   B. C. Kuo, *Linear Networks and Systems*, New York: McGraw-Hill, 1967.
[8]   M. E. Van Valkenburg, *Network Analysis*, 2nd ed. Englewood Cliffs, N.J.: Prentice-Hall, 1964.
[9]   L. A. Manning, *Electrical Circuits*, New York: McGraw-Hill, 1966.
[10]  N. Balabanian, *Fundamentals of Circuit Theory*. Boston: Allyn and Bacon, 1961.
[11]  L. P. Huelsman, *Digital Computations in Basic Circuit Theory*. New York: McGraw-Hill, 1968.
[12]  J. B. Cruz, Jr., and M. E. Van Valkenberg, *Introductory Signals and Circuits*. Waltham, Mass.: Blaisdell, 1967.

# Index